ISBN 978-0-656-50473-2
PIBN 10680337

This book is a reproduction of an important historical work. Forgotten Books uses state-of-the-art technology to digitally reconstruct the work, preserving the original format whilst repairing imperfections present in the aged copy. In rare cases, an imperfection in the original, such as a blemish or missing page, may be replicated in our edition. We do, however, repair the vast majority of imperfections successfully; any imperfections that remain are intentionally left to preserve the state of such historical works.

National Municipal Review

INDEX

1954

VOLUME XLIII

Supplement to the
NATIONAL MUNICIPAL REVIEW
February 1955, Vol. XLIV, No. 2

NATIONAL MUNICIPAL LEAGUE
542 FIFTH AVENUE
NEW YORK 36

Index

NATIONAL MUNICIPAL REVIEW
Volume XLIII, 1954

AUTHORS

TITLES AND SUBJECTS
(Main Articles in Italics)

Index for 1953 Will Be
Distributed with February Issue

The National Municipal Review

ALFRED WILLOUGHBY, Editor   ELSIE S. PARKER, Assistant Editor

Contributing Editors

JOHN E. BEBOUT, Research
RICHARD S. CHILDS
EDWARD W. WEIDNER, County and Township
H. M. OLMSTED, City, State and Nation

WADE S. SMITH, Taxation and Finance
GEORGE H. HALLETT, JR.
WM. REDIN WOODWARD
Proportional Representation

State Correspondents

H. F. ALDERFER, Pennsylvania
CARTER W. ATKINS, Connecticut
MYRON H. ATKINSON, North Dakota
CHESTER BIESEN, Washington
D. BENTON BISER, Maryland
ERNEST M. BLACK, Oklahoma
JOHN C. BOLLENS, California
WILLIAM L. BRADSHAW, Missouri
A. C. BRECKENRIDGE, Nebraska
ARTHUR W. BROMAGE, Michigan
FRANKLIN L. BURDETTE, Maryland
CHARLTON F. CHUTE, Pennsylvania
WELDON COOPER, Virginia
C. A. CROSSER, Washington
PAUL DOLAN, Delaware
D. MACK EASTON, Colorado
WILLIAM O. FARBER, South Dakota
FOREST FRANK, Ohio
DAVID FUDGE, Oklahoma
ROBERT M. GOODRICH, Rhode Island
MRS. LEONARD HAAS, Georgia
M. H. HARRIS, Utah
SAM HAYS, Arkansas
ROBERT B. HIGHSAW, Mississippi
JACK E. HOLMES, New Mexico
ORREN C. HORMELL, Maine
HERMAN KEHRLI, Oregon
PAUL KELSO, Arizona
DRYDEN KUSER, Nevada

JOHN D. LANGMUIR, New Hampshire
STUART A. MacCORKLE, Texas
RICHARD G. MARDEN, New Hampshire
BOYD A. MARTIN, Idaho
EDWARD M. MARTIN, Illinois
JAMES W. MARTIN, Kentucky
JAMES W. McGREW, New Jersey
DAYTON D. McKEAN, Colorado
EDWIN B. McPHERON, Indiana
WILLIAM MILLER, New Jersey
LENNOX L. MOAK, Pennsylvania
ANDREW E. NUQUIST, Vermont
KIMBROUGH OWEN, Louisiana
FRANK W. PRESCOTT, Tennessee
JOHN E. REEVES, Kentucky
ROLAND R. RENNE, Montana
PAUL N. REYNOLDS, Wisconsin
RUSSELL M. ROSS, Iowa
ALBERT B. SAYE, Georgia
VICTORIA SCHUCK, Massachusetts
LLOYD M. SHORT, Minnesota
GEORGE G. SIPPRELL, New York
PAUL D. STEWART, West Virginia
JOHN G. STUTZ, Kansas
HERMAN H. TRACHSEL, Wyoming
PAUL W. WAGER, North Carolina
YORK WILLBERN, Alabama
JOHN F. WILLMOTT, Florida

Published by THE NATIONAL MUNICIPAL LEAGUE

George H. Gallup, President

John S. Linen, Vice President
George S. Van Schaick, Vice President

Carl H. Pforzheimer, Treasurer
Alfred Willoughby, Executive Director

Richard S. Childs, Chairman, Executive Committee

Council

Charles Edison, West Orange, N. J., Chairman

Frederick L. Bird, New York
Arthur W. Bromage, Ann Arbor, Mich.
E. Bartlett Brooks, Dayton, Ohio
Henry Bruère, New York
William H. Bulkeley, Hartford
L. E. Burch, Jr., Memphis
Mrs. Albert D. Cash, Cincinnati
Charles E. Commander, Jr., Jacksonville
L. P. Cookingham, Kansas City, Mo.
Karl Detzer, Leland, Mich.
E. D. Dodd, Toledo
Harold W. Dodds, Princeton, N. J.
Bayard H. Faulkner, Montclair, N. J.
Arnold Frye, New York

Ewart W. Goodwin, San Diego
Thomas Graham, Louisville
Mrs. Virgil Loeb, St. Louis
Rob Roy Macleod, Buffalo
Mark S. Matthews, Greenwich, Conn.
Cecil Morgan, New York
Albert E. Noelte, Central Falls, R. I.
Mrs. Maurice H. Noun, Des Moines
H. Bruce Palmer, Newark, N. J.
Lawson Purdy, New York
Thomas R. Reid, Dearborn, Mich.
Philip K. Robinson, Milwaukee
Murray Seasongood, Cincinnati
Lee M. Sharrar, Houston

Regional Vice Presidents

Lester L. Bates, Columbia, S. C.
William Collins, New York
Ben B. Ehrlichman, Seattle
John B. Gage, Kansas City, Mo.
Carl J. Gilbert, Boston
Barry Goldwater, Phoenix
Lloyd Hale, Minneapolis

Arthur E. Johnson, Denver
Mrs. Siegel W. Judd, Grand Rapids
John Nuveen, Chicago
Ed. P. Phillips, Richmond
Charles P. Taft, Cincinnati
Alex R. Thomas, San Antonio
Carleton B. Tibbetts, Los Angeles

NEWS for League Members

Gallup Names NML Study Group

To make a continuing study of the McLean report and any other proposals regarding the League's program and activities, President George Gallup has appointed the following committee:

Cecil Morgan

Chairman, Cecil Morgan, general counsel, Standard Oil Company (New Jersey); Bayard H. Faulkner, vice president, Seaboard Oil Company; Lloyd Hale, president, G. H. Tennant Company; Frank C. Moore, president, Government Affairs Foundation, and James M. Osborn, Yale University.

In announcing the committee, President Gallup provided that the president and other officers, including the chairman of the Finance Committee, should be members *ex officio* and that the committee be free to invite any other persons to participate in its deliberations.

Appointment of the committee was in accordance with action of the Council at the Richmond Conference. The committee will consider possible changes in the League's constitution as well as studying other problems and is expected to report at the spring meeting of the Council.

Chairman Morgan has called the first meeting of the committee for 10:30 A.M. on January 9. It will be held at the Yale Club, New York.

NML Fellowship Set Up at Harvard

Establishment of a National Municipal League Fellowship at the Harvard Graduate School of Business Administration has been approved by the League's Council.

The Fellowship will help men with substantial experience in public administration in municipal or state government to participate in the Advanced Management Program of the school which heretofore has been attended largely by business executives and some administrators in the federal government.

The Advanced Management Program is an intensive course of study for mature, experienced administrators, usually between the ages of 38 and 48.

A holder of the Fellowship may attend either of two sessions, one running from the middle of September to early in December, and the other from late in February to the latter part of May. Classes are limited to 150 men in each session.

The Fellowship carries a stipend of $1,500, provided by Mr. and Mrs. Preston Farley, of Evanston, Illinois. Total costs for the thirteen-week program are approximately $2,500.

Detailed information may be obtained from Harvey P. Bishop, director, Advanced Management Program, Harvard Business School, Boston 63, or from the National Municipal League.

Random Conference Pictures . . . .

Upper left—Karl Detzer, Carl Pforzheimer and William Collins cast approving looks at the 59th National Conference on Government program at Richmond, Virginia.

Above—Sherwood Reeder (second from right) with a group of German municipal experts attending the Conference. The visitors are Fritz Littman (left), Wolfgang Jager and Konrad Simons.

Upper right—Richmond meets Richmond. Mayor Edward E. Haddock of Richmond, Virginia, receives a gold key to Richmond, California, from its mayor, Ed J. J. McKeegan.

Below—Former Governor Charles Edison shakes hands with Cadet Calvin Bailey after Armistice Day Memorial Services at John Marshall High School. With them, left to right, are Dr. Clyde Hickerson, Ed. P. Phillips and Cadet Robert W. Wray.

National Municipal Review

Volume XLIII, No. 1   Total Number 439

Published monthly except August

By NATIONAL MUNICIPAL LEAGUE

Contents for January 1954

The contents of the REVIEW are indexed in *International Index to Periodicals* and *Public Affairs Information Service*.

Entered as second class matter July 11, 1932, at the Post Office at Worcester, Massachusetts. Publication office, 150 Fremont Street, Worcester 3; editorial and business office, 299 Broadway, New York 7. Copyright 1954 by the National Municipal League.

Subscription, $5 per year; Canadian, $5.25; foreign, $5.50; single copies 50 cents.

Editorial Comment

New York's City Administrator

SOMETHING new has been added to the government of New York—a city administrator.

The nation's largest city clearly has the greatest need for competent top management and, not always deservedly, has had one of the most dubious reputations for it.

The world over, Tammany has become a word meaning a voracious appetite for favors, jobs, political plunder, payment of political mercenaries out of the public treasury.

The occasional good mayors and the high-minded actions of the not-so-good mayors have been eclipsed in memory by the antics of the spectacular personality boys who grabbed the next ship to England or chose voluntary exile in Mexico.

New Yorkers have grown a bit cynical, too, over the grandstand plays of Tammany mayors designed to persuade the public that they are unbossed.

Nevertheless, the big city experienced a genuine thrill when, shortly after his election, Tammany-supported Robert F. Wagner, Jr., announced that there would be a city administrator and that this officer would be Luther Gulick, famous authority on public administration, who directed the recent $2,000,000 management survey of the city's government. Dr. Gulick presumably knows more than anyone else about what is right and what is wrong. It takes six and one-half inches in *Who's Who* to list his accomplishments as an expert on governmental problems.

It should prove difficult for self-seeking political forces to push around a man of Dr. Gulick's stature as they have been able to do with mayors. The door may well be open for the new administration to demonstrate, in day-to-day conduct and accomplishments, the validity of the administrative proposals made by the Mayor's Committee on Management Survey (directed by Dr. Gulick), the plan of the Temporary State Commission to Study the Organizational Structure of the Government of the City of New York (created by the last legislature at the instigation of Governor Dewey), and the suggestions made during the last year or two by the Citizens Union and other civic forces.

The New York experiment may prove to be the first so-called mayor-administrator plan worthy of establishing a "trend" in large cities which some hasty observers feel they have detected recently.

A chief administrator of a city or any other operation needs adequate management tools, particularly those having to do with finance and personnel. In Philadelphia, Los Angeles and San Francisco—the cities usually cited as indicating the trend—he does not have them. He therefore is not and cannot be a true chief administrator.

New York's experience will merit the careful attention of all interested in good government.

A Mighty Oak Grows

IN 1919 the National Conference on Government turned itself into a mock state constitutional convention, debated reports brought in by specialist committees and put together the National Municipal League's first *Model State Constitution,* published in 1921 and now in its fifth revised edition dated 1948.

Espousal of untried inventions being part of the League's function, the model included the novel idea of providing a legislative council equipped with qualified researchers to explore needs and remedies between legislative sessions and bring in well matured and fact-supported bills.

Kansas in 1933 was first to pick up the idea at the instance locally of Sam Wilson, manager of the Kansas Chamber of Commerce, who stumped the state for it. Kansas' lead was followed by Virginia in 1936 and by Connecticut, Illinois, Nebraska and Pennsylvania in 1937. In the postwar period the move-ment has accelerated and legislative councils or council-type agencies have been established in 33 states.

Their usefulness has been immense in organizing and publishing orderly information, often in such array that sound policy shows inescapably on the surface. They have likewise developed a fine type of professional research worker adept in practical dealings with legislators although often inhibited from pushing their logic all the way to logical ends.

The original name "legislative council" remains the generic name of such agencies and the official name in two-thirds of the states using them. The Council of State Governments is now the source of the most systematic information about their spread and functioning.

A comprehensive review entitled "The Legislative Council Movement 1933-1953" appears in the *American Political Science Review* for September 1953. Harold W. Davey, of Iowa State College, is the author.

Jersey Coroner 'High Hats' Job

NEW JERSEY has produced a noteworthy episode to point up the REVIEW's November editorial, "Ghosts on the Jersey Ballot," which related that New Jersey counties were still electing coroners although they have no duties and no pay. The Newark *Sunday News* of November 15 reported that John B. Lawrence, a reporter living in Somerville, got some friends to write in his name on their ballots, there being no other nominees. With 21 votes, he was elected coroner of Somerset County. Thereafter he went forth with a silk hat, frock coat and lantern —and a camera man—to perform the only remaining duty left to him since the law substituted qualified appointive medical examiners for the old elective coroners. This duty was to take charge of dead bodies thrown on the shore from shipwrecks. There being no seacoast to his county, he faithfully searched the Raritan River bank without success.

The Businessman's Challenge

*Active participation in affairs of the community urged;
conflict between public interest and self-interest denied.*

By CECIL MORGAN*

NOT so long ago the voice of the businessman was not very welcome in government. At least it was not at some levels, and that feeling spread widely. As a consequence, after he had been cussed beyond what seemed to him to be all reason, the businessman began to have something of a guilt complex. His statements about public affairs often tended to be more querulous than constructive.

But lately there has been a marked change in attitude, in both the businessman's attitude and that of the public. Some reasons are fairly obvious and others can be speculated upon. Beyond a doubt the businessman's performance during and after the war had much to do with his current stature in the public eye.

One important change in attitude in recent years is that which took place in the businessman's own concept of himself. Instead of avoiding public attention, today he often seeks it. He has grown more articulate. He not only is not timid about giving an account of himself to the public but, as a rule, goes out of his way

*Mr. Morgan, a member of the Council of the National Municipal League, is counsel to the Board of Directors of the Standard Oil Company (New Jersey). This article is the text of Mr. Morgan's address before the Kiwanis Club of Richmond, Virginia, November 9, 1953, during the National Conference on Government in that city. It is reprinted with permission from the *Virginia Municipal Review*, organ of the Virginia League of Municipalities, for November 1953.

to report on his activities. He takes employees and customers and the general public, as well as shareholders, into his confidence regarding his views and his company's policies.

He may not be able to match the oratory of the professional politician, who does the bulk of the work of government, or the latter's ability to capture the spotlight and arouse enthusiasm. I don't mean by this to disparage the professional politician in the least. In fact, I think it might be a good idea if more businessmen could develop their ability to win warm personal response from people. But the businessman does have some special abilities of his own and he can contribute these to government without venturing out onto the partisan political background.

Another change in attitude concerns the businessman's acknowledgment of responsibilities which he may not have thought about too seriously before. For years he has been shouldering a large share of the burden of good causes, particularly in raising funds for a variety of educational, health and welfare activities. He now is ready to do more than to contribute to the local community chest, the TB fund and the Red Cross. But while accepting new responsibilities in theory he comes, in practice, up against this question:

"What can I do? Here I am, a citizen and taxpayer of Richmond— I have a home and family and I am interested in the welfare of this community—but I am no politician, I am busy and other people are running our government."

I'd like to make a few suggestions, first, of general nature and, later, of specific actions. To begin with I would suggest that the businessman rid himself of several notions. The ones I have in mind are as wrong, it seems to me, as they are widely held. One of them concerns self-interest versus the public interest.

Take, for example, the subject of profits. A good deal of loose talking about profits has tended to make the businessman sensitive about them. To my mind, he is unduly so. Of course, he concentrates on making profits, for they are basic to his company's continuing in operation. Certainly they represent self-interest. But they are fully as basic to the well-being of the community and, hence, fully as basic to the public interest because without them there can be no enterprise, jobs, products, revenues or public services.

Take, for example, the subject of taxes, which are one of a businessman's chief concerns. Now, if a tax cut is obtained at the expense of educational or health or protective services in the community where a company operates, it can be shortsighted indeed. On the other hand, too high taxes can ruin a business, with consequent injury to customers, employees and investors. So here again self-interest is not incompatible with the public interest.

Perhaps we might say that the best goal for the businessman in this respect is a state of balance—balance, that is, between the demonstrated needs of the community on the one hand and, on the other, the financial means that are available. As in the case of the family, one must consider requirements and desires in the order of their importance and in the sometimes grim light of one's income. Once the basic needs have been met, we can take up the not-so-basic ones in turn. In this connection, two points I would especially like to make are, first, that the good of the community should be our guide and, second, that the good of the community does not compel the sacrifice of convictions or the assumption of disproportionate burdens by the businessman any more than by anyone else. From the standpoint of self-interest coinciding with the public good, why not work for a proper equalization of the tax burden first and efficient and sound expenditure to follow?

Businessmen As Politicians

Another notion concerns participation in partisan political affairs. A few businessmen are natural politicians. They run for and hold public office and, when they do, more power to them. They have their business affairs in such shape they can give the necessary time to the office. They can contribute much to public life. But some businessmen think they can be simply businessmen in public office. They forget that there is a special skill required to get elected, stay in office and function effectively as a public servant. They forget that government financial affairs are not run on a profit and loss basis, just as politicians often forget simple business concepts of efficiency and financial control.

Here is where we need to pay tribute to the so-called professional politician. (A businessman who lacks certain of his qualities shouldn't, and usually can't, hold office. But whether he wants to or not, or whether he can or not, doesn't detract from his interest in and concern with the conduct of that office, and there is much that he can do.) Most companies shun involvement, as a business organization, in partisan political activities. This is quite natural and proper. We can see, too, why it would be difficult for certain individuals, such as the president or the chairman of a company, to engage in partisan political activity without, in the process, involving the company itself. Not all individuals, however, are so closely identified with the company. And in any event there are many nonpartisan activities which can be undertaken, or activities which we like to feel do not have strong partisan implications.

I suppose that even activity in behalf of what, in theory, is as nonpartisan as an improved city charter could turn out to be partisan in practice. However, such objectives come under the heading of the "good of the community," which was mentioned previously as a pretty good guide for action, and invite the active participation of businessmen.

In addition to the offices which are strongly political, and others which simply may demand more time than the businessman ordinarily can spare out of the 24 hours of a day, there is the area which includes the boards and commissions that oversee education, planning, zoning, recreation and the like. These, too, invite the earnest thoughts and the helping hand of the businessman.

Many employees of companies affiliated with Standard Oil Company (New Jersey), for which I work, take part in the activity of such local boards and commissions in the many states in which those companies operate, particularly in the work of the school boards. The policy of Esso Standard Oil Company, for example, which has long been active in the Richmond area, has been to encourage all employees to accept responsibility of this kind. In some situations our affiliates have approved of such activities on company time.

Duty to Schools

In this connection, you may be interested in a statement which Jersey Standard, the parent company, circulated among affiliates some time ago. It reads, in part, as follows:

"American business enterprise is aware of its great debt to the public school system of this country, because that system is essential to the survival and growth of business.

"The right and duty of the individual to support our public school system is clear. One such duty is, of course, that of paying taxes. But it seems to us clear that the obligation of each of us as an individual runs beyond mere payment of taxes.

"Over the years many Jersey Standard employees have participated actively in their local school programs. The company would like to see more of its people take an active interest in the problems and opportunities facing the public schools in their own communities. Obviously, the conditions affecting the individual's ability to participate in school activities will vary, but our company encourages its employees, as good American citizens, to undertake this important work."

I would like to turn, now, from suggestions of a general nature to some of specific action and supply some answers, if I may, to the question of "What can I do?"

First, the businessman can assist in the recruiting of competent people for specialized jobs in the government. This is a management skill. It comes only with experience and the years. One of the common complaints about the public service concerns the competence of personnel. I think you will find the answer to complaints often running to the effect that, "We do the best we can with what we can get and, if you can get us something better, why don't you?" I echo that query: "Why don't you?"

Second, the businessman can render valuable staff service to government agencies. Of course, very few if any business concerns have experts in every field. But many have experts in some line—economists, engineers, statisticians, specialists in handling and storing materials, purchasing agents and others with special intellectual equipment for special types of work. The technical skills which are thus available can be very useful to local government.

Third, the businessman can contribute money or time, or both, to citizen movements in behalf of such improvements as new city charters, research on administrative questions and the solving of needs for new educational or health or recreational or other facilities. Many a businessman

is, in effect, a successful salesman of goods or services. He may sell, also, a municipal need. What he, himself, cannot contribute, he may get others to supply. He can assist in the organization and functioning of community groups that are dedicated to the improvement of government. I think it would be in order for me to call to your attention, at this point, the . National Municipal League. This organization is ever ready, able and willing to aïd local citizens with the accumulated factual information, the political experience and the organizational suggestions that will enable groups to function effectively.

Aiding Research

The businessman may be a purveyor of facts. It is a pretty sound theory, and one on which the businessman relies in handling his own business, that a study to find facts will lead to a sound policy, investment or program. Why shouldn't that apply to government? And businessmen are often responsible for nonpartisan research organizations that have the confidence of governments and contribute enormously to good government.

Fourth, the businessman can contribute to community management some of the management principles which make a business organization efficient and progressive.

Fifth, the businessman can help the government of his community by attending the meetings at which actions are decided upon by legislative or administrative bodies of local government, or at which such actions are discussed by citizen groups. Even though he may not open his mouth, the sheer physical evidence of his interest and concern can give a lift. How discouraging it must be to work in an apparent vacuum of public interest. Yet, so often that is just about the situation in which the business of the community is transacted. Then, too, the evidence of citizen interest as attested by physical presence at meetings can act as a wholesome brake upon excesses. Who but selfish interests contact the public officials if you do not do so on a basis of the general interest? Then who should be blamed for poor local government?

Letters to Officials

Sixth, the businessman can help through letters to officials and boards, giving suggestions in writing, commending where praise is deserved, or criticizing constructively where criticism is due. He can communicate to the officials and groups and to the public through that great American forum, the newspaper. Time seldom is so scarce but what he can at least "speak up" through a letter of some kind.

These are but a few illustrations of lines of approach which the businessman might consider. They have been suggested as things to do for the good of the community. I'd like to add that they are also things to do for the good of the individual himself.

The company I work for has had some interesting experiences in this respect, in working out a program of helping employees who are approaching retirement to plan the lives they will lead after they quit work. The importance of the security and health aspects of the retirement years

Reduce the Voting Age to 18?

Shall slogan of 'Old enough to fight, old enough to vote,'
prevail over universally accepted age of maturity at 21?

By HENRY J. ABRAHAM*

DURING the first century and a quarter of our existence few, if any, United States citizens seriously concerned themselves with a question that has suddenly become a rather important one of late: should the voting age be lowered from 21 to 18? Actually not until America's entry into the First World War did the matter command more than passing attention. Since the early legislators in the various states had determined upon 21, that seemed quite good enough for those who followed.

Yet, when the first conscription into military service took place in 1917, not only affected soldiers but civic reformers began to advance the currently so frequently heard slogan, "old enough to fight, old enough to vote!" However, although lip service was paid to that cry by many a political campaigner, the states did not act to lower the voting age and the federal government likewise failed to initiate any action. Nevertheless, the issue had been conceived and from that time hence hardly a major election campaign passed which did not feature a clarion call for a lower voting age, with 18 usually pegged as the "magic" number. After all, the extension of the suffrage to youths of 18 to 21 would

increase the electorate by some 7,000,000 potential votes!

The issue diminished somewhat during the 1930s; the country was faced with far more vital problems. Yet it was raised again and with greater fervor than ever with the outbreak of the Second World War which once more saw United States citizen-soldiers under arms. Somehow, however, only one of the states took final action: Under the leadership of wartime Governor Ellis G. Arnall, then at the height of his popularity, Georgia lowered its voting age to 18, a provision that has been in existence in that state ever since. It was widely expected that at least some states would follow suit. Much talk ensued but no action. After the return of our troops the issue again subsided, yet only temporarily. It was renewed during the 1948 campaign, came to the fore again with the advent of the Korean "police action" and, in particular, in anticipation of the 1952 election battles.

By that time powerful private organizations had begun to throw their weight behind the drive to reduce the voting age, among them such strong veteran groups as the American Legion and the Veterans of Foreign Wars. In anticipation of the presidential elections Democratic National Chairmen Boyle and McKinney called for the vote at 18 long prior to the 1952 national conventions; their calls were echoed by Republi-

*Dr. Abraham is assistant professor in political science at the Wharton School of Finance and Commerce, University of Pennsylvania.

11

can Chairman Gabrielson. With the Republican National Convention but a few weeks away, Candidate Eisenhower told reporters in Denver, "I believe if a man is old enough to fight he is old enough to vote." Upon his selection in Chicago, General Eisenhower's new national chairman, Arthur Summerfield, immediately reiterated that stand.

Democrats on Record

Nor were the Democrats to be outdone. On July 1, 1952, Senator Harley Kilgore of West Virginia, ranking member of the Senate Judiciary Committee, introduced a constitutional amendment that would have given voting privileges to all those 18 years of age or over. This constitutional change, which would have applied to both state and federal elections, was approved by the full committee by voice vote and sent to the floor of the Senate where, however, it was lost in the preconvention adjournment rush. In September, Candidate Stevenson was told by a reporter, during a press conference, that his opponent had come out in favor of giving the vote to 18-year-olds. "How do you feel about it?" queried the reporter. "We had that 18-year-old plan in our platform in Illinois in 1948. I was for it then; I am for it now," replied Mr. Stevenson. The latter's newly chosen national chairman, Stephen Mitchell, seconded that sentiment during the campaign.

Unlike earlier experiences, however, the drive to reduce the voting age did not cease with the termination of the presidential campaign. In May 1953 President Eisenhower's new Republican national chairman, Leonard W. Hall, announced that both President Eisenhower and Vice President Nixon had enthusiastically endorsed a proposal by Mr. Hall for an intensified campaign to lower the minimum age from 21 to 18 years.

Mr. Hall declared it was his intention to support "all valid proposals in this direction with every effort at my command." In a press release from the Republican National Committee he stated his belief that youth had been more vigorous than older groups in support of President Eisenhower's victorious campaign—probably a valid contention, if we can adhere to statistical evidence based upon various polls.

Chairman Mitchell of the Democratic National Committee lost no time in pointing out that his party, too, was in favor of the movement. Clearly, the issue was no longer a dormant or latent one.

This brings us to the significant question of how the voting age could be lowered legally. There are two primary methods of accomplishing the desired goal: (1) by action of the federal government; (2) by action of the several state governments. In view of the present constitutional *status quo*, the federal government could bring it about only by virtue of a constitutional amendment, such as the one introduced by Senator Kilgore. The various states could act either by amending their constitutions in accordance with individual requirements or, if such is not called for in the basic document, simply by statute. Most of the states have at least "dabbled" with the problem.

Since 1952-1953 seemed to be an advantageous year for the purpose, and inasmuch as most legislatures of the states meet only in odd years, the writer conducted a survey last fall with the following results:

On the federal level proposed constitutional amendments calling for a lowering of the voting age to 18 for all federal and state elections were introduced in the Committee on the Judiciary in both the Senate and the House of Representatives of the 83rd Congress, which adjourned early in August 1953. While the two measures were accorded bipartisan support in committee, they were not called up for floor action during the session. Presumably they are still "alive" for the second session of the 83rd. In general, there is a feeling among the members of Congress that this is chiefly a state matter which ought to be handled in the same manner as Georgia did a decade ago.

Legislative Proposals

Discussion in many state legislatures was lively, indeed, but when all was said and done no state had followed Georgia's lead completely, although a number had either submitted the question to the people in a referendum or were planning to do so. South Dakota, for example, had a referendum question on the lowering of the voting age to 18 on its 1952 presidential ballot. The people rejected it by the tiny margin of 685 votes out of a total of 257,147 cast on the issue! Oklahoma put the same question to its electorate dur-

ing the November 1952 elections, but it was soundly defeated. Missouri's legislature passed a constitutional amendment last year, authorizing reduction of the voting age to 18, which will be submitted to a referendum in November 1954.

Of the remaining 44 states, 34 considered bills or resolutions during the past three legislative sessions. In the vast majority of these the suggested legislation died in committee pigeonholes of the house where it had been introduced. In a few cases it attained varying degrees of the floor stage—as in Idaho, Indiana, Illinois, Kansas, Massachusetts, Montana, Nebraska, North Dakota, Pennsylvania and Wisconsin—but failed to pass either one or both houses. No gubernatorial vetoes are on record.

What of the merits of reducing the voting age from 21 to 18, the latter apparently having become the figure upon which the proponents of the enfranchisement of now noneligible youth are agreed? The slogan most frequently heard is "Old enough to fight, old enough to vote!" Many a prominent and distinguished personage in public life has resorted to it—viz. Messrs. Eisenhower and Stevenson, as already indicated. The late Senator Arthur E. Vandenberg (Republican—Michigan) commented "If young men are to be drafted at 18 years of age to fight for their government, they ought to be entitled to vote at 18 years of age for the kind of government for which they are best satisfied to fight." Norman Thomas, the venerable Socialist leader, voiced the same opinion and added, "There is certainly no magic in 21 to give wisdom to voters."

Senator Olin D. Johnson (Democrat—South Carolina) volunteered views paralleling those of Senator Vandenberg. Mrs. Eleanor Roosevelt told a press conference during World War II: "If young men are old enough to be trained to fight their country's battles at 18 and 19, and to proceed to the battlefields, I think we must face the fact that they are also old enough to know why we fight this war. If that is so, then they are old enough to take part in the political life of their country and to be full citizens with voting powers." It was chiefly that slogan that prompted Georgia's legislators to lower the voting age.

Reasons for Change

While the equating of the privilege of the franchise with the ability to serve in the armed forces and to fight in battle has been the outstanding sloganization of the issue by far, it has by no means been the only one advanced on the part of proponents. Governor Arnall, for example, in asking the Georgia legislature for the vote at 18 advanced that argument merely as "the third" of three reasons why, in his opinion, young citizens of 18 to 21 should be given the ballot. The first reason mentioned by Mr. Arnall was that their fellow citizens "need their participation in public affairs . . . the fresh viewpoint of these unregimented voters, their idealism." The second was that, in his estimation, it was important that young people "exercise their training in citizenship at the earliest opportune time."

He felt strongly that whereas the student population of senior high school age is "deeply conscious of government and anxious to participate in it," a lapse of three or four years between classroom discussion and the exercise of citizenship "has a tendency to produce inertia in the citizen."

Those who oppose a reduction in the voting age have fastened upon the latter and similar arguments by contending that the gap between the departure from high school and the acquisition of the suffrage does not necessarily result in a loss of interest in government and politics, especially not if such an interest has been effectively developed in the schools in the first place. Moreover, it is pointed out that an ever-increasing percentage of young men and women enter college, where courses in government and politics are frequently mandatory. With respect to Mr. Arnall's emphasis upon the desirability of the "fresh young viewpoint," many opponents feel quite acutely that that viewpoint is in dire need of a bit more seasoning. Indeed, some fear that impulsive youth would be more readily inclined to further radical ends. Others fear that such youthful voters would be too unstable, too inconsistent, psychologically unfit for the ballot. One political figure who requested non-attribution commented, "A shot in the veins from youthful voting would be a shot in the dark."

Of necessity, the opponents have to concentrate their fire on the popular and powerful "old enough to fight, old enough to vote" slogan.

They point out that service to the country in a military capacity, with its demands of physical fitness and discipline, and service by suffrage with its demands upon analysis and reasoning, are hardly the same, and that, by no stretch of the imagination, does military service *ipso facto* qualify participants as voters. They argue that since this is a representative form of government, the fighting soldiers and sailors below the age of 21 can make their voices and influences felt through their elders who elect the legislators. Thus, contend the opponents, the service man is actually represented under our democratic system of government—surely his families will do their utmost to see to it that his legislative wishes are heard and his legislative interests safeguarded.

Tradition Plays Part

Finally, the opponents point to the tradition behind 21 as the accepted minimum voting age·and to its widespread acceptance throughout the world. All major countries commence their suffrage at 21, some even at a higher age limit, although Australia does automatically enfranchise its servicemen and women, but not its non-service 18- to 21-year-olds. They point to its over-all acceptance from the legal point of view, for 21 has, indeed, long been the legal age under common law almost everywhere, including the infant days of this country.

Impartial observers recognize, of course, the potency of the "old enough to fight, old enough to vote" slogan. But they also recognize that it is primarily an emotional issue

which is fraught with dangers of exploitation by political demagoguery, despite the fact that a host of its advocates have nothing but the best of intentions on behalf of the conscripted serviceman. The latter is understandably sensitive about his enforced service and, in the time-honored American tradition, is often inclined to blame his government rather than the enemy for his situation. These observers feel rather strongly that the mere presence of necessary qualifications for military service bears no direct relation upon the privilege of the suffrage. A person's body attains full development long before his mind reaches maturity, if ever.

It is acknowledged that no magic attends the age of 21. Somehow, however, it has been universally accepted in the modern civilized world as the suffrage and legal age limitation. A difference of three years may not be a great deal in the span of a lifetime of some 70 years, yet these three years may well constitute the difference between an impulsive and a more closely reasoned decision. Naturally, there is no magic in 21 and many an 18- or 16-year-old boy or girl is capable of infinitely more sane judgment than a 21- or 40-year-old, for that matter. Yet life is filled with the necessity of "line-drawing"; governmental operations are certainly no exception! Drawing the line at 21 may be no more than a necessary evil—yet, in view of all the arguments advanced and the manifold considerations involved, it would seem to the impartial observer that the line has been drawn with considerable validity.

Tax Rates of American Cities

A majority of the municipalities reporting in 1952 and 1953 have raised both tax rates and assessed valuations.

By THE CITIZENS RESEARCH COUNCIL OF MICHIGAN*

(Formerly Detroit Bureau of Governmental Research)

Copyright 1954 Citizens Research Council of Michigan

THE accompanying table (pages 19-33) is a statement of tax rates as levied against real and personal property in American cities of more than 30,000 population. This 32nd annual tabulation is made possible through the cooperation of city and county officials, governmental research bureaus, chambers of commerce and related organizations. Of the 409 cities polled, 357, or 87 per cent, returned the questionnaires from which the tabulation was made.

Summary Tables I and II indicate changes in assessed valuation and tax rates since 1952. The trend continues upward, as it has ever since the end of World War II.

Assessed valuations were reported for both 1952 and 1953 by 302 cities, tax rates for the two years were reported by 303 cities, in both cases 74 per cent of the total number of cities.

Ninety-one per cent of the cities reported increases in assessed valuations: 51 per cent reported increases of less than 5 per cent, 17 per cent increases of greater than 15 per cent.

A decrease in valuation was reported by 21 cities or 7 per cent.

A decrease in tax rates was indicated by 86 cities and an additional 32 cities did not increase rates during the two-year period. These two groups comprise 39 per cent of the responding cities. Of course, this is in part accounted for by the fact that 91 per cent of the cities increased their valuations. Twenty-seven per cent of the cities reporting increases in assessed valuation indicated a rise of more than 10 per cent in their tax rates.

The tabulation by cities includes for each of those reporting total assessed valuation, the percentage of total valuation represented by personalty, tax rates and the *estimated* ratio of assessed valuation to current market value. The total tax levy has been multiplied by this estimated ratio to provide an estimate of the total rate on the basis of 100 per cent valuation.

The estimate of the ratio of assessed value to current market value is based on the answer of the person submitting the form to the following question: "In your opinion, what per cent of the current market value of real property is the city (county) assessed valuation?" Since the replies are based on the opinion of the correspondent they may be at variance with the opinion of others in the same community.

---

*This article was prepared under the supervision of the council staff by the Lent D. Upson Fellows in public administration, as part of their field training with the Citizens Research Council of Michigan. The compilation and tabulation of the data were done by Donald A. Woolf, Fred F. Jiacoletti, Robert C. Crawford and J. Morris Hickman.

TABLE I
CHANGES IN TOTAL TAX RATE, 1952-1953—303 CITIES

Population Group*	Number of Cities in Group	Total Tax Rate	No Change	Decrease	Number of Cities Reporting Both Years — Increase			
					Total	0-5%	5-10%	Over 10%
I	5	5	1	1	3	2	1	0
II	13	11	0	2	9	4	3	2
III	23	22	5	9	8	3	3	2
IV	66	52	4	11	37	15	14	8
V	127	96	9	25	62	27	18	17
VI	175	117	13	38	66	26	18	22
Totals	409	303	32	86	185	77	57	51
Per Cent of Cities Reporting	100		11	28	61	25	19	17
Per Cent of Cities Reporting Increase					100	42	31	27

TABLE II
CHANGES IN ASSESSED VALUATION, 1952-1953—302 CITIES

Population Group*	Number of Cities in Group	Assessed Valuation	No Change	Decrease	Number of Cities Reporting Both Years — Increase				
					Total	0-5%	5-10%	10-15%	Over 15%
I	5	5	0	1	4	3	1	0	0
II	13	12	0	1	11	7	2	0	2
III	23	21	2	0	21	7	5	2	7
IV	66	51	2	3	46	26	9	4	7
V	127	96	2	12	82	53	17	3	9
VI	175	117		4	111	58	27	5	21
Totals	409	302	6	21	275	154	61	14	46
Per Cent of Cities Reporting	100		2	7	91	51	20	5	15
Per Cent of Cities Reporting Increase					100	56	22	5	17

*Census Bureau groups are used. Group I includes all cities of 1,000,000 and over; Group II, 500,000 to 1,000,000; Group III, 250,000 to 500,000; Group IV, 100,000 to 250,000; Group V, 50,000 to 100,000. Group VI is defined by the Bureau of the Census to include cities between 25,000 and 50,000 but in this study cities under 30,000 are not included.

Variations in this estimate from year to year for a particular city may be caused by the estimate being supplied by different people. This year no 100 per cent estimates were included in the table since experience has shown such estimates are reported primarily because of legal requirements and, generally, no unit of government assesses at 100 per cent of today's market value.

The estimated ratio of assessed valuation to current market value includes both city and county ratios. In those cases where separate assessment by city and county yield different ratios, the percentage reported is a weighted average of the two. It should be noted that the estimated ratio applies only to real property.

Multiplying the assessed valuation by the tax rate to derive the tax levy of a city is not a valid procedure because of varying rates on different classes of property, exemption of certain properties and the fact that special district taxes may affect only part of a city.

Tax collections for 1953 in the 246 cities reporting this figure averaged 96.69 per cent, remaining about the same as last year's figure of 96.40 per cent. The average for property exemptions in the 173 cities reporting was 18.78 per cent.

All tax rate figures reported are based on $1,000 of assessed valuation. Rates levied by special taxing units, such as park, sanitary or water districts, have been classified under the four general headings with footnotes to give necessary explanations.

It should be remembered that tax rates in themselves are not necessarily an index either of quality or quantity of government, nor do they provide an accurate basis of comparison of governmental costs between cities. One explanation for this is that many cities have substantial sources of income other than the property tax.

Although every reasonable precaution has been employed in the compilation of the tables, it is hoped that any errors found, in addition to comments or suggestions thought helpful, will be reported to the Citizens Research Council of Michigan.

(See following pages for tabulation by cities.)

TAX RATES OF AMERICAN CITIES FOR 1953

Compiled by the Citizens Research Council of Michigan from Data Furnished by City Officials and Members of the Governmental Research Association

City	Population 1950	Assessed Value	Per Cent Personalty	Actual Tax Rate as Levied per $1,000 Assessed Valuation					Estimated Ratio of Assessed Value to Current Market Value (Per Cent)	Adjusted Tax Rate On 100% Basis of Assessment
				City	School	County	State	Total		
Group I (1,000,000 or over)										
1 New York, N. Y.*	7857	$19,814,318,222	N	33.30	13.04	3.54	N	33.30	—	—
2 ago, Ill.‡*	6896	8,751,206,468	22	19.40	13.25	N	N	35.98	—	—
3 Philadelphia, Pa.‡*	2,071,605	4,199,533,199	16	17.00	13.25	N	N	30.25	57	17.24
4 Los Angeles, Calif.*	1,970,358	2,919,401,760	22	18.37	24.29	22.90	N	65.55	25	16.39
5 Detroit, Mh.	1,849,568	4,592,304,610	34	18.37 . 2	10.81	6.14	N	39.17	—	—
Group II (500,000–1,000,000)										
6 Baltimore, Md.*	9808	2,712,023,861	34	28.20	—	N	0.60	28.80	75	21.60
7 said, Mo.*	914,808	2,279,164,757	28	15.60	12.30	3.20	0.30	31.40	50	15.70
8 St. luis, M*	6896	1,408,475,835	15	18.10	11.90	N	0.70	30.70	60	18.42
9 ..., D. C.*	802,178	2,204,347,602	18	21.22†	—	—	—	21.22	75	18.9 2
10 Boston, Mass.*	801,444	1,565,666,000	9	51.67	12.50	3.04	3.49	70.70	92	65.04
11 San Francisco, Calif.*	775,357	1,884,884,826	50	45.71	16.99	N	N	62.70	50	31.85
12 Pittsburgh, Pa.*	676,806	1,065,173,432	N	2. 2	11.75	10.38	N	44.35	53	23.50
13 Milwaukee, Wis.*	637,392	1,435,773,145	23	17.58	15.81	18.73	0.38	47.50	52	24.70
14 Houston, Tex.‡*	596,163	1,172,647,660	37	20.00	12.00	12.91	4.20	49.11	28†	18.75
15 Buffalo, N. Y.*	580,132	1,018,780,980	N	22.13	8.27	13.46	N	43.86	70	30.70
16 New Orleans, La.*	570,445	740,027,755	21	21.50	10.00	5.50	5.75	42.75	30	12.83
17 Minneapolis, Minn.	521,718	Not Reported	26	14.62	12.37	4.27	0.30	31.56		
18 ti, Ohio	503,998	1,269,790,040	26	14.62	12.37	4.27	0.30	31.56	55	17.36

N = None.
— = Figures or breakdown not available.
‡ = Data applies to 1952 tax year.
† = Different assessment rat of or ... were reported. The figure shown is the ... average (to the ... integer) of the several ...

* = Footnote indicated by city number.
See also state notes at the end of ...
1 New York, N. Y. ... rate ... are as follows: Manhattan $1.00, Bronx $1.10, Brooklyn $1.40, ... $1.40, Richmond $1.30.
2 Chicago, Ill. City rate includes: library ... $35, TB ... $0.60, poor relief ... $35, park district $3.20, sanitary district $2.76, forest preserve distr ct $0.88.
3 Philadelphia, Pa. Intangible personalty rate is $3.00.
4 Los Angeles, ... rate ... titles $3.41 flood control and $2.50 water district rates. ... personalty taxed at rate of 100, $1.875 and $3.00.
5 Cleveland, Ohio. County rate includes $0.23 for metropolitan park

district. ...Washington, D. C. No ... personalty tax. Realty is taxed at the rate of $21.50. Tangible personalty at $20. Rate listed is an adjusted figure.
6 ..., Md. Ratio of assessed valuation to current ... is as fows: ... 100%, residential 76%, ... 92%, ... district 68%. Based on ... of sales between 1-1-52 and 6-30-52.
7 San Francisco, Calif. ... includes $663,511,365 ... at $1.
8 Pittsburgh, Pa. Separate ... rates are as ... personalty $10, realty, land $32, buildings $16. City rate listed is an adjusted figure.
9 Milwaukee, Wis. County rate ... includes $0.765 metropolitan sewerage districts.
10 Houston, Tex. ... rate includes: flood control $0.83, ... tin $1.01, school equalization $0.10.
11 ..., N. Y. City rate includes $1.13 for sewer authority.
12 New Orleans, La. City rate is ... against 86% of assessed valuation and includes $7.00 debt retirement, $00 sewerage, water and drainage, and $3.00 fire and police ...

City	Census 1950	Assessed Value	Per Cent Personalty	Actual Tax Rate as Levied per $1,000 Assessed Valuation					Estimated Ratio of True and Full Value to Current Market Value (Per Cent)	Adjusted Tax Rate On 100% Basis of Assessment
				City	School	County	State	Total		
Group III (250,000–500,000)										
19 Seattle, Wash.*	467,591	512,045,066	27	19.10	19.50	12.42	2.18	53.20	26	13.83
20 Kansas City, Mo.	456,622	748,297,671	39	15.00	17.80	6.70	0.70	40.20	35†	14.07
21 Newark, N. J.	438,776	700,103,000	—	21.50	18.10	—	N	77.90	48	37.39
22 Dallas, Tex.	434,462	948,209,290	26	23.40	20.80	0.50	4.20	49.40	26†	12.84
23 Indianapolis, Ind.*	427,173	714,287,060	44	23.40	20.80	6.90	1.50	51.60	30	15.48
24 Denver, Colo.*	415,786	872,715,530	33	11.71	23.60	5.74	2.71	43.76	50	21.88
25 San Antonio, Tex.	408,442	514,899,220	26	22.50	12.68	10.30	4.20	49.68	35†	17.39
26 Memphis, Tenn.	396,000	634,834,428	15	11.50	6.50	10.50	N	28.50	40	11.40
27 Oakland, Calif.*	384,575	429,528,490	9	31.12	23.78	23.70	N	78.60	50	39.30
28 Columbus, Ohio	375,901	747,215,950	22	5.34	11.86	3.50	0.30	20.40	50	10.20
29 Portland, Ore.*	373,628	642,925,735	25	19.80	22.20	11.50	N	53.50	30	16.05
30 Louisville, Ky.‡*	369,129	661,516,862	41	16.00	16.00	5.00	0.50	35.50	40	14.20
31 San Diego, Calif.*	334,387	615,114,965	—	17.40	19.80	20.70	N	57.90	30	17.37
32 Rochester, N. Y.	332,448	689,276,037	N	19.69	11.51	13.41	N	44.61	50	22.31
33 Atlanta, Ga.	331,314		39	26.00		22.75		47.75	—	
34 Birmingham, Ala.	326,037	358,972,529	32	11.50	6.50	11.50	6.50	36.00	40	14.40
35 St. Paul, Minn.	311,349	Not Reported								
36 Toledo, Ohio‡	303,616	739,313,390	27	3.45	13.48	3.17	0.30	20.40	33	6.73
37 Jersey City, N. J.	299,017	490,368,000	17					74.50	56	41.72
38 Fort Worth, Tex.*	278,778	509,229,060	27	19.90	11.00	8.50	7.20	46.60	43	20.04
39 Akron, Ohio‡*	274,605	619,000,000	23	10.87	14.98	3.15	0.30	29.30	50	14.65
40 Omaha, Neb.*	251,111	512,539,426	27	14.60	18.85	2.75	8.04	44.24	60	26.54
41 Long Beach, Calif.*	250,767	431,069,880	22	18.84	26.72	16.99	N	62.55	30	18.77
Group IV (100,000–250,000)										
42 Miami, Fla.*	249,276	440,216,810	28	23.76	17.50	11.50	N	52.76		
43 Providence, R. I.	248,674	855,873,275	45	31.00	N	N	N	31.00	70	21.70
44 Honolulu, T.H.	248,340	486,823,477	N	—	—	—	—	16.33	60	9.80
45 Dayton, Ohio	243,872	Not Reported								
46 Oklahoma City, Okla.	243,504	246,882,969	18	20.01	29.62	8.88	N	58.51	22	12.87
47 Richmond, Va.	230,310	614,625,039	16	22.00	—	—	—	22.00	72	15.84

* = Footnote indicated by city.

See also state notes at the end of tabulation.

†**Seattle, Wash.** City rate includes $3.00 for port authority.
Indianapolis, Ind. City rate includes $0.54 for township.
Oakland, Calif. City rate includes: water and sewer, $3.00; park, and flood control, $0.717.
Portland, Ore. City rate includes $2.60 port of Portland rate.
Louisville, Ky. State rate for tangible only is $5.00.
Fort Worth, Tex. City rate includes $3.20 for water district.

‡**Akron, Ohio.** City rate includes $0.256 for metropolitan park district.
Omaha, Neb. Intangible personalty total of $184,052,814 is not included. Intangible personalty rates are as follows: money $2.50, stocks and bds $3.00. School rate includes $1.60 for Omaha University. City rate includes $0.40 for utilities.
Long Beach, Calif. City rate includes $2,500 metropolitan water authority, $3,411 flood control district and $1,724 sanitation district.
Miami, Fla. City rate includes $1.00 drainage rate.

#	City	Census 1950	Assessed Value	Per Cent Personalty	Actual Tax Rate as Levied per $1,000 Assessed Valuation					Estimated Ratio of Assessed Value to Current Market Value (Per Cent)	Adjusted Tax Rate On 100% Basis of Assessment
					City	School	County	State	Total		
48	Syracuse, N. Y.	220,583	374,984,018	5	29.48	—	17.44	N	46.92	70	32.84
49	Norfolk, Va.	213,513	Not Reported		11.70	—				50	—
50	Jacksonville, Fla.	204,517	215,139,200	29						50	—
51	Worcester, Mass.	203,486	331,255,700	7	31.90	16.40	1.63	0.07	50.00	70	35.00
52	Tulsa, Okla.	182,740	238,872,756	15	12.41	32.68	7.98	N	53.07	25	13.27
53	Salt Lake City, Utah*	182,121	220,633,476	28	20.55	25.35	8.90	3.60	58.40	19	11.10
54	Des Moines, Iowa	177,965	201,410,460	22	27.56	44.60	14.23	0.47	86.86	26	22.59
55	Hartford, Conn.*	177,397	533,772,000	29	24.00	13.28	0.72	N	38.00	—	—
56	Grand Rapids, Mich.	176,515	Not Reported	21	22.00	—	20.00	N	42.00	50	21.00
57	Nashville, Tenn.	174,307	272,113,136	27	4.70	16.20	3.00	0.30	24.20	50	12.10
58	Youngstown, Ohio*	168,330	388,820,217	52	22.95	23.08	17.06	1.51	64.60	18	11.63
59	Wichita, Kan.*	168,279	363,087,294	30	21.46	13.49	0.55	N	35.50	50	17.75
60	New Haven, Conn.	164,443	406,628,893								
61	Flint, Mich.	163,143	376,494,070	23	10.00	16.60	5.90	N	32.50	48	15.60
62	Springfield, Mass.	162,399	327,488,108	12	31.51	18.29	N	N	49.80	44	19.36
63	Spokane, Wash.	161,721	160,834,107	26	16.60	17.10	8.00	2.30	44.00	44	19.36
64	Bridgeport, Conn.*	158,709	377,953,370	40	26.38	10.46	0.26	N	37.10		
65	Yonkers, N. Y.	152,793	370,148,625	N	36.96	—	—	—	36.96	60	22.18
66	Tacoma, Wash.*	143,673	108,183,878	—	19.65	23.30	23.25	2.23	68.43	23	15.74
67	Paterson, N. J.‡	139,336	193,044,705	12	22.28	24.46	9.96	N	56.70	43	24.38
68	Sacramento, Calif.‡*	137,572	234,790,840	27	21.30	25.60	21.50	N	68.40	53†	36.25
69	Albany, N. Y.‡	134,995	287,058,449	N	20.05	10.24	15.51	N	45.80	90	41.22
70	Charlotte, N. C.	134,042	357,508,540	34	10.69	4.11	—	—	14.80	50	7.40
71	Gary, Ind.‡*	133,911	188,980,910	49	26.80	27.90	7.20	1.50	63.40	30	19.02
72	Fort Wayne, Ind.*	133,607	235,500,000	45	21.80	18.30	7.40	1.50	49.00	27	13.23
73	Austin, Tex.*	132,459	—		19.90	10.20	10.30	4.20	44.60	35†	15.61
74	Chattanooga, Tenn.	131,041	194,266,744	11	19.20	—	20.40	N	39.60	35	13.86
75	Erie, Pa.	130,803	380,051,310	10	6.50	8.00	10.00	N	24.50	76†	18.62
76	El Paso, Tex.	130,485	204,816,670	31	17.50	13.20	9.50	4.20	44.40	38†	16.87
77	Kansas City, Kan.	129,553	—	46	35.16	34.71	11.37	1.51	82.75	15	12.41
78	Mobile, Ala.	129,009	Not Reported								

* = Footnote indicated by city number. See also state notes at the end of tabulation. City rate includes $1.75 water levy and $0.30 mosquito abatement levy.

[53] Salt Lake City, Utah. City rate includes $1.21 metropolitan district rate and $0.67 civic institutions rate.

[55] Hartford, Conn. City rate includes $0.10 for township.

[57] Youngstown, Ohio. City rate includes $0.10 for township.

[59] Wichita, Kan. Intangible personalty is taxed at 0.5%. City rate includes $4.609 for municipal university.

[64] Bridgeport, Conn. City rate includes $2.37 levy for welfare and $2.39 for debt service.

[66] Tacoma, Wash. County rate includes $3.00 port of Tacoma rate and $10.25 metropolitan park rate.

[68] Sacramento, Calif. City rate includes $.50 mosquito abatement, $.50 port district and $.40 flood control rates.

[71] Gary, Ind. City rate includes $3.37 township, $1.40 library rate and $1.56 sanitary district rates.

[72] Fort Wayne, Ind. City rate includes $1.50 poor relief and $1.70 library rates.

City	Census 1960	Assessed Value	Per Cent Personalty	Actual Tax Rate as Levied per $1,000 Assessed Valuation					Estimated Ratio of Assessed Value to Current Market Value (Per Cent)	Adjusted Tax Rate On 100% Basis of Assessment
				City	School	County	State	Total		
79 Evansville, Ind.*	128,636	177,750,220	44	22.90	24.10	6.50	1.50	55.00	28	15.40
80 Trenton, N. J.	128,009	176,557,268	19	29.18	26.22	12.14	N	67.54	43	29.04
81 Shreveport, La.	127,206	203,160,310	35	16.75	13.60	4.90	—	16.75	60	10.05
82 Baton Rouge, La.*	125,629	143,713,465	20	11.70	24.50	15.75	5.75	35.95	34	12.22
83 Scranton, Pa.*	125,536	98,107,158	N	25.92†	—	25.20	N	66.17	40	26.47
84 Knoxville, Tenn.	124,769	216,503,234	30	26.40	—	—	N	51.60	53†	27.35
85 Tampa, Fla.*	124,681	219,208,729	22	22.55	19.55	17.40	N	59.50	70	41.65
86 Camden, N. J.	124,555	146,708,000	9	36.45	12.15	—	N	69.20	35	24.22
87 Cambridge, Mass.	120,740	213,340,500	—	26.00	—	—	—	48.60	88	9.88
88 Savannah, Ga.	119,638	161,941,627	26		17.80	2.60	0.30	26.00	50	12.10
89 Canton, Ohio*	116,912	201,966,710	30	3.50	19.00	7.10	1.50	24.20	33	14.98
90 South Bend, Ind.	115,911	205,124,780	—	17.80	19.00			45.40		
91 Berkeley, Calif.*	118,805	142,586,105	13	17.90	26.88	28.12	N	72.90	52	37.91
92 Elizabeth, N. J.	112,817	146,825,000	—	37.41	—	—	N	71.60	37	26.49
93 Fall River, Mass.	111,963	124,440,350	12	9.87	16.39	—	N	53.80	—	—
94 Peoria, Ill.*	111,856	398,377,757	30		9.75	1.38	N	21.00	—	—
95 Wilmington, Del.	110,356	196,153,800	N	19.18	5.33	6.50	N	31.00	50	16.50
96 Reading, Pa.	109,320	145,670,550	N	14.00	19.50	8.00	N	41.50	40	15.60
97 New Bedford, Mass.	109,189	129,949,675	16	40.07	10.73	—	N	50.80	50	25.40
98 Corpus Christi, Tex.	108,287	173,908,090	23	18.00	18.00	15.00	4.20	55.20	35	19.32
99 Phoenix, Ariz.	106,818	133,762,206	26	18.50	45.40	10.80	10.00	84.70	29	24.56
100 Allentown, Pa.	106,756	202,880,970	N	9.00	14.00	7.00	N	30.00	50	15.00
101 Montgomery, Ala.	106,525	75,437,272	29	12.50	3.00	8.00	N	15.50	20	8.10
102 Pasadena, Calif.*	104,577	262,569,385	12	10.80	26.70	21.81	N	59.31	55	32.62
103 Duluth, Minn.*	104,511	52,957,679	23	51.58	68.92	40.05	6.49	167.04	25	41.76
104 Waterbury, Conn.	104,477	284,065,152	35	36.00	—	—	N	36.00	55	19.80
D5 Somerville, Mass.	102,351	130,714,000	6	36.89	18.41	—	N	55.30	—	—
D6 Edle Cek,	102,218	74,126,066	30	11.80	32.00	8.00	N	51.80	13	6.73
107 Utia, N. Y.	0&31	156,360,644	N	24.80	13.97	16.07	N	54.84	—	—

* = Footnote edited by city.
See also state taxes at the end of tabulation.
79 Evansville, Ind. City rate includes $0.45 tuberculosis hospital rate, $.15 library rate and $1.40 township rate.
83 Baton Rouge, La. City rate ... sewer tax by districts ranging from $3.50 to $6.00, and garbage tax by districts ranging from $3.50 to $5.00. The rate as listed in the table includes the lower rate.
85 Scranton, Pa. City rate includes $6.25 ... rate.
City rate is a ... average of $37 ... rate and $21.15 building rate.

85 Tampa, Fla. City rate includes $0.20 navigation district rate and $0.50 port district rate.
88 ... Mo. City rate includes $.10 township rate.
91 Berkeley, Calif. City rate includes $3.70 utility district, $.53 park and $3.18 ... rates.
94 Peoria, Ill. City rate includes $.97 township, $.68 library district, $1.16 park and $.27 airport rate.
102 Pasadena, Calif. County tax rate includes $3.411 flood control and $1.411 sanitation district taxes.
106 Duluth, Mn. County rate includes $1.879 county school rate.

	City	Census 1950	Assessed Value	Per Cent Personalty	Actual Tax Rate as Levied per $1,000 Assessed Valuation: City	School	County	State	Total	Assessed Ratio of Assessed Value to Current Market Value (Per Cent)	Adjusted Tax Rate On 100% Basis of Assessment
	Group V (50,000-100,000)										
108	Lynn, Mass.	99,738	140,775,310	11	41.63	17.17	—	N	58.80	75	44.10
109	Richmond, Calif.*	99,545	101,446,340	26	25.40	36.94	23.84	N	86.18	25	21.55
110	Lincoln, Neb.*	98,884	135,901,747	20	14.80	27.88	4.00	7.03	53.71	50	26.86
111	Jackson, Miss.	98,271	156,950,184	23	16.50	19.00	14.29	2.00	51.79	23	11.91
112	Lowell, Mass.	97,249	110,319,900	10	42.74	15.06	—	N	57.80	—	—
113	Albuquerque, N. M.	96,815	Not Reported								
114	St. Petersburg, Fla.*	96,738	296,730,909	7	18.15	—	18.50	—	36.65	60	21.99
115	Madison, Wis.	96,056	277,069,045	20	9.20	15.62	6.91	0.27	32.00	75	24.00
116	Glendale, Calif.*	95,702	153,783,000	17	11.30	25.87	20.40	N	57.57	50	28.79
117	San Jose, Calif.‡*	95,280	114,509,920	19	17.36	29.07	18.14	N	64.57	40	28.84
118	Dearborn, Mich.	94,994	437,226,780	46	15.29	20.00	6.52	N	41.81	32	13.38
119	Beaumont, Tex.	94,014	Not Reported								
120	Rockford, Ill.*	92,927	345,480,540	28	8.37	10.28	1.26	N	19.91	50	9.96
121	Saginaw, Mich.*	92,918	174,203,850	25	13.20	13.81	5.19	N	32.20	40	12.88
122	Lansing, Mich.	92,129	196,757,440	36	18.70	18.12	6.33	N	43.15	23	9.92
123	Roanoke, Va.	91,921	145,952,641	24	27.40	—	—	—	27.40	35	9.59
124	Schenectady, N. Y.	91,785	177,235,305	N	25.05	17.23	9.86	N	52.14	—	—
125	Fresno, Calif.*	91,669	121,024,085	18	21.27	28.03	14.02	N	63.31	40	25.32
126	Niagara Falls, N. Y.	90,872	180,523,790	3	21.52	17.55	10.34	N	49.41	—	—
127	Harrisburg, Pa.	89,544	120,644,260	N	14.50	19.00	9.00	N	42.50	62	26.35
128	Winston-Salem, N. C.	87,811	210,831,368	44	16.50	3.50	7.00	N	27.00	50	13.50
129	Hammond, Ind.*	87,594	129,732,685	—	24.40	35.55	7.60	1.50	69.05	—	—
130	Columbia, S. C.	86,914	Not Reported								
131	Huntington, W. Va.*	86,353	184,772,070	43	6.10	13.77	4.86	0.10	24.83	30	7.45
132	Waco, Tex.	84,706	141,259,380	31	15.50	15.00	—	N	30.50	50	15.25
133	Sioux City, Iowa	83,991	99,326,235	17	25.45	36.29	13.89	0.47	76.11	27	20.55
134	Quincy, Mass.	83,835	154,964,700	6	50.80	—	—	N	50.80	40	20.32
135	Manchester, N. H.	82,732	128,510,974	27	42.81	0.95	3.24	N	47.00	80	37.60
136	East St. Louis, Ill.‡*	82,295	179,659,748	23	13.70	13.70	2.40	N	29.80	70	20.86

* = [illegible]te indicated by city [illegible]er.

See also state [illegible]es at the end of tabulation.

[109]Richmond, Calif. City rate includes $2.69 sewer district and $2.14 hospital district rates.

[110]Lincoln, Neb. City rate includes $2.00 sanitary district rate.

[114]St. Petersburg, Fla. City rate varies from $16.05 to $18.15 in 4 districts.

[116]Glendale, Calif. City rate includes $.11 flood control rate.

[117]San Jose, Calif. City rate includes $0.48 flood control district rate. Additional tax on land only of $7.54 for Santa Clara Valley water conservation district.

[120]Rockford, Ill. City rate includes $1.52 township, $.76 sanitary district, $.42 park district and $.59 airport rates.

[121]Saginaw, Mich. City rate includes $3.20 debt service and school rate includes $4.00 school debt service.

[125]Fresno, Calif. City rate includes $.575 mosquito abatement and $1.156 library rates.

[129]Hammond, Ind. City rate includes $1.05 township, $2.96 sanitary district and $1.35 library rates.

[131]Huntington, W. Va. City rate includes $.60 park board rate.

[136]East St. Louis, Ill. City rate includes $1.055 township, $.50 health district, $3.30 sanitary district and $2.38 park district rates.

	City	Census 1950	Assessed Value	Per Cent Personalty	Actual Tax Rate as Levied per $1,000 Assessed Valuation					Estimated Ratio of Assessed Value to Current Market Value (Per cent)	Adjusted Tax Rate On 100% Basis of Assessment
					City	School	County	State	Total		
137	Newton, Mass.	81,994	226,344,950	5	27.88	16.12	—	N	44.00	—	—
138	Springfield, Ill.‡*	81,628	231,974,388	18	9.17	11.78	2.45	N	23.40	—	25.20
139	Pawtucket, R. I.*	81,436	210,254,690	35	36.00	N	N	N	36.00	70	25.20
140	Binghamton, N. Y.	80,674	126,069,017	N	27.24	16.54	7.96	N	50.74	60	30.44
141	Lawrence, Ma.	80,536	90,714,300	10	34.16	19.84	—	N	54.00	—	—
142	Portsmouth, Va.	()89	63,116,925	7	26.00	—	—	N	26.00	50	12.60
143	? 5lb, Ga.	79,611	84,943,066	25	16.00	—	—	N	16.00	80	4.80
144	East Orange, N. J.	79,340	2648	10	26.00	21.87	11.14	N	58.00	50	29.00
145	?a, Kan.*	78,791	6852	40	29.47	19.95	10.11	1.51	61.04	23	14.04
146	?ark, Calif.*	78,577	174,156,770	40	15.30	29.35	20.40	N	65.05	35	22.77
147	St. Joseph, Mo.	78,588	73,130,500	32	8.5D	19.30	8.80	0.70	47.30	45	21.29
148	Springfield, Mo.*	78,508			5.70	18.20	2.60	0.30	26.80		
149	?dd, Me.*	77,684	102,631,800	30	37.07	16.82	1.71	N	55.60	60	33.36
150	Bayonne, N. J.	77,203	148,060,000	—	—	—	—	—	77.00	56	43.12
151	Altoona, Pa.‡	77,177	75,000,000	N	12.00	18.00	14.00	N	44.00	51†	22.51
152	Wilkes-Barre, Pa.*	76,826	83,216,501	6	18.00	21.00	11.20	N	50.20	47†	23.59
153	Davenport, Iowa‡	74,599	87,385,337	15	29.00	31.80	12.19	0.48	73.46	20	14.69
154	Greensboro, N. C.	74,389	Not Reported								
155	Stamford, Conn.*	74,293	268,961,599	24	36.70	N	N	N	36.70	65	23.86
156	Amarillo, Tex.	74,246	Not Reported								
157	New Britain, Conn.	73,726	Not Reported								
158	Pontiac, Mich.	73,681	174,997,185	34	13.80	14.20	5.76	N	33.76	75	25.32
159	Evanston, Ill.‡*	73,641	218,979,505	8	15.82	15.05	4.30	N	35.17	60	21.10
160	Charleston, W. Va.	73,501	187,148,100	49	4.44	12.17	3.92	0.07	20.60	25	4.12
161	?by, N. Y.	72,311	Not Reported								
162	Cedar ?, ?	72,296	110,742,563	27	27.38	39.03	9.02	0.48	74.91	60	44.95
163	Mount ?mn, N. Y.*	7899	9850	5	18.45	20.37	8.55	N	47.37	70	33.16
E4	Lubbock, Tex.	71,747	Not Reported								
165	Santa Monica, Calif.*	7495	128,825,545	31	21.00	23.07	20.40	N	64.47	45	29.01

* = Footnote ? ?d by city number.
See ?wo state notes at the end of tabulation.

138Springfield, Ill. City rate includes $1.32 sanitary district and $.60 airport ?ax.
140Topeka, Kan. City rate includes $3.92 municipal university rate and $.45 city library rate. ?u6ity ?ate includes ?51 ?nty elementary school rate.
?46?k, Calif. County rate includes $3.41 ?d control rate. No assessed valuation reported. City rate includes $0.03 township ?ax.
149Portland, Me. City rate ? ?udes $3.84 ?ebt service and $3.88 capital ? ?ght rates.

?ap, $.59 park, $.54

152Wilkes-Barre, Pa. County rate includes $3.00 institution district rate.
159Stamford, Conn. The city is divided into three districts with respective rates of 6.80, $31.50 and $27.10. The amount varies according to the ?ber of municipal services in each district. II Four school districts have different rates causing variation in the total rate as follows: $34.72, $234 and 382, for the ?wo districts.
162Mount Vernon, N. Y. City rate includes $1.57 ?blic library ?ate.
205Santa ?ica, ?lif. City rate includes $2.60 metropolitan water district ?te. County ?te includes $3.41 ?d control rate.

City	Census 1950	Assessed Value	Per Cent Personalty	Actual Tax Rate as Levied per $1,000 Assessed Valuation					Estimated Ratio of Assessed Value to Current Market Value (Per Cent)	Adjusted Tax Rate On 100% Basis of Assessment
				City	School	County	State	Total		
166 Augusta, Ga.	71,608	Not Reported								
167 Durham, N. C.	71,311	Not Reported								
168 Racine, Wis.‡	71,193	154,942,285	22	12.96	19.06	7.69	0.42	40.13	50	20.07
169 Stockton, Calif.	70,853	95,873,200	16	25.00			N	25.00	28	7.00
170 Macon, Ga.‡	70,262	74,748,000	40	3.0●			N	13.00	33	4.33
171 Charleston, S. C.	70,174	22,851,496	39	62.00	88.00	24.00	—	124.00	8	9.92
172 Lakewood, Ohio‡	68,071	149,341,707	10	9.10	13.90	3.20	0.30	26.50	50	13.25
173 Wichita Falls, Tex.*	68,042	93,192,810	40	19.50	17.90	7.00	4.20	48.60	33†	16.04
174 Cicero, Ill.‡*	67,544	210,139,894	30	14.10	14.48	3.54	N	32.12	—	
175 Springfield, Mo.*	66,731	62,929,261	32	16.50	26.50	7.80	0.70	50.50	20	10.10
176 Galveston, Tex.	66,568	Not Reported	N							
177 Bethlehem, Pa.*	66,340	82,814,108	22	17.50	17.50	9.00	N	44.00	34	14.96
178 Decatur, Ill.‡	66,229	179,281,374	6	8.81	15.40	0.99	N	25.20	60	15.12
179 Medford, Mass.	66,113	97,424,200	N	31.14	19.66	—	N	50.80	—	
180 Chester, Pa.	66,039	67,843,548		19.15	22.00	6.50	N	47.65	51†	24.30
181 Raleigh, N. C.	65,679	Not Reported								
182 Waterloo, Iowa	65,198	94,915,928	19	23.82	28.79	7.24	0.48	60.32	50	30.16
183 Clifton, N. J.	64,511	95,981,450	10	16.60	28.30	10.00	N	54.90	75	41.18
184 Covington, Ky.	64,462	76,056,093	11	16.80	14.70	N	N	31.50	60	18.90
185 Alameda, Calif.	64,430	49,830,640	17	19.30	N	54.20	N	73.50	24†	17.64
186 Terre Haute, Ind.*	64,214	77,382,430	43	25.00	26.60	9.90	1.50	63.00	33	21.00
187 Lancaster, Pa.	63,774	102,778,750	N	9.50	15.50	4.00	N	29.00	51†	14.79
188 Pueblo, Colo.‡	63,685	64,862,500	14	29.54	27.01	6.30	2.71	65.55	40	26.22
189 Oak Park, Ill.‡	63,529	177,047,111	2	12.68	17.20	3.54	N	33.42	—	
190 Johnstown, Pa.‡	63,232	73,223,815	N	5.0●	19.00	9.00	N	43.00	56†	24.08
191 San Bernardino, Calif.*	63,058	68,334,430	13	15.40	39.40	20.60	N	75.40	23	17.34
192 Brockton, Mass.	62,860	83,749,550	10	37.01	17.59	—	N	54.60	—	
193 Alexandria, Va.*	61,787	135,000,000	26	28.15	N	N	N	8.35†	30	8.45
194 Atlantic City, N. J.	61,657	96,037,207	9	40.20	23.00	18.70	N	81.90	31	25.39
195 York, Pa.	59,963	123,850,000	N	7.00	13.50	9.50	N	30.00	55†	16.50

* = ● ●te edited by city ●●●.
See also state ●●●s at the end of tabulation.
[170]Macon, Ga. No school or county rates were reported.
[169]Wta Falls, ●●. City rate inlud● $3.50 water district rates.
School rate ●●● $3.90 junior college rate. ●●● rdam, $1.68
park district, $2.76 sanitary district and ●● valuation reported. County
[175]Springfield, Mo. No ●●al ass ●● valuation reported. County
rate includes $3.50 road and bridge and $4.30 general revenue rates.
[177]Bethlehem, Pa. The city lies in two ●des. The rate ●led is

for Northampton ●ty; Lehigh ●ty rate is $7. ●as.
[178]Decatur, Ill. City rate includes $4.23 township ●as.
●●n, Ky. City rate ●des $1.47 for bond and sinking
fund.
[186]Terre Haute, Ind. City rate ●des $1.50 ●hip rate.
[184]●●●o, ●lo. City rate includes $6.78 special ●●●.
[191]San Bernardino, Calif. ●●ty rate ●des $1.80 flood control
rate.
[193]Alexandria, Va. The city rate is a weighted average of a $27.50
levy on real ●tate and $30 on ●●l property.

	City	Census 1950	Assessed Value	Per Cent Personalty	Actual Tax Rate as Levied per $1,000 Assessed Valuation					Estimated Ratio of Assessed Value to Current Market Value (Per Cent)	Adjusted Tax Rate On 100% Basis of Assessment
					City	School	County	State	Total		
196	Malden, Mass.	59,804	98,563,650	10	39.35	16.65	N	N	56.00	67	31.62
197	New Rochelle, N. Y.	59,725	179,200,355	N	21.80	16.60	8.90	N	47.20	48	33.50
198	Irvington, N. J.	59,201	83,887,000	N	7.80	18.50	3.20	0.30	69.80	—	—
199	Cleveland Heights, Ohio‡	59,141	156,938,688	N	11.00	23.70	14.30	1.00	29.80	—	—
200	Wheeling, W. Va.	58,891	170,769,625	38					50.00	—	—
201	Muncie, Ind.*	58,479	70,601,255	—	20.20	31.50	4.80	1.50	58.00	33	19.14
202	Greenville, S. C.*	58,161	21,707,275	51	63.00		19.00		82.00	5	4.10
203	Hamilton, Ohio	57,951	130,188,580	26	5.55	14.49	2.55	.30	22.89	50	11.45
204	Kalamazoo, Mich.	57,704	120,281,800	37	10.90	20.41	5.00	N	36.31	38	13.80
205	Passaic, N. J.	57,702	95,300,138	20	24.70	25.10	10.00	N	59.80	60	35.88
206	Brookline, Mass.	57,589	162,445,800	5	28.80	12.20	—	N	41.00	50	9.00
207	Port Arthur, Tex.‡	57,530	79,999,860	19	18.00			N	18.00	25	15.79
208	Ogden, Utah*	57,112	54,697,168	25	20.25	30.40	8.90	3.60	63.15	23	8.28
209	Gadsden, Ala.*	55,725	47,508,421	28	10.00	3.00	15.50	7.50	36.00	56	48.83
210	Union City, N. J.	55,537	65,971,000	—				N	87.20	—	
211	Lexington, Ky.	55,534	81,636,160	22	14.60	12.70	5.00	N	32.30	48†	5.50
212	Cranston, R. I.	55,060	148,983,360	84	80.00		N	N	30.00	70	21.00
213	Holyoke, Mass.	54,661	85,436,460	6	81.82	11.18	N	N	43.00	55	23.65
214	Kenosha, Wis.*	54,368	100,064,430	16	13.57	24.68	15.32	0.43	54.00	50	27.00
215	East Chicago, Ind.	54,263	Not Reported								
216	Pittsfield, Mass.	53,348	104,163,380	8	25.62	16.65	2.42	0.31	45.00	50	22.50
217	Asheville, N. C.	53,000	Not Reported								
218	Green Bay, Wis.*	52,735	9,200,000	18	9.00	17.52	8.25	0.87	35.14	51	17.92
219	Sioux Falls, S. D.	52,696	77,498,635	23	22.21	28.10	6.06	N	56.37	35	19.73
220	Bay City, Mich.*	52,523	72,528,515	30	22.48	13.50	6.25	N	42.23	40	16.89
221	Orlando, Fla.	52,367	99,468,875	21	16.00	33.80	N	N	49.80	65	32.87
222	San Angelo, Tex.*	52,093	66,129,125	26	5.50	17.50	8.00	7.20	48.20	40†	19.28
223	Laredo, Tex.	51,910	81,405,558	N	24.10	17.00	N	N	41.10	80	32.88
224	Joliet, Ill.‡	51,601	145,551,001	25	8.26	18.27	1.68	N	28.21	—	—
225	McKeesport, Pa.	51,502	Not Reported								
226	Alhambra, Calif.*	51,359	30,561,780	12	11.95	26.17	21.81	N	59.93	35	20.98

* = Footnote cited by city number.
See also state rate notes at the end of tabulation.
The rate is given for Class #1.

200Wheeling, W. Va. The rate varies for different classes of property.
201Muncie, Ind. City rate includes $0.70 township and $1.80 library tax.
202Greenville, S. C. City rate includes $6.00 debt service and $2.00 library tax.
208Ogden, Utah. City includes $1.75 rate for special assessments.
209Gadsden, Ala. City rate includes $4.00 county school rate.

214Kenosha, Wis. City rate includes $1.35 township rate.
218Green Bay, Wis. City rate includes $1.52 metropolitan sewer district rate.
220Bay City, Mich. City rate includes $2.50 sewage disposal rate.
222San Angelo, Tex. School rate includes $2.60 college rate.
224Joliet, Ill. City rate includes $1.82 township, $1.10 park district and $0.05 forest preserve rates.
226Alhambra, Calif. County rate includes $3.41 flood control and $1.41 sanitation district rates.

	City	Census 1950	Assessed Value	Per Cent Personalty	Actual Tax Rate as Levied per $1,000 Assessed Valuation					Estimated Ratio of Assessed Value to Current Market Value (Per Cent)	Adjusted Tax Rate On 100% Basis of Assessment
					City	School	County	State	Total		
227	Berwyn, Ill.‡*	51,280	102,865,101	9	12.24	16.08	3.54	N	81.86	80	—
228	Lorain, Ohio*	51,202	172,711,835	N	7.39	12.49	2.36	0.30	22.54	25	8.03
229	South Gate, Calif.*	51,116	55,418,230	28	11.70	24.29	28.87	N	59.86	25	14.97
230	Jackson, Mich.	51,088	111,678,500	34	10.70	16.57	6.37	N	33.64	40	8.45
231	Hoboken, N. J.	50,676	80,919,000	21	9.79	15.62	1.18	N	85.20	56	47.71
232	Aurora, Ill.‡*	50,576	144,233,009		—	—	—	—	26.59	73	9.41
233	Lima, Ohio	50,246	Not Reported								
234	Woonsocket, R. I.	50,211	96,161,800	35	30.00	N	N	N	80.00	60	8.09
	Group VI (30,000-50,000)										
235	Warren, Ohio	49,866	117,682,842	21	—	—	—	—	—	75	—
236	Elmira, N. Y.	49,716	Not Reported								
237	Dubuque, Iowa	49,671	Not Reported								
238	Norwalk, Conn.*	49,460	125,688,590	24	23.63	15.98	0.29	—	39.90	50	19.95
239	Bloomfield, N. J.	49,307	86,683,000	—	—	—	—	—	56.90	48	27.31
240	Chicopee, Mass.	49,211	54,464,380	6	42.27	13.73	—	—	56.00	—	—
241	New Castle, Pa.	48,834	53,184,310	N	4.09	20.00	2.94	N	34.00	35	11.90
242	Rock Island, Ill.‡*	48,710	124,957,848	31	9.03	12.49	5.25	N	24.46	—	—
243	Battle Creek, Mich.	48,666	132,758,260	34	8.80	18.75	5.98	N	27.80	—	—
244	Muskegon, Mich.*	48,428	116,934,500	37	11.40	14.25	—	N	31.63	50	15.82
245	Ann Arbor, Mich.	48,251	Not Reported								
246	Compton, Calif.	47,991	49,830,690	18	13.65	36.16	25.49	—	75.31	30	22.59
247	Fort Smith, Ark.	47,942		—	10.75	32.00	9.00	—	51.75	18	6.73
248	Lynchburg, Va.*	47,727	77,697,848	17	2.09	11.50	—	—	23.50	49	11.52
249	LaCrosse, Wis.*	47,535	86,648,940	18	11.84	17.70	12.10	0.86	42.00	51†	21.42
250	Haverhill, Mass.	47,280	70,645,200	18	3.45	11.35	—	—	42.80	—	—
251	Waltham, Ms.	47,187	74,888,200	8	85.98	15.42	—	—	51.40	27	16.86
252	Royal Ok, Mh.	46,898	69,117,723	12	21.50	29. Q	10.00	—	60.60	33	8.03
253	Anderson, Ih*	46,820	61,404,365	48	21.10	25.20	6.80	1.50	54.60	—	—

* = Footnote did by city number.
See also state notes at the end of tabulation.

²²⁷Berwyn, Ill. City rate ...udes $1.42 ... phic ...th and ... ben-losis sanitarium, $0.78 ... tary district, $0.38 forest preserve, ...and $0.90 park district rates. School district rates vary between districts.

...in, Ohio. City rate ...udes $0.12 ... Imp, $2.59 bond re...., ()43 park and recreation and $0.60 police and fire pension rates.

²²⁹South ...te, ...lif. ... u...ty rate i... kes ...677 ... ther district rates.

²³⁰Aurora, Ill. City rate includes $0.72 ... Imp, $1.05 road and bridge ...xs, and $92 levy for fest preserve, ...tary district and

park district. District 181 has ...tal tax rate of $24.72.

²³⁸Norwalk, Conn. City ...ate includes $9.30 ...ther district ...xn.

²³⁹Rock Island, Ill. City rate ...udes $0.30 township and $0.95 air-port rates.

²⁴⁴Muskegon, Mh. City rate includes $1.00 city lebt law. Sobol rate in...uced $5.25 ...evy for deb...l and improvement.

...in, Calif. ...ity rate includes $8.51 special assessments.

²⁴⁹La ...se, Wis. City rate ...udes $3.78 debt ...ndce and $0.87 recreation ...xs.

...n, Ind. City rate ...des $1.00 township and $0.70 spe-c..h assessme..t ...xs.

					Actual Tax Rate as Levied per $1,000 Assessed Valuation					Estimated Ratio of Assessed Value to Current Market Value (Per Cent)	Adjusted Tax Rate On 100% Basis of Assessment
	City	Census 1950	Per Cent Personality	Assessed Value	City	School	County	State	Total		
254	Riverside, Calif.*	46,764	14	73,248,500	12.50	29.59	16.30	—	58.49	50	29.25
255	Tuscaloosa, Ala.	46,396		Not Reported							
256	Highland Park, Mich.	46,393	44	155,089,300	15.00	18.95	6.14	—	35.09		
257	Miami Beach, Fla.	46,282	14	346,569,050	16.00			N	16.00	50	8.00
258	Inglewood, Calif.*	46,185	16	68,042,730	22.95	36.89	16.99		76.83	50	38.42
259	Everett, Mass.*	45,982	20	101,084,400	26.76	12.75	1.68	3.41	44.60	50	22.30
260	Abilene, Tex.	45,570	25	102,226,780	13.00	11.00	11.00		35.00	55	19.25
261	Santa Ana, Calif.*	45,533	2	68,820,570	22.98	25.62	14.27		62.87		
262	Colorado Springs, Colo.‡*	45,472	30	61,454,200	12.50	22.43	6.61	2.71	44.25	43	19.03
263	Tucson, Ariz.	45,454	13	40,289,522	32.17	50.95	14.02	10.00	107.14	20	21.43
264	Council Bluffs, Iowa	45,429	9	32,788,456	32.27	42.57	10.60		85.44	30	25.63
265	Williamsport, Pa.	45,047		Not Reported							
266	Wilmington, N. C.	45,043		Not Reported							
267	Santa Barbara, Calif.	44,913	6	93,291,185	11.90				11.90	72	8.57
268	West Hartford, Conn.‡	44,402	20	172,597,910	29.50				29.50	55	16.23
269	Arlington, Mass.	44,353	6	69,771,500	41.42	16.18			57.60		
270	Elgin, Ill.‡*	44,223	24	120,587,194	7.61	15.35	1.18		24.14		
271	North Little Rock, Ark.	44,097	31	Not Reported	36.00				36.00	60	21.60
272	Meriden, Conn.	44,088		93,016,975	—				64.70	48	31.06
273	Montclair, N. J.	43,927		88,033,000							
274	Mansfield, Ohio	43,564		Not Reported							
275	Pensacola, Fla.	43,479		Not Reported							
276	White Plains, N. Y.	43,466	41	163,584,931	17.45	19.92	8.81		45.68		
277	Hamtramck, Mich.	43,365	51	119,494,520	20.00	11.58	6.76		38.29	76	29.10
278	Jamestown, N. Y.	43,354	N	63,423,567	25.12	21.31	7.36		53.79	84	45.18
279	West Palm Beach, Fla.*	43,162	12	94,562,490	30.00	19.00	16.38		64.38	50	32.19
280	Salem, Oregon	43,140		Not Reported							
281	Warwick, R. I.	43,028	19	108,910,020	27.50				27.50	60	16.50

* = Footnote indicated by city number.
See also state notes at the end of tabulation.

[254]Riverside, Calif. City rate includes $1.40 flood control rate.
[258]Inglewood, Calif. City rate includes $3.36 metropolitan water district and $7.59 flood, sanitation, library and west basin water supply district rates.
[259]Everett, Mass. City rate includes $1.16 debt service rate.
[261]Santa Ana, Calif. City rate includes $1.68 flood control, $0.30 harbor district, $0.12 mosquito abatement district, $0.08 cemetery and $2.50 metropolitan water district rates. County rate includes $2.77 sanitation district rate on land only.

[262]Colorado Springs, Colo. School rate includes $4.44 county school rate.
[270]Elgin, Ill. The city lies in two counties. The rate listed is for Kane County. Cook County rate is $3.54. The city rate in Kane County includes $1.82 township, $0.48 sanitary district and $0.11 forest preserve rates. City rate in Cook County includes $0.58 township rate, $0.88 forest preserve rate and $0.76 tuberculosis sanitarium rates. School rate in Cook County is $15.36. Total rate in Cook County is $26.30.
[279]West Palm Beach, Fla. Homestead rate is $5.80 up to $5,000 valuation. County rate includes $3.75 special assessment levy.

No.	City	Census 1950	Assessed Value	Per Cent Personalty	Total Tax Rate as Levied per $1,000 Assessed Valuation					Estimated Ratio of Assessed Value to Current Market Value (Per Cent)	Tax Rate On 100% Basis of Assessment
					City	School	Cnty	State	Tot		
282	West Allis, Wis.*	42,959	129,238,700	42	17.16	11.66	15.70	0.43	44.95	41	18.43
283	Fitchburg, Mass.	42,691	63,329,825	16	56.40	—	—	—	56.40	—	—
284	Plainfield, N. J.	42,366	71,467,460	13	24.50	33.30	8.60	0.87	66.40	40	26.56
285	Sheboygan, Wis.	42,365	76,900,460	16	13.97	20.22	8.91	—	43.47	50	21.74
286	Newport News, Va.*	42,358	79,000,897	24	12.90	15.60	—	—	28.50	40†	11.40
287	Meridian, Miss.	41,893	Not Reported		34.22	13.78	—	—	48.00	—	—
288	Salem, Mass.	41,880	77,161,650	26	11.45	—	—	—	11.45	35	4.01
289	San Mateo, Calif.	41,782	123,426,385	9	34.27	23.98	19.92	—	78.17	85	27.36
290	Rome, New York	41,682	38,322,153	N	—	—	—	—	—	—	—
291	Vancouver, Wash.	41,664	Not Reported	49	7.95	9.94	2.49	—	20.38	75	15.29
292	Quincy, Ill.‡	41,450	130,032,049	37	7.50	18.20	3.20	0.30	29.20	—	—
293	Euclid, Ohio	41,396	202,064,624		—	—	—	—	—	—	—
294	Perth Amboy, N. J.	41,330	59,398,000		79.30	—	—	—	79.30	24	19.03
295	Lake Charles, La.	41,272	Not Reported		—	—	—	—	—	—	—
296	Oshkosh, Wis.	41,084	75,026,575	24	12.72	21.61	4.14	0.88	39.20	60	23.52
297	Poughkeepsie, N. Y.	41,023	Not Reported		—	—	—	—	—	—	—
298	Lewiston, Me.	40,974	Not Reported		—	—	—	—	—	—	—
299	Greenwich, Conn.*	40,835	Not Reported	14	28.55	—	—	—	28.55	60	17.13
300	Zanesville, Ohio	40,517	Not Reported		—	—	—	—	—	—	—
301	Taunton, Mass.	40,109	41,335,720	6	32.84	16.56	N	N	49.40	40	19.76
302	East Cleveland, Ohio	40,047	81,108,248	10	7.60	13.80	3.20	0.30	24.90	50	12.45
303	High Point, N. C.	39,973	125,000,000		10.69	6.02	3.25	—	19.96	70	13.97
304	Kearny, N. J.	39,952	85,698,000		—	—	—	N	51.60	56	28.90
305	University City, Mo.	39,892	64,217,700	20	11.60	29.60	9.70	0.70	51.60	20	10.32
306	Champaign, Ill.‡*	39,563	98,168,460	22	8.48	13.30	1.40	—	23.18	—	—
307	Richmond, Ind.	39,539	58,689,470	42	18.60	24.20	6.40	1.50	50.70	33	16.73
308	Great Falls, Mont.	39,214	85,621,827		49.40	28.81	28.68	28.87	135.36	20	27.07
309	Tyler, Tex.	38,968	70,163,365	32	14.86	18.34	—	—	28.20	45	12.69
310	Waukegan, Ill.‡	38,946	132,180,815	22	8.64	15.96	1.69	N	26.29	60	15.77
311	Chelsea, Mass.	38,912	46,307,150	9	50.12	20.88	N	N	71.00	34	23.82
312	New Brunswick, N. J.	38,811	50,657,710	17	24.00	27.50	17.10	N	68.60	—	—

* = Footnote indicated by city number.

See also state notes at the end of tabulation.

282 West Allis, Wis. City rate includes $1.71 capital improvements rate.

286 Newport News, Va. Personal property levy is $16.90 for city purposes.

299 Greenwich, Conn. City rate listed includes school and county purposes. Sewer district rate of $0.76, included in figure listed, does not apply to entire city.

306 Champaign, Ill. City rate includes $0.30 public health, $1.09 township, $0.15 park district, $1.20 sanitary district and $0.12 forest preserve rates. Separate township rate in city is $2.81. Total rate for this district is $24.60.

310 Waukegan, Ill. City rate includes $1.52 township, $0.62 park and $0.65 sanitary rates. Separate park district within city has levy of $1.54. Total rate for this district is $27.21.

	City	Census 1950	Assessed Value	Per Cent Personalty	Actual Tax Rate as Levied per $1,000 Assessed Valuation					Estimated Ratio of Assessed Value to Current Market Value (Per Cent)	Adjusted Tax Rate On 100% Basis of Assessment
					City	School	County	State	Total		
313	Joplin, Mo.*	38,711	32,926,244	42	18.50	31.40	8.00	0.70	58.60	25	14.65
314	Kokomo, Ind.*	38,672	63,122,779	42	19.35	26.40	6.35	1.50	53.60	30	16.08
315	Monroe, La.	38,572	Not Reported								
316	Yakima, W.	38,482	30,840,680	30	6.09	15.50	10.00	2.50	44.00	23	10.12
317	Fargo, N. D.	38,256	Not Reported	N							
318	Norristown, Pa.*	38,126	24,872,700	N	16.00	30.50	1.50	N	48.00	50	24.00
319	Orange, N. J.	38,087	49,900,000				1.98	N	65.80	48	31.58
320	Danville, Ill.*	37,864	38,142,143	25	11.96	15.30		N	29.24	75	21.93
321	West New York, N. J.	37,683	49,563,847	10	39.15	32.32	16.86		88.33	60	53.00
322	Cumberland, Md.	37,679	72,268,233	28	180	7.80	10.90	0.60	32.90	60	19.74
323	Newport, R. I.	37,564	91,793,400	42	29.00	N	N	N	29.00	50	14.50
324	Biloxi, Miss.	37,425	Not Reported								
325	Moline, Ill.*	37,93	122,460,814	28	8.87	13.25	2.94	N	25.06	67	16.79
326	Watertown, Mass.	37,329	68,182,885	7					44.80		
327	Muskogee, Okla.	37,289	28,971,304	19	8.82	23.12	11.05		42.49	28	11.90
328	Pine Bluff, Ark.	37,162	Not Reported								
329	Independence, Mo.	36,963	32,371,930	25	3.9	24.00	6.70	0.70	44.90	30	18.47
330	Wyandotte, Mich.*	36,846	81,511,075	40	14.48	18.66	7.26	N	40.40	35	14.14
331	Portsmouth, Ohio‡	36,798	72,599,100	17	8.17	11.35	3.08	0.30	22.90	75	17.18
332	Spartanburg, S. C.*	36,795	14,067,487	51	61.00	43.00	25.00	N	129.00	11	14.19
333	Revere, Mass.	36,763	57,162,500	7	1.00	22.81			56.00		
334	Auburn, N. Y.	36,722	57,015,120	N	23.23	18.83	7.37		44.33		
335	Fort Lauderdale, Fla.	36,328	156,642,636	11	19.00				19.00	40	7.60
336	Hagerstown, Md.	36,260	83,844,000	30	5.00		15.00	0.60	20.60	60	12.36
337	Brownsville, Tex.	36,066	Not Reported								
338	Eau Claire, Wis.‡	36,058	80,698,115	20	9.31	14.70	10.10	0.36	34.47	55	18.96
339	Enid, Okla.	36,017	25,713,010	34	21.50	30.00	7.10		58.60	88	22.97
340	Bristol, Conn.	35,961	97,226,790	40	4.58				34.56	50	17.28
341	Eugene, Ore.*	35,879	Not Rep'ted								
342	Steubenville, Ohio*	35,872	102,178,300	20	6.50	12.85	2.25	0.30	21.40	50	10.70

* = Footnote indicated by city
See also state notes at the end of ... taxation.

288 Joplin, Mo. County rate ides $3.50 special assessment levy for roads.
289 Kokomo, Ind. City rate ludes $1.23 ship rate.
290 Yakima, Wash. City rate ides $1.00 metropolitan park district re.
291 Norristown, Pa. ...l taxes of $5.00 per ... are levied for city purposes and $5.00 per capita for school purposes.
292 Danville, Ill. City rate includes $2.46 township and $0.90 sanitary district rates. County rate includes $0.24 airport rate.
293 Moline, Ill. City rate includes $0.67 township, $0.56 street and bridge and $0.95 airport rates.
294 Wyandotte, Mich. County rate includes $0.30 drainage rate.
295 Spartanburg, S. C. City rate includes $1.00 library and $5.00 special assessment rates.
296 Eau Claire, Wis. City rate includes $0.41 library rate. County rate includes $1.13 city-county health rate.
297 Steubenville, Ohio. City rate includes $0.10 township rate.

No.	City	Census 1950	Assessed Value	Per Cent Personalty	Actual Tax Rate as Levied per $1,000 Assessed Valuation — City	School	County	State	Total	Estimated Ratio of Assessed Value to Current Market Value (Per Cent)	Adjusted Tax Rate On 100% Basis of Assessment
343	East Providence, R. I	35,871	136,852,476	26	19.50	N	N	N	19.50	90	17.55
344	Port Huron, Mich.	35,726	Not Reported	N	—	—	—	—	—	—	—
345	Elkhart, Ind.*	35,646	63,067,040	N	18.60	24.10	4.40	1.50	48.60	—	—
346	Lafayette, Ind.*	35,568	47,751,905	31	20.70	31.00	4.40	1.50	57.60	33	19.01
347	Hazleton, Pa.*	35,491	28,548,100	4	22.50	28.00	8.20	4.00	62.70	60	37.62
348	Pomona, Calif.*	36,405	49,176,480	32	28.68	32.94	16.99	—	78.61	58†	23.32
349	Easton, Pa.	35,362	41,849,278	N	16.50	18.50	9.00	—	44.00	—	—
350	Superior, Wis.‡	36,325	48,204,965	19	10.43	26.46	19.87	0.30	57.06	67	38.23
351	Danville, Va.*	35,066	112,835,048	16	25.00	N	N	—	13.23†	80	10.58
352	Petersburg, Va.	35,054	46,694,490	23	7.94	12.39	4.27	0.30	25.00	50	12.50
353	Norwood, Ohio	35,001	94,354,000	N	—	—	—	—	25.40	—	—
354	Alexandria, La.	34,913	Not Reported		—	—	—	—	—	—	—
355	Bakersfield, Calif.,	34,784	94,878,625	22	17.50	43.70	21.00	—	82.20	30†	24.66
356	Lawton, Okla.	34,757	24,094,290	13	26.03	40.26	13.27	—	79.56	30	23.87
357	Fayetteville, N. C.*	34,715	50,706,462	26	9.80	2.00	10.50	—	22.30	40	8.92
358	Nashua, N. H.*	34,669	51,573,221	33	48.47	4.00	0.13	—	52.60	—	—
359	Irondequoit, N. Y.*	34,417	56,653,300	N	17.34	22.50	—	N	39.84	40	15.94
360	Boise, Ida.*	34,393	33,060,661	16	35.70	42.00	18.80	3.50	100.00	16	16.00
361	Watertown, N. Y.	34,350	52,985,051	N	18.80	19.00	17.10	—	54.90	90	49.41
362	Newark, Ohio*	34,275	65,942,530	29	4.35	13.15	3.10	0.30	20.90	50	10.45
363	Bloomington, Ill.*	34,163	97,948,785	N	7.68	14.51	2.42	—	24.61	75	18.45
364	Manchester, Conn.‡*	34,116	92,428,563	85	32.50	—	—	—	32.50	45	14.63
365	Bellingham, Wash.*	34,112	24,492,118	85	18.50	17.54	11.83	2.48	50.35	18	9.06
366	Appleton, Wis.	34,010	87,195,525	15	7.89	15.41	8.31	0.39	32.00	60	19.20
367	Everett, Wash.	33,849	Not Reported		—	—	—	—	—	—	—
368	Marion, Ohio	33,817	Not Reported		—	—	—	—	—	—	—
369	Middletown, Ohio	33,695	109,024,056	36	8.16	11.95	2.55	0.30	22.96	50	11.48
370	Owensboro, Ky.‡	33,651	35,641,925	88	13.00	19.10	—	—	32.10	50	16.05
371	Ottumwa, Iowa	33,681	Not Reported		—	—	—	—	—	—	—
372	Hutchinson, Kan.*	33,575	58,614,604	54	18.62	27.57	10.80	1.61	58.50	35	20.48

* = Footnote indicated by city number. See also state notes at the end of tabulation.

345 Elkhart, Ind. City rate includes $1.50 township rate.
346 Lafayette, Ind. City rate includes $0.70 township rate.
347 Hazleton, Pa. City rate includes $3.00 institutional rate.
348 Pomona, Calif. City rate includes $3.67 sanitary district, $3.41 flood control and $4.80 metropolitan water district rates.
351 Danville, Va. Total rate listed is a weighted average of $11 realty rate and $25 personalty rate.
357 Fayetteville, N. C. City rate includes $0.30 cemetery rate.
359 Irondequoit, N. Y. City rate includes county rate and includes averages of sub-rates within various districts.
360 Boise, Ida. School rate includes $5.00 junior college rate.
362 Newark, Ohio. City rate includes $0.05 township rate.
363 Bloomington, Ill. City rate includes $0.90 township and $0.87 sanitary district rates.
364 Manchester, Conn. City rate includes $2.50 fire district rate.
365 Bellingham, Wash. County rate includes $2.63 port district rate.
372 Hutchinson, Kan. City rate includes $1.11 library rate.

	City	Census 1950	Assessed Value	Per Cent Personality	Actual Tax Rate as Levied per $1,000 Assessed Valuation					Estimated Ratio of Assessed Value to Current Market Value (Per Cent)	Adjusted Tax Rate On 100% Basis of Assessment
					City	School	County	State	Total		
373	Lafayette, La.‡*	33,541	17,467,540	38	19.80	—	—	—	19.80	30	5.94
374	Stratford, Conn.‡	33,428	67,733,440	27	44.40	—	—	—	44.40	52	23.09
375	Butte, Mont.	33,251	61,643,330	22	40.68	—	—	—	40.68	—	—
376	Wauwatosa, Wis.‡*	33,324	69,171,050	5	10.12	19.95	16.40	—	46.94	43	20.18
377	Burlington, Vt.*	33,155	47,166,965	14	24.95	13.20	0.25	0.47	38.40	50	19.20
378	Mishawaka, Ind.	32,913	Not Reported					N			
379	Paducah, Ky.	32,828	33,164,110	36	18.60	20.00	6.00	—	44.60	26	11.60
380	Belleville, Ill.‡	32,721	86,880,099	34	7.40	12.30	2.40	—	22.10	—	—
381	Weymouth, Mass.	32,690	90,638,052	25	—	—	—	—	39.20	—	—
382	Reno, Nev.	32,497	Not Reported								
383	Alton, Ill.‡*	32,550	91,309,276	28	5.44	12.30	2.16	—	19.90	70	13.93
384	Amsterdam, N. Y.	32,240	Not Reported								
385	Belleville, N. J.	32,019	48,369,000	—	—	—	—	—	63.50	48	30.48
386	Clarksburg, W. Va.*	32,014	79,776,950	54	5.00	9.18	4.76	0.10	19.04	—	—
387	West Haven, Conn.	32,010	Not Reported								
388	Columbia, Mo.*	31,974	18,496,710	24	12.50	23.50	10.80	0.70	47.50	28	13.30
389	Newburgh, N. Y.	31,956	Not Reported								
390	Cheyenne, Wyo.	31,935	35,618,236	—	8.35	38.15	10.31	1.50	58.31	25	14.58
391	Billings, Mont.	31,834	23,050,840	—	37.90	—	—	—	37.90	60	22.74
392	Bangor, Me.	31,558	Not Reported					N			
393	Galesburg, Ill.‡*	31,425	81,250,595	27	8.82	18.16	1.52	—	23.50	—	—
394	Wilkinsburg, Pa.	31,418	43,112,404	30	9.50	—	—	—	9.50	39	3.71
395	Albany, Ga.	31,155									
396	Ashland, Ky.*	31,181	39,478,587	24	11.35	17.95	7.00	0.50	36.80	25	9.20
397	Anniston, Ala.	31,066	Not Reported								
398	Newport, Ky.*	31,044	31,017,500	5	15.10	14.50	6.90	0.50	37.00	65†	24.05
399	Lakeland, Fla.	30,851	60,180,500	9	16.00	—	—	—	16.00	65	10.40
400	Linden, N. J.	30,644	93,930,000	—	—	—	—	—	54.70	37	20.24
401	Burlington, Iowa	30,613	25,105,786	18	26.73	45.68	12.02	—	84.43	—	—

* = Footnote indicated by city number.
See also state notes at the end of tabulation.
375Lafayette, La. City rate includes $8.80 bond issue levy.
376Wauwatosa, Wis. City rate includes $0.92 metropolitan sewer district.
377Burlington, Vt. City rate includes $2.00 pension, $1.20 salary increase, $2.00 highway, $0.50 debt service, $1.30 interest and $0.20 park district rates.
380Belleville, Ill. City rate includes $0.70 township rate. Separate school district rate of $13.70 increases total rate for that district to

$23.50.
383Alton, Ill. City rate includes $1.30 township and $0.32 airport rates.
386Clarksburg, W. Va. Rates listed are for Class 4 property. Class 1 rate is $4.76 and Class 2 rate is $9.52.
388Columbia, Mo. County rate includes $2.00 hospital, $0.30 road bond, and $3.50 road levies.
393Galesburg, Ill. City rate includes $0.97 township rate and $1.37 sanitary district rate.
398Newport, Ky. County rate includes $0.60 courthouse rate.

City	Census 1950	Assessed Value	Per Cent Personality	Actual Tax Rate as Levied per $1,000 Assessed Valuation					Estimated Ratio of Assessed Value to Current Market Value (Per Cent)	Adjusted Tax Rate On 100% Basis of Assessment
				City	School	County	State	Total		
402 New London, Conn.‡	30,551	61,791,099	21	40.00	—	—	—	40.00	67	26.84
403 Fairfield, Conn.	30,489	Not Reported								
404 Wausau, Wis.	30,414	Not Reported								
405 Clinton, Iowa	30,379	Not Reported								
406 Elyria, Ohio‡*	30,307	87,901,443	85	7.71	14.39	2.36	0.30	24.76	—	—
407 Jackson, Tenn.*	30,207	22,631,900	5	17.70	5.50			23.20	50	11.60
408 Daytona Beach, Fla.	30,187	Not Reported								
409 Marion, Ind.*	30,081	35,557,640	11	22.50				22.50	33	7.43

‡ = Footnote indicated by city number.
See also state notes at the end of tabulation.

* = Footnote indicated by city number.

406 Elyria, N. Y. City rate includes $0.07 township rate.

407 Jackson, Tenn. City rate includes $0.40 library rate.

409 Marion, Ind. No county rate reported.

STATE NOTES

Alabama. Homestead exemption: first $2,000 of assessed value of homestead is exempt from state levy only.

Arkansas. Homestead exemption: first $2,000 of assessed value of homestead exempt from state levy only.

Florida. Homestead exemption: first $5,000 of assessed value of homesteads exempt from state and all local taxes except assessments for special benefits.

Georgia. Homestead exemption: first $2,000 of assessed value of homesteads exempt from state, county and school taxes except for taxes to pay interest on and retire bonded indebtedness.

Illinois. Capital stock and railroad valuations are determined by the Illinois Department of Revenue.

Indiana. Mortgage exemption: mortgaged real estate is subject to $1,000 exemption on its assessed value.

Iowa. Homestead exemption: credit of 25 mills (per dollar) is allowed up to $2,500 valuation.

Kentucky. There are three classes of property taxed at different rates by the state as follows: real property, $0.50; tangible personal property, $5.00; intangible personal property, $2.50, per $1,000 assessed valuation.

Louisiana. Homestead exemption: $2,000 general exemption on owner-occupied residential property in Orleans Parish. Exemptions from state, parish and special taxes, not including municipal or city taxes, in the rest of the state.

Minnesota. There are five classes of property assessed at varying percentages of true value: platted real estate at 40%, except for first $4,000 of homesteads assessed at 25%; unplatted real estate at 33-1/3%, except for first $4,000 of homesteads at 20%; iron ore at 50%; and personalty in six classes at 10%, 16%%, 20%, 25%, 33-1/3% and 40%. The first $4,000 true value of homesteads is further exempt from state levies except debt service on obligations issued prior to enactment of the law.

Missouri. Intangible personal property is assessed and the tax thereon collected by the state. Railroads and other utilities are also state assessed but are payable to the county collector.

Montana. State classified property tax law levies are extended against taxable valuation of property rather than against assessed valuation thereof. Figures given represent taxable valuations which average 30% of the assessed valuation. While assessed valuation by statute supposedly represents the full and true value, in practice such assessed valuation probably represents not more than 60% of the full and true value.

New Hampshire. Veterans exemption: $1,000 of assessed valuation of homestead exempt if total taxable assets do not exceed $5,000 for anyone having served 90 days or more in the armed forces.

New Jersey. Household exemption is $100. The estimated ratio of assessed value to current market value are those reported by the local correspondents except for Atlantic City, which submitted no estimate. In this case the figure used is from the Sixth Report of the New Jersey Commission on State Tax Policy (1953), which includes the Commission's estimates for all New Jersey municipalities.

Oklahoma. Homestead exemption: first $1,000 of assessed value of homestead exempt from tax rates of all units.

Texas. Homestead exemption: first $3,000 of assessed value of homestead exempt from state property tax only.

Utah. Household exemption: $300 maximum exemption allowed on owner-used household furnishings.

West Virginia. Property is divided into four classes: Class I, all intangible personalty; Class II, owner-occupied residences; Class III, all other property outside municipalities; and Class IV, all other property within municipalities. No municipal rates may be laid against Class III property. Each class has a maximum tax rate for all purposes. The maximum rates on $1,000 assessed valuation are: Class I, $5; Class II, $10; Class III, $15; and Class IV, $20.

Wyoming. Homestead exemption: exemption is allowed from all taxes to assessed value of $500.

News in Review

Merger of City and Towns Urged at Niagara Falls

Experts' Report Gives Plan to Aid Industrial Community

AFTER an exhaustive investigation extending through seven months, Dr. and Mrs. Thomas H. Reed, governmental consultants, have rendered a report to the city of Niagara Falls, New York, and the adjoining towns (townships) of Niagara and Lewiston, recommending consolidation of the three municipalities. The small village of Lewiston, on the lower Niagara River, is included in the town of that name and would thus also be consolidated. The Reeds had been engaged by the city and the two towns to determine the best method of providing municipal services throughout the three units, including water and sewers, schools, fire protection, health activities, etc.

The report points out that the falls of the Niagara River have brought about an industrial and recreational community of which the city and the towns are integral parts. At present an overwhelming proportion both of people and industry in the area are in the city of Niagara Falls, which had a population of 90,872 in 1950 and is expected to level off at about 110,000 soon after 1960. The logical community development is the movement of industry into the town of Niagara and of population into the town of Lewiston. Niagara's 1950 population was 4,729; that of Lewiston, with a much larger area than Niagara or the city, 6,921. As said by the Reeds, "These movements cannot and should not take place without proper planning of the area as a whole and the provision of water, sewers, schools and other munic-

ipal services." These services are fragmentary in the towns and can best be provided through consolidation with the city or, in the case of schools, into a few large school districts. The towns as now organized are stated to be administratively as well as financially incapable of coping with the service problems of a rapidly growing urban community.

The city of Niagara Falls has had the council-manager plan since 1916.

The 1950 population of the total area, 102,522, is expected to increase by 1980 to 154,000 as a conservative figure and possibly to over 180,000.

As to alternatives to consolidation the Reeds say:

"A water and sewer authority embracing the city and the two towns would be financially feasible, but is objectionable because it puts the whole cost of sewer extension on the users of sewers and because of the absence of direct responsibility to the people on the part of its governing body. It would not provide the area-wide planning essential to proper community development. What is worse, it would postpone—perhaps forever—any complete solution of the whole problem.

"The so-called borough plan, in which an over-all municipality would be superimposed on present units, would increase the complexity and the cost of local government and is wholly inapplicable to the Niagara Falls community."

One large uncertain factor in the Niagara Falls situation is further development of hydro-electric power, and the present controversy as to whether such development will be by private electric power corporations, with more taxes available to the community, or by the state itself as a public enterprise.

34

The report concludes that the decision to consolidate should not be postponed until the power question is decided. "The case for it is complete, irrespective of the outcome of that dispute, and there are many problems crying loudly to be solved now, not in 1959 or 1961."

Council-manager Plan Developments

SANTA BARBARA, CALIFORNIA, (1950 population 44,913) has been placed on the list of the International City Managers' Association, which has determined that charter amendments adopted last May provide for the council-manager plan. Santa Barbara had operated under the plan for some years but reverted to the mayor-council system in 1926. The association has also placed MESQUITE, TEXAS, (1,696) on its list, a home rule council-manager charter having been adopted there.

GREENVILLE, TEXAS, (14,727) on November 21 adopted a new charter, providing the council-manager plan, by a vote of 1,164 to 928. Under it the council will be composed of five members, to be elected in April 1954, taking office the same month.

On December 14, voters of TECUMSEH, MICHIGAN, (4,020) approved a new council-manager charter, 699 to 266.

FRIDLEY, MINNESOTA, (3,796) on December 8 approved, 364 to 235, the state's optional village manager plan.

LAKE MILLS, WISCONSIN, (2,516) voted 291 to 135 on November 3 in favor of an ordinance providing the state's statutory council-manager plan.

In BETHEL, MAINE, the committee appointed by the town meeting in March 1953, to study the town manager plan, held a public discussion meeting, attended by 60 citizens, on November 12. The committee is expected to render a report soon at a special town meeting.

At a meeting of the WAVERLY, NEW YORK, Community Council on November 25, all eighteen organization delegates present voted in favor of putting the question of adopting the council-manager plan to vote of the people. A committee of seventeen persons who favor the manager plan was formed as the Citizens Committee for the Village Manager Form of Government, to promote the plan. It is expected that a petition will be circulated, asking the board of trustees to put the question to popular vote.

A recount in MT. HOLLY, NEW JERSEY, has upheld the adoption of the manager plan as originally indicated and as noted in the December REVIEW, page 565.

Two aldermen of BAMBERG, SOUTH CAROLINA, have voiced their belief that the council-manager plan should be adopted in Bamberg, as the city's business is large enough to require a trained, full-time manager.

In ELBERTON, GEORGIA, the civic clubs have organized a joint committee to promote the council-manager plan and to work for a charter change to put it in effect.

The board of directors of the Chamber of Commerce of HUNTINGTON, WEST VIRGINIA, unanimously approved a proposal of its municipal affairs and legislative committees that the home rule act be amended so that the Huntington charter can be changed to provide the council-manager plan.

ANNISTON, ALABAMA, defeated a proposal to adopt the manager plan by a vote of 1,465 to 783 on November 17.

Nearly 300 representatives from 25 ILLINOIS cities met in Decatur on November 24 to discuss the council-manager plan and methods of aiding its spread. It was reported that 600,000 people in fifteen Illinois municipalities are now under the manager plan.

The ST. LOUIS PARK, MINNESOTA, charter commission on November 12 adopted a "limited" city manager plan for use when the village becomes a city.

Hiring and discharge of city employees would require approval of the city council as well as action by the manager. A charter proposed in 1949 which did not call for council approval of employees was defeated. The charter commission is continuing its work.

JOPLIN, MISSOURI, will vote February 9 on the question of adopting a home rule council-manager charter drafted by the Joplin charter commission. If it is adopted, the new council of nine, replacing the present city commission, will be elected on April 6. It would appoint the manager, city clerk, city attorney and municipal judge.

Voters of NEOSHO, MISSOURI, on November 24, turned out in record numbers to support the city's council-manager government. The vote was 1207 to 919 for its retention.

In MISSOULA, MONTANA, where a vote on the council-manager plan had been set for December 8, 1953, the city council, by unanimous action, rescheduled the date of the election for March 22.

Petitions for a change in the form of government from the commission to the council-manager plan are being circulated in MINOT, NORTH DAKOTA.

More than 300 voters have signed petitions in SPARKS, NEVADA, asking that the city adopt the council-manager plan.

CORSICANA, TEXAS, voted 883 to 437 on November 3 against a proposal to adopt the manager plan. At the same time a proposal for an increased tax rate was defeated 1,040 to 245.

The incoming and outgoing mayor and council, alike, of OREM, UTAH, agreed to draft an ordinance to authorize the hiring of a city manager. As Orem is a third-class city, no election is needed to give the council the power to employ a manager.

The city council of TRACY, CALIFORNIA, on November 3, unanimously appointed a citizen chairman for a fact-finding committee to study the council-manager plan, the chairman to choose the other committee members. The committee is to report its findings at a public meeting about 60 days prior to the April city election. At the meeting it will be decided whether the question of adopting the manager plan shall be placed on the April ballot.

In MARYSVILLE, CALIFORNIA, a petition with more than 700 signatures, circulated by the League of Women Voters, asking that the question of adopting the council-manager plan be voted on at the January 18 municipal election, has been approved by the city clerk.

The FRESNO, CALIFORNIA, Board of Freeholders has voted fourteen to one to submit a charter embodying a compromise between the strong-mayor plan and the council-manager plan. The council would appoint an experienced chief administrative officer who may be nominated by the mayor. He may be removed by the council on 30 days' notice, with reasons, which the manager may answer. Public hearings to discuss the charter were to be held by the board of freeholders.

Citizen Advisory Board for New York City

Robert F. Wagner, Jr., new mayor of New York City, announced shortly after election that he was organizing a Mayor's Advisory Council of businessmen, industrialists, financial experts, economists and labor representatives to assist him in administering the city's affairs.

As chairman of the council he named Nathan Straus, former federal housing administrator; W. Averell Harriman, former mutual security administrator, was designated honorary chairman and is expected to participate actively.

Mayor Wagner announced that an initial activity of the council would be to help in preparing the city's fiscal program, with emphasis on devising a more favorable financial arrangement between the city and the state. He commented that in time the council would be expanded to include experts in education, housing and other areas of municipal governmental activity.

Central Cities Reach Out for Suburbs

Notable 1953 results of efforts of central cities to absorb adjoining areas before unfavorable developments unduly hampered the city's growth include Tampa, Florida, which added 100,000 to the city's population and increased its area by 45 square miles; Seattle, Washington, which added 40,000 people and nine square miles; and Midland, Michigan, which increased its population by 5,000 and its area by fifteen square miles.

Boulder, Colorado, has prepared an information sheet for distribution to residents of outlying communities, stating the pros and cons of annexation.

Merger of Police and Fire Work Studied

The question whether police and fire protection duties can be effectively performed by a single municipal department is being subjected to a year's study by Public Administration Service with aid from the International City Managers' Association. The latter will collect information about the operation of public safety programs throughout the nation through questionnaires sent out to police and fire chiefs.

To the extent that consolidation appears to be feasible and desirable the attempt will be made to develop workable plans of organization.

Representatives of several groups especially concerned with public safety will be asked to criticize the program and findings of the project.

Established authorities in police and fire work will be used throughout the

study, in addition to the regular staff. Other advisors will include prominent police and fire chiefs and experts in municipal affairs and public works. Fire protection engineers will be asked to give their views on the effects consolidation might have on the rating of cities for fire insurance. Problems of automotive equipment design, communications, training and education will also be dealt with.

Seven communities in the U. S. and Canada are reported to have protection systems under which the same staff does both police and fire work. They are Buena Park and Sunnyvale, California; Grosse Pointe Shores and Huntington Woods, Michigan; Oakwood, Ohio; Sewickly Heights, Pennsylvania; and Montreal-East, Quebec. Timmins, Ontario, (population 27,743) has such a move under consideration.

Sunnyvale, with a population of about 15,000, is the largest community to have a consolidated system, under a department of public safety. Employees are called public safety officers and are supervised by one chief. Buena Park (population 5,483) is the latest place to adopt the system, having done so in 1953.

Huntington Woods (population 4,919) has had eighteen years' experience with the same personnel serving as policemen and firemen.

Sewickly Heights (population 671), the smallest community with an integrated public safety service, has had it since incorporation in 1935.

Montreal-East, with a population of 5,000 and a business district containing 22 stores and 29 industrial plants, reports a saving of about $26,000 a year by having a combined department.

Norfolk Steps Up Traffic Law Enforcement

Disturbed by the increase in traffic accidents and determined to curb reckless driving, the city council of Norfolk, Virginia, authorized establishment of a special court, as of January 1, 1954, to deal primarily with traffic cases. It is known as Police Court, Part II, and has full police jurisdiction.

Because Police Court, Part I, which heard traffic cases one afternoon per week, was so crowded with other cases, the violators of traffic laws had been allowed to settle their cases by paying their fines ahead of court time at police headquarters. This was ineffective because most people paid their fines practically at their own convenience, and traffic law enforcement suffered. Beginning January 1, 1954, all persons charged with moving traffic violations must actually appear and stand trial in the new traffic court, which will sit six days a week. It is believed that the personal appearance of the violator in court will give the court special value.

The purpose of the court is not only to deal out punishment but also to educate offenders. The program will include movies concerning violations. Work will be done in the schools and in civic clubs toward educating the public. It is thought that such a specialized court is in a better position to work with traffic problems from an educational as well as an enforcement point of view; that liaison between the judge, traffic engineer and director of public works will be effectuated; and that the court will foster wider respect for the law and bring about a reduction in traffic law violations and highway accidents.

H. H. GEORGE, 3RD
City Manager
Norfolk, Virginia

Minnesota League Holds Meetings Throughout State

The League of Minnesota Municipalities in September and October 1953 conducted or sponsored seventeen meetings in as many municipalities in all parts of the state. These meetings provided the opportunity for widespread contacts and down-to-earth discussions of local problems, in relation to statewide interests and experience. The number of municipalities represented at the meetings was 268 and 1,151 municipal officials attended. The league staff traveled 3,000 miles in attending the meetings.

Tennessee League Has Nine District Conferences

Policies of the Tennessee Municipal League and a wide variety of local problems were discussed at nine district conferences throughout the state in October 1953. The league policy matters included the fight to preserve the Tennessee Valley Authority against its enemies in Washington and elsewhere, extension of home rule for cities, and efforts to attract further industrial development. Local issues discussed included traffic, parking and annexation problems. The conferences were attended by 176 officials of 76 cities.

State and Local Merit Systems Cooperate in Alabama

The Alabama legislature, according to the National Civil Service League, has adopted the provision of the *Model State Civil Service Law*[1] which permits cooperative arrangements between the State Personnel Department and local governments in holding examinations and establishing eligible lists. It also allows the state to furnish technical service to localities on a cost basis.

Alabama, and also Illinois, have joined New York in trying continuous recruiting and examination for hard-to-fill positions, including many of professional and technical nature.

Rhode Island Problems Discussed at Government Meet

The Sixth Annual Institute on Problems of Government at the University of

[1]Published jointly by the National Civil Service League and the National Municipal League.

Rhode Island was held in Kingston, December 1. The meeting, with about 75 progressive-minded public officials and civic workers from the principal cities, organized into five discussion groups on problems of collecting automobile taxes, pension plans for municipal employees, recruiting of local police, maintaining municipal autonomy and a municipal ordinance on personnel.

Richard S. Childs addressed a joint session on municipal home rule, a subject as to which Rhode Island is having difficulties under the new home rule constitutional amendment. The amendment has been weakened by the decision of the State Supreme Court[1] to the effect that it does not give cities the right to decide upon nonpartisan elections and elections at dates separate from general elections.

Resolutions were passed favoring formation of a League of Rhode Island Municipalities to defend the cities against the legislature and to exchange administrative information, repair of the damage caused by the court decision to home rule, and a single-house legislature like Nebraska's.

Over-all Legislative Service Agency Created in Ohio

The 1953 Ohio legislature established the Legislative Service Commission as an over-all agency to coordinate activities in the fields of legislative research, bill drafting, codification, etc. It has succeeded to the powers and duties of the Commission on Code Revision, the Legislative Research Commission and the Program Commission. The Ohio Legislative Reference Bureau retains its separate identity.

State Court Administrator Established in Michigan

The Michigan Supreme Court, under authorization by the legislature, has es-

[1]See the REVIEW, November 1953, page 515; December, page 568.

tablished the office of court administrator for the state's judicial system. His duties, according to *State Government,* include examination of court dockets and administrative systems, preparation of an annual budget for the judicial system, recommendations on assignment of judges, and collection of information pertinent to realigning and coordinating courts. The newly appointed administrator plans to study the operation of similar administrative offices in the New Jersey, Virginia and federal court systems.

Sixth Annual Legislative Service Conference Meets

More than 325 state legislators and heads of agencies serving state legislatures and Congress participated in the sixth annual meeting of the Legislative Service Conference in New Orleans and Baton Rouge, Louisiana, September 28 to October 1.

General discussion sessions were concerned with the responsibilities and methods of legislatures, organization of legislative services, new developments in the field of legislative procedure, and substantive law revision, reports *State Government.* In addition, the program included workshop sessions dealing with specialized fields—legislative research, statutory and code revision, fiscal analysis, reference and library services, work of legislative clerks and secretaries, bill drafting—and a special workshop for legislators. A revised preliminary report of the Special Committee on Organization of Legislative Services, established by the conference at its 1951 sessions, was distributed at the meeting.

New York Reapportions State Senate

At a special session on November 18 the New York legislature, by party vote, adopted a bill to reapportion the Senate and Assembly as called for by the state constitution after each federal census. The legislature determines the boundaries of Senate districts and the number of assemblymen for each county, but assembly district lines within counties are drawn by the county supervisors or, in New York City, by the council. In commenting on the bill, the New York *Times* said editorially:

> Under the present apportionment, which has been in effect since 1944, New York City, with 55 per cent of the state's population, has 44.6 per cent of the seats in the State Senate and 44.6 per cent of the seats in the Assembly. Under the new proposal it would get only 43.1 per cent of the Senate seats and 43.3 per cent of the Assembly seats. . . . A citizen should have no less rights because he chooses to live in the Bronx than in Onondaga. Yet the proposed apportionment would allocate one senator for each 340,000 citizens in the Bronx and one for each 167,000 in Onondaga. And in New York the Senate, theoretically, is the chamber where more weight is given to population than to area.

An amendment that frankly attempted to carve out three safely Republican Senate districts in Kings County (Brooklyn) was defeated.

Under the new apportionment a number of senators find themselves in the wrong district for the future. In Brooklyn, three senators now live in a single district.

Caucus Rule in New Jersey Senate Ends

At a meeting of Republican majority members of the New Jersey Senate on December 9, it was decided to end the secret caucus system that has controlled legislation for decades and to substitute a system of working committees in the 1954 legislature.

Under the caucus system, the Republican majority decided the fate of bills at closed party conferences and as a rule permitted bills to be debated on the floor only when they appeared to be assured of success.

The former Senate committees, numerous but ineffective, are to be reduced from 44 to about a dozen representative working committees, doing business in the open.

Robert B. Meyner, newly elected Democratic governor, had denounced the caucus system, as had also Senator Malcolm S. Forbes, who had unsuccessfully contended for the Republican gubernatorial nomination. Paul L. Troast, who defeated him in the primary, took no stand on the caucus.

Urge Reduction of 70 Federal Agencies to 30

The Temple University survey of federal reorganization, directed by Robert L. Johnson, president of Temple, and financed by private business, proposed reduction of the number of independent agencies of the federal government from 70 to 30 in a report to President Eisenhower made public on December 10. Numerous other recommendations were made in the effort to increase efficiency including revamping of the executive office and the Labor, Post Office, Treasury, Commerce, Interior and Agriculture Departments.

County and Township •   •   • *Edited by Edward W. Weidner*

County Officers Debate State-local Relations

Ask Return of Authority to County Governments

THE main theme of the 1953 conference of Wisconsin County Boards of Supervisors was returning authority to county government. In light of this theme, the conference passed a resolution to aid its 1954 operation by development of regional conferences and meetings of boards of supervisors to study, discuss and exchange ideas on the forms and techniques of county government administration.

The association resolved that it avail itself of the facilities of the Bureau of Government at the University of Wisconsin in developing plans for such regional conferences and institutes for supervisors with the possibility of publishing a handbook of information so that newly elected supervisors will have an opportunity to understand fully the duties, obligations and requirements of the office to which they have been chosen.

The conference heard a number of talks that stressed the theme of returning authority to county government. Two of these were by congressmen from Wisconsin, Glenn R. Davis and John Byrnes. The former predicted a gradual decline of what he called federal domination in government and the latter took the position that tax dollars now being used by the federal government should revert back to local levels when local jurisdiction is returned.

At its annual session last fall, the North and East Convention of County Judges and Commissioners of Texas passed a resolution urging more farm-to-market road assistance by the state instead of a policy of restriction which has been proposed by the State Highway Commission. It was agreed that an increase in national and state assistance to farm-to-market roads was desirable.

In stark contrast to this resolution was the general approval given to a speech by U. S. Senator Lyndon Johnson. Addressing the convention, he said in part: "We must recognize the fact that the [governmental] structure has been weakened over the past half century. . . . I think we have become so preoccupied with the problems of war and peace, the problems of our national economy, that we have failed to stop to take the necessary look at our objectives.

"Fortunately we of Texas—we of the south—have been fortified against the resulting trend toward centralized government. We have resisted the tendency to concentrate all power in Washington. We have insisted upon the rights and obligations that are due the states.

"Our attitude—despite scoffing critics —has been healthy. It can be traced, I believe, to one important factor. We have maintained our county governments as strong and functioning units. We have kept our government close to the people —as close as is humanly possible."

Road Administration

The two major problems of county highway administration are how to secure effective management at the county level and how to develop effective state-local relations. This is the theme of the November 1953 issue of *Better Roads* (Chicago). The issue is featured by an editorial, "Too Many Managers." It points out that road management at the county level has lagged 50 years behind the times and centralization in the hands of a single engineer for the entire county is way past due.

The same issue contains an article defining elements of good state-local relations. Engineers from Kansas, Minnesota, Alabama, Kentucky and Michigan highway departments comment upon the policies of their respective state agencies in their relationships with county highway organizations. The underlying theme is that a workable plan based upon common interests must be developed. These common interests should meet at the professional level in the opinions of the contributors. Joint financial responsibility was cited as one factor that aids better state-county relations.

Philadelphia Home Rule Threatened by Courts

A law passed by the Pennsylvania legislature last summer, which severely cripples Philadelphia's home rule charter (adopted in 1951 after authorization by the legislature), has been upheld by a lower Pennsylvania court.[1] In a decision that has possible far-reaching consequences the judge held that home rule was granted Philadelphia only subject to such restrictions, limitations and regulations as may be imposed by the legislature. The judge found no basis for assuming that the legislature has surrendered permanently its right to control the government of Philadelphia or that it has the constitutional authority to do so.

If this view of constitutional home rule is upheld by the Pennsylvania Supreme Court, Philadelphia will still be at the mercy of the state legislature in almost all respects. The law, now being considered by the Supreme Court, provides that the sheriff, the board of revision of taxes, the county commissioners and the registration commission shall be exempt from the city-county consolidation amendment; that these agencies are

[1]See the REVIEW, November 1953, page 518.

removed from the structure of municipal government and returned to their former preferred status of county offices, outside the bounds of the city charter and the civil service. It permits the officers and the employees of these departments to engage freely in political activities. It excludes the offices from reorganization under the city charter, the plans for which have called for the abolishment of the tax revision board, county commission and registration commission.

Commenting editorially, the Philadelphia *Bulletin* says: "The setting up of the four departments as tight political strongholds, and the vesting of tax assessment powers in a politically controlled board, are obviously opposed to the public interest.

"It has been the city's contention that the exemption bill would override an amendment to the constitution voted by the people and is thus unconstitutional. If a change is to be made in the purposes and provisions of the consolidation amendment, the city claims, it must be made by the people themselves, not by the legislature. . . .

"It is a terrible blow to decent government in Philadelphia if a legislative majority can undo in the space of a few days the reforms it has taken many years to achieve. The Supreme Court's answer in this case will have momentous consequences."

Grand Jury Recommends County Manager Plan

The most drastic change recommended by the retiring Richmond County (Augusta), Georgia, grand jury is that suggesting establishment of the county manager plan of government. The matter was presented to the county commissioners meeting in regular session, to which County Attorney Frank Pierce reported that the first step in getting the manager plan would be a petition, signed by 5 per cent of the county's registered voters, asking the Ordinary for a referendum at the polls.

Suffolk County May Consider New Charter

Serious consideration is likely to be given to a county charter form of government in Suffolk County, New York, by the board of supervisors taking office in 1954. In part this interest in county reorganization is a result of the rapid growth in population that the county has experienced during the last decade.

It is probable that if the movement toward the county charter form of government materializes it will have bipartisan support. Both Republicans and Democrats have indicated that early and serious consideration should be given the matter by the incoming board.

One of the supervisors has pointed out that Suffolk's present governmental system dates back almost to colonial times, when the county was a thinly populated rural area with a sprinkling of small hamlets.

It has been proposed that such services as law enforcement and property assessment be placed on a county basis. Also under consideration is the establishment of a county executive to which the board could delegate its administrative functions. Under such a plan the board could confine its activities to law-making and policy-making. The executive would be appointed by the board and removable by it.

University to Study Miami Metropolitan Area

A full fledged study of the metropolitan area of Miami and Dade County, Florida, is to be undertaken by the University of Miami under contract with the Metropolitan Miami Municipal Board.[1] Special attention will be given

[1]See the REVIEW, September 1953, page 407.

in the study to city-county merger possibilities. The department of government at the university will engage expert consultants and furnish an executive secretary for the board chairman to aid in the study. A library covering the field of metropolitan problems is to be established.

The board pointed out that the local nonpartisan, non-political leadership furnished by the university should help gain acceptance of any merger, federation or consolidation plan finally approved by the board.

In selecting the university, the board did not turn down previous consultant proposals submitted by the Public Administration Service and Griffenhagen and Associates. The university will be authorized under its contract to engage these or other expert consultant organizations for specific parts of the study.

Michigan Township Officials Form Organization

Township officials from 53 of Michigan's 83 counties organized the Michigan Association of Township officials. State organizations of township officers are reported to have been established in Ohio, Pennsylvania and possibly other states —whether despite or because of efforts to eliminate townships in the interest of governmental simplification.

St. Louis to Vote on Metropolitan Sewer District

The voters of the city of St. Louis and St. Louis County will vote on adoption of a proposed plan for a metropolitan sewer district at a special election February 9. An affirmative vote in both jurisdictions is necessary.

This is the first opportunity for the electorate of the St. Louis metropolitan area to utilize a new provision in the 1945 Missouri constitution which provides a device for meeting area-wide problems

(Continued on page 47)

Proportional Representation . . *Edited by George H. Hallett, Jr.
and Wm. Redin Woodward*
(This department is successor to the Proportional Representation Review)

Charter Committee Wins Majority in Cincinnati

Communism Issue, Raised by 'Machine,' Proves Boomerang

CINCINNATI voters in the November 3 election returned control of their municipal government to councilmen sponsored by the City Charter Committee, the citizens organization responsible for the adoption of the city's council-manager P.R. charter in 1924 and active in its support ever since.

Nineteen candidates—for the third time in the last three elections—again made the race, the Charter group and the local Republican party's County Courthouse machine, which has opposed the Charter group since its inception, offering full slates of nine, with one independent. The total first-choice vote was: Charter, 73,588; machine, 69,402; independent, 189; written in, 9; invalid, 9,578. The total vote cast, 152,766, was about average for the city's municipal elections, approximately 61 per cent of those registered participating.

The election campaign—Cincinnati's fifteenth under the Hare system of proportional representation—was undoubtedly the strangest and most hysterical in a long succession of remarkably controversial campaigns.

Despite a continuing struggle by the Charter candidates to direct discussion and debate at the earthy, practical issues of municipal housekeeping, the spokesmen for the machine attempted—with more than passing success—to shape the election into a referendum on the extraordinary issues of "communism" and "commie-coddling."

So amazing was this aspect of the campaign that several national publications, together with the *New York Times,* long before election day began to take interest in the results as a revealing case history in contemporary social and political trends. By the time this account appears in print, *Harper's,* the *Nation* and the *Reporter* will have carried comments on the campaign, with other publications apparently about to follow suit.

Unwitting storm centers of the campaign were three officials of the City Planning Commission, an independent board under the Cincinnati charter consisting of five members appointed by the mayor for five-year terms, the city manager and a representative of the city council.

Five weeks before the election, the council representative on the commission, who was also the floor leader of the machine delegation, emerged from a private session with the city manager charging that the chairman of the Planning Commission and a fellow member (both appointees of former Mayor and Charter leader Albert D. Cash, who lost his life in August 1952 in a Michigan boating accident) had failed to disclose that the commission's recently appointed chief executive officer allegedly had been affiliated with a San Francisco Marxist study group during 1946.

This accusation was swiftly followed by a demand for the dismissal of all three officials, resignation of the planning executive, and refusals to resign from the two commission members.

Simultaneously, although the Washington office of the FBI declared it was not the policy of that agency to volunteer information to city officials regarding the records of city employees, the city manager stoutly maintained that he had received information about the planning director from the newly appointed head of the Cincinnati office of the FBI. The manager also admitted in passing that he had "sat" on the information for eleven days before it was made public by the machine floor leader, in the meantime revealing it to the three machine representatives on the Planning Commission but not disclosing it to the three Charter members.

At this juncture, the City Charter Committee, aided by a spontaneously organized "Committee of 150 for Political Morality," denounced the sequence of events as an unwarranted interjection of unscrupulous politics into the highly important and previously non-political activity of the Planning Commission, as well as an unjustifiable attack on the reputations of two high-principled, unpaid and extremely valuable public servants.

Heated Campaign

From then until election day, the issue raged hotly with both sides employing television appearances, newspaper publicity and paid advertising on a larger scale than ever before in a council election.

The election result, which has been variously interpreted, was succinctly summed up by the *Cincinnati Post* on November 9, as the final tabulation of the vote was being completed:

"The Cincinnati council campaign began without an issue. It ended in thunder and lightning. ·

"It began with a consensus of opinion among political observers that the Republicans should take five seats readily enough. It ended with a genuine upset as the count of first-choice votes forecast, and the transfer of votes confirmed, a solid victory for the Charter candidates.

"What happened? The *Post* has its

theories. We offer them here fully aware of the perils of interpreting elections.

"The Bettman-Collett issue boomeranged against the Republicans. The reckless zeal with which the Republican campaigners pursued this subject, the demand for the heads of two good public servants for what was at most an honest mistake in judgment and the shocking effort to 'smear' the Charter candidates as 'commie coddlers,' stirred the inevitable reaction among fair-minded citizens.

"Republican Chairman Eyrich, who said before election that the Bettman-Collett episode 'has absolutely become a campaign issue', and Councilman Allen, who saw the election as 'a referendum', may well ponder their own honest mistakes in judgment, which perhaps, as much as any other factor, led their party to 'snatch defeat from the jaws of victory.'"

Perhaps as a consequence of the result, the city manager, who consciously or unconsciously had lit the fuse which exploded the campaign, on November 25 tendered his resignation, effective December 31.

The new Charter majority, taking office December 1, after electing Edward N. Waldvogel as mayor and Mrs. Dorothy N. Dolbey as vice mayor (first woman ever to serve in such a capacity among the nation's larger cities), appointed a committee consisting of the mayor, vice mayor, Theodore M. Berry (Charter majority floor leader), Carl W. Rich (minority leader), and Walton H. Bachrach (also of the minority), as a committee to recommend a new manager. The committee at once let it be known it would seek recommendations from responsible sources both locally and throughout the nation.

One of the significant features of the election is that it found the Charter group for the second time in its history successfully flouting the ancient political wheeze that "reform groups never survive defeat."

Given majorities in its first five campaigns—1925, '27, '29, '31 and '33—the Charter Committee then went into a series of three four-four-one councils which terminated in 1941 with the first election of an opposition-controlled five-four council. This situation continued until the 1947 election when the Charter group swept back into control in conjunction with a highly successful defense of the city's P.R. voting system. Returned to control in '49, the group lost out in '51 when its floor leader, Charles P. Taft, declined to stand for reelection. Its minority representation of four was further depleted a year ago with the tragic death of Mr. Cash, referred to earlier.

In the light of these circumstances, how was victory possible? Again, the Post editorial just cited gives a clue:

"In the routine, but highly valuable, political chore of 'working the precincts,' the Charter Committee appeared to have done better this year than in some recent elections. This is not to suggest, however, that the more professional organization of their Ninth Street rivals had suddenly collapsed. It hadn't; it just lacked the materials in candidates and talking points to make an effective appeal to independent-minded voters.

"And Cincinnati does have its generous share of independent-minded voters. They resent political trickery; they are not fooled into confusing national with municipal issues. They came out in good number last Tuesday. They decided the council election."

FOREST FRANK
Cincinnati City Charter Committee

Hamilton Holds Largest P. R. Election

In the largest P. R. council election ever conducted in Hamilton, Ohio, five incumbent councilmen and two new members were elected on November 3. Three local parties succeeded in filling six of seven council seats in the fourteenth election since adoption of P. R. in 1926. An independent was elected to the seventh seat. One of the new members is a former mayor and long-time councilman, William Beckett, now returned to council after a three-year absence while in military service. This is Mr. Beckett's sixth term on council.

The total number of ballots was 19,-907. Invalid ballots numbered 755 and 166 were blank, leaving 18,986 valid ballots. Invalid and blank ballots comprised 4.6 per cent of the total number. Twenty-one candidates, the smallest number since 1941, sought the seven council seats. The quota figure was 2,374. The count was completed within 46 hours after the polls closed. Actual counting required 19 hours, a record for recent P. R. elections in Hamilton. In 1947, 22 hours were required to count

HAMILTON, OHIO, COUNCILMANIC ELECTION. NOVEMBER 3, 1953

Party and Number of Candidates	Total First-choice Votes	Per cent of Total Votes	Number of Seats Won	Per cent of Total Number Council Seats
Forward Hamilton (8)	7728	40.7	3	42.8
Labor (7)	4704	24.7	2	28.6
People's (3)	2335	12.3	1	14.3
Independents (3)	4203	22.1	1	14.3
Write-ins	16			
Totals	18,986	99.8	7	100.0

16,682 ballots, and in 1945, 27 hours were used in counting 14,479 ballots.

The first candidate elected was former Mayor Beckett, who reached the quota figure on the eleventh transfer. Mr. Beckett had 2,094 first-choice votes, the highest accorded any candidate in the 1953 election. Fifteen transfers were required before the seven seats were filled. The last candidate chosen won automatically when no further eliminations were possible. The only Negro candidate stood tenth in the first-choice count with 1,023, or 5.3 per cent, of first-choice votes and was not elected. There were no women candidates.

The three local parties accounted for 18 of the 21 candidates. The Forward Hamilton ticket won three seats while the Labor and People's tickets won two and one, respectively. The percentage of first-choice votes received by party candidates as compared with the percentage of seats won is shown in the table on page 46.

The campaign was devoid of the issues which have characterized council elections in Hamilton in recent years. Neither the retention of the city manager nor strict vs. "liberal" law enforcement was debated seriously. Despite the interest indicated by the large number of voters the campaign was comparatively quiet.

During the past two years, the Forward Hamilton party has had a voting majority in council. As no party won clear control in the recent election, considerable interest and speculation center on the attitude of the successful independent candidate, Herbert Mick, a newcomer. Mick is expected to vote with the Forward Hamilton group in the selection of a mayor. There is little likelihood that any coalition between the Forward Hamilton and the Labor or People's party representatives will be effected.   ALAN C. RANKIN
Miami University

COUNTY AND TOWNSHIP
(Continued from page 43)
on a functional basis. The constitutional procedure which is being followed is essentially a home rule approach. Unlike many functional districts in other metropolitan areas, which have been established by state statute and are controlled by state officials, the proposed district is being created by a plan or charter drafted locally by a board of freeholders representing both the city and the county. The charter may subsequently be amended locally as the situation changes.

The governing body of the proposed district is the board of trustees, three appointed by the mayor of St. Louis and three by the county supervisor of St. Louis County for overlapping terms of four years. Approval of the appointments by a majority of the circuit judges in the respective jurisdictions is required. The principal administrative officers provided by the charter are the executive director appointed by the board and a director of finance and personnel director appointed by the executive director.

The metropolitan sewer district is to have the necessary powers to build, operate and maintain all sewer facilities within its area. The plan gives the district limited taxing power and authorizes it to incur indebtedness, charge rates, rentals or service charges for the use of sewer facilities, and subdivide districts into subdistricts which will bear the expense of specific localized improvements. The exact form which the financing program will take is a matter to be determined by the board subject to approval by referendum in the case of bond issues.

If this plan is accepted, it will be the first local jurisdiction to include St. Louis and urban St. Louis County since the city and county were separated in 1876.

WILLIAM N. CASSELLA, JR.

Citizen Action . . . . . . *Edited by Elsie S. Parker*

Pea Ridge — Unincorporated

Community Club Organizes Informal Town Government

YOU won't find Pea Ridge, West Virginia, on any roadside sign as you motor through the state or ride over its railroads. Neither is it in the postal directory nor on any map. Yet it has had a mayor and a set of officials since October 12, 1937.

I thought I was going to church. Several residents of the community were entering the little brick church and I followed them—into the basement. This is the "city hall."

At the foot of the stairs a lady held a hat in her hand collecting a miscellaneous dropping of coins. "Is this for the church?" I dared to ask.

"No. This is your tax collector's office," she replied.

I contributed; I wasn't sure why.

The mayor pounded his gavel and called the Pea Ridge Community Club to order. The minutes of the last meeting were read and approved. Then he began asking for reports from his twelve councilmen and from various committees —beautification, playground, voting precinct, fire department and on down the line. The recorder read the correspondence received since the last meeting. This was followed by various other items of business.

Despite the fact that no town existed, here was a full set of officials and committees functioning with a mayor at the head.

In the mid '30s many affluent residents of Huntington—West Virginia's largest city—moved out to the rolling hills beyond the border. When these influential people had comprised quite a formidable group, they decided they deserved more utility and like services than the ordinary gas, water, electric and telephone lines afforded. This feeling called for a mass meeting in the basement of the Methodist church this October day in 1937.

Among those present was Dana Shank, an oil dealer whose trucks skirted the community over U. S. Route 60. He suggested they form a municipal organization and act collectively. This they did, electing Shank mayor, with a recorder and six councilmen. In case they should become incorporated some day, they would already be in stride. Other councilmen were added through the years.

Huntington on the west and Barboursville, a small incorporated town, on the east investigated the possibility of annexation, but declined because the low residential taxes of the wide expanse wouldn't pay for its upkeep. For Pea Ridge, whose boundaries are definitely defined, is two miles wide and three miles long. The population in 1937 might have numbered 1,000. Today it would be nearer 2,500. So, since Pea Ridge was an "unwanted child," she decided to function on her own. And the head men out Pea Ridge way have found that, despite the fact they have no authority officially, the title, "mayor," carries plenty of prestige.

During the more than sixteen years of the community's existence there have been four mayors—Dana Shank, the oil man; Ira P. Baer, judge of Domestic Relations Court; William Ives, manager of Westinghouse; and Dennison Garrett, dealer in automobiles. Mr. Garrett has just been elected mayor for his fifth consecutive term. Mrs. Anthony Gebhardt has been the area's recorder almost from the beginning.

The utility companies were not hard to crack. They were, rather, very considerate. The Huntington Water Corporation tapped its line running across the hills to Barboursville in many places. Service lines were enlarged in others. The United Fuel Gas Company followed by laying adequate lines and setting private meters for residents of the Ridge, rather than keeping large meters where citizens paid the bill collectively. Electric service was greatly improved. Residents arranged for garbage disposal at $1.75 a family per month. Bus service between Barboursville and Huntington was improved. The Humane Society agreed to look after helpless dogs and cats dropped by passers-by.

Then the community turned to other matters. Lots were donated for playgrounds at either end of the "city." The business districts are at the extreme ends, east and west. The center of the city is a rural store.

Pea Ridge's Main Street was originally a stagecoach turnpike. Then it was paved for modern traffic and used as a national route until the construction of U. S. Route 60 in a more direct line. Route 60 is now one of Pea Ridge's suburban streets. Roads branching out from the old brick road form the city's streets. These streets have been beautified and markers and glares placed where Main Street crosses Route 60.

All these improvements and advancements came in answer to the call of the "city" fathers. And others are yet to come.

All the taxes necessary are the offerings used to carry on the community's correspondence, advise residents of special meetings, elections and various other matters. No one ever wants an office at election time, so there is no electioneering.

The town has no law other than the general law of the land, no police, no lockup, no salaried officers—and no parking meters.

The chief aspiration of the community at present is for a fire department. For this area of six square miles, bordered by a giant fishhook bend of the Guyandotte River and two rural roads, is building up fast. Plans are under way to finance the purchase of adequate fire-fighting equipment by the residents paying the difference between their present rate of insurance and the rate it would be with equipment. It will be operated voluntarily.

The latest addition to Pea Ridge's accomplishments is a central voting place. Heretofore, residents had to scatter to half a dozen polls—some on the Ridge, others in Barboursville or Huntington. But the voting place will be used for county, state and national elections only. Pea Ridge will still elect her officials town hall style.

FRANK BALL

Barboursville, West Virginia

Good Government Wins Again in Phoenix, Arizona

That good government is good politics, particularly if it has the backing of an alert citizens' group, was demonstrated again when the voters of Phoenix, Arizona, on November 10 gave their approval to all seven councilmanic candidates of the Charter Government Committee. It was the third consecutive victory for the Charter Government group, which has supported improvements that have put the city among the better governed municipalities of the nation. Its ticket was opposed by an Economy party which promised, if its candidates were elected, to discharge City Manager Ray W. Wilson. Only about 30 per cent of the registered voters participated in the balloting.

PAUL KELSO

University of Arizona

Financing Educational TV

A *Fund Raising Plan*, prepared for the St. Louis Educational Television Commission, is termed "applicable to any community." Twenty mimeographed pages, it contains an organization chart, describes the qualifications for the headquarters staff, officers and committees. The latter include committees on special events, labor, organizations, house-to-house, coin collectors, gifts, etc.

According to *Educational Television News* (published by the National Citizens Committee for Educational Television, Washington, D. C.), three cities —Chicago, St. Louis and Pittsburgh— have been working hard to complete fund-raising drives for educational TV stations. Civic organizations, business leaders, PTA's and other groups have combined forces to put their communities "over the top."

Jacksonville, Florida, is preparing to make a drive for a fund of $200,000 for operating its educational TV station.

There is much activity in Michigan cities. Detroit has completed plans for its finance drive. The University of Michigan's studios at Ann Arbor were the first in the state to get under way. Michigan State College expects its station to be available early in 1954.

In Dade County (Miami), Florida, the voters turned down a proposal that the school board operate a television station, 14,725 to 6,323. The vote, advisory only, was placed on the ballot at the behest of the school board, seeking the approval of the voters on whether it should spend tax money to operate such a station.

Despite the adverse vote, a request by the chairman of the county school board for a construction permit was granted by the FCC. The school board, however, has now voted to assign the permit to a non-profit foundation to be known as The Community Television Foundation of South Florida.

Cincinnati started its drive for the final $150,000 needed to complete its financing for an educational TV channel with a dinner of the financing committee held November 16. The city and its surrounding area, including school districts in northern Kentucky, have been organized into 114 geographic units, each assigned a quota of money to raise.

According to *Educational Television News* Oklahoma has prospects of getting two stations on the air by January 1955. A legal opinion states that the State Building Fund "provides adequate funds to service and retire a $5,000,000 TV Authority bond issue."

Publications on Educational TV

Recent publications on educational TV include *Tales of Seven Cities and Of Video That Teaches*. Thirty-seven pages, it is published by the National Citizens Committee for Educational Television, Ring Building, Washington 6, D. C. The communities covered include Cincinnati, St. Louis, San Francisco, Seattle, Pittsburgh, Wilmette and Philadelphia.

TV—A New Community Resource is "The story of a television workshop for community organization personnel." It is published by Wells Publishing Company, Leonia, New Jersey, 95 pages, priced at $1.00.

Community Councils

The September issue of *The Michigan Community News Letter*, distributed by the University of Michigan's School of Education and Extension Service in the interest of community adult education, describes "Community Councils of Michigan in 1953," pointing out "differences in direction." Names of the various councils in the state are listed with a short description of the activities of each.

Organizing a Community Council (24 pages) is "a manual prepared by the Committee on Community Organization Projects of the Michigan Council on Adult Education." It has been published jointly by several Michigan colleges and may be secured from the council at the Department of Public Instruction, Lansing 2, Michigan.

Know Your Community

Leagues of Women Voters in New Jersey have been educating the citizens of their communities by issuing descriptive pamphlets.

Know Your County—A Study of Monmouth County, cleverly illustrated by numerous cartoons, was prepared by the Red Bank Region League of Women Voters.

Know Your County—A Survey of Hunterdon County contains photographs of the historic county courthouse at Flemington, the county seat, and other interesting landmarks. It is published by the League of Women Voters of Hunterdon County.

Your Town: Bernardsville is a "Directory and Guide" published by the League of Women Voters of that community. *Know Your Township* has been prepared by the League of Women Voters of Ewing Township.

This Is Westfield—A Know Your Town Government Survey comes from the League of Women Voters of that New Jersey community. It is illustrated by drawings and photographs.

This is Mercer County—A Survey of the County Government was prepared and published by three Leagues of Women Voters—Trenton, Ewing Township and the Princeton Community. Included are a map of the county and a chart showing its organizational setup.

All describe the government of the community concerned. Several contain business directories. Price of each is 50 cents.

Skipping to other states, *A Handbook of Town Government,* prepared by the Lexington (Massachusetts) League of Women Voters, is available for 25 cents.

A Guide to Fairfax County (Maryland) is made up of twenty pages of staggered length crammed full of information on voting and on the county. Attractively printed in two colors—red and green—the pamphlet is sold for ten cents by the County League of Women Voters.

The Women Voters of Hammond, Indiana, with the cooperation of the local Chamber of Commerce, has made available its handbook *Hammond City Government.* Seventy-seven pages, mimeographed, it sets forth the duties of city officials, boards, courts, etc., with salaries and other pertinent data.

Minneapolis Activities

The Citizens League of Greater Minneapolis has issued a *Directory of Minneapolis and Hennepin County Officials* as a handy reference for members and other interested citizens.

The League's new president, Charles S. Bellows, has suggested that the organization might well concentrate during 1954 on countywide problems. He commented that the league hopes to complete countywide studies of assessment, park planning, hospitals, highways, education and fire and police problems during the current year.

Constitution Published

The constitution of the City Club of Portland, Oregon, has been published in the *City Club Bulletin* for October 9. The issue also contains a roster of the club's membership.

New Policy

The Lens, publication of the Massachusetts Civic League, has inaugurated a new policy. The paper will publish "authoritative articles on problems of interest and importance." The October issue carries two such stories, "District Court Reorganization," by Livingston Hall, and "Children, the Law and Psychiatry," by Thaddeus P. Krush.

Researcher's Digest . · . · . · . · . · *Edited by John E. Bebout*

Technical Assistance to Citizens Discussed

Conference Panel Reviews Programs and Techniques

TECHNICAL assistance to citizens was defined by Weldon Cooper, of the Bureau of Public Administration, University of Virginia, as the act of a civic organization, either governmentally sponsored or privately endowed, providing guidance to groups interested in better government, health projects, welfare developments, educational facilities, etc. With this definition Dr. Cooper, as chairman, opened a panel discussion of the subject at the 1953 National Conference on Government in Richmond.[1]

Harold F. Alderfer, Institute of Local Government, Pennsylvania State College, pointed to three aspects of technical assistance to citizens: (1) legal information concerning elected offices, assigned duties, limits of power, etc.; (2) aid to citizen groups interested in governmental reorganization and various community improvements; (3) basic information on government for the vast numbers of citizens whose education was deficient or devoid of this fundamental area of knowledge. The general lack of statewide citizen action groups able to use the technical assistance provided was deplored. The third aspect of technical assistance, which in effect trains the citizens for participation in public affairs and to use more specialized guidance on public issues, is extremely important.

Gladys M. Kammerer and Ruth Mc-

_____

[1]This report is based on the notes of Turpin Phillips, Jr., recorder for the session on Technical Assistance to Citizens.

Quown, both of the University of Kentucky, described the activities of the Kentucky Legislative Research Commission, which contributes materially to the understanding of governmental programs by unofficial citizen groups as well as the state legislature itself. Three principal methods for disseminating the results of the Commission's research have been used. The detailed factual monograph and critical analysis of state agency reports go to a relatively limited audience, but are used as source materials for study groups, radio and television roundtables, and editorials and feature stories in newspapers. Illustrated brochures in a more colorful format are given more general distribution.

Richard Kraft, of the Virginia Division of Planning and Economic Development, pointed out the importance of technical assistance by state agencies to local citizen groups at various stages in their efforts to promote certain programs. Allen D. Manvel, Governments Division, Bureau of the Census, referred to the fact-gathering activities of the Census Bureau as "getting bricks to lay the foundations." These facts in the form of statistics on revenues and expenditures of all levels of government, levels of public employment, indebtedness, etc., are of great use to civic groups which are making serious studies of the programs of their local governments and comparing them with other communities.

Richard S. Childs, chairman of the Executive Committee, National Municipal League, described the ready response which his survey on coroner service has received from medical and legal organizations. Victor C. Hobday, University of Tennessee, discussed the work of the Municipal Technical Advisory Service in assisting citizens who are holding public office and in helping them interpret the city's programs to the electorate.

Among the questions which received particular attention was one posed by the chairman and addressed to Miss Kammerer: "How do you know that your reports are read?" Her answer: "We find them quoted in various publications, we hear them on TV programs, radio programs, school participation panels, see them in newspaper feature articles, and in letters to the editors."

It was emphasized that the extent to which the reports were used depended in large part upon the manner in which they were presented. There was general agreement with Miss Kammerer's point that "every effort should be made to have a colorful presentation of the facts and figures and numerous graphs, charts and line drawings." In answer to a question Roscoe Martin, Syracuse University, spoke of the need for sound judgment on the part of the agency providing assistance in order to avoid political involvement in local affairs but still provide answers to practical questions involving more than academic issues.

The panel concluded that the citizen groups which utilize technical assistance provided by governmental agencies must come to the support of these agencies when legislative bodies are considering their appropriations. Parallel services rendered by extension programs in the agricultural and engineering fields have been expanded and improved as a result of strong support from the clientele which they serve. Technical assistance to citizens and local governments can be broadened in scope and improved in quality only with such support.

WILLIAM N. CASSELLA, JR.

Model Ordinances

The first set of *Model Iowa Ordinances* has just appeared in published form. This project was undertaken three years ago as a cooperative effort of the Insti-

tute of Public Affairs and the College of Law of the State University of Iowa and the League of Iowa Municipalities (Iowa City, price $10.).

The published models cover municipal government—structure and officers, storage, collection and disposal of refuse, milk and milk products, traffic code, nuisances, planning and zoning, restricted residence districts, trees.

The ordinances are published in looseleaf form and additions and corrections can be made easily. Plans call for the project to continue until models are prepared on every phase of municipal activity. Although the ordinances are designed for cities and towns of less than 5,000, many of them may be used by larger cities.

The record of cooperation which made this project possible is described by Robert F. Ray in "The League and the Institute of Public Affairs—A Working Team," League of Iowa Municipalities *Monthly Magazine,* November 1953.

Bureau Reports

An increasing number of research bureaus and associations are using a compact pocket-sized format for their annual reports. Just received are the Texas Research League's *A Progress Report—1952-53* and the New Jersey Taxpayers Association's *A Good Thing for Jerseyites.* In addition to its more elaborate annual report on its fourth year of work, the Mississippi Economic Council published a program prospectus for its fifth year, together with other information about the council.

Research Pamphlets and Articles

Alcoholism

ALCOHOLISM. Staff Report to the Alcoholic Study Commission. Frankfort, Kentucky Legislative Research Commission, October 1953. 42 pp.

Annexation

ANNEXATION—WHAT IS THE PRICE? Seattle, Municipal League of Seattle and King County, *Municipal News*, October 17, 1953. 4 pp.

Authorities

THE PHILADELPHIA AIRPORTS IMPROVEMENT AUTHORITY. Philadelphia 7, Bureau of Municipal Research, *Citizen's Business*, October 6, 1953. 3 pp.

Commission Government

GOVERNOR VETOES LEAGUE REVISION OF THE WALSH ACT—ASSEMBLY BILL 641. Veto Message Answered by League Executive Director, James J. Smith. Trenton, New Jersey League of Municipalities, *New Jersey Municipalities*, October 1953. 3 pp.

Economic Development

MECHANICS OF THE URBAN ECONOMIC BASE: THE PROBLEM OF TERMINOLOGY. By Richard B. Andrews. Madison, University of Wisconsin, *Land Economics*, August 1953. 6 pp.

REGIONAL AND COUNTY PATTERNS IN ARIZONA. As Reflected in Data Concerning Non-agricultural Employers, Employees and Wage Payments, by Quarters, 1949-1952. Tucson, University of Arizona, College of Business and Public Administration, Bureau of Business Research, *Arizona Business and Economic Review*, October 1953. 6 pp.

Education

A CRISIS IN SCHOOL SERVICES AND FINANCE. The League Analyzes the Pittsburgh School Budget for 1954. Pittsburgh 19, Pennsylvania Economy League, Inc., Western Division, *P. E. L. Newsletter*, November 1953. 7 pp.

EQUALIZING EDUCATIONAL OPPORTUNITY THROUGH ADOPTION OF COMMUNITY SCHOOL DISTRICTS. St. Paul 1, Minnesota Institute of Governmental Research, Inc., *Bulletin*, October 1953. 7 pp.

A FOUNDATION PROGRAM FOR EDUCATION. Staff Analysis of Advisory Committee Recommendations. Frankfort,

County, Minnesota, seeking new sources of revenue to speed construction of permanent-type improvements on its system of primary highways. Bond issue seen as practical solution of income problem. Forces maintaining 400 miles of bituminous roads. By L. P. Zimmerman. Chicago 2, *Better Roads*, October 1953. 3 pp.

THE LEAGUE GETS A NEW JOB. Research for the Metropolitan Study Commission of Allegheny County. Pittsburgh 19, Pennsylvania Economy League, Western Division, *P. E. L. Newsletter*, September-October 1953. 11 pp.

NEEDED URBAN AND METROPOLITAN RESEARCH. Donald J. Bogue, Editor. Oxford (Ohio), Miami University, Scripps Foundation for Research in Population Problems, and University of Chicago, Population Research and Training Center, 1953. 98 pp. $1.25.

THE WORK LOAD OF METROPOLITAN COUNCILLORS. Open letter. Toronto 5 (Ontario), Bureau of Municipal Research. *Civic Affairs*, November 13, 1953. 8 pp.

Personnel

BLANKET SURETY BONDS FOR PUBLIC EMPLOYES. Blanket Bonds Permit Broad Coverage of Municipal Employes. By Richard H. Custer. Madison, League of Wisconsin Municipalities, *The Municipality*. November 1953. 2 pp.

'LITTLE HATCH ACTS' PROVIDE ELECTION-TIME DO'S AND DON'TS FOR PUBLIC SERVANTS. New York, National Civil Service League, *Good Government*, September-October 1953. 5 pp.

Recreation

RECREATIONAL DEVELOPMENT OF PRAIRIE LAKE, HOLTON, KANSAS. Lawrence, University of Kansas, Governmental Research Center, 1953. 46 pp.

Redevelopment

A LOOK AT REDEVELOPMENT IN BOSTON. Boston 8, Municipal Research Bureau, *Bulletin*, November 16, 1953. 4 pp.

Taxation and Finance

THE AD VALOREM TAX PROCESS. By Lyle C. Kyle. Lawrence, University of

Kansas, Governmental Research Center, *Your Government*, November 15, 1953. 3 pp.

A DECADE OF MISSISSIPPI STATE TAXES. University, University of Mississippi, School of Commerce and Business Administration, Bureau of Public Administration, *Public Administration Survey*, November 1953. 4 pp.

ENGLISH LOCAL GOVERNMENT FINANCE 1930-1951. By A. H. Marshall. London, Westminster, S. W. 1, Institute of Municipal Treasurers & Accountants, *Local Government Finance*, October and November 1953. 7 and 4 pp. respectively.

PENNSYLVANIA TAX CHART. Harrisburg, Pennsylvania State Chamber of Commerce, *Bulletin*, November 1953. 6 pp.

REPORT OF CITIZEN'S FACT-FINDING COMMITTEE APPOINTED BY MAYOR OF SHREVEPORT TO STUDY THE CITY'S FISCAL NEEDS AND PROBLEMS AND RECOMMEND A LONG-RANGE SOLUTION. Shreveport (Louisiana), The Committee, June 1953. 92 pp. Charts, tables.

SPENDING CAUSES TAX BURDEN. Government Costs Need Curtailing. By Ben Hulse. Los Angeles 14, California Taxpayers' Association, *The Tax Digest*, December 1953. 6 pp.

THE STATE OF YOUR STATE'S FINANCES. Springfield, Taxpayers' Federation of Illinois, 1953. 42 pp.

STATE TAXES—HIGHER THAN EVER. Collections Top Old Marks; Enactment of Fewer New Levies May Mark Trend. By Marilyn Gittell. New York 20, The Tax Foundation, Inc., *Tax Review*, October 1953. 4 pp.

THE TAX COLLECTOR—HIS DUTIES AND RESPONSIBILITIES. By George C. Skillman. Trenton, New Jersey State League of Municipalities, *New Jersey Municipalities*, November 1953. 6 pp. 35 cents.

TAX SYSTEM IN UTAH—1953. Salt Lake City 1, Utah Foundation, *Research Report*, November 1953. 6 pp.

Books in Review

RENEWING OUR CITIES. By Miles L. Colean. New York, Twentieth Century Fund, 1953. x, 181 pp. $2.50.

In a mercifully short and readable little volume, the Twentieth Century Fund reviews the problem of blight in cities and analyzes with thoughtful care and obviously abundant information the problem of securing orderly renewal of run-down sections before they reach the stage of blight or the lower stage that calls for slum clearance.

The task of looking over the condition of a city for the purpose of identifying decaying sections, and finding means of arresting decay, deserves more attention than it gets and this book, in its examination of promising experiments in certain cities and stressing of causes and possible preventive steps, comes as a contribution of high importance.

R. S. C.

CAREERS FOR COLLEGE GRADUATES IN NEW YORK STATE GOVERNMENT. Albany, New York Civil Service Commission, 1953. 52 pp. Illus.

An attractive and readable brochure which exhibits to college graduates the attractions of working for New York State. The 76,000 full-time employees enjoy a five-day week, with four weeks' vacation with pay and one day monthly of sick leave accumulated to 150 days, some security of tenure and retirement privileges. The character of work in each department is pictorially and interestingly presented. An attractive example of recruiting procedure!

MORE POWER. Report of the Newark Public Library, 1946-1952. By Alexander L. Crosby. Newark (New Jersey), the Library, 1953. 36 pp.

Newark's famously progressive library makes clear in print and fine photography

how important, exciting and fascinating the service of such an institution can be. The story includes a candid poke at TV's competitive effects on circulation. Alexander L. Crosby, whose skill enlivens some of the National Municipal League's pamphlets, designed and authored it, as he did the earlier Newark report, *The Power of Print* (1946), which was widely hailed as the finest reporting in library history.

MUNICIPAL AND INTERGOVERNMENTAL FINANCE IN THE UNITED STATES—1932-1942-1952. Washington, D. C., United States Conference of Mayors, 1953. 32 pp. $2.00.

NEEDED—NEW MUNICIPAL REVENUES. By Simeon E. Leland. Washington, D. C., United States Conference of Mayors, 1953. 24 pp. $1.00.

These two pamphlets will serve as useful source materials for the Commission on Intergovernmental Relations. The first was prepared to provide background and factual information for the discussions of the 1953 International Municipal Congress. The second is the paper written by Dr. Leland for the 1953 meeting of the United States Conference of Mayors. The intergovernmental dimension of municipal financial problems is given particular attention.

W. N. C., JR.

OLSON'S NEW DEAL FOR CALIFORNIA. By Robert E. Burke. Berkeley, University of California Press, 1953. 279 pp. $4.00.

In his preface Dr. Burke limits the usefulness of his book to promoting "an understanding of California politics" and helping California Democrats "to see their situation a little more clearly." Actually, this story of the Olson administration (1938-42) is a grammar

56

Civic Centers

CIVIC AND CULTURAL CENTERS. A Planning Bibliography. By D. Natelle Isley and Leo J. Zuber. Atlanta (Georgia), Metropolitan Planning Commission, March 1953. 7 pp.

Civil Service

STAFF REPORT ON THE DEPARTMENT OF CIVIL SERVICE. Albany, New York Temporary State Commission on Coordination of State Activities. 1953. 750 pp.

Education

THE COMMON CORE OF STATE EDUCATIONAL INFORMATION. By Paul L. Reason, Emery M. Foster and Robert F. Will. Washington, D. C., U. S. Department of Health, Education and Welfare, Office of Education, 1953. xvi, 116 pp. 35 cents.

FLORIDA'S SCHOOL FINANCING PROGRAM. An Address by The Honorable Thomas D. Bailey before The Municipal Forum of New York. New York, The Forum, November 13, 1953. 16 pp. (Apply The Forum, c/o Bank of New York, 48 Wall Street, New York 5.)

Insurance

INSURING AGAINST THE HAZARDS COMMON IN PUBLIC ADMINISTRATION. A symposium of insurance practices and kinds of insurance commonly obtained by municipalities in Canada and the United States. Chicago 37, Municipal Finance Officers Association of the United States and Canada, 1953. 12 pp. $1.00.

STATE AND MUNICIPAL SELF-INSURANCE. By George S. Hanson. New York 38, National Association of Insurance Agents, 1953. 72 pp.

Legislation

1953 LAWS OF INTEREST TO NEW JERSEY MUNICIPALITIES. Third Annual Edition. Trenton 8, New Jersey State League of Municipalities, 1953. xi, 115 pp. $1.00.

Marinas

THE MODERN MARINA. A Sound Business Opportunity for Community, Investor and Operator. New York 17, National Association of Engine and Boat Manufacturers, 1953. 61 pp. $1.00.

Municipal Government

TOWARD A BETTER CHICAGO. By Robert E. Merriam. Address before the Junior Association of Commerce and Industry. Chicago, The Association, March 31, 1953. 15 pp.

Population Statistics

ESTIMATES OF THE POPULATION OF STATES: July 1, 1950 to 1952. Washington 25, D. C., U. S. Department of Commerce, Bureau of the Census, 1953, 4 pp. 5 cents.

FINAL REPORT OF THE JOINT LEGISLATIVE COMMITTEE TO STUDY THE EFFECT OF THE 1950 CENSUS ON CERTAIN STATUTES. Submitted to the New Jersey Senate and General Assembly. Trenton, The Committee, 1953. 57 pp.

MOBILITY OF THE POPULATION OF THE UNITED STATES, APRIL 1952 TO APRIL 1953. Washington 25, U. S. Department of Commerce, Bureau of the Census, 1953, 12 pp. 10 cents.

Public Administration

THE VALUE OF MANUALS. A comprehensive discussion of the need for manuals together with a presentation of the essential items that should be included in an administrative manual. Chicago 37, Municipal Finance Officers Association of the United States and Canada, 1953. 8 pp. $1.00.

Public Health

PUBLIC HEALTH. Thirteenth Report of the Special Commission on the Structure of the State Government, Common-

ove—Congressman J. Vaughan Gary, of Virginia, speaking at the "kick-off" of the "Youth in Civic
airs" program, which reached over 7,000 high school and college students in Richmond during the
h National Conference on Government.

ht—Mrs. J. L. Blair Buck
cond from left), George
lup and Mrs. Hiram
ighton (extreme right),
·America Cities jurists,
h the Flint, Michigan,
gation.

ow—George D. Braden speaking at the "More Responsible States" session. Left to right, W. Brooke
ves, Charles B. Coates, Charlton F. Chute, Frank C. Moore (presiding), Mrs. Tom Ragland, Mr.
den and Albert L. Sturm.

Above—Hohen Foster, mayor
of Phoenix, addresses panel
at the Richmond Conference.
Left to right, Dr. Edward E.
Haddock, John B. Gage,
Mark S. Matthews, William
T. Middleton, Norman H.
Peterson, George S. Van
Schaick, Mayor Foster,
Bayard H. Faulkner and
Cecil Morgan.

Below—L. E. Marlowe chats
with Mayor Paul Goebel of
Grand Rapids.

Right—Mrs. Siegel W. Judd
and Mrs. Maurice H. Noun
of the League, discuss the
role of women in civic campaigns with Mrs. John G.
Lee (right), president of the
U. S. League of Women
Voters.

MUNICIPAL REVIEW

BRUARY 1954   VOLUME XLIII, NO. 2

The National Municipal Review

ALFRED WILLOUGHBY, Editor   ELSIE S. PARKER, Assistant Editor

Contributing Editors

JOHN E. BEBOUT, Research
RICHARD S. CHILDS
EDWARD W. WEIDNER, County and Township
H. M. OLMSTED, City, State and Nation

WADE S. SMITH, Taxation and Finance
GEORGE H. HALLETT, JR.
WM. REDIN WOODWARD
Proportional Representation

State Correspondents

H. F. ALDERFER, *Pennsylvania*
CARTER W. ATKINS, *Connecticut*
MYRON H. ATKINSON, *North Dakota*
CHESTER BIESEN, *Washington*
D. BENTON BISER, *Maryland*
ERNEST M. BLACK, *Oklahoma*
JOHN C. BOLLENS, *California*
WILLIAM L. BRADSHAW, *Missouri*
A. C. BRECKENRIDGE, *Nebraska*
ARTHUR W. BROMAGE, *Michigan*
FRANKLIN L. BURDETTE, *Maryland*
CHARLTON F. CHUTE, *Pennsylvania*
WELDON COOPER, *Virginia*
C. A. CROSSER, *Washington*
PAUL DOLAN, *Delaware*
D. MACK EASTON, *Colorado*
WILLIAM O. FARBER, *South Dakota*
FOREST FRANK, *Ohio*
DAVID FUDGE, *Oklahoma*
ROBERT M. GOODRICH, *Rhode Island*
MRS. LEONARD HAAS, *Georgia*
M. H. HARRIS, *Utah*
SAM HAYS, *Arkansas*
ROBERT B. HIGHSAW, *Mississippi*
JACK E. HOLMES, *New Mexico*
ORREN C. HORMELL, *Maine*
HERMAN KEHRLI, *Oregon*
PAUL KELSO, *Arizona*
DRYDEN KUSER, *Nevada*

JOHN D. LANGMUIR, *New Hampshire*
STUART A. MacCORKLE, *Texas*
RICHARD G. MARDEN, *New Hampshire*
BOYD A. MARTIN, *Idaho*
EDWARD M. MARTIN, *Illinois*
JAMES W. MARTIN, *Kentucky*
JAMES W. McGREW, *New Jersey*
DAYTON D. McKEAN, *Colorado*
EDWIN B. McPHERON, *Indiana*
WILLIAM MILLER, *New Jersey*
LENNOX L. MOAK, *Pennsylvania*
ANDREW E. NUQUIST, *Vermont*
KIMBROUGH OWEN, *Louisiana*
FRANK W. PRESCOTT, *Tennessee*
JOHN E. REEVES, *Kentucky*
ROLAND R. RENNE, *Montana*
PAUL N. REYNOLDS, *Wisconsin*
RUSSELL M. ROSS, *Iowa*
ALBERT B. SAYE, *Georgia*
VICTORIA SCHUCK, *Massachusetts*
LLOYD M. SHORT, *Minnesota*
GEORGE G. SIPPRELL, *New York*
PAUL D. STEWART, *West Virginia*
JOHN G. STUTZ, *Kansas*
HERMAN H. TRACHSEL, *Wyoming*
PAUL W. WAGER, *North Carolina*
YORK WILLBERN, *Alabama*
JOHN F. WILLMOTT, *Florida*

Published by THE NATIONAL MUNICIPAL LEAGUE

George H. Gallup, *President*

John S. Linen, *Vice President*
George S. Van Schaick, *Vice President*

Carl H. Pforzheimer, *Treasurer*
Alfred Willoughby, *Executive Director*

Richard S. Childs, *Chairman, Executive Committee*

Council

Charles Edison, West Orange, N. J., *Chairman*

Frederick L. Bird, New York
Arthur W. Bromage, Ann Arbor, Mich.
E. Bartlett Brooks, Dayton, Ohio
Henry Bruère, New York
William H. Bulkeley, Hartford
L. E. Burch, Jr., Memphis
Mrs. Albert D. Cash, Cincinnati
Charles E. Commander, Jr., Jacksonville
L. P. Cookingham, Kansas City, Mo.
Karl Detzer, Leland, Mich.
E. D. Dodd, Toledo
Harold W. Dodds, Princeton, N. J.
Bayard H. Faulkner, Montclair, N. J.
Arnold Frye, New York

Ewart W. Goodwin, San Diego
Thomas Graham, Louisville
Mrs. Virgil Loeb, St. Louis
Rob Roy Macleod, Buffalo
Mark S. Matthews, Greenwich, Conn.
Cecil Morgan, New York
Albert E. Noelte, Central Falls, R. I.
Mrs. Maurice H. Noun, Des Moines
H. Bruce Palmer, Newark, N. J.
Lawson Purdy, New York
Thomas R. Reid, Dearborn, Mich.
Philip K. Robinson, Milwaukee
Murray Seasongood, Cincinnati
Lee M. Sharrar, Houston

Regional Vice Presidents

Lester L. Bates, Columbia, S. C.
William Collins, New York
Ben B. Ehrlichman, Seattle
John B. Gage, Kansas City, Mo.
Carl J. Gilbert, Boston
Barry Goldwater, Phoenix
Lloyd Hale, Minneapolis

Arthur E. Johnson, Denver
Mrs. Siegel W. Judd, Grand Rapids
John Nuveen, Chicago
Ed. P. Phillips, Richmond
Charles P. Taft, Cincinnati
Alex R. Thomas, San Antonio
Carleton B. Tibbetts, Los Angeles

NEWS for League Members

NML to Present All-America Awards

With the announcement of the eleven winning All-America Cities of 1953 (for details see page 65), representatives of the National Municipal League have been selected to make the award presentations. *Look* magazine, co-sponsor of the contest with the League, was also to be represented at ceremonies marking the occasion, scheduled between January 26 and February 11.

Those selected to make the awards are officers of the League or have been associated with it and the All-America Cities Awards for some time. Appearing at the eleven cities will be the following:

CANTON, OHIO—E. D. Dodd, public relations director of the Owens-Illinois Glass Company, Toledo, Ohio, and League Council member.

DAYTONA BEACH, FLORIDA—Laurence F. Lee, chairman of the board, Chamber of Commerce of the United States and member of the 1953 All-America Cities jury at the National Conference on Government in Richmond, Virginia.

DE SOTO, MISSOURI—At the time the REVIEW went to press the League representative had not been announced.

FLINT, MICHIGAN—Mrs. Siegel W. Judd, director of the Grand Rapids Citizens' Action group and League regional vice president.

PARK FOREST (Rich Township High School District), ILLINOIS—John Nuveen, chairman of the board, John Nuveen and Company, Inc., Chicago, and regional vice president of the League.

(Continued on page 62)

Committee Tackles League Problems

Preliminary steps looking toward a partial revision of the League's constitution were taken January 9 at an all-day meeting at the Yale Club, New York, of the Survey Committee created at the Council's Richmond meeting to make a continuing study of program and policy.

Staff was directed to prepare suggested drafts of proposed constitutional amendments for consideration at the next meeting of the committee, which was set for January 30.

Staff was also assigned to prepare suggestions on machinery for consultation and policy-making, improved communications, summary of suggestions in the McLean report, status and future plans regarding League publications.

Among other matters discussed were the locale and program of the 1954 National Conference on Government and a possible restatement of the League's program and objectives.

Members of the committee present were: Cecil Morgan, chairman, who presided, Bayard H. Faulkner, Frank C. Moore and James M. Osborn.

Others attending were: George Gallup, president; Richard S. Childs, chairman of the Executive Committee; Carl H. Pforzheimer, treasurer; Mark S. Matthews and Thomas R. Reid, members of the Council; Stanley T. Gordon, of the Ford Foundation; Alfred Willoughby, executive director; John E. Bebout and Allen H. Seed, Jr., assistant directors.

Three Civic Awards Presented by League

Ed. P. Phillips, L. E. Marlowe, both of Richmond, Virginia, and Alex R. Thomas, of San Antonio, are the recipients of the League's three Distinguished Citizen Awards for 1953. The awards were presented at the Richmond National Conference on Government.

Phillips and Thomas are both regional vice presidents of the League and Marlowe recently completed his term on the Council.

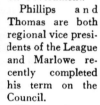

Ed. P. Phillips

The awards were presented to each man for "steadfast devotion and faithful service to his community and his self-sacrificing efforts to make a reality of self-government." The citation continues, "His demonstration of responsible citizenship above and beyond the call of duty has made his community a bet-

L. E. Marlowe

ter place in which to live and work and has given high encouragement and inspiration to the people of many other communities."

Phillips and Marlowe were leaders in the Richmond Citizens Association's fight for adoption of a modern city charter some years ago, while Thomas, as chairman of the San Antonio Citizens Committee, was instrumental in winning the council - manager form of government for his city.

Alex R. Thomas

All-America Awards

(Continued from page 61)

PEORIA, ILLINOIS—Dr. George H. Gallup, League president, foreman of the 1953 All-America Cities jury at the Richmond Conference and director of the American Institute of Public Opinion.

PETERSBURG, VIRGINIA—Ed. P. Phillips, senior partner of Phillips Machinery Company, Richmond, and League regional vice president.

PORT ANGELES, WASHINGTON—Ben B. Ehrlichman, chairman of the board, Pacific Northwest Company, Seattle, and regional vice president of the League.

RICHMOND, CALIFORNIA—Carleton B. Tibbetts, president-general manager, Los Angeles Steel Casting Company, and League regional vice president.

SCRANTON, PENNSYLVANIA—Richard S. Childs, chairman of the League's Executive Committee and chairman of the board, the Bon Ami Company, New York.

SHREVEPORT, LOUISIANA—Lee M. Sharrar, attorney for the Humble Oil and Refining Company in Houston, Texas, and member of the League's Council.

National Municipal Review

Volume XLIII, No. 2   Total Number 440

Published monthly except August

By NATIONAL MUNICIPAL LEAGUE

Contents for February 1954

The contents of the REVIEW are indexed in *International Index to Periodicals*
and *Public Affairs Information Service*.

Entered as second class matter July 11, 1932, at the Post Office at Worcester,
Massachusetts. Publication office, 150 Fremont Street, Worcester 3; editorial
and business office, 299 Broadway, New York 7. Copyright 1954 by the National
Municipal League.

Subscription, $5 per year; Canadian, $5.25; foreign, $5.50;
single copies 50 cents.

A Thought on "States' Rights"

THERE is a widespread approval of the idea that the functions of government should, in so far as possible, be performed by the governments that are closest to the people.

As in the case of economy, however, everyone is for it until the doctor gets specific about the useless parts he proposes to amputate.

There already are howls of distress in connection with current efforts to "pass back to the states"—and, let us hope, to the cities—responsibilities which for one reason or another have gravitated to Washington. The states are not being slow about asking where the money will come from.

Truth is that the services that come most readily to mind never were handled by the states because they deliberately ducked them.

Lest it be thought that this trend toward centralization in government is something recent or that it has been due to some conscious plot, it might be well to ponder the words spoken nearly half a century ago by Elihu Root, in an address delivered December 12, 1906, before the Pennsylvania Society:

It is useless for the advocates of states' rights to inveigh against the supremacy of the constitutional laws of the United States or against the extension of national authority in the fields of necessary control where the states themselves fail in the performance of their duty. The instinct for self-government among the people of the United States is too strong to permit them long to respect any one's right to exercise a power which he fails to exercise. The governmental control which they deem just and necessary they will have. It may be that such control would better be exercised in particular instances by the governments of the states, but the people will have the control they need, either from the states or from the national government; and if the states fail to furnish it in due measure, sooner or later constructions of the constitution will be found to vest the power where it will be exercised—in the national government.

The true and only way to preserve state authority is to be found in the awakened conscience of the states, their broadened views and higher standard of responsibility to the general public; in effective legislation by the states, in conformity to the general moral sense of the country; and in the vigorous exercise for the general public good of that state authority which is to be preserved.

And in a speech of acceptance of the senatorship of New York, delivered before the legislature on January 28, 1909, he said:

If the powers of the states are to be preserved and their authority is to be continued, the states must exercise their powers. The only way to maintain the powers of government is to govern.

1953's All-America Cities

Corruption, disaster and inertia in eleven communities
met by intelligent, effective citizen-inspired action.

NOTEWORTHY citizen action in 1953 armed eleven communities in the United States with the winning stories to qualify them for All-America Cities Awards.

The 1953 winners, representing ten different states, are: Canton, Ohio; Daytona Beach, Florida; De Soto, Missouri; Flint, Michigan; Park Forest (Rich Township High School District) and Peoria, Illinois; Petersburg, Virginia; Port Angeles, Washington; Richmond, California; Scranton, Pennsylvania; and Shreveport, Louisiana.

The contest has been conducted by the National Municipal League for five consecutive years. Since 1952 *Look* magazine replaced the *Minneapolis Tribune* as co-sponsor to recognize and reward progressive and purposeful civic activity in campaigns waged by citizens and citizen organizations.

"Over the years the League has had as a primary objective the encouragement of citizen action," League President George H. Gallup declared last November at the 59th National Conference on Government in Richmond, Virginia. As foreman of a jury of twelve distinguished civic, business, educational and professional leaders who picked the winners at the Conference, Dr. Gallup added: "Each of our All-America cities has its distinctive lesson and each shows what citizens can do if they want to badly enough."

What happened in the eleven winning cities that qualified them for the awards?

In some cases it was citizens as individuals and groups pushing through a successful campaign to root out corruption, vice and the concomitant maladministration of their communities. In one city, alert citizens realized that their community was behind the times, had lost its grip on its own young people, who were leaving home after graduating from high school. They surveyed the situation, got at the disease that paralyzed their town's growth and advancement and proceeded to effect community improvements on a strictly volunteer basis.

Still other towns, hit by the collapse of war industry after World War II, faced virtual economic extinction. Citizen groups of all stripes got together and embarked on programs to attract new industry and rehabilitate the entire area. One community's citizens, hamstrung by legal technicalities and the opposition of many self-satisfied residents, generated such a reaction that they built themselves one of the most up-to-date high schools in the nation.

Citizens hit by a devastating tornado organized a tremendous rebuilding program for themselves. Another city's forward-looking residents realized that one portion of the community was so much on the down grade that if something was not done the whole city would be affected. They made a thorough survey, put reforms into practice and not only helped solve an economic problem but also made important progress in easing race tensions.

The All-America Cities contest has become an American institution. It recognizes outstanding players in the game of civic progress. The National Municipal League and *Look* magazine do not pretend that the winning cities are the best governed in the United States. What they do claim is that the most significant progress in American communities results from intelligently planned citizen action. Each year the contest selects noteworthy accomplishments and awards citations to the communities in recognition of the efforts and achievements of an alert and active citizenry. They are presented on the basis of a variety of considerations, one of them generally being some evidence that the citizen action will be sustained and not stop dead when one goal is reached.

Dr. Gallup emphasized this point in Richmond, saying, "Citizen effort must be continuous. A single impressive effort followed by relaxation and return to the old, easy ways of silence is civic tragedy."

To win in a given year community action must reach a high point or a significant goal in that year, although the campaign may have begun years earlier.

One hundred and fifteen cities were nominated for the 1953 awards; 22 finalists presented their cases at the Richmond Conference before a jury comprising: George H. Gallup, director, American Institute of Public Opinion, foreman; Arthur W. Bromage, University of Michigan; Mrs. J. L. Blair Buck, former president, General Federation of Women's Clubs; Harold S. Buttenheim, editor, *The American City*; Lloyd Hale, president, G. H. Tennant Company, Minneapolis; Mrs. Hiram Cole Houghton, Foreign Operations Administration; Mrs. John G. Lee, president, League of Women Voters of the United States; Laurence F. Lee, chairman of the board, Chamber of Commerce of the United States; Vernon C. Myers, publisher, *Look* magazine; James M. Osborn, Yale University; Leo Perlis, national director, National CIO Community Services Committee; Donald H. Webster, University of Washington.

The eleven runner-up cities whose cases were presented to the jury were Corpus Christi, Texas; Fair Lawn, New Jersey; Glendale, California; Grand Rapids, Michigan; Greenwich, Connecticut; Hamilton, Ohio; Lawrence, Massachusetts; Norwich, Connecticut; Pittsburgh, Pennsylvania; Rome, New York; and Toledo, Ohio.

The following stories tell why the eleven winners were selected.

Canton Cleans Up

The Citizens Committee for Good Government of Canton, Ohio, (population 116,912) was formed in 1950 as a protest against booming vice, crime and gambling conditions in the city. The committee aggregated 600 housewives, businessmen, teachers, ministers, factory workers, doctors, nurses, Democrats, Republicans and independents, all of whom had a common area of agreement on what had to be done to clean up their home town.

First on the committee's list of objectives to counteract the miasmic moral atmosphere which had affected law enforcement, voter interest and general community progress was the election of a city administration that would execute the laws. This was no small order for a city that until then had refused to turn out and vote because of the caliber of candidates offered. But the 1951 primary was on the way and something had to be done.

The Citizens Committee took the bull by the horns and began to encourage successful men in a variety of business and professional fields to run for public office. In order to present good candidates in the general election, it was necessary to nominate good candidates in the partisan primaries. A man who had been in the real estate business for more than 22 years was urged to run for mayor, a young veteran for city solicitor, a well known manufacturer for council president. Others encouraged to do their bit for Canton were a dairy company president, a doctor, bank employees and industrial men.

The next big job for the Citizens Committee was to publicize the job to be done. Newspaper, radio station and church cooperation helped arouse qualified voters from their lethargy and get out the vote in both the primary and general elections. In addition, sample ballots were mailed to more than 53,000 persons.

Newspaper ads demanded: "Who runs Canton's biggest business?" and "What's Wrong with Canton That *You* Can't Cure?"

What were the results of all this activity?

In the 1951 primary only one Citizens Committee candidate was defeated. In the general election a new mayor and practically the entire remaining slate — seventeen out of twenty councilmen plus other key officials — s w e p t into office and cleaned out city hall.

With this new team in office, decisive action was taken immediately. The new director of public safety cracked down on gambling establishments. Ninety gambling houses were closed after 60 arrests. Police made sixteen narcotics arrests in twenty months—where before two had occurred in a total of sixteen years. A prosperous prostitution racket had thrived within a few blocks of city hall, but the new administration made almost 200 arrests, closed the bawdy houses.

The American Social Hygiene Association freed Canton of its "Vice Center" tag when it praised the cleanup. In February 1953 Stanley Cmich, the new public safety director who had led the crackdown against vice and crime, was given the U. S. Junior Chamber of Commerce award for good government. Besides being named Canton's outstanding young man of 1952, Mr. Cmich has also been honored as the outstanding young man of the state of Ohio. The Narcotics Division of the Treasury Department commended the city administration on its drug traffic crackdown.

But the Citizens Committee for Good Government did not stop there. It was mindful of its motto: "Good government is hard to get and easy to lose." The group continued to urge competent people to run for public office and exhorted all citizens to vote.

Result: Last November the re-formers won again. Canton's citizens went to the polling places and re-elected their candidates in seventeen out of nineteen offices.

Proof of the group's good work is the fact that in two years only two of the original 600 members have withdrawn from the Good Government Committee.

Daytona Beach Fights Corruption

A year ago Daytona Beach, Florida, (30,187) put in a strong bid before the All-America Cities jury in San Antonio but did not make the 1952 team. Citizen activity has continued. By 1953 the record was clear. The citizens of Daytona Beach, sparked by the Civic Affairs Committee, had put in a reform group of city commissioners, scoring a five-to-zero victory over the old guard professional politicians.

Gambling was Daytona's biggest evil. Taxes were high because of a spoils system of government. The laws were not enforced. The city's growth was stunted in comparison with other sections of Florida.

The only solution to this problem was to change the city's governing force. Accordingly, a five-year fight was initiated in 1948 by the Civic Affairs Committee. The only effective way to carry on the fight was to by-pass elected officials. This was done by invoking an almost forgotten power: Daytona citizens obtained from the state court authorization to serve writs. On the strength of this, they could personally make raids on gambling casinos and horse rooms. By closing these establish-ments, which were feeding the corrupt political machine with illegally gotten profits, the citizens threw a half nelson on the entrenched elements.

Because of election frauds, the committee and other affiliated groups, including the *News-Journal* Corporation and the Ministerial Association, both of which helped provide leadership for the Civic Affairs Committee, lost out in the 1948 elections.

The next step was the devising of a fraud-proof election bill. This was passed by the state legislature and, as a result, the election rolls were purged and "floaters" eliminated. In the 1950 election a reform majority of three to two was voted in power. And, by virtue of a last-minute write-in campaign, the machine-sponsored mayor was defeated for reelection.

But tragedy followed this temporary triumph when the new mayor switched his allegiance. The city manager was fired and a $260-a-month clerk was appointed to the $10,000 manager's post.

This was a bit too much. The Civic Affairs Committee and a host of other aroused citizens forced the resignation of the turncoat mayor by a widespread recall petition, which the mayor carried to the Supreme Court. When the court turned down his plea, he resigned and was replaced by a young businessman, a veteran of World War II.

An out-of-state professional city manager was appointed. A civic survey, entitled "What Does Daytona Beach Need — to increase beauty, improve economy, strengthen government, etc.," was undertaken. Representatives of 21 civic groups toured the city in a bus to survey conditions personally.

One of the new city manager's first actions was to fire the head of the city yards, which was a political patronage center, exempt from civil service. In reprisal, a death threat was leveled at the manager, city employees went out on strike and equip-

ment was sabotaged. But the citizents "stuck to it," backed up the manager, manned garbage trucks and maintained vital municipal services. In ten days the siege was over and the reformers had won a resounding victory.

Since the 1952 election success, citizen participation has continued to be a positive force in Daytona Beach. The city planner is now being helped by 120 citizens on a new comprehensive plan. Five men's civic clubs have met jointly to review the proposed budget with city officials. The League of Women Voters has sponsored large public budget hearings. One result: The "first full budget year for reform group started with $138,000 deficit and $175,000 unpaid bills; ended with $66,000 available surplus and bills currently paid."

Revival in DeSoto

When a small railroad town loses 44 per cent of its high school graduating class, something is wrong. So decided a majority of the alert citizens of De Soto, Missouri, (5,357). Then they began to look around and see why the city was so backward.

Most of the town's streets were unpaved. A street lighting system had been non-existent since depression days, when De Soto failed to pay its light bill. The city hall was in a dilapidated condition. Worst of all, young people had nothing to do. There seemed to be no incentive for staying around.

When the alert people around town realized why the population was

leveling off and why the town had reached a new low in all respects, they began to think about some general community improvement. In 1948 the Planned Progress Program of De Soto was formed. It was the first constructive step that had been taken in years.

The Planned Progress Program consists of two or more representatives of every organization in De Soto, which means a total of 79. The group comprises churches, clubs, unions, lodges and many other organizations, plus all interested citizens and teenagers who are willing to work toward community improvement. The names of 967 persons show on the organization's records as direct participants. But it was the executive committee of the program which laid the foundations for the work that began in 1952.

A switch to council-manager government in 1948 gave primary impetus to the program's activation. Until then the city was in a semibankrupt state. There were few municipal records and law enforcement and city pride were almost nonexistent.

By 1953 the picture had changed radically. Not only is the city financially sound, with records up to date, but efficient administration has made possible a 30 per cent tax reduction. As a result of citizen participation in community improvement programs— about 2,500 people pitched in actively — many things were accomplished. Eighty blocks of street were resurfaced by the citizens themselves. The city hall was remodeled. A new fire house was built strictly by volunteer labor. A new lighting system was installed. Voters overwhelmingly approved a new park tax and school levy. More than 1,100 people transformed an old furniture store into a club for the city's teenagers.

Over a hundred citizens are working actively in civil defense as auxiliary police and firemen and in De Soto's unique Junior Auxiliary Police Department.

The reasons why so much was accomplished? Over 1,400 citizens of De Soto canvassed, solicited and contributed to the road resurfacing job. All of the other improvements were carried out because the people in De Soto simply got out and did the job.

And in the future? A new sewage disposal plant is planned. Work on a swimming pool has already begun, and a new high school is anticipated.

The town's highest expectation is to keep the young people home in a community they needn't be ashamed of.

The city's 150th anniversary celebration brought 25,000 visitors into De Soto to watch 420 local "actors" participate in a pageant. Some called it a revival. Others knew that it was alert and intelligent citizen action which had made it all possible. Without that action, De Soto would have been just another sleepy railroad town.

Flint Rebuilds

The north end of Flint, Michigan, (163,143) was struck by a tornado on June 8, 1953. It killed 116 people, injured over 900, caused property damage amounting to millions of dollars and, in a four-mile sweep, wiped out an area one block and a half wide. About 600 families were directly affected by the disaster.

After the immediate rescue and

clearing operations were over, a lethargy set in for several weeks, and the unfortunate victims found themselves facing the enormous job of rebuilding their homes alone. It was not the best prospect in the world. Something would have to be done to arouse the whole community to its responsibility.

Then Father Henry Berkemeier,

pastor of St. Francis of Assisi Church, which served the storm area, got an idea. He brought it to the attention of Flint's civic leaders. The idea became a plan. And the plan became a fact.

What happened is no secret, since the wire services, newspapers, radio and television covered the event thoroughly. The biggest building bee in history began at 8 A.M. on Saturday, August 29. It was called "Operation Tornado," but what it did far outshone the name. On each of two days (that Saturday and the succeeding Sunday), with temperatures in the high 90s, more than 7,800 people contributed time, materials and effort to rebuild the devastated area. Some 5,000 persons worked at the job at one time.

The local group responsible for all this activity was the Central Committee of Operation Tornado—sixteen members with sixteen special assistants, a cross-section of Flint's citizenry. Forty-two civic, business, labor, church, transportation, youth, construction, hospital and innumer-able other organizations have been listed by the Central Committee as major participants in the rebuilding of 193 homes in the two-day period.

The exact total of actively participating individuals will never be known, but 7,823 persons are on record as having done their bit. More than 99,800 man-hours, together with materials, knowhow and skill, were donated toward the rebuilding of homes in the stricken Beecher area.

There have been other building bees since the two-day miracle last summer. More homes damaged by the storm have been rebuilt. Continued efforts involving civic cooperation are the facts of life in Flint, and a more wholehearted citizen concern for the welfare of the community in the future is anticipated.

The Flint story shows what a community can do for itself under stress. It also shows that there is hardly any task beyond the power of cooperative citizen action when it is organized intelligently.

Park Forest Builds a School

The citizens of Park Forest, Illinois, (8,138) had three problems to face in getting a high school for their fast-growing community, a mushrooming Chicago suburb. They had to organize a new school district. They had to win public support for a bond issue to build a new school. And finally they had to plan a superior educational program and plant.

A number of citizen committees were formed to come up with the answers. One of the big problems was to convince the people that they needed a new high school. Grade schools were no problem, since they had been constructed by not-for-profit corporations established for that purpose. But as for high schools, many residents felt they could send their children to neighboring institutions, although they were inadequate.

As the High School Organization Committee began to work on the first problem, organizing the new school district, it was confronted with the labyrinth of Illinois local governments and the opposition of farmers and residents of nearby villages, which opposed the new high school in Park Forest. A special boundary change election had to be won before the new Rich Township District could be established. Petitions were circulated in record time to beat a legal deadline. After a hard-fought, hurry-up campaign led by the committee, new boundaries were approved. The way was paved for a vote on a $1,250,000 bond issue for the school in June 1951.

A special "Get Out the Vote Committee," comprising 105 representative citizens, cooperated with the Organization Committee of 50 to produce the sought-for results. A high school publicity committee of five also helped out. But the opposition, which consisted mainly of p e o p l e who were averse to any change, became indignant, printed literature and tore down election signs of the pro-high school group.

The organizing committee and the other groups obtained color photographs of new high schools in Chicago and showed them all over the Park Forest area. Pamphlets telling the aims and purposes of the committee were issued by the thousands. The election was close at hand and, to insure a large turnout, the committee began recruiting baby-sitting teams. Sound trucks were employed to whip up enthusiasm for the idea of a new school.

By virtue of a four-to-one verdict, the school bonds were approved in what was the community's record election turnout. Only 40 per cent of the voters outside Park Forest

really wanted the school, however. Then, on the ground that the district was not operating a high school, new state legislation dissolved the district. It was a hard blow.

Undaunted, local citizens began a long court battle to reverse the effect of the legislation. They finally won. Then volunteer canvassers went out again, this time discovering that a much more ambitious school was desired. People now really felt they needed a high school. The second bond issue was approved April 12, 1952. Construction had already begun on a 56-acre site provided by the company that had developed Park Forest.

Meanwhile, a High School Study Group of 108 citizens had tackled the problem of curriculum needs. The Rich Township High School Citizens Committee, a permanent group of 24 civic-minded people. worked hand in hand with the study group. Finally, on September 14, 1953, the physical plant of the school was completed and the citizen leadership that had planned it all tasted the first fruits of victory.

Today, Park Forest has a fully accredited high school (the Rich Township High School) with 500 students, a capacity for 900 and a future expansibility to 1,800. The new school enjoys enthusiastic citizen participation and support. Some 300 lay citizens spent over 6,500 hours on behalf of the school. Volunteers are still in business as a representative advisory body. And a continuing effort to improve educational service within the district is still being carried on by the permanent township high school citizens committee.

Peoria Reforms Itself

The cue to civic-minded people in Peoria, Illinois, (111,856) came in 1951 when state legislation was enacted which enabled all Illinois communities other than Chicago to adopt council-manager government if they wanted it. Peorians for Council-Manager (PC-M), a permanent group of 250 citizens, jumped at the opportunity. Why?

The second largest city in the state was operating under an inefficient system of government, featuring an unwieldy 22-man council, elected by wards. As of last May, Peoria was in debt to 279 creditors to the amount of $350,000. Back in 1942 the city's Junior Chamber of Commerce reported over 80 brothels.

The situation, however, did not improve. As late as 1953, before the election of competent officials under a new form of government, a woman brothel proprietor pleaded guilty to evading over $200,000 in income taxes over a period of four years. Charges that vice operators were paying in the thousands weekly for "protection" were levelled by at least one investigator. Gambling houses prospered without much interference.

PC-M, which had its roots in individual and collective action by civic-minded Peorians as far back as 1915, snapped to action. Four thousand signatures were secured in four days calling for a referendum. The reformers launched a furious three-weeks campaign. They made 32,000 phone calls, urging voters to go to the polls. A speakers bureau of 30 people made 142 speeches. Pamph-

lets entitled "Mess or Management?" were dispatched to every home. On the day of election, January 22, 1952, the ice-covered streets presented an unexpected obstacle to a large vote. Accordingly, a car pool organized by the Junior Chamber of Commerce carried 2,600 voters to the polls. The result was clear victory: 15,892 for council-manager, 7,095 against.

A new form of government does not necessarily insure a community's future. The people who operate it will determine its ultimate usefulness. So PC-M, while pleased with the initial victory, squared away for round two of the fight. The most pressing matter now was to elect a city council of high caliber. An unprecedented campaign began immediately. In three months, over a quarter-million mailing items sprayed out like buckshot from committee headquarters. When election day arrived on April 7, the high-powered speakers bureau, publicity which was fed regularly to the local papers, and a phone call campaign paid off with amazing success. Five of the city council's eight members were PC-M candidates, as was the new mayor.

The results didn't stop there. The price paid for asphalt on paving jobs dropped from $12.50 to $9.45 a ton. Miscellaneous city d e b t s were lumped together in a single bond issue. Gambling and prostitution were held down by vigorous prosecution. The new police chief raided thirteen bawdy houses 35 times in six months. A payroll cut of $23,000 was effected by eliminating purely political jobs.

NATIONAL MUNICIPAL REVIEW

The new council's quality and demonstrated alertness of citizens made it possible for Peoria to hire a first-rate city manager.

PC-M wasn't alone in its fight for better government. Among the participating and supporting groups were civic, fraternal, religious, labor and business organizations ranging from the League of Women Voters to the Peoria Advertising and Selling Club.

The price of reform: time, faith and endurance. Total work over the two years: 359 speeches, 3,500 people transported to the polls in car pools, 85,000 phone calls to registered voters, 325,000 mailing pieces dispatched, poll watching and checking, publicity, coordination—the multitude of details that add up to victory. The reward: that once vague but now tangible fact called good government.

Petersburg Progress

Over 1,500 people pitched in actively to realize an old dream of Petersburg, Virginia, (35,054). They tried once before, in 1940, but the war intervened and the effort went by the board for the duration. But what they wanted was so important to the city that they tried again in 1949. The object: a new and modern city hospital. It was badly needed. The old hospital was not only short of equipment and space but it had been condemned by the state fire marshal.

Like many other cities of comparable size, Petersburg failed to carry on a comprehensive program of municipal improvements. A large backlog of community needs had accordingly accumulated. The city government realized this and decided, in a remarkable example of government-citizen cooperation, to go "all out" in 1949.

Nine prominent business and professional men composed the Hospital Authority created by the city officials. These men, forming a permanent group, carefully planned a fund-raising campaign based on subscrip-

tions. The idea began to grow. Before long a number of volunteer workers were enlisted. Many civic groups, including the Chamber of Commerce, the Rotary, Kiwanis, Lions Clubs, the Junior Chamber of Commerce, churches, civic clubs and fraternal organizations joined the bandwagon. The local newspaper and radio station gave added force to the drive. All in all, 1,500 Petersburg citizens participated actively in a Group Pledge, worked on fund-raising committees and did public speaking—all for the cause of a long-deserved hospital.

The campaign was carried on with such enthusiasm that the financial goal was exceeded by approximately 50 per cent. A modern 180-bed hospital, costing $3,000,000, was completed and occupied on January 15, 1953.

This campaign served to rejuvenate citizen interest in community needs. From 1950 to the present time the city has carried on an active program of community improvement —all of it with the continuing support of the press, radio, Chamber of

Commerce, civic clubs and the citizens generally.

Among the many results of this heightened community interest have been a $1,000,000 Negro high school, a $500,000 elementary school, an $80,000 fire station, a $250,000 farm market, improvements in the city's water distribution system, off-street parking facilities for more than 400 cars, adoption of a one-way street system in the downtown area which has involved street cutbacks and enlargement of many intersections, adoption of the sanitary land-fill method of waste disposal and, at the present time, the building of a $1,-500,000 sewage treatment system as well as a $100,000 Negro outdoor swimming pool.

In an age when self-reliance has fallen into some disrepute, Petersburg has shown what a city can do for itself, provided the will of forward-looking citizens is unified into effectively programmed action.

Port Angeles Studies Itself

For 25 years Port Angeles, Washington, (11,233) was satisfied with itself, but a few years ago some of the townspeople decided that the community needed some face-lifting. It was a bigger assignment than many expected. What actually happened in 1952 and 1953 was that over half the citizens worked for the town. Civic efforts moved on many fronts. One thousand citizens created a new YMCA Youth Center from a 45-year-old hospital building.

About 3,000 turned out rewarding results in a Community Study, which involved complete research on Port Angeles' boundaries, population, community organizations, churches, library, education, government, social agencies, agriculture, industry, trades and services, beautification, health, recreation and history. A complete community census was taken. The town held a series of 27 weekly town meetings with the research committees, and recommendations from these sessions were carried into action by citizen groups. Eighty-five volunteer typists, stencil cutters, machine operators, using donated materials, did the paper work.

Every week for a year's time an average of 250 people turned out for the self-study sessions which were the assembling point for so many of the subsequent advances. Unsightly community areas were cleaned up by citizen work parties.

One thousand people worked for the bond issues which built a new school. Additional hundreds canvassed and persuaded others to tax themselves for a badly needed arterial street paving program, the first such program in a quarter of a century. The city was brought out of the mud for the first time since its founding.

The townspeople even arranged a special caravan to go to the state capital for a legislative hearing on the Puget Sound bridge proposals, vital to the community's welfare. Over 250 people traveled to the House of Representatives from Port Angeles and accounted for that body's largest public hearing.

Other accomplishments: The Children's Hall, a home for abandoned and delinquent children, was remodeled, painted and furnished in one day by a total community effort. A $4,000 fund was raised to finance a complete freight rate study after the community claimed the rates were the highest in the nation. The new hospital was brought out of the red.

Many citizen groups helped in producing these miraculous results. They worked hard and long for the new "Y," for streets, for schools and other community improvements. There was the Citizens Advisory Board for Schools and the Community Study Group. Out of the latter has grown the "Community Action Assembly," which is currently engaged in planning a variety of new local improvements, both in and around Port Angeles. Practically every civic, church, business, fraternal, labor, youth and professional organization in town was in on the act. The change to council-manager government had been sparked by the Municipal League of Port Angeles.

The city of Port Angeles claims: "There is nothing impossible if you and your neighbors are willing to work for it yourselves—together!"

On the basis of what has been accomplished in the past year or two and what is planned for the future, the statement bears more than an element of truth. As a fitting climax to Port Angeles' civic progress, the town was selected by the U. S. Department of State as a showplace of American democracy in action for seven German students who lived and worked in the community.

Richmond Reconverts

Without World War II, Richmond, California, (99,545) would have avoided a lot of headaches. And there were considerable headaches, particularly when almost 100,-000 war jobs folded up in 1945. It was a problem, one faced by many communities which had grown with alarming rate as a consequence of war industry. Reconversion was just as much a problem for municipalities in the United States as it was for American industry.

Richmond's citizen organizations rallied to the occasion in the postwar years. Some 2,500 citizens not only proceeded to stop their city from becoming a veritable "ghost town" but set out on a long-term program of community improvement. It took eight years and it continues.

They first began work to attract industry to Richmond. As a result, they were able to bring a lot of the shipbuilding industry back to the empty Kaiser shipyards. New land was bought by the city council and before long there were almost 90 new industries and 36,000 jobs, as well as many more within a short commuting distance. The economic problem had been solved for the time being.

Next came the program of community improvement. Numerous citizen and mayor's committees pitched in, aggregating 1,000 temporary citizen-volunteers. The 100-strong League of Women Voters, the Service Clubs Council of 25 and the Community Welfare Council of 35 were the main local groups leading the campaign. The press and radio helped disseminate factual information. Industrial, labor and civic organizations helped raise funds, provided committee participation and collected endorsements. A committee of 100 of the Church Council, as well as 500 from the Merchants Association, helped in planning, displays and information distribution.

What did all these citizen groups accomplish?

They defeated a strong effort to establish a divisive "ward" system and they strengthened their council-manager government by charter revision.

They eliminated a "spoils" system by adopting new personnel rules, backing them up by a charter amendment.

An unsound general pension system was terminated by another charter amendment.

They accounted for the greatest tax cut in the city's history.

They conducted a successful fight for an off-street parking bond issue.

A twelve-man delegation of citizens flew to Washington to get the government to expedite the return of government land to private interests for industrial promotion purposes.

They met with city, county and state officials and began to rout out widespread vice conditions in an adjacent unincorporated area.

They provided leadership in a housing relocation program.

They established an industrial development group to attract more new industry and supply jobs for residents.

A citizens committee put over two large bond issues, one for a county office building, the other for a major road program. Before 1953 the most outstanding postwar citizen accomplishment was the construction of a modern, postwar civic center financed by a $4,000,000 bond issue. School, hospital and youth center buildings were also built by means of bond issues.

As for the future, many other civic improvements are contemplated. Work is already in process to revise the police and fire pension system. A continuing program to flatten 24,000 jerry-built wartime housing units has begun, and these are being replaced with modern dwelling construction.

A movie, entitled "The Story of Richmond," was filmed in 1953 to show wartorn European audiences. Ordered by the High Commissioner of Germany and the U. S. State Department, it demonstrates how citizen action in a community has helped solve the pressing problems of postwar living without federal assistance.

Scranton Diversifies

When Scranton's anthracite coal reserves became exhausted after the war, a major economic crisis threatened to hit the community. Not only was there the grim fact of 29 mines shutting down but also the loss of 30,000 jobs for miners who had worked in pits that once gave America half its anthracite.

The industrial rehabilitation and

diversification program that citizen action accomplished in Scranton after the war has come to serve as a model to other communities. And it was accounted for mainly by a hundred Scranton businessmen who were not particularly pleased with the 15,000 drop in population over the ten-year period 1940-1950. Among the other contributing citizen factors were 2,000 members of the Scranton Chamber of Commerce, 150 incorporators of the Lackawanna Industrial Fund Enterprises and a group of non-profit civic organization members.

The Chamber of Commerce group began the task of attracting new industry. Community non-profit corporations within the Scranton Chamber of Commerce tackled the job of providing the requisite financial support. Citizen bond drives and outright capital contribution campaigns were waged throughout the Scranton area. Labor leaders, churchmen, veterans' organization leaders, small income wage earners and everyone else joined with big and small business representatives, bankers, civic leaders to raise a fund of over $4,000,000. The banks came through with credit support amounting to additional millions.

All the money raised was used by the non-profit companies to build new industrial plants. As soon as they were ready they were offered to new industries at attractive rentals—with an option to buy.

Fifty-five new factories and 75 plant expansions have resulted from this well planned activity. The unemployed have been reduced substantially and by this coming spring it is expected there will be a job for everybody. Once a great coal producing area, Scranton now is manufacturing everything from cigars to children's wear. Coal miners have become shoemakers, carpenters, textile weavers. Formerly unemployed diggers have found work in producing building materials, women's and children's wear, household fixtures and auto batteries.

In economic-threatened Scranton "jobs-for-men" bond selling drives had chalked up unprecedented success a few years after the war when most communities throughout the nation were prospering.

The "Scranton Plan" is a model. Surrounding towns have patterned programs to attract new industries along the same lines. Chambers of commerce from Missouri, South Carolina, Florida and Oklahoma, among many states, have sought details from Scranton as to how they did it.

Back in 1949 the *Wall Street Journal* put it this way in a story on the "Scranton Plan": "Citizens here have proved a recession-hit city can pull itself up by its bootstraps." Scranton people claim their story outstrips any other community-generated industrial development program in the country. The U. S. Department of Labor and the Chamber of Commerce of the United States point to it as a stellar example of community cooperation and community action.

A basic task force of a hundred put over the program, but it involved the active participation of 250,000 people in a united effort to resurrect

Scranton and the Lackawanna Valley. Ground-breaking ceremonies for new plants under the community program continue.

Shreveport Survey

When part of a community lives in substandard conditions and suffers from poor educational facilities, no private hospital facilities and extremely poor health facilities, the rest of the community, sooner or later, is going to suffer. The realization of this fact by a group of civic-minded white citizens in Shreveport, Louisiana, (127,206) served to arouse enough interest in the city to begin one of the most unusual surveys ever undertaken in the deep south. Without the facts, it was obvious that nothing could be done.

The Council of Social Agencies, a permanent organization with 53 members, decided that a survey of the Negro population and its problems would be the only answer to the many questions that had gone begging for so long. They began work in 1949. Their survey was concluded last April.

More than 1,000 people contributed to the job. Before the actual interviewing began, a comprehensive educational program was undertaken. As a result, a house-to-house canvass of 11,002 dwelling units—almost 100 per cent of all Negro housing—was made by 700 trained Negro volunteers, 400 of whom were teachers. The finest specialists in each area of study—population, education, employment, health, medical care, housing, law enforcement, recreation, religion, transportation and welfare—gave generously of their time and talent.

The survey told some grim facts: There were thirteen Negro slums breeding crime and disease; toilet facilities in substandard housing were deplorable; banks were unwilling to extend loans to Negroes who could afford better housing; Negro schools were overcrowded and many of them needed to be torn down; 2,000 Negro adults couldn't read or write; no private hospital facilities existed for Negroes, and Shreveport's five Negro doctors were barred from the hospitals.

When these facts were brought to light, action was initiated immediately. A $20,000,000 bond issue passed in an election—$11,000,000 would be spent for eighteen Negro schools. Night classes were begun for Negro adults. The banks started to extend housing loans to Negroes. At the present time almost 800 housing units are under construction. The down payment on two-bedroom houses is currently $330, while rental units cost $47.82 per month. Negro doctors can now be admitted to a white hospital, which also provides private rooms for their patients. Many other improvements were begun on the basis of survey findings.

One of the highest tributes to the survey was made by the Negro doctor who headed the house-to-house canvass. He said: "The chasm which has always existed between my people and the white citizens of Shreveport has been closed. Never again will we be alone or shut off."

In addition, the survey has been publicized by the press, radio and television so well that it will prob- ably stimulate similar efforts in other southern communities where the problem is equally pressing.

Eleven Runner-up Cities

The eleven runner-up cities were cited for the following examples of citizen action:

Corpus Christi, Texas —
For the Better Government League's campaign for a recall election and a subsequently successful municipal election campaign in which the league's candidates were elected by an almost two-to-one majority.

Fair Lawn, New Jersey —
For the activities of the Citizens School Committee and the Nonpartisan League in promoting better school facilities and better understanding and support for the borough's council-manager charter.

Glendale, California —
For the activities of various local organizations engaged in a number of community improvement programs, among them charter revision, an off-street parking program and a traffic safety campaign.

Grand Rapids, Michigan —
For citizen action sustained over a ten-year period, directed towards charter amendment and revamping of the city administration, which in turn provided for scientific, nonpolitical citywide reassessment. Grand Rapids was an All-America City in 1949.

Greenwich, Connecticut —
For efforts of the Republican Citizens Committee and Town Republican Club, as well as other participating citizen groups, and their successful fight for the enactment of a municipal direct primary law and the elimination of political patronage as a factor in party candidate selection.

Hamilton, Ohio —
For the combined efforts of several citizen groups in securing the passage of bond issues for school and street improvements, organizing an annexation program, launching a revision of the city's building code and undertaking a novel approach to raising charity funds.

Lawrence, Massachusetts —
For the organization of the Citizens' Committee for Industrial Development which, over the last two years, has succeeded in attracting new industry and thereby relieved unemployment problems created by a recession in the woolen-worsted textile industry.

Norwich, Connecticut —
For the seven-year drive conducted by the Citizens' Committee for Better Norwich Government to obtain adoption of a new, modern charter for a consolidated city and town government and commensurate administrative efficiency in the new government.

Pittsburgh, Pennsylvania —
For the long sustained effort for fundamental area-wide improvements led by the Allegheny Conference on Community Development, the Pitts-

(Continued on page 110)

News in Review

Manager Plan Gains 93 in 1953

List Now Numbers 1,229 in the U. S. and Canada

NINETY-THREE additional communities in the United States and Canada were added to the list of those using the council-manager form of government in 1953. Total number of local governments using the plan is now 1,229.

The record rate of adoptions each year since World War II indicates the council-manager plan will become the prevailing form of local government within the next decade. Adoptions in 1953 were exceeded since the war only in 1948 when there were 95.

About 40 per cent of all American communities with populations over 25,000 now have the plan, as do about one-third of those between 10,000 and 25,000.

California led all states in adoptions last year with ten communities added to the list. Florida and Illinois were second and third. Three Alaskan cities adopted the plan.

Largest city to secure the plan was Savannah, Georgia, with a population of 119,600 (s e e b e l o w). Cincinnati (504,000) is the largest council-manager city today; Teterboro, New Jersey, (28) the smallest.

Although council-manager government is most popular in Maine, where 120 communities have the plan, California is a strong second with 113. Texas is third with 98, followed by Michigan with 93, Florida with 67, Virginia 65, Pennsylvania 58, North Carolina 50 and Oklahoma 47.

SAVANNAH, GEORGIA, (1950 population 119,638) has been granted council-manager government by the state legislature. A bill to that effect passed the House of Representatives on November 23 and the Senate on November 28. It was expected that a city manager would take office in February 1954, by appointment of the existing city council. The present mayor and the twelve aldermen are to serve out their terms in 1954. On the second Tuesday of January 1955 an election for mayor and six aldermen will be held. At an advisory referendum on March 28, 1951, Savannah voted 8,369 to 5,983 for the council-manager plan, but efforts to make it effective had failed until now.

BETHEL, MAINE, (1,067) at a town meeting held December 17, voted 135 to 30 for adoption of the council-manager plan.

LATHRUP VILLAGE, MICHIGAN, adopted a council-manager charter on December 7 and elected its first council, which took office December 14.

The International City Managers' Association reports the following adoptions of the council-manager plan in 1953 not previously reported by the REVIEW: in FLORIDA, HALLANDALE (3,886), FORT WALTON (2,463), and JUPITER ISLAND (Hobe Sound); in KENTUCKY, MOREHEAD (3,102); in MICHIGAN, ROSEVILLE (15,816); in TENNESSEE, DAYTON (3,191); in TEXAS, KERMIT (6,912); in UTAH, CLEARFIELD (4,723); in WASHINGTON, NORMANDY PARK. The Association also added ELK CITY, OKLAHOMA, (7,962); HOLLY, MICHIGAN, (2,663) and LYNN HAVEN, (1,787) and BAY HARBOR ISLANDS, (296), FLORIDA, which adopted the plan before 1953. It has removed TEMISCAMING, QUEBEC, because it has not appointed a manager for over a year.

A bill has been filed in the MASSACHUSETTS legislature calling for a local referendum in the town of RANDOLPH on the question of establishing the selectmen-manager plan of government.

Judge Jesse Morton of the Suffolk Superior Court has approved a request of the BROCKTON, MASSACHUSETTS, Taxpayers Association that Brockton registrars of voters provide more specific information on why they turned down the association's petition for a referendum on the question of adopting the council-manager plan. A bill to authorize such a referendum in 1954, despite the rejection of the petitions, has been filed with the legislature.

In NATICK, MASSACHUSETTS, a town manager committee, appointed at the last town meeting, is making a study of the manager plan and has held a public meeting for discussion of the plan.

A bill has been introduced in the MASSACHUSETTS legislature under which appointments by city managers would require council confirmation. As criticized by the *Worcester Gazette,* this would subject such appointments to patronage under the council and break down the safeguards against interference between administrative and legislative functions in the council-manager plan.

At the annual session of the Barnstable County Selectmen's Association on December 4 in Hyannis, Massachusetts, on Cape Cod, a member warned his brethren against town manager and executive secretary forms of town government "creeping onto the Cape."

In EAST PROVIDENCE, RHODE ISLAND, a charter based on the strong mayor principle was submitted and defeated in November 1953 by the opposition of the local citizens' league. The latter then spearheaded a drive for election of a new charter commission dedicated to the manager plan. It was successful on December 9 in electing five candidates definitely committed to council-manager, three uncommitted as yet and one member of the former commission who favors the strong mayor form. East Providence now has the old town form of government.

In PEEKSKILL, NEW YORK, the newly formed City Manager Committee has set up three subcommittees to gather information on the functioning of the council-manager plan in other cities.

In WAVERLY, NEW YORK, petitions for a vote on the council-manager plan have been circulated by the Citizens Committee for a Village Manager Form of Government, which has also formulated a program of popular education.

KINGS MOUNTAIN, NORTH CAROLINA, recently voted to abandon the manager plan.

In THOMSON, GEORGIA, as a result of study by a committee appointed by Mayor Darrell Johnson, proposed charter amendments, including appointment of a city manager by the mayor and council, have been incorporated in a bill for introduction in the state legislature. The manager would have charge of all departments; however, his appointments of department heads and employees would be subject to approval of a majority of the mayor and council.

The city council of BECKLEY, WEST VIRGINIA, has proposed various charter changes, subject to public reaction, one of them calling for appointment of a so-called city manager by the mayor with council approval.

The village of AMBERLY, OHIO, a suburb of Cincinnati, recently elected a charter commission to draft a council-manager charter.

In SPRINGFIELD, ILLINOIS, the Manufacturers and Employers Association points to the success of Peoria in establishing the council-manager plan and emphasizes the need for vigorous community-wide action for the same purpose in Springfield.

In DULUTH, MINNESOTA, a vote on adoption of the council-manager plan is being urged, possibly as early as April of this year.

A campaign for the council-manager

plan has been in preparation in SEDALIA, MISSOURI.

The first public hearings on the council-manager charter drafted by the WEBSTER GROVES, MISSOURI, charter commission were held in December. An election thereon is scheduled for March 23. Mayor John H. Cassidy has announced that he does not favor the charter.

The November REVIEW (page 517) erroneously reported that VINTON, IOWA, defeated a proposal to adopt the manager plan. As correctly stated in May (page 184) the Vinton city council established the office of manager and made an appointment March 1, 1953.

The MISSOULA, MONTANA, Chamber of Commerce polled its membership on the council-manager plan; 79 per cent voted in its favor.

Members of the FLAGSTAFF, ARIZONA, Chamber of Commerce voted 87 to 25 for the council-manager plan.

In SAN ANTONIO, TEXAS, a petition calling for an election on charter amendments to replace the council-manager plan by the strong-mayor plan was filed with the city clerk on December 2. The movement is supported by the group that has unsuccessfully sought the recall of six council members.

LOVINGTON, NEW MEXICO, is reported to be preparing to vote at the next election to become a city under the council-manager plan.

A petition calling for a referendum on the question of adopting the manager plan has been filed with the city council of SPARKS, NEVADA. A referendum is expected in the spring.

ROSEVILLE, CALIFORNIA, rejected a proposed council-manager charter at an election on December 1.

The city council of PORT HUENEME, CALIFORNIA, established the position of chief administrative officer by ordinance effective September 24, 1953, and made an appointment to the office on November 18. The ordinance describes as his primary duty, "To execute on behalf of the city council its administrative supervision and control of such affairs of the city as may be placed in his charge." He is directed to prepare and administer the budget, to coordinate departmental operations and to make various studies; but no appointive power is specified.

Municipal Policy Statements at AMA Convention

At the 1953 American Municipal Congress, held by the American Municipal Association in New Orleans early in December with a registration of nearly 750 officials and representatives, several policy statements codifying various resolutions and statements of the AMA in recent years were adopted.

The statement on municipal finance asked the federal government to consider the requirements of local governments when drafting national tax proposals. The need of payments in lieu of taxes was stressed in connection with federal installations requiring municipal expenditures, particularly in connection with an influx of military or industrial defense personnel. The states were asked to grant a broad tax base to cities and to help stabilize municipal finances and services by state aid. State municipal leagues were urged to submit comprehensive revenue plans to the legislatures.

As to highways, the need of more adequate allocation of federal aid for use in urban areas was reiterated; the Bureau of Public Roads was asked to continue its present level of planning; state highway agencies were urged to establish urban road sections, with further technical assistance to municipalities and development of over-all highway plans.

Municipal objectives in intergovernmental relations were stated to include: The federal government should not enter fields of state and local activity unless there is a well defined national interest therein; federal agencies should make greater use of advisory councils of

ysis of the New York State Department of Civil Service and its activities, with many recommendations for improvement.

The commission is headed by Senator Walter J. Mahoney and includes two other senators, three assemblymen, State Tax Commissioner A. J. Goodrich, Dr. Paul Studenski, fiscal consultant to the State Division of the Budget, and Lawrence E. Walsh, then counsel to the Public Service Commission. The staff work on the civil service report was headed by William J. Ronan as director of studies and Arthur J. Schwartz as counsel.

One of the chief recommendations resulting from the study was that there should be a single administrative head for the department, heretofore headed by the Civil S e r v i c e Commission. This change has already been authorized by statute, and Governor Thomas E. Dewey recently appointed a high-level business executive to the position. The commission remains as a board to hear appeals and make rules, which is in line with another recommendation in the report.

Other conclusions reached by Dr. Ronan and Mr. Schwartz as to civil service needs are:

Better integration of the personnel bodies now in the state government, realignment of their functions and clarification of their relationship to the Department of Civil Service.

More definite establishment of responsibility of the governor for personnel management in the state.

Substantial reorganization of the department, with streamlining of its procedure so as to render better service to the operating departments, to applicants for positions and to the general public.

Greater flexibility in administration than tradition, present practices and procedures and, in some instances, the interpretation of the law permit.

More emphasis on positive personnel activity that can be achieved without sacrificing essential safeguards of the merit system.

Some decentralization of personnel management, in view of the size of the state government and its departments. •

A more systematic spelling out of personnel policy in the rules of the commission, to provide guidance for the operating departments as well as for the Civil Service Department itself.

Restatement and amendment of the civil service law, to provide a better base for efficient administration of a personnel system comprising more than 70,000 persons.

Arizona's Apportionment Amendment Held Constitutional

The Arizona Supreme Court in December upheld a constitutional amendment adopted in September which was challenged on the ground that, in limiting the House of Representatives to 80 members and giving two senators to each of the state's fourteen counties, it violated the provision of the constitution requiring measures to deal with one subject only.[1] The plaintiffs were opposed specifically to the Senate provisions of the amendment. Though the Senate section did not contain an effective date, the court inferred from the specific date of the House section that the change in the Senate was to begin in January 1955, with the 22th legislature.

PAUL KELSO

University of Arizona.

Use of Census Tracts Urged in Redistricting

Legislation in Michigan, following adoption of the reapportionment constitutional amendment in November 1952, assigned 38 of 110 state representatives to Wayne County, including the city of Detroit. It directed the county board of

[1]See the REVIEW, December 1953, page 565.

supervisors to divide the county into representative districts and also to arrange the seven senatorial districts (out of 34 statewide) allotted to Wayne County by the amendment.

The board's special reapportionment committee completed the task in December 1953, closely following ward boundary lines in Detroit. The Detroit Citizens League has pointed out that there is little justification for even maintaining the present ward boundaries. It commended a proposal of the Citizens Research Council of Michigan for the use of federal census tracts in establishing legislative districts, as the best aid in making the districts substantially equal in population, per legislator, compact in area and relatively homogeneous in socioeconomic characteristics.

N. Y. State Chamber of Commerce Supports P.P.R.

At its regular monthly meeting in New York City on January 7, the New York State Chamber of Commerce, reversing its previous position, took a stand for permanent personal registration on a statewide basis. The chamber traditionally supports Republican measures. Governor Thomas E. Dewey, in his annual message to the legislature on January 6, gave his support to P.P.R. but on a local option rather than a statewide basis.

Wisconsin Retirement Fund Integrated with OASI

Wisconsin has pioneered in the integration of a state retirement fund with federal old age and survivors' insurance (OASI).[1] Congress was persuaded, in August 1953, to pass a special act authorizing integration of the Wisconsin retirement fund, created by the 1943 legislature, with OASI. Now that this

[1] See "State, Local Retirement Plans Need Clarifying," the REVIEW, November 1953, page 533.

has become operative, some 30,000 state, county and municipal employees continue under the state retirement fund on an integrated basis and are also brought under OASI. In addition 10,000 or more persons in over a thousand local governments are under OASI only.

FREDERICK N. MACMILLIN
Executive Secretary
League of Wisconsin
Municipalities

New York Studies Ethics Code for Legislators

Senator Thomas C. Desmond has introduced in the New York legislature a series of bills relating to ethics of legislators. They would bar legislators from taking fees for representing clients before state departments; bar state, city or county chairmen of political parties from serving as paid lobbyists at the capitol during their terms of party office and for five years thereafter; ban political contributions from holders of liquor or race track licenses, road contractors and other purveyors to states and cities; ban race tracks and professional baseball clubs from giving lawmakers season passes.

Governor Dewey also has a program toward such ends and has appointed a commission on ethics of legislators where such measures will probably be reviewed.

R. S. C.

Interstate Forest Fire Compact for Southeast

State foresters and commissioners on interstate cooperation, meeting in Nashville, Tennessee, last fall, approved a new Southeastern Interstate Forest Fire Protection Compact, according to *State Government* for December. Integrated forest fire plans and provisions for mutual aid in fighting fires are objectives. The member states were expected to be Alabama, Florida, Georgia, Kentucky, Mississippi,

North and South Carolina, Tennessee, Virginia and West Virginia.

Limit on New U. S. Senatorships Proposed

A constitutional amendment to restrict representation of new states in the United States Senate to the population average for the existing states is advocated by John R. Pillion, Republican member of the House of Representatives from Lackawanna, New York. He urges that action on admission of Hawaii or Alaska as states be deferred until such an amendment is adopted. If they are admitted under the present system they would have four senators, for only 628,437 people, while the average for the United States is four for 6,456,000. In the Electoral College they would have seven votes, an average of one for 89,000 people, as compared to the national average of one for 287,000.

Representative Pillion's proposal would permit a new state one senator after its population attained one-half of the national average population per senator. This minimum, based on the 1950 census, is 794,646; and neither Hawaii, with 499,794, nor Alaska, with 128,643, would rate one senator. For two senators one and one-half times the average, or 2,383,938, based on 1950, would be required.

Admission of Hawaii alone, Mr. Pillion asserted, would lay the Republican Congress open to the charge of Senate-packing, as Hawaii would probably elect Republican senators. This would strengthen the demand for statehood for Alaska, expected to go Democratic, and the disproportion caused by admission of Hawaii would be made much worse, he commented.

Canada Struggles with Representation Inequalities

The Canadian House of Commons on December 7, 1953, by unanimous resolution, empowered its standing committee on privileges and elections to seek an improved method for the redistribution of parliamentary seats. The Citizens Research Institute of Canada (in Toronto, Ontario) has urged such action and recently issued in a brief bulletin results of a study of parliamentary representation. This shows that inequalities of representation that plague the United States are also found in Canada.

In the Canadian Senate each province has a fixed quota of seats, but in the House of Commons seats have been apportioned among the provinces according to population, as shown by the decennial census, with certain exceptions because of constitutional changes that have weakened the strict population principle. These have not greatly distorted the representation of provinces as a whole; but as the constitution does not require an equitable distribution of parliamentary seats within each province, the actions of the House of Commons in redistricting provinces have provoked widespread criticism and have produced gross inequalities. A table in the bulletin shows that under the 1952 redistribution the constituency populations, per member, vary from less than 10,000 to over 90,000, as compared to an average of 52,844. As in the United States, the urban areas are generally much under-represented.

The institute emphasizes that the House committee has a unique though difficult opportunity to develop standards for controlling the redistribution process, both as to populations and boundaries of constituencies.

County and Township . . . . *Edited by Edward W. Weidner*

County Seen as Key in Metropolitan Areas

Simultaneous Studies Urged to Test Alternate Patterns

EDITOR'S NOTE.—The article below is made up of excerpts from an address by Frank C. Moore, former comptroller and former lieutenant governor of New York State, before the Buffalo and Erie County Planning Association, December 11, 1953.

MORE than half the people of our nation live in its 168 metropolitan areas. In each of these areas we are witnessing a centrifugal movement of people as well as business and industry.

Despite gloomy predictions to the contrary, I believe the core cities will retain their preeminent importance as the cohesive centers, which hold the region together. They will continue to be the best location for some types of activity but the outlying areas will increase in importance for other purposes.

With intelligent planning and action, each part of the area will develop the activities for which it is best fitted. There will be increasing interdependence of each section upon the rest of the area.

In recent years, quite a few attempts have been made to find solutions by isolated, duplicating and uncoordinated studies of fragments of the total problems of the great metropolitan areas.

It seems to me that time and money can be saved and the chances of success greatly increased by attacking these problems on a nation-wide and coordinated basis. This could be accomplished by pooling the efforts and resources of outstanding organizations of citizens and public officials, the research agencies, the universities and the foundations interested in our federal, state and local governments.

By selecting ten or fifteen typical metropolitan areas, we could find the common denominators of problems and possible solutions to the advantage of all areas. For best results, it would still be necessary to custom tailor the general conclusions to fit the specific community.

We have in Buffalo and Erie County one of the great metropolitan areas of the nation.

In population, Erie County is the largest unit of government in New York outside of New York City. Its boundaries include a large portion of the territory of this metropolitan area. It now provides important services to most of the people of the area.

Within the last decade, we have observed considerable change in the county government of New York State. There is evidence of its continued expansion in the period ahead.

If there is to be a decentralization of federal and state governments, the county is the natural heir to any powers that may be surrendered by the central governments. It has the geographical size and the potential resources to take on additional duties.

The counties of New York State cannot escape their destiny of the dominant role among our local governments, outside of New York City.

To predict the ultimate effect of the development of this metropolitan area upon the county of Erie, I would have to anticipate the results of studies not yet started. But I can list the governmental routes to the development of this area, assuming that our citizens are not content with the somewhat leisurely pace of past progress.

In enumerating routes, I intend no inferences of priority of preference except as I specifically indicate. I have included some methods I frankly believe impossible and unwise solely because other areas have employed them—although under what I believe to be differing circumstances and conditions.

Here is a list of these possible and impossible routes.

1. A new over-all government—perhaps some type of borough government—could be established for the metropolitan area in place of the present municipalities and districts. A borough plan like that of London (not New York) has been suggested recently for Cincinnati.

2. The rest of the metropolitan area could be annexed to the city of Buffalo and the county and city governments merged as in New York.

3. The present city of Buffalo could be set apart as a separate county and a new county of Erie established including the remainder of the present county.

4. A federation of local governments could be created as in the Toronto metropolitan area.

5. Our present system of local governments could be continued with the county providing certain services now supplied through separate local governments.

6. Our present system of local governments could be continued with the elimination of the obstacles—constitutional and otherwise—which prevent the cooperation of our localities in meeting the common needs of their citizens.

7. A new type of suburban community could be created which would eliminate the overlapping of town and village governments.

8. We could siphon off functions of normal local government and exercise them through public authorities, outside the control of the electorate, sometimes created when we do not trust ourselves or those whom we choose to represent us in municipal government.

Frankly, I prefer the continuation of our present system of municipalities and school districts with these provisos:

1. We should eliminate the obstacles to cooperation among municipalities in providing a common service.

2. We should reappraise the role of the county and strengthen it wherever necessary to meet its expanding responsibilities.

3. We should recognize that our suburban towns are no longer mere administrative subdivisions of the state and county but municipalities providing most of the services of cities and villages through the old-fashioned medium of "special districts." The time has come to revamp the town law and town government to meet the present needs of suburban communities.

4. We should find the answer to the conflict between towns and villages over the alleged double taxation of village real estate for town and village services.

FRANK C. MOORE, *President*
Governmental Affairs Foundation

Albemarle County Executive Cites Accomplishments, Aims

A new county executive has been elected in Albemarle County, Virginia, M. Maupin Pence, formerly finance director for the city of Charlottesville. Mr. Pence has outlined some of the plans and progress of the county in the October 1953 issue of *Virginia and the Virginia County*. The construction of a joint city-county airport is proceeding as well as the creation of a central fire department which embraces considerable territory. The county is also taking action in providing area dumps for rural residents and has developed a seven-year school building program.

Wayne County Committee Studies Reorganization

The board of supervisors of Wayne County (Detroit), Michigan, has set up a ten-member study committee to report on the "feasibility of abolishing, altering and/or merging certain functions of government within Wayne County," according to *The Civic Searchlight* of the Detroit Citizens League.

A number of proposals have already been placed before the committee for consideration. Merger of the following functions of the county and of the city of Detroit has been suggested: purchasing, building and maintenance, tax collection, property assessment, civil service, election commission, public health and hospitals, social welfare, water and sanitation, and parks and recreation. Such consolidations might well pave the way for other municipalities and townships in the county to purchase services on a contractual basis if they can be furnished more economically.

Two proposals deal with the judiciary. One would consolidate the Recorder's Court Jury Commission with the Wayne County Board of Jury Commissioners; the other would merge the various offices collecting court fees and provide for a careful audit of them.

Philadelphia Coroner Duties under Non-medical Examiner

The elective office of coroner in Philadelphia has been abolished, together with several other county offices,[1] and his functions divided. The coroner's legal duties have been placed under the district attorney and his remaining functions transferred to an examiner in the Department of Health.

Old ways persist, however. The new title was made "examiner" rather than "medical examiner" and the equivalent of inquests, without juries however, still lingers in the new office. The examiner is not required to be a doctor or to have any particular medical or experience qualifications and holds hearings and investigates deaths in a manner similar to inquest procedures.

Efforts are being made in the city

council to restore to the new examiner former legal functions of the coroner, turning the hands of the clock backward again by the mingling of legal and pathological duties.

R. S. C.

Suggests Virginia Counties Set Up Sanitary Districts

A suggestion that counties take advantage of the provisions of Virginia law permitting establishment of sanitary districts has been made by Dr. E. S. Overman, assistant director of the Bureau of Public Administration at the University of Virginia. An article in *Virginia and the Virginia County* (October 1953) points out that sanitary districts are devised for providing service where service is desired and needed without creating an additional unit of local government. Once established in a county, a sanitary district is under the complete control of the county board of supervisors. The board may provide the following services in such districts: water supply, sewage disposal, garbage removal and disposal, heat, light, fire fighting, power and gas systems, and sidewalks.

Dr. Overman points out that there are 191 incorporated towns in Virginia, of which 167 have a population of less than 3,500.

Riverside County, California, to Study Charter Plan

Accord has been reached by the County Farm Bureau and the Associated Chambers of Commerce in Riverside County on the proposed study of the suitability of a charter plan of government for the county.[1] Both organizations have now come out as backing a study, results of which would be presented to the board of supervisors in April. It is recommended that the study be made by a private group rather than by an officially

---

[1] See the REVIEW, November 1953, page 518.

[1] See the REVIEW, October 1953, page 466.

appointed committee. If the proposal for a board of freeholders should be accepted by the board of supervisors in April, an election must be called for the purpose of selecting its members.

In addition to the Chambers of Commerce and Farm Bureau, the idea of a charter plan for the county was backed by a recent grand jury and is supported by the Riverside *Enterprise.*

"I venture to say that with the right kind of cooperation between the people in these towns and the boards of supervisors and especially with a sincere desire on the part of county officials to provide the services needed, most of these towns would be better served as sanitary districts. I would even go so far as to say that there are cities in this state which would be more appropriately governed as sanitary districts."

The latest information available indicates that, in 1948, 21 districts had been created but 14 were already inactive. Many instances of inactivity were caused by the annexation of district territory by cities.

Dr. Overman concludes, "Here is one area of government where the board of supervisors can be master in its own house. As long as the provisions of the statutes are complied with, the counties can go their own way in operating sanitary districts."

City-county Building Proposed for El Paso

Under a proposal recently made by the county judge of El Paso County, endorsed by the mayor of the city of El Paso, the county and city plan to join forces to improve and enlarge the court house as a general government building. The present city hall would be vacated.

In addition to the general over-all economies obtained by having the two units of government in the same building, there will be specific improvements in law enforcement as a result of a system of cooperation between the sheriff's department and the city police.

Virginia Local Government Officials Hold Conference

The second Virginia Local Government Officials' Conference was held at the University of Virginia in September. The conference was so successful that this training session will become an annual event. Rendering technical assistance was the Bureau of Public Administration at the University of Virginia. A large number of sessions were held and both academic and public officials spoke and chaired sessions. Attendance was 477 persons, as compared with 357 in 1952.

Arizona County Joins State Retirement System

Cochise County became the first county of Arizona to adopt a retirement plan for its employees when its board of supervisors in December voted to join the state retirement system.

PAUL KELSO

University of Arizona

Manuals Prepared for County Officials

A new manual for county supervisors in Virginia has been issued and a manual for clerks of boards of supervisors in New York is well on its way to completion. Preparation of the Virginia manual was supervised by Dr. E. S. Overman, assistant director of the Bureau of Public Administration at the University of Virginia, and was drafted by Jo Desha Lucas, assistant professor of law, at the University of Chicago Law School.

Preparation of the Virginia manual required nearly three years. Preliminary drafts were revised in accordance with suggestions from ten state and twelve local government officials. It has been hailed as an outstanding contribution to a better understanding of county government in Virginia.

(Continued on page 97)

Proportional Representation .   .   *Edited by George H. Hallett, Jr.*
and Wm. Redin Woodward
(This department is successor to the Proportional Representation Review)

Worcester Elects Civic Group Majority

But Mayor Is Chosen on Partisan Lines

WORCESTER'S new city council took a step toward partisanship in the wake of the city's third P.R. election.

The nine councillors who were elected November 3 didn't campaign on party lines. Nor were there any party labels on the ballot. But when the councillors-elect met in December to choose a mayor, a majority agreed that he would have to be a Democrat. The new council included two Republicans, six Democrats and one independent who attended the few Democratic caucuses that have been held. The previous council had three Republicans, five Democrats and the same independent.

The new council was deadlocked for 270 ballots on the choice of a mayor. On the 271st, six of the Democrats agreed to elect Councillor James D. O'Brien to the post. He is the senior member of the city government, having served a dozen years in the old city council and the past four years under the council-manager plan adopted in 1950. He has been neutral toward P.R., saying that he has been elected under both P.R. and plurality voting and would not argue with the public's choice of an election system.

As mayor, he succeeds Andrew B. Holmstrom, a Republican, who has held the job for the past four years. Mr. Holmstrom was unanimously chosen vice-chairman of the new council.

Most councillors insist the vote on mayor was not the opening gun in an effort to make the administration of city affairs openly partisan. But one or two frankly admit they favor such a move.

In the P.R. election, Mayor Holmstrom led the field, as he did in the first two under that election system. This time, he polled 11,710 first-choice votes, a decrease from the 13,290 he received in 1949 and the 14,752 credited to him in 1951. His total was still substantially above the quota of 5,677.

Councillor O'Brien also topped the quota on the first count, with 5,940 first-choice votes, 1,500 more than he received two years ago. It was the first time two council candidates had exceeded the quota in Worcester's three P.R. elections.

In addition to Mr. Holmstrom and Mr. O'Brien, four councillors were reelected. A fifth sought reelection and was the last man counted out. Two councillors did not run for another term.

Citizen Support

The Citizens Plan E Association, non-partisan civic organization which led the fight for council-manager government, endorsed nine council candidates out of the 38 running. Seven of those endorsed by the association were elected, as was the case in 1951.

The association continued its policy of not trying to keep councillors rigidly in line once they are elected. It did not campaign openly for any particular candidate for mayor. Mayor O'Brien, who received the votes of five councillors endorsed by the Citizens Plan E Association, was not one of the candidates endorsed by the group in the election. He was approached at the time, but declined the endorsement.

Although it has not taken a firm stand on most issues, the association has expressed concern at the trend toward partisanship. If this trend continues, the association is expected to become more vigorous in combatting it.

A six-member school committee was also elected November 3. Mayor O'Brien automatically becomes chairman and seventh member, with full voting privileges.

For the second election in a row, School Committeeman Edwin Higginbottom was the only member to exceed the quota on the first count. He received 9,062 first-choice votes. The quota was 8,112.

The three other school committee members who sought reelection won it. One other member did not run. Another ran for the council and was defeated. In all, there were sixteen candidates for the school committee.

A Mild Campaign

The election campaign, for both the city council and school committee, was a mild one. The turnout of voters reflected it. For the second straight time, there was a decrease in the number of votes cast, with only 59,710 going to the polls.

But that was substantially more than pre-election forecasters had expected. It compared favorably to the 61,397 of two years ago, although it was well under the 76,390 who voted in the first P.R. election in 1949. In 1949, however, there were 152 candidates for the council and 36 for the school committee.

As the number of voters went down, the number of invalid votes went up. Some 2,843 council ballots were found to be improperly marked this year, as compared to 2,719 in 1951 and only 1,584 in 1949. There was not an intense educational campaign this year on how to mark P.R. ballots, as there had been before the two previous elections.

There were three ballots this year—one for the council, one for the school committee and one for a referendum. But this apparently caused no particular confusion. Nor did it slow the count.

The ballots were counted in the fastest time yet, under the direction of George H. Hallett, Jr. The council count began Wednesday morning and was completed Friday night. The school committee count began Saturday morning and ended Monday night, with time out Saturday afternoon and Sunday. Referendum ballots were counted at opportune moments during the council count. The entire counting procedure went off without a hitch and without criticism from any quarter.

Election Information

As a result of a change in state law, more detailed information on the election results has been kept than in the past. City Clerk Robert J. O'Keefe has published a pamphlet showing not only first-choice votes and transfers, but the first-choice votes received by each candidate in each precinct and the number of votes from each polling place finally counted for each of the elected candidates.

There was nothing in the election results to indicate any weakening of support for P.R. Unless those who are disturbed by growing partisanship turn against the election system, it would seem as strong as ever.

An attempt by some Democratic leaders to put the repeal of P.R. on the November ballot as a referendum fizzled when they failed to collect enough valid signatures. They needed only 5 per cent of the registered vote but couldn't quite muster it. A similar effort failed a year before. As the state law now stands, the question cannot be put on the ballot again before 1955.

ROBERT C. ACHORN
The Evening Gazette
Worcester, Massachusetts

Tax-free U. S. Industrial Property a Problem

Loss in Income a Serious Setback for Communities

EDITOR'S NOTE: The following is an excerpt from a paper delivered before the panel on "Cities and the National Government" at the National Conference on Government of the National Municipal League, Richmond, Virginia, November 9, 1953, by George H. Deming, director of technical assistance, American Municipal Association.

THE problem of payments to state and local governments on account of federal real and personal industrial property has received considerable attention for a number of years. While it is not a new problem, it has merited increasing thought more recently for two reasons: (1) the competition for revenues to meet the cost of governmental services; and (2) the increased defense program and property acquisitions by the federal government, which have taken valuable property off local property tax rolls.

The situation is made more complex by the fact that some agencies pay taxes while other agencies pay no taxes or payments in lieu of taxes on similar pieces of property. Similarly, one federal agency may pay taxes on a property as long as it is owned by it—when the property is transferred to another agency, it becomes tax-exempt.

From the standpoint of local government, the problem is particularly acute because it brings a more extensive defense burden to bear on some units of local government than upon others. Indeed, the officials of the Defense Department are willing to admit that, to the extent that a unit of local government can be made to support a tax-free industry, so the national defense budget is stretched

out. This attitude was brought out in no uncertain terms in a congressional hearing last winter when the acquisition of an aircraft plant in southern California was under consideration.

The effect of the loss of taxes on industrial property can be appreciated best perhaps by detailing a few cases resulting from the transfer of taxpaying RFC property to a tax-exempt status.

In Southington, Connecticut, a town of 6,000 persons, a tax loss of $60,840 was suffered when an industry became tax-exempt. In Riverbank, California, a community of 2,200 persons, a tax loss of $55,512 was suffered when a metals processing plant went off the tax rolls. In Madison, Illinois, a tax loss of $66,196 was suffered when a small parts plant went off the tax rolls. These are three of scores of similar cases throughout the nation.

Tax loss of this magnitude is nearly a catastrophe in such communities since in most cases they must continue to provide school facilities, streets, municipal utilities, welfare services and the like to those employed by the tax-exempt industry.

In addition, there is a growing tendency on the part of federal defense agencies to phrase contracts so as to exempt raw materials, implements, equipment, machine tools and goods in the process of manufacture from local taxation. This is accomplished by immediately transferring title to such property to the federal government, or an agency thereof, upon small partial payment of the purchase price by the contracting federal agency.

The holders of such contracts constitute a large segment of private enterprise in the nation. They require and receive all the protective and other services of local government without which they could not operate during the process of manufacturing material under federal contract. The cost of such removals means an annual loss of a quarter of a million dollars in tax revenue to the city of Detroit. In San Diego, about $80,000,-000 worth of personal property is tax-exempt.

Present legislation assumes the primary responsibility for meeting needs of critical areas because of defense activities to be that of municipalities unless they are demonstrably fiscally incompetent. This assumption is contrary to the premise that the cost of defense is a "national" responsibility that should be extended over the complete tax base of the nation.

The basic question would seem to be whether or not the costs of national defense should be borne by the whole nation on an equitable basis or whether particular communities because of their industrial abilities should be asked, indeed ordered, to bear more than their fair share.

GEORGE H. DEMING
American Municipal Association

State-local Borrowing at New Peak in 1953

State and local governments of the United States set a new record in long-term financing in 1953, selling their bonds to a total of more than five and a half billion dollars. The year's total was one-fourth higher than in 1952, and included seven hundred and seventy million dollars of bonds sold in December 1953, an all-time monthly record. The annual totals, as compiled by *The Daily Bond Buyer*, have been as follows for the last five years:

State-local Long-term Financing

1949	$2,995,525,049
1950	3,693,604,165
1951	3,278,153,053
1952	4,401,317,467
1953	5,551,317,269

The 1953 total included $1,566,244,570 of revenue bonds, a figure which also set an all-time record for annual issuance of this type of obligation. The other $3,-985,072,699 includes bonds payable from ad valorem taxes, assessments or from water, light and similar service enterprise revenues but with the pledge also of the issuer's general taxing power. The total also includes bonds of local public housing authorities, supported under federal statutes from rentals and federal contributions.

Voter approvals of new state and local bonds in 1953 were lower than in either of the two preceding years, although the voters approved nearly as large a proportion of the dollar aggregate submitted to them as they had in 1952. In 1953, bonds aggregating $1,851,594,000 were approved, while proposals defeated aggregated $388,769,450, approvals thus representing 83 per cent of the total submitted. In 1952, approvals had totaled $2,353,970,000 and defeated issues $458,-278,500, approvals accounting for 83.8 per cent of the amount submitted. By months, approvals in 1953 were lower in nearly every instance than in 1952, but the largest difference was for November. The November 1953 approval total amounted to $929,130,000 compared with $1,285,864,000 in November 1952. Approvals in the full year 1951 had been $2,249,602,000 and in 1950, $1,537,517,000.

A large number of governmental units at the state-local level do not require the approval of voters to issue bonds, or at least to issue bonds for particular purposes, so that voter approvals do not provide a complete guide to prospective state-local borrowing. As 1954 got under way, it appeared that this year's long-term financing would press closely on the 1953 record and might, especially if the federal government undertook to promote a state-local public works program to help take up the slack in unemployment, considerably exceed last year's high level.

As the year began, state-local borrowing costs were again at a level likely to attract public officials who keep an eye on the money market so as to bring their bonds to market at the most advantageous time. *The Daily Bond Buyer's* index of yield on twenty representative long-term bonds, after dipping to 2.38 per cent during the forepart of 1953, rose to a July peak of 3.09 per cent, a twenty-year high, and then moved irregularly downward to show a slow decline during the closing months of the year and end at 2.58 per cent the last week in December.

By early January 1954, the index stood at 2.54 per cent. To an issuer of $1,000,-000 of bonds maturing in annual installments in one to twenty years, the 1/2 of 1 per cent decline in interest cost from the 1953 peak represented an interest saving of about $50,000, while to the issuer of the same amount due in one to twenty years on a level debt service arrangement the saving was more than $60,000.

Arizona League Studies City-county Tax Relations

The Arizona Municipal League, at its fall meeting at Mesa in November, authorized a study of county taxation of property within municipalities, the proceeds from which are largely spent to provide services for outside areas. The league hopes the study will be helpful in obtaining a reduction in the amount of property taxes which counties can collect within cities. The league also endorsed bills to be introduced in the next regular session of the state legislature which would provide alternative annexation methods and permit formation of improvement districts in downtown areas, with power to acquire property and make improvements for off-street parking.

PAUL KELSO

University of Arizona

COUNTY AND TOWNSHIP

(Continued from page 92)

The New York Manual for clerks of boards of supervisors will include the following chapters:

Computation of equalization (with concrete examples), establishment of tax rates (with concrete examples), calendar for clerks of board plus check list, calendar for supervisors, uniform Rules of Procedure, taking accurate minutes without shorthand, indexing "Journal of Proceedings," caption writing for resolutions —working of resolutions—reference to proper section of law, what annual reports are mandated by law and what additional information is generally published, editing annual reports to retain essential features but reduce cost of printing, handling of insurance problems in general, calendar for assessors, and the mortgage tax.

More Powers for Counties Proposed in Saskatchewan

The Saskatchewan Association of Rural Municipalities has again proposed a plan for replacing the more local rural units by enlarging the scope and power of county governments. Speaking before the Royal Commission on Agricultural and Rural Life, a representative of the association said, "Area in itself is not a major factor in the efficient functioning of rural municipal units and no justification is seen for a general reorganization of boundaries."

The association's position is that the specific weakness in the municipal system is in the lack of equity in the present system of taxation based on land values. Proposed as an alternative to enlarging rural local government boundaries or placing in the county control of rural government were the suggestions to broaden the sources of income to rural-local units and to stabilize agricultural income. Perhaps this might be done in part through a system of equalizing grants.

Citizen Organization in Small Communities

Volunteer Groups Can Do Much Without Paid Staff

IT'S about time that counsel and guidance were given citizens in the hundreds of smaller communities who want to form a civic or municipal league but cannot afford a full-time secretary.[1]

There are some 3,600 cities between 2,500 and 50,000 population whose organized citizens generally cannot afford to support such a full-time secretary. In many of these, civic leagues or government betterment associations have been formed, but scores have died after a few gallant gasps and resolutions.

The reason for their early demise is that they were all dressed up with an organization but knew no place to go. They were formed in the heat of some civic betterment campaign to chase out public scalawags, to put over a new city charter or some such stirring project. When this job was accomplished, the citizens' group had the best of intentions of continuing its endeavors, but didn't know how to go about it.

Every community has as much need for a citizens' group to watch and help its city officials as a motor car has for its warning horn. Such an association serves as a rallying place where citizens can

[1]See also The Citizen Association—How to Organize and Run It and The Citizen Association—How to Win Civic Campaigns. (National Municipal League, 1953, 75 cents each, both for $1.20.) These pamphlets have been prepared to meet the needs of citizen organizations in cities of all sizes. While they contain material on staff and financing applicable to groups in large cities, most of their suggestions are equally applicable to citizen organizations in small communities.

volunteer their talents for the betterment of their city and the protection of the advantages they already have.

A newly organized civic group is like a fine, coiled spring which needs only some useful mechanism to set it working. So, assuming we have a basic civic organization already formed, let us take off from there.

It is desirable to have a larger rather than a smaller board of trustees—say in the twenties. Better decisions on civic matters are likely to come from many good minds than from a few—provided members who vote on the minority end of a decision cheerfully bow to the majority. Presumably, there is a small executive committee with power to act rapidly between monthly board meetings.

There must be a secretary to act as the spark-plug of this organization. Assuming that a trained civic expert is beyond the organization's means, the secretary could be a young lawyer paid for a few hours time weekly, a full or part-time young woman who can nudge members to action and make them like it, a retired or semi-retired citizen with time on his hands and civic experience at his fingertips, or simply a man or woman citizen whose zeal for civic betterment outweighs his personal sacrifice of time and energy.

Committees are the motive-power of the organization. Members can have the most interesting civic adventures of their lives. They can consist of board and general members. These should be permitted to choose the group on which they wish to serve—with the assent of the president, who should be alert to weed out too many special pleaders on any committee. For a small organization, these groups can be: committee on city affairs, committee on school affairs, committee on county affairs.

If the agency has enough members for more committees, these groups could be constituted by broad functions such as: city budget and finance committee, county budget and finance committee, city and county planning committee, public safety committee, public health and welfare committee, public works committee, public schools committee.

Each committee should number not less than half a dozen and preferably fifteen or twenty. About half can be depended upon for faithful attendance after the league gains momentum and public respect.

Noon luncheon meetings will probably bring out the largest attendance—folks have to eat somewhere. Adjournment should not be later than 1:30 P.M. even if a shotgun is necessary to disperse them. Otherwise members won't come back. If a matter of major importance requires lengthy discussion, occasional night meetings will be productive but will not be appreciated by families of members.

Each committee should have a chairman, vice chairman and secretary, who are appointed by the president and confirmed by the board. Committee secretaries should be expected to keep minutes of their meetings which they will send to the agency secretary to be included in the files of the organization. It is important to preserve comprehensive minutes for future reference.

Checking the Budgets

Next to voting for officials, the most important yearly public transactions of a community are adoption of the annual city, county and school budgets. This operation brings to public attention these paramount matters—the level of property taxes for the coming year, the degree of solvency or insolvency of the public body, and the only real discussion in the year relating to the performance or services rendered by public bodies.

Provisions of budget laws in most states are miles ahead of the interest of citizens. In most states, such laws provide: (1) that cities, counties and school districts must make available to citizens by publication in a newspaper or in printed or mimeographed form, copies of a proposed or preliminary budget for the coming year and (2) that, on a certain day at a certain time, there must be a public hearing on the budget. So, the welcome mat is legally out for any citizens who really want to study and discuss their local budgets.

Here are several time-dishonored budget traps and tricks for the layman scrutinizer to watch out for.

Most common one is to inflate next year's revenue estimates far above any possibility of collection in order that they may equal—on paper—the planned expenditures, so that the city fathers can piously announce, "Our budget is balanced."

This trick can be detected by comparing every individual estimate of income—parking meter fees, building permits, licenses, occupational tax and the city's score of other revenues—with the actual collections during a recent twelve-month period. If the "guesstimates" for the coming year are not too much larger than the recent actual collections—after allowing for normal gains—the former may be approved as a reasonable revenue estimate for next year's budget.

Next, subtract the proposed total estimates of expenditures for next year from the total revenue estimate, and note the all-important resulting figure. If it is minus, showing excess expenditures over income, the investigating committee should start sending up distress rockets of public protest about an "unbalanced budget with a probable deficit."

Next, ascertain the number of additional employees asked for in next year's budget. If one or two new building inspectors are proposed, though the trend of building construction is downward, such additional help can be challenged.

Similarly, any increases in employees should be compared with current trends and requirements of city services, to meet the test of their necessity.

Many other checks and explorations of city budget items will occur to good businessmen on the investigating committee. Keep pelting city officials with questions. The good ones love to answer them to show citizens how much they know about their duties.

The *Municipal Year Book,* published annually by the International City Managers' Association, is a gold mine of statistical information by which your city's operations can be compared with others. If your public library doesn't have it, this volume should be purchased by your civic organization. It presents statistics for most cities on salaries of major groups of city officials and employees, number of employees and their working conditions, basic financial statistics, planning statistics, fire-fighting facilities and losses, police facilities and many others. These are invaluable for budget-checking, but should be used with care, only after reading the introductory chapter on "How to Use the *Year Book.*"

As a word of caution, watch out for the committee member who, at the outset, announces with flat finality, "We all know that our city budget is full of waste, duplication and probably graft. There's no reason why we can't cut 25 per cent from it and not hurt city services a bit." He can do the investigating committee a great disservice and hinder its progress. If his views reach city hall, the lay group will not find it easy to extract enlightening information from city officials who won't feel disposed to discuss matters with a gentleman who is out to cut their throats. Furthermore, the average American city is not so filled with waste that any 25 per cent can be cut from its budget without seriously impairing present services.

But, if this committee approaches city, county and school officials at budget time

in a spirit of cooperation and helpfulness, the chances are that it can finish its project with contributions to the budget-framing which will more than justify the time its members donated and make them glow with satisfaction at a job well done.

The other big periodical job which calls for doing by the civic league is the pre-election appraisal of candidates. To some members, this may seem like a hot poker. "We mustn't get tarred with politics," they protest.

But, in most communities, citizens might as well vote for ghosts as for the numerous candidates about whom they know nothing. Numerous slates of recommended candidates fill the press—those of Pro-America, the A. F. of L., the C. I. O. and so on. How much more helpful to the ordinary voter would be the appraisal of candidates by a respected group of his fellow-citizens whose viewpoint is generally agreed to be reasonably objective?

Supporting Candidates

From another standpoint, what sense does it make for the league to condemn the mayor sharply for the illegal purchase of a piece of equipment and yet stand dumbly by when he seeks reelection?

A number of civic leagues do this job with success and public appreciation, including the Seattle Municipal League, Cleveland Citizens League, Detroit Citizens League, New York Citizens Union, East Detroit Civic League, Sioux City Good Citizens League, Council-manager Association of Iowa City, and others. More than half the 5,000 members of the Seattle Municipal League joined out of appreciation of the reports on candidates for local and legislative offices which it furnishes them.[3]

[3] See "They Don't Vote for Ghosts," by C. A. Crosser, the REVIEW, June 1951, page 294; "How One Group Selects Candidates," the REVIEW, October 1952, page 471; *The Citizen Association—How to Organize and Run It,* pages 38-40.

If these two jobs don't keep the civic league busy, there are plenty of others calling for attention.

The civic league should keep itself alerted during the session of the state legislature. The officials of its city may be seeking passage of a bill to benefit the community—or the opposite. Both sides of the proposal should be studied by the appropriate committee of the league which, after coming to a decision, should throw its weight to help or hinder its passage. Maybe it can concoct and push a measure of its own in the interests of economy and efficiency.

A new zoning ordinance is under consideration by the city council. It should be studied by the appropriate committee, which could make helpful suggestions. In fact, in the average city there are one or more public transactions afoot at all times which need citizens' attention.

In searching for items of economy and efficiency for the civic agency to work on, here are a few civic "medicines" which are as sure-cure as penicillin. They have been tested in actual practice in many cities and counties.

We by-pass the means by which these projects can be accomplished because of different procedures in different states. Some will require changes in the state constitution, state statutes, city charter, city ordinances or a county resolution or by-law.

Here are a few—by no means all of them.

If registration of voters is required before each election, a more economical permanent registration system can be substituted under which a voter registers only once provided he votes regularly. Also, voting by machine can be cheaper and more foolproof than by paper ballot.

Fees to the sheriff for feeding jail prisoners, to county attorneys for certain kinds of cases, to assessors for listing dogs and in fact perquisites of all kinds

should be abolished and adequate salaries granted.

City or county purchasing now performed by many department heads could be combined under a single purchasing agent or some existing official. Big items like election ballots and tax bills can be bought more economically on competitive bid.

Labor-saving business machines and similar devices can be installed to eliminate long-hand record-keeping and will save substantial sums. Recording of mortgages, deeds and other legal documents could be done quickly by photostat instead of by laborious typing. The annual listing of taxpayers and their properties on the tax roll, the calculation of the taxes they owe and the preparation of annual tax statements, could be combined in one operation by machine at big savings. Installation of one or more of these economies would add laurels to the league's crown and attract members.

Long-term Goal

Besides its immediate objective to patch and mend the imperfect fabric of local government, the league should have a "cause"—some grand goal which will arouse the ardor of members and bind them together in the fellowship of an inspiring common aim. This could be a new city or county charter or some form of consolidation of the county and city governments. Most of these major projects would require tedious preliminary steps such as a state constitutional amendment, a state enabling statute or the election of a charter-drafting commission which might take years.

Time passes rapidly, however, and with a few daily nudges given to the main project, along with the other day-to-day missions, its consummation before long will become a gratifying reality.

A civic agency, no matter how small, should issue some kind of regular bulletin. For many members who do not

serve on committees, this would be their
only contact with the central office outside of the yearly dun for dues. This
bulletin should describe the activities of
the board and committees and interpret
important current public transactions in
a confidential vein which gives the member the feeling he is being let in behind
the scenes at city hall. Also, this newsletter should give the member a feeling
that he is getting something for his membership dues.*

The question as to the amount of annual membership dues is one to be decided
by each agency. Generally speaking, dues
can be of two kinds—a regular membership for a modest fee of a few dollars a
year, and subscriptions or contributions
of larger amounts by individuals and
business concerns.*

Lastly, what should the members and
the community expect from this civic
agency? It will behave much like a human being because it is the sum of the
temperament and talent of many human
beings. It can fade like a finished candle
or it can become firmly established as a
fixed and respected institution in the
community. It can turn in prodigies of
civic accomplishments. It should finish
each year with half a dozen completed.
Its very existence will have a salutary
effect on the scamps in public office and
reinforce the good motives and aspira-
tions of conscientious officials.

This civic agency can have an impact
on its community far greater than its
physical numbers and resources if its efforts and strategy are well planned and
directed. Above all, officers and members should remember that sometimes
civic reforms move only with the speed
of a glacier but their progress is just

---

*See also "Don't Mislay Your Best
Tool—Publicity," by C. A. Crosser, the
REVIEW, July 1953, page 359.
*See *The Citizen Association—How to
Organize and Run It*, pages 50-60.

direct citizen control—home rule, primaries, methods of amendment and constitutional review, the initiative, referendum and recall. The last dealt with the executive branch and the courts.

Citizenship in the Schools

The Municipal League of Seattle and King County, Washington, has completed an appraisal of the training for citizenship undertaken in Seattle public schools. Titled *The Making of a Seattle Citizen* (nine pages mimeographed), the study represents the work of one of the league's committees, which has been looking into the situation for the past five years. Committee members have read textbooks used in civics courses and visited classes in both elementary and high schools. The report finds that citizenship training in Seattle schools is much better than it was a generation ago but recommends additional instruction in local government. A supplement of six pages makes short reports on citizenship training in other city school systems.

'City Council — In Three Acts'

"Among its many activities, it appears the Citizens Union puts on a good show, 'The City Council,'" says the union's bulletin *Across from City Hall*. At least that is the impression one gets from a booklet, *How to Make a Little Go a Long Way*, which describes free and inexpensive entertainment in the world's largest city. Here is what it says:

"NEW YORK CITY COUNCIL MEETINGS: City Hall, Chambers Street near Broadway. The public is welcome to attend meetings of New York's own legislative group, the city council. As newspaper accounts have indicated in the past, sessions can be quite interesting, sometimes stormy. Meetings are held in City Hall, usually on Tuesday afternoon, around 2 P.M. Telephone the Citizens Union, at BA 7-0342, to make certain of time and date."

City Projects

Nine "projects for a progressive city" are listed by the Citizens League of Kansas City, Missouri, in its *Kansas City Citizen*. The list includes completion of trafficways, modernization of street lighting, erection of a railroad station, reassessment of all property, annexation of certain areas and increased pay to police and fire department personnel, with both departments removed from politics. "Where there is no vision, the people perish," quotes the bulletin.

Library Educates Voters

In anticipation of the November elections, the public library in Haverhill, Massachusetts, where the question of retaining the council-manager plan was on the ballot, assembled pertinent material as background reading. Publications of the National Municipal League and the local branch of the League of Women Voters, as well as government textbooks and the laws setting up the two plans of government being debated, were available to the public.

Rendering an Accounting

The Municipal League of Seattle and King County, Washington, has published an *Inventory of Municipal League Accomplishments from 1945-53 and Basic Services Rendered*, for distribution to its chairmen of committees and subcommittees. A second memorandum, *What Makes the League Tick*, lists committees, subcommittees and their missions.

Home Rule for the Capital

The Washington Home Rule Committee, an affiliate of the Central Suffrage Conference, and its *Home Rule News* are working actively to secure "restoration of the maximum possible local self-government for local Washington, D. C."

State, Local Studies of Federal Aid Needed

Handbook Provides Guide for Local Study Groups

IMPORTANT national decisions regarding federal aid may soon be made. Public understanding of the issues involved is vital. There is particular need for local participation in presenting the facts on which the national decisions will be made, local consideration of the effects of possible changes and local planning for action needed." In these words the American Parents Committee of Washington, D. C., in its newly published *Handbook on Federal Grants-in-Aid* (216 pages, $1.50), emphasizes the need for citizen awareness of the basic pattern of federal assistance to the states and localities.

The Commission on Intergovernmental Relations is to give federal aid programs the closest scrutiny to determine whether or not such aid is justified in its present form, whether some programs should be extended, altered or reduced, or whether the states and localities should be given greater financial responsibilities. No matter what recommendations are forthcoming from the commission many significant policy determinations will be made shortly on problems of federal aid.

This means that people in the states and localities will be studying the specific implications of federal aid upon their governmental programs. The findings of such studies may well influence any change which may be made in federal aid policy. *The Handbook on Federal Grants-in-Aid* is "designed to be of assistance in the making of such community studies of health, education, social welfare and other services which are aided by federal grants-in-aid."

Twenty-eight federal grant-in-aid programs are described under the following headings: services, general appropriations, state and local contributions and administration. Tabulations showing the amount of the grants to each state for the fiscal years 1953 and 1954 are included. For each state the agencies administering the federally aided programs are listed with complete addresses. This will encourage local groups to contact the appropriate state departments.

A word of warning seems appropriate, however. As valuable as local research will be, it would be unfortunate for citizens interested in particular functional programs in particular localities to pursue their interest with no reference to broad questions of public finance and governmental structure.

What is really needed in each state is a comprehensive review of the fiscal structure of the state and its localities similar to that which is being made of the government of the state of New York by the Temporary Commission on Fiscal Affairs. Research of this order and breadth is required if adequate facts are to be made available in the consideration of a realignment of federal, state and local responsibilities.

Another useful statewide summary is *Federal Grant-in-Aid Programs in Kansas* (45 pages), published in November 1953 by the Kansas State Chamber of Commerce (Topeka). Again it must be remembered that federal aid policy ultimately must be considered in relation to the whole range of fiscal problems at all levels of government. Individual state and local studies of aid programs will provide but fragments of the data vitally needed as the questions of intergovernmental fiscal relations are considered.

WILLIAM N. CASSELLA, JR.

University of Iowa, Institute of Public
Affairs and College of Law, in cooperation with the Iowa Commission on Children and Youth, 1954. 55 pp.

Debt

DEBT PROBLEMS OF FLORIDA MUNICI-
PALITIES. By Wylie Kilpatrick. Gainesville, University of Florida, Public Administration Clearing Service, 1953. 20
pp.

REFUNDING BONDS. Baton Rouge,
Louisiana Legislative Council, October
14, 1952. 7 pp.

Education

FIVE YEARS OF THE MINIMUM
FOUNDATION PROGRAM. Tallahassee,
Florida Legislative Council, 1953. 59 pp.

LOUISIANA TEACHER RETIREMENT SYS-
TEM. Baton Rouge, Public Affairs Re-
search Council, *PAR Research Brief,*
December 17, 1953. 10 pp.

STATE UNIVERSITY GOVERNING BOARDS.
Baton Rouge, Louisiana Legislative
Council, June 19, 1953. 15 pp.

UNIVERSITY EXTENSION IN THE
UNITED STATES. A Study by the Nation-
al University Extension Association,
Made With the Assistance of a Grant
from the Fund for Adult Education. By
John R. Morton. Birmingham, Univer-
sity of Alabama Press, 1953. xiii, 144 pp.
Cloth bound: $2.25, Paper bound: $1.00.

Elections and Voting

QUALIFICATIONS TO VOTE: LOUISIANA
AND OTHER STATES. Baton Rouge,
Louisiana Legislative Council, December
14, 1953. 6 pp.

Fire

REPORT ON THE FIRE DEPARTMENT. By
Griffenhagen & Associates. Chicago, The
Committee on City Expenditures, Sep-
tember 1953. Variously paged.

Home Rule

THEY'RE POSSIBLE NOW: LOCAL CON-
TROL, HOME RULE, CONSOLIDATION. Nashville, Tennessee Municipal League, *Tennessee Town & City,* December 1953.
2 pp.

Incentives to Industry

MANUFACTURERS' TAX EXEMPTIONS IN MARYLAND. Baltimore 2, Maryland State Planning Commission, October 1953. 27 pp. 25 cents.

Judiciary

SEPARATE CRIMINAL COURTS. Baton Rouge, Louisiana Legislative Council, December 7, 1953. 9 pp.

WHO PICKS OUR JUDGES? New York 38, Citizens Union of the City of New York, *The Searchlight,* December 1953. 7 pp.

Legislative Bodies

THE LEGISLATIVE PROCESS IN LOUIS-IANA. Baton Rouge, Louisiana Legislative Council, February 1953. vi, 98 pp.

LEGISLATIVE REORGANIZATION IN MINNESOTA. Minneapolis 3, League of Women voters of Minnesota, November 1953. 20 pp. 20 cents.

Legislative Councils

PROGRESS REPORT. Topeka, Kansas Legislative Council, November 1953. 10 pp.

Medical Education

MEDICAL EDUCATION. Does Kentucky Need a State-supported Medical School? Frankfort, Kentucky Legislative Research Commission, 1953. 98 pp.

Metropolitan Areas

GUIDE BOOK 1954—METROPOLITAN ST. LOUIS AREA DEVELOPMENT. St. Louis, Metropolitan Plan Association, 1953. 43 pp.

MUNICIPAL FRINGE AREA PROBLEM IN ALABAMA. By Robert T. Daland. University, University of Alabama, Bureau of Public Administration, and the Alabama League of Municipalities, 1953. 72 pp.

Personnel

THE ADMINISTRATIVE STRUCTURE OF THE CENTRAL OFFICE OF THE DIVISION OF EMPLOYMENT SECURITY. Baton Rouge, Louisiana Legislative Council, September 1953. 48 pp.

WAGE AND SALARY SURVEY. Chicago 3, Citizens' Civil Service Association of Illinois, October 1953. 31 pp.

Police

REPORT ON THE DEPARTMENT OF POLICE. By Griffenhagen & Associates. Chicago, Committee on City Expenditures, September 30, 1953. Variously paged.

Primaries

NONPARTISAN PRIMARIES. Baton Rouge, Louisiana Legislative Council, June 30, 1953. 8 pp.

Public Welfare

REVIEW OF PUBLIC ASSISTANCE IN LARAMIE COUNTY. Cheyenne, Wyoming Taxpayers Association, December 1953. 58 pp.

Reapportionment

REAPPORTIONMENT OF SEATS IN THE HOUSE OF REPRESENTATIVES. Baton Rouge, Louisiana Legislative Council, September 11, 1953. 5 pp.

Records

MICROFILMING PUBLIC RECORDS. State Microfilm Service Available to Municipalities at Cost. By Paul Weiss. Madison 3, League of Wisconsin Municipalities, *The Municipality,* December 1953. 1 p.

Retirement Systems

A COMPREHENSIVE RETIREMENT PROGRAM FOR THE EMPLOYEES OF THE CITY OF PHILADELPHIA. Philadelphia 7, Bureau of Municipal Research, October 1953. 72 pp.

REPORT ON THE PHILADELPHIA FIREMEN'S PENSION FUND. Philadelphia 7, Bureau of Municipal Research, August 1953. 51 pp.

Sanitary Districts

CHICAGO SANITARY DISTRICT. Springfield, Illinois Legislative Council, 1953. 34 pp.

Streets and Highways

SOME PROBLEMS OF HIGHWAY COST ASSIGNMENT with Special Reference to the Trucker's Share. By Richard M. Zettel. Minneapolis 14, League of Minnesota Municipalities, *Minnesota Municipalities,* November 1953. 8 pp.

A SURVEY OF MINNESOTA HIGHWAYS.

A Report to the Minnesota Highway Study Commission. By M. J. Hoffman. Minneapolis 14, League of Minnesota Municipalities, *Minnesota Municipalities,* November 1953. 3 pp.

Taxation and Finance

FINANCIAL STATISTICS OF NEW JERSEY MUNICIPALITIES AND SCHOOLS. Trenton 8, New Jersey Taxpayers Association, September 1953. 43 pp.

HOW HIGH WILL YOUR CITY TAXES BE IN 1954? Woonsocket (Rhode Island), Taxpayers Association, *Your Business,* December 1953. 4 pp.

NEW TAX LAWS OF PENNSYLVANIA— 1953. Harrisburg, Pennsylvania State Chamber of Commerce, *State Affairs Bulletin,* December 1953. 8 pp.

1953 WISCONSIN TAXES. State and Local Taxes Exceed 530 Million Dollars; Seven Dollars More Per Person Than Last Year. Madison 3, Wisconsin Taxpayers Alliance, *The Wisconsin Taxpayer,* December 1953. 6 pp.

OPERATION FINANCE. HOW THE CITY SPENDS ITS MONEY. Hartford, Governmental Research Institute, *Budget Alert,* December 1953. 3 pp.

PITTSBURGH MAKES THE BIG SWITCH. The Earned Income Tax and Future City Finance. Pittsburgh 19, Pennsylvania Economy League, Western Division, 1953. 11 pp.

SALES TAXES AND THEIR APPLICATION TO FARMERS. By W. P. Walker and F. E. Hulse. College Park, University of Maryland, Agricultural Experiment Station, *Bulletin,* June 1953. 36 pp.

THE STATE GENERAL PROPERTY TAX. Baton Rouge, Louisiana Legislative Council, December 1, 1953. 14 pp.

TRIPLING OF TAXES SINCE 1946 FOR MILWAUKEE'S SIX PUBLIC RETIREMENT SYSTEMS INDICATES NEED FOR CURRENT CITY STUDY AS TO INTEGRATION WITH SOCIAL SECURITY. Milwaukee 2, Citizens' Governmental Research Bureau, Inc., *Bulletin,* December 18, 1953. 5 pp.

Traffic

ADMINISTRATIVE STUDY OF THE BUREAU OF TRAFFIC ENGINEERING OF THE CITY OF SPRINGFIELD, MASSACHUSETTS. Springfield, Future Springfield, Inc., 1953. 12 pp.

OUR FUTURE FREEWAYS. LET'S PLAN COUNTY ROADS. Houston 2, Tax Research Association of Houston and Harris County, Inc., *TRA Journal,* August 1953. 3 and 4 pp. respectively.

Training for Public Service

SEVENTH ANNUAL PEACE OFFICERS TRAINING SCHOOL. A Report. Lawrence, University of Kansas, Governmental Research Center, 1953. 99 pp.

SEVENTH SHORT COURSE FOR ASSESSING OFFICERS. Ann Arbor, University of Michigan, Institute of Public Administration, Bureau of Government, 1953. 52 pp.

TRAINING FOR BETTER PUBLIC SERVICE. An Outline of the Tokyo Metropolitan In-service Training Institute. Tokyo (Japan), Council on Liaison with Foreign Cities, *Tokyo Municipal News,* November 1953. 2 pp.

Water Pollution

THE CHALLENGE OF WATER POLLUTION. By Mark D. Hollis. Charleston, West Virginia League of Municipalities, *West Virginia Municipality,* July-August-September 1953. 2 pp. 25 cents.

POLLUTION ABATEMENT IN VIRGINIA— Past, Present and Future. By Ross H. Walker. Richmond 19, *Virginia Municipal Review,* September 1953. 3 pp. 25 cents.

Books in Review

COUNCIL-MANAGER GOVERNMENT IN IOWA. By Clayton L. Ringgenberg. Iowa City, State University of Iowa, Institute of Public Affairs, in cooperation with the League of Iowa Municipalities, 1953. 96 pp. $1.00.

THE COUNCIL-MANAGER PLAN IN FLORIDA: THEORY AND PRACTICE. By William F. Larsen. Gainesville, University of Florida, Public Administration Clearing Service, 1953. 15 pp.

The first of these publications is a comprehensive recital of information about every council-manager municipal government in Iowa, including some discussion of the achievements claimed under the plan by local councils and managers. It constitutes a complete report to date for the benefit of any other Iowa city where the manager plan is contemplated.

The second is a pocket-size review of the council-manager plan in 57 cities in Florida, including a sketch of the council-manager movement throughout the country and a candid description of how Florida cities have functioned under the plan. It constitutes an adequate introduction to the whole subject, connecting the literature of the National Municipal League with the local scene.

These pamphlets are the latest of a growing series of such state pamphlets of great usefulness in the promotion and correct understanding of the council-manager plan. Previous ones include studies of manager communities in Maine, Pennsylvania, South Dakota, Utah, New Hampshire and Illinois.

R. S. C.

NIMLO MUNICIPAL LAW REVIEW (successor to MUNICIPALITIES AND THE LAW IN ACTION). A Record of Municipal Legal Experience in 1952. Edited by Charles S. Rhyne and Brice W. Rhyne. Washington 6, D. C., National Institute of Municipal Law Officers, 1953. 462 pp. $10.

A change in title and a broadening of scope characterize this sixteenth annual Proceedings of the Annual Conference of the National Institute of Municipal Law Officers. Familiar to those concerned with municipal affairs as *Municipalities and the Law in Action* the 1953 edition is entitled *NIMLO Municipal Law Review*. Included for the first time are specialized papers submitted to the association on matters of interest to municipal attorneys in addition to those delivered at the NIMLO conference.

Forty-seven provocative articles and committee reports are represented. They cover such a wide range of subjects as intergovernmental relations, civil defense, public utilities, water fluoridation, parking and mass transportation, civil liberties, ordinance codification, public records, municipal bonds, revenues and expenditures, torts and contracts, and zoning. Adding to the usefulness of the volume is a comprehensive index.

JOHN P. KEITH

THE RAT RACE. By Edward Rager. New York, Vantage Press, Inc., 1952. 288 pp. $3.50.

The author, an attorney in New York and at one time recording secretary of the National Republican Club and a member of the New York City Council, has written a novel, which obviously reflects his own experience and dealing in disguise with important public characters, with the freedom which a novelist can enjoy. He makes a dismal picture of New York politics and politicians on both sides, unredeemed by any cases of men of good character except the hero, which one suspects is the author himself. People who know part of the picture and suspect more will find here confirmation of their darkest fears if they share the cynicism of the author.

R. S. C.

Additional Books and Pamphlets

(See also Researcher's Digest and other departments)

Constitutions

AMERICAN CONSTITUTIONAL CUSTOM: A FORGOTTEN FACTOR IN THE FOUNDING. By Burleigh Cushing Rodick. New York City, Philosophical Library, 1953. xx, 244 pp. $4.75.

Disaster Preparedness

DISASTER PLAN AND WARNING PROCEDURE FOR CITY OF MANHATTAN. Manhattan, Kansas, Office of City Manager, 1953. 7 pp.

Education

SALARY SCHEDULES OF PUBLIC SCHOOL TEACHERS IN MASSACHUSETTS as of September 1953. Boston 8, Massachusetts Teachers Association, 1953. 16 pp.

Employee Suggestions

EMPLOYEE SUGGESTION SYSTEMS. By Robert Batson. Chicago 37, Civil Service Assembly of the United States and Canada, 1953. 7 pp. $2.00.

Federal-state-local Relations

ARE THE STATES YIELDING TOO MUCH POWER TO THE FEDERAL GOVERNMENT? Broadcast of December 15, 1953. Moderator: James F. Murray, Jr.; Speakers: Charles B. Brownson and Richard Bolling. New York City, Town Hall, Town Meeting of the Air, 1953. 15 pp. 25 cents.

HIGHWAY CONSTRUCTION—FEDERAL-STATE RELATIONS. Washington 6, D. C., Chamber of Commerce of the United States, Construction and Civic Development Department, 1953. 11 pp. 10 cents; discounts on quantity orders.

INTERGOVERNMENTAL COOPERATION IN HIGHWAY AFFAIRS. A Recommended Action Program for Effective Relation-ships. Washington, D. C., Highway Research Board, 1953. 7 pp. 30 cents.

Inflation

INFLATION. What inflation has done to the purchasing power of the dollar and what you can do about it. New York City, Columbia University, Graduate School of Education, The American Assembly, 1952. 23 pp.

Initiative and Referendum

NEBRASKA AS A PIONEER IN THE INITIATIVE AND REFERENDUM. By Adam C. Breckenridge. Lincoln, Nebraska History, September 1953. 9 pp.

Juvenile Delinquency

YOUTHFUL OFFENDERS COURT AND COMMUNITY—Their Reciprocal Needs. Report of the Chief Justice. New York City, Court of Special Sessions, 1953. 27 pp.

Legislative Committees

CHRONOLOGICAL LIST OF CALIFORNIA LEGISLATIVE INTERIM COMMITTEES AND THEIR REPORTS—1937-1953. Sacramento, Legislative Auditor, 1953. 88 pp.

Mediation

A GUIDE TO STATE MEDIATION LAWS AND AGENCIES. Washington, D. C., United States Department of Labor, Bureau of Labor Standards, 1953. 57 pp.

Municipal Government

BUSINESS ACTION FOR BETTER CITIES. A Complete Report on the Businessmen's Conference on Urban Problems, Portland, Oregon, June 23 and 24, 1952. Washington 6, D. C., Chamber of Commerce of the United States, 1953. 185 pp. $1.00; discounts on quantity orders.

Personnel

A SUPERVISORY GUIDE FOR THE PREVENTION AND HANDLING OF THE PROBLEMS OF EMPLOYEES. By Arthur O. England. New London, Connecticut, National Foremen's Institute, 1953. 23 pp.

Public Works

PUBLIC WORKS ADMINISTRATION. Papers Presented at the 1953 Institute for Public Works Officials. Madison 3,

League of Wisconsin Municipalities, 1953. 29 pp. $1.00.

Shopping Centers

ESTIMATING PRODUCTIVITY FOR PLANNED REGIONAL SHOPPING CENTERS. By James W. Rouse. Washington 6, D. C., Urban Land Institute, *Urban Land,* November 1953. 4 pp.

Snow Removal

SNOW REMOVAL MANUAL. New York City, Department of Sanitation, Bureau of Street Cleaning and Waste Collection, 1952. 79 pp.

Streets and Highways

MUD AND MUDDLE OR MOBILITY. A Presentation at the National Project Adequate Roads (PAR) Conference. Washington, D. C., June 15, 1953. 32 pp.

Toll Roads

INDIANA TOLL ROADS. By Albert J. Wedeking. (Address before the Municipal Forum of New York.) New York, the Forum, 1953. (Apply the Forum, The Bank of Wall Street, 48 Wall Street, New York 5.)

Traffic

MODEL TRAFFIC ORDINANCE. By Department of Commerce, Bureau of Public Roads. Washington 25, D C., United States Government Printing Office, 1953. 41 pp. 20 cents.

Traffic Safety

THE COST OF TRAFFIC CONGESTION AND TRAFFIC ACCIDENTS IN THE CITY OF NEW YORK. New York 38, Citizens Traffic Safety Board, Inc., 1953. 20 pp.

OPERATION SAFETY. Program Kit on Traffic Safety Promotion. Theme for March 1954: MOTOR MANNERS. Chicago 11, National Safety Council, 1954. Variously paged.

STATE TRAFFIC SAFETY. Its Organization, Administration and Programming. By Maxwell Halsey. Saugatuck, Connecticut, Eno Foundation for Highway Traffic Control, 1953. xi, 280 pp.

azarus Named to League Staff

Andrew J. Lazarus, for the past three ears an assistant information officer th the United States Information rvice in Helsinki, Finland, has joined the staff of the National Municipal League as information associate.

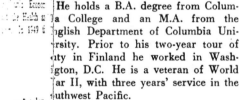

From 1946 to 1948 Mr. Lazarus served as a university and foreign correspondent for the New York *Herald Tribune* in New York and andinavia. He has also worked as a porter on two other newspapers and research assistant in election campaigns.

Andrew J. Lazarus

He holds a B.A. degree from Columa College and an M.A. from the nglish Department of Columbia Unirsity. Prior to his two-year tour of ity in Finland he worked in Washigton, D.C. He is a veteran of World ar II, with three years' service in the uthwest Pacific.

eague Staffer Speaks New Jersey

John Keith, League senior associate, cently talked before two Bergen ounty, New Jersey, civic groups—the len Rock Civic Association and Inpendents for Good Government. Bere both groups Keith advocated a ounty manager appointed by the ounty governing body.

He argued against the proliferated, ulti-layer government of Bergen Coun-, which comprises an area two-thirds e size of New York City and has 70 parate municipalities averaging three and one-third square miles in area with about 7,500 inhabitants each. The duplication of police work and other governmental activities, he said, is wasteful and inefficient. He added that Bergen County was one place that city-county consolidation was badly needed.

If the first two steps were to be taken, Keith said that Bergen County would then have to strive for constitutional or legislatively imposed home rule so as to have the necessary powers to carry out its functions.

Dodds Heads Hoover Task Force

Dr. Harold W. Dodds, president of Princeton University and former League secretary and president, has been named head of a ten-member task force to study problems of federal service for the Commission on Organization of the Executive Branch of the Government. Among many aspects of the federal personnel picture, the task force will review Civil Service Commission programs and practices.

Commission Chairman Herbert Hoover described Dr. Dodds, who is a life member of the League's Council, as a man who brings to his new job "a wealth of experience in personnel, political science and related fields."

The new Hoover commission was established by President Eisenhower several months ago to study and recommend means of making the executive branch more modern and efficient.

Dr. Dodds was editor of the NATIONAL MUNICIPAL REVIEW from 1920 to 1933 and served as the League's president from 1934 to 1937. He was secretary from 1920 to 1928.

League Dines Visiting Authorities

A dinner session of the League's "continuing seminar on government" was held from 5:30 to 8:00 P.M. on January 8 at Columbia University, in connection with the university's first Bi-Centennial Conference, "The Metropolis in Modern Life." The seminar devoted itself primarily to the League's proposed program in metropolitan area problems. Attention was also given to the developing state government project.

Attending the seminar were: William Anderson, professor of political science, University of Minnesota; Ernest A. Englebert, professor of political science, University of California, Los Angeles; Martin L. Faust, professor of political science, University of Missouri; Victor Jones, professor of government, Wesleyan University; John M. Kernochan, associate professor of law and secretary of the Metropolis in Modern Life Conference, Columbia University; Charles M. Kneier, professor of political science, University of Illinois; Albert Lepawsky, professor of political science, University of California; Allen Manvel, chief, Governments Division, Bureau of the Census; Hugh R. Pomeroy, director, Westchester County (New York) Department of Planning; Edward W. Weidner, director, Governmental Research Bureau, Michigan State College; and Harold Zink, professor of political science, Ohio State University.

Representing the League were Alfred Willoughby, executive director; John E. Bebout, assistant director; Richard S. Childs, chairman of the executive committee; and staff principals William N. Cassella, Jr., and John P. Keith.

NML Models Useful in Filipino Elections

Word from Dr. Harold F. Gosnell who has recently returned from a trip to the Philippine Islands, indicates that League publications were helpful in administering the Filipino elections last fall.

Professor Gosnell, research consultant and lecturer at American University, reports that two League models—the *Model Registration System* and the *Model Election Administration System* —were of substantial use to Commissioner Perez, of the elections commission, and that he was "very happy to have them." Professor Gosnell, who says that the Philippine election code has many sound features and that its administration was in capable hands during the contest in which Ramon Magsaysay emerged triumphant, had requested the League publications from Manila.

Cassella Counsels Newark Women Voters

William N. Cassella, Jr., League Staff Fellow for 1953-54, addressed a group of leaders of the Newark (N.J.) League of Women Voters in January on a proposed short course, "Organizing Government for Good Administration." The Newark League plans to run the course in eight sessions during February and March. It is designed to inform Newark citizens of their responsibilities under the newly adopted city charter.

Professor Cassella, on leave for a year from the University of Missouri, spoke to the group on the context and arrangement of the course of study.

REVIEW

The National Municipal Review

ALFRED WILLOUGHBY, Editor   ELSIE S. PARKER, Assistant Editor

Contributing Editors

JOHN E. BEBOUT, Research
RICHARD S. CHILDS
EDWARD W. WEIDNER, County and Township
H. M. OLMSTED, City, State and Nation

WADE S. SMITH, Taxation and Finance
GEORGE H. HALLETT, JR.
WM. REDIN WOODWARD
Proportional Representation

State Correspondents

H. F. ALDERFER, *Pennsylvania*
CARTER W. ATKINS, *Connecticut*
MYRON H. ATKINSON, *North Dakota*
CHESTER BIESEN, *Washington*
D. BENTON BISER, *Maryland*
ERNEST M. BLACK, *Oklahoma*
JOHN C. BOLLENS, *California*
WILLIAM L. BRADSHAW, *Missouri*
A. C. BRECKENRIDGE, *Nebraska*
ARTHUR W. BROMAGE, *Michigan*
FRANKLIN L. BURDETTE, *Maryland*
CHARLTON F. CHUTE, *Pennsylvania*
WELDON COOPER, *Virginia*
C. A. CROSSER, *Washington*
PAUL DOLAN, *Delaware*
D. MACK EASTON, *Colorado*
WILLIAM O. FARBER, *South Dakota*
VICTOR FISCHER, *Alaska*
FOREST FRANK, *Ohio*
DAVID FUDGE, *Oklahoma*
ROBERT M. GOODRICH, *Rhode Island*
MRS. LEONARD HAAS, *Georgia*
M. H. HARRIS, *Utah*
SAM HAYS, *Arkansas*
ROBERT B. HIGHSAW, *Mississippi*
JACK E. HOLMES, *New Mexico*
ORREN C. HORMELL, *Maine*
HERMAN KEHRLI, *Oregon*
PAUL KELSO, *Arizona*

DRYDEN KUSER, *Nevada*
JOHN D. LANGMUIR, *New Hampshire*
STUART A. MacCORKLE, *Texas*
RICHARD G. MARDEN, *New Hampshire*
BOYD A. MARTIN, *Idaho*
EDWARD M. MARTIN, *Illinois*
JAMES W. MARTIN, *Kentucky*
JAMES W. McGREW, *New Jersey*
DAYTON D. McKEAN, *Colorado*
EDWIN B. McPHERON, *Indiana*
WILLIAM MILLER, *New Jersey*
LENNOX L. MOAK, *Pennsylvania*
ANDREW E. NUQUIST, *Vermont*
KIMBROUGH OWEN, *Louisiana*
FRANK W. PRESCOTT, *Tennessee*
JOHN E. REEVES, *Kentucky*
ROLAND R. RENNE, *Montana*
PAUL N. REYNOLDS, *Wisconsin*
RUSSELL M. ROSS, *Iowa*
ALBERT B. SAYE, *Georgia*
VICTORIA SCHUCK, *Massachusetts*
LLOYD M. SHORT, *Minnesota*
GEORGE G. SIPPRELL, *New York*
PAUL D. STEWART, *West Virginia*
JOHN G. STUTZ, *Kansas*
HERMAN H. TRACHSEL, *Wyoming*
PAUL W. WAGER, *North Carolina*
YORK WILLBERN, *Alabama*
JOHN F. WILLMOTT, *Florida*

Published by THE NATIONAL MUNICIPAL LEAGUE

George H. Gallup, *President*

John S. Linen, *Vice President*
George S. Van Schaick, *Vice President*

Carl H. Pforzheimer, *Treasurer*
Alfred Willoughby, *Executive Director*

Richard S. Childs, *Chairman, Executive Committee*

Council

Charles Edison, West Orange, N. J., *Chairman*

Frederick L. Bird, New York
Arthur W. Bromage, Ann Arbor, Mich.
E. Bartlett Brooks, Dayton, Ohio
Henry Bruère, New York
William H. Bulkeley, Hartford
L. E. Burch, Jr., Memphis
Mrs. Albert D. Cash, Cincinnati
Charles E. Commander, Jr., Jacksonville
L. P. Cookingham, Kansas City, Mo.
Karl Detzer, Leland, Mich.
E. D. Dodd, Toledo
Harold W. Dodds, Princeton, N. J.
Bayard H. Faulkner, Montclair, N. J.
Arnold Frye, New York

Ewart W. Goodwin, San Diego
Thomas Graham, Louisville
Mrs. Virgil Loeb, St. Louis
Rob Roy Macleod, Buffalo
Mark S. Matthews, Greenwich, Conn.
Cecil Morgan, New York
Albert E. Noelte, Central Falls, R. I.
Mrs. Maurice H. Noun, Des Moines
H. Bruce Palmer, Newark, N. J.
Lawson Purdy, New York
Thomas R. Reid, Dearborn, Mich.
Philip K. Robinson, Milwaukee
Murray Seasongood, Cincinnati
Lee M. Sharrar, Houston

Regional Vice Presidents

Lester L. Bates, Columbia, S. C.
William Collins, New York
Ben B. Ehrlichman, Seattle
John B. Gage, Kansas City, Mo.
Carl J. Gilbert, Boston
Barry Goldwater, Phoenix
Lloyd Hale, Minneapolis

Arthur E. Johnson, Denver
Mrs. Siegel W. Judd, Grand Rapids
John Nuveen, Chicago
Ed. P. Phillips, Richmond
Charles P. Taft, Cincinnati
Alex R. Thomas, San Antonio
Carleton B. Tibbetts, Los Angeles

NEWS for League Members

1954 Conference Set for Kansas City

Kansas City, Missouri, will be the site of the 60th National Conference on Government next fall, it has been announced by the National Municipal League. The Conference is slated for November 7, 8, 9 and 10.

John B. Gage

In announcing the selection of Kansas City, League President George H. Gallup said the Executive Committee was accepting an invitation which had been tendered jointly by John B. Gage, former Kansas City mayor and currently regional vice president of the League, and Clinton W. Kanaga, Jr., president of the Citizens Association of Kansas City, at the annual membership meeting during the Richmond Conference last November.

The Executive Committee also gave serious consideration to an invitation from Phoenix, Arizona, which was presented by a delegation from that city led by Mayor Hohen Foster.

Kansas City was the winner of two All-America City Awards—in 1950 and 1951—in recognition of its citizens' successful efforts to maintain clean nonpartisan government and to rehabilitate areas inundated by flood waters.

Survey Committee Continues Reappraisal

The Survey Committee, created at the Richmond meeting of the NML Council last November to review suggestions in the McLean report and recommend appropriate action to the spring Council meeting, has held three more all-day Saturday meetings since its initial session January 9.

The Committee has reviewed staff reports on various aspects of League policy and procedure and has consulted a number of other persons.

The League's constitution has been given a thorough going-over and a proposed revision, based on experience since the present document was adopted in 1932, probably will be submitted to the Council along with other Committee recommendations.

League Awarded Honor Medal

The George Washington Honor Medal will be awarded in the near future to the National Municipal League for its "All-America Cities" program in which the League honors eleven communities annually for progress achieved through intelligent citizen action.

Freedoms Foundation, donor of the honor medal, termed the "All-America Cities" program "an outstanding achievement in helping to bring about a better understanding of the American way of life."

Look magazine, co-sponsor of the program, was similarly honored by the Foundation.

All-America Cities Receive Awards

Local pride hit new highs with the presentation in recent weeks of All-America City Awards in eleven winning communities. Top honor cities in the 1953 contest, sponsored by the National Municipal League and *Look* magazine, accepted the national recognition given to their local citizen efforts with elaborate ceremonies which attracted wide attention.

Nation-wide publicity brought news of the winners to radio listeners and television viewers all over the country. Associated and United Press and International News Service wires put the 1953 contest into many news columns, and regional wire services made impressive showings in the press of six middle western and eastern states.

Peoria, Illinois, one of the larger winning cities, was responsible for a good share of the country-wide publicity on radio and TV, thanks to comedians Fibber McGee and Molly and sports commentator Jack Brickhouse, all loyal Peorians. Don McNeill's morning breakfast club show, originating in Chicago, featured interviews with residents of Park Forest, another winning community.

Look, printing the story in its February 9 issue, reported record sales in the winning areas, while both the League and the magazine have received orders for reprints running into the thousands.

Peoria's Award was presented by George Gallup, League president and director of the American Institute of Public Opinion, to Mayor Robert D. Morgan at capacity-filled Shrine Mosque Auditorium on February 5. Jack Star,

114

midwest editor of *Look* and writer of the magazine's story, and Fred Bauer represented the magazine at the ceremonies. The entire Peoria city council was present.

Petersburg, Virginia, received its award on February 5 from Ed. P. Phillips, regional vice president of the League, and Mrs. Jane Douglas, of *Look,* who presented it to Mayor Churchill Dunn at the country club. A large delegation from Richmond turned out for the occasion and that city's *Times-Dispatch* gave the event thorough coverage. The Petersburg *Progress-Index* put out a 28-page special edition marking the Award.

In Canton, Ohio, Mayor Carl F. Wise received the Award on February 11 from E. D. Dodd, League Council member of Toledo. Participating in the ceremonies at Timken High School Auditorium were Dr. L. R. Elson, pastor of the National Presbyterian Church in Washington, D. C. (known as "President Eisenhower's pastor"), Martin Frank, chairman of the Chamber of Commerce public relations committee, and Jean Herrick, assistant to *Look's* general manager. Governor Frank Lausche of Ohio was present at the event, which featured music by an all-star high school band.

On January 31 at Flint, Michigan, Rev. Henry Berkemeier received the Award from Mrs. Siegel W. Judd, League regional vice president. Vernon C. Myers, publisher, represented *Look*. Main speaker was Arthur S. Flemming, national director, Office of Defense Mobilization. Co-recipient of the award was M. F. Borgman, general chairman of "Operation Tornado," Flint's historic building bee. The celebration took place in the Industrial Mutual Association Auditorium with 1,500 present.

(Continued on next page)

Winners in Shreveport display their new flag — left to right, William A. Peavy, co-chairman of the survey committee; Mrs. Elsie Larson Wilson, director of the Council of Social Agencies; Mayor Clyde E. Fant; Thomas A. Wimberly, president of the Chamber of Commerce; and Harold J. Bryant, general manager of the Chamber.

All-America Cities
(Continued from preceding page)

At Park Forest, Illinois, Herbert Emmerich, former Council member of the League, and Jack Star presented the award to Lester B. VandeBerg, president of the permanent Rich Township High School Committee, in the school gymnasium on January 29. Over 100 people attended the special dinner, which was followed by a concert of the Mexican Boys Choir. Park Forest received a commendatory letter from Mrs. Oveta Culp Hobby, U. S. secretary of Health, Education and Welfare.

Scranton, Pennsylvania, received its Award on February 9. It was presented by Richard S. Childs, chairman of the League's Executive Committee, to Ted V. Rodgers, Sr., president of the Chamber of Commerce. The ceremony, which followed a parade through the city, was held in the Masonic Temple before an audience of 900 at the annual Chamber of Commerce dinner.

Ceremonies were televised over WARM-TV, Scranton's new television station.

On January 31 Daytona Beach, Florida, held its celebration. The award was presented by Laurence F. Lee, chairman of the board, U. S. Chamber of Commerce, to Mayor Jack Tamm in the Peabody Auditorium. A concert by the Daytona Beach Symphony Orchestra and singing by a Negro group from Bethune-Cookman College were features of the event. The local program listed the All-America Cities jury, the winning team and the runners-up.

Lee Sharrar, Council member of the League in Houston, presented the Award to Mayor Clyde E. Fant, of Shreveport, Louisiana, at a ceremony on February 2. The program preceded dinner in the Crystal Ballroom of the Washington-Youree Hotel and special arrangements were made in the Booker T. Washington High School for Ne-

(Continued on page 168)

League President George H. Gallup presents "All-America Cities" Award to Peoria's Mayor Robert D. Morgan. Eight Peoria councilmen also participated in receiving the award.

National Municipal Review

Volume XLIII, No. 3   Total Number 441

Published monthly except August

By NATIONAL MUNICIPAL LEAGUE

Contents for March 1954

The contents of the REVIEW are indexed in *International Index to Periodicals* and *Public Affairs Information Service*.

Entered as second class matter July 11, 1932, at the Post Office at Worcester, Massachusetts. Publication office, 150 Fremont Street, Worcester 3; editorial and business office, 299 Broadway, New York 7. Copyright 1954 by the National Municipal League.

Subscription, $5 per year; Canadian, $5.25; foreign, $5.50; single copies 50 cents.

Editorial Comment

The English Are Tougher

IN the *Model City Charter* all the powers of the city are located in the city council and the council is carefully required to do its work as a unit, expressing composite representation and composite judgment and eliminating all one-man power and individual caprice. But councilmen who have been accustomed under prior structural regimes to help manage departments as commissioners or as committee members oftentimes continue their intervention into departmental management to the distress of the manager and the impairment of his proper authority. Tactfully combatting such intervention and persuading councilmen to exert their proper powers only through channels is a problem of some city managers.

In England, councils are large and committees of council practically run departments. It would seem reasonable enough, therefore, that a councilman might ask the town clerk to explain his authority for carrying out certain work. Such an inquiry, reported in the *Municipal Journal* (London), did not carry with it any direction or intervention but, according to the *Journal,* it provoked a sharp reply in which the clerk said, "I cannot accept the principle that I need account to anyone other than the city council, or in certain cases a committee of the city council, for the action I take on behalf of the city council."

The conflict was referred to a special committee of council which reported that "the town clerk's responsibility, like that of all other officers, was to the city council and not to an individual member."

Municipal Journal editorializes, "We think the town clerk in this case dealt with the matter with correctness . . . and express the hope that in the interest of proper local government others will follow his example."

In the United States, a city manager would undoubtedly find nothing to object to, but the English are tighter in the restriction of councils and administrators to their respective spheres.

Lobbying in New Hampshire

THE fact that the Rockingham Race Track supported the private free bar room that has been operating in a room at the Eagle Hotel [Concord] during the past several years during legislative sessions has been admitted publicly.

The spokesman for the race track stated the group wanted to withdraw from this activity but that pressure had been brought to bear on it and it had continued their support. What the pressure was was not disclosed, but it must be obvious to anyone that the pressure, in order to be effective, must have originated with members of the General Court [legislature].

Only pressure that was directly connected with the right to vote on legislation that would affect racing could be strong enough to influence the race track with enough force to have it carry on an activity it would like to discontinue.

The maintenance of the bar room, with free drinks for any legislator, is a form of lobbying that self-respecting lobbyists would not take part in nor, in most cases, would their employers countenance such action.

It is far from a healthy condition and the free liquor at the Eagle is only part of the entertainment offered by the race track to legislators.

A weekly dance is held during legislative sessions at the Princess Ball Room, on the Daniel Webster Highway north of Concord, during legislative sessions and it is understood that the race track group picks up the check.

Further, a dinner for members of the Ways and Means Committee and their friends is held during each legislative session, with the expense assumed by the race track group, according to reports. In 1953 more than two hundred attended this dinner and enjoyed the food and liquor as well as dancing to the music provided by a "live" band, without being called upon to spend one red cent.

Many courageous, self-respecting legislators refuse to accept any of the gratuitous entertainment offered, some others accept all that is offered.

The acceptance of any free articles or entertainment by a member of the General Court, from a group whose business activities depend in any way on that individual's vote, is undeniably wrong.

Other interests provide liquor through free bar rooms at the Eagle but we do not have definite proof as to who the interests are nor have any of them admitted publicly that they supported such free entertainment. We have been informed by a member of the 1951 General Court that the beer interests paid all the expenses of a large group of legislators for a trip to Boston, dinner and attendance at a ball game. The particular legislator who furnished this information stated he had refused to attend as he did not feel it was good practice for legislators to accept such entertainment when, sooner or later, they would be called upon to vote on legislation affecting the donor.

The whole situation smells to high heaven and it is to be hoped that Rockingham, having admitted its participation in this pernicious practice, will withdraw from all of its "free" activities and allow legislation affecting its interests to be decided upon its merits alone, and that other lobbyists will follow suit.

In the meantime, Mr. Taxpayer, ask YOUR representative these questions:

1. Do you patronize the race track bar room at the Eagle?

2. Do you attend the weekly dances at the Princess?

3. Do you attend the Ways and Means Committee party at the Princess?

4. How did you vote on the proposed increase in the state's percentage of the race track "take" in 1951? in 1953?

The *New Hampshire Taxpayer*, publication of the New Hampshire Taxpayers Federation, January 1954.

Filipinos Hold Free Election

Despite limitations of communication systems, election code, based on NML model election laws, operates well.

By HAROLD F. GOSNELL*

UNTIL WE stand back and look at the operation of modern democracies, we fail to realize how important a role is played by modern means of communication and transportation. In the United States, one candidate wins by means of a citizens' telephone campaign, another makes a successful appeal over radio or television, still a third wins in a primary election because of strong press support. On election day an alert press and radio report important events immediately and thus help insure an honest and fair election.

In the Philippines the backwardness of communications makes the operation of democratic devices difficult. It is hard for many of the voters to learn about the qualifications of candidates. Safeguarding the casting and counting of ballots r e q u i r e s extraordinary vigilance since there is no floodlight of publicity to illuminate the dark areas. What happens in a remote precinct on election day may not be known for days or even weeks.

The extent of the handicap under which the Filipinos suffer can be shown by a few figures. Whereas in

the United States every other person has a radio and every third person buys a daily newspaper, in the Philippines only one out of every 100 persons has a radio and only one out of every 50 persons buys a daily newspaper.

It is possible for the party in power, with its vast central control over local administration, to exert great influence over the results of an election should it choose to do so. It was this possibility which created apprehension regarding fraud and terror prior to the November elections. The memory of padded registration, flying voters and intimidation in the 1949 national elections, which returned President Quirino to office, kept the citizens on the alert.

Apparently, in 1949, the powers of the executive over the Philippine constabulary, provincial treasurers, municipal mayors and other local officials were used to terrorize the voters and manipulate the result of the elections. In contests which followed these elections several Liberal congressmen lost their seats. The Nacionalista party was taken by surprise. Its candidate for president, José Laurel, never admitted that he had been rightfully defeated. While frauds were greatly reduced in the 1951 elections, they were not entirely eliminated.

During the 1953 campaign certain actions taken by the government were interpreted as preparatory to the commission of election frauds

*Dr. Gosnell has recently returned from the Philippine Islands, where he witnessed the November 1953 elections for president and national legislature. With the University of Chicago from 1922 to 1946, Dr. Gosnell is professor at the American University. He is author of numerous publications in the field of politics, the most recent of which is *Champion Campaigner: Franklin D. Roosevelt* (1952).

and terror. The last-minute transfers of Philippine constabulary commanders, provincial treasurers and other officials were held to indicate that these officials refused to go along with the government and were being replaced by officials who would "cooperate."

Reports were also printed in the press to the effect that surplus ballots had been printed, that ink eradicator had been distributed, that large campaign funds had been raised to buy votes, and that opposition voters and candidates had been intimidated. These reports were played up in scare fashion. The country was threatened with dire consequences if the elections were "stolen." It was intimated that a revolution might be in the making.

Democracy Demonstrated

On November 10, 1953, the Filipinos demonstrated that in spite of the obstacles which they had to overcome they could successfully use democratic methods to choose their president and national legislature. They voted out of power a regime that seemed ready to use the great powers it had to perpetuate itself in office. Nacionalista candidate Ramon Magsaysay decisively defeated President Elpidio Quirino, running for reelection on the Liberal ticket. The elections were free and the forebodings about fraud and terror proved to be wrong. How was this happy result achieved?

The Philippine election code has many sound features and its administration was in capable hands. The use of the signature to identify the voter, the use of ballot stubs to keep track of ballots, the procedures guaranteeing secrecy, the provisions against treating and bribery, the use of bipartisan boards of inspectors and partisan watchers and the careful regulations governing the reporting of the count are to be found in the *Model Election Administration System* of the National Municipal League and in many state laws.[1]

Unique features of the Philippine election code are the centralization of election administration for the entire country in a Commission on Elections, the use of the right thumb print for identification, the requirement that each voter write the names of the candidates for whom he wishes to vote, the procedures for prompt recount in cases where fraud is suspected, and the use of roving inspectors or representatives of the commission who can go at once to trouble spots. As one watches these provisions in operation, their wisdom grows apparent.

I thought that the requirement of writing out the names of persons voted for could lead to endless haggling and possibly to manipulation. Couldn't the party in power direct the chairmen of boards of inspectors to be excessively technical with all voters who oppose them? In practice the Philippine courts have been very liberal in interpreting voters' intent.[2] The main point to remember is that it is much more difficult, if not impossible, to alter a whole

[1]The author is indebted to the League for the prompt delivery of the *Model Registration System* and *Model Election Administration System* to him in Manila. The Commission on Elections was most grateful to receive them.

[2]Commission on Elections, *General Instructions*, Manila, 1953; José Aruego, *Philippine Government in Action*, Manila, 1953.

name than to alter or erase a cross mark. The count is slowed up but the voter is protected. In addition, the device is one way of enforcing the literacy requirement for voting. It is a spur for improving the educational system.

Not only does the law have some fine features but the commission has some fine public servants. For intelligence, energy, far-sightedness and devotion to public duty it would be hard to duplicate the Commission on Elections in any country.

The commission, able though it is, could not have done the job by itself. An alert body of citizens is always necessary to make election laws work. The Filipinos were organized to protect their voting rights. In the cities where their influence was direct, the Philippine press and radio did a magnificent job. Their crusade for free elections was carried to the remote areas by word of mouth. Travellers would carry back word of the efforts to secure an honest poll. The National Movement for Free Elections (NAMFREL), the League of Women Voters, Catholic Action and other civic groups recruited volunteer workers to canvass the precincts for illegal voters, to watch the casting of ballots and to watch the count. Partisan workers were also well trained for the occasion. The Magsaysay-for-President Movement (MPM), the Women's Magsaysay-for-President Movement, the Magsaysay-Garcia Youth League, and the National Students' Movement for Democracy filled their ranks with enthusiastic young people who were determined to safeguard their suffrage. Election

corruption had been widespread in 1949, but in 1953 the citizens were organized to combat it.

A word or two about NAMFREL. It was led by a veteran, a former guerrilla, who learned to appreciate democracy during the bitter period of occupation. The other leaders were recruited from the veterans' organizations, jaycees, rotarians and similar nonpartisan groups. Charges of partisanship were made against NAMFREL during the campaign but the organization lived them down.[3] If fighting for honest elections was "partisanship" then they were partisan. It is perhaps too much to ask all the officials of NAMFREL to follow the rule that a member of the Commission on Elections adopted for his family. He told his wife and his son that under no circumstances should they engage in any political activity. Anything they did for any political party would endanger his claim to being nonpartisan.

Election Literature

NAMFREL published a newsletter and a series of pamphlets on how to make the election clean. One pamphlet was entitled *The Ballot Is Your Sacred Heritage* and another, *Here's How We Can Have Free, Honest and Orderly Elections*. Literature of the organization was transported free of charge by individuals connected with various

(Continued on page 164)

---

[3] The situation was complex. MPM appealed to some of the same groups that had formed NAMFREL. The heads of the two organizations were brothers-in-law. The Liberal candidate for vice president, José Yulo, refused to speak at a NAMFREL meeting. The Philippine press raked him over the coals for this.

How Can Voters Understand?

Clearer, uniform methods of informing citizens on costs of state government urged by ex-businessman now official.

By ROGER A. FREEMAN*

OUR system of government, a government not only for but by the people, rests on the belief that the people are capable of judging vital public issues. The wisdom of the far-reaching decisions they are called upon to make depends largely upon the extent of their knowledge of public affairs.

Americans like to pride themselves on being the best informed nation. How much do we know about our government? In a study on citizen interest in government, the Council of State Governments reported in 1952: "Public opinion surveys consistently reveal a high degree of illiteracy about government." Each of us could probably quote dozens of examples from his own experience as to how little citizens know about state government.

Madison wrote in a letter to W. T. Barry on August 4, 1822: "A popular government without popular information, or the means of acquiring it, is but a prologue to a farce or a tragedy, or perhaps both. Knowledge will forever govern ignorance; and a people who mean to be their own governors must arm themselves with the power which knowledge gives."

*Mr. Freeman, formerly in the merchandising business, is special assistant to Governor Arthur B. Langlie of the state of Washington. He is author of *Your Dollar's Worth of State Government*, an official report on finances in his state written for popular consumption, as well as numerous articles on similar topics. This article is his address before the ninth annual convention of the National Association of State Budget Officers.

Why should American people be ignorant about their state governments? State fiscal agencies publish voluminous reports regularly, with hundreds of tables showing all the minute details of state revenues and expenditures. Some states publish abbreviated versions of the big reports. It seems that little of that information gets through to our citizens. The public professes interest but pays no attention to the material prepared for it. There must be something wrong, either with the public or with the material.

I used to be in the merchandising business before I was called into state government; I was a buyer for Macy's for some years. It happened occasionally that we'd have some goods which the public would not buy. The management had a very obnoxious policy in those cases. They never blamed the public.

With all the efforts many states have put into their reports, they do not seem to be able to clarify for the citizens the relationship between the financial plan and the working program of the state. Even "budgets in brief" do not meet the citizens' demand or need for knowledge of the essential facts on state government. We confuse disclosure with information and publish abbreviated transcripts of our books.

Years ago, corporation annual reports were like our abbreviated budgets: terse, technical, forbidding documents. But some companies would not accept "stockholder ignorance" or "stockholder indifference" as unconquerable. They went to a great deal of trouble to find out what the people wanted to know — and what they would read. Recent annual reports of major industrial corporations are attractive, informative and invite reading. The *Financial World* grades 5,000 stockholder reports each year and awards "Oscars of Industry" for the best one. Weston Smith, vice president of the *Financial World*, who runs those contests, has said his publication would be glad to run a category for states or for governments in general — if they had competitive entries. There aren't any now.

Reports Too Technical

What's wrong with government reports? They consist largely of technical terms and figures. Figure-statements mean something to finance officers, because they are used to working with them. But to most others they are dull, even frightening. We must translate figures into a language which nontechnical people can understand. The real trouble lies, I believe, in the approach: we view the budget from the official's angle, not from the public's angle. From where the official sits the budget has two sides, revenues and expenditures. That's not the way the public looks at it.

What the public puts into state government is taxes; what it gets back is not expenditures but services. Service to people is the ultimate purpose of government; and people are more interested in people than in anything else. They prefer a "ren-

dition of the melody to a copy of the music score."

The high point of a corporation annual report is the chapter that talks about the dividends, the return which the stockholder gets on his investment. A state cannot express its dividends in dollars per share. The dividends which the taxpayer gets are not "per capita expenditures." They are children educated, aged and disabled supported, patients in hospitals cared for or cured, handicapped made self-supporting, highways constructed and maintained, roads patrolled and accidents prevented.

The most important lesson a state financial report can and should drive home is that taxes are payments for services which the people buy collectively through government. The way to cut the bill is to order less.

Now, all this is not new. It is basically the philosophy of the "performance type" budget, based on functions, activities and services, which the Hoover Commission recommended a few years ago.

No matter how much narrative we have, or how many graphs, a financial report must contain many figures. The human brain cannot absorb series of unrelated figures without a yardstick by which it can judge them. What is a yardstick of state costs? Since there is no objective standard, comparisons are the only means of arriving at relative judgments. The only comparisons we show in our budgets are data for the preceding year or biennium. What makes last year a standard? Maybe it was too much because that interest group had a glib advocate, or maybe it was too little. "The assembly of a mass of financial data is of no avail unless the professional or amateur analyst can look past the figures and recognize the major forces which have produced the ends."[1]

How do corporate managers, bankers, investors or creditors evaluate the financial and operating data of a company? Through the industry approach. Trade associations serving management, investment services and credit bureaus prepare industry surveys in which they show various ratios and percentages of the companies in the same line of industry side by side. That is one of the most useful and informative services they render their clients.

Can we compare financial data of various states with each other? The committee on Uniformity of Reporting Revenues and Expenditures of the National Association of State Budget Officers reported in 1949, "At the present time state budget systems and accounts present a bewildering variety when comparisons are attempted." Interstate fiscal comparisons cannot be based on our present state budgets or financial reports. States may use the same terms — but those terms don't always mean the same things. Remember what Humpty-Dumpty said? "When I use a word, it means just what I choose it to mean, neither more nor less." "The question is," said Alice, "whether you can make words mean so many different things."

In state accounting we can. The

[1] *Annual Reports to Stockholders*, by N. Loyall McLaren. New York, 1947.

same term may mean 48 different things in the 48 states. No two states use the same system of funds, departmental organization or account classification. Some states include federal grants-in-aid in their budgets and some do not; some include agencies which are supported from license fees and user charges and some do not; some count transfers of funds to other state agencies as expenditures and some do not; some include certain revolving or trust funds and some do not.

Whenever legislative study committees set out to investigate major areas of state operation they try to obtain interstate comparisons. They know there is no better way to judge a state's work program than to view it in the light of the standards, practices and experiences of other states. They usually base their revenue and expenditure data on the only source which is now available for such interstate comparisons — the statistics of the U. S. Bureau of the Census. The Census Bureau has for many years gathered financial statistics of states. It pays no attention to fund or agency breakdowns but reclassifies revenues and expenditures by functions — education, public welfare, highways, public safety, natural resources, health and hospitals, etc.

The Census Bureau shows as state expenditures all payments made by agencies and instrumentalities of state governments, including self-sustaining, proprietary and insurance and trust fund operations, monopoly systems and independent authorities. That is the total of all external disbursing transactions of state governments. It is not the cost of state government. The liquor purchases of a state monopoly system, for example, are a disbursement of state funds, but they do not constitute cost of government.

There is a widespread, legitimate demand for interstate comparisons of the cost of state government which cannot be satisfied from any presently available source. It seems that the fiscal officers of the states could render a valuable service by defining "cost of state government" and agreeing on a uniform system of reporting it.

Unsolvable Problem

Some years ago the National Association of State Budget Officers set up a committee to explore the possibilities of uniform financial reporting. The committee held several meetings between 1947 and 1949. It has not been active since. "Its members felt that they were up against an unsolvable problem; that though association members might agree on a set of standard classifications, so many changes in state laws would be necessary that the ultimate goal could not be reached."

To design a standard state accounting system would be the most desirable way to accomplish uniformity of reporting. But it would at best take many years to have it adopted by all states. The other possibility is to continue with our diverse accounting systems and reclassify their products to fit uniform reporting requirements. That is a clumsy and laborious method. But it may be the only practical way at this time.

Experience in other fields has shown that uniform reporting often leads eventually to uniform accounting. No law forces industrial enterprises to use uniform accounting. But they must submit uniform reports to the Securities and Exchange Commission, the Internal Revenue Service, stock exchanges, credit bureaus and regulatory commissions. Most of them gradually adjust their books to fit those requirements.

The American Institute of Accountants and the American Accounting Association have promulgated certain generally accepted accounting principles. Many industries have gone farther than that. They realized that uniform accounting could produce an extremely useful management tool and adopted standard terminology and classification.

Can governments agree on uniform procedures? A large number of uniform state laws, particularly in the fields of commercial law and crime control, have found their way onto the statute books of many states since 1892, under the sponsorship of the National Association of Commissioners on Uniform State Laws and more recently the Council of State Governments.

Can that be done in the field of financial statistics? Within the last year the Canadian provinces agreed on a uniform system of financial reporting. State departments which handle federal aid must now observe uniformity in some of their statistical reporting. May we not assume that states will be able to agree among themselves on a mutually beneficial program without federal compulsion?

Our legislators may be more agreeable or even enthusiastic over the idea of uniformity than we think. They find it more difficult to grope their way through state financial reports than do finance officers. Initiative and leadership for such a program must obviously come from fiscal officials.

Use of Per Capita Data

The amounts dealt with in state budgets are so enormous that they defy the understanding of people who are not used to wading casually through hundreds of millions of dollars. Multi-digit figures can be reduced to manageable size by the use of per capita data. For purpose of comparison between states or over a period of years, however, it is preferable to express revenues and expenditures in percentages of the income of the residents of the state (state income payments). State taxes of $60 per capita impose a lighter burden in a state with a per capita income of $2,000 than in a state with an average income of $800. Public welfare expenditures of $15 per capita do not mean the same thing in a state with an average weekly wage of $46 and one with a wage of $86. Most important though, per capita taxes or expenditures of $60 in 1952 are not the same as $60 in 1940.

All these variables — the different income level and financial capacity of states and the shrinking value of the dollar — are automatically considered when we express taxes and expenditures in percentage of state income payments. It seems to be the most effective way to present the huge sums in their right perspective

for either historical or interstate comparisons. What counts is not how many millions of dollars we pay in taxes but how large a share of our income we have to shell out. Just as we say that we spend 29 per cent of our income for food, 21 per cent for housing and household operation, 9 per cent for clothing and 4 per cent for recreation, we may say that we spend 6.2 per cent of our income to buy certain services through our state governments — 1.6 per cent goes to education, 1.3 per cent to highways, etc.

Over-all comparisons of the size of state expenditures need to be supplemented with a description of the relative share of financial responsibility borne by state and local governments in each state. Cost accounting should provide a variety of unit data — how much it costs to educate a child, to maintain a patient in a hospital, to build a mile of concrete road, to process a tax return, to patrol 100 miles of highway, etc. Those unit data have, of course, only limited value for interstate comparisons until we can establish quality standards and uniform methods of cost accounting. While those standards of cost accounting are a desirable objective, it seems to me that priority should be accorded to a project of uniform reporting of revenues and expenditures.

To agree on a pattern of uniform reporting is not just a question of compromising on some accounting rules. Uniform reporting may in some cases result in an expenditure total which is several hundred million dollars higher than that shown in the budget. That will take a lot of explaining to the newspapers and to the public.

Two principles should guide a uniform financial reporting system:

1. It should be comprehensive;
2. It should strive to achieve comparability between states according to substance rather than according to legal form.

The summary statement might be fashioned after the consolidated statement of a corporation with many subsidiaries which are engaged in a great variety of activities and which are wholly or partially controlled by the parent company. The reporting system should include all agencies and instrumentalities created by the state for state purposes, whether or not they are subject to legislative appropriation, gubernatorial control or quarterly allotments by the budget office.

What Is Cost of Government

The Census Bureau code is an excellent starting point. A series of adjustments will be necessary to exclude non-cost disbursements and bring various classifications into conformance with cost concepts.

Some items may cause a little difficulty. The Census Bureau treats state employee and teacher retirement systems as "trust fund operations." Most fiscal officers will probably regard state contributions to retirement systems as cost expenditures.

The treatment of so-called self-sustaining activities may not be so easy to settle. Many regulatory agencies in the field of public utilities, banks, insurance companies, professions, agriculture, game and fish, recreation, motor vehicles and drivers, etc., are financed from license fees or direct service charges and receive no support from general tax revenues. But they use the police power of the state and are carried on as governmental functions. They probably constitute "cost of government."

Several states have created authorities to construct state office buildings or other public works from the proceeds of revenue bond issues. Other states finance those undertakings from current funds or by issuing regular state bonds. Is there a basic difference to the citizen between the two methods? Is a state office building constructed from current funds "cost of government" while an authority-financed building is not? Is state aid to districts for public school construction "cost of government" while construction of school buildings by a state authority is not? Are self-sustaining state insurance systems for workmen's compensation and disability cost of state government?

In recent years it has become increasingly popular to create state highway authorities for the construction of certain roads and bridges. Some states are now doing the greater part of their road-building through authorities. Are those authorities part of state government or are they independent, self-sustaining enterprises?

It may not be easy to solve those controversial questions to everybody's satisfaction. It is to be hoped though that an agreement will be reached and a start made soon toward uniform reporting, although the system may not be perfect in the beginning. It will be helpful to consult with banking and investment groups, financial analysts societies, the American Institute of Accountants, Controllers Institute of America and Municipal Finance Officers Association.

Need for Information

Investors have for a long time complained about the lack of information on governments. Julius Grodinsky, in his recent book, *Investments*, (Ronald Press Company, New York) says:

> Another significant difference between private and public securities is sufficiently important to merit consideration. Private corporations publish information that is comparable and, subject to numerous qualifications, can be readily interpreted. For some industries — railroads, electricity, gas, telephone, automobiles and steel among others — there is available industry-wide information. The investor can compare the figures as a whole. It is difficult, and frequently impossible, to make such comparisons in the field of public securities. Budgets are bulky and complex documents. . . . The investor has little grist for his analysis mill.

Most states depend for their major improvement programs on the investment market. It would be in the state's interest to make available to investors the kind of information which they are used to getting from other applicants for funds.

It will be helpful to enlist the support of the press and civic groups. They will doubtless welcome and aid efforts to improve state reporting. They have long demanded more meaningful and understandable information on governmental costs. Close cooperation between state financial officers, the staff of the Council of State Governments, the Bureau of the Census and the U. S. Bureau of the Budget could produce tangible results within a reasonable time.

The success of a project of uniformly and understandably reporting the financial operations of state government can greatly enhance the standing of state budget officers. A budget officer holds a position similar to the controller of a business corporation. It has been said repeatedly that the most important function of a controller is not to gather and summarize detailed figures, or to accomplish minor savings here and there, but to interpret operating results and financial statements to the other executives.

State fiscal offices submit more minute details to legislatures than corporations give to their boards of directors or to their stockholders. But corporation management receives more significant information to guide it in its policy determination than our governors, our legislators and our citizenry.

Attention must be given to making state costs meaningful to the average citizen because popular information on government is probably the most important factor in maintaining and strengthening government by the people.

Lawmakers Take Initiative

Louisiana's new legislative council, in first year of operation, encourages legislators to assume leadership.

By WILLIAM C. HAVARD*

THE Louisiana Legislative Council, created by the 1952 legislative session, made Louisiana the 29th state to set up such an agency. On August 1, 1953, the council completed a year of actual operation. This article attempts to report the human and political problems of organizing such a council as found in one state.

During this first year the new organization has run the full gamut of experience in so far as its activities are concerned: one major research report, *The Legislative Process in Louisiana,* was completed by the staff; a special session was held in July 1953, during which the staff provided the usual professional services; two outside research projects—on highways and education—were authorized to be carried out under the council's general supervision; and literally a flood of committee, council and private member reports were begun, many of which are now completed.

Given this background of experience, it is possible to review the Louisiana Council's operations with an eye to the special problems that such an organization is likely to encounter in its early stages. It is well to bear in mind that Louisiana has not as a state been noted for the use

of technical aides for its legislature and judiciary. Until recently there has been little interim budgetary activity on the part of the legislature, and only this year has a system of permanent registration gone into effect for part of the state.

These are merely random illustrations, but they serve to point up the major problem of securing acceptance for totally new governmental devices such as a legislative council. Other states with political patterns similar to Louisiana are likely to encounter precisely the same difficulties manifested in this state as they move in the direction of bringing their governmental operations into line with recommendations made by proponents of reform.

The provisions of the act creating the Louisiana Council are fairly typical. The council itself is composed of the speaker of the House, the lieutenant governor and eight members from each of the two houses. The eight members from each house are distributed geographically on the basis of one member from each of the state's eight congressional districts.

The council is permitted to employ an executive director who in turn selects, with the council's approval, the agency's clerical and professional staff. The total staff has varied from about six to ten members, its usual composition being from four to six researchers and two to four cleri-

*Mr. Havard, assistant professor in the College of Arts and Sciences of the University of Florida, was with the Legislative Council of Louisiana, during the summer of 1953, as a research associate.

cal assistants. The legislature appropriated $60,000 for the expenses of the agency for each fiscal year of the 1952-54 biennium. This figure was supplemented by an additional allocation of $20,000 for fiscal 1953-54.

Duties of Council

The legally defined functions of the council, like its composition, are fairly typical of the practice elsewhere, with perhaps slightly more emphasis on research assistance to individual legislators than is usual. The law permits the council to provide bill-drafting services, make long-range studies of problems for future legislative consideration, give research assistance to individual legislators, engage in fiscal analysis, prepare reports on pending legislation, produce manuals and directories and perform all the duties that it may deem essential to the efficient working of the legislature. With the single exception of fiscal analysis the staff has been active in all these functional areas.

The major problems encountered by the council have been political rather than legal or administrative. That is to say, the difficulties of staffing, performance and conformity to the legal basis of the agency have been less noteworthy and of less interest than the problems of carrying on effective relations with the legislature and the administration.

The first of these problems of effective relations derives from the strong tendency on the part of the state's political officers to assume that no governmental activity is free from political influence. In Louisiana the governor has long maintained undisputed leadership of the legislature. At the same time, state politics are characterized by the presence of two factions which, in terms of organization and program, closely resemble a two-party system, although without the responsibility and permanent clarity of line of two-party government. Consequently, since the council was created during a new administration's first legislative session, it immediately became associated in the minds of many legislators with that administration. Sides were chosen accordingly and the council and its staff were forced to adopt a wary defensive position in the attempt to prove absolute impartiality.

The events of the special session of 1953 did much to shake the dedicated political partisan's confidence in the supposition that every state agency belongs body and soul to one of the two state factions. The council staff prepared an analysis of the twelve administration bills introduced at that session. As a result of the interpretation of several of these bills, the administration leaders were forced to defend their program with more care than usual and even to accept floor amendments to some of their bills. The council was thus placed in the peculiar position of being the temporary hero of its former opponents. A number of legislators remained unconvinced, however, that the staff of the council was a fact-finding body rather than the promoter of factional interests, and a few were even heard muttering that the council and the administration had better get together on their bills. The council is, nevertheless, impartial in all its findings and has actually been quite successful in avoiding partisanship.

It is an interesting sidelight on this situation to note that the deviousness of factional politics in this one-party state may have militated against the acceptance of impartial professional legislative services much more than if the political division were clearly manifested in a two-party system. The attempt to commit the council to a definite stand on current political issues is a practice that seems to be accepted as a legitimate part of the state's political "gamesmanship."

Legislative Employees Critical

Closely related to the difficulty of demonstrating the nature of its function to politicians and public alike is the problem of securing acceptance of the council's staff by the older, established legislative employees. The fear of loss of prerogative and influence on the part of a few persons who occupy traditional legislative staff positions precipitated the most overt attack on the Louisiana Legislative Council which has yet occurred. The occasion for the explosion was the publication of the legislative process study. This thorough report, though widely praised both in and out of the state for its accuracy and impartiality, was openly attacked in a letter from a legislative employee to members of the legislature, a letter which was given fairly widespread press coverage. Although the criticism of the study was in vague and general

terms, it was grist to the mill of the small group who had already categorized the council as a political agency in their own minds. In consequence, the unusual step was taken by House Resolution 9 of the special session of 1953 of inviting the legislative employee responsible for the attack to explain his position.

It is probable that the remarks made by the critic on the floor of the House strengthened rather than weakened the position of the council since the sole point of his speech was that the report was insulting to the legislators because it referred to certain standing committees as "minor." The fact that a number of these "minor" committees had not met at all during the life of the present legislature made the comment of the council on them a truism obvious to all members present. Further assault of this type on the council and its functions has probably been forestalled by the lack of effect that the employee's address had on the legislature.

Perhaps even more important to the future of the council than these evidences of personalized attitudes toward government agencies and the process of government is the inability of most of the legislators to make proper use of this new agency. In order to avoid the charge that the council was set up to usurp the legislative function, the council has bent over backward in proffering staff services to individual members of the two houses. As a result, the council itself has probably not taken the initiative comparable to that in some other states in providing for larger research studies, and the director has been flooded with unchanneled direct requests from non-council members.

Many of these requests hit at important problems which cannot be solved with the ease that the legislator would like. In other cases the member is not quite sure what information he is seeking and sometimes has to apply for assistance several times before he even discovers the full implications of the legislative project that he is trying to get under way. It is difficult for legislators in all states, accustomed as they are to using a subjective approach to governmental problems, to adapt themselves to the current necessity of securing specialized reports on technical and involved subjects.

Legislators Take Initiative

Fortunately only a few members demonstrate their inability to appreciate the importance of unbiased research to the legislative process by indulging in caprice. One Louisiana legislator did, however, request an extensive study and, when the completed material was delivered, commented that he had not really desired information on the subject but only wanted to find out what that "outfit" was doing. It is hardly necessary to remark on the reaction of the trained and well paid professional personnel who had put weeks of work into that particular report.

As the council continues to function, its operations, both internally and in relation to other state agencies, should smooth out. The council probably will begin to give more effective direction to the staff in terms of work-load, and the requests from individuals are likely to decline as the initial volume of piled-up need for information is satisfied. Already there are encouraging signs. Many a skeptic in the legislature has become convinced of the value of such an organization because of the practical services which have been performed for him by the staff.

More than this, some of the oldest antiques in the legislative closet are being hauled out for inspection. For the first time in many years the legislature has become concerned with what it should do to maintain continuous review over the budget; and the legislative process study has furnished the impetus for statewide committee hearings on the need for changing outmoded legislative procedures.

Although not directly connected with the council, a series of interim study committees has been formed on the fundamental problems of the state, with most of the services being provided for these committees by the council staff.

In brief, the council has in large part been the inspiration for reawakening the initiative of the legislators in the lawmaking process, thereby altering the past practice of allowing all leadership to go by default to the governor. In large part, the very problems with which the council has had to wrestle most vigorously are evidence of the need for such a legislative service agency in Louisiana.

News in Review

Politicians Attack
Philadelphia Charter

Many Weakening Changes
Are Submitted to Council

THE HOME rule charter that Philadelphia achieved in 1952 after a long struggle, marked at the end by the overthrow of the entrenched Republican regime by reform Democrats, is under heavy attack by leaders of the old-time organizations of both Democrats and Republicans.[1] Twenty amendments, tending to weaken the charter in various ways and to various degrees, have come before the city council, fourteen by petitions, representing the wishes of Democratic City Chairman William J. Green, Jr., and six offered by two Democratic councilmen, for possible submission to popular vote on May 18. This would be at the primary election, on which occasion the political machines hope to dominate. As a "compromise," it was proposed to defer a vote until the November general election and appoint a committee to study proposed amendments.

The especially harmful and controversial proposals, included in both groups, would remove from the civil service system the employees and subordinates of all elected officers, other than the mayor, and the members and employees of various boards, and would permit political activity by employees of elected officials and of various boards.

Opponents of these amendments assert that they would remove from the charter the provisions intended to keep the city hall from becoming "a haven for political drones and a center of political activity."

[1] See the REVIEW, February 1954, page 85.

Mayor Joseph S. Clark, Jr., has warned their sponsors that they would "never be forgiven by the electorate of Philadelphia." District Attorney Richardson Dilworth, team-mate of Mayor Clark in the 1952 campaign but who has been reported as favoring more political activity by city employees, is joining in the fight to preserve the charter and, when looked to as a Democratic candidate for governor of Pennsylvania, has announced that his first duty is to the city in its present danger.

The six amendments proposed by councilmen would, in addition: Permit city officials to seek other elective offices without resigning the posts they hold; allow the council to fill vacancies in elective offices; deprive the civil service commission of the right to waive residence requirements for municipal employees and place that power in the council; and give the council final authority in determining water and sewer rates now fixed by the water commissioners subject to standards that may be set by the council.

The fourteen proposals sought by petition, which may be deferred indefinitely, include the following additional provisions:

Require councilmanic confirmation of the mayor's appointment to the positions of managing director, director of finance and city representative; appointments by the managing director and the director of finance; and the appointment, by the civil service commission, of the personnel director;

Repeal the provision that no councilman shall solicit or recommend the appointment of any person to any position in the civil service, nor interfere with the performance of the duties of the police or other city employees;

Remove the Fairmount Park Com-

134

mission (a city agency) from under the charter, and prevent the city council from reorganizing former county offices—thus largely nullifying city-county consolidation;

Require a line-item budget for personal services, instead of making appropriations to city agencies by major classes in lump sums;

Eliminate the requirement that the city's pension systems be actuarially sound;

Remove the managing director's right of appeal to the civil service commission if dismissed;

Decentralize the city's legal activities, now under the city solicitor;

Provide for an elective rather than an appointive city solicitor;

Remove the present requirement of minimum mandatory appropriations for the civil service commission.

Council-manager Plan Developments

JOPLIN, MISSOURI, (1950 population 38,711) adopted the council-manager plan on February 9 by a vote of 4,750 to 3,769.

PONCA CITY, OKLAHOMA, (20,180) put the council-manager plan into effect on February 1 as provided by ordinance adopted December 21, 1953. The city has had a modified manager plan for many years, not considered adequate until now by the International City Managers' Association.

OKMULGEE, OKLAHOMA, (18,317) adopted a council-manager charter on January 26 by a vote of 1,704 to 1,163. It was drafted by President Charles F. Spencer of East Central State College of Ada, Oklahoma, working with a committee of the Okmulgee Junior Chamber of Commerce, and is expected to go into effect on April 13 of this year.

FERGUSON, MISSOURI, (11,573) adopted the council-manager plan by a vote of 1,859 to 587, on February 2, to take effect after the April election.

In ARLINGTON HEIGHTS, ILLINOIS, (8,768) a council-manager ordinance passed by the village council and vetoed by the mayor was repassed by the council, four to two, on January 5, to override the veto.

COMMERCE, TEXAS, (5,889) on January 30 voted 525 to 310 in favor of a council-manager charter, effective April 1. It provides for five commissioners or councilmen, to serve without pay. In the course of the campaign a questionnaire survey by C. A. Bonham, as to 50 Texas council-manager communities ranging up to 10,700 population, showed general satisfaction with the plan. Out of 27 manager towns smaller than Commerce, fourteen had lower tax rates, ten the same and three higher rates. Manager salaries in the 27 ranged from $2,400 to $8,000. In the entire group of 50, the salary ranged up to $10,000. Twenty places reported that the manager was a local man; 25, a man from out of town.

The MASSACHUSETTS House of Representatives, by a vote of 118 to 105, on February 1 rejected a bill that would have required city managers to submit all appointments to city councils for approval. The House also rejected, by voice vote, a bill that would guarantee the right of a city councilman to seek information from department heads.

A committee to study the town manager form of government and a system of limited representative town meetings has been proposed in a report of the public works committee of WARE, MASSACHUSETTS.

The BRIGHTON, MICHIGAN, *Argus* urges the council-manager plan for that city, which now has the mayor-council form.

The city council of ELGIN, ILLINOIS, has set April 6 as the date for a special election on the question of adopting the council-manager plan.

The new city council of CHARLES CITY, IOWA, voted to abolish the office of city manager.

KIRKSVILLE, MISSOURI, defeated a proposed council-manager plan by a vote of 1,530 to 550 on February 2.

It is expected that a new charter being drafted for EL PASO, TEXAS, will provide the voters with a choice between the council-manager and the mayor-council forms.

The government committee of the PUEBLO, COLORADO, charter convention voted four to one on January 20 to recommend the council-manager plan, and the convention itself voted for it twenty to one. Pueblo has had a form of commission-manager government since 1950, but without full authority for the manager, according to the Pueblo *Chieftain*, which urges adoption of a complete council-manager form. It states that under the present charter the manager can only be a "glorified executive secretary for the city council," which consists of fourteen members elected by districts.

A proposed council-manager charter has been filed with the mayor and city commission of TULSA, OKLAHOMA, by a committee that has been working on the matter since April 1953. Another committee submitted a charter based on the strong mayor principle. The manager charter specifies a nonpartisan council of seven, including the mayor, with four-year terms but with elections at two-year intervals—four members at one time and three at the following election.

LA GRANDE, OREGON, voted 354 to 118 to approve a newly drafted council-manager charter at a special election on December 1, 1953. Manager government was originally established in La Grande in 1913.

MARYSVILLE, CALIFORNIA, defeated a proposed council-manager charter 1,424 to 502 on January 18.

In FORTUNA, CALIFORNIA, a study committee has recommended the council-manager plan to the city council, which has placed the question of its adoption on the ballot for April 13.

Greenwich, Connecticut, Makes First Test of Model Primary

As previously related[1] Greenwich, Connecticut, (population 43,000) obtained from the legislature a party primary procedure for its partisan elections closely following the National Municipal League's *Model Direct Primary Election System*.

The first trial under the new law came on October 14, 1953, and resulted in an unprecedented outpouring of voters for the selection of nominees in both the Republican and Democratic parties.

Ironically, the old guard faction of the Republican party, which had bitterly fought reform in nominating procedures, was able to use those procedures in successfully contesting three of the 21 choices submitted by the insurgent Town Committee responsible for the reform. Their proposals for the Republican nomination for two selectman posts and the office of registrar of voters defeated the reform faction's choices. The other eighteen were uncontested. Members of the Democratic party—a 30 per cent minority in Greenwich—under the new rules of procedure were able to present and successfully campaign for a member of the bipartisan board of education who many felt had been dropped by the party management for purely political reasons.

This demonstration of a healthy citizen interest in the selection of party candidates for public office climaxed a long struggle by various citizen groups in Greenwich. Connecticut is the only state without a primary system. Nominating procedures in Greenwich, as in many other towns and cities, had been determined by town committees, the management of local political parties. Through its control of party rules and the use of an antiquated caucus system, each party committee not only effectively discouraged opposition proposals but perpetuated itself in power.

---

[1]See the REVIEW, July 1953, page 346.

Citizen groups had long recognized the need for reform. In 1949 the Greenwich Legislative Council and the Greenwich League of Women Voters supported a bill which would have required the town committees to give party members a more adequate opportunity to study their nominations and to propose others. The bill was killed in a committee of the legislature because of opposition from party leaders then in control of the Republican Town Committee.

If reform was to be brought about, local Republican leadership, it was apparent, would have to be changed. A "Republican Citizens Committee" of about 400, faced with the certainty that the incumbent members of the Republican Town Committee would again rename themselves as candidates, put together a full slate of petition candidates well in advance of the caucus date. These candidates campaigned on a platform calling for the enactment of a direct primary law for Greenwich, the liberalization of rules governing participation in party affairs, and an end to estates-appraisal patronage. Nonpartisan groups endorsed the objectives of the reform movement.

Thirty-four of the 37 reform candidates were elected. The new Town Committee secured enactment of the special primary bill in the 1953 legislature. It amended the rules of the Republican party so that members of its governing board, the Republican Town Committee, are elected by district, with ample time and opportunity for candidates to be presented in opposition to the slate selected by the Town Committee after that slate is brought out. The committee's candidates are identified as such on the primary ballots.

The new leadership is now engaged in efforts to change an archaic state estate-appraisal system which in many Connecticut towns and cities is an important source of patronage.

Old guard forces, supported by the only newspaper with a town-wide circulation, are complaining about the cost of the primary, now a municipal function. Indications are that a strong effort will be made to unseat the present Republican Town Committee and check a rising tide of sentiment in favor of further reform in Greenwich.

Greenwich's nonpartisan representative town meeting of 230 members is considering reports proposing creation of a town manager under the board of selectmen.

R. S. C.

Cincinnati Council on Radio and TV

Weekly radio broadcasts of meetings of the Cincinnati city council are being presented by station WSAI. A microphone is placed on the desk of each councilman and a complete recording of each regular Wednesday meeting is made. It is subsequently edited by the radio station so that the broadcast will take only 15 minutes, when presented on the same evening at 6:15. The necessary equipment is provided by the station at no cost to the city. Television broadcasts of council meetings are also occasionally given.

State Commission Ends Study of N. Y. City Government

The Temporary State Commission to Study the Organizational Structure of the Government of the City of New York[1] submitted its final report on February 2 and called for broad city charter revision "to meet the city's serious managerial crisis" and to place its government on a sound basis in budget, personnel and top-level administration. It reiterated its previous recommendations for a strong "city administrator" in addition to a deputy

[1]See the REVIEW, November 1953, page 517.

mayor, a personnel administrator and a performance budget. As to the city administrator, an office now established and held by Dr. Luther Gulick, it expressed disappointment over the limitations on his powers. It noted that a first step has been taken by the city towards a true performance budget, but said that no definite action has been taken to improve the personnel system or to expand and redefine the deputy mayor's functions.

Connecticut Municipalities Form Organization

A constitution and by-laws for the Association of Connecticut Towns and Cities were adopted at a meeting in Cheshire in December and plans were made for an annual meeting in May. Representatives from 50 towns and cities were present and the chief executives of 25 other local units wrote to the temporary chairman, Mayor Stephen Bailey of Middletown, indicating their interest in becoming members.

Georgia to Vote on Five Amendments

At a session held in November and December 1953, the General Assembly of Georgia passed five constitutional amendments to be submitted to the people at the next general election:

Home Rule. This amendment provides that the provisions of Article XV of the Georgia constitution dealing with home rule be deleted in their entirety and replaced by the following: "The General Assembly is authorized to provide by law for the self-government of municipalities and to that end is hereby expressly given the authority to delegate its powers so that matters pertaining to municipalities upon which, prior to the ratification of this amendment, it was necessary for the General Assembly to act, may be dealt with without the necessity of action by the General Assem-

bly. Any powers granted as provided herein shall be exercised subject only to statutes of general application pertaining to municipalities."

A municipal home rule act passed by the General Assembly of Georgia in 1951 was declared void by the State Supreme Court in September 1953.[1]

Educational Funds to Citizens. Governor Herman Talmadge advocates abolition of public schools in Georgia if the United States Supreme Court rules against "equal but separate" schools for the white and colored races in cases now pending. Upon his recommendation, the General Assembly passed an amendment to the state constitution designed to prepare the way for grants to citizens for private education. It reads as follows:

"Grants for Education: Notwithstanding any other provision of this constitution, the General Assembly may by law provide for grants of state, county or municipal funds to citizens of the state for educational purposes, in discharge of all obligation of the state to provide adequate education for its citizens."

Additional Taxation by Counties for Education. The Georgia constitution places a 15-mill limitation on taxation by counties for educational purposes. A proposed amendment would permit individual counties, upon a favorable vote in a referendum on the question, to exceed this limitation.

Slum Clearance. This amendment declares slum clearance to be a governmental function and authorizes the exercise of the power of taxation and eminent domain in furtherance of slum clearance.

Annual Legislative Sessions. This amendment provides that the General Assembly shall meet annually for a session of 40 days. Georgia has experimented a great deal with constitutional provisions on sessions of the legislature.

[1]See the REVIEW, October 1953, page 462.

Since 1877 the state has tried, in the order listed, biennial sessions, annual sessions, split annual sessions and biennially-adjourned sessions. Now it appears that it will return to annual sessions.

. One argument advanced for the need of a new constitution in 1945 was the hodge-podge of amendments, numbering 301, to the constitution of 1877. If the tempo of recent years is continued, the constitution of 1945 will soon have been amended as many times as the former constitution. In the six-year period from 1946 to 1952 a total of 101 constitutional amendments passed the General Assembly and 83 of these were ratified by the people.

When the constitution is cluttered up with numerous provisions statutory in nature that require frequent revision the basis for the distinction between constitutional and statutory law is destroyed.

ALBERT B. SAYE
University of Georgia

Alabama Eases Poll Tax Requirement

An amendment to the Alabama constitution, to allow persons to vote upon payment of two years' back poll taxes—a maximum of $3.00 instead of $36 as formerly, was approved by the voters on December 28.

Partisan Legislative Setups Sought in Nebraska

The political party leaders who last year announced a plan to restore the bicameral legislature in Nebraska,[1] if the voters would act favorably on a constitutional amendment at the general election in 1954, have announced a change in their proposed initiative petition. They will seek instead to restore the partisan features and enlarge the membership of the single house.

[1]See the REVIEW, December 1953, page 563.

If these plans materialize, and the voters approve the constitutional amendment, the nonpartisan feature which has characterized the legislature since 1937 would come to an end and partisan lines would be restored in legislative campaigns, elections, programs and organization. Additionally, the present membership, which is set at 43 (it may range between 30 and 50 members), would be subjected to new minimum and maximum ranges, probably double the existing numbers. There appears to be far greater support among various political groups for this proposed change than the one which would have restored the bicameral legislature in addition.

A. C. BRECKENRIDGE
University of Nebraska

California Civil Service Committee Reports

The Senate Interim Committee on Civil Service, established by the California Senate in 1951 to investigate the state civil service system, recommended various changes to the 1953 Senate. Its final report has recently become available in printed form.

A primary question considered by the committee concerned policy and procedure as to dismissal of incompetent employees. The report sympathetically discussed a proposal by civil service consultants to authorize removal of permanent employees by department heads but concluded that this would be too drastic a revision of the present system. It urged that supervisors should take greater responsibility with regard to personnel, including better utilization of performance reports, which in 1951 and 1952 showed only 0.1 per cent of all employees, or about 38, as graded "unsatisfactory," although 434 disciplinary actions were taken against permanent employees in the two years. It was also pointed out that 66 per cent of state employees responding to a questionnaire felt that it should be made easier to remove unsatisfactory employees.

Three bills were submitted: one calling upon the State Personnel Board to recommend a uniform schedule of penalties to guide supervising officials; one providing that hearing officers submit findings and recommendations to the board, instead of the present requirement that the latter have a full transcript of all testimony in disciplinary actions before final decision, which is thus delayed; and a three-year statute of limitations for disciplinary proceedings.

The Board was also urged to recommend appropriate grievance procedures to the individual agencies, and to report from time to time as to their adoption.

Six Fellowships Offered in Public Administration

The Citizens Research Council of Michigan (Loren B. Miller, executive director, Farwell Building, Detroit 26) announces the offering, for the fifth year, of six Lent D. Upson fellowships. They provide for graduate training in public administration at Wayne University in Detroit, for twelve months beginning in September 1954. The course includes on-the-job training with the research council of not less than 1,080 hours. A fellowship carries a grant of $1,800 plus graduate tuition and fees and G. I. rights.

Special Districts Increase 48% in Ten Years

The Bureau of the Census issued in January its report on *Special District Governments in the United States,* dealing with 1952 data. It states that "the growth in number of special districts—from about 8,300 in 1942 to some 12,300 in 1952—has been one of the most striking developments in American governmental structure during the past decade." This is an increase of 48 per cent. The count of special districts includes only units having substantial autonomy and thus excludes many local authorities

closely related to other governments. School districts are not involved.

The total of 12,319 special districts is classified into the following groups, as to functions: natural resources (soil conservation, irrigation, drainage, etc.) 5,224; fire protection, 2,272; housing, 863; highways, 761; water supply, 665; sanitation, 429; health, 228; nonhighway transportation, 159; hospitals, 156; utilities other than water, 105; all other, 1,457. Non-water utilities account for the largest percentage (29.3) of all revenues received; but housing districts or authorities account for 39.7 per cent of total expenditures and 30.4 per cent of long-term debt.

Michigan Holds Traffic Conferences

Two conferences on highway safety were held at Michigan State College in January. The first was a traffic court conference sponsored jointly by Michigan State, the Traffic Institute of Northwestern University, American Bar Association, Michigan Justices of the Peace Association, Michigan Prosecutors Association, Michigan Municipal Judges Association and Michigan Association of Municipal Attorneys. The conference was on the theme that the judge is the key to traffic safety. Representatives of various associations sponsoring the conference met to study scientific techniques, promote uniformity in procedure, build public confidence and respect for the courts, propose model legislation, discuss and confer on problems relating to courts and traffic enforcement.

A second conference was held on highway safety and was sponsored by the Michigan Safety Commission. Those present included members of the legislature, state officials, and representatives of business, industry, utilities, universities, schools, social agencies and courts. The object was to propose a program to reduce traffic deaths and traffic accidents of all kinds.   E.W.W.

County and Township .   .   .   . *Edited by Edward W. Weidner*

The Tail That Wags the Dog

Mississippi Counties Dominant Local Unit

THE 1950 Census shows 72 per cent of Mississippians living in rural areas. The state, with a 1950 population of 2,178,914, has only one city of over 50,000—the capital city of Jackson with 100,000 inhabitants. In 1950 there were 54 cities of 2,500 or more population. Total population of these urban places was only 607,914. The rural complexion of the state combined with organization on the Virginia county model continues to highlight the county as the dominant local government unit.

The state is divided into 82 counties, each composed of five supervisory districts. Only one county has taken advantage of the statutory option of operating road systems on a county unit basis. The clinging to an extreme of local home rule leads to criticism that for all practical purposes the state has 400 "counties," rather than 82. Municipal dwellers are not exempt from the county system since all cities lie within one or more county districts.

The state is without any form of effective home rule. The five county supervisors are elected from their individual districts. As a board of supervisors they have general jurisdiction over county affairs. But, except for the one true unit system county, each supervisor manages road operation within his district. Several more counties, however, are moving toward the unit system, especially for capital improvements. The citizen of the local county district is likely to view his supervisor as the closest representative of government. His feelings of loyalty or antagonism are intensified by the need for farm-to-market roads which the supervisor largely maintains. The supervisors, as a county board, are confronted with three major elected officials: chancery clerk, sheriff–tax collector and tax assessor. The chancery clerk also serves as auditor, treasurer and clerk to the board of supervisors. The ballot is lengthened by the circuit clerk, county attorney and justices of the peace with their accompanying constables. Fourteen counties have created county courts, but in doing so they have not been permitted to abolish justice of the peace courts. To make matters more confusing boards of supervisors in many counties employ private attorneys as counselors rather than use the elected county attorney. The boards and segments of the public plead that the elected attorneys are not sufficiently competent to act as legal advisors. The county attorney is relegated to prosecuting attorney for the most part.

The office of chancery clerk is the focal point of county administration. The clerk's administrative and fiscal functions are large, but unfortunately he must devote much of his energies to court duties, which supply the bulk of the income of his combined offices. By all odds chancery clerks are the most respected of county officials. It is a rule of thumb that an honest and efficient clerk is the strongest guardian of the local treasury. The common complaint of the clerks is that the diversity of their several offices prevents their doing the best total job. Perennial attempts to separate the offices of sheriff and tax collector flounder on the bulwarks of the "fee system." All county officials except tax assessors, supervisors, county attorneys and county judges are compensated through many and diverse fees. Sheriff–tax collectors, unlike other county officials, may not be elected for consecutive terms. This restriction, together with reliance on tax-collecting fees for the major source of office income, makes many sheriffs inefficient, if not unwilling, law enforcers.

Many sheriffs urge the separation of the two offices. These advocates of reform would normally prefer this separation after they left office, for the legislature is not overly generous in establishing county salary schedules.

State attempts to regulate county affairs are weakened by the barriers of traditional love of local self-government and the entrenched "fee system." The voter's wish to retain the maximum of local self-government is often in opposition to his expressed desire for efficiency when the facts of the state-local arrangement in Mississippi are faced. His praiseworthy attachment to local self-rule is reinforced by the local officeholder's pecuniary interest in retention of an outmoded method of conducting local government.

Moves to reorganize the structure of county government, so as to provide more efficiency while retaining essential rights of the voter, meet the hard question of which offices will be eliminated. Reorganization in Mississippi, as elsewhere, may become less a question of proper structure and more one of whose ox will stand goring most quietly.

The state has become in part a tax-collecting agency for the counties. In 1952 the state's general revenue totaled $154,944,000, of which 24.7 per cent was revenue received from the federal government. In the same year the state returned to local governments $61,080,000, of which $48,588,000 went to the counties. The largest portion of this return was for the road systems managed by the district supervisors. Fortunately, the state some years ago created a state department of audits which makes annual audits of all county operations.

The combination of supervision of a large bulk of state-collected revenues and the relative secrecy of the "fee system" tends to make many county officials impervious to public clamor. State law requires that county fee officials submit annual reports on their receipts and disbursements to the secretary of state, an elected official. Lack of effective enforcement of the law has led to its virtual disuse. A sheriff–tax collector with an annual income, after payment of his employees, of $30,000 is hesitant to reveal the "pay" of the job to the voters. What are some of the results of this pattern of local government? First the counties are divided into areas too small for effective road building and maintenance. Supervisors compete with each other for available revenue with little reference to over-all county needs.

Sheriff–tax collectors, with only one term of office, concentrate on collection of taxes and neglect the police function. Where law enforcement is pushed, it is for the most part a stand-off between the untrained and poorly staffed sheriff's office and the law violators.

Officials Like Fee System

Each fee official dislikes surrendering functions which return revenue to his office. Recommendations to combine the circuit and chancery clerks and create an effective fiscal officer with the present chancery clerk's fiscal and administrative duties collapse when cutting the "fee pie" is approached. Moves to abolish the justice of the peace system are legion. Yet it would be a brave rural legislator who would want his name on the "bill." Back home are five justices of the peace and their constables. These, together with their families and friends, make a healthy voting bloc in a county of a few thousand population.

What can be done to change from such a system to one more suited to present conditions and needs? Certainly not academic studies of the problem alone. Twenty years ago the state launched an exhaustive study of the entire structure of state-local government. The Brookings Institution report came to many conclusions and recommendations. The report was shelved by the legislature because of the state's lack of readiness to accept such bitter medicine unattractively packaged. Failure to sell the report to the people contributed to its rejection. Further, its attempt to solve all problems in one bite created few friends but many enemies.

The chances for reorganization of county affairs are much better now. Creation of strong statewide business and citizen groups has been accomplished. Reorganization is in the air. County officials are now banded together in state associations. These associations may look long and carefully at attempts to change the setup. But they have brought county officials together and serve as forums to inject new ideas. Many county officials see the clumsiness of the structure of government in which they must work. The combination of an increasing number of thoughtful county officials and forceful citizen groups will certainly bring changes in old ways of doing county business.

S. R. JEFFERS
Jackson, Mississippi

St. Louis Metropolitan Sewer Plan Approved

At a special election on February 9, the voters of St. Louis and St. Louis County approved by majorities of three to one the creation of a Metropolitan St. Louis Sewer District.[1] The six-member board of trustees will be appointed by the mayor of St. Louis and the supervisor of St. Louis County before March 15. The district will acquire title to all sewer facilities in the city and the populous parts of the county on July 1. The date upon which the district will take over

actual operations must be determined by resolution of the board of trustees.

The citizens committee which conducted an active campaign on behalf of the plan was made up of representatives of civic organizations, business institutions, labor unions, both major political parties, schools and churches. The mayor of St. Louis expressed gratitude that the results of the election would afford the people of the city and county their first opportunity to work together in solving a major metropolitan problem. He said: "I hope that this is just the first step in a continuing program of area-wide efforts to seek metropolitan solutions to many of our complex problems of the day."

The plan for the new metropolitan sewer district was drafted by a board of freeholders representing both the city and the county. A significant feature of the plan provides "for the functional administration of other services common to the area within the district when authorized by amendment to this plan."

WILLIAM N. CASSELLA, JR.

Counties Set Up Urban Districts under Two State Laws

The legislatures of both California and North Carolina last year gave counties authority to set up special or urban districts outside incorporated areas, where such areas are in need of urban services.

Until passage of the California law, counties have been furnishing services to unincorporated urban areas in that state from taxes collected from incorporated municipalities as well as the unincorporated areas. This practice has brought violent protests from the cities.[1]

The measure sets forth a complete procedure for establishing county service areas, for determining the extent to which municipal-type services are already

[1]See the REVIEW, January 1954, page 43.

[1]See the REVIEW, January 1951, page 44.

provided, for determining the nature and costs of services to be provided and for abandonment of such areas if desired. Proceedings may be initiated by the board of supervisors or by a petition signed by not less than 10 per cent of the registered voters in the area to be served. Services include fire and police protection, parks and recreation, road construction, libraries, public health and numerous others.

The need for urban services in built-up areas outside city limits has resulted in a number of campaigns to create special districts in counties of North Carolina. According to *Popular Government*, published by the Institute of Government of the University of North Carolina, one such district, the first under Chapter 69 of the General Statutes, was created north of Greensboro in December. Residents of the district voted almost ten to one in favor of its formation. Shortly thereafter a second district was created in an adjacent area. These districts are officially labeled fire districts.

Union County and Buncombe County have been considering enlarging or creating sanitary districts to provide services for suburban areas within their boundaries. Under Article 6 of Chapter 130 of the General Statutes such districts may perform a wide variety of municipal-type functions.

Maryland Counties Zone for Industry

In 1953 the Maryland legislature extended the act enabling every county in the state to set up a planning and zoning commission[1] and many counties have begun work on new zoning ordinances and subdivision regulations.

Talbot County has become the first on the eastern shore to have a county-wide zoning ordinance. It was enacted in May 1953 after twenty months of study by the planning and zoning commission. The

[1]Chapter 19, Laws of Maryland, 1953.

county is now making an industrial site survey to determine what type of industry it needs and which would be the best sites for the location of new industry.

Anne Arundel County has rezoned much of its area as industrial or commercial since it is being drawn increasingly into the Baltimore metropolitan industrial area. Another county with a suburban problem is Howard County, which finds it has a continual increase in the number of commuters from both Baltimore and Washington, D. C., who are building homes in its territory.

Harford County has drawn up an interim zoning ordinance pending completion of a master plan for future development.

Grand Rapids and Kent County Make Fire Compact

The city of Grand Rapids and Kent County, Michigan, have recently drawn up a contract for mutual cooperation in fighting fires. Under the agreement the city will send equipment to fight fires at county institutions outside the city at a given rate per hour. At the present time Kent County pays the city the actual cost of sending equipment to fires. The new contract is based on the total annual city fire budget and takes in such matters as the depreciation of fire department equipment.

Kentucky Aids Counties on Reassessments

The Kentucky State Department of Revenue has now given reassessment aid to fourteen counties. This has been done under a law passed in 1950, which provides that counties may petition the department for reappraisal of their assessments. In the case of six projects, contracts were let with private firms to conduct the property value study. In other instances the projects have been conducted by the state. In most cases the surveys have been paid for entirely out of state funds, but in a few of the wealthier counties the work has been jointly financed.

Many Wisconsin Counties Decrease Taxes

Property tax rates for Wisconsin seem to be leveling off. Thirty-four county boards have voted lower levies to finance budgets for 1954; 36 have made increases, many of them rather small; and one made no change.

The *Wisconsin Tax News,* published by the Public Expenditure Survey of Wisconsin, comments that the new budget law of 1953 was partly responsible for taxes leveling off: "Following the urging of taxpayer organizations the local budget law was strengthened to provide that all surplus funds and balances be recorded in budget documents. Apparently this change has had the effect of putting an increased amount of idle funds to work and thus of confining local government demands more closely to essentials."

Los Angeles County Adopts New Recruiting Devices

A vigorous recruiting drive by Los Angeles County was put into effect when the county found itself short some 471 engineers on a huge program to design and build storm drains. Specifically, the county has adopted five measures which differ considerably from the usual procedures of public service recruitment, says the Civil Service Assembly:

1. The county decided to go directly to colleges and universities in search of promising engineering graduates.

2. It took note of the fact that students applying for professional jobs find written tests an encroachment on their study time and shun taking them, especially since they can get good jobs without that bother.

3. It prepared promotional literature to show prospective employees the advantages of living in the Los Angeles area and working for the county.

4. It recognized that few students have enough money to make long trips for interviews with supervisors in the hope of getting a good job, while many are glad to accept an offer made when they are in school.

5. It sent on recruiting assignments the best qualified and best informed persons available.

The Engineering Recruitment Service of the County Civil Service Commission has now ended a year's operation, which has been considered a success.

Kansas County Clerks Hold School

A School for County Clerks was held at the University of Kansas last January, sponsored jointly by the Governmental Research Center of the university and the County Clerks Association. It covered a wide variety of topics, including the question of the clerks' political and administrative responsibility and the question of county government reorganization.

The December 15 issue of *Your Government,* bulletin of the Governmental Research Center, outlines rather extensively the case for the county manager plan in Kansas. Following this up, one of the dinner meetings of the conference was devoted to the topic of reform in county government, including administrative change.

Proportional Representation . . *Edited by George H. Hallett, Jr. and Wm. Redin Woodward*
(This department is successor to the Proportional Representation Review)

New South Wales Provides P. R. for Municipalities

Elections Held in Sydney, 136 Other Communities

ON NOVEMBER 10, 1953, an act to provide for the use of either proportional representation or the alternative vote system in all local elections in the Australian state of New South Wales became law. Previously, only the town of Armidale used P.R. The new law applies to the 240 municipalities and shires (rural districts) within New South Wales. In 137 of these, mostly municipalities, where three or more members are chosen in an election district, P.R. is provided. In the remaining 103 areas, mostly shires, where only one or two persons are chosen at a time, the alternative vote system, called preferential voting in Australia, is provided.

More extensive changes were made for electing the city council of Sydney, the state capital and largest city. There the ten wards, which formerly returned three aldermen each, were eliminated and the total membership of the council was reduced from thirty to twenty. These twenty are chosen by P.R. on an at-large basis on a single ballot. The mayor of Sydney, previously selected by the council, is now elected by popular vote by means of preferential voting. Elections under the new law were held throughout New South Wales on December 5 and will be reported in a forthcoming issue of the REVIEW.

Prior to this election, local elections were conducted by ordinary plurality voting, using X-marks.

Democrats Poll 51.7% of N. Y. Votes; Seat 92% of Candidates

Since proportional representation dropped out of the picture in New York, two city councils have been elected under the plurality system and the first has now completed its four-year term. The election of the second council on November 3, 1953, provides an opportune occasion for assessing the choice of legislators under the district system.

The most arresting fact is that the Democrats, whose mayoralty candidate polled something less than a majority, seated 92 per cent of their councilmanic candidates with a bare majority of the votes. The table below tells the story.

Certainly these figures prove that the

NEW YORK CITY COUNCILMANIC ELECTION, NOVEMBER 3, 1953

Party	Votes Total	Percentage of Votes	Council Seats Earned	Seats Actually Obtained	Percentage of Seats Obtained
Democrats	1,057,543	51.7%	12.9	23[a]	92%
Republicans	596,425	29.2%	7.3	2[a]	8%
Liberals	339,515	16.6%	4.2	0[a]	0
American Labor	51,315	2.5%	0.6	0	0
Totals	2,044,798	100.0%	25.0	25	100%

[a]One of the two Republicans and two of the Democrats elected were endorsed by the Liberals. One of the Democrats elected was endorsed by the Republicans.

Democratic leaders who initiated the campaign for repeal of P.R. in 1947 knew precisely what they were about. In five P.R. elections, from 1937 to 1945, their candidates never won more than 66.5 per cent of the seats—and to obtain these they had to poll approximately 65.5 per cent of the vote. In 1949, the first year councilmen were elected under the district system, they made almost a clean sweep—obtaining 96 per cent of the seats with 52.6 per cent of the vote. This year's results may be likened to a second dividend on the investment they made in the P.R. repealer campaign six years ago.

The Republicans gained slightly. In the last election they seated one candidate with 21.6 per cent of the vote. This year, with 29.2 per cent of the votes, the minority party in New York elected two councilmen—8 per cent of the total. In addition one reelected Democratic incumbent was endorsed by Republicans as well as Democrats. Now the minority leader will not have to rely on Democrats to second his motions. Nevertheless, it is hardly likely that a minority of two will prove more effective than a minority of one.

No Liberals Elected

Although they received more than a third of a million votes, not one of the Liberals' nominees was elected. This bitter pill was slightly sweetened by the fact that one Republican and two Democrats whom they endorsed and gave places on their line were elected. Each of these three, however, could have won easily this time without Liberal endorsement, a fact they are hardly likely to overlook. All told, the Liberal party polled one-sixth of the councilmanic vote; yet it is excluded from direct representation in the city legislature.

The most telling argument in the anti-P.R. campaign of 1947 was that it had given the Communists representation in the city council. This year the party did not even offer candidates. The left-wing

American Labor party, which endorsed an avowed Communist in the 1949 councilmanic race, obtained only 2.5 per cent of the total vote this year and elected no one. Even if P.R. had remained in effect, none of its candidates would have been seated. For the smallest number of ballots that ever elected a candidate in New York's P.R. elections was 39,052 (except for the borough of Richmond, which contains a relatively small proportion of the city's population and elects a single councilman). But the most votes the A.L.P. could muster in any one borough was 20,540. These returns demonstrate that it was unnecessary to discard P.R. to remove the left-wingers from the city council. The voters would have repudiated them under any electoral system.

Since World War II, a great mass migration has taken place out of the centers of our cities into outlying districts and suburbs. In New York, which shared this trend, the political district lines which were drawn a decade ago did not reflect this population movement. So it happened that 404,000 votes were cast for councilmen in Manhattan and six were elected; in the fast-growing borough of Queens the candidates for council received 453,000 votes, but only four councilmen were elected. In the current session of the council, the average Manhattan legislator will represent 67,000 voters, his counterpart in Queens 113,000.

Within individual constituencies the differences were even more pronounced. One Manhattan district polled an aggregate of 45,000 votes, while the voting machines in two Queens districts registered 128,000 and 143,000 respectively. A defeated candidate in Queens obtained 46,000 votes, more than 15 candidates out of the 25 successful candidates obtained that day.

The reapportionment passed late in 1953 will iron out the worst of these discrepancies, but if the state has to wait another 26 years for the next redistrict-

(Continued on page 155)

Taxation and Finance • • • • *Edited by Wade S. Smith*

Bid to End Local Tax Immunity Halted

House Committee Decides Not to Alter Reciprocity

PROPOSALS of the House Ways and Means Committee, to limit the traditional intergovernmental tax immunity by making the interest on future issues of certain local and public housing authority bonds subject to federal income taxes, had undergone drastic change by mid-February, when the committee announced abandonment of the proposals. The original recommendations, made at the beginning of the present session of Congress, had been that so-called local industrial-aid bonds, when secured solely by rentals etc. from the industrial concerns occupying the plants, be subject to the income tax and that local housing authority bonds be similarly treated. In neither case would bonds already outstanding or authorized be affected.

The proposal as to the housing bonds was opposed by public housing groups, which pointed out that the tax exemption feature is an important factor in holding costs at a level which permitted effectuation of the low-rent policies of public housing. Further, since the federal subsidy payments are based on cost factors, the additional federal income resulting from taxation of the interest on the bonds would have been offset by the added cost in subsidies.

The proposal as to industrial aid bonds was opposed as a matter of principle by most of the associations of state and local officials and governmental units, which feared it might be an entering wedge for recurrent efforts to make all state and local bonds subject to the federal income tax.

Industrial aid bonds have been used mainly in the south, where plants have been constructed with public credit to attract manufacturing industry as part of "balance agriculture with industry" programs. Over the last several years the use of so-called revenue bonds for the purpose has attracted wide attention. These have been secured not by the full faith and credit and taxing power of the issuing community but solely by a lien on the plant rentals, usually based on long-term leases with manufacturing concerns.

The use of revenue bonds for such purposes, and in fact the use of the public credit in any form, has been censured by various groups in the local government finance field[1] and the committee's recommendations reportedly were the result of criticism by New England groups of this "unfair competition" for industry.

The Ways and Means Committee, in dropping its recommendations that the two classes of bonds be made taxable as to future issues, proposed alternatively that the income tax laws be amended to provide that rentals paid by concerns on plants built with industrial aid bonds should not be deductible by such concerns in computing their taxable income. Said Chairman Daniel A. Reed of the committee, such action "will correct the same evil against which the original amendment was directed and will do so more effectively."

The two proposals originally made by the committee were of immediate concern to groups interested in the preservation of the tax-free status of state and local government bonds because such groups feared the recommendations raised the likelihood of another prolonged battle

[1]See the REVIEW, January 1952, page 50.

in Congress over the whole matter of tax immunity. Had the committee implemented the recommendations by causing appropriate bills to be introduced, some observers saw the possibility of extended litigation to clarify at least two constitutional features of the problem.

Foremost, of course, was the possibility of a reexamination by the courts of the whole question of intergovernmental tax immunity. Marshall's famous *dicta*, paraphrased generally as "The power to tax is the power to destroy," was delivered, it must be recalled, in *Mc-Culloch v. Maryland*, in which the power of a state to tax a federal instrumentality was at issue and the main question was the implied powers of Congress. The doctrine of reciprocal tax immunity which flowed from this case has been by no means a placid stream. In general, over the years the courts have construed the doctrine strictly to prevent any state taxation impinging on federal activities but have inquired more broadly into the precise circumstances and the impact of the tax when the levy was made by the federal government.

The Saratoga Spa Case

In the most recent case, in fact, that involving New York's Saratoga Spa, decided by the Supreme Court in 1946, a federal excise tax on the bottled water sold by a state agency was upheld. The present tax exemption of state and local bonds is statutory, and there are some authorities at least who profess inability to foresee the result should there occur contemporaneously a full-dress argument before the highest court on the constitutional question.

A secondary question, sure to have gotten before the courts had the committee's recommendations as to taxation of interest on industrial aid bonds been enacted, was the judicial construction of "governmental" as contrasted with "proprietary" functions. For more than

a century the tendency of the courts to take a narrow view of local governmental activities, particularly in the fiscal field, had been an impediment to the effective assumption of responsibility at the local level.

Such a narrow view was expressed in the judicial predilection to apply the property tax as a test in determining whether a function was a proper governmental one. Such a test might have been appropriate in the days when the general property tax yielded the great bulk of state and local income, but it became nonsensical when the use of other revenues became widespread. None the less, the test persisted to the present generation, and has been repudiated by the Supreme Court only in the last fifteen years. (In the Saratoga Spa case, Mr. Justice Stone wrote: "We regard as untenable the distinction between governmental and proprietary activities.") The proposal to tax the industrial aid bonds was made, however, not only on the basis of the type of local government activity which they were issued to finance but, even more importantly, on the basis of the type of instrument used—a revenue bond as contrasted with a general obligation or "tax" bond.

The committee's experience appears to demonstrate again that the several aspects of intergovernmental tax immunity cannot successfully be tackled piecemeal. The industrial aid bond, whether revenue or general obligation, does raise special problems of tax avoidance, but so does the whole matter of tax exemption of state and local evidences of indebtedness. So, also, does the vast immunity of the federal government from taxation of its great real estate holdings as well as on industrial properties and materials ostensibly federally-owned but actually in the possession of private concerns.

Obviously, what is called for is a thorough study by qualified students sufficiently informed to see the whole problem, and to see it in a perspective undistorted by sectional or political considerations.

Study on Intergovernmental Relations Gets under Way

A deep and comprehensive inquiry into the ramifications of mid-twentieth century fiscal and administrative problems, as they penetrate and interact vertically through federal, state and local government, appeared imminent last summer when Congress enacted the legislation to create the President's Commission on Intergovernmental Relations.

Delays in staffing the committee—sixteen persons are said to have declined the chairmanship before an acceptance was secured—made it evident that no more than a preliminary report would be available by March 1, the reporting date under the statute. More disappointing, however, has been the severely restricted scope of inquiry as indicated thus far by press reports of the committee's activities. Hence, the March 1 report to Congress will be awaited eagerly by those interested in local governmental aspects of the problem, especially for what it may indicate as to the fields in which the commission intends to employ its effort.

So far, four fields have received prominent mention by the press as being the matters of most pressing concern to the committee. They are: federal aid for highways, disaster relief, administration of unemployment compensation, and payments by the federal government in lieu of taxes to local governments, the subcommittee to study the latter reportedly now being organized.

The commission's initial inquiries are in the form of so-called "impact studies," to be made in five states under contract by private management research organizations and to require about three months each. According to press reports, the studies will be made in Kansas, Michigan, Mississippi, Washington and Wyoming. The studies will concentrate on the effect on the states and their local units of some 22 federal aid programs.

The committee's slow start was more or less inevitable in the light of the wide scope and complexity of the subject. The chairman, Dr. Clarence E. Manion, former dean of the School of Law of Notre Dame University, was criticized as having been too active in accepting speaking engagements after his appointment in which he expressed sentiments antagonistic to established conceptions of the federal structure in the United States. The chairman reportedly was asked for his resignation and it was submitted and accepted February 17. Whether a change in the chairmanship will further delay the committee's work remains to be seen.

Reassessment Almost Pleases Taxpayers

When Erie, Pennsylvania, shifted the basis of assessing property in the city from a 1932 price level to a 1953 price level, the assessed valuation rose 130 per cent, from $165,000,000 to $380,000,000. Newspapers and the city government kept the property owners informed of the reasons for bringing the city's tax base up to date, however, and according to the National Association of Assessing Officers appeals were filed on only about 3,000 parcels out of a total of 38,000.

Teenagers Urged to Civic Effort

Speaker Issues Challenge to High School Audience

EDITOR'S NOTE: The article below is the address of Former Governor of New Jersey Charles Edison, chairman of the Council of the National Municipal League, before the student body of John Marshall High School in Richmond, Virginia. The address was made November 11, 1953, during the National Conference on Government of the League, held in that city.

HOW fortunate you and I are that we live in a land in which we are citizens first and soldiers second. May it ever be so. And it will be, provided you and I and all of us accept our civic responsibilities. In these perilous times, military training is necessary. But training for citizenship is even more necessary.

Civic competence is not something that you just acquire, like a new watch, when you reach the ripe old age of 21. Like any other skill that is worth anything, it requires practice—and more practice—and it is never too early to start.

In these important days in which you are laying the foundations of your house of life, be sure you build firmly and soundly. The education you are receiving is offered both for your own good and for that of the state. Thomas Jefferson combined these two reasons for the importance of public education in one sentence: "No other sure foundation can be devised for the preservation of freedom and happiness."

The great truth here is that in our country active citizenship is part and parcel of the full life; consequently, public education has no meaning unless it is education for the life of the active citizen. So, take all that you can from the education which is offered and remember that with the privilege of education comes civic responsibility. Upon you in a few short years will be thrust the full responsibilities of world leadership. But you cannot lead the world unless you can first lead your own home town.

High adventure is not limited to the battlefield or exploration of new lands. Adventures in politics—in good government—can be as exciting as those in the fields of sport and combat. And they can serve a much higher purpose. Some of you may regret that you were born too late in Virginia's history to fight the redcoats with Washington, to explore the west with Lewis and Clark, or to fly to the poles with Richard Byrd.

I assure you, nevertheless, that the opportunity for adventure is never lost. Only its method of expression changes from one generation to another. Let me offer you what has been called "the endless adventure of governing men." Only recently Governor Dewey was quoted as saying that politics is the most challenging and difficult of the sciences.

Politics is just as interesting as people are interesting, as various as people are various, as old as the pyramids and as new as this morning's paper. Politics is something you can watch—it is all around you all the time. How did this school building get here? By votes of the people, by bonds and taxes, by school boards and building inspectors, by licensed architects—in other words by government, by politics.

Have the decisions on street paving, sewage disposal, welfare and all the other governmental functions been well made? What do you think? If so, you will want to support and defend those who have done the good work. If not, you will say "it is time for a change."

Politics is part of your life and of

mine. Don't be afraid to play the great game. I invite you to "come in, the water's fine!" Form opinions on political matters, even though you can't yet vote. See to it that your opinions are heard. If your ideas have merit, those who are of age to cast a ballot will listen and translate what you propose. In the give and take of opinion formulation you will exert immediate influence and get valuable exercise for future political activity.

Ways to Help

No one is entitled to claim exemption from the universal draft for active citizenship. It doesn't matter whether you already have decided to be doctor, lawyer, merchant—I won't conclude the rhyme! If you cannot devote your whole time to politics, you can devote spare time to it. No party ever has as many workers as it wants. The political parties need people of varying talents—people who can write, speak, type, drive cars—and even baby-sit. You can help and so influence your country to make it a finer and better place in which to live.

Registration a n d get-out-the-vote drives are tailor-made for youthful participation. So are certain other projects. Have you ever thought what useful citizens you might be if you were to become solicitors for the Community Chest? Inter-high school competition on solicitation in a block-by-block canvass would be a stimulating activity; and I am willing to venture that you would put your elders to shame in "going over the top."

The League of Women Voters conducts "Know Your Town" studies in which students your age sometimes help as the field men who gather and analyze facts about their town's government. Participation in such an effort is the finest way to find out how things are really run. You have to know your facts before you can be politically effective.

Loyalty to truth is in the finest American tradition.

For those of you who want to prepare for politics or concern with government as a life work let me urge you to inquire into the fine college courses available to you. Scholarships and fellowships are increasingly being provided for those interested in government service. If your vocational counselor wants assistance, or if you want to handle the problem by yourself, write the National Municipal League for information.

Get to know the National Municipal League as I did when I returned to New Jersey from Washington, after a tour of duty as Secretary of the Navy. When the people of my state elected me governor, it was to the League that I turned for help and advice. If you are going to be an effective citizen you must have information. Get in the habit of using the resources available to you at the National Municipal League and other national, state and local organizations working in the public interest.

Georgia has pioneered in extending the right to vote to eighteen-year-olds. This is a subject that you young people should debate among yourselves. It is a controversial subject, with much to be said on either side. Learn the facts for yourself—take a position—and then work earnestly to win your objective, whether that be for or against granting the right to vote to eighteen-year-olds.

We have only to look to history to realize that any great cause worth fighting for is not impossible of achievement. Property qualifications for voting, for instance, once were common, and such stalwarts of the "Old Dominion" as Marshall, Monroe, Madison and Randolph once stoutly upheld them. In most of the states they are no more. Then, too, it is not so many years that women have had the right to vote.

These are provocative and challenging times in which we live. I envy you the opportunity for greatness that lies before you. The American system has met every attack with the vitality of youth. Don't listen to those who predict futility and failure for your efforts. When you are tested you will not be found wanting. It is only the challenge and the test that bring out the best in a people.

One of my predecessors in the governor's office in New Jersey, who later became president of the United States, was born in Staunton. At a young age he wrote on his visiting cards "Thomas Woodrow Wilson, Senator from Virginia." Don't be afraid to dream greatly and then to put forth the effort to make those dreams a reality. It may be that a statesman, in the tradition of the young "senator" who became president instead, sits with us today.

CHARLES EDISON

Chicago Citizens Complete First Year

Citizens of Greater Chicago, formed a year ago, have won the praise of the *Chicago Daily News.* An editorial, dated December 14, reads:

"The Citizens of Greater Chicago came into being on a wave of public indignation over lawlessness in Chicago. The murder of Charles Gross was the spark that ignited long-smoldering resentment over the many defects in civic and governmental affairs.

"Too often, reform movements of this nature lose their momentum when it develops that improvements do not come about with a few luncheons and inspirational speeches. The CGC, we are glad to report, shows no signs of this creeping apathy.

"At its annual meeting last week, it was announced that membership of civic organizations which send delegates has grown in one year from 54 to 225. It is well financed, despite erroneous reports to the contrary. It has a concrete, practical program.

"Its principal immediate objectives are reform of the city charter and reorgani-

zation of the state's judicial system. Substantial progress has been made toward these goals. Most importantly, it recognizes that sustained effort is required to bring about such far-reaching changes.

"The CGC thus becomes one of the most hopeful developments to rise on the Chicago horizon in decades. Its influence will grow with success, and we venture to forecast that the day will come when association with its early efforts will be a badge of honor in Chicago citizenship."

Chicago Activities

Two recent leaflets from the Chicago group tell its story. One, a folder of six pages, describes the organization's method of operation and lists all its member organizations; the other, *The Significance of Senatorial Reapportionment,* discusses the "dictatorship of minority" and points up the need for reapportionment.

The first annual report of the group's executive director, Fred K. Hoehler, was presented at the annual meeting in December. It lists numerous activities, reporting on the work of the field staff, education programs set up, discussion groups developed, number of publications distributed, legislation worked for (including a bill providing amendments to the city charter which, though it failed to pass, secured great editorial support), first delegates assembly, and the CGC's role in the November "get-out-the-vote campaign." On the latter, the report points out that 310,000 tabs, "I Will Vote November 3," were distributed via other organizations, business and manufacturing plants and volunteers. The latter distributed 48,000 tabs in the loop, at railroad and elevated stations on "Citizens Day," November 2.

Livonia Citizens Committee

Livonia, Michigan, boasts a 51-member Mayor's Advisory Committee, which is aiding the city in meeting the many problems caused by its growth. Appointed in 1951, to study the policies and plans of the city government and offer suggestions, subcommittees of the larger group have investigated various phases of the city government. Many suggestions made by the committee have been accepted by the voters and public officials.

Rebirth for Two Groups

The Citizens Committee of San Antonio, Texas, which several years ago did yeoman service in securing the council-manager plan for the city, has recently been reorganized, "as a prelude to broadening its base and getting set for municipal contests to come," according to the San Antonio *News*. Sixty members of the organization heard Dr. Max E. Johnson, new chairman, call on them to remain "vigilant and alert and to defend the good government program against the selfish interests which are now throttling San Antonio."

The Hartford (Connecticut) *Courant*, in an editorial of January 14, comments, "It is too early to say that the Citizens Charter Committee has been reborn. But, under the leadership of John C. Parsons, it is struggling to be reborn. And if the outstanding good government Hartford has had for six years is to survive, it must be done. First is the fact that the CCC is using its recent defeat[1] as the occasion for more, not less, energy and activity. Second is the fact that it is simply not always true that, in American cities, reform flowers briefly and then dies."

Supporting Manager Plan

Prior to the Ferguson, Missouri, election on the council-manager plan, successfully concluded on February 2, the

[1]The Hartford Citizens Charter Committee, for the first time since the council-manager plan went into effect, failed to elect a majority of the city's council at the November 1953 elections.

local League of Women Voters maintained a booth in a drug store where it dispensed information on the proposal. The league also conducted workshops which made a thorough study of forms of city government.

Civic Awards

Recipient of the third annual award presented by the LaGuardia Memorial Association, in honor of the late Fiorella LaGuardia, mayor of New York from 1934 to 1945, was deLessups Morrison, mayor of New Orleans, "in recognition of his constant and successful struggle to secure decent, responsible government for New Orleans despite seemingly overwhelming odds."

The City Manager Advocates of Brookfield, Illinois, received the annual Lane Bryant group award for 1953, because of the interest the organization took in improving the government of its small village. It worked eight years to form a stable government.

Edmund Orgill, chairman of the executive committee and board of directors of the Civic Research Committee of Memphis, Tennessee, has been named that city's outstanding citizen for 1953. The award, made by the Memphis Civitan Club, was "specifically for his work on the Civic Research Committee."

LWV Information Center

The League of Women Voters of Chicago, in 1953, created the Metropolitan Civic Information Service—a nonpartisan organization established to reach as many people as possible in the Chicago area with information on civic matters. "It is a center and source of basic, accurate and unbiased information concerning the citizen and his responsibility in the affairs of government," according to a six-page folder describing the organization. It makes election information available, provides original resource materials, publications, a speakers bureau, personal information service and offers citizenship training.

Adult Education Aids

The Fund for Adult Education, with national offices in Pasadena, California, has presented its story in *The Challenge of Lifetime Learning*. Freely illustrated with photographs, on slick paper, the pamphlet tells of the accomplishments of the fund, created by The Ford Foundation in April 1951, "as an independent organization to advance and foster adult education. The fund was assigned as its special responsibility the improvement of methods and opportunities in that part of the educational process which begins when formal schooling is finished."

Recent issues of *Adult Leadership*, published by the Adult Education Association (Chicago), include pointers for those furthering adult education. That for October is devoted to "Social Inventions for Learning" and discusses such matters as finding time for citizenship, why social inventions?, learning through role playing. The November issue discusses a "Workshop on Handling Controversial Issues," and also publishes an article by Lyman Bryson on "The Meaning of Community Leadership." December's issue is devoted in part to a "Workshop on the Dynamics of Work Groups," with articles by H. L. Keenleyside on "Education or Catastrophe"; Paul L. Witty, "To Become a Better Reader"; and Sir Richard Livingstone, "The Quality of a Democracy."

The Council of National Organizations of the Adult Education Association has issued a *Program Guide—1954*, setting forth "current adult education activities and emphases of organizations participating in the council." It may be obtained from the council, Cooper Union, Fourth Avenue at 7th Street, New York 3.

Adult Education on the March is the report of the second year of AEA, featuring what has happened during the past year with "A Look into the Future."

Strictly Personal

The board of directors of the Citizens' Plan "E" Association of Worcester, Massachusetts, has elected Jeremiah F. Gallo as president. Mr. Gallo served as vice president during the previous year. He succeeds Thomas S. Green, Jr.

Francis V. Rudnicki has been chosen as the new membership secretary for the Municipal League of Seattle and King County.

PROPORTIONAL REPRESENTATION

(Continued from page 147)
ing, as it did between 1917 and 1943, they are bound to reappear. One of the features of P.R. as it was used in New York City was that it automatically reapportioned the members to the different boroughs at each election on the basis of the numbers of votes cast. The 1953 elections demonstrate once again that the district system in New York can and does create "rotten boroughs" and distortion of the will of the electorate in the political complexion of the legislature.

FREDERICK SHAW
Board of Education of the City of N. Y.

Massachusetts Legislature Upholds P. R.

The Massachusetts legislature, by a roll-call vote of 116 to 112, has approved a bill to permit cities which repeal or have repealed proportional representation voting to readopt the system by referendum after four years.

A bill to raise the number of signatures necessary for a P. R. repeal from 5 per cent back to the original 10 per cent of the voters was favorably reported by the Committee on Cities but defeated on the floor of the House of Representatives.

A bill to abolish P. R. for any city in the state, including those already using it, introduced in the House by Charles McGlue of Boston, former head of the Democratic State Committee, was defeated in both the Senate and the House.

Researcher's Digest .   .   .   .   . *Edited by John E. Bebout*

Citizen Survey
Methods Suggested

But Further Research Needed on Tools for Making Studies

AS citizen interest in the affairs of
local government increases, a frequent question which is raised in the
meetings of citizen groups is "How do
I know whether my town is well run?"
This query is often referred to the National Municipal League. If the local
group making the inquiry is interested in
a thorough-going administrative survey
of a particular public function, or the
over-all structure of the community's
government, there are able consultants
who conduct the type of survey desired.

A more difficult type of inquiry comes
from the citizen group which wants a
relatively simple yardstick or series of
criteria upon which to judge the quality
of public administration found in the
home town. Often the inquiry suggests
the possibility of comparing per capita
expenditures or tax rates with those of
other cities of comparable size. Immediately a warning must be sounded.
As every researcher knows only too well,
tax rates, assessed valuations, per capita
revenues and expenditures have an il-
lusory preciseness.

The complexity of the measurement
problem can be seen by a glance at the
standard work, *Measuring Municipal
Activities—A Survey of Suggested Cri-
teria for Appraising Administration,* by
Clarence E. Ridley and Herbert A.
Simon (International City Managers'
Association, Chicago, 1943).

The criteria suggested by Ridley and
Simon and the questions which they raise
have served as guides for the more
searching appraisals of public performance. However, many citizens want an

introduction to the process of community
appraisal. They want some tentative
answers to their questions on whether or
not their community is well run and well
served. They want to point up quickly
the weak spots which must be given
more careful scrutiny.

Any preliminary survey must be
designed to avoid erroneous conclusions
drawn from unqualified statistical comparisons. Probably the most useful device is a relatively short check list
designed to stimulate greater interest
in public affairs and giving sufficient in
dication of the quality of the perform
ance of governmental functions to sug
gest basic weaknesses.

Any number of such check lists have
been prepared. One of the most recent
appeared in the September 1953 number
of *Changing Times—The Kiplinger
Magazine* (page 12). Thirty-five questions based upon the International City
Managers Association's *Check List on
How Cities Can Cut Costs* (1949) highlights the most significant areas of local
governmental activity. For a short list
it contains a reasonable balance in emphasis between the standards of efficiency
and adequacy in the performance of
public functions. No attempt is made to
construct an exact score for purposes of
comparison. However, if many of the
questions result in negative answers,
deficiencies are readily apparent.

In its annual report published in 1947,
the Municipal League of Seattle and
King County presented yardsticks by
which the citizens could measure the
services being provided. These were
used to compare Seattle with a composite
of twelve other cities of similar size.
In 1951 the same organization prepared
a rating scale for community "diagnosis."
In parallel columns it rated the standard
of service and the comparative cost of

various governmental programs. A column headed "improvement needed" tended to highlight deficiencies. The risks inherent in such an evaluation were noted.

A *Scoreboard for Your Town* was prepared by the New York Citizens' Council in 1948. Ten "scoring standards," covering most phases of community life and government, were to be rated as good, fair or poor. Citizens using this scoreboard were encouraged to follow up with further study and surveys of the areas where weakness was indicated.

The Project on the American Community sponsored by New York University is in the process of preparing a "comparator" which is "a device for use by a community in measuring itself against a recognized norm, standard or national average." No extravagant claims are being made concerning the precision of the "comparator" as a measuring instrument. It is rather a "study-provoking and discussion provoking" technique for giving citizens the enlightening experience of gathering facts about their communities and encouraging more exhaustive local studies, alertness and concentrated concern upon the part of citizens and citizen groups with respect to community problems. "Comparator is not designed to be an end in itself, but a means to an end: the end being alert, intelligent and responsible citizens." Undoubtedly this device, when available, will prove useful to many citizen groups which are attempting to evaluate community services.

Surveys by Citizen Groups

Citizens· in many communities have engaged in various self-surveys which have brought to light the facts of community life, the quality of governmental service and the need for sound future development. Among these are the surveys conducted by Connecticut towns and cities under the guidance of the Connecticut Public Expenditure Council.

A remarkably thorough citizen study was carried on recently by the citizens of Port Angeles, Washington. The three-year-long self-survey of the Negro community of Shreveport, Louisiana, was an unusually significant demonstration of the capacity of citizens to engage in community self-appraisal. Both Port Angeles and Shreveport received 1953 All-America City Awards, partly as a result of the citizen effort which went into these surveys.

Leagues of Women Voters in cities in all parts of the nation have studied and reported upon the governments of their localities, following patterns set by the national office. Some of the L. of W. V. "Know Your Town" reports give a searching analysis of the performance of public functions and lead the way toward action to effect improvements.

From time to time local chambers of commerce have developed useful survey techniques. An *Outline for a Master Community Survey*, prepared by the Civic Development Department of the Chamber of Commerce of the United States, would ordinarily require some paid staff work but includes many suggestions that could be carried out by volunteers.

Some years ago the Tax Foundation issued a series of civic guides to economy in municipal government, covering budgeting, purchasing, police and fire, public utilities, personnel and public welfare. State taxpayers' organizations also have prepared somewhat similar materials for the guidance of local taxpayer groups.

Although the presently available check lists, scoreboards, study techniques, etc., all assist the active citizen in answering some of the questions which occur to him, there is a distinct need for further research into the possibility of developing tools for citizens who are trying to evaluate their communities. These tools are needed to point the direction of more concentrated effort. Often such preliminary evaluation must precede any comprehensive administrative studies.

It is to be regretted that many conscientious and completely well intentioned diagnostic and survey efforts have been reluctant to come to grips with issues involving government and politics. As a result social and economic conditions have been studied without reference to needed changes in public policy and the political and governmental climate in which it is made and executed.

There undoubtedly are other examples of citizen surveys which have stimulated improvement in the performance of the governmental functions.

The League is anxious to keep its files on research and experiments in the field as nearly up-to-date and complete as possible. All suggestions would be appreciated.

WILLIAM N. CASSELLA, JR.

Chicago Civic Federation Presents Budget Views

The statements made by representatives of the Civic Federation of Chicago at the 1954 budget hearings of the various local jurisdictions in metropolitan Chicago emphasized the need for various administrative reforms. The reorganization and strengthening of the Department of Finance of Chicago was urged. Consolidation of all Chicago Sanitary District fiscal administration in a proposed Department of Finance was recommended. The federation urged abolition of township collectors and transfer of their duties to the Cook County treasurer.

The eventual consolidation of Park District and city police forces was suggested. Immediate merger of police pension plans was urged as a first step. Park District personnel administration by the Chicago Civil Service Commission was recommended.

A single salary schedule for teachers in the Chicago schools has been advocated.

Bureau Note

The executive board of the Washington State Taxpayers Association has announced the opening of permanent headquarters for its research department at 1059 Capitol Way, Olympia, Washington.

Strictly Personal

Dr. George C. S. Benson, president of Claremont Men's College, Claremont, California, has been appointed research director of the Federal Commission on Intergovernmental Relations.

Edward J. Steimel has been named assistant executive director of the Public Affairs Research Council, Baton Rouge, Louisiana. He has assumed the active direction of the council during the leave of absence of Dr. Robert W. French, who has been named vice president of Tulane University.

Research Pamphlets and Articles

Annexation

MUNICIPAL ANNEXATION OF TERRITORY—A COMPARISON OF PRINCIPAL METHODS. By William O. Winter. Ann Arbor, Michigan Municipal League, *Michigan Municipal Review,* January 1954. 4 pp.

Billboards

REGULATION OF BILLBOARDS. Springfield, Illinois Legislative Council, November 1953. 27 pp.

Budgets

CHECK LIST FOR A MODEL MUNICIPAL BUDGET AND ITS COMPARISON WITH THE WORCESTER CITY BUDGET. Worcester, Massachusetts, Citizens' Plan "E" Association, 1954. 7 pp.

MUNICIPAL BUDGET MAKING AND ADMINISTRATION. By John Alexander McMahon. Chapel Hill, University of North Carolina, Institute of Government, April 1952. 69 pp. $1.00.

POSSIBLE WORK UNITS. Prepared in conjunction with the development of a program budget for the town of Manchester. Hartford, Connecticut Public Expenditure Council, February 1953. 13 pp.

A REPORT ON WEST VIRGINIA MUNICIPAL AND COUNTY BUDGETS 1953. By Harold J. Shamberger. Morgantown, West Virginia University, Bureau for Government Research, 1953. 28 pp.

Business and Industry

LEGISLATION AFFECTING BUSINESS AND INDUSTRY IN SOUTH DAKOTA. By Robert F. Patterson. Vermillion, University of South Dakota, School of Business Administration, Business Research Bureau, May 1953. 39 pp.

Child Welfare

LET'S TALK ABOUT CHILDREN. A Review of Mississippi's Youth Court Act . . . How It Works . . . Why It Needs Wider Use. Jackson, Mississippi Economic Council, Committee on Social Legislation, April 1953. 11 pp.

Education

ANALYSIS OF RECENT CHANGES IN UTAH'S PUBLIC SCHOOL LAWS. Salt Lake City 1, Utah Foundation, *Research Report,* January 1954. 6 pp.

EDUCATION. A CHALLENGE AND AN ANSWER FOR MISSISSIPPIANS. Jackson, Mississippi Economic Council, June 1953. 23 pp.

Federal-state Relations

FEDERAL-STATE RELATIONS IN UTAH. Salt Lake City 1, Utah Foundation, December 1953. 4 pp.

REALLOCATION OF FEDERAL-STATE FUNCTIONS AND TAX SOURCES. A Staff Report Outlining Four Alternative Programs and Indicating How Each Would Affect the Finances of the Federal Government and the State of New York.

Albany 10, Empire State Chamber of Commerce, Department of Governmental Affairs, August 1953. 33 pp.

Hospitals

REPORT OF A STUDY OF MINNEAPOLIS GENERAL HOSPITAL. Prepared at the Request of Mayor Eric G. Hoyer. Minneapolis 2, Citizens League of Greater Minneapolis, August 1953. 62 pp.

Housing

STATE HOME OWNERSHIP PROGRAM RUNNING DEFICIT. (Connecticut's mortgage housing fund.) Hartford 3, Connecticut Public Expenditure Council, *CPEC Special Bulletin,* January 1954. 4 pp.

Legislative Committees

SIXTY INTERIM COMMITTEES. State Legislators Study Many Problems. By Frank Irwin. Los Angeles 14, California Taxpayers' Association, *The Tax Digest,* November 1953. 9 pp.

Licensing

STUDY OF ADMINISTRATIVE PROCEDURE BEFORE EXAMINING AND LICENSING BOARDS IN NORTH CAROLINA. By Max O. Cogburn and Ernest W. Machen, Jr. Chapel Hill, University of North Carolina, Institute of Government, January 1953. 115 pp. $2.00.

Metropolitan Areas

WHERE'S FLINT GOING? The Metropolitan Area—A Look at Problems Confronting Flint and Its Neighbors. (A series of articles appearing in the Flint *Journal.*) Flint (Michigan), *The Journal,* 1953. 36 pp. Illus.

Motor Vehicle Insurance

FINANCIAL RESPONSIBILITY IN MOTOR VEHICLE ACCIDENTS. Springfield, Illinois Legislative Council, October 1953. 37 pp.

Personnel

EMPLOYEE TRAINING PAYS IN CINCINNATI. By Robert G. Sarvis. Chicago 37, American Public Works Association, *Public Works Engineers' News Letter,* January 1954. 3 pp.

LOCAL GOVERNMENT'S RECRUITING CRISIS. By Norman W. Bingham. London, N. W. 1, National and Local Government Officers Association, *Public Service,* December 1953. 2 pp.

Police

GEORGIA MUNICIPAL POLICE. A Study of Salaries and Working Conditions in Municipal Police Departments of Georgia. Athens, University of Georgia, Bureau of Public Administration, in Cooperation with The Peace Officers Association of Georgia. December 1953. 36 pp. $1.00.

Public Welfare

WASTEPROOFING WELFARE LEGISLATION. States Tighten Assistance Laws to Bar Unscrupulous and Undeserving. New York 20, The Tax Foundation, *Tax Review,* December 1953. 6 pp.

Reapportionment

PARLIAMENTARY REPRESENTATION. Toronto 5, Citizens Research Institute of Canada, *Effective Government,* December 9, 1953. 6 pp.

REAPPORTIONMENT IN MINNESOTA: DEMOCRACY DENIED. Minneapolis 3, League of Women Voters of Minnesota, November 1953. 22 pp. 20 cents.

Sewage Disposal

LEGAL ASPECTS OF SEWERAGE AND SEWAGE DISPOSAL. By Ernest H. Campbell. Seattle 5, Association of Washington Cities in cooperation with the University of Washington, Bureau of Governmental Research and Services, December 1953. 15 pp.

Social Security

SOCIAL SECURITY ENABLING ACT. By E. W. Busch. (Address before Annual Convention of the Illinois Municipal League.) Springfield, the League, November 1953. 3 pp.

State and Local Government

KNOW YOUR STATE AND LOCAL GOVERNMENTS IN FLORIDA: A BRIEF SURVEY. By J. E. Dovell. Gainesville, University of Florida, Public Administration Clearing Service, 1953. 24 pp.

State Government

CLASSIFICATION OF THE FUNCTIONS OF STATE GOVERNMENT. (United States Bureau of the Census classifications as adapted to the administrative structure of the state of Montana.) By David W. Smith. Bozeman, Montana State University, Department of Political Science, December 1953. 5 pp.

AN OUTLINE OF THE DEVELOPMENT AND GROWTH OF STATE ADMINISTRATION IN MONTANA. 1890-1953. By David W. Smith. Bozeman, Montana State University, Department of Political Science, September 1953. 34 pp.

THE STATE DEPARTMENT OF ADMINISTRATION. By Leonard H. Axe. Lawrence, University of Kansas, Governmental Research Center, *Your Government,* January 15, 1954. 4 pp.

State-local Relations

STATE-LOCAL CONFLICT CAN LEAD TO PROGRESS. State-county relations are basically human relations, and are approached in terms of attitudes. Differences can be resolved without needing to give up anything essential on either side. By Clint Burnes. Chicago 3, *Better Roads,* January 1954. 4 pp.

Taxation and Finance

ASSESSMENTS AND THE TAX PROBLEM. By Harold Riegelman. (Address before the New York Town Hall.) New York 17, Citizens Budget Commission, Inc., December 1953. 11 pp.

CALIFORNIA'S TAX SYSTEM. $2 Billion Plus Revenue in 1954. By J. Roy Holland and Donna D. Spragg. Los Angeles 14, California Taxpayers' Association, *The Tax Digest,* January 1954. 18 pp.

A "CAPITAL FINANCING GUIDE" FOR PHILADELPHIA? Philadelphia 7, Bureau of Municipal Research, *Citizens' Business,* January 25, 1954. 4 pp.

COUNTY FINANCES. A Fiscal Background for the Study of County Government in New Jersey. Trenton 8, New Jersey Taxpayers Association, Inc., 1953. 12 pp.

Books in Review

THE STATES AND THE NATION. By Leonard D. White. Baton Rouge, Louisiana State University, 1953. x, 102 pp. $2.75.

This small volume contains the Edward Douglass White lectures delivered by Professor Leonard D. White at the Louisiana State University in the spring of 1953. These lectures were primarily intended to assess the place of the states in the American federation.

White views the background and present status of the states in the light of his long and varied experience both as teacher and as public official. He presents an interesting and graphic account of what he believes are the strengths and weaknesses of the states as partners in the federal system. To the vitality of this partnership he applies the test of Elihu Root, who said in 1909 that "if the powers of the states are to be preserved and their authority is to continue, the states must exercise their powers."

Being persuaded, as was Root, that "the only way to maintain the powers of government is to govern," White ventures to take a look at what the states can do in the next quarter century to improve their effectiveness and standing in the federation. He thinks that they should do something immediately "to clear out the constitutional and administrative rubbish of the last century," which continues to clutter up their several domains.

He believes that the states should make valiant and persistent efforts to modernize their structures and procedures and to raise their official capacities and personnel standards, if they are not to continue to lose power and influence to Washington. He thinks it is possible for the states to achieve a "new federal-state balance" by insisting on the return to the states of some functions now carried on or financed in whole or in part by the federal government, by modifying the federal grants to give more freedom of action to the states, by a wider use of the interstate compact idea to avoid going to Washington, and by making more energetic use of the powers the states already possess.

He is of the opinion that there should be a joint standing committee on federal-state relations for continuous review of federal-state problems, and a commission of inquiry to conduct a searching examination of American federalism (the Commission on Intergovernmental Relations has since been established for this purpose).

And so White believes that "it is possible within limits to mold the shape of things to come" in revitalizing the state governments. If not, "the next quarter century promises to be one of strain and tension, conducive to the continued march of power away from the state capitals."

A. E. BUCK

TEXAS PRESIDENTIAL POLITICS IN 1952. By O. Douglas Weeks. Austin, University of Texas, Institute of Public Affairs, 1953. 116 pp. Paper bound, $1.25; Cloth bound, $2.00.

This is a very comprehensive and tightly documented story of what happened in both political parties in Texas in 1952. It begins with discussion of presidential candidates, the unprecedented functioning of the precinct caucuses in both parties with large turnouts, the county conventions which selected delegates to the big state conventions choosing the delegates subject to the split-offs which sent up contesting delegates for a battle before the credentials committees. It exhibits clearly the influx of life-long Democrats into the skeleton Republican party, as permitted by the law, and the fraudulent methods that the latter sometimes used to turn aside that invasion. The tale is finished with the part which the Texas delegations, as finally seated, played in the national conventions and the pre-election campaign in the state.

The study is an elaboration of the necessarily condensed account of the same events which will be found later in the American Political Science Association's spacious compilation of similar reports from all the states due for publication in May 1954.

R. S. C.

Additional Books and Pamphlets

(See also Researcher's Digest and other departments)

The Aged

PERTINENT FACTS ON "EARNING OPPORTUNITIES FOR MATURE WORKERS." (Kit compiled for the University of Michigan Sixth Annual Conference on Aging, July 8-10, 1953.) Ann Arbor, the University, 1953. Variously paged.

Annexation

ANNEXATION??—CITY OF JANESVILLE, WISCONSIN. Janesville, Office of the City Manager, 1953. 9 pp.

SHALL THE CITY OF JANESVILLE EXPAND ITS CORPORATE LIMITS? A Report to the City Council on the Implications of Accepting or Rejecting Petitions Asking that the River Valley and South Janesville Areas be Annexed to the City. By Warren C. Hyde. Janesville, Wisconsin, Office of the City Manager, 1953. 15 pp.

Auditing

AUDIT REPORTS OF GOVERNMENT CORPORATIONS AND AGENCIES. Washington, D. C., Eighty-Third Congress, Senate Committee on Government Operations, 1954. 97 pp.

City Managers

DIGEST, CITY MANAGERS' CONFERENCE, 1953. Sponsored by the Bureau of State and Community Service and the

Colorado Municipal League. Boulder, the League, 1953. 9 pp.

DIRECTORY OF ADMINISTRATIVE ASSISTANTS TO CITY MANAGERS. (Reporting name, title, age, education, date appointed, annual salary.) Chicago 37, International City Managers' Association, 1954. 7 pp.

Constitutions

YOUR RUGGED CONSTITUTION. By Bruce and Esther Findlay. Stanford (California), Stanford University Press, 1952. 282 pp. $1.00.

Education

FACTS ABOUT SCHOOL DISTRICT DEBT LIMITATIONS. Trenton, New Jersey State Federation of District Boards of Education, 1953. 7 pp.

HINTS ON SELLING SCHOOL BONDS. Trenton, New Jersey State Federation of District Boards of Education, 1953. 5 pp.

LET'S EXAMINE OUR SCHOOL DISTRICTS. Lincoln, Nebraska State Committee for the Reorganization of School Districts, 1953. 13 pp. Illus.

SCHOOL ENROLLMENT: October 1953. Washington 25, D. C., U. S. Department of Commerce, Bureau of the Census, 1954. 10 pp. 10 cents.

THE LICENSE STATUS OF A SAMPLING OF SOCIAL STUDIES TEACHERS IN INDIANA. Terre Haute, Indiana State Teachers College, 1953. 10 pp.

Federal Government

ACTIVITIES OF THE SENATE COMMITTEE ON GOVERNMENT OPERATIONS. Washington, D. C., Eighty-Third Congress, Senate Committee on Government Operations, 1954. 14 pp.

Government Publications

A POPULAR GUIDE TO GOVERNMENT PUBLICATIONS. By W. Philip Leidy. New York 27, Columbia University Press, 1953. xxii, 296 pp. $3.00.

Immigration

THE STRANGER AT OUR GATE—America's Immigration Policy. By Hubert H.

Humphrey, Jr. New York 16, Public Affairs Committee, 1954. 28 pp. 25 cents.

Interstate Trade Barriers

BARRIERS TO THE INTERSTATE MOVEMENT OF AGRICULTURAL PRODUCTS BY MOTOR VEHICLE IN THE ELEVEN WESTERN STATES. By J. S. Hillman and J. D. Rowell. Tucson, University of Arizona, Agricultural Experiment Station, 1953. 47 pp.

Milk Control

MILK ORDINANCE AND CODE. 1953 Recommendations. Washington, D. C., Federal Security Agency, Public Health Service, Division of Sanitation of the Bureau of State Services, 1953. 242 pp. 75 cents. (Apply Superintendent of Documents, Washington 25, D. C.)

Municipal Government

NATURE AND ORGANIZATION OF MUNICIPAL CORPORATIONS IN KANSAS. By Nick N. K. Kittrie. Reprinted from *Kansas Law Review*, January 1953. Topeka, University of Kansas, Government Research Center, 1953. 21 pp.

Parking

CURB PARKING. Washington 6, D. C., Chamber of Commerce of the United States, Transportation and Communication Department, 1953. 16 pp. Illus.

CHICAGO'S NEW OFF-STREET PARKING AND LOADING ORDINANCE. By Evert Kincaid. Washington 6, D. C., Urban Land Institute, *Urban Land*, December 1953. 3 pp.

Personnel

CIVIL SERVICE ADMINISTRATION IN THE EMPIRE STATE. "According to Merit and Fitness." Albany, New York State Civil Service Commission, 1953. 28 pp. Illus.

GETTING DIVIDENDS FROM PERSONNEL ADMINISTRATION. By Wallace S. Sayre, Austin J. Tobin and James P. Mitchell. Chicago 37, Civil Service Assembly, 1953. 17 pp. $2.00.

GUIDE TO PERSONNEL ACTIVITIES OF PROFESSIONAL AND TECHNICAL ASSOCIATIONS. By Dorothy W. Otten. Chicago 37, Civil Service Assembly, 1953. 55 pp. $2.00.

Population

NUMBER OF INHABITANTS—U. S. SUMMARY. Totals for Regions, States, Cities, Metropolitan Areas. (Volume 1 of U. S. Census of Population: 1950.) By Bureau of the Census. Washington 25, D. C., Superintendent of Documents, U. S. Government Printing Office, 1952. 84 pp. 40 cents.

Ports

PORT OF MILWAUKEE. Chicago, *World Ports*, March 1953. 7 pp.

Public Administration

A SHORT INTERNATIONAL BIBLIOGRAPHY OF PUBLIC ADMINISTRATION. New York 27, Columbia University Press, 1953. 20 pp. 30 cents.

Public Health

STATE LAWS GOVERNING LOCAL HEALTH DEPARTMENTS. Washington 25, D. C., U. S. Department of Health, Education, and Welfare, Public Health Service, Bureau of State Services, Division of State Grants, 1953. iv, 68 pp. 40 cents.

Public Opinion

PUBLIC OPINION AND STRIKES. By Allan Weisenfeld. (Reprinted from *Labor Law Journal*, July 1953.) Chicago, Commerce Clearing House, 1953. 13 pp.

TO VOTE OR NOT TO VOTE? "What Are the Opinions of Young People Regarding the Extension of the Voting Privilege to 18, 19 and 20 Year Olds?" An Opinion Survey Conducted for the Common Council by the Mayor's Committee on Children and Youth. Detroit, Michigan, The Committee, 1952. 31 pp.

Taxation and Finance

COMPARATIVE COSTS OF STATE GOVERNMENTS, 1948-1951. By Robert F. Steadman. Lansing 13, Michigan Department of Administration, Office of the Controller, 1953. 5 pp.

THE MUNICIPAL INCOME TAX—A JANUS IN DISGUISE. By Robert A. Sigafoos. Sacramento 8 (California), National Tax Association, *National Tax Journal,* June 1953. 6 pp.

PROPERTY TAX TABULATIONS OF SELECTED CITIES. Manhattan (Kansas), Office of City Manager, 1954. 11 pp.

TOTAL GOVERNMENT EXPENDITURES IN 1952. Princeton (New Jersey), Tax Institute Inc., *Tax Policy,* October 1953. 8 pp. 25 cents.

Traffic

THESE TRAFFIC FACTORS ARE INVOLVED IN INTERSECTION DESIGN. By Fred W. Hurd. Saugatuck (Connecticut), Eno Foundation for Highway Traffic Control, Inc., *Traffic Quarterly,* July 1953. 14 pp.

TRAFFIC VIOLATIONS BUREAUS— NOTES, ORDINANCE AND RULE. Minneapolis 14, League of Minnesota Municipalities, Municipal Reference Bureau, Information Service, 1953. 17 pp.

Traffic Safety

OPERATION SAFETY. Program Kit on Traffic Safety Promotion. Theme for April 1954: CHILD PEDESTRIAN AND BICYCLE SAFETY. Chicago 11, National Safety Council, 1954. Variously paged.

Units of Government

MINOR CIVIL DIVISIONS AND PLACES OF THE UNITED STATES: 1950. Washington 25, D. C., U. S. Department of Commerce, Bureau of the Census, 1953. 4 pp.

FILIPINOS HOLD FREE ELECTION

(Continued from page 122)

public carriers. The substance of the articles was also disseminated by special features in the press. Volunteer help was relied upon for aiding at the headquarters, addressing envelopes and distributing literature. Coordinators were placed in charge of the different regions and, prior to the election, prepared provincial reports on those provinces where it appeared that election irregularities

were most likely to occur. These reports pointed out that both major parties had in the past committed election code violations. The findings were released to the press, submitted to the Commission on Elections and furnished guidance for watchers on election day.

While the elections were not entirely free from violence and fraud, in all but a few of the nation's 28,072 voting precincts conditions were calm and peaceful on election day and during the count that followed. Five persons were killed in Cavite and fatalities were reported in two or three other provinces. In 1949, 24 persons were killed on election day. Cavite has a reputation for violence that goes back for centuries. Incomplete demobilization of guerrillas after the war, unemployment and corruption have perpetuated this tradition.

Ballots were snatched by force in ten precincts in Pasay, a suburb of Manila. As soon as the Commission on Elections and the Philippine constabulary could act, this situation was brought under control. Nacionalista candidates and voters were intimidated by provincial and local officials in Ilocos Sur, President Quirino's home province. These and a few other incidents were localized.

Everywhere else the voting was free. The Filipinos demonstrated to the world that they could bring about a change in administration by the peaceful method of the ballot box in spite of the limitations of their communications system and the powers of the executive that might be used to thwart the will of the people.

?forzheimer Diamond Birthday

The 75th birthday of Carl H. Pforzeimer, for 32 years treasurer of the ational Municipal League, was observed on January 29 with many tributes to one of the League's most devoted long-time friends.

At a birthday party in Mr. Pforzeimer's New York home, Richard S. hilds, chairman of the League's Executive Committee, presented a folder containing letters om eight of the [ational Munici]al League's past nd present officers—Lawson Pury, George H. Galp, Murray Seangood, Harold '. Dodds, Henry ruère, Richard S. hilds, Charles Edon and Alfred 'illoughby.

The letters exessed apprecian of Mr. Pforzeimer's service to e League. The rty brought toether 300 friends nd associates of Mr. Pforzheimer. John Maloney, chairman of the Westchester County Council of Social Agencies, ıc., presented a "First Citizen of Westıester" tribute to Mr. Pforzheimer, who treasurer of the Westchester group. ıe citation honored Mr. Pforzheimer's ork on behalf of the Council. He was ıairman of the Commission on Govnment, 1934-36, which guided the delopment of the Westchester County ıarter.

Among many other tributes was a

Carl H. Pforzheimer

letter from Ralph Beals, director of the New York Public Library. Mr. Pforzheimer's rare book and manuscript collection is one of the significant libraries of English literature in private hands. His collection of Shelley's writings is second only to that in the British Museum.

John Brownlee, Metropolitan Opera baritone, sang at the party, which followed a reception at the Horace Mann School in Riverdale, the Bronx, two days before, at which Mr. Pforzheimer, chairman of the school's administrative board and board of trustees for 30 years, was presented with an honorary diploma. He also became an honorary member of the school's alumni association. A special birthday edition of the school paper, *The Horace Mann Record,* was issued.

Mr. Pforzheimer has been chairman of many League Committees, among them the Committee on Organized Citizens' Participation in City Government, the Committee on A Model Municipal Indebtedness Law, and the Committee on A Model Municipal Budget Law. He has been a member of the advisory committee, Consultant Service, as well as a member of the National Finance Committee and the Executive Committee.

New Publications Get

Three new League publications—*The Citizen Association* manuals and *A Model County and Municipal Bond Law* —have received favorable comment throughout the country from newspapers, magazines and national organization officers.

The *Citizen Association* manuals, published in November, were described by the *Philadelphia Evening Bulletin:* "Summing up the experience in many communities that have won notable civic victories, these two booklets should bring a wealth of helpful suggestions to groups struggling for better government."

The *Chicago Daily News* wrote: "The National Municipal League, which in its 60 years has participated in many successful fights against entrenched political machines, has performed a notable public service in the publication of two manuals for citizens who are interested in getting better local government. . . . More than 30 active citizen groups over the country contributed facts and ideas aimed at making the pamphlets practical and effective civic tools. Leaders of better government movements in every community can use these manuals with profit."

Samuel A. Wright, director, American Unitarian Youth, wrote: "The efforts of the National Municipal League for better government through these manuals should be one of the best contributions for citizens who ask, 'What can I do?' in these days of tension and frustration."

"The National Municipal League has made a real contribution to better municipal government with these publications," said the *Passaic (N.J.) Herald-News.*

The *Model County and Municipal*

Bebout Advises Erie Group

Assistant Director John E. Bebout participated in a recent meeting at Erie, Pennsylvania, which considered the problems involved in obtaining legislation which would permit Erie and other cities of the third class in the state to adopt the council - manager form of government.

John E. Bebout

Called by the Erie Junior Chamber of Commerce, the conference included two other outside consultants, from the Institute of Local Government at Penn State University and the Pennsylvania Chamber of Commerce.

The State Chamber of Commerce and other civic groups have for many years been trying to get such legislation. These attempts have been blocked, however, by officials of cities of the third class. Erie has been one of the more active leaders in the drive to obtain council-manager government.

Alaska Calling

Victor Fischer, executive secretary of the League of Alaskan Cities, will be the League's first Alaskan correspondent. Mr. Fischer recently informed Elsie S. Parker, assistant editor of the NATIONAL MUNICIPAL REVIEW, that he would submit news on nearly 30 cities in Alaska.

Mr. Fischer, who is also city planning director of Anchorage, paid a visit to the League offices last fall, during which he had extensive talks with all staff members. He was given pamphlets on council-manager government for use by Alaskan organizations.

Col. George H. McCaffrey Dies; Active in NML

Colonel George H. McCaffrey, a member of many League committees in the 20s and 30s, died in January. He was 63 years old and had served as a military government officer in Italy, Austria and Japan and later was assigned to the United Nations Civil Administration Commission for Korea.

Colonel McCaffrey, who lived in Montclair, New Jersey, was the first director of the Municipal Administration Service, which was operated in connection with the League's office for six and a half years.

George H. McCaffrey

Committees on which he served included the Committee on Metropolitan Government (1924), the Committee on Non-voting in Municipalities (1924), the Committee on Organized Citizens' Participation in City Government (1929), and the Proportional Representation Committee in the 1930s.

While Colonel McCaffrey was military governor of Palermo, a Sicilian province, a bridge was named Ponte Caffreo in his honor.

Colonel McCaffrey served at various times as military governor of five Italian and Sicilian provinces. In John Hersey's *A Bell for Adano*, a novel of the conflicts between a military government officer and a combat general, Colonel McCaffrey figured as Colonel Sartorious.

All-America Cities

(Continued from page 116)

groes in Shreveport to view the event as televised over Station KSLA.

Port Angeles, Washington, received its award from League Regional Vice President Ben Ehrlichman of Seattle at a ceremony in the high school gymnasium on February 4. Governor Arthur B. Langlie spoke. Radio station KONP broadcast the proceedings. After the presentation a large meeting for leaders of all civic organizations and out-of-town guests was held in the Lee Hotel.

Visiting mayors from sixteen surrounding cities and guests and officials of the San Francisco Bay area comprised an audience of over 600 on February 5 at the largest luncheon ever held in Richmond, California, to witness the presentation of the city's All-America Award. Carleton Tibbetts, regional vice president of the League, and Jack Sayre, of *Look*, made the presentation to Dana Murdock, chairman of the Citizens Committee, and Mayor Ed J. J. McKeegan in Richmond's Memorial Auditorium. Thousands of "All-America City" window stickers were distributed. A sixteen-foot button and ribbon were displayed on city hall announcing the award.

In De Soto, Missouri, Mrs. Virgil Loeb, League Council member from St. Louis, presented the Award to Mayor Vernon Young at a banquet on February 20. Main speaker was Powell B. Heney, president of the General America Insurance Company. Simultaneously, the Union Electric Company awarded a prize of $1,000 in recognition of the city's Planned Progress Program.

Stories describing citizen efforts which netted the awards for the eleven winners appeared in the February REVIEW.

The National Municipal Review

ALFRED WILLOUGHBY, Editor   ELSIE S. PARKER, Assistant Editor

Contributing Editors

JOHN E. BEBOUT, Research
RICHARD S. CHILDS
EDWARD W. WEIDNER, County and Township
H. M. OLMSTED, City, State and Nation

WADE S. SMITH, Taxation and Finance
GEORGE H. HALLETT, JR.
WM. REDIN WOODWARD
    Proportional Representation

State Correspondents

H. F. ALDERFER, *Pennsylvania*
CARTER W. ATKINS, *Connecticut*
MYRON H. ATKINSON, *North Dakota*
CHESTER BIESEN, *Washington*
D. BENTON BISER, *Maryland*
ERNEST M. BLACK, *Oklahoma*
JOHN C. BOLLENS, *California*
WILLIAM L. BRADSHAW, *Missouri*
A. C. BRECKENRIDGE, *Nebraska*
ARTHUR W. BROMAGE, *Michigan*
FRANKLIN L. BURDETTE, *Maryland*
CHARLTON F. CHUTE, *Pennsylvania*
WELDON COOPER, *Virginia*
C. A. CROSSER, *Washington*
PAUL DOLAN, *Delaware*
D. MACK EASTON, *Colorado*
WILLIAM O. FARBER, *South Dakota*
VICTOR FISCHER, *Alaska*
FOREST FRANK, *Ohio*
DAVID FUDGE, *Oklahoma*
ROBERT M. GOODRICH, *Rhode Island*
MRS. LEONARD HAAS, *Georgia*
M. H. HARRIS, *Utah*
SAM HAYS, *Arkansas*
ROBERT B. HIGHSAW, *Mississippi*
JACK E. HOLMES, *New Mexico*
ORREN C. HORMELL, *Maine*
HERMAN KEHRLI, *Oregon*
PAUL KELSO, *Arizona*

DRYDEN KUSER, *Nevada*
JOHN D. LANGMUIR, *New Hampshire*
STUART A. MacCORKLE, *Texas*
RICHARD G. MARDEN, *New Hampshire*
BOYD A. MARTIN, *Idaho*
EDWARD M. MARTIN, *Illinois*
JAMES W. MARTIN, *Kentucky*
JAMES W. McGREW, *New Jersey*
DAYTON D. McKEAN, *Colorado*
EDWIN B. McPHERON, *Indiana*
WILLIAM MILLER, *New Jersey*
LENNOX L. MOAK, *Pennsylvania*
ANDREW E. NUQUIST, *Vermont*
KIMBROUGH OWEN, *Louisiana*
FRANK W. PRESCOTT, *Tennessee*
JOHN E. REEVES, *Kentucky*
ROLAND R. RENNE, *Montana*
PAUL N. REYNOLDS, *Wisconsin*
RUSSELL M. ROSS, *Iowa*
ALBERT B. SAYE, *Georgia*
VICTORIA SCHUCK, *Massachusetts*
LLOYD M. SHORT, *Minnesota*
GEORGE G. SIPPRELL, *New York*
PAUL D. STEWART, *West Virginia*
JOHN G. STUTZ, *Kansas*
HERMAN H. TRACHSEL, *Wyoming*
PAUL W. WAGER, *North Carolina*
YORK WILLBERN, *Alabama*
JOHN F. WILLMOTT, *Florida*

Published by THE NATIONAL MUNICIPAL LEAGUE

George H. Gallup, *President*

John S. Linen, *Vice President*   Carl H. Pforzheimer, *Treasurer*
George S. Van Schaick, *Vice President*   Alfred Willoughby, *Executive Director*
Richard S. Childs, *Chairman, Executive Committee*

Council

Charles Edison, West Orange, N. J., *Chairman*

Frederick L. Bird, New York
Arthur W. Bromage, Ann Arbor, Mich.
E. Bartlett Brooks, Dayton, Ohio
Henry Bruère, New York
William H. Bulkeley, Hartford
L. E. Burch, Jr., Memphis
Mrs. Albert D. Cash, Cincinnati
Charles E. Commander, Jr., Jacksonville
L. P. Cookingham, Kansas City, Mo.
Karl Detzer, Leland, Mich.
E. D. Dodd, Toledo
Harold W. Dodds, Princeton, N. J.
Bayard H. Faulkner, Montclair, N. J.
Arnold Frye, New York

Ewart W. Goodwin, San Diego
Thomas Graham, Louisville
Mrs. Virgil Loeb, St. Louis
Rob Roy Macleod, Buffalo
Mark S. Matthews, Greenwich, Conn.
Cecil Morgan, New York
Albert E. Noelte, Central Falls, R. I.
Mrs. Maurice H. Noun, Des Moines
H. Bruce Palmer, Newark, N. J.
Lawson Purdy, New York
Thomas R. Reid, Dearborn, Mich.
Philip K. Robinson, Milwaukee
Murray Seasongood, Cincinnati
Lee M. Sharrar, Houston

Regional Vice Presidents

Lester L. Bates, Columbia, S. C.
William Collins, New York
Ben B. Ehrlichman, Seattle
John B. Gage, Kansas City, Mo.
Carl J. Gilbert, Boston
Barry Goldwater, Phoenix
Lloyd Hale, Minneapolis

Arthur E. Johnson, Denver
Mrs. Siegel W. Judd, Grand Rapids
John Nuveen, Chicago
Ed. P. Phillips, Richmond
Charles P. Taft, Cincinnati
Alex R. Thomas, San Antonio
Carleton B. Tibbetts, Los Angeles

NEWS for League Members

NBC to Dramatize Citizen Action

A series of radio broadcasts, dramatizing the stories of successful citizen action in American communities, will be presented Sunday afternoons beginning April 18 under the joint auspices of the National Municipal League and the National Broadcasting Company.

The half-hour shows will originate in New York and will be broadcast from 1 to 1:30 P.M., Eastern Standard Time. Most local stations will broadcast the program when received. Others will rebroadcast it at a later time.

Stories already chosen for dramatization by script writers include those of Daytona Beach, Florida; Scranton, Pennsylvania; Richmond, California; Brookfield, Illinois; Canton, Ohio; Kansas City, Missouri; and Columbia, South Carolina, all winners of the All-America Cities Awards given by the League and *Look* magazine, and Greenwich, Connecticut, which was a runner-up in the 1953 competition. Several other programs may be added.

The programs are under the direction of Wade Arnold, executive producer for the National Broadcasting Company.

The current broadcasts are the second instance of League joint action with NBC in producing civic education programs. In 1932 Dr. Thomas H. Reed, chairman of the League's Committee on Citizens' Councils for Constructive Economy, was chairman of many programs presented by the League in cooperation with the Committee on Civic Education by Radio of the National Advisory Council on Radio in Education and the American Political Science Association.

Twelve series of these weekly broadcasts, under the general title "You and Your Government," were produced on time donated by NBC from 1932 to 1936. Broadcasts in several series were presented in connection with the League's Pay-Your-Taxes Campaign. Among the topics covered in these series were "Planning," "Trends in Government," and "Taxation For Prosperity."

All twelve series were compiled and distributed in bound volumes, as well as more than 50,000 printed copies of the individual broadcasts. Many scripts were printed in the official publications of other national organizations, and much of the material was used for re-broadcast purposes. In 1935 the "You and Your Government" radio programs received the award of the Women's National Radio Committee for the best non-commercial and non-musical program.

Goodwin Leads San Diego Conference

Ewart W. Goodwin

Ewart Goodwin, League Council member and president of the Percy H. Goodwin Company, was chairman of a discussion entitled "The Urban Problem" at the Fifth National Businessmen's Conference on Urban Problems, March 4, in San Diego, California.

The two-day conference, sponsored by the Chamber of Commerce of the United States, had as its theme: "A Brighter Future for America's Cities."

Bankers Briefed on Model Bond Law

The League's new *Model County and Municipal Bond Law*, which had an enthusiastic reception in financial and legal publications at the turn of the year, was the subject of the February 25 meeting of the Municipal Forum of New York.

Dr. Frederick L. Bird, League Council member and director of municipal research, Dun and Bradstreet, Inc., and John S. Linen, vice president of the League and of the Chase National Bank, were the main speakers at the forum's luncheon meeting held at the Lawyers Club. Topic of the session was "Better Laws Make Better Bonds."

Both Dr. Bird and Mr. Linen are members of the League's Committee on a Program of Model Fiscal Legislation for Local Governments.

Dr. Bird, who wrote the introduction for the law, discussed the objectives and philosophy behind the model and the League's entire program. Mr. Linen spoke on those aspects which are of special concern to investment houses bidding on bond issues.

Staff Members Attend ASPA Conference

Three League staff members attended the annual conference of the American Society for Public Administration in Chicago, March 19-21. In addition to attending meetings League representatives met with the Committee on the National Municipal League Staff Fellowship to consider applicants for the fellowship for the 1954-55 period.

Participating from the League were Alfred Willoughby, executive director; John Bebout, assistant director, and William N. Cassella, Jr., NML staff fellow for 1953-54.

The NML Staff Fellowship Committee

Conference Plans Progress In Kansas City

Plans for the 60th National Conference on Government moved forward with the visit of Allen H. Seed, Jr., assistant director, to Kansas City, March 21-24.

Allen H. Seed, Jr.

Mr. Seed conferred with local civic leaders concerning preliminary arrangements for the Conference, which will be held November 7-10. He also addressed a meeting of the board of directors of the Kansas City Citizens Association. Representatives of cooperating organizations attended.

The Hotel President has been designated Conference headquarters. John B. Gage, League regional vice president and former mayor of Kansas City, will be chairman of the local arrangements committee. Clinton W. Kanaga, Jr., president of the Citizens Association, will be vice chairman.

consists of Roscoe C. Martin, chairman of the Department of Political Science, Syracuse University, chairman; Winston W. Crouch, director, Bureau of Governmental Research, University of California at Los Angeles; Lee S. Greene, director, Bureau of Public Administration, University of Tennessee; Joseph E. McLean, Woodrow Wilson School, Princeton University; Edwin O. Stene, University of Kansas, and Edward W. Weidner, director, Governmental Research Bureau, Michigan State College.

National Municipal Review

Volume XLIII, No. 4   Total Number 442

Published monthly except August

By NATIONAL MUNICIPAL LEAGUE

Contents for April 1954

The contents of the Review are indexed in *International Index to Periodicals* and *Public Affairs Information Service*.

Entered as second class matter July 11, 1932, at the Post Office at Worcester, Massachusetts. Publication office, 150 Fremont Street, Worcester 3; editorial and business office, 299 Broadway, New York 7. Copyright 1954 by the National Municipal League.

Subscription, $5 per year; Canadian, $5.25; foreign, $5.50; single copies 50 cents.

Editorial Comment

Distance Makes for Inertia

PERHAPS a new law of political physics should be written. It would read something like this: the interest of a given voter is aroused in inverse proportion to his distance from the elective office. The closer he is, the greater his indifference; the more removed, the greater his use of the ballot.

If such a law has not been formulated, there are good grounds for its existence on the basis of three special elections for assemblymen conducted recently in the city of New York.

In the fourteenth Manhattan Assembly District, 2,810 votes were cast where, during the 1952 presidential election, 22,569 people voted for presidential electors and assemblyman; 90 per cent unquestioningly accepted the choice of the party. Another way of looking at it —90 per cent of the citizens elected not to choose their own representative. In the fifth Kings County Assembly District, 4,164 voted this year, 32,580 two years ago. In the nineteenth Kings A.D. 67,943 voted in 1952—but this year under 5,000 figured it was worth the effort.

Light voting means lightly considered responsibilities. Inertia at the polls makes no community—whether it be a city, county, state or nation —a better place in which to live.

Great strides have been made in improving municipal and federal government, but what of the states? If the states are to be given some of the responsibilities now borne by the federal government, it is vital that citizens increase their interest in state affairs—in direct, rather than inverse, proportion to their distance from the state capital.

No Place Here for Corruption

WHAT are you doing about graft and corruption in your South Oakland County area?" several out-of-state newspapermen asked me.

They had been describing how their newspapers are trying to clean up graft-ridden police departments and city governments in vice-rotten "wide-open" towns. The occasion was an exchange of newspapermen's experiences at the American Press Institute Seminar, Columbia University, New York City.

"We just don't have that problem in South Oakland County," I declared flatly.

"That's a pretty broad statement," one of them challenged.

"I don't mean that South Oakland County doesn't have crime—and too much of it. We have murders, robberies, burglaries, book-making and vandalism. But these crimes are individual acts, not part of an organized vice or crime network and not covered by 'protection' from lax or corrupt police departments or city governments," I told them.

"Your area is unusually fortunate," these other newspapermen stated—and they wondered why.

"It's because of the people themselves and the way in which they

172

have set up their local governments. The citizens of each community," I explained, "are very much interested in their own community and in their local government. They take an active part in community affairs and a keen interest in the way in which their city is governed. They are willing to render all sorts of service to their community without the thought of what they can get out of it. They will not stand for anything which is not honest and aboveboard.

"Since ours are all relatively new communities, the people have had a chance to put in the type of government which they, through careful study, have thought to be the most advantageous.

"In the case of each city, this has turned out to be the city manager-council type of government.

"The mayor and council are elected directly by the voters and are responsible to them. They form the 'board of directors.' The actual administration of city affairs is done by the city manager, who is a professional and career man. He keeps his job only when he sees that the city gives the best type of service and protection to its citizens. This system provides a series of checks and balances which makes it pretty hard for any group to seize control of the city government and to riddle it with graft and corruption.

"Perhaps," I told them, "the fact that the nearby city of Detroit is relatively free of organized crime has helped us considerably. It's pretty hard to live next door to a corrupt city and not have some of the evils creep into your community.

"One evidence of the people's interest in keeping their community clean has been the interest and action taken in the elimination of crime-comic books from our communities. It was only necessary for us to point out and emphasize the dangers of this type of literature. The people, in all sorts of community groups and through their local governments, have taken definite steps to rid this area of this undesirable element.

"If the people ever go to sleep on the job and lose their interest in local affairs, things could change. But as long as the citizens in each community are interested in and active in community affairs and local government, the chances are pretty good that we can preserve clean, corruption-free communities."

PHILIP F. MILLER, *Vice President*
The Daily Tribune

Reprinted with permission from *The Daily Tribune*, Royal Oak, Michigan, February 17, 1954.

Broader Inquiry Advocated

Current intergovernmental relations studies inadequate to solve overlapping; states blamed for big government.

By CHARLES S. RHYNE*

TWO NEW federal commissions have just launched investigations which could lead to far-reaching changes in federal, state and local relationships. These are the Commission on Organization of the Executive Branch of the Government (Hoover Commission No. II) and the Commission on Intergovernmental Relations. The Hoover commission is to whittle down the size of the federal government by recommending elimination of functions found to be unnecessary and by devising means for increasing the efficiency of other functions. The intergovernmental commission is to study the grants-in-aid programs involving federal funds for state and local governments. This then is a most appropriate time to take a look at this important field.

Some authorities estimate that today we have approximately 175,000 separate legal entities or units of government in the United States. These range downward from the federal government to the states, territories, counties, cities, towns, boroughs, parishes, townships, special districts, commissions, boards and authorities of many kinds. The relationships embraced in so many units of government are practically unending in number, complexity and

*Mr. Rhyne, member of the Washington, D. C., Bar, is general counsel of the National Institute of Municipal Law Officials. This article is reprinted, in part, from *The Daily Bond Buyer* (New York) for December 14, 1953.

variety. Each governmental unit acts and reacts upon the other for no government can operate in a vacuum.

The vast increase in intergovernmental relationships is an increase which has flowed directly from the basic demands of an expanding nation. When this nation came into being the pattern of intergovernmental relationships was a comparatively simple one. In the eighteenth and nineteenth centuries there was little need for extensive contact between levels of government.

To assess the problems created by this increase in intergovernmental relations it seems well to state the major problems which exist at each level of government and then to relate these problems to the entire field of intergovernmental relations.

The Federal Government

As for the federal government, the problem is one of "bigness" and what to do about it, with its accompanying load of burdensome taxation which funnels one out of every four dollars earned into the national treasury. From 592,000 employees in 1932 the federal government has grown to 2,666,000 employees; from a total budget of $4,700,000,000 in 1932 to a total budget of about $72,000,000,000 in 1953; from a total of $1,889,000,000 in tax collections in 1932 to more than $65,-000,000,000 in 1952.

With the expansion in forms of

business organization in this country and improvements in our systems of communication and transportation, "bigness" in commerce and industry made "bigness" in our national government inevitable. You cannot set up great corporate powers that reach out into each of the 48 states and into foreign countries without setting up great power in government to insure fair play and to protect against the hazards of our economic system. You cannot via air transportation shrink nations to neighborhoods and via radio and television provide still another means of lessening vast distances without having a government which, to be effective, must be equal in size to the problem with which it is dealing.

The problem is one of elimination of unnecessary functions, a shrinking of personnel and budget to fit present needs, a more businesslike performance of functions and a giving up of functions, powers and sources of revenue so as to allow the states and cities to perform services they are best able to perform. Federal functions and services now number in the thousands. Inability or unwillingness of the states to face up to the needs of our people under modern conditions has chiefly caused this great growth in the federal government.

State Government

States dragged their feet for years as the federal government grew into a giant in comparison. State governments are for the most part dominated by rural interests and these interests have stubbornly refused to recognize the urbanization of our nation. Antiquated state constitutions which give this unfair control to rural minorities have acted as a brake on state leaders who recognized the needs of urban areas. Since Congress and the federal administration are responsive to majority control, it was a natural development that the people went to those who could and would help solve the problems of our modern society. And the fact that through local government lies the quickest and surest approach to the people has not been overlooked by federal officials interested in electoral votes.

Modern economic and other problems now overflow local and state lines. And the only place a solution can be found is often in federal action. Also, modern money needs are often so large, as in the case of the depression during the 30s, that only the federal government has the fiscal resources to meet the requirements of such needs.

The states now seem to have decided that if they are not to become mere conduits between the federal and local governments they must exercise their governmental authority and act to meet modern problems on a state level. Undoubtedly many of these problems can best be solved there. But to do so states must allow reapportionment of their legislatures so as to give city residents and rural residents representation based upon principles of equality. Minority control must end or the states will never grow up to do the job they must do if their importance in our governmental system is not to continue to dwindle and fade.

The chief development in state government has been the rise of determination by the states to prove that they can meet the challenge of current-day problems. By adoption of facilitating legislation the federal programs covering many fields, such as housing, banking, deposit insurance, social security and civilian defense, have been implemented. State commissions on interstate cooperation and interstate compacts have done much to solve metropolitan area and other problems on a state level and thus avoid federal action. Uniform laws have done much to standardize and improve state government in many fields.

Thus one finds the major problems in the states arise from antiquated constitutions, statutes and governmental organization directed toward assurance of rural control. Modernization of state government machinery and thinking to meet current needs is vitally needed. Denial of "home rule" to cities, refusal to share taxes contributed by city residents with city governments, and failure to give city residents equal representation in state legislatures with rural residents, create the major problems here.

County Government

There are a few who contend that our 3,000 county governments have outlived their usefulness and should be abolished. On the other extreme one finds advocates of solving our problems of overlapping jurisdictions of local governments by abolishing all local units of government except counties. In between are the arguments of those who say that certain functions should be taken over by the states and that others should be handled on a metropolitan area basis by consolidation of certain functions under a regional or other metropolitan authority.

A sharpening of the tools of county government to meet the needs of modern urban society today, rather than the throwing of those time-tested tools into the waste can, could solve the problem here. We should find out what county government can do best and give it the powers and funds to perform those functions. Home rule, police powers and funds to pay for essential services have done wonders in some counties—note the experience in Montgomery County, Maryland, for example.

On county consolidation one hears reports of real success as, for example, the case of Georgia's Fulton County (Atlanta) absorbing Milton and Campbell. Denver, San Francisco and Baton Rouge are examples of city-county consolidations which are working well. Undoubtedly in spite of strong opposition there will be further consolidations. Some counties and cities are so small in area, or so weak in financial status, as to warrant such action for the good of their inhabitants.

As steps toward consolidation one finds a combination of health, police and other public services in some metropolitan areas whose economic, health and other problems overlap innumerable units of local government. Notable progress has been made in the Louisville, Philadelphia and other areas in this field. But the caution with which progress has been made in consolidating counties, or in consolidating cities and counties, indicates how jealous our people are of their local government and its functions.

City Government

In city government one finds the chief problems arise from inability to finance adequately many of the modern-day services which their residents now demand. Denial of "home rule" and state usurpation of local powers and sources of revenue leave cities legally and financially incapable of proper solutions to many pressing problems. Few cities are coterminous with the metropolitan area of which they are a part, so many have so-called "fringe" area problems. Often residents of adjacent areas enjoy city services but pay none of the costs. Here, too, one finds many of the same arguments and suggestions which have been directed against counties applied to cities, often coupled with attacks upon the antiquated and inadequate legal powers most cities have with which to cope with modern problems.

The trend toward urbanization in our nation has been great. And the pronounced movement of recent years toward the suburbs has not been enough in volume to affect the over-all problems resulting from this urbanization. It has been said that in 1790 our first census found our people 80 per cent rural and 20 per cent urban, but that the 1950 census found almost the reverse. Cities today are not only gigantic in size, but the ever increasing services they operate, from airports to housing, garbage, sewage, water and transportatiou, are tremendous in scope and variety.

Since the chief problem of cities is money with which to pay for essential services it was only natural that they looked for that money in Washington when the states failed to meet their needs. But any real assessment of the problems of cities today will blame their major problems not upon a slackening of that aid but upon continued failure of the states to give cities essential powers, and failure of the states to share with cities the taxes the states have collected from city residents. Some state governments boast of their surpluses, while their cities are near bankruptcy.

While many illustrations exist as to the causes of specific city fiscal woes, let us examine the gasoline tax situation, and the admitted inability of many cities to finance essential street improvements. Here it is admitted that most of these taxes are paid by city residents. But this tax money is spent chiefly on rural roads. "State maintenance ends here" is still a familiar sign at the corporate limits of many cities. State highway departments are still political vehicles in some states and quite naturally favor the rural areas as there lies political control of the state governmental machinery.

Thus, one finds that lack of "home rule" and lack of equal representation with that of rural residents in state legislatures are in fact the causes of most of the major city problems today.

Federal-state Relations

Perhaps any consideration of federal-state relations should logically begin with federal grants-in-aid. While the states created the federal government and have an inter-relationship so vast as to almost defy adequate description in the fields of regulation, law enforcement, etc., such grants have become one of the most important aspects of government finance in our country and are a good starting point because of the current inquiry now being undertaken by the Commission on Intergovernmental Relations.

Prior to 1932 federal grants-in-aid were made to the states in the amount of about $100,000,000, of which $80,000,000 was for highways. The other $20,000,000 was for agricultural colleges, experimental stations in the agricultural field, forest fire protection and public health. Contrast this with the growth almost yearly since then of federal grants-in-aid programs until an estimated $2,294,000,000 was available this year in some 40 such programs—and that sum is much smaller than the amount available in past years.

Range of Studies

The Commission on Intergovernmental Relations is to study and investigate the following: The present activities in which federal aid is extended to state and local governments; the inter-relationships of financing this aid; the sources of financing governmental programs; whether justification exists for federal aid in the various fields in which such aid is extended; whether federal control with respect to these activities should be limited and, if so, to what extent; whether there are other fields in which such aid should be extended; whether federal aid should be limited to cases of need; and all other matters incidental to such federal aid, including the ability of the federal government and the states and local governments to finance governmental activities. Out of this study may come far-reaching rearrangement of functions and programs in the fields in which federal aid is, or was, or should be, a dominant factor.

The Hoover commission will recommend elimination of federal services and functions which it believes states and cities can best perform. Already many utility interests have released propaganda evidently aimed at convincing this commission that certain federal regulatory powers over specific utilities should be given over to the states. In nearly every instance the reason for the adoption of federal regulatory statutes was inability of the states to control these utilities. The natural gas industry is a good example. There the constitutional inability of the states to control interstate rates caused adoption of a federal regulatory act. Now the natural gas interests want certain federal regulations scuttled, knowing full well that the states cannot step into the regulatory void thus created.

The elimination of unnecessary federal functions is a desirable thing, but such elimination where state and local governments are powerless to protect the public could be disastrous.

Unfortunately, the powers of the Hoover commission do not seem to reach over into the fields where increased federal-state cooperation could be helpful. And in some instances it would be in the public interest to increase federal-state relations.

One must conclude that the Hoover and intergovernmental commissions will take only small bites at the overall picture in the field of federal-state relations. Neither commission is authorized to evaluate the whole field of government in our nation and recommend a comprehensive program looking toward the performance by each level of government of the powers and functions it can best perform in our modern society.

Federal-local Relations

Beginning in 1932 with the emergency relief loans, one finds in federal statutes, regulations and orders a gradual increase in this relationship until today it exists in some 40 federal grants-in-aid programs for purposes ranging from aid to dependent children and airports to water pollution control. In addition there are more than a hundred services available to aid local governments on subjects ranging from specifications for abattoirs (prepared by the Department of Agriculture) down the alphabet to a zoning ordinance (prepared by the Department of Commerce).

It is certainly true that from the first mention of local government in federal legislation in 1932, in the emergency relief act of that year, direct relationships between federal and local government have increased tremendously. And, as already stated, it is generally conceded that these direct federal-local relations were a natural development from the failure of state governments to meet the problems of our times.

If the intergovernmental commission recommends that certain grants-in-aid programs be abandoned the effect on local government should not be ignored. For any abandonment of federal aid must be accompanied by a corresponding relinquishment of tax sources now preempted by Congress, and relinquishment in such a way that the tax sources can be reached by local government. If experience is any guide it will take years of effort for local government to wrest any new revenues, or new revenue sources, from the states, or to secure state grants-in-aid to replace those abandoned by the federal government.

The whole story of federal-local relationships is not secured by an examination of the federal grants-in-aid programs. Cities appear constantly before such agencies as the Federal Power Commission, seeking fair treatment of their residents on natural gas and electrical rate matters, before the Federal Communications Commission on telephone rates, radio and television matters and before innumerable other agencies on hundreds of subjects. Here again there are fields where more federal-local cooperation would be fruitful. One example is in the field of enforcing regulations prohibiting interference with radio and television reception.

And it must not be forgotten that since the chief problem of cities is that of finding the money with which to finance essential local services, the fact that the federal government siphons off the chief tax resources of each city may not be overlooked. It has been pointed out, for example, that residents of Kansas City, Missouri, pay $250,000,000 in federal income taxes alone but only $27,000,-000 to the city for all local services.

In carrying out the laudable goal of restoring a balance to the relationships between federal, state and local governments by whittling down federal bureaucracy and lessening centralized government, it is therefore submitted that the meat-ax approach cannot be used. There is a danger that the shifting of responsibility without an adequate and timely redistribution of functions and areas of potential revenue may do serious damage to essential governmental services. The Hoover and intergovernmental commissions are delving into highly complex, intricate and, in some respects, sharply controversial fields with respect to activities, sources of revenue and countless other factors and actions which have confused the basic and constitutional relationship of our triple-layer form of government. These commissions have important, pressing and gigantic tasks. It is to be hoped that in their desire to cut down the size and functions of the federal government—a goal which all applaud—they will not ignore the effect on local government. And their evaluation of this effect should take into consideration the relative inability of local government in most states to secure fair treatment from state legislatures.

State-local Relationships

The fortunes of local government are inextricably entwined with those of the state. State action or inaction can mean success or failure for local government in many ways. Over and over again it has been emphasized that disuse of powers by the states forced federal action to meet social and economic problems of the past twenty years—even forcing the federal government to go beyond what many of us would conceive as national areas of concern. That inaction by the states on these problems forced action on a national level can hardly be disputed. Where the problems were too great for local solution and the states did not act, the federal government was the only instrumentality available to act. At times local government had to go directly to the federal government because it was upon the city and county officials that the demands of the people were made. These local officials are easiest for the people to reach and the first to realize local needs.

And the states are awakening to the fact that they cannot continue to roll up surpluses (as some have) while their local governments are poverty stricken. We find today on the state level a tremendous increase in so-called "shared taxes." A total of $4,702,000,000 was returned to local government by the states last year. State governments have been driven by the demands of local officials—chiefly by the excellent and ever growing state leagues of cities —to a realization of the fact that they must utilize their more facile powers of taxation to raise revenues and funnel those revenues back to local government if the needs of their people in the world of today are to be met. The only trouble is that in many states the idea of "shared taxes" has not been accepted to any appreciable extent.

"Home rule" for local government is the most needed development in the field of local-state relationships. State officials who cry out against centralization in Washington when they are centralizing everything in their state under themselves are inconsistent to say the least. The principles apply equally in each case. Centralization of government is fatal to personal liberty. And democracy cannot be imposed from the top—it must well up from the bottom.

Existing home rule clauses in constitutions have been weak barriers against the state's inroads on local rights. Constant attempts to emancipate local government from state control have often been scuttled by the courts. A model "home rule" constitutional provision which cannot be destroyed by any process of erosion is one of the great needs in this field. The recent draft prepared by Dean Jefferson B. Fordham, of the University of Pennsylvania Law School, for the American Municipal Association offers an answer.[1]

Perhaps the most fundamental reason for inequity in treatment of local government is found in the disproportionate representation of urban and rural elements in our state legislatures. A great step forward would be taken if this inequity and one-sidedness in representation were corrected. Local autonomy will remain only a dream for most local governments so long as this situation stands as it is now (in most states).

Our big problem today is to de-

velop a map for the road ahead for government on each level.

Government is as old as people. But the machinery of government has not kept pace with the people it serves. The last twenty years have been a period of swiftly changing emphasis in the apportionment of authority among the different levels of government. The development has been haphazard—often from one emergency to the next. No clear line of policy has emerged with respect to the distribution of authority.

What we need to bring order out of the maze of overlapping and conflicting intergovernmental relationships is a study of our whole governmental structure, a study not limited to the federal government, as is the Hoover commission, or to federal aid programs, as is the intergovernmental relations commission.

It has been truly said, "Where there is no vision, the people perish." This proposal is one for the development of an informed vision on this business of government in our nation. Tremendous changes are taking place. No one knows more than a small part of what is happening in government along a dozen fronts. Present efforts are being made by the slow and expensive methods of trial and error. Important consequences are incidental and even accidental. There is no plan. And there should be one to guide the course of events in the whole field of intergovernmental relations in the future.

But before any plan can be made we must secure much more basic information than we have now. Hence, the proposal for this over-all study of government in the United States.

[1] *Model Constitutional Provisions for Municipal Home Rule.* Washington, D. C., 1953.

Indiana Still Seeks Home Rule

Constitutional amendment, adopted by 1953 legislature, must be passed again in 1955 and submitted to voters.

By CARL L. HEYERDAHL*

THE INDIANA legislature has taken an initial step toward giving home rule powers to the state's cities and towns. At present local governments are permitted no choice in the form of government they may have. They derive all their powers from state laws which specify the form of government for the several types of local political subdivisions. Counties must operate under boards of county commissioners, townships and towns under a trustee system and cities are limited to the mayor-council form of government. These laws also provide in detail for the powers and duties of local public officials.

Local units must take many issues which concern them alone to the General Assembly for legislative action. It goes without saying that time spent by legislators over local questions cannot be devoted to issues of statewide importance. Furthermore, if a problem demanding attention arises shortly after the end of a legislative session, the community must wait nearly two years to get the necessary authority to deal with it.

The arguments advanced in other states for home rule apply equally to Indiana. In the first place, home rule would introduce the generally accepted principle of self-determination. Cities differ in many ways. They vary in size of population and area, in their need for governmental services, in their local customs and traditions and in their interests. A charter suitable for a large city is not feasible for a small one. Cities located on rivers may have problems of flood control while others may be suffering from water shortages. Problems relating to schools, recreation, traffic, crime, sanitation and others vary from city to city. It seems a reasonable argument that the residents of a community have the greatest interest and are best equipped to solve their special local problems and thus satisfy their local needs and desires.

In the second place, home rule applies the federal principle to state government. Since this principle has worked advantageously in many respects on a national scale, why not also on a state basis? Various experiments in local government would then be possible. And if constitutional home rule were established it would militate against too much centralization of power in the state government. It should also increase popular interest and participation in governmental affairs.

In the third place, home rule would give the legislature more time for matters of statewide importance. This is especially true in Indiana where biennial sessions are limited to a period of 61 days.

*Professor Heyerdahl, who teaches courses in state and local government and constitutional law at Purdue University, is author (with Robert Phillips) of a case book in constitutional law, *Decisions of the Supreme Court*, as well as numerous articles in his field.

An analysis of the work of the 1953 General Assembly well demonstrates the importance of this third argument for home rule. A total of 874 bills was introduced in the two houses of the legislature. Of these bills, 297 passed both houses, 577 failed and 14 were vetoed by the governor and not repassed by the legislature. Thus, 283 laws were enacted.

While in some laws it is difficult to draw the line exactly between what is state and what is local, an analysis of the 1953 acts indicates that 161 deal with state affairs or matters of statewide concern and 122 relate to local matters pertaining to counties, cities, towns, townships and schools, including many which are the equivalent of special laws for particular localities only.

Legislature in Local Affairs

A number of examples can be found to point up the loss of precious time to the legislature. Required under the present arrangement to act as a super-board of county commissioners, the General Assembly authorized counties to establish and operate dumps; authorized them to require licensing of all horse-drawn vehicles, except agricultural implements, at an annual fee of one dollar; permitted the coroner of St. Joseph County to hire deputies, investigators and office employees; empowered county surveyors to order repair, cleaning or spraying of any public drain or ditch and to assess the land owners benefiting therefrom; authorized county councils to appropriate money from general funds to reimburse county treasurers for money lost as the result of burglaries;

allowed county commissioners of any county to contribute up to $500 to join with a city in construction of a dog pound; authorized county plan commissions or county commissioners to erect signs showing numbers of county roads and to prepare maps or charts designating county roads.

Forced to act as a super-city council the legislature passed laws permitting city clerk–treasurers in cities of the fourth and fifth classes to be paid extra for keeping records of parking meter collections; granted the Evansville city council and school board permission to raise the appropriation for the city's public museum; allowed the city of Hammond to establish a cumulative sinking fund to pay for its portion of grade separation or alteration costs; reduced from 2,000 to 1,500 the population necessary for a town to become a fifth class city (this was primarily to permit Butler to become a city); allowed slum clearance in cities through the creation of a redevelopment commission similar to the one already existing in Indianapolis; and increased Indianapolis police pensions to make them equal to firemen's pensions.

Obligated to act as a super-township trustee or super-town board, the General Assembly permitted such local officials to have Canadian thistles destroyed and to charge ten dollars a day plus expenses if the owner of the land failed to destroy them; granted township trustees power to buy real estate for cemetery use and to raise the amount of the perpetual care fund to maintain such cemeteries (town boards were given similar powers); established a salary range of $1,200 to $3,600 per annum for the justice of the peace of Center Township, Howard County, and a salary range of $800 to $2,400 for the constable of the same township; increased the salary of the justice of the peace of Center Township, Delaware County, and raised his allowance for supplies; and increased from eight feet to eight feet, six inches, the width allowed for buses operated in cities and towns or counties of more than 160,000 population.

Is it not obvious that a county is capable of deciding whether or not to establish and operate a dump or to join with a city to construct a dog-pound? Cannot a fifth-class city itself determine whether to pay an official extra for keeping additional records? Surely a township is able to deal with the problem of removing thistles. It should not be necessary to burden the state legislature with questions of such strictly local concern. A session of 61 days is brief enough to deal with matters of state-wide interest.

Home Rule Law

The movement to secure some form of home rule in Indiana is not a recent development. In 1921 advocates of the council-manager form of government were successful in getting the General Assembly to enact a law permitting cities to adopt this type of government. Michigan City adopted it and operated under the plan until 1929. Evansville and Indianapolis were in the process of selecting this type of government when the law was challenged in the courts. A case from Evansville questioned the procedure for calling an election in that city to decide the question of adopting a manager form of government. The court early in 1929 held the law valid.

Later, in the same year, another attack was made on the law, this time from Indianapolis, and in this case the law was declared invalid by a divided court. The issue involved was the procedure used in calling the election to determine whether Indianapolis should adopt a council-manager form of government. The city clerk was authorized to check the petition of those asking an election to see whether the signers were duly qualified electors. He was given only five days for this examination and the court held that the clerk could not check 19,000 signatures in so short a period. This impossibility of checking 19,000 names in five days made the law special in form in the eyes of the court and therefore unconstitutional.

Ten years later, primarily in response to pressure from the Junior Chamber of Commerce and the League of Women Voters, the General Assembly passed a resolution setting up a City Manager Study Commission. The commission, composed of seven members, was duly organized and held ten meetings, one of them an open meeting at which individuals and representatives of organized groups appeared to present their views. After examining the plans of other states the commission recommended adoption of a constitutional amendment providing for home rule rather than the enactment of a new law which would have to be carefully framed to meet the objections of the State Supreme Court. The text of the amendment submitted by the commission, much short-ened in form, was passed by the 1941 General Assembly. But in Indiana amendments to the constitution must be passed by two successive legis-latures and, in 1943, the foes of home rule succeeded in defeating the second passage of the proposal.

The issue was not pressed during the war years but in 1949 the original amendment drafted by the 1939 study commission was introduced into the General Assembly. It was referred to a committee and not reported on until the last three days of the session, which proved too late to get action.

In 1951 nothing further could be done by the legislature since other amendments were pending, and in Indiana no new amendments may be introduced while others are awaiting second passage.

Legislature Acts

But an indication that legislative thinking may be inclining to a more favorable attitude toward home rule is evidenced by the action of the 1953 General Assembly, which passed and referred to the 1955 legis-lature a joint resolution incorporat-ing, verbatim, the home rule consti-tutional amendment proposed by the 1939 City Manager Study Commis-sion. This amendment would permit cities and towns to choose their own form of local government by holding charter conventions to draft and adopt charters. To preserve the principle of popular government the amendment requires that the voters must decide the question of holding a charter convention, select the mem-bers thereof and approve the charter

after it is prepared by the conven-tion.

Provision is also made for local amending of the charter, once it is formulated and adopted. The amend-ment lists five groups of powers which may be exercised by cities and towns subject only to the restrictions im-posed by the constitutions of Indi-ana and the United States. These powers authorize any city or town to prescribe its form of government, to exercise control over its personnel, to determine the organizational setup by which to carry out its municipal functions, to determine its own rules relative to selection, term, compen-sation, hours of work, and dismissal of officials and employees, and to provide for recall of elective officials.

Unlike home rule amendments in a number of states, the proposed amendment does not permit a city or town to determine which functions of local self-government it cares to exercise. The determination of these functions still remains with the Gen-eral Assembly. In addition, the amendment does not extend to all units of local government—it does not apply to counties or townships. It will not relieve the legislature from dealing with all local problems. It is a long way from complete home rule.

But it is a step in the right direc-tion and it is to be hoped that the proposed amendment will be agreed to by the 1955 General Assembly and approved by the voters at the general election in 1956.

Most recent development in the problem was the appointment by Governor Craig in December 1953 of a commission of 21 members,

(Continued on page 207)

Pre-primary Trial Dropped

Nebraska's nominating experiment, designed to foster party responsibility, has been repealed after ten years.

By ADAM CARLYLE BRECKENRIDGE*

NEBRASKA'S pre-primary convention statute, which its supporters had hoped would combine some of the better features of the old nominating convention with the more democratic features of the direct primary, was repealed by the legislature last year.

What this statute actually did during its short life—enacted in 1943 and effective for the elections of 1946, 1948, 1950 and 1952—was to take control over nominations a step away from the voters and make it difficult for any candidate who could not get a party endorsement to get the party nomination. As its supporters hoped, it appears that this feature did produce a greater measure of party discipline and responsibility for making nominations. It did so without supplanting final control by the rank and file of the voters. There is some evidence, however, that it may have made some contribution to party disunity.

Thus, after a brief experiment, Nebraska found the cure for the uncertainties of the direct primary more unpalatable than the disease.

From the beginning there has been a struggle to make our political institutions as truly representative as possible. Effort has centered upon making these institutions more re-

sponsible to the people. The search to improve election machinery has centered often upon solutions to some of the abuses of the political party caucus. From this has come the direct primary, the presumed ultimate at the time it swept the country.

The political party convention was a natural outgrowth of the caucus, but it failed, as did its predecessor, in the task of designating candidates for ultimate voter selection. It, too, was run by the masters of the political arts, or at least near masters, most of the time. Frequently these individuals were unscrupulous and turned their position of control over the party machinery to their own advantage. Some of these abuses were brought into check during the latter part of the nineteenth century. The major shortcomings of the caucus, convention and indirect primary were routed for a time by the direct primary. Here, it was claimed, was a system wherein the voters, as party members, would make the selections for and in the name of the party. The powers of the party leaders who dominated the c o n v e n t i o n s were presumably doomed.

But the direct primary did not succeed in erasing all the objections of the caucus or convention. The hope was that men with qualities of leadership, high purpose and integrity, men whose interest was the public interest, would be selected, *i.e.,* nominated. Critics of the direct

*Dr. Breckenridge is associate professor of political science and chairman of the Department of Political Science at the University of Nebraska. He has been with the university since 1946.

186

primary believed that inferior candidates would be selected and, indeed, there is no conclusive evidence that these critics were entirely wrong.

The chief complaint against the direct primary was that it would destroy party responsibility or that, under the most favorable conditions, responsibility would be weakened. If party responsibility was broken, the people would not be able to select between or among political parties or place properly responsibility for the actions of the officials so elected who wore the party label. Why? Because the primary permitted anyone meeting the most limited requirements to be put on the party ballot as its nominee. The party leaders and spokesmen for the "organization" of the party, those with the feel of the party pulse, would not have any great influence over the nominee or his decisions. Or, at best, their influence might be strictly limited. So, how could the voter complain to the party? It seemed that the voters were defeating themselves.

Convention Abuses

One of the abuses of the conventions was that the bosses and factions controlled the party machinery and thereby controlled nominations. But with the direct primary there was nothing to prevent the leaders of the party from meeting, exchanging views and, following some agreement, announcing their preferences to the voters by whatever medium was available.

The primary enhanced rather than diminished intra-party conflicts. Party responsibility was demanded, indeed necessary, and there was no effective substitute for it.

Some of the party leaders realized that the direct primary was here to stay and they looked to other methods to modify what they considered its undesirable features. But the trend was against them. Indeed, they found the demand strong for a "free" primary ballot.

Some legislatures provided the open primary, others liberalized it by removing requirements for party loyalty. Elsewhere the nonpartisan primary was introduced for some state and many local offices. Minnesota and Nebraska now have legislatures nominated and elected on a nonpartisan ballot. California authorized the cross-filing method, whereby a candidate can file not only for the nomination of his own party but also for any other party and receive the nomination from each of them. Washington has the blanket primary which breaks down party lines even more.

Thus political party leaders found themselves beaten at almost every encounter.

But all was not hopeless. Why not have a pre-primary convention? Apparently South Dakota is credited with the first effort at combining some of the features of the old nominating conventions and the direct primary with a pre-primary convention. A statute of 1917 provided that candidates could be designated by such a convention and placed on the primary election ballot. This was abandoned in 1929. In Minnesota, a pre-primary convention can make nominations. There the convention endorses candidates who are to be voted upon "by voters of the entire state." This endorsement does not appear on the ballot, nor are the endorsed candidates given any position preference. Other candidates may seek nomination by means of petitions.

Massachusetts adopted a similar law in 1932, abandoned it in 1937, and readopted it in 1953, to be effective in 1954. This law provides for nominating candidates for offices to be filled by "all the voters of the commonwealth." The conventions which are authorized may place candidates in nomination without the necessity of the usual filing papers such as the petition requires. This law goes further than the statutes of the other states indicated above. The name of the endorsed candidate is openly favored for against his name on the ballot are the words "Endorsed by (name of political party) Convention." This law was used during the primary elections of 1934 and 1936 and will be used again commencing with the primary of 1954. Here, as in Minnesota, other candidates may file through the use of petitions.

Colorado provides for a single ballot at a pre-primary convention and the names of all those receiving 20 per cent or more of the votes of the convention are put on the ballot. Utah provided for a pre-primary convention in 1947. But the ballots do not carry any indication of the endorsement, a feature which is not essential in Utah since the two candidates for each office receiving the highest number of votes at the party convention are the only ones which appear on the ballot. No provision is made for nomination by petition.

Rhode Island enacted her first direct primary law in 1948 and it

has some of the features of the earlier Nebraska law. In Rhode Island the names of candidates having the endorsement of their political party committees are printed "in the first column at the right of the title of the offices they seek" and each is identified with an asterisk. In the 1948 campaign the endorsed candidates were referred to as the "first column" candidates and the unendorsed candidates were called the "insurgents" or "second column" candidates.[1]

Pre-primary Authorized

In 1943 the Nebraska legislature adopted a statute authorizing a pre-primary convention which was to endorse candidates and adopt a program at the same time. After the name of each candidate so selected the words "Endorsed by the —— (party) Convention" would appear on the ballot. There was nothing to prevent other aspirants from filing for a place on the ballot, however, and many did so. The difference was in the identification by the party convention appearing on the primary election ballot.

Beginning with the primary election of 1946 each of the two major parties—Republican and Democrat —held a pre-primary convention, as well as district conventions, biennially, "on the eighth Tuesday preceding the holding of the general state-

[1]For an account of this primary see "Rhode Island Tries Primary," by Richard S. Childs, the REVIEW, March 1949, page 126. For a detailed analysis of the various state schemes for nominations, see "A New Primary System," by Joseph P. Harris, *State Government*, July 1948, page 140, and his report for the National Municipal League, *A Model Direct Primary Election System*, 1951.

wide primary election." This convention was authorized to make endorsements for "all party, state and national officers for which nomination or election at large is to be made at the forthcoming primary election." The candidates who were chosen under this plan would be the endorsed candidates of the convention for the statewide offices.

A district convention, held at the same time for each congressional district, was provided to perform the same functions for members of the House of Representatives and delegates and alternates to the national party convention.

The statute permitted the endorsement of not more than two candidates for each office, provided they received at least 25 per cent of the votes cast at the convention. This 25 per cent provision was raised to 35 per cent in 1949 and the restriction of nominating not more than two candidates for each office was eliminated. The chairman of the Republican state committee said at the time these changes were made that the best features of the pre-primary convention were ended. Apparently he believed it would put too many endorsed candidates in the field. Actually, it did not do so.

In the preparation of the ballots, the names of the unendorsed candidates, if any, were to be rotated, but the pre-primary convention choices retained their respective places at the top and in the order of convention preference.

The critics of the endorsement plan claimed that it reduced the direct primary to a secondary and perfunctory role. But the absence of an endorsement on the ballot does not prevent a strong party organization from bringing decisive influence to bear upon the voters in the primary. It is obvious that the party managers will have substantial influence upon the voter regardless of any endorsement feature. They have done so for many an election long before the endorsement feature was known.

Nebraska election statistics show that organization candidates sponsored by the pre-primary convention almost always won the nominations. It is true, however, that of opposition candidates filed, some won and others showed s u r p r i s i n g strength. But it is not conclusive that the endorsement label on the ballot alone was the key to success. The system did not operate long enough. Many of the candidates were incumbents and got endorsements easily. Most of them would have won anyway. They were better known to the voters and, if the formality of the pre-primary had not existed, it is altogether likely that the state party committee, for example, would have given the "nod" to those candidates it preferred and that such information would have trickled down to the party workers throughout the state.

Passing the Word Along

Is it not desirable that the voter know these preferences of the party leaders? Is it not better to have these desires known openly and unmistakenly than to presume upon rumor? Is not the open endorsement more plausible and desirable than the whispered word passed down to the faithful? There is plenty of evidence that this was the standard practice without the pre-primary convention: for the party leaders to assemble, discuss candidates, the platform, party strategy and then agree upon those hopefuls they would support in the coming primary. The extent to which this support was transferred to the voters is not easily determined. Similarly, there is no conclusive evidence that the undesirable features of the old convention system did dominate the pre-primary conventions in Nebraska as some have claimed. There is some evidence, of course, that some endorsements were so controlled, but the restrictive features of limiting them to two candidates for any one office were removed in 1949.

In some elections no more than one candidate for a particular office was given an endorsement. During the last two primaries, 1950 and 1952, any candidate receiving 35 per cent of the convention support was to receive such an endorsement. Yet, there was nothing to force the delegates to give that much support however great the field of aspirants. Even so, there were choices most of the time for the voter from among the endorsed candidates.

Did the pre-primary endorsement plan strengthen the political party where it had been weakened presumably by the direct primary? It seems to have strengthened the Influence of the party managers, if no other.

The endorsement feature removed the system of tacit understandings and gave wide berth to those candidates favored by the party organization. The decisions of candidate pref-

erences were announced and the vote reported as required by the statute. Finally, of course, the endorsement appeared on the ballot below the candidate's name.

The failure of a candidate to receive the required percentage of convention votes did not prevent him from having his name on the ballot. He could obtain a place on the ballot through petition. But the Democrats, for example, usually would endorse but one candidate for each office. This caused some dissatisfaction in that party. Without the endorsement most candidates fell by the wayside either by withdrawing or by defeat at the polls after a limited campaign.

One close observer of the pre-primary endorsement feature stated prior to the repeal of the law that "whatever may have been the original objectives, say a sincere effort to eliminate 'name' candidates and to give more effective expression to responsible party leadership, the fact remains it simply has not worked out."[2]

Convention Choices Win

The preferences of the convention usually won in the four elections where the pre-primary convention was used in Nebraska.[3] But the first choice did not always win. There are instances where a candidate with an endorsement, even a reluctant

[2]Editorial in *The Lincoln Star*, April 6, 1953, page 4.
[3]Statistical data compiled from various issues of the *Omaha World-Herald*, *The Lincoln Star* and *The Nebraska State Journal*. The primary election vote data is contained in the *Official Report of the Nebraska State Canvassing Board*, compiled by the Secretary of State for each election in question.

Commission but he was defeated in the primary by the unendorsed candidate, McReynolds. Schlater ran third with second place going to another unendorsed candidate.

In the last election, 1952, the first choice of the Republican convention for lieutenant governor, Hoyt, received 245 votes to 171 for the incumbent, Warner. Warner won the nomination 135,881 to 55,339. The same year, for secretary of state, the incumbent Pittenger, who was filling out a term by appointment, received 334 votes to 39 for Marsh who was the son of the recently deceased secretary. But although Marsh did not receive the endorsement he won the nomination by 108,437 to 86,086. Here, in this case, a "name" candidate won. For attorney general, the incumbent, Beck, received 188 votes to 195 for Towle, with Beck winning by 116,161 to 68,150.

Thus, preference by the pre-primary convention does not insure success. Perhaps with some of the familiar incumbents passing from the scene in a few years, the endorsement feature might have suffered more defections than it did. But the legislature would not have it that way.

Since the Republican party is usually dominant in Nebraska the primary election has become a real battleground. It seems that many voters affiliate with that party in order to have their ballots affect the outcome of the general election. Just how many of these additional voters in the Republican party are temporary, only to switch in Novem-

(Continued on page 222)

News in Review

Government Ethics Code Proposed in New York
Regulations Drafted for Inquiries and Officials

A CODE of fair procedure for legislative investigations and similar special inquiries, and a code of ethics for legislators and public officials, were recommended to the New York State legislature on March 8 and 10, respectively, by the Special Legislative Committee on Ethics in Government, comprised of eight legislators and four "public" members appointed by Governor Thomas E. Dewey. It is headed by Charles C. Lockwood, former state judge.

The code for investigations would be incorporated partly in the civil rights law and partly in the legislative law. The latter would include a provision that no temporary state commission having more than two members shall have power to take testimony at a public or private hearing unless at least two of its members are present.

The remaining portions, to be added to the civil rights law, would:

Afford a witness the right at any hearing to be accompanied by counsel who would be permitted to advise the witness of his rights, subject to reasonable limitations to prevent obstruction of or interference with the orderly conduct of the hearing.

Afford a witness the right to file a brief sworn statement relevant to his testimony for incorporation in the record.

Afford any person whose name was mentioned at a public hearing and who believed the testimony adversely affected him the right to testify or file a statement of facts under oath relating solely to material relevant to the testimony of which he complained.

Permit a witness to obtain a copy of his testimony given at a public hearing and his testimony given at a private hearing, if available, where the testimony became relevant in a criminal procedure or subsequent hearing, provided that the furnishing of such copy would not prejudice the public safety or security.

Make it a misdemeanor for any member of an investigating agency, its counsel or employees, to make public the testimony taken at a private hearing without the consent of a majority of the investigating committee or, in the case of a single-member agency, without the consent of the head of the agency.

Substantial non-compliance by any agency as to major provisions of the code would relieve a witness of the compulsion to testify.

The *New York Times* stated editorially on March 10 that this code, despite some omissions and possible defects, "sets a fine example for Congress, where it is more needed than it is in this state."

A proposed bill prohibiting certain acts or practices would:

Forbid any officer or employee of a state agency, or any legislator, to appear in any manner before a state agency wherein his compensation would be based on a contingent fee;

Forbid any such person to sell goods to any state agency unless after public notice and competitive bidding;

Forbid for two years after leaving a state agency any former officer or employee to appear before that agency in matters in which he was directly concerned or in which he personally participated during his public employment.

No code for the conduct of officers of political parties was recommended but the committee proposed legislation barring them from serving as judge of courts of record, attorney general, district attorney or assistant district attorney.

Besides these specific prohibitions, a violation of which would constitute a misdemeanor, the code of ethics, a separate bill, sets forth the following rule with respect to conflicts of interest:

"No officer or employee of a state agency, member of the legislature or legislative employee should have any interest, financial or otherwise, direct or indirect, or engage in any business or transaction or professional activity or incur any obligation of any nature, which is in substantial conflict with the proper discharge of his duties in the public interest."

This is further detailed by setting up ten standards dealing with various types of conflicts of interest, and condemning disclosures of confidential information gained in the course of official duties, and the use of official position to obtain unwarranted privileges or exemptions. They include a provision that any state official with a direct or indirect financial interest of $10,000 or more in any activity subject to jurisdiction of a regulatory agency should file a statement to that effect with the secretary of state, to be open to public inspection.

The legislature was asked to adopt resolutions to make committees of four members of the Senate and Assembly, respectively, responsible for the effectiveness of the code. An Advisory Committee on Ethical Standards would be formed by the attorney general to check on the conduct of officers and employees of state agencies, and recommend dismissals in case of code violations. The legislative committees could recommend prosecution for misdemeanors or votes of censure by either house if a member is found guilty of misconduct.

Senator Thomas C. Desmond of Newburgh, veteran watchdog of governmental practices, criticized the committee for not completely barring legislators from taking pay for representing clients before state agencies, and asserted it was "unrealistic" to call upon the Senate and Assembly to sit in judgment on the conduct of their members.

U. S. Senate Leaders Suggest Fair Play Code

A uniform code of procedure for committees of investigation was put forward on March 10 by Republican Senate leaders as a guide for such committees. No method of enforcement was proposed. It provides that no committee or subcommittee should hear a subpoenaed witness or take testimony unless a majority of its members is present, or unless the committee decides that a majority member and a minority member together constitute a quorum; and that no confidential testimony or material presented in an executive hearing of an investigating committee or subcommittee, or any report of the proceeding, shall be made public unless authorized by a majority of the members.

No investigating subcommittee would be established except by the majority of the main committee. No investigating committee or subcommittee could delegate authority to issue subpoenas except by a vote of such body; and no hearings would be initiated without specific authorization by the body. A hearing outside of Washington would require a majority vote.

Any witness summoned to a hearing could be accompanied by counsel, who would advise him of his legal rights.

Following these suggestions, Democratic Senators Douglas and Humphrey and independent Senator Morse proposed, as matters of ethics, that members of Congress and all other federal officials who are paid $10,000 or more per annum file sworn public statements of outside income; that no former congressmen or officials should appear before government agencies to seek contracts, other business or favors; and that former congressmen should not go on the Senate or House floors to lobby. Special restrictions were proposed as to officials handling government contracts, loans, licenses, etc., and to prevent the use of gifts or favors to obtain special treatment or confidential information.

A commission of fifteen members—nine from outside the government—to study and report on the moral standards of official conduct of officers and employees, was also urged.

State Reorganization Makes Slow Progress in Minnesota

A report of the Minnesota Citizens Committee for the Little Hoover Report is concerned with past and prospective legislative action on recommendations of the Minnesota Efficiency in Government Commission. It states that few bills in line with the recommendations were adopted by the 1951 and 1953 legislatures but that much educational groundwork was done and that efforts will be continued in preparation for the next legislative session, in 1955.[1]

Pointing out that the commission had made 205 recommendations, the report announced that several of its minor policy recommendations have become law and some departmental reorganizations have been completed by executive orders. In particular, the health and agriculture departments were mentioned as having been revamped along lines suggested by the commission. A major victory was achieved in the 1953 session when the Public Institutions and Social Welfare Departments were consolidated into a Department of Public Welfare, at an estimated annual saving of $100,000.

The Legislative Research Committee was assigned a study of the Little Hoover Report along with its other duties but,

[1]See also "A Blueprint for Minnesota," by Leroy F. Harlow, the REVIEW, April 1951, page 190.

in accordance with its established policy, it made no recommendations.

The Citizens Committee report urges that the next legislature, early in the session, set up a special committee on reorganization, to give study and impetus to desirable plans, and that the finance and appropriations committees should not rehear all the reasons for and against reorganization measures. It was also suggested that an interim committee of legislators be established in the future to study such matters and sponsor bills for consideration in the legislature—especially as there were no legislators on the Little Hoover Commission.

Connecticut Redistricting Two Years Too Late

By a three-to-two decision on February 15, the Connecticut Supreme Court of Errors declared unconstitutional the bill to redraw State Senate districts, passed in March 1953 by the Republican-controlled legislature. The bill had been challenged by the Democratic party on the grounds that action should have been taken in 1951 and that the 1953 district lines discriminate against the Democrats.

Connecticut law requires redistricting to be done by the legislature meeting "next after" completion of a federal census. The state attorney general argued that the last census was not fully completed until November 1951; but the court majority agreed with the Democratic contention that the census was completed by October 30, 1950.

The State Senate in 1951 was controlled by the Democrats.

No valid redistricting has occurred for 50 years. The next must now wait until 1961. Present district populations range from 25,000 up to 129,000.

Ohio and Maryland Adopt Laws for Open Meetings

The Ohio legislature has recently enacted a law requiring that all meetings of any state board, commission, agency or authority shall be open to the public at all times, and that no resolutions, rules, regulations or formal actions of any kind shall be adopted at executive sessions.

The city council of Columbus, Ohio, followed suit by requiring that all meetings of any board, commission, department or any city agency or authority shall be open to the public at all times.

Maryland's 1954 legislature has enacted a law which goes a step farther than that of Ohio. It provides that all meetings, regular and special, of state commissions, boards and agencies, as well as all county and city boards, agencies and councils, shall be open to the public at all times.

It is reported by *Editor and Publisher* (March 6, 1954) that in 1953 seven states enacted laws providing for open public meetings of governing bodies, thus making a total of nine in little more than a year.

Massachusetts Bill for Open Meetings Loses

A bill before the Massachusetts legislature to require city government meetings in Springfield to be open to the public was rejected in the State Senate on March 2 by a vote of 24 to 9. Reconsideration was defeated on the following day, 18 to 4. The original proposal would have applied throughout the state, but it had been narrowed to Springfield only. The defeat was charged in part to lack of positive support by Mayor D. B. Brunton, although he announced, "As far as I'm concerned, we will have open meetings in Springfield."

Senator S. O. Conte of Pittsfield, a supporter of the bill, said that if he returns to the Senate next year he will offer a general bill to require open meetings of boards, commissions and committees in all cities and towns in accordance with the "democratic principle of the people's right to know about their government."

Automatic Vote Recording Used in Ohio Lower House

Members of the Ohio House of Representatives used machines for voting at the last special session, instead of undergoing roll calls. All 136 members voted simultaneously and their votes were recorded both on tape in the machine and on illuminated boards on opposite walls. This improved, speedy system was estimated to save as much as $15,000 a week.

The Cleveland Citizens League, in reporting the change, notes that it had urged it more than fifteen years ago.

Reapportionment Amendment Urged in Illinois

Two co-chairmen for the Illinois Committee for Constitutional Revision, which will conduct a campaign for a reapportionment amendment to the state constitution, were elected on February 11 at a meeting of 25 statewide organizations at the Chicago Bar Association. Illinois legislative districts have not been changed since 1901, despite a constitutional requirement for redistricting after each census. It was pointed out that 2,900,000 people live in the nine largest districts and only 585,000 in the eight smallest. It is hoped that the proposed amendment will be adopted at the November 2 election.

New Jersey Building Code Makes Progress

The first two parts of a six-part state building code, in the course of preparation in New Jersey by the State Standard Building Code Advisory Committee since 1950, have been adopted by Commissioner Charles R. Erdman, Jr., of the State Department of Conservation and Economic Development at the committee's recommendation. The state code can be adopted by municipalities by reference ordinance, thus avoiding the expense of reprinting and publishing.

. The two parts are: (1) general provisions and definitions and (2) structural, fire and general safety requirements. The other parts, dealing with less general matters, are still in preparation.

The code itself embraces administrative provisions, articles of enforcement and terms of required performance. It is accompanied by a manual presenting standards of design and construction provisions currently considered reasonable and adequate.

A code survey in 1952 showed that 418 of the state's 567 municipalities had some type of building code, the largest group having codes of local character.

Registration Bill Adopted in N. Y. State

Permanent personal registration is authorized in New York State, on an optional basis as to the city of New York and each upstate county, in a bill of the Republican administration 'which the State Assembly approved on March 17 after similar action by the Senate.

A voter where the plan is adopted would remain on the election rolls after once registering, if his address remains unchanged and he votes once in every two years. Safeguards in the bill have been criticized as so rigorous and costly as to militate against wide adoption of permanent registration.

Training for Southern Public Personnel Officials

The Southern Regional Conference of the Civil Service Assembly and the Bureau of Public Administration, University of Tennessee, are sponsoring a four-day training institute for public personnel officers, June 8-11, at the University of Tennessee in Knoxville. It includes a two-day session on position classification and pay, a two-day program on recruitment and classification and two evening meetings on the problems of employee relations and training programs.

Tennessee River Pollution Control Compact Drafted

Representatives of the Tennessee River basin states—Alabama, Georgia, Kentucky, Mississippi, North Carolina, Tennessee and Virginia—met in Chicago in December and drafted for submission to the state legislatures a Tennessee River Basin Water Pollution Control Compact. According to *State Government,* this compact is similar in some respects to the Ohio River Valley Water Sanitation Compact and is designed in part to supplement it. There are to be three commissioners from each state and three non-voting representatives of the United States government.

The commission would have power to assist the states of the basin in developing cordinated pollution control plans and in enforcing them. Provision is made for party states to handle special pollution control problems within the compact framework, such as in the case of Kentucky and Tennessee with respect to the Cumberland River.

Council-manager Plan Developments

WEBSTER GROVES, MISSOURI, (1950 population 23,390) adopted a council-manager charter on March 23. The vote was 3,528 to 774, the charter carrying in all precincts.

Voters of the village of MONTICELLO, NEW YORK, (1950 population 4,223) have adopted the council-manager plan by popular referendum. The plan went into effect March 17.

In a hearing in February before the MASSACHUSETTS legislative committee on towns, general legislation to permit selectmen-manager town government was urged by various speakers but was opposed by the Massachusetts Selectmen's Association. The same committee held a hearing in RANDOLPH on February 17 on a proposed manager bill for that town.

A referendum in March on adoption of

the selectmen-manager form of government in SCITUATE, MASSACHUSETTS, lost by a vote of 1,506 to 1,030.

The town manager government in operation for the past three years in IPSWICH, MASSACHUSETTS, was repealed by a 79-vote margin in March. The vote was 1,657 to 1,578.

The town of CONCORD, MASSACHUSETTS, voted 1,543 to 1,383 against adoption of the selectmen-manager plan of government on February 22. The question will be voted upon again at next year's town election in February.

Charter commissioners in EAST PROVIDENCE, RHODE ISLAND, voted six to three on March 3 to draft a council-manager charter for the town. They also adopted a resolution, seven to one, asking the town's legislative representatives to introduce legislation for off-year nonpartisan elections.

The representative town meeting in GREENWICH, CONNECTICUT, voted on March 2 to retain the board of selectmen form of administration but recommended that it be supplemented by a trained, full-time chief administrative officer. Permission of the state legislature is said to be needed. This plan represents a compromise from the town manager plan proposed by the former reorganization committee.

A bill has been introduced in the VIRGINIA legislature to amend the charter of BIG STONE GAP so as to provide for a manager, appointed by a five-member council, superseding the present mayor-council form. The bill was introduced at the request of the present six-man council, but much local opposition is reported.

In an election on March 2, voters of LEBANON, MISSOURI, retained the council-manager plan by a vote of 1,045 to 728.

A group of citizens in MINOT, NORTH DAKOTA, has revived the question of a change from council-manager government to the commission form. Such a move was defeated in 1950 by a vote of 3,355 to 2,253, and under state law four years must elapse before another election on the subject.

On March 18 the voters of SIOUX FALLS, SOUTH DAKOTA, defeated a proposal that the city employ a city manager, by a margin of five to three.

Petitions have been circulated in LEXINGTON, NEBRASKA, asking an election on the question of abandoning the council-manager plan.

The city council of SPARKS, NEVADA, has postponed until January 18, 1955, a special election on adoption of the council-manager plan, proposed in petitions sponsored by the chamber of commerce. The latter is reported to have acceded to the delay.

The PORT TOWNSEND, WASHINGTON, *Leader* reports much interest in the possibility of a change to council-manager government.

The voters of SAN CLEMENTE, CALIFORNIA, will pass upon the question of adopting the council-manager plan at the April 13 municipal election.

Boston Reorganization Fosters Efficient Administration

The city council of Boston, Massachusetts, has approved a reorganization plan embodied in three ordinances that will be in full effect by June 30, 1954. The number of city departments responsible to the mayor is compressed from 36 into 21, and a new administrative services department is set up as a topside management control agency for the mayor.

This new department, which became effective January 1, 1954, has taken over the city's budget, personnel and purchasing activities. It is under an administrative services board consisting of the director of administrative services, the supervisor of personnel, the purchasing agent and, ex-officio, the city auditor and city treasurer. The director is the real head of the department through his powers over personnel and finances, despite the direct appointment of the other members of the board by the mayor. The administrative services board does, however, determine the internal organization of the department.

The director and the board are empowered to make "studies and recommendations with respect to the organization, activities, policies and procedures of all departments, boards and officers so that the administration thereof shall be economical and efficient." The director is a kind of vice mayor in charge of operations, and is the mayor's chief budget officer.

One of the most potent tools of the director is his power to review all personnel transactions—appointments, transfers, promotions, reinstatements, increases in compensation, changes in title or pay. His approval is final except where the mayor orders otherwise in writing.

The supervisor of personnel, a newly created office, maintains personnel records, studies personnel problems, employment conditions and economic changes affecting city departments, makes recommendations for improvements in personnel matters, supervises the city's compensation plans and the classification and compensation plan for county employees, and aids the director in his budget duties.

The city printing plant, now an independent department, has been placed under the purchasing agent.

The mayor's original plan for assessment organization provided for a single assessor to supervise the basic assessment operation. The reorganization ordinance provides for an assessor of taxes who will also be the chairman of a three-man board of assessors. The assessor will have administrative control of the assessing department and will administer poll and motor vehicle excise taxes, but the board of assessors will deal with property taxes under the general laws of the state. The mayor's proposal for an independent

board of review of three members, to handle the abatement of property taxes, is retained. Occupational requirements—law, real estate management and engineering—for the positions on this board were eliminated in its final draft.

Other departmental changes, effective May 1, include combining the collecting and treasury departments into a single treasury department under a collector-treasurer. The board of street commissioners is abolished and its functions are transferred to the public works department. The health department absorbs the present separate departments of registry and weights and measures. Three city hospitals are placed in a single hospital department, under an unpaid board of five trustees.

A public safety commission is set up to coordinate inspectional activities of the building, fire and health departments; it consists of the related department heads. A single real property department replaces the public buildings department and the board of real estate commissioners, which handles property acquired because of non-payment of taxes, and also administers the off-street parking program. The new department is headed by a board with a paid chairman and assistant. A new parks and recreation department takes over the present park department and the board of recreation; it is under a commission with a paid chairman.

JOSEPH S. SLAVET, *Secretary*
Boston Municipal Research Bureau

Philadelphia Council Defers Charter-Wrecking Amendments

Proposals to submit six charter amendments, designed to weaken the merit system and encourage political activity by city employees,[1] at the May 18 primary election, lost out in the Philadelphia city council on February 25, although receiving ten votes to seven. A two-thirds vote

[1]See the REVIEW, March 1954, page 134.

of twelve was necessary. Eight Democrats and two Republicans voted for the proposals; six Democrats and one Republican voted against them. The amendments had been offered in the council by two organization Democrats with the support of Congressman W. J. Green, Jr., Democratic city chairman. They had been vigorously attacked in the press and by good government groups. Action on them is now deferred until the November general election, when they may be submitted to popular vote.

Annexation Efforts Aided by Arizona Court Decision

Circulators of petitions for the annexation of municipal fringe areas in Arizona are not required by existing law to include in their annexation petitions a precise description of the bounds of the area to be annexed, according to a decision of the Arizona Supreme Court in February. Persons circulating petitions in the urban fringes of Phoenix and Tucson have found that the absence of exact boundary definitions gives them a greater chance of circumventing opposition within the general area whose annexation is sought. Officials of Phoenix and Tucson, defendants in the court action, welcomed the decision because of the vigorous annexation programs of the two cities and the possible effect of an adverse ruling upon areas already annexed.

PAUL KELSO
University of Arizona

Arizona City Administrators Hold Annual Meeting

Problems of municipal management were discussed at the second annual conference of the Arizona City Administrators' Association held at Mesa in February. Clarence E. Ridley, executive director of the International City Managers' Association, addressed the conferees. Administrative officials of approximately 30 cities were present. Ray W. Wilson,

city manager of Phoenix, was reelected president; J. A. Petrie, city manager of Mesa, vice president; and E. M. Pederson, city clerk of Casa Grande, secretary.

Another Bay County Poll on Voter Awareness

Professor Donald S. Hecock of Wayne University has repeated his 1950 poll in Bay County, Michigan, to measure the extent to which voters know the names of elective public officers. The 1950 poll[1] tested the voters' knowledge of such minor elective state offices as secretary of state, state treasurer, attorney general and superintendent of public instruction.

The new findings, not yet published, confirm the 1950 study. Shortly before the state election, on October 18, 1952, 401 voters were asked the names of nine elective and appointive statewide officers. In 1950 only 4 per cent could name the elective state treasurer; in 1952, 7.2 per cent did so. In 1952 only 5.5 per cent knew the name of the elective attorney general and 5.9 per cent knew the name of the elective superintendent of public instruction. In general, only about two thirds knew whether a given office was elective or appointive although most of them had been voting for candidates for some of the offices for years. Only 43 per cent knew that the superintendent of public instruction was elective.

When asked, after the interviewing, for ideas of improvement of government, voters freely admitted their usual lack of information but only 21 per cent complained that too many officers were elective, although that is the inference which most political scientists would draw.   R. S. C.

[1]The results of the 1950 poll are embodied in the 1951 report of the Michigan Legislative Committee on Reorganization. The report is available as one of the readings in *Civic Victories* by Richard S. Childs. See also "Too Many Elective Officials?", by Donald S. Hecock, the REVIEW, October 1952, page 449.

County and Township . . . . *Edited by Edward W. Weidner*

Texas County Official Advises Fellow Judges

Stresses Cooperation at All Levels of Government

EDITOR'S NOTE.—The responsibilities of county officials were described in unusually broad terms in the keynote address by County Judge J. N. DICKSON of Grayson County, Texas, at the 1953 convention of the County Judge and Commissioners' Association of Texas. The county judge in Texas is chairman of the county governing body. Judge Dickson stressed the importance of intergovernmental cooperation. He indicated that county judges are in a strategic position which gives them a special responsibility to inform the citizens not only about the conduct of county business but also about the working of state legislation and institutions with which the judges come in contact. Pointing out that the official oath binds county judges to preserve and protect the constitution of the United States as well as of the state, he declared that their highest duty was to preserve the rights guaranteed by the constitution and "maintain our individual freedom and preserve the American way of life." Excerpts from Judge Dickson's speech, as published in *County Progress*, official publication of the County Judges and Commissioners' Association of Texas, follow.

WE county judges should be especially interested in the state institutions for the mentally ill. The state builds these mental institutions. County judges, by commitments, furnish the inmates.

We county judges know the following statements to be facts: the mental institutions are overcrowded; hospital facilities are inadequate; institutions do not have sufficient numbers of doctors, nurses or attendants to give the patients the necessary attention; salaries paid are far below those that doctors and nurses receive in private practice.

These conditions should not exist in this great state of Texas. No one is personally responsible for this condition. Apparently no one has ever successfully championed the cause of the poor, unfortunate inmates of these institutions. These inmates are placed in the mental institutions upon commitments authorized by the state of Texas and issued by the county judges. The entire citizenship of Texas is responsible for the conditions under which these inmates live and the treatment which they receive. When the citizens are properly informed as to these conditions they will demand that they be remedied. Your legislature is faced with the responsibility of properly financing these institutions. The people must provide the funds. Tell your senators and representatives how you feel in this matter. Give them your support. . . .

Keep your people informed. The strength of a democracy is the knowledge of its people. In a democracy, wisdom is power, ignorance is destruction. No governmental agency, whether it be national, state or local, has the right to withhold from its citizens records or information which it possesses and which is vital to their welfare unless to divulge such information would imperil the safety of the nation. . . . Give the people the facts, and do not be afraid to risk their judgment.

Secrecy in democratic government leads to suspicion and suspicion leads to distrust. Only through an informed public can we hope to retain our freedom and our liberty.

Work with the press—you will find the reporter wishes to report the facts. Help him to interpret the orders of your commissioners court. Left to his own interpretation he may interpret wrongly and thereby embarrass both the court and the press, especially the court.

In addition to the duties you owe your county and state governments, you have a duty to your national government. In your official oath you swore you would, to the best of your ability, *"Preserve, protect* and *defend* the constitution and laws of the United States and of this state."

As a nation we have risen to the undisputed leadership of the world. This has been accomplished under the principles and guarantees of the greatest manmade legal instrument the world has ever produced, the constitution of the United States of America. . . .

Today there are good citizens in this country who without proper thought are suggesting destroying certain provisions of this constitution, provisions which protect all the citizens, in order to more easily prosecute those who would destroy all freedom. This danger is so grave that it and what it portends should be called to the attention and thoroughly explained to the American people lest, in angry frustration and disgust at Communist spies who hide behind the provisions of the fifth amendment of the constitution and refuse to give their party affiliations under the excuse that to do so might incriminate them, the American people themselves by amendment might inadvisedly relinquish a part of their guaranteed rights. . . .

The fifth amendment is the basic law which protects a person from brutally forced confessions, that prevents the prosecution from using information obtained by brutality, eaves-dropping and wire-tapping. . . .

It was proposed and adopted as one of the guarantees of freedom and has served this purpose for more than 160 years. Are the people now to decide they know more about freedom and freedom's laws than those patriots who framed the constitution and who had known the tyrants' lash?

No! To do so would be to adopt the same tactics in dealing with criminals or suspected criminals and/or political opposition as is now the practice in totalitarian countries. The Communists must be driven out of our government, but not at a sacrifice of our individual rights.

The treatment of the individual and the recognition of his individual right is the difference between slavery and freedom. . . .

We must, above all, preserve our constitution and the rights thereunder guaranteed to us. We must, as officials of county government, cooperate with the officials of the other governments under which we live, work for the general welfare, maintain our individual freedom and preserve the American way of life.

Texas Conference Concerned with State-local Relations

At its conference in December the Texas County Judges and Commissioners' Association passed resolutions concerning forest management and state-local relations.

On the former subject it resolved: "That we believe the sale of our national forests in Texas to private interests would be unwise and against the best interests of the economy and welfare of the people of this state and the United States; and we do respectfully urge our United States senators and all members of Congress from Texas to oppose any legislation which would result in the sale of our East Texas National Forests."

The association also vigorously opposed "any and all legislation which would provide for new offices and positions and for a mandatory pay raise for any clerk, auditor, reporter or any other county official or assistant to any county official except with the concurrence of the governing bodies affected."

City-county Consolidation in the News

Consideration of city-county consolidation is widespread throughout the country. In Toledo the Municipal League and the city manager have taken leadership in suggesting creation of a countywide committee to study the needs of all parts of Lucas County. There is a general feeling among local government officials that some harmonious program should be worked out to serve the best interests of all districts in the county. The needs throughout the county vary but all of them are related to the needs of neighboring communities. Extension of water lines and sewer lines, school district reorganization and expansion, and planning and zoning are suggested.

A study of possible advantages and the feasibility of consolidating city and county boundaries, services and governments has been authorized by the Arizona Legislative Council, according to *State Government*. Primary objective of consolidation proposals is economy. Representative Alvin Wessler, who presented the project to the council, indicated that some authorities have estimated that combining municipal and county governments and their functions would save up to 25 per cent of the costs of independent governments.

Under consolidation as suggested, municipalities within a county would retain their own names and entities, but multiple government setups would be replaced by a single governing authority. Each area would be given representation on that authority, probably on a population basis. There would be varying tax rates, based on the number and types of public services given and on other factors.

According to the *American Municipal News*, consolidation of the governments of Memphis and Shelby County, Tennessee, has been urged in an initial planning report prepared for the city by a consultant.

In Louisville, Kentucky, Mayor Andrew Broaddus is seeking uniform closing hours for taverns in the city and county to aid the enforcement of liquor control laws and stop confusion. Indiana's Supreme Court last month upheld a law

under which the health departments of Indianapolis and Marion County may be merged into a joint operation.

A county grand jury has urged creation of a centralized coordinated police force for St. Louis County, Missouri, and the numerous suburbs of the city of St. Louis. The city lies adjacent to, but is not within, St. Louis County. The city has transferred property at Jefferson Barracks to the county for health or educational use.

Kansas City, Missouri, is negotiating with surrounding Jackson County for allocation of county road and bridge tax funds to improve city streets. City residents pay 83 per cent of this tax. Cooperative planning and financing of major mutual-benefit projects is envisioned. In Detroit a joint city-county building is being completed.

Mecklenburg County, North Carolina, has acted in conjunction with Charlotte city officials in appointing a committee to study the problem of acquiring school sites in the fringe areas of the city. Another committee is working on the merger of city and county boards and still another is studying consolidation of the county and city tax collection agencies.

The city of Petaluma and the county of Sonoma, California, have decided upon a city-county courthouse and city hall. The city is putting up 78 per cent of the money, the county 22 per cent.

Long Ballot Operates in Cuyahoga County

The voters of Cuyahoga County (Cleveland), Ohio, elect 32 officials including 21 judges, auditor, treasurer, prosecuting attorney, engineer, coroner, recorder, sheriff, clerk of courts and three county commissioners. An analysis of the rather complicated organization of the county was recently published by the Cleveland Bureau of Governmental Research in its publication *Greater Cleveland*.

Most of the elective offices are carried over from nineteenth century practices or ideas. However, a number of departments with appointive heads have been established, including the welfare, sanitation, airport, building and civil defense departments, as well as a general agency of budgeting and purchasing. In 1952 the board of county commissioners established the position of county administrative officer in an attempt to facilitate its supervision of these departments.

Highway Problems Discussed by County Officials

The problem of building and maintaining roads and highways of adequate standards and of facilitating highway safety continues to absorb a good portion of the time of county officials. In Wisconsin the County Boards Association has appointed a special committee to study that state's traffic law enforcement problem in an attempt to work out cooperative patterns between local and state agencies that will help reduce the death toll on highways. One suggestion under consideration is expansion of the state traffic patrol force but also under consideration is a reexamination of all state laws relative to highway safety, regulation and enforcement.

A large portion of the recent convention of the Wisconsin Association was devoted to the highway problem. Wisconsin has begun a long-range road construction planning program with emphasis upon developing a master plan built around the more than 2,000-mile state trunk highway system.

Oakland County, Michigan, Builds County Center

Oakland County, Michigan, has taken the initiative in planning an extensive county government service c e n t e r. Already the county has in operation at the center buildings housing the welfare department, agriculture and extension service, central stores, juvenile home, juvenile cottages, nurses home, contagious disease hospital and infirmary. It is proposing to add to it a new courthouse and office building.

If these steps are carried out it will be possible for a citizen to go to the center and transact any county business he may have all in county-owned buildings with a central campus and grounds.

New York Issues Manual for County Supervisors

A manual outlining rules of order and procedure of the Board of Supervisors in New York State has been issued by the Association of Clerks and Boards of Supervisors. Much of the work on this manual was done by Professor A. M. Hillhouse, of Cornell University, in connection with the expanded services the university is providing county officials.

Township Official Protests Loss of Assessment Duties

The executive director of the Michigan Township Association has come out strongly against a bill which would remove the assessing of property from township officials and place it in the hands of county officers. Editorializing in *Official Michigan* he says:

"This is a dangerous bill, and we must fight it with all the facilities and strength of our organization. This bill, if enacted, would be the opening wedge in the program of abolishing township government. We have already had many of our functions taken away from us. We must not let them take this vital function away from the township supervisor."

Commission Studies New York Finances

State in Good Financial Condition, Experts Report

THE New York Temporary Commission on the Fiscal Affairs of State Government, created by the 1953 legislature, rendered its first report February 15. The report outlined the method of approach adopted, summarized the progress of studies to the report date, and recommended continuance and initiation of additional intensive investigations in specific study areas. Later in the month, the legislature extended the commission for another year.

The commission was authorized to "make a comprehensive study and appraisal of the fiscal affairs of the state government including its relationships with the federal government and the units of local government." The commission was given broad instructions to study the state's fiscal policies, practices and procedures, the relationship of federal, state and local revenue programs, trends in existing state programs of expenditures, the adequacy of the state's capital construction programs, the equity and adequacy for present and future needs of the state's revenue structure, the effect of the state's constitutional limitations on fiscal policies, the adequacy of the tax stabilization reserve funds and such other subjects as the commission should deem appropriate.

The commission's report discloses that, following its organization in August of last year, it considered whether to make concentrated studies in a few areas, in view of the limited time, or whether to make "diagnostic' studies of as many areas as possible. It determined on the latter procedure, since "all the areas

specified by the legislation could be given consideration. Inter-relationships among all the study areas could be kept in focus" and "once the entire field was reviewed, it would be possible to initiate detailed examination of individual major problems without loss of perspective and proportion. The commission believes that this method . . . permits the greatest long-term contribution to the state. It provides the means of making a comprehensive review of the state's fiscal affairs and establishes an over-all program of study within which all fiscal matters can be examined in a consistent and coordinated manner."

To carry out its studies, the commission adopted a method of approach involving the identification and definition of the major fiscal problems facing the state, determination of the causes of these problems and development of an over-all program of study, with concentration initially on the areas where findings are prerequisite to the study of other areas. For purposes of the study, the fiscal affairs of the state were classified in three major areas: the state's own fiscal activities, federal-state relationships and state-local relationships.

The commission had initiated studies in each of the broad areas defined by its method of approach, and reported advanced progress in its studies of state expenditure trends and revenues. It found that a major problem faces the state over the next decade in the possibility that required expenditures may increase more rapidly than revenues. Assuming no change in the value of the dollar, no extension in the scope of state services, no increase in cost levels—and specifically in salary levels—and that external trends, such as population, proceed at rates indicated by the actual experience of recent years, it was estimated that state general fund expenditures, covering almost all activities provided from current revenues, would rise from $1,054,000,000 in 1952-53 to $1,315,000,000 in 1962-63, an increase of $261,000,000. In addition, it was estimated that capital outlays may be required at an average annual rate of $270,000,000 to $340,000,000.

Revenue yields from the existing revenue structure were estimated on the basis of three assumptions. Assuming that they rise at the 2.1 per cent average annual rise at which income payments to individuals in the state increased in 1929-52, revenues in 1962-63 would be $296,000,000 higher than in 1952-53. Assuming that they rise at the 1.6 per cent annual increase in income payments to individuals shown in 1947-52, the total by 1962-63 would be $264,000,000 higher than in 1952-53.

Finally, assuming that the revenue increase is merely the same as the estimated increase in population—1 per cent per year—the total in 1962-63 would be $176,000,000 above 1952-53. All these estimates are in constant dollars, without the addition of new revenue sources. Each increase in revenues is less than the estimated increase in expenditures on the basis cited above.

The commission noted that the state had three alternatives in meeting the budget problem posed by the gap between expenditures and revenues: control of expenditures within the existing revenue structure, increasing the yield of the present revenue structure, or increasing taxes or finding new sources of funds.

The commission found New York State in a good position to cope with its fiscal problems. It commended such major achievements as the executive budget system, separation of state-purpose and local-assistance budgets, modernized system of state aid grants, centralized tax collection and improvements in both capital financing and state debt administra-

tion. It recommended further intensive studies in various areas to maintain the state's position in pioneering in fiscal administration and techniques. Among its proposals was that experiments should be made in one or two departments to develop the most effective cost systems and operating controls.

Chairman of the commission is Dr. Frederick L. Bird, director of municipal research of Dun and Bradstreet, Inc., and a member of the council of the National Municipal League. Vice chairman is State Budget Director T. Norman Hurd. Other members include Frederick W. Ecker, president of the Metropolitan Life Insurance Company; Edward S. Foster, executive secretary of the State Conference Board of Farm Organizations; Weston Vernon, Jr., New York City tax attorney; State Senators Austin Erwin and Samuel L. Greenberg; State Assemblymen Julius J. Gans and Edmund R. Lupton; Allen J. Goodrich, president of the State Tax Commission; and State Comptroller J. Raymond McGovern.

The commission's director of studies is Gilbert H. Clee, of the management consultant firm of McKinsey and Company. Other staff members include Ralph F. Bischoff, John A. Bryson, A. E. Buck, Clarence Heer, Ernest Kurnow, Robert T. Lansdale, Herman C. Loeffler, James A. Maxwell and Paul Studenski.

Cincinnati Levies Earnings Tax

Cincinnati's city council on February 10 adopted as an emergency measure a seven-months one per cent earnings tax, effective from April 1 to October 31, thus becoming the eleventh Ohio city to resort to taxation of income in order to maintain solvency.

Designed to meet a crisis created by the disapproval last November of a request for the renewal of extra property taxes expiring at the close of 1953, the emergency tax is earmarked to provide:

(1) administration costs, (2) $5,500,000 for general operations, (3) $525,000 for the University of Cincinnati and (4) $300,000 for rebates. Any surplus received after these allocations is to be devoted to a reduction in the city's bonded debt.

The tax is imposed on Cincinnati-earned earnings of businesses as well as individuals and on non-residents as well as residents. A reciprocity feature, however, allows credits to be taken for similar taxes imposed by other municipalities on the earnings of Cincinnati residents. It does not apply to pensions, annuities, dividends or similar payments.

The tax has had one dramatic though not entirely unexpected result. Councilman Albert C. Jordan, United Steelworker representative, whose regional superior, Al Whitehouse, has vehemently opposed earnings tax legislation throughout his region, though with dubious success to date, has resigned as a member of the City Charter Committee's delegation in council. In a formal announcement February 24, Jordan declared that henceforward he will vote as an "independent."

FOREST FRANK, *Executive Director* Cincinnati City Charter Committee

Recommend Governments Census Be Resumed

The Intensive Review Committee, appointed last October to review the operations of the Bureau of the Census, has reported to the Secretary of Commerce with recommendations that a broad range of traditional statistical reports of the bureau be continued and improved and that major studies abolished or severely restricted in the last year or so be resumed.

Among the recommendations was one that the complete census of governments, last taken in 1932, be taken in 1956 to cover the year 1955, and that a complete census of government be taken every tenth year thereafter. It also recommended that, during the intercensal period, a biennial sampling survey be conducted to provide up-to-date trend information and that the present program of limited quarterly and annual reporting be continued.

The committee noted that while Congress in 1950 had authorized a complete census of governments to be taken for 1952 and every fifth year thereafter, no funds for the purpose had been provided by Congress. It described the census of government's function as bringing together statistics concerning the federal government, the 48 states and upwards of 115,000 local governmental units, under a program begun in 1850. It found that, "The collection and publication of such information are vital for sound governmental policies affecting intergovernmental relations" and that "local governments and private business . . . find these facts indispensable."

The committee also recommended resumption of compilation and publication of the census of business, the census of manufactures and of various of the publications whose emission had been curtailed in recent years, including the annual *Foreign Commerce and Navigation of the United States* and the *Monthly Summary of Foreign Commerce.* It was urged that appropriations be made on a regular basis to support the planned census program so that the bureau might advantageously utilize its highly specialized man power and the various segments of our society might be able to plan on the availability of the basic data. Specific improvements in the presentation of various of the statistical series was also recommended.

In a sharply critical commentary on the "erosion" of sources of basic statistical data, the committee noted that: "Business executives, farmers, labor leaders, professional men, scholars, scientists, government officials and administrators in all phases of the society are dependent on census records or on economic indicators based on census records." Regarding the record of these programs in recent years, it stated, "In plain, unvarnished truth, it is a disturbing record of retrogression."

The 80th Congress took a constructive step in 1948, when the programs of the Census Bureau were reviewed and Public Law 671 was enacted to provide for a carefully planned and staggered program of quinquennial economic censuses—manufactures; retail, wholesale and service trades; mineral industries and transportation. The 81st Congress, in 1949 and 1950, supplemented this program by authorizing a decennial census of housing and a quinquennial census of governments. But what followed? In the words of the committee:

"The first of these carefully planned and rescheduled censuses to come up for budgetary consideration after 1948 was the census of governments, first taken in 1850 and scheduled to be taken this time early in 1953 on 1952 figures, and each fifth year thereafter. Great care had gone into the planning of that census by an advisory committee of outside experts and the bureau staff. Despite the fact that the last good census of that type had been conducted for 1932 at the bottom of the great depression (the 1942 census having been seriously deficient because of unavoidable wartime reasons), funds were denied."

Thereafter, Congress refused to provide funds for the scheduled 1954 census of manufactures. Instead limited spot-check funds were provided. Next to fall by the wayside for lack of funds was the census of business (retail, wholesale and service trades), scheduled for 1954 on 1953 business. Similarly defaulted was the congressional obligation to appropriate funds for a 1954 census of mineral industries and the census of agriculture, scheduled to be taken for 1954. In addition, the foreign trade statistics program was virtually

starved, "to the detriment of our foreign traders, government agencies and analysts; and to the embarrassment of the world's chief trading nation."

The Intensive Review Committee comprised nine businessmen and economists appointed by the secretary of commerce last year. Ralph J. Watkins, director of research of Dun and Bradstreet, Inc., was chairman. Other members include Murray R. Benedict, of the University of California; John W. Boatwright of Standard Oil Company (Indiana); Stephen McK. DuBrul, of General Motors Corporation; Peter Langhoff, of Young and Rubicam; J. A. Livingston, financial editor of the Philadelphia *Evening Bulletin;* Myron S. Silbert, vice president of Federated Department Stores, Inc.; Lazare Teper, research director of the International Ladies' Garment Workers' Union; and Merrill Watson, executive vice president of National Shoe Manufacturers Association, Inc.

INDIANA STILL SEEKS HOME RULE

(Continued from page 185)

designated at the time as "Indiana's Little Manion Commission." Its purpose is to study overlapping federal-state and state-local functions. In the field of state and local relations Governor Craig believes the commission might inquire into the possibility of giving more authority to local governments to carry out some functions now handled by the state, and of finding relief for the fiscal plight of Hoosier cities and towns. This program would not be a substitute for the home rule amendment but rather a basis for legislation to implement the amendment if and when it is added to the constitution.

Citizen Action .   .   .   .   .   . *Edited by Elsie S. Parker*

The 'Do-gooder' in Politics

Novice Spokesman Needs New Approach to the Politician

THE average politician does not know how to deal with the "do-gooder." The lobbyist, the person sponsoring a cause from which he will directly gain economically, the political figure who is attempting to align power centers to his own or his party's advantage—all these are commonplace to the politician. But the individual or the volunteer representative of a citizen's group motivated solely by the desire to achieve better government is an enigma. For want of a better term, the politician refers to him as a do-gooder and treats him with suspicion.

The legislator, the councilman and the administrative head of a large department are all at the vortex of competing forces which demand their making decisions. Like judges depending upon counsel to point up the possible courses of action through their briefs, so, too, the politicians rely upon the charges and countercharges forthcoming through the interplay of pressures brought to bear upon them.

In the courtroom, the judge tends to discount courtroom histrionics and to seek the legal logic inherent in the case. The politician, too, goes right to the heart of the matter and wants to know "what's in it for you?" Knowledge of the personal motivation somehow serves as a catalyst which permits him to weigh the justice of a claim through a peculiar type of logic which also assigns importance to voting strength, symbolic appeal, political associations and the like.

A civic-minded group is characterized by the intensity of its feeling in the righteousness of its cause. It tends to be idealistic to a fault. The politician knows that sheer idealism in a power-politics world may itself become a power to be reckoned with just so long as it has or may attract battalions of supporters. Thus the politician may not cavalierly disregard the do-gooder. He is an unknown factor and is potentially dangerous; as such he is to be feared. And fear and hate are frequently siblings.

Recently, two legislators were overheard discussing a group interested in better government. Apparently one of the legislators had been approached to obtain his assistance in staging a public forum. The spokesman for the group had explained that the purpose of the meeting was to allow the pros and cons on a current issue to be presented. "What pros and what cons?" was the legislator's inquiry. In scorn he related to his colleague the generality of the response, the failure to detail the arguments which would be raised. That a group should be interested merely in establishing a forum for presentation of all views was incomprehensible to him.

The do-gooder tends to be ignorant of all this. It never occurs to him that the politician is suspicious of the person with a cause and simon-pure motives, that the politician may even dislike him from the time of the first meeting just because he is a do-gooder. Cloaked with the justice of his cause and confident that right will triumph as soon as the politician allows himself to have an open mind, he makes his initial contact. He is listened to politely without any outward manifestation of disapproval. Perhaps he is met with a seemingly sympathetic response in which the difficulties of effectuating the request are outlined. The first meeting he follows up with additional calls, all the while developing his argument along derstanding the position of the politician on a matter of current interest, and even flattery through acknowledgment that his political utterances and actions have been followed as a matter of course are all within this category.

Once rapport has been established, the politician will feel more at ease with the do-gooder. The latter will still remain somewhat the enigma, but only because he has identified himself with a civic movement without demonstrable selfish motives for doing so. He has taken on a new character as a good fellow, and this over-shadows his original characterization; it is only then that he first becomes effective as a spokesman for his cause. It is to this point that he should bend his initial efforts and, paradoxical as it may seem, until then he will have given more attention to selling himself than to selling his cause.

NORMAN MELLER
University of Hawaii

Citizenship Clearing House Reports on Progress

Bulletins of the Citizenship Clearing House, affiliated with the Law Center of New York University, report that ten citizenship clearing houses were established during recent months, bringing the total number of state and regional affiliates to sixteen. Among the new groups are those in Michigan, with headquarters at Michigan State College, Massachusetts at Amherst College, Ohio at Miami University, Harvard for the Boston metropolitan area, Indiana at Wabash College and Iowa at the University of Iowa. Other state clearing houses include those in Connecticut, Illinois, Kansas, Maine, Minnesota, Missouri, New York, Oregon, Pennsylvania and Washington.

At a meeting of the directors of local affiliates and representatives of institutions considering their establishment, held in New York, primary objectives for state clearing houses were developed: (1) Emphasis will continue to be placed on referring interested college students and graduates to the political party of their choice; (2) effort will be made to encourage greater political participation by outstanding graduates of the last five to ten years; (3) one-day conferences of students, faculty and political leaders will be held for the purpose of introducing students to practical politics. Other activities, such as the development of new teaching techniques and interdisciplinary courses on political behavior, the encouraging of student unions and political clubs, and the publishing of local newsletters, were also suggested. It is anticipated that each local affiliate will prepare a program to meet the particular requirements of the state or area which it serves.

The fourth in the 1953-54 series of conferences on college training for effective participation in politics was held at Marshall, Indiana, December 11 and 12, according to the Clearing House *Bulletin*. Professor Philip Wilder, of Wabash College, organized the conference, which was under the sponsorship of Wabash and the Citizenship Clearing House. One of the chief speakers was Congressman Charles B. Brownson, of Indianapolis, who urged that young people "burst their way into politics." He commented that college graduates can make a place for themselves in the political parties and that the way to learn is through practical application.

The Political Science Department of New York University is conducting a program (1) to interest students in active participation in politics and (2) to observe the difference in degree of participation between students who have completed the social science course and those who take the traditional required courses in government.

The University of Florida and the Citizenship Clearing House sponsored a Florida conference in January. Some 50 political and civic leaders, college administrators, and political scientists attended.

The Clearing House is continuing to make available, in a limited number of instances, a "selected group of political scientists to consult with departments which are interested in evaluating their courses in the fields of American government and political parties with special reference to incorporating in these courses greater emphasis on training college men and women for practical politics." Inquiries should go to the Citizenship Clearing House, 40 Washington Square South, New York 3.

Grants for Training

The Maurice and Laura Falk Foundation has renewed its grant to Boston University for its Citizenship Training Project. Increased to $16,000, the grant is to support the second year of "grass roots training" in the practical operation of local, state and national government. Director of the project will be Professor Troy E. Westmeyer.

A bequest has been made to the New Jersey College for Women to establish the Wells Phillips Eagleton and Florence Peshine Eagleton Foundation. Income from the $1,000,000 gift is to be used for "the advancement of learning in the field of practical political affairs and government to the end that the study of actual administration of government, especially in the municipality and state, may be encouraged."

The Carnegie Foundation has made a grant of $90,000 to Northwestern University to extend over three years. The money is to be used to reorganize the political science curriculum, both graduate and undergraduate.

Citizenship on TV
"Citizens Union Searchlight," a radio program of the Citizens Union of New York City, broadcast every Sunday

the weekly program, "Town Meeting of the Air" on "Do Our States Dominate Our Cities?" Among the speakers were Governor George N. Craig of Indiana and Mayor David Lawrence of Pittsburgh. Several past presidents and charter members were honor guests.

In an address before the Chicago City Club in December, Civic Director Guy D. Yoakum "urged that the City Club take special cognizance in its next half century of the need for bringing the forces of education and religion into closer harmony with true democracy, which translates itself into making our educators and cultural leaders, our ministers and churches, more responsive to the great needs of our increasingly complex civilization," reports the *City Club Bulletin.* "Through the years it has been in the realm of education and morals that the club has won its greatest success, said Mr. Yoakum. It has exalted intelligence and integrity as the requisites of good citizenship." The next 50 years presents an even greater challenge, he concluded.

The Commonwealth Club of California, which held its golden jubilee celebration in May of last year, has published a Golden Jubilee number of *The Commonwealth,* its weekly publication. Front and back covers comprise a photograph of the 500 members and friends attending the banquet. Speakers included Robert Gordon Sproul, president of the University of California, on "The Most Famous Forum of the West," and J. E. Wallace Sterling, president of Stanford University, on "The Commonwealth and the State," as well as Justice Homer R. Spence and Max Thelen, former presidents of the Club, and others. Music and motion picture presentations were featured.

Illinois Manager Plan Conference

An all-day conference on the council-manager plan was held in November in

Peoria, Illinois. Sponsored by the Illinois State and Peoria Chambers of Commerce, the meetings were attended by delegates from numerous Illinois cities, particularly those which have recently adopted the council-manager plan. Reports on how the plan has worked in Bloomington, Peoria, Rock Island and elsewhere were heard; the act under which cities may secure the plan was explained.

Community Councils Celebrate

Four community councils in Kansas City, Missouri, celebrated their tenth anniversaries last fall. These councils are composed of neighborhood groups and were among the first organized after the inception of the city's Community Service Division. According to the Kansas City *City Managers' News Bulletin*, three new neighborhood councils are in process of organization.

Work on 30 Projects

There are 30 projects listed in the *News Bulletin* of the Citizens League of Greater Minneapolis for its 1954 program. Each is being promoted by one of the league's committees.

The league's *Report of Two Years of Growth and Action* (twelve pages) shows that the membership has passed 2,200; adequate broadly based financial support has been developing; a solid record of contribution to better city and county government has been established; a sound organization has been set up and good procedures for tackling problems have been adopted; top grade volunteer personnel has been enlisted and a capable staff has been employed; the league has been well received generally.

A six-page folder describes the league in popular terms, winding up with an appeal for membership.

'Who Picks Our Judges'

This is the title of a pamphlet recently issued by the Citizens Union of New York City. The report cites evils of the present system, taking its evidence from the *Second Report* of the New York State Crime Commission, and advocates for New York City a new method of judicial selection.

The method includes important features of the so-called Missouri Plan, advocated by the American Bar Association and the American Judicature Society, but does not require constitutional amendment. Also it is not open to the objection often made to the Missouri Plan that under it there is no way to get a good judge if the governor or mayor who names the judges persistently declines to name a good one, though a bad judge can be turned down by the electorate at a referendum on his continuance after a short period of service.

Cleanup for Streets

The Reduction of Litter on the Streets of New York City is a report of the Municipal Affairs Committee of the City Club of New York. The report concludes that "at best there are problems connected with the collection of refuse in New York which are almost impossible of solution. . . . However, the City Club believes that a combination of rigid enforcement, a continuous public relations program including community organization, more effective control of parking, industry cooperation and the concentration of collection and cleaning facilities in offending areas are best calculated to achieve lasting results. Above all, the will to have a clean city must come from the top of the city administration and it must be vigorously and increasingly felt at all levels of the city's personnel whether in the sanitation, police and health departments or in the courts."

Researcher's Digest .   .   .   .   .   *Edited by John E. Bebout*

'The People's Right to Know' Reviewed

Access to Public Records Discussed by Harold Cross

"YOU can't print that" is a reply not unfamiliar to newsmen in search of reputedly public records. As government has grown, many newspapermen, researchers and interested citizens have found it increasingly difficult to gain first-hand access to records of the public's business. And yet, "Public business is the public's business. The people have the right to know. Freedom of information is their just heritage. Without that the citizens of a democracy have but changed their kings."

Here is the attitude of journalists involved in the problem of what is and what is not public information. The words are those of Harold Cross in opening his book, *The People's Right to Know*,[1] which is an invaluable source of knowledge on the subject. Commissioned by the American Society of Newspaper Editors (ASNE) as a report on laws affecting access to public information, the book is at once a well organized report, a legal reference work, a textbook and a spirited account of what remains a misty no-man's-land between government on all levels and the people.

Mr. Cross has specialized in newspaper law for many years, principally as counsel to the *New York Herald Tribune* and as a lecturer at Columbia University on laws affecting journalism.

Excepting military and atomic energy censorship, the book gives the ASNE's answer to the question, "Where can we get organized material on this subject with actual experiences recorded and

[1]Columbia University Press, New York City, 1953. 405 pages, $5.50.

lines of action indicated?" In the preface, Mr. Cross expresses the hope that the book will be of especial use in smaller communities where newspaper law experience or books in which the law may be found are not available.

The need for a composite work on "Legal Access to Public Records and Proceedings," the book's subtitle, is emphasized by recent activity in the field of governmental research as well as in journalism. Last year a report to the Michigan Joint Legislative Committee on Reorganization of State Government said that certain of the regulatory agencies being studied were ignoring the laws under which they were operating, sometimes circumventing them, and often applying them unequally. In culling data for the report the roadblock of "That's confidential information!" was met more than once. Final recommendations include the need for "full and complete records of public hearings" by the agencies under scrutiny.

More recently, the Virginia Press Association adopted a resolution urging the General Assembly to make records of juvenile offenders available to the public through the press. The VPA argued that secrecy of arrest and trial of juveniles in many instances has served to encourage delinquency rather than to protect the good name of the accused.

On the other hand, the Civil Rights Committee of the New York State Bar Association recently proposed for adoption by the state legislature a resolution which would make it unlawful in any criminal case for prosecutor, defense attorney or any official connected with the case to make public any information about the defendant before trial.

Again, Frank S. Hogan, Manhattan district attorney, in commenting on his refusal to disclose the contents of criminal confessions, said last month: "I'll agree that it is a postponement of the people's right to know, but it is only done in an effort to preserve the traditional rights of a defendant under our system of law."

In his book Mr. Cross notes a heavy increase in the trend toward secrecy in several fields, chiefly in financial dealings between government and citizens. This trend toward changing transactions between government and citizens from the status of public business to one of "privileged, confidential relationships has been spreading into the field of taxes, penalties, settlement of claims and the like."

Judicial proceedings, records and official action affecting various phases of family relationships have also tended toward secrecy by virtue—or by the evil—of bureau regulations and recent statute law. In other respects the law has improved generally on the matter of public records, particularly in the states and municipalities. Louisiana is cited as one of the states in which the statutes are most clear.

Mr. Cross swings his axe most effectively in commenting on federal government regulations. Provisions in the U. S. Code are taken to task for the present state of affairs in which people must trust primarily to "official grace" and other non-legal considerations for their information. Qualifications in other acts of Congress have allowed agencies "to withhold practically all the information they do not see fit to disclose." He also criticizes the 1951 executive order which, while providing uniform standards for classifying and protecting security information, at the same time deprives the courts of their jurisdiction to sit in judgment on issues of "right."

"Most of the existing rights to inspect state and municipal records, imperfect as such rights are in the absolute sense," are "strikingly superior . . . to the federal scene," Mr. Cross comments.

In a chapter on "State and Municipal

out the information in Mr. Cross's book was reported in an *Editor and Publisher* editorial on March 6. Ohio is cited as the eighth state to join the ranks of those which have laws providing that "all meetings of any board or commission of any state agency or authority are declared to be public meetings open to the public at all times." Columbus, Ohio, immediately climbed on the bandwagon as its city council followed the state's lead with an ordinance which in effect forbids secret sessions for the public's business. By mid-March Maryland had become the ninth state to adopt an "open meeting" law. The Maryland Press Association was largely responsible for promoting adoption of the legislation.

"Eventually, every state should make such guarantees by law to its citizens," the editorial concludes. "Newspapers, as a general policy, should back these measures. Only their sustained interest and support will convince legislators."

ANDREW J. LAZARUS

Metropolitan Study Center at Northwestern University

Northwestern University has established a Center for Metropolitan Studies which will investigate the prospects and problems of metropolitan areas, giving special attention to metropolitan Chicago. It will function as a cooperative program integrating the work of specialists in several schools and departments of the university.

"The center," Dr. J. Roscoe Miller, Northwestern president, emphasized "is for both teaching and research in a field of study clearly vital to the welfare of us all."

The program of the center will include a continuation of a series of lecture discussions on metropolitan Chicago questions which was initiated in 1948 and conducted under the name of the Metropolitan Chicago Research Center. This series provides a forum for the exchange of information and policy opinions among members of the Chicago area business community, city and suburban officials and Northwestern University personnel.

New York Group Makes Awards for Service

The Citizens Budget Commission's annual awards for service to the city of New York were recently announced:

For high public service by an individual, Devereux C. Josephs, chairman of the Temporary State Commission to Study the Organizational Structure of the Government of the City of New York;

For a career that has exemplified the best in municipal civil service, Charles Gilman, administrator of business affairs of the Board of Education.

For the most noteworthy contribution by a newspaper during 1953 to an understanding of the significance of good management in achieving efficient and economical administration of the city of New York, *The New York Times* for articles written by Peter Kihss on the capital plant of New York.

Bureau Notes

The Municipal Technical Advisory Service of the University of Tennessee has received its 1,000th request for assistance from a Tennessee city. This request, typical of the other 999 received in the MTAS's four-year history, is for a "charter and code of ordinances" for Columbia. MTAS has received requests for technical assistance from approximately 190 different cities during the past year. Assistance to cities has involved almost every phase of municipal governmental activity.

The Associated Institutes of Government of Pennsylvania Universities has changed the name of its publication from *Municipal Administration* to *Horizons for Modern Pennsylvania Local Government.* "The change in name indicates the change of emphasis. The former publication directed the attention of local government officials to technical subjects in the field of public administration. *Horizons* will try to lift the eyes from day-by-day routine to over-all problems that need to be solved if Pennsylvania local government is to continue to adjust itself to the needs of the modern day." The January 1954 issue was the first number in the new series.

Research Pamphlets and Articles

Aged

HOMES FOR THE AGED. Story No. 1— BACKGROUND FOR ACTION; Story No. II— A PROJECT AND A PROBLEM. (A problem of the Toronto Metropolitan Federation). By Eric Hardy. Toronto 5, Bureau of Municipal Research, *Civic Affairs,* January 28 and February 12, 1954. 5 and 4 pp. respectively.

Alcoholism

ALCOHOLISM. Public Health Problem No. 4. Frankfort, Kentucky Legislative Research Commission, November 1953. 20 pp.

Budgets

BUDGETS, SURPLUSES — DEFICITS AHEAD??? Michigan Expects to Balance its Budget this June, But There is Possibility of Another Deficit in 1956. Detroit 26, Citizens Research Council, *Council Comments,* February 12, 1954. 4 pp.

FURTHER STEPS TOWARD A BALANCED MUNICIPAL RAILWAY BUDGET. San Francisco, Bureau of Governmental Research, *Bulletin,* February 26, 1954. 2 pp.

Business and Government

CLINIC ON STATE GOVERNMENT. By Jack B. Mackay. Chicago 37, Council of State Governments, *State Government,* December 1953. 4 pp. (Excerpts appear as "Minnesota's Novel Experiment. Business and Government Figures Convene to Discuss Common Problems."

New York 20, Tax Foundation, *Tax Outlook,* February 1954. 4 pp.)

Capital Improvements

FINANCING PHILADELPHIA'S FUTURE CAPITAL IMPROVEMENTS. (Revised Edition.) Philadelphia 7, Bureau of Municipal Research, August 1953. 22 pp.

County Government

A COUNTY EXECUTIVE OFFICER. By Samuel K. Gove. Urbana, University of Illinois, The Department of Agricultural Economics and the Institute of Government and Public Affairs, *Local Government Notes,* November 1953. 6 pp.

Drunken Driving

TESTS FOR DRUNKEN DRIVING. Baton Rouge, Louisiana Legislative Council, February 2, 1954. 17 pp.

Education

5000 CITIZENS REPORT ON THEIR SCHOOLS. Kentucky's Education Puzzle. Frankfort, Kentucky Legislative Research Commission, August 1953. 13 pp.

LOCAL PUBLIC SCHOOL EXPENSES AND STATE AID IN CONNECTICUT. Including Data for the School Year, 1952-1953. Hartford 3, Connecticut Public Expenditure Council, January 1954. 33 pp.

Efficiency

MEASURING EFFICIENCY FACTORS IN LOCAL GOVERNMENT. By S. Sugden. London W.C.2 (England), *The Municipal Journal, Public Works Engineer and Contractors' Guide,* February 19, 1954. 1 p.

Federal-local Relations

FEDERAL-CITY LEGISLATIVE DEVELOPMENTS. A Report from Washington. By Albert Rains. Montgomery, Alabama League of Municipalities, *Alabama Municipal Journal,* February 1954. 3 pp.

Flood Control

THE CENTRAL AND SOUTHERN FLORIDA FLOOD CONTROL PROJECT. By William F. Larsen. Gainesville, University of Florida, Public Administration Clearing Service, 1954. 24 pp.

Handbooks

A HANDBOOK FOR TEXAS VOTERS. (Revised Edition.) Austin, University of Texas, 1953. 60 pp. 50 cents.

Legislative Bodies

LEGISLATIVE REORGANIZATION IN MINNESOTA. Minneapolis 3, League of Women Voters of Minnesota, November 1953. 20 pp. 20 cents.

Liquor Control

IMPACT ON ALCOHOLIC BEVERAGE CONTROL OF TAXATION AND MARK-UP. Cleveland 14, Joint Committee of the States to Study Alcoholic Beverage Laws, 1953. 59 pp.

STATE VS. LOCAL LIQUOR CONTROL. San Francisco 19, Commonwealth Club of California, The Commonwealth, Supplement, March 1, 1954. 36 pp. 25 cents.

Mining

STRIP MINING. A 1954 Kentucky Legislative Problem. Frankfort, Kentucky Legislative Research Commission, January 1954. 15 pp.

Municipal Government

MUNICIPAL GOVERNMENT IN NEW JERSEY. By Stanley H. Friedelbaum. New Brunswick (New Jersey), Rutgers University Press, 1954. 63 pp.

REPORT OF THE PROCEEDINGS AT THE 68th ANNUAL GENERAL MEETING AND CONFERENCE. London, Westminster, S. W. 1 (England), Institute of Municipal Treasurers and Accountants, 1953. 134 pp.

Probation and Parole

PROBATION AND PAROLE IN THE UNITED STATES. Baton Rouge, Louisiana Legislative Council, January 13, 1954. 45 pp.

Public Safety

THE PUBLIC SAFETY DEPARTMENT. A Study of Integrated Police and Fire Services. Martinez (California), Contra Costa County Taxpayers' Association, December 1953. 4 pp.

Public Welfare

BIENNIAL ROUND TABLE CONFERENCE ISSUE. Chicago 37, American Public Welfare Association, Public Welfare. January 1954. 44 pp. $1.00.

Purchasing

ONE YEAR UNDER THE NEW CITY PURCHASING SYSTEM. Houston 2 (Texas), Tax Research Association of Houston and Harris County, TRA Journal Newsletter, January 1954. 4 pp.

Reapportionment

LEGISLATIVE REAPPORTIONMENT. 1955 Legislature to Have Unusual Senate Districts. Four Counties Without Senators. Madison 3, Wisconsin Taxpayers Alliance, The Wisconsin Taxpayer, February 1954. 6 pp.

Recreation

THE MUNICIPAL RECREATION SURVEY —ITS NATURE, ITS PURPOSE, ITS VALUE. By William G. Robinson. Ann Arbor, Michigan Municipal League, Michigan Municipal Review, February 1954. 2 pp.

State Aid

THE PROPOSED REVISION OF STATE AID IN MASSACHUSETTS. By Troy R. Westmeyer. Boston, Boston University, School of Law, Law Review, January 1954. 18 pp. $1.00.

State Government

MICHIGAN REGULATORY AGENCIES. Part I—AN OVER-ALL VIEW WITH FINDINGS AND RECOMMENDATIONS. Part II—INDIVIDUAL AGENCIES. Lansing, Michigan Joint Legislative Committee on Reorganization of State Government, 1953. 74 and 136 pp. respectively.

STATE ADMINISTRATIVE AGENCIES. Constitutionally Prescribed Powers and Duties. By University of Oklahoma, Bureau of Government Research. Oklahoma City, Oklahoma State Legislative Council, 1953, xiii, 86 pp.

State Printing

PRINTING BY STATE AGENCIES. Baton Rouge, Louisiana Legislative Council, January 26, 1954. 25 pp.

Taxation and Finance

GRAND LIST TRENDS. Hartford (Connecticut), Governmental Research Institute, Budget Alert, February 1954. 2 pp.

THE INCOME TAX AMENDMENT: A STRAIT-JACKET FOR SOUND FISCAL POLI-

CY. By William L. Cary. Chicago, *American Bar Association Journal*, October 1953. 4 pp.

1954 PROPERTY TAX TRENDS IN MILWAUKEE COUNTY LOCAL GOVERNMENTS. Milwaukee 2, Citizens' Governmental Research Bureau, Inc., *Bulletin*, February 18, 1954. 7 pp.

PAYMENTS IN LIEU OF TAXES. Digest of proposed laws introduced in 83rd Congress, 1st Session, prepared by the Washington office of The National Association of County Officials, Englewood (New Jersey), National Association of County Officials, *The County Officer*, February 1954. 2 pp.

REPORT ON LOCAL PUBLIC FINANCE IN CONTRA COSTA COUNTY—1953. Martinez (California), Contra Costa County Taxpayers' Association, January 1954. 16 pp. $1.00.

SALES TAX DIVERSION AND THE CONLIN PLAN. Detroit 26, Citizens Research Council, *Council Comments*, February 5, 1954. 4 pp.

$72 MILLION FEDERAL AID FOR STATE IN '53. Boston 8, Massachusetts Federation of Taxpayers Associations, *Taxtalk*, January 1954. 2 pp.

STATE AND LOCAL GOVERNMENT SPENDING: HOW FAST WILL IT RISE? Evidence Indicates Outlays Will Continue to Mount. By Roger A. Freeman. New York 20, The Tax Foundation, Inc., *Tax Review*, February 1954. 4 pp.

STATE INCOME TAX WITHHOLDING. Chicago 37, Federation of Tax Administrators, November 1952. 35 pp.

STATE SUPPORT AND GRASS ROOTS: CITY FINANCE. University, University of Mississippi, School of Commerce and Business Administration, Bureau of Public Administration, *Public Administration Survey*, January 1954. 6 pp.

TAX-EXEMPT PROPERTY AT RECORD PEAK. Boston 8, Municipal Research Bureau, *Bulletin*, January 1954. 2 pp.

TRENDS IN PUBLIC FINANCE—As They Affect Citizens and Taxpayers in Tennessee. Significant Aspects of Federal, State and Local Government Finance. Nashville 3, Tennessee Taxpayers Association, January 1954. 39 pp.

A TWO-YEAR ANALYSIS OF MINNESOTA'S STATE FISCAL OPERATIONS. St. Paul 1, Minnesota Institute of Governmental Research, Inc., February 1954. 8 pp.

UTAH STATE GOVERNMENT FINANCIAL SUMMARY, 1953-55 Biennium. Salt Lake City 1, Utah Foundation, *Research Report*, February 1954. 4 pp.

Trailers

TAXATION AND REGULATION OF HOUSE TRAILERS. Philadelphia 4, University of Pennsylvania, Associated Institutes of Government of Pennsylvania Universities, *Municipal Administration*, December 1953. 2 pp.

Urban Decentralization

ARE NEW YORK'S BUSINESS OFFICES ON THE WAY TO THE SUBURBS? New York, The Bowery Savings Bank, 1953. 13 pp.

Urban Redevelopment

TOWARDS A NEW BIRMINGHAM. SLUM CLEARANCE AND REDEVELOPMENT. London, *The Municipal Journal*, December 4, 1953. 27 pp.

Water and Sewer Service

THE WATER AND SEWER PROBLEMS OF METROPOLITAN COLUMBUS. Columbus 15, Citizens Research, Inc., 1954. 4 pp.

Water Systems

LEGAL PROBLEMS AND RESPONSIBILITIES IN ADMINISTERING WATER SYSTEMS. By Ernest H. Campbell. Seattle 5, Association of Washington Cities in cooperation with the University of Washington, Bureau of Governmental Research and Services, January 1954. 21 pp.

Workmen's Compensation

THE KANSAS WORKMEN'S COMPENSATION ACT. By Harry O. Lawson. Lawrence, University of Kansas, Governmental Research Center, *Your Government*, February 15, 1954. 5 pp.

Books in Review

STUDY KIT ON MICHIGAN LOCAL GOV-ERNMENT. Ann Arbor, University of Michigan, Bureau of Government, Institute of Public Administration, 1954. Variously paged. 75 cents. (Discounts on quantity orders.)

This kit will constitute an extremely useful tool for both citizen groups and schools in their study of local government. It consists of a series of eleven carefully prepared charts illustrating local government and an information pamphlet supplying descriptive detail in an easily readable style.

The charts and descriptive sections deal with specific cities as illustrations of the basic governmental forms. This gives the presentation a reality which is so often absent from abstract descriptions of organization or structure.

In addition to city governments, the village, rural township and urbanized township are described. The existing government and a model county manager plan for a moderate sized county are charted and discussed.

A chart dealing with the judiciary presents in graphic form the route of appeals and the jurisdiction of the several levels of the court system. The descriptive comment concludes with a discussion of elected versus appointed judges.

The final chart shows the tax calendar for counties, townships and school districts. The accompanying description defines a number of terms used in the chart, points to the importance of the property tax as a revenue source and suggests ways of improving the property tax process.

A particularly useful feature of the kit is the list of ways "to learn about . . . ," following each chapter of the explanatory pamphlet. If those who use this kit follow these suggestions they will have an invaluable series of field trips and interviews which cannot help but be informative.

Although the kit deals with structure, in the introduction it instructs those who use it: ". . . remember that it is *people* that make government good or bad. The best structure in the world cannot operate without competent officials backed by informed and interested citizens."

WILLIAM N. CASSELLA, JR.

PRESIDENTIAL ELECTION REFORMS. Edited by Walter M. Daniels. New York, H. W. Wilson Company, 1953. 200 pp. $1.75.

This timely compendium of recent discussions regarding the election of the president reflects the agitation developing in many quarters for less disorderly and more controllable procedures than those we now use in those vast private organizations which we call Democratic and Republican. Parties are essential in filling the gap left by the virtual elimination of discretion of presidential electors, but their internal methods are complex and in large part are unrealistic and only in nominal use. The idea that substantial numbers of party members will turn out at a precinct caucus to elect delegates of a county convention which, in turn, would elect delegates to a state convention of a thousand members, which will meet for a day and elect delegates to the national conventions is only about 5 per cent true to the facts as will presently be disclosed by a great study of the American Political Science Association covering the 1952 nomination processes in all the states.

This little volume brings together the most useful of recent comment and material.

R. S. C.

POLITICS, PRESIDENTS AND COATTAILS. By Malcolm Moos. Baltimore, Johns Hopkins Press, 1952. 237 pp. $4.50.

This is a statistical study of the degree to which congressional elections run

219

parallel to the presidential vote. It points out a growing disparity between the district votes and those of presidential candidates ranging from an average difference of 5.3 per cent from McKinley's election down to 1916 to 11.9 per cent for the period 1916-1948. Special attention is given to close districts and there is a large reduction of the facts to maps, tables and graphs. A source book and an important one with some fresh evidence for students of congressional phenomena and of our political parties at the national level!

Additional Books and Pamphlets

(See also Researcher's Digest and other departments)

Aged

A BIBLIOGRAPHY FOR MATURE READERS. New York 16, *Lifetime Living Magazine,* 1954. 25 pp.

HOW TO LIVE FROM 40 ON. By *Lifetime Living Magazine* in cooperation with Senator Thomas C. Desmond, chairman, New York State Joint Legislative Committee on Problems of the Aging. New York 16, *Lifetime Living Magazine,* 1954. 24 pp.

THE NEEDS OF OLDER PEOPLE AND PUBLIC WELFARE SERVICES TO MEET THEM. An analysis and Description of Public Welfare Experience. By Elizabeth Wickenden. Chicago, American Public Welfare Association, 1953. 148 pp. $2.

Annexation

ANNEXATION PROBLEMS AND SUGGESTIONS FOR ADOPTING AN ANNEXATION POLICY. REPORT ON PROPOSED CHRISTIANSEN ANNEXATION. Beloit (Wisconsin), Office of City Manager, 1953. 7 and 9 pp. respectively.

Assessors

PROCEEDINGS—1952 AND 1953 INSTITUTES FOR MUNICIPAL ASSESSORS. Madison 3, League of Wisconsin Municipalities, Assessors' Section, 1953. 126 pp.

County Government

COUNTY GOVERNMENT IN ESSEX, NEW JERSEY. An Outline of Its Origin, Its History and Its Functions Today. Compiled from Information Collected by Its County Supervisor Walter S. Gray. Newark, Essex County Board of Chosen Freeholders, 1953. 108 pp. Illus.

Directories

ILLINOIS MUNICIPAL DIRECTORY. Officials of Illinois Municipalities over 1,000 population. Mayors, Village Presidents and Clerks of Illinois Municipalities of Less Than 1,000 Population. Springfield, Illinois Municipal League, 1953. 96 pp. $5.00.

Economics

ASPECTS OF THE LOUISVILLE AREA ECONOMY. By James W. Martin and Will S. Myers. With the cooperation of *The Louisville Courier-Journal and Times,* Louisville Chamber of Commerce and Agricultural and Industrial Development Board of Kentucky. Frankfort, Agricultural and Industrial Development Board of Kentucky, 1953. 47 pp.

Housing

HOUSING CONSERVATION ROUND TABLE. Report and Recommendations. New York 20, *House & Home,* October 1953. 16 pp.

PUBLIC HOUSING. By Paul L. Poirot. Irvington-on-Hudson (New York) Foundation for Economic Education, 1954. 36 pp. Single copy free; 8 copies $1.00; 25 copies $2.50.

Judiciary

BAR SURVEYS OF TRIAL COURTS. Homer S. Cummings Lecture on Judicial Administration. By Murray Seasongood. New York 3, New York University, School of Law, 1952. 12 pp.

Juvenile Delinquency

UNDERSTANDING THAT BOY OF YOURS. By Melbourne S. Applegate. Washington, D. C., Public Affairs Press, 1953. 52 pp. $1.00.

DELPHIA, 1943-1952 (Ten-year Issue). Philadelphia 7, City Planning Commission, *Public Information Bulletin,* July 1953. 8 pp.

Recreation

SCHOOL-CITY COOPERATION IN THE PLANNING OF RECREATION AREAS AND FACILITIES. By George D. Butler. (Reprinted from *Recreation,* April, May and June, 1953.) New York 10, National Recreation Association, 1953. 12 pp. Illus. 75 cents.

Refuse Disposal

REFUSE COLLECTION AND DISPOSAL FOR THE SMALL COMMUNITY. Chicago 37, American Public Works Association, November 1953. vi, 39 pp.

Retirement

RETIREMENT COVERAGE OF STATE AND LOCAL GOVERNMENT EMPLOYEES. Washington 25, D. C., Department of Commerce, Bureau of the Census, 1953. 12 pp. 10 cents.

Service Charges

SEWAGE SERVICE CHARGES IN CITIES OVER 5,000 POPULATION. Chicago 37, American Public Works Association, 1953. $2.00.

Slum Clearance

A NEW FACE FOR AMERICA. A Program of Action Planned to Stop Slums and Rebuild Our Cities. Washington 6, D. C., National Association of Home Builders, 1953. 25 pp. Illus.

SELECTED CHARACTERISTICS OF LOCAL PROGRAMS AND PROGRAM OPERATIONS as of June 30, 1953. ASPECTS OF COSTS: 42 PROJECTS WITH LOAN AND GRANT ALLOCATIONS as of September 30, 1953. Washington, D. C., Housing and Finance Agency, Division of Slum Clearance and Urban Redevelopment, 1953. 6 and 12 pp. respectively.

Taxation and Finance

THE NEW YORK STATE AND LOCAL TAX SYSTEM 1953. Albany 1, New York State Department of Taxation and Finance,

State Tax Commission, Research and Statistics Bureau, 1953. 32 pp.

OKLAHOMA SALES TAX INCLUDING OPERATIONS OF THE USE TAX AND COIN DEVICE LICENSES. Statistical Report for the Fiscal Year Ending June 30, 1953. Oklahoma City, Oklahoma Tax Commission, Division of Research and Statistics, 1953. 37 pp.

TAXES, NATIONAL SECURITY AND ECONOMIC GROWTH. New York 22, Committee for Economic Development, Research and Policy Committee, 1954. 44 pp.

THE TAX INSTITUTE AND POSSIBILITIES OF FUTURE SERVICE. By Herbert M. Kelton. (Presidential Address, December 4, 1953) Princeton (New Jersey), Tax Institute, Inc., *Tax Policy*, January 1954. 8 pp. 25 cents.

Unemployment Relief

THE PROBLEM OF ABUSE IN UNEMPLOYMENT BENEFITS—A STUDY IN LIMITS. By Joseph M. Becker. New York City, Columbia University Press, 1953. xx, 412 pp. $6.50.

Urban Redevelopment

TOWARD A NEW FACE FOR AMERICA'S CITIES. Cities Organized Reconstruction. (Based on New Orleans activities.) Washington, D. C., National Association of Home Builders, Department of Housing Rehabilitation, 1953. 16 pp. Illus.

Youth

FROM SCHOOL TO JOB: GUIDANCE FOR MINORITY YOUTH. By Ann Tanneyhill. New York 16, Public Affairs Committee, 1953. 28 pp. 25 cents.

Zoning

SUGGESTED MUNICIPAL REGULATIONS FOR ROADSIDE ZONING ALONG NEW JERSEY'S BLUE STAR MEMORIAL HIGHWAY. Trenton 7, State of New Jersey Department of Conservation and Economic Development, Planning Section, 1953. 12 pp.

PRE-PRIMARY TRIAL DROPPED
(Continued from page 191)

ber, is difficult to determine. That many do so is a fact.

The recent repeal of the pre-primary convention statute ended a brief experiment. It was an interesting chapter in the politics of the state. To some it was quite satisfactory. But to its opponents it was unacceptable from the beginning. It was adopted through the urging of party leaders in order that they might give the voters their announced preferences. It did serve as a guide, but whether it did more than that is difficult to appraise.

There was more than mere lip-service given to the idea that political party leadership was essential and that it could not maintain itself with the unrestricted use of the direct primary. Where the average voter may not have much information about the maze of candidates he finds when entering the voting booth he may earnestly want to know party preferences. Beginning in 1954 the Nebraska voter will find his party primary ballot with names only and must rely upon the tacit understandings of preferences by the party managers.

It is unlikely that the law will be re-enacted in the near future, if ever. But it had many friends, most of them apparently outside the state legislature. The fact that the Nebraska legislature is nominated and elected on a nonpartisan ballot may have had some bearing on the repeal during the 1953 session, but the legislature which enacted it ten years earlier was similarly elected.

INSIDE THE OFFICE . . .

Theodore White of *The Reporter* magazine and author of Book-of-the-Month-Club selection *Fire in The Ashes*, walked into the office two weeks ago in

Theodore White

search of information about American cities and states. Home from a fifteen-year stint as foreign correspondent in the Far East and Europe, White believes that some of the most dramatic stories of the day are brewing in the U.S.A. right now. . . . **Thomas Graham,** president of the Bankers Bond Company in Louisville and new NML Council member, paid a call to the office recently. He expressed interest in the League's evolving program in state government. . . . **Franklin A. Lindsay** of the Ford Foundation talked with staff members about the League's work. . . .

Miss Helen H. Abreu, chief attorney of the Philippines' Commission on Elections, conferred recently with John Bebout on her study of American election administration. She is currently studying at New York University. . . . **Arthur Glover,** director of the Schenectady (New York) Bureau of Municipal Research, came to the NML for advice on a state conference on county government

Sherwood Reeder

Belle Zeller

ment to be held in Schenectady. . . . **Radio Free Europe** and the **Voice of America** have checked with the staff regarding the All-America Cities Awards and other recent citizen action stories. Both stations are planning a number of programs, based on the winning cities' experiences, for overseas broadcast. . . . **Sherwood Reeder,** president of the Pennsylvania Economy League, was a caller at the office. . . .

The **National Federation of Business and Professional Women's Clubs** has ordered 2,300 Citizen Association manuals for incorporation in its study kits to go to affiliates all over the country. Also ordered were reprints of the *Look* article on the All-America Cities Awards and a leaflet describing the contest. . . . John Keith, League senior associate and trustee of the **Governmental Research Association,** met with the GRA trustees and GRA conference committee on plans for the organization's 1954 conference. . . .

John M. Kernochan

Professor **Belle Zeller** of Brooklyn College, Professor **John Kernochan** of Columbia University, and **Herbert**

(Continued on next page)

223

Conference Panel Report Available

A report entitled *More Responsible States* has been issued by the League. The report is a mimeographed transcript of a panel session held in November during the 59th National Conference on Government at Richmond, Virginia.

Chairman of the session was Frank C. Moore, former lieutenant governor of New York, now president of the Government Affairs Foundation. Participating in the discussion were W. Brooke Graves, Library of Congress; George D. Braden, town counsel, Plainville, Connecticut; Mrs. Tom Ragland, Democratic National Committeewoman for Tennessee; Charlton F. Chute, Pennsylvania Economy League, Southeastern Division; Albert L. Sturm, West Virginia University; and Charles B. Coates, general manager, Citizens' Committee for the Hoover Report.

The report, which covers 33 pages, is available from the League's office for 50 cents, or may be obtained on request without charge by sustaining members.

New Directory-Report to Be Issued Soon

The League will shortly issue a new directory of its officers and council for the current year in conjunction with a report covering operations for 1953.

First part of the 64-page booklet will contain the report, while the main section will comprise biographical sketches of the League's principal officers, regional vice presidents and council members.

Survey Committee Revises Constitution

The NML Survey Committee has prepared a proposed revision of the League's constitution which will be distributed to officers and Council for consideration at the spring meeting of the Council. Accompanying the revised constitution will be a tentative draft of the Survey Committee's report dealing with its recommendations regarding the study of the League's operations and future opportunities prepared by Dr. Joseph E. McLean of Princeton University.

Upon the Council's approval, the revision will be circulated to League members. Final action will occur in November at the annual membership meeting during the 60th National Conference on Government in Kansas City, Mo.

The revision reflects more clearly, fully and explicitly the extent and nature of the League's program. It puts greater emphasis on the educational nature of the League's work and on its service being primarily directed to citizens. Classes of membership are omitted, being left for the Council to decide. Other proposed revisions deal with the government of the League and are aimed to bring the constitution more in line with current practice and needs. One proposal allows for a larger Executive Committee, which will provide for more flexible government as well as sufficient quorums to conduct the League's business during the year.

(Continued from preceding page)

Wiltsee and B. E. Crihfield, Council of State Governments, met with League staff members. . . . Over 3,000 copies of a new leaflet describing the All-America Cities Awards and a reprint of the *Look* article have been requested by the Chamber of Commerce of the United States.

224

MAY 1954   VOLUME XLIII, NO. 5

The National Municipal Review

ALFRED WILLOUGHBY, Editor   ELSIE S. PARKER, Assistant Editor

CONTRIBUTING EDITORS

JOHN E. BEBOUT, Research
RICHARD S. CHILDS
EDWARD W. WEIDNER, County and Township
H. M. OLMSTED, City, State and Nation

WADE S. SMITH, Taxation and Finance
GEORGE H. HALLETT, JR.
WM. REDIN WOODWARD
Proportional Representation

STATE CORRESPONDENTS

H. F. ALDERFER, *Pennsylvania*
CARTER W. ATKINS, *Connecticut*
MYRON B. ATKINSON, *North Dakota*
CHESTER BIESEN, *Washington*
D. BENTON BISER, *Maryland*
ERNEST M. BLACK, *Oklahoma*
JOHN C. BOLLENS, *California*
WILLIAM L. BRADSHAW, *Missouri*
A. C. BRECKENRIDGE, *Nebraska*
ARTHUR W. BROMAGE, *Michigan*
FRANKLIN L. BURDETTE, *Maryland*
CHARLTON F. CHUTE, *Pennsylvania*
WELDON COOPER, *Virginia*
C. A. CROSSER, *Washington*
PAUL DOLAN, *Delaware*
D. MACK EASTON, *Colorado*
WILLIAM O. FARBER, *South Dakota*
VICTOR FISCHER, *Alaska*
FOREST FRANK, *Ohio*
DAVID FUDGE, *Oklahoma*
ROBERT M. GOODRICH, *Rhode Island*
MRS. LEONARD HAAS, *Georgia*
M. H. HARRIS, *Utah*
SAM HAYS, *Arkansas*
ROBERT B. HIGHSAW, *Mississippi*
JACK E. HOLMES, *New Mexico*
ORREN C. HORMELL, *Maine*
HERMAN KEHRLI, *Oregon*
PAUL KELSO, *Arizona*

DRYDEN KUSER, *Nevada*
JOHN D. LANGMUIR, *New Hampshire*
STUART A. MacCORKLE, *Texas*
RICHARD G. MARDEN, *New Hampshire*
BOYD A. MARTIN, *Idaho*
EDWARD M. MARTIN, *Illinois*
JAMES W. MARTIN, *Kentucky*
JAMES W. McGREW, *New Jersey*
DAYTON D. McKEAN, *Colorado*
EDWIN B. McPHERON, *Indiana*
WILLIAM MILLER, *New Jersey*
LENNOX L. MOAK, *Pennsylvania*
ANDREW E. NUQUIST, *Vermont*
KIMBROUGH OWEN, *Louisiana*
FRANK W. PRESCOTT, *Tennessee*
JOHN E. REEVES, *Kentucky*
ROLAND R. RENNE, *Montana*
PAUL N. REYNOLDS, *Wisconsin*
RUSSELL M. ROSS, *Iowa*
ALBERT B. SAYE, *Georgia*
VICTORIA SCHUCK, *Massachusetts*
LLOYD M. SHORT, *Minnesota*
GEORGE G. SIPPRELL, *New York*
PAUL D. STEWART, *West Virginia*
JOHN G. STUTZ, *Kansas*
HERMAN H. TRACHSEL, *Wyoming*
PAUL W. WAGER, *North Carolina*
YORK WILLBERN, *Alabama*
JOHN F. WILLMOTT, *Florida*

Published by THE NATIONAL MUNICIPAL LEAGUE

George H. Gallup, *President*

John S. Linen, *Vice President*
George S. Van Schaick, *Vice President*

Carl H. Pforzheimer, *Treasurer*
Alfred Willoughby, *Executive Director*

Richard S. Childs, *Chairman, Executive Committee*

COUNCIL

Charles Edison, West Orange, N. J., *Chairman*

Frederick L. Bird, New York
Arthur W. Bromage, Ann Arbor, Mich.
E. Bartlett Brooks, Dayton, Ohio
Henry Bruère, New York
William H. Bulkeley, Hartford
L. E. Burch, Jr., Memphis
Mrs. Albert D. Cash, Cincinnati
Charles E. Commander, Jr., Jacksonville
L. P. Cookingham, Kansas City, Mo.
Karl Detzer, Leland, Mich.
E. D. Dodd, Toledo
Harold W. Dodds, Princeton, N. J.
Bayard H. Faulkner, Montclair, N. J.
Arnold Frye, New York

Ewart W. Goodwin, San Diego
Thomas Graham, Louisville
Mrs. Virgil Loeb, St. Louis
Rob Roy Macleod, Buffalo
Mark S. Matthews, Greenwich, Conn.
Cecil Morgan, New York
Albert F. Noelte, Central Falls, R. I.
Mrs. Maurice H. Noun, Des Moines
H. Bruce Palmer, Newark, N. J.
Lawson Purdy, New York
Thomas R. Reid, Dearborn, Mich.
Philip K. Robinson, Milwaukee
Murray Seasongood, Cincinnati
Lee M. Sharrar, Houston

REGIONAL VICE PRESIDENTS

Lester L. Bates, Columbia, S. C.
William Collins, New York
Ben B. Ehrlichman, Seattle
John B. Gage, Kansas City, Mo.
Carl J. Gilbert, Boston
Barry Goldwater, Phoenix
Lloyd Hale, Minneapolis

Arthur K. Johnson, Denver
Mrs. Siegel W. Judd, Grand Rapids
John Nuveen, Chicago
Ed. P. Phillips, Richmond
Charles P. Taft, Cincinnati
Alex R. Thomas, San Antonio
Carleton B. Tibbetts, Los Angeles

NEWS for League Members

Kansas City Plans Conference

Representatives of 50 Kansas City civic organizations met recently at the Continental Hotel in that city at the invitation of John B. Gage, regional vice president of the League, to make plans for the November 7-10 National Conference on Government.

Allen H. Seed, Jr., League assistant director, talked to the group about the Conference and upon his return to New York reported enthusiasm for the League's 60th meeting, which will be held in the Hotel President.

Mr. Gage was chosen chairman of the sponsoring and arrangements committee. Clinton W. Kanaga, Jr., president of the Kansas City Citizens Association, and Mrs. Gil Miller, president of the League of Women Voters, were elected vice chairmen. Cliff C. Jones, president of R. B. Jones and Sons and member of the League finance committee, will serve as treasurer.

Mr. Kanaga said the committee would be enlarged to include representatives of civic groups from all of Missouri and Kansas as well as Kansas City itself.

Among the organizations represented at the meeting were the Kansas City Citizens Association, Parent-Teachers Association, Community Councils, Citizens Regional Planning Council, Chamber of Commerce, Women's and Junior Chambers of Commerce, Kiwanis and Rotary Clubs, League of Women Voters, Kansas City University, University of Kansas, Boys Club, radio stations and others.

Allen H. Seed, Jr., addressing the organization luncheon in Kansas City, Missouri, on March 24. Seated at the speaker's table are, left to right, Winifred Wilder, executive secretary, Citizens Association; Blanche Barnett, former president, Women's Chamber of Commerce; Richard Righter, Chamber of Commerce; Mr. Seed, Clinton Kanaga, Jr., chairman, Citizens Association; Mrs. John B. Gage, Mrs. Gil Miller, president, League of Women Voters; Harold Mann, president, Community Councils; Hayes Richardson, director, Kansas City Department of Welfare.

League Council Holds Mid-year Meeting

An old NML custom has been revived in the all-day spring council meeting scheduled for May 7 at the Waldorf-Astoria Hotel in New York. The meeting was called by President George Gallup in accordance with instructions voted by the Council at the meeting in Richmond last November.

Main business of the session is consideration of the report of the Survey Committee chaired by Cecil Morgan. The Committee's report, based on recommendations in the "evaluation" of the League's program and operations by Dr. Joseph E. McLean of Princeton University, was mailed to council members in March. A major feature of the report is a revision of the League's constitution, to be submitted, subject to Council approval, for adoption at the November membership meeting in connection with the National Conference on Government in Kansas City. The proposed constitution includes a new statement of League objectives.

In the early years, the Council regularly held two meetings annually. The last spring meeting was held in Chicago in May 1933. Since that time, the Executive Committee has acted for the Council on all matters coming up between annual meetings.

Larsen Awarded Staff Fellowship

William F. Larsen, assistant professor of political science and director of the Public Administration Clearing Service, University of Florida, has been awarded the National Municipal League Staff Fellowship for 1954-55. He will join the League staff in July on a one-year leave of absence from the university.

William F. Larsen

Mr. Larsen earned his B.A. and M.A. degrees from the University of Tennessee, and has completed all his Ph.D. requirements, save his thesis, at the University of California. During World War II he served with the army in Europe. He has taught at the University of Tennessee and The Citadel in Charleston, South Carolina. He is currently educational consultant to the Florida civil defense director and is on the board of directors of the Florida Planning and Zoning Association.

Meeting of the NML Staff Fellowship Committee at the American Society for Public Administration Conference in Chicago, March 20. Left to right, John E. Bebout, League assistant director; Joseph E. McLean, William N. Cassella, Jr., present Staff Fellow; Edwin O. Stene, Winston W. Crouch, Edward W. Weidner, Guthrie S. Birkhead, former Staff Fellow; Roscoe C. Martin, chairman; Lee S. Greene, and Alfred Willoughby, League executive director.

National Municipal Review

Volume XLIII, No. 5   Total Number 443

Published monthly except August
By NATIONAL MUNICIPAL LEAGUE

Contents for May 1954

The contents of the REVIEW are indexed in *International Index to Periodicals* and *Public Affairs Information Service.*

Entered as second class matter July 11, 1932, at the Post Office at Worcester, Massachusetts. Publication office, 150 Fremont Street, Worcester 3; editorial and business office, 542 Fifth Avenue, New York 36. Copyright 1954 by the National Municipal League.

Subscription, $5 per year; Canadian, $5.25; foreign, $5.50; single copies 50 cents.

Editorial Comment

Pledges Against the Future

This guest editorial is extracted from a report under the same title prepared by the Pennsylvania Economy League. The report says very well some important things that apply to state government in general. —EDITOR.

PENNSYLVANIA'S government, not unlike other states, has a built-in habit of acting first and facing the consequences later. By the terms of the constitution the governor cannot succeed himself and, humanly, is most concerned with what will happen in his own four years of administrative responsibility. Each legislative session is an organism unto itself, with only one-half of the Senate's membership certain of returning to legislate again. The sessions are held only every other year, and the lapse of time works against continuity of policy. By ancient custom, the legislators adjourn in the high spirits that come from a sense of relief—that session's days of responsibility are over!

No one in official life has the obligation of observing the long-term trends in state government in Pennsylvania, particularly in the growing involvements of the state with local governments. In theory, the state has its jobs to do and the local governments have theirs. In practice, the state now devotes a major share of its total revenues to local purposes and the legislature's liveliest issues are the ones which relate to local governments, their powers and their finances.

A citizen's organization whose purpose is better government at less cost everywhere in Pennsylvania does have such an obligation, and the Pennsylvania Economy League accepts it fully.

Because the league has a state office which deals directly with the state government at all times and with the legislature during sessions, it is able to grasp the problems of state administration and to understand and interpret the state official's approach to them.

Because the league is also a local organization, with branches in 23 populous counties of the state, it is able to make true estimates of the effect of state programs in the municipalities and to understand and interpret the local official's problems and decisions.

To the league, the interaction of state policies and local administration is one of the continuous processes which we clock and test and predict. We are able, as few others are, to see it through its whole development—in legislation, in state administration and in local government.

We are also able to take our time. The elected official is a crowded man, racing against the calendar, the next election and the momentary pressures. The league has permanence. We have our pressures too—the multitudinous things that must be done in a hurry—but we are conscious that, every so often, we must stop to look at the long-term trends in the governmental areas which we service.

As it seems to the league, the strongest pressures against state finance will arise from the state's obligations to education, public health and stream purification. The pattern is one of increasing support by the state of locally-administered functions, usually because the state has chosen to enforce certain standards by law or to encourage their adoption by offers of financial aid.

Obviously, there will be an effect on the state's budgets in future years. Obviously, too, it should not creep up on us as a surprise. The programs should be estimated as to cost and value, and the citizens of the commonwealth should know what they are in for in terms of money and what they will get in terms of service. The Pennsylvania Economy League has charted this area of intergovernmental action as a major field of exploration.

It should be made very clear that the league's listing of these areas where state finance is affected by commitments to local governments does not indicate opposition to the theory of state matching funds, or necessarily to the purposes to which the various programs are dedicated. We do strongly believe that intelligent fiscal planning for the state and for its local governments must take these programs into consideration, not only as they now affect the state's budget but as they are likely to do so in the future.

There should be no blanket condemnation of them as "give away" programs on the part of the state, but there should be constant reexamination of them from the standpoint of effectiveness, economy and equity in distribution. The large cities believe that state aid programs are usually weighted against their interests. There is a steady tension in all grants-in-aid programs as to how much jurisdiction the higher unit of government should exercise over the expenditure of the funds it distributes. There is the danger of the state making commitments beyond its ability to pay. And, above all, there is the lack of a coordinated long-term understanding of the range of these problems, a lack of continuity in the state's observation of them, and a lamentable failure to relate them one with the other with respect to their final impact on the state's finances.

The commonwealth of Pennsylvania is sadly in need of an official planning body, reporting directly to the governor and the legislature, with an overlapping membership that will give it a sense of allegiance to the state and not to any particular administration. The existing State Planning Board is obviously limited by its subordination to one department of the state government and by a relatively narrow field of operations. A properly established planning agency would accept responsibility for projecting and constantly evaluating the long-range objectives and needs of the commonwealth.

Municipal 'Charm School'

*Milwaukee teaches its public servants how to get along
with their bosses, the taxpayers, during the day's work.*

By MICHAEL COSTELLO*

A MILWAUKEE man named Johnson telephoned city hall one afternoon last winter with a complaint. He was an honest, hardworking citizen, a taxpayer, a home owner. At the moment he also was the maddest man in Milwaukee.

"This the tax commission?" Johnson yelled. "You bet there's something you can do for me. I'm warning you I'm not going to keep on paying taxes and have you . . . ."

"What seems to be the trouble, sir?" the calm voice at city hall asked.

"Trouble? Listen, mister, and I'll tell you! You're not going to get away with it. Not for a minute! I just get home from work and what do I find? My wife shows me what you blankety-blank fools have been doing to my property today. With the taxpayers' money, yet. Bunch of surveyors come out on account you're going to blacktop the street. So what do they do? They raise the curb line nine inches! So when it rains the curb will push the water back in my lawn and down my basement windows! I tell you, I'm not going to stand . . . ."

"Just a moment, sir," the city hall voice, still unruffled, broke in. "You have the wrong department, but . . . ."

"That's it! Always give the taxpayer the run around!"

"Not at all, sir. Give me your address and I'll take it up with the engineers at once. I'm sure they'll come out to see you right away."

Johnson gave him the address and hung up. What good did it do to argue with a fellow who refused to argue back? And within two hours a young city engineer was rapping politely at the Johnson door. It turned out he was the sensible sort of engineer who would listen to a practical man. The two stood in the street and studied the curb line. Johnson had taken out his own steel rule, just in case there might be an argument. The engineer borrowed the rule, asked Johnson to help him measure. Thus it was Johnson who discovered that the curb was not nine but four inches too high.

"This curb settled since it was put in four years ago," the engineer said pleasantly. "Built on a fill over an old celery farm, just like your lot. If you want, when we make the cut in the next block, we'll dump a couple of loads in your yard. You can smooth it off yourself. That will protect your property and not cost anybody anything. I certainly want to thank you for calling it to our attention. Wish more people would do that."

"Come in and have a glass of beer," Johnson said.

Taxpayer Johnson and thousands of other Milwaukee citizens each

---

*Michael Costello is a pen name used at times by Karl Detzer. Mr. Detzer, writer and former newspaper publisher, is a member of the council of the National Municipal League. This article may not be republished, in whole or in part, without permission.

day encounter this cheerful, co-operative attitude on the part of their public servants. Librarians and garbage collectors, telephone operators and tax assessors, museum guards and water department clerks, top officials and lowly employees in every branch of the city government go out of their way to give their ultimate bosses, the taxpayers, the best possible service in the friendliest possible manner. The voters love it.

For generations the people of the beer city by the lake have been accustomed to good public service. In spite of an obsolete municipal government structure and unwieldly, outgrown methods, Milwaukee has been one of the best run cities. But of late something new has been added.

'Charm School'

The people call it the "Charm School"—a unique institution operated by the city to teach its employees how to deal pleasantly and efficiently with the public and with one another. In six years more than 1,000 municipal workers (about one in five), ranging from common laborers to department heads, have been graduated from the course. The clerk who took Johnson's telephone call and the engineer who borrowed his rule to measure the curb both were graduates. Eventually all city employees must take the course, except policemen—who have their own excellent training program—and teachers in the public school system.

The Charm School is the brain child of Mayor Frank P. Zeidler, a smart, rigidly honest 41-year-old administrator. Graduated from local schools, he•is the son of a local

barber. His brother was mayor before him, left office to join the Navy in World War II, and died in the Pacific.

Shortly after Frank Zeidler took office in 1948 he attended a picnic at which he heard several irate citizens discussing what they called "the run-around at city hall." Investigating, he found that several city employees, when faced with taxpayers' complaints, had tried to shunt them off on other departments. That is not hard to do in Milwaukee, which lists some 50 boards, commissions, departments and divisions of government in its municipal directory. Zeidler decided then and there that the practice must stop.

For aid he went to his old friend, William F. Rasche, director of Milwaukee's outstanding vocational school.

"I'm having trouble, Bill," the mayor said. "Do you have any courses that teach people how to get along with one another?"

"No," Rasche admitted, "but it sounds like a good idea."

That's how the Charm School was born. The two men planned it together and Zeidler set it up in the municipal civil service division, which hires and keeps the records of all employees. In charge he placed the assistant director of civil service, a pleasant, enthusiastic public servant named Ovid B. Blix. From the vocational school faculty, Rasche sent Miss Evelyn Shaw, whose training in psychology seemed to fit her for the job, to act as teacher.

The school term is four weeks. Classes run one hour each, two mornings a week, with from 18 to 25 students to a class. They attend on city time. It would be hard to find a more diverse group anywhere than the men and women of a typical class—accountants, labor foremen, telephone operators, engineers, stenographers, bridge tenders, public health nurses, planning analysts, tree surgeons, architects, garbage collection supervisors, punch-machine operators. Veterans and new employees quickly find that no matter what their jobs they face the same problems.

Conduct of Classes

"The more diversified, the better the class," Miss Shaw explains. "The laborer digging a hole in the street in front of some unhappy citizen's home and the girl answering a complaint on the city hall telephone may seem to have nothing in common, but underneath we find the same knotty human equations. In our classes we show how common courtesy makes everyone's job easier."

Time and again the school has proved that a librarian, by sharing what she has learned while dealing with the public at a check-out desk, can help the garbage collector, and that the garbage man in turn can assist the librarian. Architects, accountants and sewer workers, by pooling their wisdom and practical knowledge, solve headaches for one another. The youngsters supply enthusiasm, the old-timers solid judgment based on experience.

Classes are most informal. There are no lectures. Miss Shaw merely acts as discussion leader. One of her tasks is to keep everyone from talking at once when some problem common to all departments comes up for solution. Each member of each class brings personal experiences and convictions he wants to share.

At a recent session a museum guard brought up an awkward situation that long had troubled him. "I hate to talk about this here," he said, blushing hard and looking at the ceiling, "but a museum, it's a big place, with all kinds of shadowy corners and the like, and a fellow can't be everywhere at once. So these kids . . . well, there's too many of them and, when you do catch 'em, why they . . . I tell you, you've no idea."

"Oh, yes, we have a very good idea," a young librarian said. "Have you ever been in the stacks of a public library? The necking that goes on back of the biology shelves. . . ."

No one laughed. This was serious business. After a moment a park department laborer spoke.

"What if you had 40 acres of shrubs and bushes and flower beds? Me, I keep an elm club handy. When these kids begin to give me their lip, well, I chase 'em."

A public health nurse said suddenly, "I know how you feel about it, and why. But you're not going to drive young love out of a museum or a library or a park with a club. You just enrage these kids when you chase them. Why don't you say, 'Look, kids, I don't want you to get into trouble,' and act friendly. Be on *their* side. Pretty soon you'll find they're on yours."

One of the things stressed in every class is the opportunity all city employees have to help citizens save face. Milwaukee's police department has used this psychology for years with excellent results. Now the city is trying to make it universal.

"No matter how wrong a person may be, give him a loophole through which he can salvage his self-respect," Miss Shaw tells her students. "No one likes to be told he's 100 per cent wrong. And in even the most unreasonable man's argument there must be some point on which he is right. Watch for it. Agree heartily with it. That way you save his face and he will listen with less hostility to what you have to say."

New Type Class Book

At the first meeting of each class, every member receives the "Charm School Textbook," a small blue card on which the entire course is printed in 100 words. One side lists four steps to take in every public contact; on the other side are "tips for a city employee to remember."

The "tips" are these:

"My time is the taxpayers' money, entrusted to my care. I must invest it well. Service to the public is my duty. The public is made up of individuals who must be understood and dealt with as such. It is always smart to be courteous."

The four steps are just as simple:

1. GREET individual or group promptly, pleasantly, courteously, sincerely.

2. LISTEN attentively and patiently. Get the facts.

3. PROVIDE information, material, service, or . . . .

4. REFER to proper authority. Do everything possible to close the interview on a friendly note. Follow up when necessary.

The students often pair off, after the first few meetings, and bring their problems to class in dialogue form, one impersonating a taxpayer, the other a harassed city employee. When they have finished they ask the class what they have done wrong, how they could have done better. Lively discussions follow.

The school teaches the employee to listen attentively and carefully, to be sympathetic but cautious, to promise nothing that he isn't positive he can deliver. Because any municipality is bound up in red tape and hedged in by legal restrictions, many citizens have a hard time understanding why certain seemingly reasonable things cannot be done. The Charm School pounds home the necessity of explaining simply, patiently and at length, until even the most obtuse taxpayer understands.

The good effects of the school can be felt even among employees who have not yet attended a class. Participants go back to their departments full of enthusiasm and share it with their fellow workers. The fire-alarm office is an example. So far, only the supervisor has "been to school," but the dispatchers who man the switchboards reflect school training.

As in most cities, bewildered Milwaukee residents call the fire department with requests for all kinds of services and assistance which the city for many obvious reasons cannot be expected to render: there's a dead rat in a house wall, a landlord is stingy with his heat, a toilet will not flush, there's a cat up a tree, a neighbor has a barking dog, small boys are making life hideous in a quiet street. In most towns these complaints get short shrift.

"This is the fire department," the dispatchers say. "Is anything burning? Then why call us?"

The Milwaukee dispatchers listen patiently, sympathize properly, offer suggestions, and volunteer to refer the matter at once to the proper department.

The city instructs employees in how to deal pleasantly not only with the public but with each other. Any organism as complex as a city administration contains overlapping jurisdictions that lead to departmental quarrels. Too often employees "pass the buck" on difficult decisions.

The Charm School teaches city workers how to avoid this whenever possible, and why. Recently a truck driver, employed by one municipal division, applied for reinstatement after he had been discharged following an accident. The discharge may have been a mistake for there was nothing in the record to show that this driver had been at fault. But his application for reinstatement came in too late. Under the law he had three days to apply, but in typing the man's notice a stenographer had written "30 days" and then erased the zero imperfectly. It was a fine chance for a row.

"I read that for 30 days!" the driver insisted, "and this is only the seventh day."

"I'm sorry," the Charm School graduate said. "The law is specific.

But maybe we can fix it up some other way." She carefully avoided blaming the driver for being late or the stenographer for carelessness. Instead, she looked up the driver's record, found that in seven years he had been involved in no other accident. Then she helped him apply for a different job in another department—one that paid lots more than the lost job.

"It was the polite thing to do," she later said.

Mayor Zeidler has placed graduates on around-the-clock duty at city hall telephones to answer questions or receive and act on complaints. No matter what hour of the day or night an irate or unhappy citizen calls his city government, he gets courteous attention. Usually the specially trained complaint clerks are able to answer questions immediately or to set in motion the machinery to handle the matter promptly.

Hope Comments

Milwaukee's visitors detect this new sense of civic responsibility engendered in employees by the school. Comedian Bob Hope, reading of the school in the paper, was much impressed by the politeness of the public servants.

"When one garbage collector meets another in a Milwaukee alley these days," Hope said to his radio audience a few nights later, "he takes off his hat, bows from the waist and says, 'Sir, it's your turn to pour!'"

The taxpayers love it.

New York Area Still Stymied

Despite some consolidation and the use of palliatives,
metropolitan region does little to solve its problems.

By PAUL STUDENSKI*

AFTER AN interval of a quarter of a century there is a conspicuous renewal of interest in the problems of government of metropolitan areas. Inquiries into possible ways of improving existing organization and procedures are being considered in many areas.

In the efforts made in the New York region along these lines two periods stand out, that of the 1890s and that of the 1920s. Whether the region is on the threshold of another active period of attack upon this problem remains to be seen.

During the 1890s a comprehensive and highly imaginative, but still only partial, solution for the problem of organization of metropolitan government in the region was devised and applied. This was the consolidation of more than a hundred local governments, comprising what was then known as Greater New York, into the present City of New York.[1] It

was only a partial solution, however, inasmuch as it applied only to that portion of the area that lay within the borders of the state of New York and did not touch upon the New Jersey and Connecticut portions.

Consolidation was only a partial solution because it did not provide a practical pattern for future treatment of further extensions of the area. The consolidation could not be repeated indefinitely for, meanwhile, a strong reaction against their absorption by the central city had developed among the communities not embraced in the consolidation.

The borough form of government, adopted as the cornerstone of the consolidation, did not reserve enough self-government to the annexed communities and even this small measure was further curtailed in succeeding revisions of the city charter, so that the consolidated city ended up with having a fairly unitary type of government. At the same time the administration of this fairly centralized city did not always prove to be competent and free from corruption. Many suburban communities in the area could boast of better governments. The consolidation was unquestionably beneficial and no sane person ever proposed to undo it. But its benefits were somewhat marred by a loss in citizen participation in government. The advantages

---

*Dr. Studenski is professor of economics at New York University and fiscal consultant to the Division of the Budget of the State of New York. He has advised many federal, state and municipal agencies on problems of public finance and administration and is author of numerous works in the field, the latest of which (in collaboration with H. E. Krooss), is *Financial History of the United States* (McGraw Hill Book Company, New York, 1952).

[1]For a fuller account of the manner in which the consolidation was carried out and the government of the consolidated city reorganized later, see *Regional Survey of New York and Its Environs*, Volume II on *Population, Land Values and Government*, Chapter 6, by the author. Committee on Regional Plan of New York and Its Environs (now Regional Plan Association), New York, 1929.

of extending the boundaries of the city still further appeared to be dubious to most citizens who gave any thought to the subject.

All these considerations eventually prompted suburban communities in the New York and other metropolitan regions in the state to institute a move which would protect them against similar forcible annexation by a central city. An amendment to the state constitution, submitted to the people and adopted in 1927, prohibited annexation by a city of any territory against that territory's will. Thus a death knell was sounded to any future attempt, either in the New York or in any other metropolitan region in the state, to repeat the feat of the New York City consolidation of 1898.

Period of the 1920s

During the 1920s altogether different approaches to the problem were initiated. The war and the postwar boom had brought to the New York Port and to every other central and suburban segment of the region a tremendous increase in industry and population and, along with it, colossal traffic congestion and other problems requiring action on a grand scale.

New York and New Jersey were impelled to act jointly upon some of these problems, creating first the joint Bridge and Tunnel Commission and next the Port of New York Authority, while also acting separately upon other problems affecting the comfort and well-being of the populations of their respective sections of the region. Several *ad hoc* authorities and commissions, such as the North Jersey District Water Supply

Commission, the Long Island Park Commission and the Jones Beach Park Authority,[2] were set up by the two states.

At the same time, private civic effort brought about the organization of the Committee on Regional Plan of New York and Its Environs, predecessor to the Regional Plan Association, for a thorough study of the resources of the region and their best utilization for the benefit of all its people. It was the hope of the founders of the association to provide a pattern of development of the region which could serve as a guide to the local governments in their future individual or joint work.

The rapidly growing suburban populations of Westchester and Nassau Counties in New York and Hudson and Essex Counties in New Jersey began to turn to their county governments as the most suitable agencies for the care of some of their broader and most urgent needs. To enable these governments to do this job effectively, power to modernize county structures was sought.

During this period, the National Municipal League set up a Committee on Metropolitan Government to make a comprehensive study of the problem of metropolitan government in every major metropolitan area in the country. In the course of this study, the various solutions devised and applied up to that time, or being currently undertaken, were indicated, explored and appraised.[3] By crystal-

---

[2] For a fuller account of the genesis of these and other special authorities, see chapter 5 in the above-mentioned Volume II of the Regional Plan Association.

[3] *Government of Metropolitan Areas.* Report prepared by Paul Studenski with

lizing the thinking on the problem by civic leaders and students up to that time, the study laid the foundation for more enlightened action in the future.

All in all, the period of the 1920s was highly productive of new ideas and approaches to the problem. The solutions applied were of partial nature but they were quite effective within their p a r t i c u l a r narrow spheres.

Among the individuals who made great contributions to these developments were Julius Henry Cohen, architect of the Port of New York Authority; Frank H. Sommer, dean of the New York University Law School, one of the creators of the North Jersey District Water Supply Commission and chairman of the Committee on Metropolitan Government of the National Municipal League; Professor Charles E. Merriam of the University of Chicago; and Dr. Thomas H. Reed, a member of the League's Committee on Metropolitan Government, who has made a number of significant metropolitan government studies.

The Past Quarter Century

The outbreak of the depression of the 1930s interrupted this buoyant local activity by diverting public attention to critical national economic and financial developments. The outbreak of World War II similarly tended to detract public attention from the continuance of any major endeavor along that line. It would be a mistake, however, to conclude that all further activity in this field

the assistance of the Committee on Metropolitan Government, National Municipal League, New York, 1930, 405 pp.

was suspended in the 1930s and the greater part of the 1940s and that no progress towards the solution of the problem was made in either the New York or other metropolitan regions. P r o g r e s s merely became slower. It consisted mainly in the elaboration on a moderate scale of the partial solutions indicated or applied during the earlier period. But there were also some new approaches of no small importance. Progress has proceeded along seven major lines.

First, the federal government has assumed a larger share of responsibility for certain problems in the area, both by direct administration of certain functions and by the extension of grants-in-aid to certain local functions. Examples are WPA, PWA, FHA and public housing activities during the depression and development of extensive services and aids to veterans as well as aids to civil defense, highways, airports, welfare, school lunches and other local projects and activities during the war and postwar periods. Most of these activities were carried on by the federal government everywhere in the country. But, in their application to the New York and other metropolitan regions, they were necessarily planned and carried on, to some extent, with a view to the needs of the region as a whole.

Second, the state governments of New York and New Jersey have expanded administrative services and grants-in-aid considerably in their respective segments of this area, as exemplified by the construction and operation of extensive parks, parkways and other recreational facilities, mental hygiene hospitals and clinics, institutions of higher learning, maintenance of unemployment insurance and employment offices, and provision of facilities for civilian defense, as well as by furnishing increased state aids to arterial highways, health departments, hospitals, schools, welfare and like local functions.

Even though these services and aids were not devised exclusively for metropolitan regions, they filled important needs and furnished a binding and coordinating element for the activities of the individual communities in these particular fields.

Third, the functions of the New York Port Authority were expanded considerably as they came to embrace a vast variety of transportation problems. Its status as an agent of the two states has enabled it to concern itself with the problems of the whole area in a manner not available to any other governmental agency in the region. This extension has taken place both through the absorption by the Port Authority of the functions of the New York and New Jersey Bridge and Tunnel Commission more than twenty years ago and by other means. The Port Authority today operates bridges and tunnels, marine and inland freight terminals, airfields, bus terminals, docks and certain other port facilities. By such vesting of responsibility in the Port Authority, the multiplication of special interstate and intrastate *ad hoc* authorities has fortunately been avoided. The only factor which has kept the Port Authority from extending its functions even further is its lack of taxing powers and limitation to the strictly business type of undertaking.

Fourth, some county governments in suburban sections of this area have been modernized; and all county governments therein have been charged with additional administrative and fiscal responsibilities. In this way the smaller geographic units —towns, cities, villages and boroughs —have been relieved of some of the responsibilities which they could not adequately perform.

Fifth, many school districts and improvement districts in rapidly growing suburban areas have been consolidated over the past 25 years. The formation of central school districts particularly has gone apace under special financial encouragements from the state. It represents an exceedingly wholesome development of particular importance in a metropolitan region.

Administrative Improvement

Sixth, the administrative structure and fiscal powers of New York City, and of some of the other cities, towns, villages and boroughs in the region, have been improved and strengthened considerably through their own efforts and through encouragement by the state government. This has made it possible for these governments to handle more effectively the various problems peculiar to a metropolitan population.

Seventh, closer cooperation has developed among federal, state and local administrative officials engaged in the same type of activity in the area—public health administrators, highway officials, social security and welfare administrators, and so on. This cooperation has been exceedingly fruitful even though carried on in a quiet and unspectacular way.

On the other hand, during the last 25 years no progress has been made along the lines of any substantial annexation by a city of adjoining territory or of any consolidation of cities, towns and villages into a larger city. Nor has there taken place any consolidation of a city and county government. New Jersey is, perhaps, the only segment of the region in which some accomplishments along these lines may still be expected. But at the moment there is little sign of activity.

A Comprehensive Solution?

No progress has been made towards any comprehensive solution of the problem. The idea of the formation of some type of federated or dual metropolitan government—the dream of any student of the question—has not advanced a step.

Manifestly, before any such comprehensive solution could be seriously attempted, some type of informal consultative assembly of the representatives of the constituent communities would have to be instituted. This undoubtedly could come about cnly through the initiative of the communities themselves, encouraged possibly by the authorities of the two states. And this, in turn, would require a fairly strong awareness among the peoples and officials of these communities in both New York and New Jersey of the essential community of their interests.

But such a strong consciousness of metropolitan unity is still lacking in this region. North Jersey particularly considers itself to be somewhat apart from the New York segments of the area; and Westchester, Nassau and Suffolk Counties, New York, have a strong self-consciousness of their own. The situation in this respect is no different from that obtaining in any other metropolitan region, except that it is much more complicated. It explains why the hope expressed 25 years ago in *The Government of Metropolitan Areas,* that there would be in the metropolitan regions of this country "considerable experimentation in the near future with various plans for federated or dual metropolitan government," has remained unrealized both in New York and elsewhere.

In assaying the possibilities for achieving results along these lines in the New York area, consideration needs to be given to the difficulties which would be encountered in securing approval by the legislatures of the two states to any formalized type of federated government which would transcend state lines. Clearly, practical steps towards the realization of any such comprehensive solution of the problem in this region must await a more propitious time and the emergence of more inspiring civic leadership than has been available so far.

Prospects for the Future

It seems likely, therefore, that progress towards the solution of this governmental problem will continue to be made for some time mainly along the lines of a further elaboration of the various partial solutions so far indicated and applied or of the initiation of new similarly partial solutions. Even this will require considerable leadership on the part of civic groups and public bodies in this region as well as the two state govern-

(Continued on page 242)

Conference Values to a City

Richmond's civic batteries charged, interest in public
affairs sharpened by League's meeting, city leaders say.

By JULIAN C. HOUSEMAN*

RICHMOND business and civic leaders who asked the National Municipal League to bring the National Conference on Government to Richmond last November were looking for something more precious than dollars. A survey of opinion among these leaders three months after the Conference reveals that they feel they got what they wanted: wide ranging discussion of modern municipal government and effective citizenship that gave the community a needed shot in the arm.

Five years earlier Richmond had experienced a spectacular civic awakening which had done away with a cumbersome, old-style city government, built on a two-house legislature, and replaced it with a modern council-manager system. The people who had been chiefly responsible for that awakening felt the time had come to appraise the progress made against a background of knowledge and experience in other communities.

In the 25 Conference sessions and in corridor discussions at the Jefferson Hotel, November 8-11, Richmond people found themselves comparing notes and trading experiences and ideas with hundreds of the most

*Mr. Houseman is executive director of the Richmond Citizens Association. Formerly a news reporter for the Richmond *News Leader,* he was director of public relations for the Virginia Transit Company from 1945 until 1952 and winner of the 1949 Pall Mall Award for achievement in journalism.

effective civic leaders and forward-looking public officials drawn from all parts of the country. The people of the city responded eagerly to the opportunity offered. Registration at the Conference exceeded all previous meetings held by the National Municipal League. Newspapers and radio and television stations were estimated to have broken all previous records in giving space and time to the meeting. Almost ten solid newspaper pages of type—more than 77 inches—were devoted to the conference; there were sixteen radio and three television programs.

Many of the sessions had been planned in consultation with local people to meet particular needs, for example, those on "Effective Citizens' Associations," "Municipal Public Relations" and "The Citizen and Juvenile Delinquency." Sessions on "Relationships of Council and Manager" and "Policy-making Machinery in the Council-Manager Plan" brought outstanding city managers and members of city councils together for discussion of many of the problems that Richmond's city manager and councilmen had been working out together since the new charter went into effect. Other sessions of special local interest were spotted by the executive director of the Chamber of Commerce, who said: "Tops in interest were the discussions dealing with business and professional men in civic affairs, annexation, a live question in our city, the future conservation policies and the youth program which took in both high schools and colleges."

The success of the Conference and its deep impression on the city were not unexpected. In fact, it was more or less taken for granted when the team of L. E. ("Duke") Marlowe and Ed. P. Phillips took over as co-chairmen of the Arrangements and Sponsoring Committee. Both veterans in civic affairs, leaders in bringing good government to their city, these men do not seem to know the meaning of the term "second rate." Phillips is a National Municipal League regional vice president, Marlowe a member of the Council.

As a first step, they set about interesting every men's and women's organization in Richmond in the Conference. Then they went to the business and civic leaders to gain further support. By Conference time they had succeeded in tying every phase of the meeting together as meticulously as a watchmaker assembling his timepiece.

While Marlowe organized the adult meetings, Phillips began some pioneering and came up with a youth program which brought Conference facilities directly into Richmond's high schools and colleges.

The timing of the Conference proved to be even more fortunate than its sponsors had originally expected. Just as the city was completing its first five years with its new charter, its first city manager, popular and efficient Sherwood Reeder, had resigned to take over direction of the statewide governmental research activities of the Pennsylvania Economy League. The new government was in effect being tested; even while the Conference was going on, Richmond was looking for a new manager. The time also coincided with a period of increasing attention on the part of the schools to the importance of good citizenship among the students.

Local business turned out at the meetings, and attendance was not confined to top executives. Junior executives, department heads and up and coming business youngsters were given time off from work to participate in the Conference.

This participation by business paid off in big dividends. Some men, who had prided themselves on "keeping abreast" of things, frankly admitted that they carried from the meetings an intense desire to learn more about city affairs. Some others frankly admitted that previously they had only a passing interest in civic affairs, confined chiefly to voting in city council elections every two years. Now they found themselves reading every word in newspaper accounts of council meetings.

Youth Plays Part

The "Youth in Civic Affairs" portion of the Conference was a great success. Conceived by Ed. Phillips the program had the complete cooperation of school and college officials and the active participation of more than 5,000 students. George Gallup, Charles Edison and other League officers and top Conference program personalities addressed eight meetings in senior high schools and colleges.

The students themselves were largely responsible for the success of the program. They introduced speakers, spoke themselves and surprised the visitors and other older people with their knowledge of government and its functions and, more important, their place in it. More than one of the outsiders who took part in the program reported that it had been their most inspiring Conference experience and that the young people seemed quite capable of accepting the challenge thrown out by Congressman J. Vaughan Gary, who said: "I hope your generation will do a better job of running the world than mine has."

H. I. Willett, superintendent of public schools, has summed up the Conference: "We feel that this was an outstanding experience for our teachers and pupils and that the Conference in general made a great contribution to civic education."

Virginius Dabney, editor of the *Richmond Times Dispatch* and one of the country's leading editorial writers, probably described the Conference's impact on the entire population better than any other person. He said: "The fact that the Conference was held in Richmond and the large amount of newspaper, radio and television coverage were bound to make the local citizens conscious of the nation-wide interest in municipal government. Even if these newspaper accounts were not fully read, the large amount of space they occupied had to have a psychological effect to the point that there should be more interest in local affairs. The Conference served to bring modern municipal government into virtually every home in our community."

Richmond has a city council elec-

tion in June and here a true measurement of the Conference's impact may be seen. The Richmond Citizens Association, which helped bring the new form of government to the city, will certainly capitalize on the opportunity to get out the biggest vote yet in the city's history.

The League's eighteenth Annual Conference was held in Richmond in 1912. Richmond hopes it will not take 42 years to bring the Conference back again.

NEW YORK AREA
STILL STYMIED
(Continued from page 239)

ments. How much progress, if any, will be made towards a comprehensive solution will depend upon factors which are wholly unpredictable.

More than a quarter of a century ago, the author concluded the volume which he prepared with the Committee on Metropolitan Government of the National Municipal League with the following words:

The present chaos in many metropolitan areas is a summons to a broader view and higher statesmanship than has generally been displayed. The state and even the nation as a whole are concerned in the proper governmental organization and development of the great metropolitan regions. These larger interests cannot be sacrificed to the inertia or selfish interests of the smaller political divisions of that region. In the last analysis even state boundary lines will not be able to bar the rational treatment of regional difficulties.

In closing this brief review of the present situation in the New York region, he can not do better than conclude upon this same note.

News in Review

South Dakota Bolsters Legislative Council

Appropriation for Research Increased $35,000 in 1953

THE 1953 session of the South Dakota legislature was research-minded. The germ had been planted in 1951 with an appropriation of $25,000 for a Legislative Research Council. Council activities may have aided in convincing the legislature, lobby groups and the public of the value of more information on governmental problems.

Without any substantial dissent, the 1953 legislature increased the appropriation for the Legislative Council from $25,000 to $60,000 and authorized the council's executive board to make: (1) Little Hoover studies and (2) a survey of the care and treatment of the senile, with additional funds of $20,000 and $25,000, respectively. In another important act, the legislature authorized counties to make a levy "for the conduct of research on local government, employment of research and other personnel, publication of research studies and provision for office expense." State-supported educational institutions could be given financial assistance to conduct research under the terms of this legislation.

These actions by the legislature are now beginning to bear fruit. Griffenhagen and Associates were engaged to make studies of: (1) over-all administrative organization, (2) higher education, (3) the Division of Taxation, and (4) care and treatment of the senile. All four reports have now been released. The first three studies are under the supervision of a Little Hoover Committee and the last named study is supervised by the Senile Survey Committee. Both

are Legislative Research Council committees and consist of seven legislators each.

The comprehensive report on over-all administrative organization proposed an administrative structure of 26 principal agencies—consolidating, combining or reallocating some 125 existing agencies. The survey on higher education makes a total of 72 recommendations, including one for a chancellor system.

All South Dakota legislators are members of the Legislative Council. This makes possible continuous contact between legislators and administrative agencies.

On March 29 the Little Hoover Committee began a series of meetings to consider various Griffenhagen recommendations, with heads of state institutions and agencies present. Written comments were submitted by agency heads and, in some cases, where administrative action only was required, recommendations are being put into effect.

Other council activities have included meetings on water law revision, a proposed county assessor system and financing of elementary and high school education. A four-state conference of legislators from Minnesota, Wisconsin and North and South Dakota was arranged for April 29 and 30 in Pierre, with panels on such subjects as reorganization of state government, regional educational compacts, non-resident hunting regulations, state finance, truck regulation and school district reorganization.

In pursuance of the county research bill, over half South Dakota's 67 counties have made appropriations for research purposes, which as presently organized would provide about $3,700 annually if all counties participated. The state university has been designated to carry on the research studies. Plans are being made for the early publication of a handbook for county government and a magazine on county government to be issued on a monthly basis.

WILLIAM O. FARBER
University of South Dakota

Maryland to Vote on Home Rule Amendment

Maryland will have home rule for its incorporated cities and towns if the voters, at the November 2 election, approve the General Assembly's recent action in granting home rule.

In the past, the only one of Maryland's 140 incorporated cities and towns to enjoy home rule has been Baltimore City. Every other incorporated place has had to depend on the General Assembly for even the most trivial alteration of its laws.

The constitutional amendment authorizes municipalities to amend their charters and local laws so long as such action does not contravene general state law. The cities and towns are not permitted to impose new taxes, and the General Assembly retains authority to enact laws placing maximum limits on local property tax rates and debts. But the General Assembly is prohibited from enacting any law relating to the affairs of a municipality which will be purely local in its effect rather than statewide.

This home rule legislation has long been sought by practically everyone except the legislators and in recent years its passage has been pressed by the Maryland Municipal League, an organization made up of the elected officials of most of the towns and cities, which has been rapidly gaining strength.

By freeing the General Assembly from a flood of local legislation and removing the legislators from the field of surveillance over the affairs of the towns and cities, it is anticipated that they will be able to deal more thoughtfully and thoroughly with statewide matters in the General Assembly.

D. BENTON BISER
Commission on Governmental Efficiency and Economy
Baltimore

Anchorage, Alaska, Annexes Large Area

Annexation of an area of three and one-half square miles to Anchorage, Alaska's largest city, was approved at the polls on February 9 and became official in March, when a final order was signed by the judge of the Federal District Court after denying a series of motions to stay the order of annexation. The area has a population of 3,500, to be added to some 17,000 in Anchorage.

According to the Alaska annexation law, after 30 per cent of the qualified property owners in an area have signed a petition, it is presented to the council of the city to which annexation is desired and then submitted to the district court for a public hearing on the adequacy and justice of the petition. If all is found correct the judge orders an election within the annexation area and within the city and, if a majority of those voting in each area is in favor, the annexation order is signed by the court.

The people outside the city, beginning in 1949, formed three separate public utility districts designed to meet some of their basic needs—no other means appearing available, short of annexation. Alaskan public utility districts are empowered to provide all utilities, fire protection, recreation facilities, road construction and maintenance, etc. It has been contended that such a district is a municipality and that no portion thereof can be annexed to a city. The districts adjacent to Anchorage have not accomplished substantial improvements.

Annexation of an area known as Eastchester (not a public utility district), with a population of about 7,000, was voted on in 1952 but was defeated in Eastchester. Another section, known as Annexation Area No. 4, included mostly within a public utility district, began to move toward annexation. Petitions from this area and a new petition from Eastchester were submitted and a court hearing on both was held in September 1953. After various moves pro and con, and an intensive campaign, elections were held on February 9, 1954, on both. Eastchester again turned down the proposal by a 55-45 margin, while in the other area annexation was favored by 74 per cent of the voters. In the city both proposals carried by approximately 85 per cent.

After the election the city immediately proceeded to extend services into the newly annexed area, despite several judicial appeals pending in the Circuit Court of Appeals in San Francisco. Road maintenance, police protection and firefighting services were extended immediately. Zoning, building and other protective codes likewise took immediate effect.

In order to acquaint citizens with the operation of their new government, a pamphlet for general distribution was prepared by City Manager George C. Shannon.

Revision of Law Proposed

The League of Alaskan Cities has approved a preliminary draft of a new annexation enabling law. Most of the changes are designed to provide for greater flexibility and less cumbersome procedure.

The league program calls for several alternate methods of initiating and carrying out annexation. The present petition method is to be retained but provision is also made for municipal initiative in annexation. It is also proposed that the elections be set by the city rather than requiring preliminary court hearings. Concurrent elections within the city are to be eliminated, the council being enabled to act for its citizens.

A separate method is designed to provide for annexation of uninhabited or sparsely settled territory by not requiring any elections if 50 per cent of the property owners sign a petition for annexation.

The problem of public utility districts would be resolved by providing automatic exclusion from such a district of any part annexed to a municipality. The Alaska Legislative Council is cooperating on this phase of the program.

VICTOR FISCHER, *Executive Secretary* League of Alaskan Cities

High Court Upholds Philadelphia Charter

Exemption of four offices from control of Philadelphia's home rule city-county charter by the 1953 state legislature was held unconstitutional by the Pennsylvania Supreme Court voting four to three on March 29. The four offices are those of the sheriff, the board of revision of taxes, the registration commission and the city commission. The 1953 legislation attempted to exempt employees of these offices from civil service requirements and to permit political activity by them. The court ruled that this exemption was invalid because it established an arbitrary classification for certain m u n i c i p a l workers and granted special or exclusive privilege and immunity to the four departments.

The court did not clearly decide that the legislature could not enact laws regulating the city. Three dissenting justices took the position that the legislature has full power to alter or revoke a charter at its pleasure.

It also remained uncertain whether complete consolidation of these four offices in the municipal structure could be accomplished by the city council or whether state legislation was required.

Personnel Director Provided for City of New York

An amendment to the charter of the City of New York, to reorganize the civil service commission, has been approved by the legislature and signed by Governor Dewey. It provides for a three-member nonpartisan commission, the chairman of which will be the personnel director in charge of the administration and personnel affairs of the department. He and the two other commissioners are to be appointed by the mayor, with their salaries to be fixed by the board of estimate. The commission has rule-making, appellate and policy-making powers.

Ethics Code Becomes Law in New York State

Governor Dewey on April 14 signed the last of several bills putting into effect the state code of ethics and standards of investigative procedure as worked out by the Lockwood committee[1] and amended to a minor degree in the legislature.

One change was to insert a $25 exemption in the prohibition against the sale of any goods to a state agency by a legislator or an officer or employee of any state agency except by award or contract let after competitive bidding. It was pointed out that the complete prohibition would, for example, prevent a gasoline station, owned by any person affected by the plan, from selling gasoline to state trucks.

The legislative law has been more broadly amended to provide that no committee of either house, or a joint committee, or a subcommittee of such committees, may take testimony at any public or private hearing unless at least two members are present. The civil rights law as amended provides similarly as to temporary state commissions of more than two members, as well as incorporating the code of fair procedure referred to in this section last month.

[1] See the REVIEW, April 1954, page 192.

The code of ethics is made part of the public officers law. The executive law is amended to authorize the attorney general to establish an advisory committee on ethical standards and also to require every regulatory agency to keep a record of attorneys and agents appearing before it as representatives of individuals, corporations, etc., for a fee.

The legislature adopted resolutions establishing committees on ethical standards in each house.

The new laws take effect January 1, 1955.

Council-manager Plan Developments

ELGIN, ILLINOIS, (1950 population 44,-223) adopted the council-manager plan by a vote of 6,085 to 5,105 on April 6, to go into effect May 1, 1955. Elgin is the first of 74 commission-governed cities in Illinois to adopt the council-manager plan by referendum. Rochelle, a commission city, adopted the plan by ordinance last year. With Elgin, Illinois is now reported to have 34 municipalities that have adopted the manager plan—eighteen by referendum, sixteen by ordinance. Their total population is given as 662,654.

WHITTIER, CALIFORNIA, (29,265) adopted a council-manager charter on April 13 by a vote of 2,721 to 2,450. The plan is scheduled to go into effect in January of next year.

MISSOULA, MONTANA, (1950 population 22,485) voted 3,465 to 2,836 on March 22 to adopt the council-manager plan, under the state optional law. The plan will go into effect after election of the council on June 24.

BRECKENRIDGE, TEXAS, (6,610) adopted a council-manager charter on March 19, 902 to 427. The plan was scheduled to go into effect May 4.

The city council of PRATTVILLE, ALABAMA, (4,385) adopted an ordinance on January 19, providing for employment of a city manager as administrative head of the city government, with powers as provided by state law. These include the appointment and employment of all city employees, except the police chief, fire chief and superintendent of municipal utility plant, who are to be appointed by the council. The ordinance provides, moreover, that the manager's term is to be coextensive with that of the council, except that he may be discharged on 60 days' written notice following a two-thirds vote of the council.

On April 13 BROKEN ARROW, OKLAHOMA, (3,263) by a vote of 381 to 363, adopted the statutory council-manager form of government, to go into effect in May 1955.

The town of HAMPTON, NEW HAMPSHIRE, (2,847) voted 441 to 437 for the manager plan at the town meeting on March 9. A similar proposal was defeated last year 518 to 380. The board of selectmen was expected to act soon on the matter of hiring a manager. The meeting rejected a proposal for a nonpartisan ballot 592 to 270.

ROCKPORT, MAINE, (1,656) adopted the council-manager plan, at its annual town meeting in March, by a vote of nearly nine to one. The plan is scheduled to go into effect in 1955.

Additional cities adopting the council-manager plan in 1954 include: MIAMI, ARIZONA, (4,329) ; APALACHICOLA, FLORIDA, (3,222) ; CLARE, MICHIGAN, (2,440) ; MIFFLINBURG, PENNSYLVANIA, (2,259) ; ORRINGTON, MAINE, (1,895).

EXETER, NEW HAMPSHIRE, at its annual town meeting on March 9 defeated a town manager proposal, 1,070 to 575.

NEWPORT, NEW HAMPSHIRE, at its annual town meeting on March 9, voted 905 to 510 to retain the manager plan, which was adopted in 1948. ASHLAND, in the same state, also voted for retention, 433 to 91.

The VILLAGE of BENNINGTON, VERMONT, voted 652 to 643 on March 16 to abandon the manager plan. The TOWN of BENNINGTON abandoned the plan a year ago and at its annual town meeting on March

2, 1954, it voted 1,047 to 965 against a proposal to reestablish the plan. Both the town and village had adopted the plan in 1950 and for a while shared the same manager. The town engaged a separate manager in 1952.

The town of UNION, MAINE, defeated a proposal to adopt the manager plan, 57 to 47.

The WARREN, RHODE ISLAND, Real Estate Taxpayers' Association has established a committee to investigate the suitability of the town manager plan for Warren.

A campaign for adoption of the council-manager plan has been started in PLATTSBURG, NEW YORK.

By a vote of 29 to 2, COBLESKILL, NEW YORK, discontinued its village manager plan, which has been in operation since 1950.

THOMSON, GEORGIA, voted 290 to 253 on March 12 against adoption of the manager plan.

Appointment or election of a charter commission has been proposed in JACKSONVILLE, FLORIDA, with strong support in the city council. Both the commission plan and the council-manager plan have been suggested as alternatives to the present mayor-council plan.

Professor Arthur W. Bromage has recommended the council-manager plan to the Charter Study Commission of ANN ARBOR, MICHIGAN.

EDINA, MINNESOTA, will vote on adoption of the statutory village council-manager plan at the September 14 primary.

A petition has been circulated in MANKATO, MINNESOTA, calling for reversion from the council-manager plan to the commission plan.

Voters of MARINETTE, WISCONSIN, rejected a proposal to abandon their council-manager government, in operation since April 1952, in favor of the mayor-council plan. The vote for retention was 2,858 to 1,355.

EVANSVILLE, WISCONSIN, has rejected a proposal to adopt council-manager government 407 to 405.

On April 6 LARNED, KANSAS, voted 1,021 to 699 for retention of its council-manager government.

Voters of PUEBLO, COLORADO, adopted a new charter, providing the council-manager plan, on April 6. The city has had manager government since 1950, when the plan was provided by charter amendment.[1]

In ABERDEEN, SOUTH DAKOTA, the voters defeated a proposal to adopt the council-manager plan by a vote of 3,460 to 3,101.

The Junior Chamber of Commerce of TULSA, OKLAHOMA, has issued a special edition of its magazine, the *Durick*, endorsing the council-manager plan. A committee recommended the plan after a year's study and the chamber overwhelmingly approved the recommendation.

In ORANGE, TEXAS, Mayor Caillavet favors a change to the council-manager plan.

On April 6, WACO, TEXAS, voted 4,378 to 3,329 to retain its council-manager plan of government.

The EL PASO, TEXAS, charter commission voted on March 1 to submit a council-manager charter to popular vote without a mayor-council alternative as formerly contemplated.

In WALLA WALLA, WASHINGTON, in an advisory vote on March 9, the council-manager plan was favored, 4,709 to 2,521. A board of freeholders to draft a charter is expected to be elected in the fall.

In the unincorporated community of RICHLAND, WASHINGTON, a vote was taken March 9 on preferences as to form of municipal government; the council-manager plan received 1,043 votes, the mayor-council plan 427 and the commission plan 87. Richland serves the Hanford Atomic Works and all land is owned

[1]See the REVIEW, January 1950, page 37.

by the Atomic Energy Commission. The advisory Richland community council (elected) expects to draft a charter for possible use by a charter commission whenever the AEC may dispose of its residential and commercial holdings and the community ·is incorporated. In the election, at which community council members were also voted on, ballots were in the form of cards, with spaces for marking with a special pencil, and the counting was done on IBM machines.

Adoption of the manager plan for WALNUT CREEK, CALIFORNIA, has been urged in an address by H. L. Morrison, Jr., of the Contra Costa County Taxpayers Association.

Two CALIFORNIA cities approved the council-manager plan in an advisory vote taken at the April 13 election. In LAGUNA BEACH the manager plan was favored 1,550 to 456; in San Clemente, 915 to 163.

MELBOURNE, AUSTRALIA, is reported to be considering a proposal to appoint a city manager.

Housing and Planning Congress to Meet in Edinburgh

The next congress of the International Federation for Housing and Town Planning will be held in Edinburgh, Scotland, September 20-26, 1954. The main subjects for discussion are slum clearance and rehousing, housing density and national land use planning. H.v.d. Weijde, Paleisstraat, The Hague, Netherlands, is the secretary-general.

Government Public Relations Movement Widespread

An international movement to increase the role of public relations in governmental practice was announced recently by Mrs. Pan Dodd Wheeler, executive director of the Government Public Relations Association. The Committee on an International Public Relations Association is headed by T. Fife Clark of the

Institute of Public Relations in London, England. Other members of the committee include R. Wimbush, Great Britain; J. A. Brongers, The Netherlands; Etienne Bloch, France; and Ed Lipscomb, United States.

A larger, provisional group met in England last year and recommended that the committee proceed with plans for establishing the international group, which would push ahead on three fronts to: gain professional recognition, garner professional skills including the pooling of most recent experience and research, and establish a code of professional ethics which would link codes being developed in several democratic countries.

Mrs. Wheeler, adviser on municipal information for the Municipal Technical Advisory Service at the University of Tennessee, reported that MTAS is developing some statements of experience and workable plans for the integration of the citizen into municipal government (especially for the small and medium-sized city) which, when completed, will be made available to the international group.

The Government Public Relations Association, which cooperates with the international group, is affiliated with the American Municipal Association. Its recently elected president for 1954-55, David R. McGuire, Jr., who is public relations officer for New Orleans, said recently that he wants "no one to confuse the trained, well informed governmental public relations official with the old-style press agent or publicity man." He asserted that the new type of such official, instead of attempting to "gloss over the mistakes of government and its officials," undertakes to interpret public facts to the public, to explain and inform and, at the same time, to help government officials "understand what people think about the policy and activity of government so these may be responsive to public opinion."

The GPRA estimates that approximately a hundred United States cities and most quasi-governmental organizations maintain public relations officials or departments.

ANDREW J. LAZARUS

Congress of Municipalities to Meet in Puerto Rico

The fifth Inter-American Congress of Municipalities is to meet in San Juan, Puerto Rico, December 2-7, 1954. Several main topics will be considered: human relations in municipal government, between government and its personnel and the citizens, respectively; good municipal administration as an incentive toward greater municipal autonomy; and urban redevelopment.

The American Committee for International Municipal Cooperation met on April 13 at its headquarters in Chicago and discussed preparation for the Congress of Municipalities, among other matters.

Michigan League Sets Up Regional Organization

A regional organization for the Michigan Municipal League has been approved by the league's board of trustees, and election of regional officers will take place during the 1954 series of regional meetings, which runs from April 15 to June 25, in ten regions.

For each region there will be a chairman, vice-chairman and secretary, who will be primarily responsible for coordination of league activities within the region.

County and Township ·   ·   ·   · *Edited by Edward W. Weidner*

Petroleum County Thrives with Manager

Costs Much Less Than Those of Other Montana Counties

EDITOR'S NOTE.—The story below is taken from the *Montana Taxpayer*, published by the Montana Taxpayers Association, for March 1954.

HOW CAN county government meet rising costs without burdensome increases in taxes upon property? At least one Montana county, Petroleum, found the answer to this $64 question by instituting the manager system. A glance at its fiscal record on a "before and after" basis emphasizes this fact.

At the time the manager system was instituted (January 1943) the county had outstanding warrants of $20,706, a bonded debt of $40,000 and only $12,000 in cash on hand. Expenses of the nine elected officers and their staffs came to $16,930 annually but tax revenue from the maximum general fund levy of 16 mills would produce only $13,800. So successful was

the manager system that by 1946 the county's bonded debt was extinguished and surplus cash amounted to $38,000.

In that year the county had the unusual record of making no levy whatever for the county general fund. Surplus in the fund was sufficient to pay all expenditures for the current year.

Costs of county government are paid from the county general fund and were originally centered in the seven major elective offices—county commissioners, clerk and recorder, treasurer, assessor, district court (clerk of the court), sheriff and superintendent of schools. In 1941-42, the last full year before the manager system went into effect in Petroleum County, the cost of these offices totalled $16,930. In 1952-53, the last completed fiscal year, despite rising costs the corresponding total was $18,698, an increase of only $1,768, or 10 per cent. In contrast, the increase for the same functions in all other counties of the state during the same period was 68 per cent.

Under the manager system, only the county commissioners and the county at-

COMPARISON OF ADMINISTRATIVE COSTS

| | Petroleum County | | All Counties | |
	1941-42	1952-53	1941-42	1952-53
Commissioners	$ 1,527	$ 795	$ 254,430	$ 321,319
Clerk and Recorder	4,389	4,652	443,477	705,702
Treasurer	4,374	4,403	470,555	761,314
Assessor	2,236	2,617	304,237	701,773
District Court	2,084	1,750	387,220	612,134
Sheriff	2,320	1,963	478,291	832,401
Superintendent of Schools	—a	1,318	204,273	328,102
County Manager	None	1,200b	None	None
Total	$16,930	$18,698	$2,532,483	$4,362,745
Increase Over 1941-42		$ 1,768		$1,730,262
Per cent Increase		10.4		68.3

aCombined with assessor.

bPart of salary charged to other activities. For example, he acts as director of finance.

torney are elected. The commissioners serve as a board of directors to formulate policy, approve budgets and fix tax levies. They select a county manager and fix his salary.

The manager, administrative head of the county government, must devote full time to his work, shall be appointed on merit only, and need not be a resident of the county. No member of the county board or other person then filling an elective office can be chosen as manager. The manager is not appointed for a definite tenure but is removable at the pleasure of the county board. He appoints all officers except county attorney. Salaries of all officers and deputies are fixed by the county board but neither the county board, nor any of its members, can direct or request the appointment or removal of any officer or deputy. The powers of the county manager are broad; he has general supervision and control over all departments, officers and deputies.

The activities of the county are divided into the following departments: finance, public works and public welfare. Additional departments may be established by the county board on recommendation of the manager. The manager appoints a director for each department and he may, with the consent of the board, act as the director of any one department himself or appoint one director for two or more departments.

The department of finance includes all activities belonging to the county treasurer and county assessor and those of the county clerk now having to do with the budget, accounts, etc. The department of public works has charge of the construction and maintenance of county roads and bridges, drains and other public works, construction and care of public buildings, storerooms, warehouses, equipment and supplies. The department of public welfare includes all activities connected with the poor, hospitals, charitable and correctional institutions, parks, playgrounds and public health.

Petroleum County had a 1950 population of only 1,026, the lowest of any county in the state. Its taxable valuation, now as in 1941, is the lowest in the state. The manager system has proved to be the ideal solution for Petroleum County. It would have been unable to continue in existence without it. In addition to economies in administrative costs, centralized purchasing for all departments and maximum use of personnel can be achieved under the manager system. The plan has worked well in a small county with limited resources. Consideration of the system in other counties may help solve acute financial problems especially when the county general fund tax levy automatically reverts to a maximum limit of 16 mills on June 30, 1955.

Procedure for adopting the manager system in Montana is as follows: A petition must be filed with the board of county commissioners, signed by not less than 20 per cent of the number of voters who voted at the last general election, asking that a referendum be held on the question. The board of county commissioners may call a special election or may submit the question at the next general election. Notice of the referendum must be published twice a week for three consecutive weeks. If a majority of the votes cast at the election shall be in favor of the county manager form of government it shall go into effect at the date designated in the petition or resolution, but no elected officer then in office shall be retired prior to the expiration of his term of office.

Clackamas County to Vote on Manager Plan

The county manager plan of government will be submitted to the voters of Clackamas County, Oregon, for the third time on May 21. The League of Women Voters circulated petitions to force the proposal on the ballot since county officials refused to act on the matter. Under the proposal the new form of government would be established on January

1, 1955. The manager would be a well paid professional administrator under the direct supervision of a five-man commission, which would meet not oftener than four days in any one month.

A joint committee meeting of the County Grange, the Farmers Union, the C.I.O. and the A.F.L. unanimously opposed the idea and recommended that all members of the four organizations vote against the proposal.

Manager Plan Discussed in Riverside County, California

The discussion on a manager form of government for Riverside County, California, is continuing. The County Farm Bureau held a debate recently between Dr. John Vieg, head of the department of government of Pomona College, and Irwin Hayden, one of the county supervisors.

Dr. Vieg strongly supported the manager form. Supervisor Hayden suggested that the Farm Bureau be wary of the proposal, that it should "stop, look and listen" before adopting it.

City-county Fiscal Relations Studied

In Maryland the legislature has requested the governor to establish a commission to study city-county financial relationships. The resolution setting forth the proposal was part of the program of the Maryland Municipal League. The league felt that many residents of incorporated municipalities were apparently bearing more than their just share of county taxes since the services they received from the counties were limited.

The study commission will consist of thirteen members appointed by the governor. Four members will be nominated by the Maryland Municipal League, four by the County Commissioners Association, and the Senate and House will nominate others. A report of the commission is due in the 1955 session of the General Assembly.

In Tennessee the board of directors of the Tennessee Municipal League has decided to gather full information on the tax and fiscal relationships of counties and municipalities.

King County Abolishes Office of Constable

By action of the board of county commissioners of King County (Seattle), Washington, the office of constable has been abolished. Hereafter the deputies of the sheriff will process legal papers. A slight monetary saving for the county will be made and the ballot will be shortened.

Contra Costa Committee Studies County Government

Contra Costa County, California, has recently appointed a committee on county government, which is making a study of all California counties with an eye to improving Contra Costa's administration and organization. The committee is investigating the office of the county coroner and plans to extend its studies to other offices.

New York Legislature Passes County Amendment

A constitutional amendment on county government was passed by the 1954 New York legislature which would clarify, implement and rearrange the county government provisions of the constitution and in addition would give counties outside New York City the power to draft, adopt and amend their own charters as cities and first-class villages now may do.

This home rule amendment was originally passed two years ago[1] but failed to pass the legislature again last year because of the large number of amendments that were up for consideration. It must now be adopted by the 1955 legislature before it can be submitted to the voters of the state.

[1]For a description of its provisions see the REVIEW, April 1951, page 217.

Proportional Representation . . *Edited by George H. Hallett, Jr.*
and Wm. Redin Woodward
(This department is successor to the Proportional Representation Review)

Tasmania Provides Hare System for Cities

Follows Action Recently Taken by New South Wales

THE USE of the single transferable vote has been made general for elections in Tasmanian municipalities, following the recent example of New South Wales,[1] by action of the Tasmanian House of Assembly.

In the election of several representatives to the local councils at large in a single district, the result will be to institute the Hare system of proportional representation, whereas in single-member district elections it will result in what is called the alternative vote or the Hare system of majority preferential voting. The latter has been optional for a long time but little used thus far.

Tasmanians are very familiar with the Hare system of P. R. It has been used to elect this Australian state's House of Assembly since 1907.

Governor Herter Signs Massachusetts P. R. Bill

On March 4 Governor Herter of Massachusetts signed into law a bill to permit restoration of P.R. by referendum in cities which have voted P.R. out. The legislation, by specific exception, does not apply to the city of Quincy, so that at present it appears to apply only to Medford. These two cities voted to abandon P.R. in November 1952. Of course it also serves to prevent any possible future abandonments of P.R. from being irreversible.

[1] See the REVIEW, March 1954, page 146.

Belgian Parliament Chosen by List System

Belgian voters in their national election April 11 deserted the governing Christian Social party in sufficient numbers to deprive the party of its parliamentary majority, although that party remains as the largest both in terms of popular vote and in terms of parliamentary seats held.

The candidates for the Belgian House of Representatives on the Christian Social ticket polled 44.1 per cent of the votes cast and obtained 92 of the 212 seats (43.4 per cent). In the previous election four years ago they obtained 46.7 per cent of the vote and 108 seats (50.9 per cent). A party list form of P.R. is used in these elections.

The Socialist party showed the greatest gain, obtaining 39.3 per cent of the votes and 91 seats (42.9 per cent). In the previous elections, four years ago, the Socialists polled 36.4 per cent of the votes and secured 76 (35.8 per cent) seats. The slight deviations from proportionality in the apportionment of seats results from the fact that the Belgian election system applies P.R. on a district basis only.

The Liberal party also gained ground in the recent election, obtaining 12.8 per cent of the votes and 25 seats (11.8 per cent). At the last election the Liberals polled 11.1 per cent of the votes and obtained 21 seats (10 per cent). The Communists elected four (1.9 per cent), losing three of their previous seven seats, and gathered only 3.8 per cent of the votes.

Premier Jean Van Houtte and his cabinet resigned the day after the election. The chief change in policy expected from a new government, according to the Associated Press, is a reduction in the term of compulsory military service from 24 to 18 months. The results of the elec-

ELECTION OF BELGIAN HOUSE OF REPRESENTATIVES APRIL 11, 1954

Party	Votes Cast	Percentage of Votes	Seats Won	Percentage of Seats
Christian Social	2,121,978	44.1	92	43.4
Socialist	1,891,126	39.3	91	42.9
Liberal	615,922	12.8	25	11.8
Communist	184,098	3.8	4	1.9

tion are summarized in the accompanying table.

Finland Elects New Rigsdag by P. R.

Small changes in distribution of strength among parties, but the substitution of many new and younger faces, resulted from the election of a new Rigsdag (parliament) in Finland on March 7. This unicameral body is elected by a party list form of proportional representation. Almost two million voters went to the polls. The election was precipitated, according to a dispatch to the *New York Times,* by the refusal of the preceding parliament to trim appropriations to match the government's limited fiscal resources.

The distribution of seats among the parties represented is as follows, with the change over the outgoing parliament indicated in parentheses: Social Democrats 54 (+ 1), Agrarians 53 (+ 2), Communists 43 (no change), Conservatives 24 (—4), Swedish Minority 13 (—2) and Finnish People's party 13 (+ 3). The Social Democrats and the Communists are (separately) opposed to the government formed by the other parties together. The governing coalition now has an edge of 103 to 97, whereas in the outgoing parliament it had 104 seats opposed by 96.

Ireland to Choose Dail Eireann in May

A national election will take place in Ireland on May 18. The membership of the Dail Eireann (Irish Parliament) is chosen by the Hare system of proportional representation on a district basis. The country districts return relatively few members each but in the city districts a moderate number of representatives are elected at large by P.R.

A. G. Huie, New South Wales Proportionalist, Retires

A. G. Huie, of Sydney, Australia, one of the original members of the Proportional Representation Society of New South Wales, its secretary for many years and author of its first pamphlet on P. R., has retired.

Mr. Huie combines an intense interest in P. R. with an early-acquired and steadfastly pursued interest in the principles advanced by Henry George relating to taxation. He served as secretary of the Free Trade and Land Values League from its founding in 1901 until his retirement and founded that group's monthly publication, *The Standard,* in 1905. This publication, which carries news of P. R. developments in the island continent, published on December 15, 1953, Mr. Huie's farewell editorial.

The efforts of Mr. Huie and the Proportional Representation Society in New South Wales have recently borne fruit, with the system being adopted for practically all local government elections in the state.[1]

[1] See the REVIEW, March 1954, page 146.

Taxation and Finance　•　•　•　•　*Edited by Wade S. Smith*

New York Revalues Local Tax Bases

Equalization Changes Raise Fiscal Powers

NEW YORK State's local governmental units are experiencing a needed expansion of fiscal capacity this year as the State Board of Equalization and Assessment announces the results of its five-year study and revision of property tax assessment equalization rates. Typically, new rates are increasing taxing and borrowing power compared with that under the old rates.

The equalization rates are represented by the percentage of full value at which real estate is assessed for taxation. They are of particular importance in New York State because, under constitutional amendments effective in 1950 and 1952, city tax rate and debt limits are calculated on full value, as determined by the state equalization rates, rather than by assessed valuation without adjustment. Moreover, the base for fixing the limits is the five-year average of full value, not just the current or last year's total.

The ratios of equalization fixed by the state had self-evident shortcomings for many years and in 1949—in anticipation of the constitutional change in calculating debt and tax limits—the legislature had the state board undertake a restudy of the entire state. Literally hundreds of thousands of real estate sales were studied and tens of thousands of appraisals were analyzed. And, as expected, it turned out that full value in nearly every instance was much greater than the old equalization ratios had indicated.

The new rates are being announced for the largest cities first. Those for the upstate rural areas will not be forthcoming in time to be used before next year.

Of the first eighteen cities announced, all of 40,000 population or more, only one had a new equalization rate unchanged from the old; it was Troy, which had recently completed a reassessment on a 100 per cent of full value basis and was equalized by the state board at 100 per cent also. For other cities, the new ratios will have the effect of up to doubling present taxing and borrowing power.

One of the most drastically affected of the upstate cities was Rome. This city's former equalization rate was 75 per cent, the new rate 35 per cent. Elmira, another upstate city also formerly equalized at 75 per cent, has a new rate of 40 per cent. By and large, the further downstate the community, the less violent the readjustment: White Plains, with an old ratio of 99 per cent and a new one of 68 per cent, was an example.

New York City ratios confirmed widely held opinion that the outlying boroughs were assessed more leniently than Manhattan, but the range was wider than many persons had expected. By boroughs, the old and new ratios were: Manhattan, 100 and 99; The Bronx, 96 and 93; Brooklyn, 98 and 83; Queens, 93 and 69; and Richmond (Staten Island), 96 and 59.

The promulgation of the new state equalization ratios will affect only the total amount of taxes which the communities may levy and the amount of debt they may incur within their debt limits; it will not eliminate or correct disparities and inequalities such as those between the boroughs in New York City. Furthermore, since the taxing and debt incurring limits are based on a five-year average, the use of the new ratios will not be fully reflected in expanded fiscal capacity until five years have passed. New York City, for example, had its taxing power increased by $12,000,000 or so the first year and about $60,000,000 over the five-year period, based on current assessed valuations. The new rates would mean for White Plains an added $205,000 in taxing power this year and $1,500,000 over a five-year period.

The full value of realty as determined from assessed valuations and the state equalization ratios are used for other purposes than calculating taxing and borrowing power, and the state legislature consequently found it necessary to make special provisions to preserve the status quo while the new ratios are being installed throughout the state. Net returns under the state rent control laws are based on full value for tax purposes, as are some of the state aids to local units for education and highways. A 1953 legislative act provides that the old ratios are to be continued in use for rental calculations and education and highway aids, for another year at least.

County Seeks Federal Aid to Put River under Bridge

A crisis in local finance usually has an interesting story behind it. Hence, the plight of the holders of $1,970,000 toll bridge revenue bonds of the Burt County, Nebraska, Bridge Commission discloses a situation which is both interesting and unusual. Briefly, the commissioners have a bridge with a river running past instead of under it.

The bridge connects—or rather was intended to connect—Decatur, Nebraska, and Onawa, Iowa, which lie on opposite sides of the Missouri River north of Omaha. Without the crossing, residents of either town had to travel 80 to 100 miles to reach each other; with the bridge, the connection would be reduced to eight miles or so.

Plans for the bridge were begun after World War II, and application was made in 1946 to the U.S. Army Engineers for the necessary permit, required because the Missouri is a navigable waterway under Army jurisdiction. Approval was finally given in 1949.

Before construction was started, however, a shift of the river's channel to the east was noted, and the bridge commission's consulting engineers suggested that either of two alternative sites be used. The Army Engineers demurred, however, and construction of the bridge at the original site was begun on their assurances that the flow of the river would be returned to its original path.

Thus, the bridge was deliberately constructed on dry land, with the river flowing in a channel east of the bridge approach. Initial efforts to get the river back into its former channel were not effective, however, and in 1953 a $2,500,-000 appropriation was recommended for inclusion in the federal budget for a stabilization program to return the river to its course under the bridge. Congress eliminated the item. Again this year, $2,000,000 was included in the executive budget to get the river back under the bridge. Instead, the House appropriations committee made the sum available generally for river bank stabilization between Omaha and Sioux City, including the Decatur area.

Meanwhile, residents of Decatur and Onawa make their 100-mile detour to reach each other, and the holders of the toll bridge revenue bonds hopefully wait for the river to be replaced so that traffic can move and the toll booth cash registers start to clatter. Nebraskans say Congress has a moral obligation for the acts of its creature, the Army Engineers, who reaffirmed the permit for a bridge without a river, but Congress has more pressing interests.

State Payments to Local Units Reviewed

One of the highly useful special studies of the Governments Division of the Bureau of the Census is that providing

(Continued on page 266)

Citizen Action .   .   .   .   .   . *Edited by Elsie S. Parker*

Seattle Stimulates Vote with Gold Feathers

Secretary of State Announces Same Plan for Fall Elections

MARCH 9 was a very special day in the annals of Seattle citizens. For the second time the Seattle League of Women Voters and the Municipal League of Seattle and King County promoted operation "Gold Feather" at the general city elections held that day in Seattle and five other cities in the county.

The campaign was aided by two daily newspapers which published a page 1 editorial, cartoons, pictures, stories, etc.; radio stations gave spot announcements as did two TV stations. One of the latter contributed some $30,000 in time. Small community newspapers also helped.

The result was a turnout of 45 per cent of the registered voters at a non-mayoralty election—an increase of 3 per cent over 1950 when similar officials were chosen.

Envelopes containing 200 feathers each were packaged by some twenty volunteers from the League of Women Voters, one package for each of the 1,050 voting precincts. Approximately 225,000 gold feathers were used. Distribution was made by the county auditor through the election superintendent. The Municipal League paid for the feathers and envelopes.

Each voter, as he cast his ballot, received a gold feather, which he was requested to wear throughout the day, first, to show that he had done his duty as a citizen; second, to remind others that they should do likewise.

Laymen and city and county officials alike voiced their approval of the idea. It was first introduced into the city for

the 1952 election, when 63 per cent of the total registered vote turned out in contrast to 39 per cent in 1948.

Secretary of State Coe has announced that he plans to distribute gold feathers at the fall election on a statewide basis, as he did in the 1952 general election.

The gold feather "get-out-the-vote" idea was first launched in Richmond, Virginia, where it was originated by Ed. P. Phillips, local businessman and civic leader, who instigated it for the city's local elections of 1948.[1] The idea has now spread to other cities.

Chicago Celebrates Citizenship Week

On the proclamation of Mayor Martin H. Kennelly, signed March 8, Chicago celebrated "Citizenship Week" from April 5 to 12, in preparation for the April 13 county-wide primary election. The mayors of four other cities in Cook County and the president of the Cook County board also issued proclamations.

During this period, the Citizens of Greater Chicago, representing some 243 member organizations in the Chicago area,[2] sponsored "a series of public events designed to stimulate better understanding of the duties of citizenship." Citizenship meetings were held in churches, schools, clubs, etc.

Keynote of the week was set forth in CGC's Citizens' Pledge:

"I will vote in every election.

"I will know my community and its government, and work to make them better by studying issues and candidates so that I can vote intelligently, by participating in precinct and ward political

[1] See "Drama Gets Out the Vote," the REVIEW, March 1949, page 116.
[2] See the REVIEW, March 1954, page 153.

affairs and neighborhood and area civic movements.

"I will seek no special services or privileges.

"I will respect the rights of my fellow man."

The organization's get-out-the-vote campaign was participated in by schools, churches and synagogues, and civic organizations. On April 9 a great mass meeting was held at which noted Chicagoans paid tribute to great citizens of the past and present in a dramatic documentary, *Chicago Challenge—The Fabulous Years.* Merit awards were presented to four elementary and eight high schools for achievements in citizenship efforts.

Monday, April 12, was "tab" day, when a thousand women and Boy Scout volunteers distributed "I WILL VOTE" tabs on the streets and at meetings. Costumed young men of the Junior Association of Commerce toured the "Loop" in this connection in an auto-cavalcade. The Jaycees used signs and electronic megaphones to call the crowd's attention to election day and tab distributors on the street corners.

One of the important actions of Citizens of Greater Chicago was the questioning of candidates as to their stand on various important questions. Replies were tabulated and published by the organization.

Wanted: A Thousand Volunteers

Led by Harold K. Goldstein as general chairman, the drive to finance the work of the Cincinnati City Charter Committee for 1954 got off to a good start early this spring. The committee in charge has set a goal of a thousand volunteer workers. In addition to Mr. Goldstein as general chairman, Mrs. Albert D. Cash is chairman of the Initial Gifts Section, Mrs. Robert A. Lyon is chairman of general solicitation, Mrs. Robert P. Goldman of the Women's Division rummage sale, and James M. Nelson of publicity and education.

Legislative Program Fares Well

The Citizens Union of the City of New York reports that its program fared very well indeed in the 1954 session of the state legislature. "Despite the disheartening fiasco on compulsory automobile insurance, the 1954 legislature was one of solid accomplishment," announced the union's news release of March 25. Among the accomplishments cited were advances in election reforms. The legislature provided for optional permanent personal registration, direct election of district party leaders, simplification of petition procedure—removing "booby traps" from nomination procedure—and permitting the use of voting machines in primaries, heretofore used only at the final election.

Among other bills passed by the legislature, sponsored or favored by the union, were two affecting civil service,[1] one on extension of low-rent public housing and one on uniform rules of the road and compulsory car inspection, also a constitutional home rule amendment for counties.[2]

Students Study Courts

Some 80 senior students from Maumee High School in Toledo have studied the operation of municipal and state courts. Municipal court judges played the role of teachers, according to the *Toledo City Journal.* "Conditions remained unchanged," reports the *Journal,* "as the courts followed their regular daily proceedings, giving the students a true picture of Toledo's courts in operation." Some students attended the criminal court, others the traffic court, where a film on traffic accident prevention is shown daily to all traffic offenders.

50 Years of Accomplishment

While "only" 50 years of age, "Seventy has acquired a lot of experience and political know-how," says *Civic Affairs,* bulletin of the Philadelphia Committee

[1]See page 246, this issue.
[2]See page 252, this issue.

of Seventy. "The record shows that throughout our long history the members of the committee have been realistic and practical men working together as a non-partisan group. They have been as willing to support the sincere politicians and the good public servants as they have to condemn those who betray or fail in their public trust. We have learned, through shirt-sleeve experience, that political groups, like reform groups, develop the good and bad, side by side. The problem in the past, as it will be in the future, is to separate them, support and encourage those serving the public interest and help to abolish from public life the ones who use politics, municipal government, or a party label to further their own ends alone."

The committee lists numerous notable achievements in Philadelphia: a new city charter, which took from 1917 to 1949 to secure, permanent registration, uniform voting laws, the voting machine, etc.

"Seventy," continues the bulletin, "as a nonpartisan organization of civic-minded volunteers, expert in municipal and political affairs, will continue as an alert, persistent public conscience. We will tell you when things go wrong and what you can do about it. We will also continue to tell you when things go right and where credit belongs. With your help, we plan to do even more to better insure yesterday's progress, protect today's gains and secure greater improvements for tomorrow."

Citizen Publications

Citizens' Handbook of Montgomery County, Maryland, 1953, has been published by the Allied Civic Group, Inc., at Silver Spring, Maryland. The group plans to make the publication an annual project. The pamphlet gives "in one document a considerable body of financial and economic data believed to be of interest to the citizens and public officials in and around Montgomery County." •

Let's Work Together in Community Service, by Eloise Walton, published by the Public Affairs Committee of New York, is a summary of *Community Planning for Human Services,* by Bradley Buell and Associates, "a comprehensive statistical study of the human problems and the community services in St. Paul, Minnesota." Twenty-eight pages, it may be purchased for 25 cents from the Committee, 22 East 38th Street, New York 16.

The *American Planning and Civic Annual* (164 pages), edited by Harlean James (American Planning and Civic Association, Washington, D.C.,) is "a record of recent civic advance in the field of planning, parks, housing, neighborhood improvement and conservation of natural resources, including addresses delivered at the National Citizens Conference on Metropolitan Planning held at New Orleans, March 11-14, 1953, and several addresses delivered at the 33rd annual meeting of the National Conference on State Parks."

University-Community Cooperation

At its annual meeting the New York State Citizens' Council adopted a University-Community Cooperation Project, which would attempt to find the answers to such questions as these: How much and in what ways do colleges serve communities? How well are they preparing students for active participation in community affairs? The Association of Colleges and Universities of the State of New York and the State University will supply funds for a preliminary study and work closely with the council. A report on the study, with recommendations as to the next steps to be taken, has been placed on the agenda of the association's December meeting.

The council has now published *College-Community Relationships in New York State—A Report of Activities in Twenty-six Colleges and Universities,* prepared by H. Curtis Mial in consultation with The Advisory Committee of the University-Community Cooperation Project. A limited number of copies are available (mimeographed, 101 pages) at one dollar from the New York State Citizens' Council, 613 East Genesee Street, Syracuse 2.

Local Party Formed

A new group, to be known as the Economy party, has been formed in Waverly, New York. The party is emphasizing the importance of urging young men to take an active interest in the local affairs of the village. It named a slate of candidates for the March 16 election.

Manager Case Histories

The League of Women Voters of Illinois, in a recent issue of its *Illinois Voter*, has set forth "City Manager Case Histories" for "those Illinois Leaguers who are either considering or already undertaking local action on the council-manager form of government." The cities covered include Bloomington, Homewood, Oak Park and Rock Island.

Volunteers Aid Commissioners

Member organizations of the Citizens' Council of Fort Wayne, Indiana, at the request of the Allen County commissioners, furnished volunteers who, on March 9, assisted in gathering data relating to the volume and type of traffic on county roads. The data will be used by Purdue University in its preparation of a classification of the county's roads and will serve as a priority system for road improvements.

Annual Meetings

The Medford (Massachusetts) Plan E Association, at its annual meeting in February, elected James S. Castellucci as president. Mr. Castellucci has promised "a more vigorous and active pro-gram through the coming year." Speakers at the meeting included City Manager James F. Shurtleff, Mayor John C. Carr, as well as councilmen and school committee members.

Hon. Henry S. Stout, mayor of Dayton, Ohio, addressed the annual meeting of the Hamilton County (Cincinnati) Good Government League on "Dayton's Experience with the City Income Tax."

The Citizens National Conference on Metropolitan Planning, sponsored by the American Planning and Civic Association, will hold its 50th anniversary in Columbus, Ohio, May 16-20. "The Columbus conference should serve as a demonstration of citizen responsibility for getting plans prepared and seeing that they are realized," says *Planning and Civic Comment*.

Governor Christian A. Herter and his son, Christian A. Herter, Jr., were the principal speakers at the annual meeting of the Massachusetts Federation of Taxpayers Associations on April 10 in Boston. Governor Herter's topic was "Massachusetts—Gaining or Losing Its Fight for Jobs and Lower Taxes?"; that of his son, special assistant to the vice president of the United States, "Asia—The Key to Future World Peace or Conflict?" More than 1,200 representatives from local taxpayer associations throughout the state attended.

The Lake County (Waukegan, Illinois) Civic League held a successful annual meeting in March, addressed by State Auditor Orville E. Hodge. Numerous organizations in the community sent delegations to the meeting, including the Lake County Farm Bureau, Third Lake Improvement Association and the Libertyville Homeowners Association. Represented also were the Lake County Real Estate Board, various Leagues of Women Voters, Chambers of Commerce, as well as city and school boards and other public officials.

Researcher's Digest . ● ● ● ● *Edited by John E. Bebout*

Metropolitan Study Started in Toledo

150 Officials and Citizens Reviewing Area's Problems

A HUNDRED and fifty citizens and public officials from thirty-four local government jurisdictions are taking the lead in an effort to study and appraise governmental problems of the Toledo metropolitan area. Basically, the problem is one of modernizing the governmental organization and raising the standards of public service to fit the changing needs of community life.

The Toledo Municipal League, in December 1953, announced its intention of sponsoring a citizen study project aimed at implementing the master plan recently completed by the Toledo-Lucas County Plan Commission. Immediate expressions of interest in participation by the Toledo city council opened the door to cooperative development of a joint citizen and public official study.

A city council committee on metropolitan affairs was created. It reviewed the nature, scope and methods of seeking solutions to the many metropolitan headaches.

Among the many current problems are those related to:

(1) Defeat on three occasions of proposals to incorporate a 23-square-mile township adjacent to the city;

(2) Unsuccessful efforts of this area to obtain annexation to Toledo by public vote;

(3) Annexations of sixteen small areas to Toledo since 1949 by petitions of district residents;

(4) The need for thirty-two new elementary schools and four new high schools in the Toledo urban area, plus enlargement and modernization of another

thirty-seven elementary schools and eight high schools—all by 1980;

(5) The immediate urgency of establishing financial responsibility and obtaining voter approval of financing to construct four elementary schools and one high school at desirable locations which now practically straddle the boundary between township and city school districts;

(6) Answering delayed demands for extending water lines beyond city boundaries to the north, east, south and west to meet rapid residential and industrial expansion in the fringe areas, where water levels are receding and deeper wells frequently hit impotable water;

(7) Meeting needs for vast extensions of sanitary sewer lines to eliminate dangerous ground pollution outside incorporated areas;

(8) Rendering urban services in the rapidly developing fringe areas;

(9) Restudying financial capacity, tax equality, authority and organizational efficiency of the county and townships to render varying degrees of urban services in unincorporated areas;

(10) Coordination of planning, zoning and building code enforcement between county, city, village and township areas including some without adequate enforcement or even without zoning or building codes;

(11) The potential impact of the Ohio Turnpike, certain expressway developments, location of a class V express airport;

(12) The effects of the St. Lawrence Seaway upon the Toledo port;

(13) The need to develop industrial sites outside the central city to meet defense requirements.

These and other matters established for the Toledo city council the need for an over-all cooperative study of the community. After exploratory conferences at the various levels of local government, a steering committee was named by the council to present a project plan and organization. Named to the steering committee were the city manager of Toledo, the president of the board of commissioners of Lucas County, the superintendents of the city and county boards of education and the executive secretary of the Toledo Municipal League.

Project Outlined

The scope of the project was defined in general terms to include all phases of local public service in the metropolitan community. More specifically, the varying conceptions of the term "metropolitan area" were reduced for purposes of this study to approximately 155 square miles including the central city and a five-mile band around it. This area, designated by the master plan as the Toledo urban area, includes parts of two counties, two cities and seven villages, all or part of nine townships, fourteen school districts and a mosquito control district. Slightly less than 60 square miles are within some incorporated area and approximately 30 more are on the verge of either annexation or incorporation.

The Toledo area consists of less than half the land area of Lucas County and about 3 per cent of Wood County. On the other hand 94 per cent (400,000) of Lucas County's population, plus 20 per cent (12,000) of Wood County's population are in the Toledo urban area. The planning base for 1980 population is 500,000.

A compromise was reached on the question of making this a citizen or a public officials' study. During recent annexation and incorporation campaigns officials had taken rather definite stands on some subjects. In the interests of freedom to explore all ideas, it became desirable to excuse public officials from sponsoring any significant change during the study period. The compromise called for appointing representative citizens to serve on all study committees except that on research and resources. To it public officials representing all local governing jurisdictions were selected so that research data, public know-how and experience might be available to all other committees.

The plan of organization was approved by the metropolitan affairs committee of the city council and the steering committee was advised to nominate organizational chairmen. This done, the council passed a resolution officially creating the Toledo Area Study Committee. The chairmen and members of the committee were appointed.

The importance of obtaining qualified persons and assuring balanced participation should not be underestimated. TASC is designed to include persons qualified in three respects: first, to make a constructive contribution to the task of the committee to which assigned; second, to reflect prevailing attitudes in one or more areas toward the public jurisdictions serving the area; and third, to be a civic leader in his residential community in order to assist in the dissemination of the results of the study.

Committee Setup

TASC is headed by a general chairman who, with the chairman of the nine subcommittees, serves on an executive committee. The first level of organizational structure is based upon five functional subcommittees: schools, utilities and transportation, health and welfare, urban services, and zoning, planning and recreation. Each committee has nine members except schools, which has fifteen. The second level consists of four coordinating subcommittees: ways and means, organization and legislation, publicity and civic education, and research and resources. Except for the last, each committee has seven members.

The research and resources subcommittee is composed of 70 public officials, not including key staff personnel who may be called upon for specific needs. A balance is maintained between part-time elected officials, e.g., presidents of school boards and weak mayors and full-time elected officials and professional administrators, e.g., strong mayors, managers and school superintendents.

The subcommittee's policy section, composed of elected officials from all jurisdictions in the area, would give guidance on policy determination and public acceptability. Its technical section, composed of administrative and technical officials, would provide factual data and evaluation of administrative, procedural and technical questions.

The ways and means subcommittee would coordinate the fiscal sections of the work of other groups. It would study revenue sources, taxable capacity, debt, limitations and other financial problems.

The organization and legislation subcommittee would study the strengths and weaknesses of different types of government and the interdependence of units. Methods for correcting or improving forms and powers would be prepared. Legal matters raised by other groups and all proposed legislative changes would channel through this unit.

The publicity and civic education subcommittee would plan, prepare and release information, organize speakers' bureau and information outlets, and prepare adult and school information material.

The first round of general and subcommittee meetings has been held to initiate and orient the project and its many phases. Temporary financing of committee expenses was volunteered by the Toledo Municipal League.

Annexations Held Up

The first accomplishment may be said to be a moratorium on annexation, incorporation and district reorganization until January 1, 1955. The purpose is to assist in the establishment of a calm and cooperative climate during the period of critical study. Toledo's city council initiated a resolution for this purpose which, by its terms, became effective when the Lucas County, Toledo and Washington township boards of education, Lucas County Board of County Commissioners and the Washington Township Board of Trustees agreed to support the moratorium proposal.

Thus, the first phase of another experiment in self-evaluation of a metropolitan area is completed. In it may be a pattern for others who wish to strengthen and improve urban living democratically, and who wish to abate, if not escape, the pressures within a population center too compressed, too confined, too regimented, too impersonal, too uncharitable and too taxed.

RONALD E. GREGG, *Executive Secretary*
Municipal League of Toledo

Denver Economic Research Council

An Economic Research Council has been organized in Denver, Colorado, to collect and analyze statistics dealing with growth and other changes in the Denver metropolitan area. Members of the council are from the city government, school system, other taxing jurisdictions, business and industrial firms and the Bureau of Business and Social Research. The research program will include compilation and evaluation of a wide range of social and economic statistics. Information about Colorado as a whole will be gathered because of the effects which developments in other parts of the state have upon Denver.

Members of the council will pay a fee that will entitle them to all publications and make it possible for them to call on the university's Bureau of Business Research for basic information.

GRA Reporter

The Governmental Research Association has undergone some far-reaching changes in recent months. The impact of these developments is spelled out in an article by the association's president, Harland C. Stockwell, to be found in the GRA *Reporter*, First Quarter, 1954.

Publication of the *Reporter* is now the assignment of an association publications committee. The first issue under the committee was edited by Alvin K. Peterjohn of the Institute of Public Administration, New York. Articles on Newark's new charter, welfare administration in Louisiana and New York, and the use of aerial mosaics in the preparation of tax maps will interest researchers.

Research Pamphlets and Articles

Assessment

EFFORTS TO IMPROVE ASSESSMENT ADMINISTRATION IN NEW JERSEY. Trenton 8, New Jersey Taxpayers Association, *It's Your Business*, March 1954. 4 pp.

EQUALITY IN PROPERTY ASSESSMENTS. Santa Fe, Taxpayers' Association of New Mexico, *Tax Bulletin*, March 1954. 2 pp.

OREGON'S STRUGGLE TO EQUALIZE PROPERTY TAXES. By Louise L. Humphrey. Portland 4, Oregon Business and Tax Research, *Special Tax Report*, January 1954. 4 pp.

22 ASSESSMENT DEPARTMENTS IN MILWAUKEE COUNTY; 11 Chief Assessors will be elected at the April 6th Election. FIRST $4 BILLION EQUALIZED ASSESSED VALUATION OF MILWAUKEE COUNTY. Milwaukee 2, Citizens' Governmental Research Bureau, Inc., *Bulletin,* March 13 and 25, 1954. 3 and 5 pp. respectively.

Budgets

THE FEDERAL BUDGET SYSTEM. How it works . . . How it can be improved. . . . Washington 6, D. C., Chamber of Commerce of the United States, Committee on Government Expenditures, 1954. 13 pp.

NO CRISIS IN THE COUNTY. The

League Analyzes Allegheny County's Budget for 1954. Pittsburgh 19, Pennsylvania Economy League, Inc., Western Division, *P. E. L. Newsletter,* March 1954. 9 pp.

THE ROLE OF PERFORMANCE BUDGETING IN MUNICIPAL MANAGEMENT. By Lynn F. Anderson. Austin 1, League of Texas Municipalities, *Texas Municipalities*, March 1954. 9 pp.

Business Districts

THE MADISON CENTRAL BUSINESS AREA. A Case Study of Functional Change. By Richard U. Ratcliff. Madison, University of Wisconsin, School of Commerce, Bureau of Business Research and Service, 1953. 69 pp. $1.15.

Education

WHY IS A SCHOOL BOARD? Miami 32, Dade County Research Foundation, *News Letter*, March 18, 1954. 3 pp.

Fringe Areas

MUNICIPAL SERVICES TO FRINGE AREA RESIDENTS. A Survey of Tennessee Practices. Water, Sewer, Fire Protection, Garbage Collection. By Harlan Mathews. Nashville 3, Tennessee State Planning Commission, 1953. $1.00.

SOCIAL CHANGE AND AN URBAN FRINGE AREA. Ithaca, New York, A Case Illustration. By W. A. Anderson. Ithaca, State University of New York, New York State College of Agriculture at Cornell University, 1953. 28 pp.

Grants-in-aid

FEDERAL GRANT-IN-AID PROGRAMS IN MICHIGAN, 1941-1953. Lansing 13, Michigan Department of Administration, Budget Division, 1953. 133 pp. (Copies not available for distribution.)

Home Rule

HOME RULE IN NEVADA. Carson City, Nevada Legislative Counsel Bureau, December 1952. 45 pp.

Intergovernmental Relations

INTERGOVERNMENTAL RELATIONS. By Robert C. Hendrickson. (Address before Annual Convention of the New Jersey State League of Municipalities.) The

League, *New Jersey Municipalities*, January 1954. 2 pp.

Legislative Bodies

LEGISLATIVE REFORMS. By Charles W. Shull. Winfield (Kansas), *Social Science*, January 1954. 5 pp.

Management

THE INSTITUTE ON MANAGEMENT IN GOVERNMENT AND BUSINESS. By Morton Kroll. Chicago 37, Civil Service Assembly, *Public Personnel Review*, January 1954. 7 pp.

Municipal Law

FLORIDA MUNICIPAL LAW–A SYMPOSIUM: THE CHALLENGE OF CONTEMPORARY URBAN PROBLEMS, by Jefferson B. Fordham; LEGAL ASPECTS OF FLORIDA MUNICIPAL BOND FINANCING, by Giles J. Patterson; MUNICIPAL TORT LIABILITY —A CONTINUING ENIGMA, by Hugh Douglas Price and J. Allen Smith; LEGAL PROBLEMS IN FLORIDA MUNICIPAL ZONING, by Ernest R. Bartley; DEVELOPMENTS IN REVENUE BOND FINANCING, by William Alfred Rose; MUNICIPAL COURT PRACTICE, by Harry W. Fogle; MUNICIPAL CHARTERS IN FLORIDA, by Manning J. Dauer and George John Miller. Gainesville, University of Florida, *Law Review*, Fall 1953. 206 pp. $2.00.

Prisons

SURVEY OF THE JAIL NEEDS OF KENT COUNTY. A Report to the Board of Supervisors of Kent County, Michigan. Detroit 26, Citizens Research Council of Michigan, October 1953. 39 pp.

Recreation

RECREATION IN KANSAS. By Larry J. Heeb. Lawrence, University of Kansas, Governmental Research Center, *Your Government*, March 15, 1954. 3 pp.

SUGGESTED PARK AND RECREATIONAL ORDINANCES. Park Boards and Departments. By Ernest H. Campbell, William B. Pond and Ruth E. Pike. Seattle 5, Association of Washington Cities in cooperation with the University of Washington, Bureau of Governmental Research and Services, 1954. 35 pp.

Refuse Disposal

GARBAGE COLLECTION AND DISPOSAL. Methods and Practices in Washington Cities. By Bert Balmer. Seattle 5, Association of Washington Cities in cooperation with the University of Washington, Bureau of Governmental Research and Services, 1954. 38 pp.

GARBAGE—ITS COLLECTION AND DISPOSAL. A Field Survey of Incinerators and Methods of Municipal Garbage and Refuse Collection and Disposal Employed in 27 Major Cities Throughout the United States. By Philip N. Royal. Seattle, City Department of Engineering, 127 pp.

Research Bureaus

PROCEEDINGS OF THE THIRTEENTH ANNUAL CONFERENCE OF THE WESTERN GOVERNMENTAL RESEARCH ASSOCIATION, Santa Monica, California, October 1-2, 1953. Berkeley, University of California, Office of the Secretariat, 1954. 30 pp. $1.00.

Salaries

SALARY RATES OF OFFICIALS AND EMPLOYEES IN 187 OREGON CITIES. Eugene, University of Oregon, Bureau of Municipal Research and Service in cooperation with The League of Oregon Cities, 1954. 20 pp.

State-local Relations

HOW THE GENERAL ASSEMBLY CAN STRENGTHEN LOCAL GOVERNMENT. Philadelphia 4, University of Pennsylvania, Associated Institutes of Government of Pennsylvania Universities, *Horizons for Modern Pennsylvania Local Government*, March 1954. 3 pp.

STATE-CITY RELATIONS. A Review of Kentucky Constitutional Provisions. Frankfort, Kentucky Legislative Research Commission, 1954. 81 pp.

States' Rights

STATES' RIGHTS AND VESTED INTERESTS. By Robert J. Harris. Gainesville, Southern Political Science Association in cooperation with University of Florida,

The Journal of Politics, November 1953. 15 pp.

Taxation and Finance

LAND VALUE TAXATION IN CANADIAN LOCAL GOVERNMENT. Being Constructive Criticism on Reports on Provincial-municipal Relations by British Columbia, Alberta, Saskatchewan, Manitoba. By Herbert T. Owens. Westmount (Quebec), International Committee for Land Value Taxation and Free Trade and the Henry George Foundation of Canada, Inc., 1953. 48 pp. $1.00.

LOCAL INCOME TAXES IN WESTERN PENNSYLVANIA. The League Makes Some Timely Observations. Pittsburgh 19, Pennsylvania Economy League, Inc., Western Division, *P. E. L. Newsletter,* January-February 1954. 8 pp.

MISSISSIPPI STATE FINANCIAL AID TO COUNTIES. University, University of Mississippi, Bureau of Public Administration, *Public Administration Survey,* March 1954. 5 pp.

MUNICIPAL AND INTERGOVERNMENTAL FINANCE, 1930-1951. A Survey and Report on the distribution of federal, provincial and municipal government revenues and expenditures with an analysis of the financial problems of municipal governments in Canada. Montreal 2, Canadian Federation of Mayors and Municipalities, 1953. 59 pp. $2.50.

MUNICIPAL FINANCE. A Study of Nine First-class Cities. By Harry O. Lawson. Lawrence, University of Kansas, Governmental Research Center, December 1953. 35 pp.

MUNICIPAL REVENUE PROBLEMS. Report to the 68th General Assembly—1953. Springfield, Illinois Legislative Commission on Municipal Revenue, 1953. 102 pp.

PAPERS ON MUNICIPAL NONPROPERTY TAXES IN MICHIGAN. (Admissions and income taxes.) By Arthur M. Wisehart. Ann Arbor, University of Michigan, Institute of Public Administration,

Bureau of Government, 1954. 103 pp. $2.00.

Zoning

ZONING ADMINISTRATION AND ENFORCEMENT. By Ernest H. Campbell, Merrill Wallace, Charles Lyness and Murray E. Taggart. Seattle 5, Association of Washington Cities in cooperation with the University of Washington, Bureau of Governmental Research and Services, 1954. 27 pp.

TAXATION AND FINANCE
(Continued from page 256)

summary details, based on the 1952 fiscal year, on state payments to local governments.[1]

The study includes comparative statistics on payments to local governments for each of the 48 states, classified to the extent practicable by functions and by type of local government receiving the payments. Variations in state practice are emphasized in the tabulation, but it is of interest that, of some $5,044,000,000 paid by all the states to their local units, roughly half was for education and nearly one-fifth for public assistance, with highways accounting for about one-seventh.

An especially valuable part of the study is an extended table summarizing the principal grants, shared taxes, etc., on which the local aid payments of each state are based. Data are arranged to show in some detail the state tax or fund involved, the basis of apportionment and the purpose of the grant and type of local unit receiving it. Some 57 of the publication's 76 pages are devoted to this summary, which shows the status as of 1952, and a supplementary table summarizes major changes effective after the 1952 fiscal year.

---

[1] *State Payments to Local Governments in 1952.* Washington, D. C., U. S. Department of Commerce, Bureau of the Census, 1954. 76 pp. 45 cents.

Books in Review

FREEDOM AND PUBLIC EDUCATION. Edited by Ernest O. Melby and Morton Puner. New York City, Frederick A. Praeger, Inc., 1953. x, 314 pp. $4.00.

FORCES AFFECTING AMERICAN EDUCATION. 1953 Yearbook of the Association for Supervision and Curriculum Development, a department of the National Education Association. Washington, D. C., the Association, 1953. xv, 208 pp. $3.50.

Modern education and its more acrimonious critics are the subject matters of both these books. *Freedom* is a collection of articles by some 40 authors in varied fields expatiating on viewpoints, policies and problems affecting modern education, in a range from the thoughtful to the impassioned. The material is well organized in five major sections and there is a helpful continuity of editorial interpolation. *Forces*—a yearbook of an NEA department—is an educators' appraisal of the schools' position in and relation to the controversy and is at once explanation, defense and program for counteraction.

Both books ably set forth the role of public education in a democracy and the difficulties imposed on the schools by the very way of life we profess and by the character of the times. *Freedom* presents perhaps the better perspective on the problem, largely by drawing on a wider range of speakers, although "The People and Their Schools," by W. E. Goslin, in *Forces* is one of the ablest articles in either volume. To stick to citing educators, Gordon McCloskey, in "Meeting Attacks on Public Education" in *Freedom*, also gives solid food for thought—and to educators as well as to the interested layman.

There is a curious admixture in each book of jargon and plain talk, of negative —or defensive—argument and positive program. "Honest criticism" of the schools is often welcomed, but is never,

for this reader, satisfactorily defined or exampled. And the layman gains no appreciable insight into the aims of modern education as set forth in passages such as this one from *Freedom*: "These leaders [in the field of mathematics] propose that in the modern curriculum, mathematics should include not only the function of teaching skills in computation but other related skills which have a direct application to present-day living." What these related, yet presumably non-computational, skills are apparently awaits a fuller development of communication skills. And so here and there, unfortunately, the layman asked to agree with the educator is forced to respond, "I might, if I felt I clearly understood what you were talking about." Unfortunately, too, much of this sort of thing has been seized on by extremists as a convenient vehicle or pretext for attack.

The student of government, treating education as an important, but by no means the only, demand on tax-supported services, may also be mildly surprised to find himself often implicitly regarded as one of the "enemy" for having the temerity to question "adequate" school budgets. As for federal aid for education, the need is often established by little more than assertion, which will weigh little with a substantial group of fairly respectable people who do not feel that the need is either manifest or indisputable. Public education can never escape certain essential processes of the "democratic way" so long as the adjective "public" remains. This is clearly recognized by authors in both books but, in erecting their defenses, some educators appear to beg the question of the fiscal wherewithal, whether local or federal.

Points such as these could be offset many times, however, if space permitted. The value of each book lies not in the detailed review of the attacks on education. It lies in the evidence of a growing realization on the part of educators and the friends of education of the need, in the democracy, for explanation and understanding as the basis for approval and consent. Both books, read with a wary eye, present a well stated historical and philosophical commentary on the purposes, problems, pitfalls and promises of modern public education in America.

TILDEN B. MASON
Citizens Research Council of Michigan

KNOW YOUR STATE. A Handbook for Citizens of New York. New York 16, League of Women Voters of New York, 1954. 125 pp. $1.00.

Steadily the Leagues of Women Voters in the various states build up the literature of civil government for the laity and the output of *Know Your State, Know Your County* and *Know Your City* material has become immense and important for all civic workers. Perhaps the most ambitious of these is this new handbook which covers comprehensively and vividly all the phases of New York State's government, its relation to local government and to the federal government and a highly practical fact-packed chapter on the working of the political parties and their internal mechanisms. A superb job and of obvious competence.

R. S. C.

PRIMARY ELECTIONS IN THE SOUTH. A Study in Uniparty Politics. By Cortez A. M. Ewing. Norman, University of Oklahoma Press, 1953. xii, 112 pp. $2.75.

This little source book analyzes 3,800 primary contests in eleven southern states in an endeavor to detect patterns of voter behavior and party management. Small differences are found in such respects as number of candidates between the single primary contests and those in which failure to produce a majority at the first primary brings about a second primary

to select from among the two top candidates.

Other statistics show a high percentage of unopposed nominations in the Democratic party, of which a high proportion are caused by the presence of satisfactory incumbents who are willing to run again for local offices which are not too attractive in terms of salary and power and in which competent routineers may be content to stay for a lifetime.

The low turnout of voters in southern primaries is exhibited and compared with the turnout at the final one-sided elections.

Southern Democratic primaries, being a rather unorganized scramble for office by individuals, would provide an interesting analogy for a similar study of non-partisan elections in cities throughout the country where, in about half the cases, there is almost no organized or factional activity or continuing leadership.

R. S. C.

CURRENT TRENDS IN STATE LEGISLATION, 1952. Ann Arbor, University of Michigan Law School, 1952. xvii, 580 pp. $7.50.

This massive volume is the first of a series from the Legislative Research Center of the University of Michigan Law School. It has been prepared with the aid of the staff of graduate research associates with special financial support from the William W. Cook Endowment Fund. Further volumes are anticipated biennially.

It deals only with state statutes of the type which it calls private law statutes and rounds up the 1949, 1950 and 1951 output of new statutes covering ten subjects of special interest to lawyers such as "Defamation by Radio," "Right of Dissenting Shareholder," "Reciprocal Support Legislation," and "Photographic Copies as Evidence" with a thoroughness which makes each one a considerable book in itself.

Additional Books and Pamphlets

(See also Researcher's Digest and other departments)

Accounting

A STANDARD CLASSIFICATION OF MUNICIPAL ACCOUNTS. Chicago 37, National Committee on Governmental Accounting, 1953. ix, 129 pp. $3.00. (Apply Municipal Finance Officers Association, 1313 East 60th Street, Chicago 37.)

Budgeting

AN ADMINISTRATIVE CASE STUDY OF PERFORMANCE BUDGETING IN THE CITY OF LOS ANGELES, CALIFORNIA. By George A. Terhune. Chicago 37, Municipal Finance Officers Association, 1954. 32 pp. $1.25.

Building Codes

STATE BUILDING CONSTRUCTION CODE APPLICABLE TO MULTIPLE DWELLINGS. GENERALLY ACCEPTED STANDARDS APPLICABLE TO STATE BUILDING CONSTRUCTION CODE. New York 19, New York State Building Code Commission, 1953. 132 and 15 pp. respectively.

City Councils

YOUR GUIDE TO THE COUNCIL OF THE CITY OF PHILADELPHIA. Philadelphia, Bureau of Public Information and Service, Office of the City Representative, October 1953. 11 pp. Illus.

Codification

THE CODIFICATION OF SCHOOL LAWS. Washington 6, D. C., National Education Association of the United States, Research Division, *Research Bulletin*, February 1954. 47 pp. 50 cents.

Cost of Living Adjustments

COST OF LIVING PAY ADJUSTMENT PLANS. By Ismar Baruch. Chicago 37, Civil Service Assembly of the United States and Canada, 1953. 6 pp. $2.00.

Council-manager Plan

A MODEL COUNCIL-MANAGER ORDINANCE FOR BOROUGHS AND TOWNSHIPS IN PENNSYLVANIA. Pittsburgh, University of Pittsburgh, Institute of Local Government, 1952. 10 pp.

RECENT COUNCIL-MANAGER DEVELOPMENTS AND DIRECTORY OF COUNCIL-MANAGER CITIES. Chicago 37, The International City Managers' Association, 1954. 32 pp. $1.00.

Democracy

BROWNSON ON DEMOCRACY AND THE TREND TOWARD SOCIALISM. By Lawrence Roemer. New York, Philosophical Library, 1953. xvi, 173 pp. $3.75.

A FREE SOCIETY: AN EVALUATION OF CONTEMPORARY DEMOCRACY. By Mark M. Heald. New York, Philosophical Library, 1953. xii, 546 pp. $4.75.

Employment

EMPLOYMENT TRENDS 1942-1951 IN THE NEW JERSEY–NEW YORK–CONNECTICUT METROPOLITAN REGION. New York 17, Regional Plan Association, *Regional Plan Bulletin*, March 1954. 16 pp. $5.00.

Federal Government

ORGANIZATION OF FEDERAL EXECUTIVE DEPARTMENTS AND AGENCIES. Report of the Committee on Government Operations. 84 pp. Organization of Federal Executive Departments and Agencies (chart 176" x 93"). Washington, D. C., United States Government Printing Office, 1954. 25 and 20 cents respectively.

Home Rule

CONSTITUTIONAL CITY HOME RULE IN NEW YORK. By W. Bernard Richland. (Reprinted from *Columbia Law Review*.) New York City, Columbia University, March 1954. 27 pp.

Judiciary

JUDICIAL ADMINISTRATION—1953. By Sheldon D. Elliott. (Reprinted from *1953 Annual Survey of American Law*.) New York 12, Institute of Judicial Administration, 1953. 15 pp.

SUMMARY OF STATE PRACTICES IN PUBLISHING OFFICIAL STATE REPORTS. (Results of survey on problems connected with publication and distribution of official state reports on court decisions.) AR-

RANGEMENTS IN THE STATES FOR PUBLI-
CATION OF OFFICIAL REPORTS OF COURT
DECISIONS — SUMMARY OF COMMENTS
FROM RESPONDENTS IN STATE COURTS OF
LAST RESORT. Chicago 37, Council of
State Governments, 1953. 5 and 11 pp.
respectively.

STATE COURT SYSTEMS (Revised). Chicago 37, Council of State Governments,
1953. 30 pp. $1.00.

Nominating Petitions

THE CASE FOR AMENDING THE LAW
ON DESIGNATING AND NOMINATING PETI-
TIONS. (Submitted to the Members of the
New York State Legislature.) New York
5, Election Reform Committee, 1954.
13 pp. (Apply the Committee, 1 Wall
Street, Room 1338, New York 5.)

Politics

ESSAY IN POLITICS. By Scott Buchan-
an. New York, Philosophical Library,
1953. xiii, 236 pp. $3.75.

Population

THE POPULATION OF PHILADELPHIA
AND ITS METROPOLITAN AREA. General
Characteristics and Trends. Philadelphia
7, City Planning Commission, 1953.
16 pp.

President

COMPLETE HANDBOOK ON SELECTION OF
PRESIDENTS. Vol. I: THE BASIC HAND-
BOOK; Vol. II: THE DEBATE HANDBOOK;
SUPPLEMENT. By J. Weston Walch.
Portland, Maine, J. Weston Walch, 1953
and 1954. 188, 220 and 70 pp. $3.00,
$3.00 and $1.50 respectively.

Records

RECORDS MANAGEMENT PROGRAM—
RULES AND REGULATIONS. RECORDS RE-
TENTION SCHEDULE FOR MUNICIPAL AND
COUNTY OFFICES (Revised). Trenton 7,
New Jersey State Department of Educa-
tion, Division of the State Library,
Archives and History, 1953 and 1954.
15 and 4 pp. respectively.

Roadside Development

TRENDS IN ROADSIDE DEVELOPMENT. By
Park H. Martin, Patrick J. Cusick, Jr.,
and Wesley H. Hottenstein. (Addresses
presented at Roadside Conference, Pittsburgh 1953.) Media (Pennsylvania),
Pennsylvania Roadside Council, 1954.
13 pp.

State and Local Government

PLEDGES AGAINST THE FUTURE.[1] A
Review of the State's Standing Commitments to its Local Governments. Harrisburg, Pennsylvania Economy League,
Inc., 1954. 17 pp.[1]

STATE AND LOCAL GOVERNMENT IN
UTAH. A description of the structure,
operations, functions and finances of all
branches of state and local government in
Utah—their departments, commissions
and agencies. Salt Lake City 1, Utah
Foundation, 1954. 202 pp. Clothbound:
$2.00, Paperbound: $1.50.

Statistics

STATISTICAL ABSTRACT OF THE UNITED
STATES 1953. Washington 25, D. C.,
Superintendent of Documents, U. S. Gov-
ernment Printing Office, 1953. 1041 pp.
$3.50.

Taxation and Finance

THE LIMITS OF TAXABLE CAPACITY.
By Dan Throop Smith, Rowland R.
Hughes, etc. (Symposium, Tax Institute,
November 1952) Princeton, New Jersey,
Tax Institute, 1953. viii, 184 pp. $5.00.

1955 FISCAL YEAR LONG-TERM CAPITAL
IMPROVEMENT PROGRAM, State of Maryland. Baltimore 2, Maryland State Planning Commission, 1953. 88 pp. 50 cents.

PAYROLL DEDUCTIONS MADE BY MU-
NICIPALITIES. A Survey of the Practices
of Selected Cities in the United States
and Canada. Chicago 37, Municipal Finance Officers Association of the United
States and Canada, 1954. 4 pp. 50 cents.

SHOULD THE FEDERAL GOVERNMENT
ADOPT A UNIFORM MANUFACTURERS' EX-
CISE? (Forum Pamphlet Seven.) By
Robert S. Ford, Fred Maytag II, Chester
M. Edelmann, E. C. Stephenson and
Alexander Wiley. Princeton, New
Jersey, Tax Institute, 1954. 32 pp. 50
cents.

---

[1]See editorial, page 228, this issue.

INSIDE THE OFFICE . . .

Herbert Emmerich, director of the Public Administration Clearing House and former League Council member, called on Alfred Willoughby and Richard S. Childs recently. . . .

Alfred Willoughby, Herbert Emmerich and Richard S. Childs.

William H. Bulkeley, new League Council member and president of the Kellogg & Bulkeley Division, Connecticut Printers, Inc., conferred with the staff about gaining broader financial support in the Hartford area. . . . On his recent trip to Kansas City, to make preliminary arrangements for the November Conference on Government, **Allen H. Seed, Jr.,** traveled 5,000 miles to visit Tulsa, New Orleans, Shreveport and Dallas.

L. P. Cookingham, city manager of Kansas City, Missouri, and League Council member, paid a call recently. . . . **Jack Wilson and Bob Cenedella, NBC script writers** working on the Scranton and Daytona Beach stories for the weekly series of **League-sponsored radio broadcasts,** consulted with the staff on their scripts. The series began on Sunday, April 25, and will continue through mid-June, originating in New York at 1 P.M., Eastern Daylight Time. Most stations are broadcasting the program when received, others rebroadcasting later on Sunday. New Orleans has been added to the list of nine cities whose stories of citizen action are being dramatized.

Spencer Miller, Jr.

Spencer Miller, Jr., former assistant secretary of labor and former League Council member, visited the office recently. He said that after his stay in Washington he realized how important it is for America to improve its local and state government. . . . **Alfred Willoughby** attended meetings of the board of the **Public Administration Service** and of the **American Committee for Intermunicipal Cooperation** in Chicago.

J. W. Baker, president, Commercial National Bank of Shreveport, and **Lester W. Kabacoff** of New Orleans will assist the League's finance committee in developing business interest in the NML in their areas. . . . Assistant director **John Bebout** spoke recently before the **Paterson, New Jersey, Junior Chamber of Commerce** on forms of municipal government. He also addressed the **Charter League of New Rochelle, New York,** on municipal politics and its relationship to state and national politics.

Alfred Willoughby and L. P. Cookingham.

Metropolitan Problem Discussed

A discussion of the metropolitan area problem and its continuing relationship to the National Municipal League was held on March 27 at the Statler Hotel.

The group considered the specific projects in this field the League might undertake both alone and in cooperation with other groups. It also explored the areas of basic research necessary for a thorough understanding of the metropolitan area problem.

Attending the meeting were Coleman Woodbury, author and consultant; Victor Jones, associate professor of government, Wesleyan University; Charlton F. Chute, vice-president, Southeastern Division, Pennsylvania Economy League; and Joseph E. McLean, Woodrow Wilson School, Princeton University. Alfred Willoughby, executive director; John E. Bebout, assistant director; John P. Keith, senior associate; and William N. Cassella, Jr., League Staff Fellow, represented the League.

League Moves Uptown

After fifteen years at 299 Broadway, the National Municipal League moved its offices to a more central and convenient location at 542 Fifth Avenue, New York 36, on April 24. The new offices are on the fourth floor of a building at 45th Street and Fifth Avenue, three blocks from Grand Central Station.

The League was "bumped" by the New York City Housing Authority, which will occupy ten floors of the Broadway building.

Max E. Friedmann Dies Suddenly

Max E. Friedmann, 64, who served two terms on the League's Council, died suddenly on March 31. He was returning from a vacation in the Virgin Islands and was stricken on a train bringing him back to his native Milwaukee.

Max E. Friedmann

Mr. Friedmann was on the League's Council from 1947 to 1949 and from 1951 to 1953. He was a member of the Finance Committee and largely responsible for initiating a drive to obtain business support for the League's program. As the immediate past president of the Citizens' Governmental Research Bureau in Milwaukee, he was an important civic force in his city.

Mr. Friedmann was president of Ed. Schuster & Company, Incorporated, operators of three department stores. He was a trustee of the Milwaukee Art Institute for 32 years and a member of the Community Welfare Council of Milwaukee County. He was succeeded on the League's Council by Philip K. Robinson, vice president, Northwestern Mutual Life Insurance Company.

Considering the metropolitan area problem are, left to right, Coleman Woodbury, Charlton Chute, John Keith, John Bebout, Joseph McLean, Alfred Willoughby, Victor Jones and William Cassella.

NEWS for League Members

Council Okays Constitution Changes

At its all-day meeting May 7, at the Waldorf-Astoria Hotel in New York, the Council approved a revision of the League's 22-year-old constitution. The revision prepared by the Survey Committee under the chairmanship of Cecil Morgan will be submitted to the membership for final action at the annual meeting in Kansas City. The document will be printed in the REVIEW at least 30 days before the meeting.

The Council also established a standing Advisory Committee on Program and Policy, adopted most of the recommendations of the Survey Committee "as a general policy guide for officers, committees and staff" and took steps that may lead to a permanent home for the League.

The Survey Committee's report as amended and adopted by the Council is available to League members on request. It reviews and generally endorses most of the McLean "appraisal" submitted to the Council last November and makes various recommendations to facilitate more active participation by Council members and others. The purposes of the new Advisory Committee on Program and Policy, described by Mr. Morgan as "the key recommendation of the Survey Committee," are set forth in the report.

The Building Committee reported that a five-story house described by an architectural firm as "ideal for the purpose of national headquarters for your organization" has been offered to the League on generous terms. The Council authorized the Executive Committee to investigate the financing problem and to acquire the building if it proves feasible.

Listen to "Citizens at Work" — NBC Radio Network

June 6, Kansas City, Mo. ● June 13, Brookfield, Ill.
June 20, New Orleans ● June 27, Roanoke, Va.

At the League's spring Council meeting in the Waldorf-Astoria Hotel, New York, are, left to right around the table: Arthur W. Bromage, George S. Van Schaick, Mrs. Albert D. Cash, William H. Bulkeley, Bayard H. Faulkner, John Bebout, Cecil Morgan, William Collins, Alfred Willoughby, President George H. Gallup, Richard S. Childs, Carl H. Pforzheimer, Murray Seasongood, Thomas R. Reid, H. Bruce Palmer, Mark S. Matthews, Henry Bruère, John S. Linen and Allen H. Seed, Jr. Arnold Frye, who attended the afternoon session, not in picture.

Representatives of the League meeting with eleven experts at the Hotel Statler, New York, to discuss a possible model state planning law.

Model State Planning Law Discussed

Eleven authorities on state and local planning problems have recommended that the League take the lead in developing model state planning legislation. Meeting at the Hotel Statler in New York on April 17, by League invitation, the group reviewed inadequacies in existing state laws and programs and stressed the importance of strengthening them as one way to help solve metropolitan area problems.

Carl Feiss, of the Housing and Home Finance Agency, said the pro-

Foundation; Joseph E. McLean, Princeton University; Hugh Pomeroy, planning director, Westchester County, New York; William L. C. Wheaton, University of Pennsylvania; Edward Wilkens, Rutgers University; and Coleman Woodbury, author and consultant of South Kent, Connecticut.

Alfred Willoughby, executive director; John Bebout, assistant director; John Keith, senior associate, and William Cassella, Jr., Staff Fellow, represented the League.

Conference Leaders

Mayor William Kemp of Kansas City, Missouri, and Governors Edward F. Arn of Kansas and Phil M. Donnelly of Missouri have accepted honorary chairmanships of the local arrangements committee for the 60th National Conference on Government in Kansas City, November 7-10.

National Municipal Review

Volume XLIII, No. 6   Total Number 444

Published monthly except August

By NATIONAL MUNICIPAL LEAGUE

Contents for June 1954

The contents of the REVIEW are indexed in *International Index to Periodicals*
and *Public Affairs Information Service.*

Entered as second class matter July 11, 1932, at the Post Office at Worcester,
Massachusetts. Publication office, 150 Fremont Street, Worcester 3; editorial
and business office, 542 Fifth Avenue, New York 36. Copyright 1954 by the
National Municipal League.

Subscription, $5 per year; Canadian, $5.25; foreign, $5.50;
single copies 50 cents.

Editorial Comment

Opportunity Appears in Strange Disguise

CIVIL defense is undoubtedly one of the most unloved babies ever deposited on the American doorstep. Yet, like most new babies, it bears great promise for the future if only it is taken up and cherished.

This is why "Planning for Civil Defense," by Dr. Joseph E. McLean, appears on page 278 of this issue of the REVIEW. Dr. McLean's article will be followed later by the printing of excerpts from the reports of *Project East River*, the civil defense study with which Dr. McLean's article deals.

The sober yet imaginative findings of this cooperative study of the possibility and the requirements of a meaningful civil defense in the atomic era have been outrageously neglected by many public authorities and almost completely ignored by citizens generally.

There can be no doubt that Americans are worried about the forces that scientific knowledge has unlocked. Too much of this worry expresses itself in political unreason and in mutual recriminations. Too little of it has been channelled into the hard but much more rewarding business of working together to control these forces and to protect ourselves against their most destructive potentialities. Project East River demonstrates that civil defense, conceived on an adequate scale and carried out with determination, can make a major contribution not only to the common defense but also to the general welfare.

As Dr. McLean points out, "re-duction of target vulnerability is an essential function of civil defense." To put it another way, effective civil defense as ordinarily thought of depends upon and must include a national program designed to reduce the concentration and therefore the attractiveness and vulnerability as targets of the industrial and population centers that have become characteristic features of the American scene.

Nobody seriously proposes that our big cities and metropolitan areas be suddenly broken up and scattered across the face of the land. Actually what is proposed is an intelligently planned decentralization which would accelerate and give sound direction to trends already discernible.

Writing of measures recommended for industrial defense, William J. Platt, chairman of industrial planning research at the Stanford Research Institute, remarked that most of them "make good sense apart from the risk of enemy attack. Many of the actions constitute preparedness for natural disasters such as tornadoes, earthquakes, floods or fires. Dispersion will contribute to national welfare by cutting down congestion, and its toll in blighted areas and in traffic accidents. Other actions, such as alternates for key jobs and alternative suppliers, are sound management practice."[1]

---

[1]*Industrial Defense: A Community Approach.* By William J. Platt. Chicago 37, University of Chicago Press, *Bulletin of the Atomic Scientists*, September 1953. 4 pages.

276

The same observation could be made regarding the way in which the project deals with city planning and zoning. In general, as Dr. McLean points out, the application of standards such as those proposed by Project East River for reducing vulnerability "would result not only in a stronger national defense but in more viable communities as well."

It is high time that local, state and national officials and citizens who care about the future well-being, not to mention the very existence, of American communities took a good and friendly look at the civil defense baby that the scientists have left at the door.

Again and again the report points out that civil defense requires a combination of individual and community responsibility, intergovernmental cooperation and federal leadership. It also makes clear that lessening of urban vulnerability depends absolutely upon a very substantial strengthening of the provisions for and acceptance of state and metropolitan planning. Specifically, the project recommends "the establishment and the financing of metropolitan area planning commissions for each metropolitan area," each commission to "prepare land use plans in cooperation with municipal authority."

What all this really means is that civil defense simply makes more urgent the kind of far-sighted collaboration between citizens and all their governments that is essential to the sound functioning of our system whether in peace or at war. Thus, civil defense adds a new and compelling reason for doing better and more expeditiously what we should be doing anyway to demonstrate the capacity of the American way for self-improvement in a changing world.

The central problem of Project East River was to show what can be done to reduce the task of civil defense to manageable proportions. This is of great psychological as well as administrative importance, because the national allergy to civil defense is largely the result of a deep-seated suspicion that there is really nothing effective that can be done about it.

The Project arrives at the hopeful conclusion that the problem can be reduced to size. Paradoxically, however, this can be achieved only by bolder action to improve the military defenses of the continent and accelerate the deconcentration of people and industry. When citizens and officials are ready to face up squarely to these imperatives, they will be ready to take civil defense in general much more seriously.

That some progress in this direction is being made is indicated by the note on the defense plan of the Rock County, Wisconsin, board of supervisors at page 300 of this issue of the REVIEW.

Planning for Civil Defense

*Hydrogen, atomic, other weapons add urgency to search
for plan of concerted action among levels of government.*

By JOSEPH E. McLEAN*

PROJECT EAST RIVER, a government-sponsored study of civil defense, completed its ten-volume report during the summer and fall of 1952.[1]

While segments of the East River report were in the publication process, a dramatic footnote—Operation Ivy—was being written in the far Pacific with the explosion of the hydrogen device that destroyed Elugelab Island at Eniwetok, November 1, 1952.

The recent release of information, including a televised film of Operation Ivy, has brought to millions of Americans an awareness of the awesome threat posed by atomic and hydrogen bombs. At the same time, Operation Ivy has heightened the sig-

nificance both of the East River findings and of the laborious and often thankless job being performed by the Federal Civil Defense Administration and by state and local civil defense agencies and personnel.

Project East River was sponsored by the Federal Civil Defense Administration, National Security Resources Board and Department of Defense to evaluate and recommend nonmilitary measures that would assist: (1) the FCDA in discharging its responsibilities for preparing to minimize the effects of attack by atomic, biological, chemical or other weapons on the population and industry of the United States; (2) the NSRB in discharging its responsibilities of advising the president concerning the strategic location of industries, services, government and economic activities, the continuous operation of which is essential to the nation's security; and (3) the Department of Defense in collaborating with FCDA and NSRB in discharging their responsibilities. The project was undertaken by Associated Universities, Inc., with Otto L. Nelson, Jr., as director.[2]

*Dr. McLean, professor of politics and public affairs at the Woodrow Wilson School of Public and International Affairs, was consultant to Project East River. The views expressed in this article are his own, however, and are not intended to represent those of the project.

[1]All but two volumes (Parts III and IV) were released in January of 1953. The titles of the various parts of the final report give some indication of their scope and nature: I: *General Report;* II: *Measures to Make Civil Defense Manageable;* II-A: *Military Measures Precedent to a Manageable Civil Defense;* II-B: *Federal Leadership to Reduce Urban Vulnerability;* III: *The Destructive Threat of Atomic Weapons;* IV: *Civil Defense Aspects of Biological, Chemical and Radiological Warfare;* V: *Reduction of Urban Vulnerability;* VI: *Disaster Services and Operations;* VII: *Warning and Communications for Civil Defense;* VIII: *Civil Defense Health and Welfare;* IX: *Information and Training for Civil Defense;* X: *Selected References for Civil Defense.*

[2]The cooperative nature of the undertaking is indicated in several ways: Associated Universities is a cooperative enterprise of nine universities; there were three sponsoring agencies of the federal government; the project staff was recruited from industry, government, the universities and other sources; and, in the course of the study, the staff consulted with federal, state and local government officials and with representatives of many private firms and agencies.

"The ten-volume report of Project East River might well have been entitled, *Survival in an Atomic Age.* In this report are possible answers to such vital, if implicitly raised, questions as: To what extent is America's 'glass jaw' showing? Can defensive measures be developed to cope with new and terrifying unconventional weapons? Can the teamwork of government, science and industry that produced the atom bomb produce effective countermeasures? Can a free people organize and discipline themselves, on both an individual and collective basis, to avoid paralysis by fear, defeat through despair and the fatal inaction and indecision induced by apathy? Is the problem of civil defense inherently unmanageable?"[3]

In its answers, Project East River evidenced a cautious optimism with respect to our capabilities. Its basic thesis is that the complex civil defense task is manageable, provided it is divided into well defined parts and responsibility for each part is assigned to a competent organization with a "stipulated standard of performance." Development of a manageable and effective civil defense organization depends particularly upon: (1) Improvements in the military defenses of continental United States and (2) initiation of a national program for reduction of vulnerability.

The Atomic Age

As improvements are effected in these two major areas, the civil defense task should increasingly be

brought within manageable limits. Project East River concluded that it was feasible to build a military defense of such a character as to prevent a "saturation attack." In the second area, PER recommended a program for the reduction of urban vulnerability, to be initiated by federal leadership under which federal funds would be spent only when certain standards relating to vulnerability were met.

The problems that gave rise to Project East River have not diminished in importance in the past year. The world continues to shrink; every farm, village, town and metropolis is open to possible enemy attack; and it is difficult to measure the deterrent influence of our "new look" military policy based in large part upon our stockpile of nuclear weapons and the threat of "massive retaliation." Will the threat of retaliation lose much of its force as a deterrent whenever the U.S. stockpile of nuclear weapons is *effectively* matched by the enemy's stockpile?

The basic conclusions of East River retain validity despite the H-bomb. In the event of attack, the "major item in the enemy's arsenal of weapons would undoubtedly be one or several types of nuclear devices. As to the number and types chosen, the answer would probably adhere to the rough formula that a million deaths require an expenditure of approximately a thousand kilotons of TNT or its equivalent. . . . Fusion or so-called hydrogen bombs will not change the situation markedly. One may recall[4] that the

[3]Joseph E. McLean, "Project East River —Survival in the Atomic Age," *Bulletin of the Atomic Scientists,* September 1953, page 247. This entire issue is devoted to "Project East River—The Strategy of Civil Defense." •

[4]U. S. Government Printing Office, *The Effects of Atomic Weapons,* June, 1950.

detonation of a nuclear bomb at an optimum height above the target area produces an over-killing from the ground-zero out to some distance, which varies roughly as the cube root of the bomb blast and, from that distance on, the number of casualties and the physical damage decrease to a negligible amount. An extrapolation of these known effects to greater bomb energies and a test against the principal U.S. cities lead to the conclusion that few cities merit the attention of a fusion bomb."[5]

Aside from the threat of nuclear devices, there are the weapons of biological and chemical warfare whose effects are not competitive with those of nuclear bombs. These exotic forms of warfare provide a means of attacking our food supplies (of animal and vegetable origin); along with incendiary attacks on our forest areas, they directly involve rural America. The defense against these forms of warfare involves our federal and local agricultural experts, forest rangers, public health specialists and others who have vital peacetime responsibilities.

Along with weapons, one must consider weapon carriers. An obvious means of delivering nuclear bombs is the long-range strategic bomber. More than a year ago, the late General Vandenberg stated that the Soviet air force then numbered many hundreds of B-29-type long-range bombers "capable of carrying atomic bombs from the growing Soviet stockpile on one-way flights to targets anywhere in the United States."[6] Whether the attack should come from

bombers or from some form of rockets or guided missiles launched from submarines, it is important to remember that a perimeter zone—a few hundred miles in depth—contains a majority of our concentrations of population and industry. True, intercontinental missiles would, of course, increase the threat and almost undoubtedly reduce the amount of early warning that could be given to civil defense.

Should the enemy attack without warning and in the absence of adequate civil defense, the consequences would be devastating. For example, Project East River made casualty estimates for attacks with nuclear weapons. "One estimate involved a nighttime raid without warning or other civil defense preparation; the result, death for 50 per cent of the population within the city limits of each target area. Thus, a hundred bombs dropped on the hundred most populous cities would result in an estimated 19,347,000 deaths."[7]

Manageable Civil Defense

If such casualty estimates are used as fear techniques in a campaign to stimulate public interest in civil defense, the result will probably be failure. A more positive campaign based upon adequate information and a realistic approach to a manageable civil defense is more likely to succeed.

Project East River has largely advanced the cause of the latter. Its approach particularly emphasized the feasibility of relevant military measures and a program to reduce vulnerability. With respect to the

[5]See McLean, loc. cit., page 248.
[6]Flying, March 1953.

[7]See McLean, loc. cit., page 249.

former, the measures concerned the military effort to turn back, stop or reduce the force of the enemy attack, as well as the military role in the provision of warning and advisory information to the civil defense organization and, hence, to the public.

Military capabilities in this regard are, of course, dependent upon technological advances: "Up to two years ago no one was willing to say that an effective defense could be made, for no one knew how to do it. But, early in 1951, scientists close to military problems began to realize that a series of technological break-throughs had occurred that might make a defense reasonable and possible."[8] If the frontier of our warning system is pushed out far enough to provide early warning, a true defense in depth becomes possible.

In the second major area—that of reducing vulnerability—Project East River emphasized the need for the application of defense standards of construction, spacing and density, particularly in our metropolitan areas.[9] Actually, the application of the PER or comparable standards would result not only in a stronger national defense but in more viable

communities as well. The elimination of slums, for example, is a legitimate peacetime goal; if, at the same time, both reduction of congestion and provision of open areas (which may serve as fire breaks) can be attained, then the values to national defense are an added return on the normal investment.

The PER proposals do not offer a "quickie" solution to urban problems. Indeed, the annual gains to be derived from the application of the proposed standards would be relatively small. Over the long pull, however, the cumulative effect would be substantial: "The total physical structure of this country's major cities increased about 25 per cent in size during the past decade, a net addition to our urban structure of 2.5 per cent per year. . . . Had we begun in 1946 to build according to defense standards, we should already have gained substantial protection for three million people living in the central cities of our largest metropolitan areas. . . . The application of defense standards to new building only during a ten-year period could have reduced urban vulnerability by approximately 20 per cent."[10] The injection of some elements of planning and control—for defense purposes—should serve both defense and healthier peacetime living.

Leadership, however, is necessary to overcome the natural inertia of individuals and institutions toward the changes required by any program for the reduction of vulnerability. The federal government is in a position to exercise much of that leadership

[8]Lloyd V. Berkner, address to the Minnesota World Affairs Center, September 29, 1952.

[9]See Donald Monson, "City Planning in Project East River," in *Bulletin of the Atomic Scientists*, September, 1953, page 265. Mr. Monson analyzed the Project East River volumes, specifically: Part II-B, *Federal Leadership to Reduce Urban Vulnerability;* sections 1, 2, 3, of part V, *Reduction of Urban Vulnerability;* and Appendix V-B to Part V, *Minimum Density and Spacing Requirements for Metropolitan Dispersion; Forces Making for Concentration in the Cores of Metropolitan Areas.* ●

[10]PER, Part II-B, page 4.

should it choose to use the leverage that it has through its own direct construction activities and through its financial, credit and contract policies, especially those affecting highways, housing, urban redevelopment, and the location of defense industry. If the federal government were to apply defense standards to its own activities, its example would encourage private institutions and individuals to pursue a similar course.

Basic Principles and Concepts

Although space does not permit adequate discussion, it seems desirable to list some of the basic principles and concepts that were formulated by Project East River as long-term guides and as a framework upon which an adequate civil defense can be built:

1. Civil defense must be a permanent partner in national defense.

2. Civil defense must be organized and operated on the principle that existing agencies and facilities should be used to the greatest extent possible.

3. Civil defense must be accomplished, in the main, as an extension of the normal duties of various officials at all levels of government, assisted by volunteers and volunteer organizations.

4. Civil defense functions must be clearly defined and responsibility for each function precisely assigned.

5. Dual use of equipment and facilities for civil defense should be encouraged to the maximum practical degree.

6. All areas of the United States are not of equal vulnerability to the several elements of the threat, and civil defense programs must be adjusted to the requirements of the individual area.

7. Reduction of target vulnerability is an essential function of civil defense.

8. The civil defense program must place first reliance on the efforts of the individual and of the community to increase chances of survival, to minimize damage, and to recover as quickly as possible in the eventuality of an enemy attack.

Civil Defense Organization

Since civil defense is so complex and involves all layers of government, it is inevitable that its organization should be an additional problem in federalism. There is a necessary and desirable emphasis in civil defense upon the roles played by governmental agencies and professional employees who have normal responsibilities with a civil defense potential. A variety of professionals should play vital roles in civil defense—firemen, policemen, public health doctors, highway engineers, school teachers, county agents and what-not. These same fraternities of specialists have already been playing a vital role in the development of a functional federalism that has cut across the traditional layer-cake concept of our federal system.

Some individuals have approached the problem of civil defense organization from the points of view of "normal federalism"—whether that would mean "states' rights," "municipal home rule," or national centralization. Many—regardless of argument—have held the implicit assumption that, when the chips were really down, the army would have to take over. Project East River rejected this last assumption and explicitly concluded that a *civilian* civil defense is the preferable solution. Military control would offer no magic solution; indeed, the military might well be diverted from its primary missions if a civilian civil defense were lacking.

Some Recommendations

Although it is not possible to review here all organizational issues involved in civil defense, a few of PER's recommendations[11] may be suggestive:

The federal civil defense regional director should be prepared to provide additional support when the situation is beyond the capacity of state and local governments;

The placing of unreasonable burdens upon state governments [should] be avoided;

The officials of fifteen top priority urban target areas [should] be permitted to consult and plan with both federal, regional and state civil defense officials;

The establishment in the Federal Civil Defense Administration of an office or division of urban defense.

Many organizational suggestions assumed that civil defense should be based upon the existing and traditional ways of government under our federal system. This pattern, however, "has serious limitations; it is not suitable for saturation attacks; it is best adapted to cope with small scattered attacks."[12] The greater the potential emergency, the greater is the need for large-scale realistic planning and probably the greater is the need for national leadership on a command basis.

The Federal Civil Defense Administration and many state and local government officials have recognized

[11]PER, Part I—*General Report*, Section 3, *Organization*, page 31.
[12]*Ibid.*, page 21.•

the values of the East River report. Yet, Congress has not been persuaded to appropriate any significant funds; and many state and local governing bodies are reluctant to plunge into large-scale civil defense programs. East River is at least partially responsible, however, for the assignment to FCDA of responsibility for the handling of peacetime disasters. In the military defense field, some progress is reported on the pushing out of our frontier of early warning, and the H-bomb revelations have stimulated thinking in favor of tactical dispersal (or evacuation) of urban populations as opposed to a large shelter program.

Many of the discussions of East River and much of the hesitation and indecision reflect basic issues in our government and society. For many years, the student and the lay citizen have moved from one dilemma to another in their approaches to the problems of federalism; metropolitan areas; urban underrepresentation in state legislatures; housing, slum clearance and urban redevelopment; new tax sources; and many others. These "normally insoluble" problems have been raised anew by the imperatives of civil defense.

The inertia and resistance to change are evident in a recent New York *Times* article dealing with resolutions proposed for discussion at the U.S. Chamber of Commerce's annual meeting. Some of the resolutions related to measures that might be necessary for national defense in an atomic age. One, for example, regarding the location of industry, provided that "in certain instances vital

(Continued on page 322)

Councilman Learns His Job

*Serving on councils is a headache, says novice politician,
but worth it if our local governments are to be preserved.*

By M. NELSON McGEARY*

YOU won't be worth much on the town council for the first two years. It will take you that long to learn the job."

Such was one comment offered to the writer when he won a council seat in the municipal election of 1951 and began practicing what for years he had been preaching.

Having now weathered half the four-year term, I can only feel that the warning was a distinct understatement; over two years have gone by but the amount still to be learned far outweighs the knowledge accumulated to date.

Within such a period, however, one does gain at least some impressions of how representative democracy works in the community. Some of my conclusions, even though only those of a freshman, are reported for what they may be worth.

Ours is a small town. Of 20,000 residents, somewhat more than half are college students without a vote and without any tax-paying responsibilities. They have little direct interest in what happens in the city government—unless a parking ticket or similar annoyance brings them briefly to city hall. Realistically, the elected council has about 9,500 constituents—men, women and children —in permanent residence.

The following observations on the job of a councilman are neither startling nor world-shaking, but they are fully supported by one man's experience:

1. One of the most difficult tasks of a councilman is trying to determine the public's real opinion on a controversial issue. A few people clearly reveal where they stand but the multitude is quiet. Last year the great debate in our town concerned a proposed public airport. Some citizens were vehemently for it. Others didn't want to spend the money. Still others objected to the possible noise or, frightened by the series of plane crashes in Elizabeth, New Jersey, stressed the safety angle. At least three petitions on the subject were circulated, and two of them were signed by sizable groups.

On several occasions, however, when my phone would ring in the evening, a citizen would quietly apologize for having signed a particular petition—"I really don't care much one way or the other." When one man wrote a lengthy letter to be published in the local newspaper and I mentioned to him that we were pleased to know exactly how he felt, he stunned us by explaining that his letter to the editor did not express his "real feelings." It is logical to suppose that a legislator in Washington, or in the state capital, or in a large city will often find it hard to

*Dr. McGeary has been with the Pennsylvania State University (formerly Pennsylvania State College) since 1939 and professor of political science since 1948. In 1951 he was elected to the council of the borough of State College, serving as its president.

gauge opinion. I was surprised to find that the same is so true in a small town.

2. A councilman has to learn to roll with the punches. Punches are as inevitable for the councilman as are "boos" for a baseball umpire. There's no question that all councils make some mistakes for which they deserve censure. But it's the snap criticism, from persons who are willing to form judgments on the basis of only a little evidence, that the councilman must learn to absorb and still maintain his resiliency.

Criticism Inevitable

Presumably in every municipality, as in ours, there are some citizens who start with the premise that anyone willing to run for council is a species of pillager—maybe not a bad one—but at least he's a man with some sort of axe to grind and will, when he finds an opportunity, maneuver things to his own advantage. Sometimes, of course, this suspicion is justified. If it's generally true, we might as well give up democracy as a bad job. Fortunately, it isn't so.

A councilman must cover himself with thick padding in order to withstand the unfailing darts, but at the same time must not so insulate himself that he becomes insensitive to constructive criticism and to useful opinions and suggestions. Perhaps it is one sign of a good councilman if his conscience forces him occasionally to lie awake at night pondering the comments of a disgruntled citizen.

All this to the contrary, however, I have not found "unfair" criticism so powerful as to justify a man's refusing to run for a council seat. When I started to serve I was steeled for the worst. I knew that on certain issues I would make some people mad whichever way I voted. That has happened and I haven't enjoyed a few of the things which have been said and which, of course, I thought were unjustified. But the striking thing, frankly, has not been the censure, but rather the surprising number of words of encouragement and sympathy for the "dirty job you've taken on." Other councilmen, I think, share with me the conviction that, if you work hard at being scrupulously fair, the citizens will be fair with you.

3. The burgess (or mayor) in our borough has few executive duties; textbooks would call him a weak mayor. To fill the gap, we employ a manager. A person needs to sit on a council only a short while to realize the downright value of having some such executive to carry out the policies that council decides upon. Members of small-town councils have their regular full-time jobs. Council work is an extra task for which we receive no pay. The time which all of us give to council is considerable but, if we had to make up the budget, do all the necessary negotiating, keep contact with state and even federal agencies, and perform the host of other duties that a manager handles, the councilman's job would seem, at least to me, to be overwhelming.

If every voter could have the experience of serving for a period of months as a non-paid part-time councilman, the opposition to the manager plan in such municipalities would crumble.

4. A councilman must take a good many things on faith. He can't be

an expert in all the matters with which he has to deal. So, wisely, his judgment is guided by experts. The shade-tree expert says that extensive trimming will help preserve the trees, so the councilman votes more funds for the purpose than he had hoped would be necessary. But the trouble begins when the experts can't agree. Our town is suffering today as a result of mistakes made, for example, by "expert" engineers in the past. At the present time council is taking steps leading toward the construction of a new sewage disposal plant. Some of the best experts disagree markedly on what can and should be done. Who's right?

Along this same line of thinking, councilmen have to be wary of original estimates of the costs of big projects. One hears many current complaints from United States congressmen that, let us say, a dam is authorized by them on the assumption that it will cost so much, but before it is finished the expenses have soared. Washington has no monopoly on low original estimates. A realistic councilman does well to blow them up for purposes of his own calculating.

Public Relations

5. One of the most perplexing problems of a council is to let the people know what it is doing and why. To a considerable extent this is the job of the manager, but council must help. Talks before citizen groups and on the radio are worthwhile, but such activities may take more time than councilmen can or are willing to spare. Our council has not managed to institute a radio program, but we do discuss local problems before clubs and other groups.

Most information on the doings of council reaches the people through the local newspaper. Our experience with the press, which has been happy, has proved to us that no secrets should be kept from it. We make special efforts, in fact, to give the press a complete picture. Although all council meetings are open to the public, there are a few extraordinary occasions when we feel the need to spend a little time in executive session for purposes of discussion. When we do so, the press is invited to sit with us. Only in this way can the reporter have the full background of a problem which is facing us. If, as on rare occasions, material must be off the record, the paper scrupulously cooperates.

I do not mean to imply that a newspaper should always be on council's side. Ours isn't. And sometimes an editorial will slap us. But because the editor has full information on our problems, and does not have to rely on rumor or gossip, the reporting of our city affairs has been unbelievably accurate and fair. Maybe we are merely lucky but I have an idea that our gold-fish-bowl tactic with the press is a wise one.

Of course, accurate as the information may be in the paper, many people won't read it. That's discouraging to both us and the editor, but there's not much that council can do about it.

6. I often think how much easier it must be to vote for higher taxes, or bigger outlays, in Congress than in a local council. In Congress, the representative is only one of 531 legislators and he is relatively far

removed from the voters; hardly anybody will blame him personally for higher taxes. Congress as a whole will be hissed at, but not one man. In our situation, on the other hand, the councilman is one of only seven persons, and a few of his friends or neighbors are in the council hall when he casts his vote. Every time he goes to a drug store or the post office he runs into people who are keenly aware that *he* is responsible for the increased tax rate. People in a community seem to be more disturbed about a local one-mill boost in property taxes (average of $2 a year per home) than a 10 per cent national income hike.

Restraining Force

As a matter of fact, it's a mighty healthy atmosphere in a local area; a legislator should find a tax increase a bitter medicine to be taken only when there is dire necessity. The close contact between councilmen and the persons being governed is a valuable restraining force and is a potent argument for the retention of strong local government. Much of the value is lost, however, if the reluctance of local councils to increase taxes and expenditures simply means a shifting of functions to state or nation where restraints are less compelling.

7. Our community is not divided into wards. Members of council are elected at large. For a small community this arrangement seems wise. Compared to some of our neighboring municipalities, where wards are used, we seem to have fewer disputes marked by geographical lines. And our councilmen definitely tend to think of the community as a whole rather than of one particular sector.

8. It seems to be the part of wisdom for a councilman not to take a position too quickly on a major issue. All the arguments for and against a particular proposal may not be apparent in the first one or two discussions. Light thrown on the subject in later debate may change the color of the picture considerably. No important issue is completely black or completely white.

It is not meant here to encourage a member of council who seeks delays merely to avoid making up his mind. But a councilman seems to command respect, and may save himself considerable embarrassment, if he takes a definite position only after all the facts are in.

These random thoughts may be valid for only one town. But different communities, like different television sets, although vastly dissimilar in outward appearances, show striking likenesses within the "cabinets." A generalization that applies to one city may apply equally well to another.

At least one conclusion probably would be uncontested: serving on council is a headache. But democracy is based on the supposition that some citizens will be willing to endure headaches. Actually the travail is not unbearable. And sometimes, for brief periods, it is forgotten—believe it or not—in the knowledge that some little service is being offered.

If the reader agrees with the writer that local government needs to be preserved, aren't the headaches worth it?

Nomination by Money Deposit

Michigan, only state where this method is used, finds it fails to keep plethora of hopeless candidates off ballot.

By HAROLD M. DORR[*]

OTHER English-speaking nations do not use the type of nominating petition generally in vogue in the United States but permit candidates to get on official ballots by depositing a sum of money returnable if the candidate gets a certain percentage of the vote.

The *Model City Charter* of the National Municipal League, however, has provided such procedure since 1941, but the only experience in this country has been in Michigan, especially in connection with the long ballot of Detroit.

The filing of a money deposit as a method of qualifying for a place in primary elections was introduced to Michigan office-seekers 22 years ago. Early experiences with the deposit system have been reviewed.[1] The latest article summarized the legislative history and experiences with the money deposit through 1947.

The money deposit was inaugurated in Michigan in 1931 by two separate legislative enactments. The first, an act of the state legislature, authorized the deposit as an alternative method for qualifying for a place on the primary ballot for all county and state legislative offices in Wayne County. The second, an amendment to the Detroit city charter, extended the optional deposit plan to the city's municipal primaries.

In 1935 the basic laws were amended to abolish the nominating petition and to make the money deposit mandatory in these jurisdictions. The mandatory features have been retained under the charter, but the 1935 amendment to the state law was declared unconstitutional. Subsequently, in 1947, the state legislature extended the optional money deposit to all county offices in the state's 83 counties and to seats in both houses of the state legislature in those counties entitled to elect one or more representatives or senators. The privilege was not extended to candidates seeking legislative positions in districts created by combining two or more counties.[2]

Undoubtedly many factors contribute to the flood of office-seekers, and there are no reasons to conclude that these factors continue to hold the same relative significance over the years. Certainly the ease or the difficulty of qualifying is but one of these factors. When confined within reasonable limits, it may not be a

*Dr. Dorr, with the University of Michigan since 1929 and formerly acting chairman of its Department of Political Science, is professor of political science and director of the university's Summer Session. He is author of numerous publications and articles in his field.

[1]"Tightening the Direct Primary," by Harold M. Dorr, *American Political Science Review*, June 1936, pages 512-522, and February 1937, pages 58-65. See also, "Candidates Won't Stay Out," by Harold M. Dorr, NATIONAL MUNICIPAL REVIEW, May 1949, pages 224-229.

[2]As currently apportioned, candidates seeking nomination to 20 House seats and to 21 Senate seats must file nominating petitions.

significant one. A review of the evidence demonstrates that the money deposit plan, in either its optional or mandatory form, has not been a deterrent to ambitious office-seekers. On the other hand, there is reason to believe that the deposit plan, especially in urban areas, actually gives encouragement to publicity seekers and other nuisance candidates.

Many Candidates in Detroit

An earlier study of Detroit municipal primaries reported an average of 4.3 candidates for each council seat during the effective period of the optional law—1931-1935. Over the ensuing fifteen years, under the mandatory law, the average number of candidates increased to 7.5, with an average of 10.6 candidates in the last reported primary, 1947. In the two subsequent primaries, 1949 and 1951, the pressure of office-seeking was not abated. A new peak for a regular primary was reached in 1949 when an average of 11.7 candidates qualified for each council position. In the 1951 primary the average dropped to 7.9. But in a special primary, held in February 1953 to fill one vacancy, 29 persons deposited $100 each to see their names in print. Twenty-six of these were required, for lack of popular support, to forfeit their deposits. Of the 176 council candidates standing in the primaries of 1949 and 1951, 110, well over 60 per cent, likewise forfeited.

Optimism among candidates is overpowering, or else the fear of forfeiture is not an effective deterrent. Election statistics support the political prognosticators who with regularity select the top winning candidates.

A knowledge of the rapid decline in vote popularity after the first five or six places have been filled encourages the flood of unknown and unacceptable office-seekers.

In 1951 the last candidate nominated polled less than 20 per cent of the votes recorded for the most popular candidate. The weakest candidate, in a list of 71, polled less than 10 per cent of the vote given the eighteenth. This is similar to the voting pattern of the 1949 primary. The 105th, the last, candidate polled less than 6 per cent of the vote of the last candidate to be nominated and only 1.03 per cent of the vote cast for the leading candidate. Other fancied advantages may have prompted these defeated candidates to file. All but the most stupid and politically naive must have known at the time of filing that defeat and forfeiture were certain.

Deposit investment policies of candidates for the office of mayor, clerk and treasurer are equally baffling. The results of the primary contests for mayor, in 1949 and 1951, confirmed the predictions of political observers: Cobo over Edwards in 1949, and Cobo over the field by a wide margin in 1951, with Branigin the second nominee. The two candidates nominated in these primaries polled 78 and 89 per cent of the total vote. Not one of the fifteen defeated candidates garnered sufficient support—50 per cent of the vote cast for the last candidate nominated—to save his deposit. Moreover, only one of the defeated candidates, a former mayor, was conceded an outside chance of winning nomination or of salvaging his deposit.

The primary returns in the contests for clerk and treasurer were of the same pattern. In 1949 the two candidates nominated for treasurer polled between them 80 per cent of the total vote. Fifty-three per cent was cast for the leading candidate. The fifteen defeated candidates forfeited their deposits. The incumbents, treasurer and clerk, were renominated in 1951 by majorities of approximately 75 and 80 per cent, respectively. With the remainder of the vote somewhat equally divided among the nine defeated candidates, only one deposit was forfeited.

Money No Object

Whatever factors encourage long lists of candidates to seek nomination to public office, the chances of winning and the fear of loss of money investment appear in many cases to be insignificant. Some, it is known, are honestly seeking eventual election to public office. They anticipate years of campaigning and numerous disappointments. It is known, also, that the $100 deposit required to qualify a "James Kenyon Jones" by a candidate whose leading opponent is "James Kennedy Jones" can be a good political investment. Other types of nuisance candidates can be identified.

But what about the average candidate? Is the deposit widely regarded as an investment in status, respectability and standing in the community, or do many believe "political lightning" will strike? How many are entitled to honest hopes? There is only enough evidence to raise the questions. It is reported that a defeated candidate—one who polled less than one-half of one per cent of the total vote—appeared to request a retabulation to assure him that he had been defeated, that there was no mistake!

The optional deposit plan permits Wayne County candidates for county offices and seats in the state legislature to file traditional nominating petitions or to make the money deposits. In present circumstances, especially in metropolitan areas, "petition-pushing" requires a financial sacrifice in excess of the money deposit. Its value in these areas as a campaigning device is questionable. Yet, among the arguments mustered against the mandatory deposit plan in the mid-'30s were those inherent in the cries "undemocratic" and "class legislation."

The courts restored the nominating petition by eliminating the mandatory provisions of the law. Even so, in the past two primaries, candidates in Wayne County have favored the deposit plan. Of a total of 795 candidates, 498—approximately two-thirds—qualified by making money deposits. Just short of 50 per cent of all deposits were forfeited. In the off-years—1949, 1951 and 1953—primaries were held to nominate candidates for the Wayne County Board of Auditors and to offices which may have become vacant. In the three years the ballots carried the names of 78 candidates, 53 of whom made deposits. Forty-one deposits were forfeited. Obviously candidates with $100 bills are numerous, and contributions to the general fund are generous.

The pattern outstate is different. The differences in part may be attributed to more discriminating notions

of the value of a dollar and a persistent belief in the merits of the
nominating petition as a campaigning device. As reported earlier, the
first outstate opportunities for deposit filing, 1948, attracted relatively
few candidates. The returns for the
two subsequent primaries, 1950 and
1952, indicate some increase in popularity of the deposit plan, yet outstate candidates risking cash are far
outnumbered by those for whom petitions are circulated. The deposit
plan has been almost completely dis-
regarded by the strictly rural sections
and the "back counties" of the state.

Few Money Deposits Outstate

In the 1950 primary elections only
47 of the reported 1,626 candidates
for county offices qualified by making money deposits. In the outstate
legislative districts to which the optional deposit plan had been extended, six of every seven candidates
filed nominating petitions. In a total
of 62 deposit-paying candidates there
were only four forfeitures in 1950.

In the most recent primary, 1952,
1,448 candidates for county offices
were reported to have qualified in
the 82 outstate counties. Sixty-eight
of these candidates, confined to eighteen counties, made deposits. All the
counties in which deposits were made
are located south of a line across the
state, usually designated as the
Muskegon–Bay City line. Forty-
seven of the deposit-paying candidates were seeking office in mixed
economy counties, i.e., agricultural
counties, with major industries or
housing industrial workers. Of the 21
candidates making deposits in predominantly agricultural counties,
seven were from Montcalm County.

The explanation for this atypical situation throws some light on the attitude of outstate candidates. In this
county all candidates were running for reelection and faced no
contests within their own or the opposition parties. The alleged campaigning merits of "petition-pushing"
were inconsequential and forfeitures
were impossible.

The optional deposit plan is available to candidates seeking election
to the lower house of the state legislature in 31 outstate counties electing
a total of 53 members, and in three
such counties electing a total of four
senators. In the most recent primary
election at least one candidate for the
Senate qualified under the deposit
plan in each of these three counties,
two in Genesee.

Of the 172 candidates for house
seats in the 31 counties, 29 made
deposits in ten counties. In the remaining 21 counties, all 95 candidates filed nominating petitions. This
evidence does not necessarily support
a thesis of increasing popularity for
the deposit. Eleven of the 29 deposits were made in Genesee County
(Flint). In one county the incumbent, a candidate for reelection, had
no opposition, and for candidates
making deposits in two other counties there were no primary contests.
With one exception—one candidate
for a house seat in Marquette County—all candidates seeking legislative
seats north of the Muskegon-Bay
City line qualified by filing signature
petitions.

It has been suggested that outstate candidates place a higher value
on cash in hand, are therefore unwilling to risk the deposit, and have

great faith in the campaign merits of signature solicitation. The recent primary elections lend credence to these claims. The rural-minded candidates, on the whole, filed nominating petitions or made deposits only in shrewdly calculated situations. Not one deposit was forfeited in a strictly agricultural county. There were thirteen outstate forfeitures; ten of these were in Genesee County. In the 1951 and 1952 primaries, 94 per cent of all forfeitures were in Wayne County.

Tentative Conclusions

In spite of 22 years of use in Michigan, the money deposit as a method of qualifying for a place on the primary ballot is still in its experimental stages. The evidence to date is inconclusive and will not support broad conclusions of potential merit or wide acceptance. Some tentative conclusion may, however, be stated. The plan, in either its mandatory or optional form, has caused no diminution in the numbers of candidates. In fact, there are reasons to believe that the ease of qualifying through the depositing of a relatively small sum of money may actually be an encouragement to certain types of nuisance candidates. In Detroit, Wayne County and, probably, in other highly industrialized areas the high rate of forfeiture is not a deterring factor.

The optional plan has been cautiously tested outstate, but acceptance is generally limited to those counties with relatively large industrial developments. Seventy-seven per cent of all deposits in the 1951 and 1952 primaries were made in Wayne County, including the Detroit municipal primaries. Of a total of 101 outstate deposits, 64 were made in five counties.[3] Yet in these five counties the frequency of use was approximately 50 per cent of that under the optional plan in Wayne County. In the general primaries of 1952, 65 per cent of all candidates for county and legislative offices in Wayne County made deposits. In the same primaries, in the two outstate counties of highest frequency of use, Genesee and Macomb, only 38 per cent of the candidates chose to make money deposits.

There are currently demonstrable differences in attitudes between the urban and rural areas of the state. With its moderate filing fees and the accompanying high risk of forfeitures, the Detroit mandatory deposit plan had little vociferous opposition. The readoption of a mandatory plan for Wayne County would evoke only mild criticism. But the mandatory plan is wholly unacceptable in the outstate areas where money enjoys a value premium over time, and "petition-pushing" is still regarded as a productive campaigning device.

---

[3]Montcalm County, designated above as atypical, is not included in this tabulation.

News in Review

City, State and Nation • • • • Edited by H. M. Olmsted

U. S. Employees Down as States, Cities Increase

But 1953 Public Payrolls Show Increase Over 1952

CIVILIAN public employees of the federal, state and local governments totaled nearly 7,012,000 in January 1954, as against 7,066,000 one year before, according to data on public employment recently issued by the Bureau of the Census. There was a decline of 208,000 in federal employees, largely offset by an increase of 153,000 for state and local.

Federal civilian employees in January were 2,360,000, or 34 per cent of all public employees; a year ago this was 36 per cent. State employees constituted 1,133,000, or 16 per cent. Local government employees as a whole increased 4.0 per cent in number during the year, and state and local together increased 3.4 per cent.

In January 1954, some 678,000 state and local employees, included in the total of 4,651,000, were part-time employees who, according to the Census Bureau, could be considered equivalent to 142,000 full-time employees, making a total of 4,115,000 for full-time or equivalent state and local employees; the corresponding number in January 1953 was 4,023,000.

An analysis of public employment by functions was not given for January 1954; but the Census Bureau publication, *State Distribution of Public Employment in 1953*, issued April 19, 1954, gives such an analysis for October 1953, when total public employees were 7,047,000. Percentagewise the analysis is as follows:

| | | Civilian Employees | | |
Functions	Total	Federal	State	Local
All functions	100.0%	100.0%	100.0%	100.0%
National defense	16.7	49.2		
Postal service	7.1	21.0		
Education	27.8	0.5	30.2	45.5
Highways	6.6	0.2	16.5	7.9
Public welfare	1.7	1.2	3.5	1.5
Health and hospitals	8.9	6.9	19.6	6.8
Police	3.7	0.6	1.9	6.4
Local fire protection	2.5			5.0
Natural resources	4.0	7.0	7.9	0.7
All other	20.9	13.5	20.4	26.1

ment employees, numbering 3,519,000, were divided as follows: cities, 1,360,000; counties, 547,000; school districts, 1,318,000; other, 294,000. State and local together comprised 4,651,000.

State employees showed an increase of 1.8 per cent over January 1953; city employees 4.8 per cent; county employees 5.8 per cent; and other local employees a decline of 0.3 per cent. Local government

On the basis of estimated population of 158,375,000 for the 48 states at July 1, 1953, and excluding from total civilian employees of 7,047,000 some 154,000 federal employees working outside the United States, federal employees represented 1.41 per cent of the population, state and local employees 2.94 per cent, and all public employees 4.35 per cent.

Public payrolls for the calendar year

1953 are reported as $23,300,000,000, or about $900,000,000 more than in 1952. The federal portion of this (restricted to civilian personnel, as with other data given) was $9,800,000,000 in 1953 and $10,000,000,000 in 1952. State and local payrolls were $13,500,000,000 in 1953 and $12,400,000,000 in 1952.

In the last decade the number of federal civilian employees increased from 3,182,000 in January 1944 to 3,450,000 in January 1945 (both 1944 and 1945 being war years), dropped to 1,976,000 in January 1950 and increased to 2,360,000 in January 1954. The ten-year decrease was 26 per cent. In the same period, the corresponding monthly payroll increased from $693,000,000 to $763,000,000, or 10 per cent.

During the same decade the number of state and local employees rose from 3,097,000 to 4,651,000, or 50 per cent, while the payroll tripled from $403,000,000 in January 1944, to $1,227,000,000 in January 1954.

Michigan Civil Service Commission Supported

A proposed amendment to the Michigan constitution, intended to deprive the State Civil Service Commission of its power to fix state salaries and to increase the number of positions outside the merit system, has been defeated in the State Senate, according to the National Civil Service League. The league states that Michigan has the only Civil Service Commission with sole constitutional authority to fix salaries. The commission had announced plans for increases totaling six million dollars a year to the state's 23,500 competitive employees. The Senate vote was fifteen to ten.

Wisconsin Reduces School Districts 29 Per Cent

A sharp drop in the number of school districts in Wisconsin is shown in figures for the 1952-53 year, recently presented by the State Department of Public In-

struction. The number is given as 4,908; compared with 6,936 in 1943-44, this is a decline of 2,028 or 29 per cent in the nine years. Thirty years ago, in 1922-23, there were 7,739 districts. One-teacher schools also declined, from 6,475 in 1922-23 to 5,063 in 1943-44 and 3,242 in 1952-53—the nine-year drop being 1,821 or 36 per cent.

Colorado to Vote on Legislative Districts

A proposed constitutional amendment on the subject of apportioning the state into districts for election of state legislators will be acted upon by the voters of Colorado at the November 1954 general election. At the same election the 65 members of the House of Representatives and 17 of the 35 members of the Senate will be chosen on the basis of an apportionment statute passed by the legislature in 1953.

The proposed amendment will fix the number of senators at 35 and the number of representatives at 65. These are the present numbers, which represent the upper limit now allowed by the constitution.

As to the Senate, the amendment will also establish and define 25 districts in the constitution, whereas the legislature now determines the makeup of districts. The new proposal would establish the same districts as provided by the 1953 statute, except for shifting one minor county from one district to another. The largest district in population is the city and county of Denver (1950 population, 415,786), with eight senators; its average population per senator is 51,973, which is exceeded by only two other districts—the eighth, Jefferson County, with 55,687, and the 22nd, Arapahoe and Elbert Counties, with 56,602. These two districts adjoin Denver.

In contrast, the proposed sixth district, comprised of five counties mostly in the central mountain region, would have only 16,684 people (at present it has

19,438, including Teller County, which is proposed to be shifted to the ninth district, which would thus have 22,693 instead of 19,939 as at present). The average population of the entire state, per senator, is 37,860. Eight districts, for sixteen senators, exceed this average, while seventeen districts, for nineteen senators, are below it and are thus over-represented, on a population basis.

The present constitutional provisions do not specifically call for representation in proportion to population, as to either the Senate or the House, although this may be implied from a requirement that the apportionment for senators and representatives shall be revised by the legislature after each enumeration (census) "on the basis of such enumeration according to ratios fixed by law"—no county, however, to be divided. It also provides for a state census midway between federal censuses. The proposed amendment, while freezing senatorial districts with little regard to population, provides that the legislature shall divide the state into districts for representatives so as "to give representation, so far as practicable, in equal proportion to population"; apportionments to be after the 1960 federal census and every ten years thereafter. The first election under the plan would be in 1962.

This requirement would call for very substantial changes in the House districts. The 1953 apportionment, ostensibly based on the 1950 census, shows wide variations, from 27,844 per representative in Jefferson County (just west of Denver) to 9,362 in the district composed of Cheyenne and Lincoln Counties (on the eastern plains). The average for the state is 20,386; for 38 of the representatives the figures are higher and for 27 lower. The average for seventeen representatives from Denver is 24,458; for two from Arapahoe County (east of Denver), 26,063; for three from El Paso County (containing Colorado Springs) 24,841; and for Las

Animas County (containing Trinidad), 25,902. On the other hand there are seven districts with less than 12,000, four of which are under 11,000.

The proposed amendment contains a provision that, if the legislature fails to reapportion, it is made the duty of a committee appointed by the chief justice of the Supreme Court to make a reapportionment within three months after the legislative session.

Governor Lausche Favors Shorter Ohio Ballot

Frank J. Lausche, running again for governor of Ohio in the Democratic primaries, has told the League of Women Voters that he favors the short ballot in Ohio—which has the longest ballot in the world. He adds, however, "I don't contemplate making it the issue in the campaign."

"In my opinion," the governor comments, "our state government could be reorganized in the direction of efficiency and economy by making the several presently elective offices, except the auditor of state and the lieutenant governor, of the state government appointive.

"The Council of State Governments and the Governors' Conference have gone on record urging that the various states give consideration to the reorganization of their government by making all offices dealing with executive matters appointive rather than elective.

"While the present elective attorney general has cooperated fully with my office, it is, nevertheless, illogical to have the chief executive and his other departmental heads subject to the possible whims of an attorney general over whom the governor has no direction or control. The secretary of state and the treasurer of state perform executive duties prescribed by the statutes. Under the law they have very minor discretionary powers, if any.

"In my opinion the lieutenant governor's office ought to continue to be elective because the lieutenant governor becomes the successor to the governor in the event of a vacancy. The people ought to make that choice.

"The auditor of state's office ought to continue to be elective because it is his duty to audit the books of the executive department. He ought to be free from any control or domination of the chief executive."

Governor Lausche declined to take a stand on how the new State Board of Education, authorized by constitutional amendment in November 1953, should be set up, there being a State School Survey Commission at work on that question, except to oppose the idea of having it appointed by the legislature as in New York.

R. S. C.

Council-manager Plan Developments

Voters of TRACY, CALIFORNIA, (1950 population 8,410) on April 13 adopted the council-manager form of government by a vote of 1,097 to 763.

The city council of OREM, UTAH (1950 population 8,351) adopted the manager plan by ordinance in January and appointed a city manager.

The WATERVILLE, MAINE, *Sentinel* of April 16 noted two changes in that city's governmental organization which point in the direction of the manager plan. One was the taking of preliminary steps toward the establishment of a public works department headed by a trained engineer; the other was making the city treasurer-tax collector a full-time city employee. The editor said, "These moves show a business-like procedure in city hall, which is one of the arguments in favor of a city manager."

The MASSACHUSETTS Senate, by a 17-16 vote on April 14, rejected a bill to allow city councils, by two-thirds vote, to increase city budgets for pay increases or other items; the present law allows

no additions to the budget after submission by the mayor or city manager.

DANVERS, MASSACHUSETTS, at a special election on May 3, participated in by 45 per cent of the voters, decided 2,414 to 895 to retain the town manager plan, which was adopted in 1950.

HAZELHURST, GEORGIA, on March 1 began operating under a commission form of charter that contains an optional provision for a city manager. This provision has not been taken advantage of thus far.

The legality of the election of April 21, 1953, at which MARYVILLE, MISSOURI, voted 852 to 693 to adopt the council-manager plan, has been upheld by the State Court of Appeals in affirming a similar decision of District Judge J. D. Green. The mayor and council had refused to canvass and certify the result of the election on the ground that Maryville, as a fourth-class city, could not adopt the manager plan. The court pointed out that state law authorizes the adoption of the manager plan either by a third-class city or by one with a population entitling it to become third class, and pointed out that Maryville had sufficient population, although it had not taken steps to enter the third class.

A petition calling for an election on the question of adopting the manager plan has been circulated in ORANGE, TEXAS, and is reported to have received sufficient signatures.

Voters of MINOT, NORTH DAKOTA, on April 5 rejected a proposal to change from the council-manager plan to the commission plan. The manager plan was adopted in 1933.

At the request of the city council of KENNEWICK, WASHINGTON, which adopted a resolution on April 6 calling upon the mayor to set a date for a special election on the matter, the city will vote November 9 on the question of adopting the council-manager plan.

Election of a board of fifteen free-holders to draft a new charter for WALLA WALLA, WASHINGTON, has been set for

June 1 by the city commission, following the advisory popular vote on March 9 favoring the council-manager plan two to one.

In MONROVIA, CALIFORNIA, at the municipal election on April 13, three candidates favoring the abandonment of the manager plan were defeated.

A proposed city charter to provide the council-manager plan for ROSEVILLE, CALIFORNIA, defeated at the polls on December 1, has been resubmitted to the city council with only a few changes of importance. At the conclusion of public hearings, the draft will be submitted to a charter expert for his legal opinion.

On April 13 voters of BURLINGAME, CALIFORNIA, rejected a proposal to establish the position of city administrator. The vote was 3,178 to 2,979.

Voters of FORTUNA, CALIFORNIA, defeated a council-manager proposal on April 13 by a vote of 370 to 93. On the same day MONTEBELLO, in the same state, also defeated a manager proposal, 2,189 to 1,751.

In the early spring, several state or regional meetings of city managers and students of city management were held. As reported by the International City Managers' Association these included:

Rocky Mountain area, April 1-3, at the University of Colorado, in Boulder; seventeen managers from Colorado, six from Utah, two from Nebraska and one from Wyoming;

Florida, March 28-31, at the University of Florida, in Gainesville, with 39 managers present;

Georgia, South Carolina and Alabama, April 1-2, at the University of Georgia, in Athens, with 25 managers present;

Missouri, in Springfield, with twelve managers present;

Ohio, April 8-9, at Ohio State University, in Columbus, with nineteen managers present;

Oklahoma, April 22-23, in Ponca City, with 25 managers present;

Texas, April 25-27, in Austin, with 83 managers present.

Boston Charter Placed in Danger

The Massachusetts House of Representatives in April passed a bill authorizing a referendum vote in Boston in November on the question of replacing its present Plan A strong-mayor charter by a new document. The present council of nine members elected at large would be superseded by one of eleven members, each elected from a "borough" consisting of two city wards. The proposed charter would also abolish the preliminary or primary election for mayor, council and school committee, which is followed by a run-off election to insure majority selection. Furthermore, it would take away the present right of the people of Boston to initiate an election on the question of adopting council-manager plans D or E. If approved by the Senate and the governor it will, however, impose upon the people a disruptive referendum without any convincing evidence of a widespread demand for one.

John Brigante, executive secretary of the New Boston Committee, a citizen organization which supported the present charter at the time of its adoption, has pointed out "the complete lack of any popular demonstration of interest in a charter change." The committee has received no communications in favor of the change and no supporting letters have appeared in local newspapers.

Charter Commissions for New Jersey Municipalities

Belleville and West Orange, New Jersey, voted May 11 to elect charter commissions to examine the organization and operation of the municipality and to recommend changes as called for, with a view to a possible referendum in November. Charter commissions are also to be voted on in November in the city of Passaic, Ewing Township and Livingston Township.

Organized activity is reported in a number of other municipalities, including Bloomfield, Clark Township, East Paterson, Hillside Township, North Brunswick, Perth Amboy, South Hackensack, Union City and Union Township.

New Washington Mayors and Councilmen Attend School

In the state of Washington newly elected mayors and councilmen taking office in June had the opportunity to acquaint themselves with the duties and responsibilities of their positions at a one-day school sponsored by the Association of Washington Cities—an annual service provided by the association. The school was planned in two sections, one for eastern Washington on May 4, in Moses Lake, and one for the western portion in Seattle on May 6.

Municipal finance was a dominant topic, including sources of revenue, capital outlay, borrowing and use of bonds, long-range budgeting, central purchasing and cumulative reserve funds. Planning and its role in the physical development of the city was another outstanding element in the program.

Award Made for Southern Mayor of Year

Mayor de Lesseps S. Morrison of New Orleans, Louisiana, has been designated the south's outstanding metropolitan mayor for 1953-54 by the "Southern Mayors of the Year" selection committee of the Tennessee Municipal League. The award was bestowed on May 14 at the annual banquet of the league's 1954 convention in Nashville. The selection committee was composed of the mayors of Tennessee's four largest cities.

Mayor Morrison, who recently was elected to his third four-year term as mayor of New Orleans, reached two of his major goals this year. One was the obtaining for New Orleans of a new charter giving the city home rule. The city also completed its new union station, the first municipally-owned railroad passenger terminal in the nation and also the first to be completely air-conditioned.

New Orleans also has a new traffic system, including elimination of the more than 144 main-line railroad grade crossings which formerly blocked city streets and provided one of the south's major traffic headaches. The committee further emphasized the city's progress in modern budgeting, centralized purchasing, improved personnel practices and development of one of the nation's most comprehensive municipal recreation programs.

Direct Election Fostered for N.Y.C. District Leaders

The New York legislature has adopted a new law clearing the way for direct election of district leaders in all party primaries in New York City. Hitherto, in Tammany Hall, the popular name given to the executive committee of the Democratic party in Manhattan, the law had permitted the party to make its own rules. These rules set up an elaborate buffer system between the party voters and assembly district leaders, who constitute the principal characters of the political party machinery.

The buffers consisted of a great array of as many as a thousand so called county committeemen, several of them elected in each voting precinct, who supposedly met in conventions to select the district leader. The leader in his turn appointed the precinct captains who collected the party committeemen to vote for the same leader next time.

This mutual admiration society was difficult for any insurgent candidate for leader to break and, in the occasional contests, half the campaign money would be spent in pointing out to the voters which of the unlabeled groups of county committeemen on the paper ballot would support the insurgent candidate if they were elected and sent to the next convention of the district.

The new law permits direct election of district leaders, and party voters will be enabled to know exactly what they are doing if they attend the party primary in a leadership contest.

Several other amendments to the law remove booby traps in the procedures for handling independent nomination petitions. The board of elections is composed of two Republicans and two Democrats chosen from the party managements and they have joined hands in making life hard for insurgent petitioners in either party. They rely on the throwing out of nominating petitions by cancelling signatures for trivial reasons which were supported by law, such as use or non-use of the middle initial, failure to register for the coming election, etc. Such technical quibbling made the board of elections a graveyard for nominating petitions. Even Mayor Impellitteri and an important candidate for Brooklyn borough president were thrown out of the contest in 1953 in spite of having produced petitions with signatures far exceeding the minimum required number. A number of these booby traps are now removed.

The original situation was described in the NATIONAL MUNICIPAL REVIEW of July 1950 by Justin N. Feldman, "How Tammany Holds Power," and the recent changes constitute major improvements in the situation there described.

R. S. C.

Alabama Cities Extend Powers Past Boundaries

The jurisdiction of Alabama cities in certain matters has been extended one and one-half miles beyond the city limits in the case of small cities and three miles in the case of larger ones, according to *Tennessee Town and City* (Tennessee Municipal League). This so-called "police jurisdiction" includes the power to build streets, assess adjacent property

for street costs, enforce building standards and exercise control over subdividers.

The Tennessee Supreme Court has declared invalid an extension of "all governmental powers and police powers" in a two-mile zone around a city but has recognized that "a limited police power" may be granted to a city outside its corporate limits (*Malone* v. *Williams*, 118 Tennessee 390, 420).

Arizona Municipal League Makes Self-survey

At its spring conference May 7-8 at Flagstaff, the Arizona Municipal League adopted the report of a special committee which recommended that steps be taken to effect drastic changes in the league's administrative organization and program. The special committee which framed the report was appointed as a result of the spirited criticism of various delegates to the conference, who charged that the league was not sufficiently effective with respect either to legislation of concern to municipalities or to the administrative problems of Arizona cities.

In accordance with one section of the report, a committee was appointed to "effect the reorganization of the Arizona Municipal League both with respect to the activities of the league and with respect to administration." The committee was instructed to submit its recommendations within 60 days to a special meeting. The report asked the committee on reorganization to consider the following suggestions for possible inclusion among its recommendations:

1. That a highly qualified director, secretary and adequate office facilities be secured;
2. That the program, including legislative, of the league be presented to all elected officials, city attorneys, city clerks and city managers for their study and consideration prior to the annual fall conference;
3. That consideration be given to
(Continued on page 302)

County and Township   •   •   • *Edited by Edward W. Weidner*

Wisconsin County Board Suggests Defense Plan

Says State Is Smallest Unit Capable of Handling Problem

RESPECT for the H-bomb has evoked considerable interest in legal and administrative problems in Wisconsin government. Calling a constitutional convention to solve some of the local and interlocal problems was recently proposed by an assistant city attorney of Milwaukee. Interest in intercounty relationships in the handling of evacuees has been expressed by the State Office of Civil Defense, which is making preliminary plans for a joint conference of administrators and county district attorneys to outline the types of legal problems that need legislative action.

A more specific plan has already been outlined by the Rock County Board of Supervisors. At its April meeting the board recommended that a network of industrial-residential districts be created by the state. A resolution sent to the governor and to the national government states in part:

> Maximum dispersion of our nation's industry and people appears to offer the most practical method of survival. . . . Comprehensive long-range planning, combined with appropriate enabling legislation is required to effectuate this type of dispersion. . . . The smallest political unit in our nation capable of effectuating such a program of dispersion is the state.

"We thought the county could handle the A-bomb but when the H-bomb came along we decided the state ought to take over!" is the explanation offered by one Rock County official for asking the state to create this special layer of districts above the county.

The board of supervisors proposed the following membership for a state dispersion committee: a director of regional planning (to be created), the "chief planner" of every municipality having a planning commission, a representative of the university's School of Commerce, a representative of the Wisconsin Manufacturers Association, two members at large appointed by the governor, and a representative from the state legislature, who must be a "lawyer by profession and who is not only thoroughly familiar with the current tax laws of the state, including those of all its political subdivisions, but those of the federal government and the state and their mutual relationships."

LLOYD W. WOODRUFF
University of Wisconsin

Information on Urban Counties Made Available

Beginning with its 1954 edition, the *Municipal Year Book,* published by the International City Managers' Association, will contain information on urban counties on a regular systematic basis. Information on metropolitan counties will include: population, land area, dwelling units built between 1940 and 1950, number of employees, amount of payroll, type of governing body and services performed by the county in unincorporated areas. In addition there will be considerable data on county government functions and activities such as planning and zoning and county-owned and operated utilities.

A preliminary analysis of the data reveals that a large proportion of the metropolitan counties are responding as urban governments to the needs of suburban residents. Thus 36 counties report they provide a measure of fire protection, at least 26 provide street lighting, 24 engage in garbage collection and disposal service, 17 in public housing and 72 in library service.

Professor Victor Jones, writing in the May issue of *Public Management*, notes that the urban counties are still organized poorly if they are to continue to assume municipal functions. He points out the need for a managerial form of government before these urban units can function successfully, including a representative and responsible county legislative body, creation of a county executive and the organization of county work in units responsible through the executive to the county legislative body. Of the 174 counties surveyed 18 had a central executive.

Maryland Counties Make Zoning Changes

The planning commission of Baltimore County has approved a revised and modernized set of regulations for its zoning code. Before it is legally effective it must be approved by the Board of County Commissioners also. The principal recommendation is for the establishment of thirteen use-zones in the county.

The planning and zoning commission of Anne Arundel County, Maryland, has approved a set of rules for strict control of signs and billboards on the county's highways. They would restrict billboards to commercial or heavy industrial districts, limit the number of signs, restrict the size of billboards and make it illegal to place billboards on dual-lane highways.

California County Seeks Better Planning

The agencies of Contra Costa County, California, are cooperating with construction companies in an effort to get better planning. Steps taken include: the development of a slope chart, land use chart and a traffic flow map. The general objective is to have over-all coordination of heavy construction work by public agencies and to work out the best possible arrangement for the governmental agencies concerned and for the construction companies in the contracts that are made.

Iowa County Government Reorganization Suggested

There is a growing sentiment throughout Iowa for the creation by the 1955 General Assembly of a commission to make a thorough study of county and township government and to recommend such measures as may be expected to increase efficiency, according to *The Iowa Taxpayer*, published by the Iowa Taxpayers Association. The periodical says this issue will be of crucial importance since the county is the one local unit of government that stands between the citizen and the centralized control exercised by state and national governments.

Los Angeles County Intern Program 20 Years Old

One of the oldest and best conceived intern programs in public administration in the United States is that operated by Los Angeles County. An analysis of this program is contained in the January issue of *Trojan in Government*, publication of the School of Public Administration of the University of Southern California.

The program was inaugurated in 1933 by Harry A. Scoville, a well known management expert who worked for the county for many years. Seventy-five interns have served during the twenty-year period; nineteen graduated from the University of California at Los Angeles, thirteen from the University of Southern California, and eleven each from the University of California and Stanford University.

The former interns have gone on to hold top positions in local, state and national government. One of the graduates is the city manager of San Diego; 28 graduates hold top administrative or management positions while sixteen are in research and administrative analysis.

Kansas Interested in County Manager Plan

Interest in the manager plan for county government is developing in Kansas, according to the Leavenworth *Times*. The paper comments editorially that Kansas "offers several systems of government to the city dweller, but no alternative for the counties." It then asks the question whether consideration ought not be given to alternative forms for county government as in several other states that have already started to experiment.

The present county government in Kansas is rather typical of that in many states in which most county officials are elected and hence are independent of each other. As a result, county government has become complicated and lacks coordination.

CITY, STATE AND NATION

(Continued from page 299)

having the director visit each member city at least once every year;

4. That each member city in cooperation with the league inaugurate a program of public education with respect to municipal problems and accomplishments;

5. That a schedule be prepared designating regular meetings for the executive committee;

6. That the program protecting municipalities against adverse legislation be strengthened;

7. That all candidates for legislative offices be questioned by each city as to their stand on municipal problems prior to their nomination.

Meetings of the Arizona Municipal Administrators Association, Arizona Association of City Clerks, Arizona City Attorneys Association and Arizona Police Chiefs Association were held in conjunction with the spring conference of the league.

PAUL KELSO
University of Arizona

Pennsylvania Local Groups Form General Organization

Six organizations of local officials in Pennsylvania have organized a local government conference to consolidate their efforts, particularly in the direction of bolstering home rule. An organizational meeting was held in Harrisburg on February 17, attended by representatives of the State Association of Boroughs, League of Cities of the Third Class, County Commissioners Association, Township Commissioners Association, Association of Township Supervisors and State School Directors Association. According to *The American City* the group elected officers under the chairmanship of John H. Doherty, president of the State Association of County Commissioners, appointed a by-laws committee to complete the organization of the conference, and arranged for a further meeting.

Correction

The article, "Reduce the Voting Age to 18?", the REVIEW, January 1954, pages 11-15, was in error in stating that "Missouri's legislature passed a constitutional amendment last year authorizing reduction of the voting age to 18, which will be submitted to a referendum in November 1954." The proposed amendment passed only one house and therefore cannot be submitted to the voters.   EDITOR

Taxation and Finance • • • • *Edited by Wade S. Smith*

Local Sales Taxes Boosted in Los Angeles

New York City Asks Its Extension to Services

PRESSURE for additional revenues caused municipalities to give renewed attention to local sales taxes during the forepart of the year. Los Angeles raised the rate of its existing tax, while New York City's new administration sought legislation from the city council to extend the existing sales and use tax to services. In Illinois, however, at least seven cities which had not had sales taxes voted down proposals to impose them.

Los Angeles raised its sales tax rate from the present one-half of one per cent to a full one per cent. The increase will be for a two-year period through June 30, 1956, with the increased collections to be used in part for capital improvements. The two-year period for the one per cent rate is intended to permit observation of the effects of the increase on trade relative to surrounding communities, where the rate is one-half of one per cent. Neighboring Glendale, however, is reported to have announced that it would increase its sales tax to one per cent if Los Angeles did so.

In New York, where the sales and use tax is at a rate of 3 per cent and the city is deep in the annual struggle to balance the budget, Mayor Robert A. Wagner has announced that extension of the tax to commercial services is "inevitable." The extension would provide an estimated $60,000,000 of additional revenue. Opposition by business interests to the proposal is intense, and there has been revived talk of moving the stock exchanges out of the city.

In Illinois, four cities submitted proposals for a one-half of one per cent city sales tax to their voters and all four proposals were defeated. The cities were Cairo, Mount Vernon, Peoria and Springfield. The voting was generally light. The Mount Vernon proposal lost 2,042 for to 2,195 against, but elsewhere the vote against the proposals ran from two to one to better than four to one. Earlier, referenda had been held and similar proposals defeated in Danville, East St. Louis and Kewanee. Proposals were submitted under a state law authorizing municipal sales taxes if approved by the local voters.

Industrial Aid Programs Stir More Controversy

Use of public funds to subsidize manufacturing industry at the local level continues a highly controversial subject at both the national and state levels.

Target of criticism from several southern states, and of concern throughout the country, was a proposal by the House Ways and Means Committee to curb use of local revenue bonds for construction of plants for lease to manufacturers.

The committee had originally proposed, it will be recalled, that interest on revenue bonds issued for such purposes be made subject to federal income taxes. Later, it substituted a proposal that the amounts paid as rent on such plants by their manufacturer-tenants should not be allowable deductions as operating expenses in determining net income for income tax purposes.

Affected at present would be tenants in a relatively few plants erected by cities in three states—Alabama, Kentucky and Tennessee. Noting that the effect of the proposal to disallow the rent deductions would be to destroy local programs, the Tennessee Municipal League said in an official statement on the plan:

"If the federal government thus declares one type of public function 'unsound,' and effectively prohibits its continuance, then a similar policy can be enforced in the case of other public functions of states. There are strong and vocal groups who vigorously insist at national, state and local levels that government should not undertake, through public ownership, the provision of electricity, gas or water and many other services.

"Heretofore, the decisions on such issues have been left to the . . . states or delegated by states to local subdivisions and their citizenship. . . . But if the . . . proposal is enacted . . . pressure groups will appear at the doors of Congress insisting that punitive and prohibitive legislation be enacted to prevent a state or local government from entering upon some new public enterprise, or to force some minority of states and communities to withdraw from what is to them a desirable and essential field of public service."

It is to be noted that in addition to Alabama, Kentucky and Tennessee, five other states permit their local units to issue bonds to construct plants for lease to manufacturers. They are Illinois, Louisiana, Mississippi, Nebraska and Pennsylvania. These use general obligation bonds, however, backed by the full faith and credit of the municipality, rather than revenue bonds backed only by the rentals paid by the manufacturer-tenant.

Texas Legislature Tackles Financial Problems

On March 15, Governor Allan Shivers presented to a special session of the Texas legislature a program which included, on the expenditure side, a suggestion that the state raise $25,000,000 to pay larger salaries to teachers and state employees. The governor also recommended an $11,000,000 building program which included improvements costing $3,500,000 each for the Southwestern Medical School

of the University of Texas and the prison system, $2,500,000 for the State School for the Deaf, and $1,187,500 for the University of Texas Dental School.

The big item of the spending program was a $402-per-year increase for public school teachers. The proposed increase represented a compromise worked out by a 24-member committee appointed by the governor and the Texas State Teachers' Association after the 1953 legislature had disapproved a $600 increase demanded by the teachers.

The building program was to be financed from a surplus in the general revenue fund. To finance teacher and state employee salary increases, it was the governor's recommendation that increased taxes be levied on natural gas, beer and corporations. It had been hoped that the legislature could meet for a spending session without having to face the problem of taxes. The hope was that the proposed expenditures could be financed by a gas-gathering tax levied by the 1951 legislature but which had been in litigation since that time. However, the U. S. Supreme Court, on February 8, 1954, in a unanimous decision, invalidated the gas-gathering tax as unconstitutional.[1] The court declared that the tax was not levied on the capture or production of the gas but rather on its taking into commerce after production, gathering and process. Thus it was held to be contrary to the constitutional provision against state interference with interstate commerce.

When the special session closed on April 13, it had enacted the governor's recommendations in their entirety. The compromise proposal on teachers' pay was accepted by the legislature with minor opposition and resulted in an increase in base pay of from $2,403 to $2,804 per year. As a result of this increase, it is estimated that teachers' salaries will aver-

---

[1] *Michigan-Wisconsin Pipe Line Company* v. *Calvert*, et al., 347 U.S. 157.

age $3,600 per year starting September 1, when the raise is effective. State employees were given a blanket $120-per-year increase in pay to supplement a $180 increase voted by the regular session in 1953. The building program was approved.

The tax bill as finally passed increased the rate on natural gas production from 5.72 per cent to 9 per cent of market value at the wellhead. The rate will be reduced to 8 per cent in 1955 and to 7 per cent a year later. This tax is expected to yield $14,000,000 annually. The beer tax was raised from $1.37 to $2.00 per barrel to provide an additional $3,000,000 per year and the franchise tax on corporations was raised from $1.25 to $2.00 per $1,000 to yield an estimated $8,600,000 in additional revenue.

With these major pieces of legislation out of the way, other topics were submitted by the governor within the last week of the session, but few passed because of the shortage of time.

STUART A. MACCORKLE, *Director*
Institute of Public Affairs
University of Texas

Pennsylvania Act 481 Yields $38,000,000 to Local Units

Pennsylvania's famous omnibus local tax law, Act 481, passed in 1947 to enlarge the authority of local units to impose a variety of special taxes and charges, yielded $38,196,687 to 2,305 local units in the last fiscal periods for which data are compiled, according to the Pennsylvania Department of Internal Affairs. Of the total, $18,265,447 represented receipts in fiscal 1952 of cities, boroughs and townships, and $19,931,240 represented receipts in fiscal 1952-53 of school districts. The city-borough-township total was $1,564,969, or 9.4 per cent higher than in the preceding fiscal period, while the school total was up $3,000,225, or 17.7 per cent.

The 2,305 units using the act compared with 5,049 eligible to use it under the law. The largest cities levying taxes under the act were Pittsburgh and Scranton. In addition, 45 of the 47 third-class cities were using it, 446 of the 942 boroughs, 36 of the 70 first-class townships, 301 of the 1,500 second class townships and 1,475 of the 2,488 school districts. In all, there were 2,988 separate taxes being levied under the act: 93 by cities, 650 by boroughs, 57 by first-class townships, 356 by second-class townships and 1,832 by school districts.

The per capita tax was levied more often than any other tax available under the act. It was levied by 1,129 school districts and 479 other units. Some 380 units used the amusement tax in some form, 345 used the income tax and 272 used the deed transfer tax. In terms of productivity, however, the income tax was the leader, with the per capita tax second; the dollar figures were $13,210,963 and $10,073,578 respectively, while mercantile and business privilege taxes yielded $5,285,704.

Yield of the amusement tax was $4,215,011, of the deed transfer tax $4,108,913, and of all other taxes $1,302,518. More than half ($797,805) of the "all other" collections was Pittsburgh's collection of the personal property tax, whose use was restricted to that city only by a 1949 amendment to the act.

Act 481 was enacted to supplement the established general property tax and usual system of licenses, fees and miscellaneous charges available to Pennsylvania local units. Additional use is constantly being made of the act. According to the Department of Internal Affairs, a number of units adopted income taxes in 1954, including a wage tax imposed by the city of Pittsburgh, and about 30 taxes of this type have been imposed in Allegheny County alone during February-March, 1954.

Chairman Appointed for Federal Tax Study Group

The U.S. Commission on Intergovernmental Relations got its replacement chairman on April 22, when Meyer Kestnbaum, president of Hart, Schaffner and Marx, Chicago clothing manufacturers, was sworn in at the White House. Mr. Kestnbaum, at the time of his appointment, was also chairman of the Committee for Economic Development and is a director of the Community Fund of Chicago.

The commission had been without a chairman since mid-February, when Professor Clarence Manion resigned. The new chairman met with the commission on April 26 and expressed confidence that "we can turn out a report that will reflect credit on the commission and its members." It was reported that the "impact studies" now under way in a number of states would begin to reach the commission between the middle of May and the first of July.

Uniformity Clauses Reviewed by Assessing Officers Agency

A current review of the provisions of state constitutions to determine the present prevalence of the so-called uniformity clauses has been completed by the National Association of Assessing Officers. The association found that, in the last ten years, only one state had changed its constitutional provisions on uniformity of taxation. This was Missouri, which in 1945 provided for different tax treatment for real estate, tangible personal property and intangibles. Its legislature was also authorized to make additional subclassifications of tangible and intangible personal property.

The constitutions of half the states now allow the legislature to make any reasonable classification of property for tax purposes. Those states are Rhode Island, Connecticut, Vermont, New York, Pennsylvania, New Jersey, Virginia, North Carolina, Kentucky, Alabama, Louisiana, Oklahoma, New Mexico, Arizona, Colorado, Michigan, Iowa, Minnesota, North Dakota, South Dakota, Montana, Idaho, Oregon and Delaware.

Eleven state constitutions require that each taxing district impose its taxes in uniform proportion to the value of all taxable property within its jurisdiction. Thus, intangible property, like money, bonds, accounts payable and mortgages, must be taxed at the same rate as tangible property like livestock, real estate or land. The states having this restriction, which is known as a "uniformity clause," are New Hampshire, Massachusetts, Tennessee, Arkansas, Indiana, Illinois, Wisconsin, Texas, Wyoming, Nevada and Mississippi.

The constitutions of seven states stipulate that all tangible property must be uniformly taxed but explicitly allows special tax rates for intangible property. Those states are Utah, Nebraska, Kansas, Maine, South Carolina, Georgia and Florida.

Constitutions of four states require uniformity only with respect to real estate. They are California, Washington, Missouri and Ohio. Maryland requires uniformity only in regard to land.

West Virginia's constitution divides taxable property into four classes and sets a low, over-all tax rate limitation for each class.

In dividing the states into six groups, the association noted that for simplicity's sake the authority of the legislatures of several states to provide special methods of taxation for natural resources, public utilities or motor vehicles was not considered. The association also pointed out that selection of the proper category for some states—such as Alabama, Massachusetts, New Hampshire and New Jersey—was based largely on state court interpretations of the constitution.

Citizen Action • • • • • • *Edited by Elsie S. Parker*

Why Not More Women in Public Office?

Voluntary Group Work Tends to Keep Them Out of Politics

EDITOR's NOTE.—The comments below represent excerpts from the remarks of Mrs. John G. Lee at a panel discussion during the National Conference on Government of the National Municipal League, Richmond, Virginia, November 10, 1953.

INVARIABLY foreigners who visit the U.S. and are interested in government ask why there aren't more women in public affairs—boards of education, town councils, state legislatures, Congress, etc. There are many angles to this question but I want to suggest the one which to my mind is most significant.

Our unique system of voluntary associations takes out of the hands of government many enterprises of a public character. For example, hospitals, churches, charitable institutions, independent schools and colleges, Girl and Boy Scouts, YM and YWCA's etc. The number of such things is legion, as is the number of volunteer man- and woman-hours they absorb.

I used to think we greatly overdid this sort of thing in the U.S.—that all our communities were over-organized. I see it differently now and I believe this multitude of voluntary associations constitutes a tremendously important safeguard in American life. They prevent the imposition of conformity, they promote experimentation, they assume responsibility for the common good which obviates to a great extent the necessity of government operation in certain fields.

They do, however, in a very real sense keep out of politics many worthy people. The average woman today is carrying a large load of public service

quite outside of government. I wish the census taker had collected data on the numbers of volunteer hours women were devoting to this sort of public service. I think it would have been staggering and, had it been computed into dollar earnings, the word "housewife" might have acquired a new and more real value.

Be that as it may, I still would like to see more women get out and seek political positions. Although most women have family obligations which preclude running for an office which would take them very far from their home towns, more women can and should run for local and state offices. I think that many women would find that being a member of the city council or of the school board or even the state legislature would not be any more of a drain on her time and energies than many of the volunteer activities in which she had previously engaged.

As a matter of fact a heartening number of women are graduating from volunteer roles into active politics. Often, because of their varied experience in the public services outside of government, they bring to their elected positions a knowledge of their cities few men have the time to acquire.

This matter of time is an important consideration. Increasingly, it seems to me, certain types of campaigns are being spearheaded more and more by women. Though men still dominate the party caucus and in most cases control the selection of candidates, campaigns on issues are very often run and won by women. In many cases it is the women of the community who get behind a movement for the council-manager form of government, or for a new state constitution, or for reapportionment of state legislative districts. They have become old hands at organizing the community as they would for a community chest campaign, making sure that every doorbell is rung and every voter reached.

Sometimes, not often enough, civic campaigns such as these lead women into active politics. A member of the PTA does an outstanding job on a school bond issue. As a result, she is asked to run for the school board. A member of a woman's club leads her group in a study of rubbish disposal problems, so the mayor appoints her to a commission to recommend a new plan for the city. A member of the League of Women Voters is a faithful attendant at city council meetings and learns a great deal about the way the city is run. A citizens' group looking for a candidate thinks she would be an excellent choice. Thus the transition is made—the "graduation" from volunteer public service to appointive or elective office.

Then, after they have learned political "know-how" in the community, where standards of behavior, political and otherwise are set, they can graduate again. As their children grow older and their family responsibilities become less they can go on to national office. I am hopeful that these graduates of our civic organizations will increase in number as the years go on and that more and more women will take part in the local, state and national affairs of their government.

PERCY MAXIM LEE, *President*
League of Women Voters
of the United States

Voters Seek Increase in Tax Rate!

Over two hundred citizens of Parsippany–Troy Hills, New Jersey, crowded into a school auditorium—so many turned out the meeting was transferred from the town hall—and stayed five hours in an effort to raise the community's budget. The budget, as submitted by the outgoing township committee, provided for a 50-point cut in the tax rate. This, one citizen declared, "puts a strait-jacket on the members of the new council-manager group whomever they may be." Numerous other citizens criticized the cut, charging that "the committee, by draining surplus, was deliberately out to make the task of the new council-manager administration difficult, if not impossible," according to a report in *The Citizen*, a weekly newspaper of Morris County.

Despite the protests, the township committee passed the budget as it had been submitted.

Modernizing New York Personnel

A New York City Conference on Public Personnel, sponsored by the Civil Service Reform Association, the Citizens Budget Commission, Citizens Committee on Children, Citizens Union, Commerce and Industry Association, League of Women Voters, City Club and Women's City Club, was held February 18. The conference was planned to support the mayor's campaign pledges, to learn the views of city officials and employees, and to focus attention on present conditions and needed changes, according to *Good Government*, publication of the National Civil Service League. The March-April issue of *Good Government* presents a digest of the discussions, including the remarks of Mayor Robert F. Wagner, William S. Carpenter of Princeton University, Wallace S. Sayre of the Temporary State Commission to Study the Organizational Structure of the Government of the City of New York, Edward J. Walsh, manager of personnel services of General Foods Corporation, and others.

Citizens Committee for Ferguson

The newly formed Citizens Committee for Ferguson (Missouri), where the voters adopted a council-manager charter in February, is seeking new members. John M. Hannegan, chairman of the committee, announced: "We feel it is of the utmost importance that Ferguson's first council-manager government under the charter should be given every possible chance to succeed. We think we can best insure this by actively working for the election of a council which favors the charter and the council-manager government. Because the election of councilmen will come up annually, we thought it wise to set up a permanent organization."

Home Rule for Chicago

A series of discussions on home rule for Chicago is being conducted by the Local Government Committee and the Committee on Constitutional Revision of the Chicago City Club. At the first meeting, on April 13, Fred K. Hoehler, executive director of the Citizens of Greater Chicago, talked of the present plight of Chicago, most of which is due to its lack of municipal powers. One of the matters discussed concerns the manner and extent of cooperation possible with other agencies working to the same general ends, including the Home Rule Commission set up last year by ordinance of the city council. It is expected that bills to provide home rule will be drafted for presentation to the 1955 legislature.

Citizen Committees

A nine-man Citizens' Study Committee will survey the financial needs of all the tax-supported agencies in New Orleans, according to the *Louisiana Municipal Review*. The panel has been selected by the temporary chairman of a large citizens' standby committee set up originally to survey the financial needs of the city's public school system. Panel members are free to decide on the specific phases of their study.

The Chicago Citizens Committee to Fight Slums has submitted its *Housing Action Report of 1954* to Mayor Martin H. Kennelly. The report presents a four-point program to fight slums: (1) An effective and diversified program to pre-

vent further slums from developing; (2) certain departmental reorganizations accompanied by determined enforcement of adequate housing, building and zoning laws; (3) acceleration of the program of slum clearance and residential redevelopment, to eliminate the blight which surrounds the central city; and (4) a sharp increase in the supply of standard housing available to families at all economic levels.

With the LWV

The Intelligent Voter, published by the League of Women Voters of Nebraska, reports that the league will approve and work for adoption of an amendment to the Nebraska state constitution improving the method of selecting judges and will continue working for improved election laws. A two-year study of "the basic tax policies of the state, exploring the possibilities of broadening the tax base" has also been decided upon.

"Does the Oregon Constitution Need Revision?" was the topic of discussion at an April 20 meeting of the League of Women Voters of Corvallis, Oregon.

The League of Women Voters of Atlanta, Georgia, continues its investigation of citizens' boards and the part they play in the government of Atlanta and Fulton County. The League's March issue of *Facts* is devoted to a "1954 Political Directory" for both the city and the county.

Members of the Wausau (Wisconsin) League of Women Voters undertook the task of addressing over 10,000 postcards to Wausau voters, reporting changes in wards, precincts and polling places—doing the job in five days and evenings.

LWV Publications

The League of Women Voters of the U. S. (Washington, D. C.) has issued numerous publications on the national and international fronts, among them: *Mr. Congressman . . . His Moneybags and Watchdogs*, twelve pages, fifteen cents;

The Citizen and International Trade, 32 pages, fifteen cents; *World Trade Affects You*, twelve pages, 100 for $2.75; *What's the U.N. to Us?*, sixteen pages, ten cents. Discounts are available on quantity orders.

Local leagues continue to publish descriptions of their governments for the use of the citizen: *Know Your County— A Survey of Northampton County*, 76 pages, 50 cents, comes from the League of Women Voters of Easton, Pennsylvania; *Darien Our Town*, 76 pages, (no price listed) has been compiled and published by the League of Women Voters of Darien, Connecticut; *The League Looks at Lafayette*, 28 pages, 25 cents, is by the Lafayette, Louisiana, League; *Know Your City Government*, 43 pages, 50 cents, comes from the league of Lynn, Massachusetts.

From the New York State League comes *What About the Primary—A Brief for League Members*, ten pages, five cents. The New York City League has issued *How Our City Laws Are Made*, eight pages, ten cents, and the 1954 edition of *They Represent You—in Washington, Albany, New York*, sixteen pages, fifteen cents, wherein are listed federal, state and local officials.

Conference on Citizenship

The United States Department of Justice and the National Education Association have announced the Ninth National Conference on Citizenship, to be held in Washington, D. C., September 15-17. The theme is "The Three Branches of the Federal Government—Yesterday, Today and Tomorrow." The conference brings together representatives of hundreds of organizations from all parts of the country. Sunday, September 17, designated Citizenship Day by act of Congress, will be celebrated by the conference "to commemorate the formation and signing of the constitution in 1787 and to honor those citizens becoming of voting age and

those recently naturalized." An elaborate ceremony is being planned.

Annual Institute

The tenth annual Institute of Community Leadership of the New York State Citizens' Council will meet at Hobart College, Geneva, New York, June 17-20. Theme of the conference will be "Training for More Effective Community Action and Development." It is planned "for people—lay and professional—who want to work more effectively for their community in their council, committee, board, industry, club, association, union— as member and as leader" and will consider such questions as: "How can communities train more people for community action and development?" with material drawn from experience in various communities; "What can be done through university-community cooperation? through adult education?"; "How can community education be tied to the live, important issues of today?"

Working groups are planned in cooperation with the Advisory Committee of the council's university-community cooperation project, the Bureau of Adult Education of the State Education Department, the Foreign Policy Association, New York State Citizen's Committee for the Public Schools and other organizations.

Voters Guides

Spring elections find civic organizations busily issuing voters' directories for the guidance of members and other interested citizens. The *Voters' Directory* compiled by the Civic Club of Allegheny County (Pennsylvania), for the May 18 primary, covers Pittsburgh, Clairton, Duquesne and McKeesport as well as boroughs and townships in the county. The Citizens League of Cleveland made its *Report on Candidates* for the May 4 primary. The league's candidates' committee, composed of 88 members, interviewed some 250 candidates prior to issuance of the report.

A nonpartisan *Voters' Guide* was prepared and issued by several units of the Church Federation of Greater Chicago: the Department of Citizenship Education and Action, The Citizenship Committee of the Council of Church Women of Greater Chicago and the Citizenship Committee of Greater Chicago Churchmen.

The League of Women Voters of Ohio has published a four-page newspaper spread describing candidates for state office; in the same state, the Dayton and Shaker Heights leagues offered information on candidates running for Congress in those communities. In Portland, Oregon, the league discussed both issues and candidates in a sixteen-page pamphlet of newspaper format.

The League of Women Voters of Hoboken, New Jersey, questioned congressional candidates on various matters of national and international interest and made replies available to members.

Teaching Citizenship

C. A. Crosser, executive secretary of the Municipal League of Seattle and King County, in an address before the Social Science Teachers' Conference at the University of Washington, set forth three paramount goals of a course in local government:

"(1) *Do you know your city?* This involves implanting knowledge in pupils about the structures and services of local governing bodies including the city, school, county, port and others.

"(2) *How good is your city?* This involves implanting knowledge in pupils of some basic yardstick for measuring whether or not local public services are good, average or inferior.

"(3) *Do you appreciate your city?* This involves arousing in the pupil an appreciation of the 'blood, sweat and tears' which went into the evolution of local public services, rights and privileges we now enjoy, from their history."

Mimeographed copies of Mr. Crosser's remarks (seven pages) are available from the Seattle Municipal League, 316 Marion Building, Seattle 4.

Recent Publications

The Chamber of Commerce of the United States (Washington, D. C.) has issued an attractive leaflet, *Community Citizenship Policies—Background for Action.*

Is "Non-group" Prepaid Health Service Adequate comprises a report of the Public Health Section of the Commonwealth Club of California (San Francisco).

The Institute of International Education (New York) has published its *34th Annual Report* (69 pages). Its objectives are "to increase understanding between the United States and other nations through the exchange of promising college students and of advanced specialists in many fields" and "through these educational exchanges to help develop leadership to deal with the basic problems of the world's peoples."

Strictly Personal

The Citizens' Association of Kansas City, Missouri, has appointed Carl B. Short, Jr., as its new executive secretary. Mr. Short succeeds Mrs. Charles G. Wilder, who is moving to Oak Ridge, Tennessee. Mr. Short, just released from the Navy, has been commanding officer of the Naval Reserve Training Center at Topeka, Kansas.

The Connecticut Merit System Association has elected Dr. Paul W. Stoddard, principal of the Housatonic Regional High School, as its president for 1954. Dr. Stoddard succeeds William E. C. Bulkeley, who has been president since 1949.

Researcher's Digest   •   •   •   •   *Edited by John E. Bebout*

Local Groups Study Metropolitan Seattle

City, County Are Asked to Set Up Official Advisory Council

SEATTLE is bursting at the seams— and is trying to do something about it. The signs of strain appear in snarled traffic and mushrooming suburbs, in insatiable demands for public services and in tightening municipal budgets. Every day in some new fashion we are reminded that the young city of twenty years ago has, almost overnight, become a metropolitan giant.

Area and Population.—Seattle's population now exceeds half a million. The city's metropolitan area contains nearly 750,000 persons and is likely to pass the million mark before 1970. Rapid growth is no stranger to a city that remembers gold rush days and timber booms, but the recent war and postwar expansion has had an explosive new twist. Today's growing pains spring not only from a great population increase but from a revolution in urban living. We demand a view from our picture windows and consider the family car an absolute necessity. This urban revolution has spread our enlarged population over an area of nearly 150 square miles including some two dozen cities, towns and unincorporated communities and about 180 junior districts, i.e. fire, water, sewage, etc.

Terrain and Setting.—Because of its unusual terrain and setting, Seattle has many problems which do not exist to the same degree in most other major cities. Shaped like an hourglass, the city is flanked on the west by Puget Sound and on the east by 21-mile-long Lake Washington. The narrow neck of this hourglass city is in the business section. The city rises in a series of short but steep hills from the sound and the lake and, like Rome, has seven prominent hills. There are but six major arterials giving access to the city. Three are on the north, two on the south, while the famous floating bridge is the only entry on the east.

Because of its shape, hills and lack of major access roads, Seattle has perplexing sewer and drainage problems. The transit system has many headaches because of the hills and the fact that all bus routes in the central city have to be channeled down a few streets. Traffic control, planning, water supply and other services are also affected by these hills and the shape of the city.

Seattle's Future.—Although various public officials and civic leaders have from time to time pointed to this or that serious unresolved problem in metropolitan Seattle, it remained for James Ellis, one of the city's rising young attorneys, to set forth clearly, in an address before several committees of the Municipal League of Seattle and King County, a detailed list of these problems and their possible solutions. The board of trustees established a committee of league members to investigate the problems and frame possible solutions.

The Committee.—Because of the complex nature of the proposed study, this hand-picked committee was made up of members from league committees on city planning, county planning, governmental research, city budget and county budget. Key members of a subcommittee which had been studying annexation were also included.

Basic Principles.—These are the basic principles which the committee is using as a guide in its study:

1. The urban revolution has created a greatly enlarged metropolitan area which is one city economically and socially. Proper development and planning require

that this area be unified governmentally.

2. The principle of local responsibility and self-determination should be recognized wherever possible within a framework of sound over-all development.

3. Certain functions demand area-wide administration while other functions may be county-wide and others may be local. A functional reorganization should assign work to the unit of government best able to perform it. Such a functional reorganization is the key to more efficient local government.

4. Changes in existing internal governmental structures and shifts of functions should be advocated only if required to eliminate wasteful duplication or to provide more efficient operation. If changes are kept at a minimum, the probability of ultimate adoption of the plan will be greatly enhanced.

Plan of Operation

Work Begins.—The committee's first task was to acquaint itself completely with city functions and services as they exist now. Therefore, three subcommittees were formed: one to study sewer, water and drainage, a second to study traffic and transportation and the third to study police and fire protection and miscellaneous subjects as they might arise.

The Experts.—To obtain a comprehensive and practical knowledge of metropolitan problems, experts in the various fields were invited to meet with the subcommittees to present the situation as it exists now and also to voice their views on possible remedies. These included the chief of police, the assistant fire chief, a fire insurance rating bureau official, the superintendent and assistant superintendent of the city water supply, the county engineer, the executive secretary of the Washington State Taxpayers Association, a representative of the city engineer's office who is an authority on sewage and water pollution and a representative of the State Highway Commission.

All these meetings were informal. The subcommittees consisted of six to eight people and the topics were dealt with on a question-and-answer basis after the guest speaker had outlined his views.

Concurrently, subcommittee members also briefed themselves on what other cities had done and were doing to solve their metropolitan problems. This was accomplished by assembling material on such topics as the Toronto plan,[1] the Cincinnati study,[2] etc., which was passed around to members.

Once the subcommittees had concluded their respective studies, the full committee then held sessions at which speakers outlined various forms of metropolitan government. To date this committee has heard from speakers describing the Toronto plan, county-city consolidation, the Atlanta plan, the Baton Rouge plan and a talk by the executive secretary of the State Association of County Commissioners, who presented his views on possible solutions to metropolitan problems through the use of existing county government.

The committee is now attempting to reach conclusions. There are seven possibilities which they will consider. These are:

1. *A continuation of the present system* with the city of Seattle encompassing part of the metropolitan area and with a suburban fringe governed by a number of small cities and special districts (status quo).

2. *Direct annexation* of substantially all the metropolitan area by the city of Seattle.

3. *Performance of metropolitan functions and services by the city of Seattle*

---

[1] See "Metropolitan Area Merges," by Eric Hardy, the REVIEW, July 1953, page 326.

[2] See *The Cincinnati Area Must Solve Its Metropolitan Problems*, by Doris D. Reed and Thomas H. Reed. A Report to the Stephen H. Wilder Foundation. Cincinnati, 1953.

throughout the metropolitan area with only limited direct annexation.

4. *Creation of a series of metropolitan special districts* to handle certain serious problems (water, sewer, etc.) common to the metropolitan area.

5. *Creation of a single metropolitan government* charged with the duty of handling common problems within the area while leaving local functions to the individual cities and towns.

6. *Consolidation of the city and county governments* within the metropolitan area and the performance of all governmental functions within that area by the consolidated government.

7. *Performance of a limited number of functions* by combined city-county agencies while leaving the balance of functions to be performed by existing governmental units.

When the Municipal League decided to make a study of the Seattle metropolitan area and its problems it was as though it had suddenly turned on a faucet. Instead of water this faucet is gushing forth a torrent of ideas and enthusiasm.

Formation of a metropolitan advisory council to study Seattle's fringe area problems and suggest possible remedies has been recommended to Mayor Allan Pomeroy, the city council and the board of commissioners of King County by the Municipal League's board of trustees. The trustees suggest that the advisory council consist of fourteen persons, seven from the city and seven from the county. Mayor Pomeroy has already agreed to the suggestion.

DON BECKER, *Publicity Director*
Municipal League of Seattle
and King County

Parking as a Business Factor

The results of the first phase of the research project on *Parking as a Factor in Business,* directed by the Highway Research Board, have been made available

in published form.[1] This is the first fundamental research effort addressed to the relationship between the adequacy of parking and the use of the automobile upon retail trade and real estate values. The detailed studies were made at the Universities of Michigan, California and Washington and Ohio State University. The second phase will include studies of shopper and merchant attitudes in two additional cities and analysis of business trends in areas which have added parking accommodations.

Michigan Summer Forum

To bridge the gap between theory and practice in politics, the Ninth Annual Summer Forum in State and Local Government in Michigan will be offered for graduate and undergraduate credit by the Departments of Secondary Education and Political Science at Michigan State College, July 6-23, 1954.

Sponsoring or cooperating groups include the Department of Public Instruction, the Michigan Institute of Local Government, the Michigan Municipal League, as well as Michigan's leading colleges and universities.

Over one hundred of Michigan's political and academic leaders will meet in panel sessions to discuss current governmental affairs. Topics to be aired include:

[1] *Parking as a Factor in Business: Preface, Foreword* (A Review of Major Findings), *Table of Contents;* Part 1. *Attitudes Toward Parking and Related Conditions in Columbus,* by C. T. Jonassen; Part 2: *Economic Relationships of Parking to Business in Seattle Metropolitan Area,* by Louis C. Wagner; Part 3: *Relationship Between Downtown Automobile-Parking Conditions and Retail-Business Decentralization,* by William J. Watkins; Part 4: *Central City Property Values in San Francisco and Oakland,* by Paul F. Wendt; Part 5: *Trends in Economic Activity and Transportation in San Francisco Bay Area,* by David A. Revzan. *Summary.* Washington, D. C., National Research Council, Highway Research Board, 1953. xxv, 321 pp. $6.00.

Are states' rights threatened by the developments of the last two decades?

What is being done to solve the "fringe" area problems?

Do we need to broaden the base of participation and financing of our political parties?

How adequately is Michigan meeting the needs of education at the primary, secondary and higher education levels?

What is the role being played by the President's and Governor's Commissions on Intergovernmental Relations?

As a special feature of the forum this summer, state, national and local officials of the two national parties and interest groups will discuss party organization, nominations, elections and lobbying in the afternoon sessions.

Programs listing discussion topics and participants are available.

Recreation Research

The National Recreation Association has established a national clearing house on research in recreation, at the urgent request of its National Advisory Committee on Recreation Research, composed of 48 recreation and park executives and educators. The chief function of the clearing house is to serve as a center where information concerning research is assembled, classified, appraised, tabulated and made available. Only items relating to the field of recreation (including parks) will be recorded, primarily those of interest and value to persons concerned with community recreation. The association's address is 315 Fourth Avenue, New York 10, N. Y.

Strictly Personal

The American Social Hygiene Association awarded a life honorary membership to Edward G. Conroy, executive vice-president of the San Antonio Research and Planning Council, "in recognition of his indispensable leadership for better government and a more wholesome environment for San Antonio."

Annual Reports

22ND ANNUAL REPORT. CITIZENS BUDGET COMMISSION. For the Year Ending December 31, 1953. New York 17, The Commission, 1954. 36 pp.

Research Pamphlets and Articles

Accounting

A MANUAL OF ACCOUNTING AND FINANCIAL PROCEDURES IN IOWA TOWNS AND CITIES. By Warren E. Marley. Iowa City, State University of Iowa, Institute of Public Affairs, in cooperation with the League of Iowa Municipalities, 1954. 96 pp. $2.00.

Annexation

MUNICIPAL ANNEXATION IN FLORIDA. By William C. Havard. Gainesville, University of Florida, Public Administration Clearing Service, 1954. 20 pp.

Budget

ANALYSIS OF THE 1954 HARRIS COUNTY BUDGET. A SURVEY REPORT. By John G. Brendel. Houston, Tax Research Association of Houston and Harris County, Inc., March 1954. 26 pp.

Daylight Saving Time

DAYLIGHT SAVING TIME IN THE U.S. Madison 2, Wisconsin Legislative Reference Library, October 1953. 7 pp.

Education

SCHOOL SPENDING AND SCHOOL GROWTH. Use of New State Funds Further Studied. By E. Maxwell Benton. Los Angeles 14, California Taxpayers' Association, The Tax Digest, February, 1954. 14 pp.

A UNITED EFFORT ON A COMMON PROBLEM. The School Boards of Glenolden and Norwood Jointly Analyze Their Future School Building Needs. Philadelphia 7, Pennsylvania Economy League, Inc., 1954. 78 pp.

U. S. PUBLIC SCHOOLS: How WELL DO THEY TEACH OUR CHILDREN? New York 36, Newsweek Club and Educational Bureaus, *Platform*, January 1954. 23 pp. 25 cents.

Election Handbook

GUIDEBOOK FOR COUNTY AND PRECINCT ELECTION OFFICIALS for Use in the 1954 Primary and General Elections. By Henry W. Lewis. Chapel Hill, University of North Carolina, Institute of Government, 1954. 96 pp. $1.00. .

Hospitals

ADMINISTRATIVE S U R V E Y OF THE WAYNE COUNTY GENERAL HOSPITAL AND INFIRMARY—ELOISE, MICHIGAN. Detroit 26, Citizens Research Council of Michigan, March 1954. 217 pp.

Incentives to Industry

MUNICIPAL INITIATIVE IMPERATIVE IN INDUSTRIAL PROMOTION. By J. T. Benoit. Nashville, Tennessee Municipal League, *Tennessee Town & City*, February 1954. 3 pp.

Local Legislation

REPORT ON A SURVEY OF THE PROBLEM OF CURTAILING EXCESSIVE LOCAL LEGISLATION. Montgomery, Alabama, Legislative Reference Service, December 1953. 11 pp.

Metropolitan Areas

A CASE FOR SATELLITE TOWNS. A presentation made by the Community Planning Association of Canada to the Fifteenth Annual Conference of the Canadian Federation of Mayors and Municipalities at Calgary, July 3, 1952. Ottawa, Community Planning Association of Canada, 1953. 24 pp. 25 cents.

Migration

PEOPLE COME—AND PEOPLE GO. 23-Year Migration Pattern for California. By Hugh H. Brown. Los Angeles 14, California Taxpayers' Association, *The Tax Digest*, March 1954. 7 pp.

Municipal Government

THE GOVERNMENT OF UNIVERSITY CITY: A PROGRESS REPORT. St. Louis 1, Governmental Research Institute, *Dollars and Sense in Government*, March 17, 1954. 4 pp.

Municipal Insurance

INSURANCE PROGRAMS IN MICHIGAN MUNICIPALITIES. Ann Arbor, Michigan Municipal League, 1954. 79 pp. $3.50.

Population

POPULATION PATTERNS IN THE MARYLAND-WASHINGTON REGIONAL DISTRICT. Silver Spring (Maryland), The Maryland-National Capital Park and Planning Commission, 1954. 13 pp.

Primary

THE DIRECT PRIMARY AND PARTY STRUCTURE: A Study of State Legislative Nominations. By V. O. Key, Jr. Washington, D. C., American Political Science Association, *American Political Science Review*, March 1954. 26 pp.

Public Administration

PUBLIC ADMINISTRATION IN INDIA. Report of a Survey. By Paul H. Appleby. New Delhi, India, Manager of Publications, Delhi, 1953. 66 pp. As.-/8/- or 9d.

REFLECTIONS OF A LAW PROFESSOR ON INSTRUCTION AND RESEARCH IN PUBLIC ADMINISTRATION: AN EXCHANGE. By Joseph P. Harris. (Discussion by Joseph P. Harris of Kenneth Culp Davis' article which appeared on pages 728-52 of September 1953 issue, followed by Kenneth Culp Davis' reply.) Washington, D. C., American Political Science Association, *American Political Science Review*, March 1954. 12 pp.

Public Health

HEALTH AND HOME RULE. Philadelphia 4, University of Pennsylvania, Associated Institutes of Government of Pennsylvania Universities, *Horizons for Modern Pennsylvania Local Government*, April 1954. 2 pp.

ILLINOIS PUBLIC HEALTH ORGANIZATION. Springfield, Illinois Legislative Council, 1954. 45 pp.

Public Welfare

FEDERAL PARTICIPATION IN UTAH'S PUBLIC ASSISTANCE PROGRAMS. Salt Lake City 1, Utah Foundation, *Research Report*, March 1954. 4 pp.

PUBLIC WELFARE PROGRAMS IN NORTH

CAROLINA. A Guidebook for County Commissioners. By John Alexander McMahon. Chapel Hill, University of North Carolina, Institute of Government, 1954. 122 pp. $1.50.

REPORTS ON WELFARE: SIZE AND SCOPE OF THE PROGRAM. BASIC WELFARE POLICY CHANGES ARE NEEDED. RELATIVE RESPONSIBILITY—LIEN, RECOVERY NEEDED. Baton Rouge, Public Affairs Research Council of Louisiana, Inc., *PAR*, January 15, March 5, and March 12, 1954. 16 pp. each.

Retirement

SUMMARY OF A COMPREHENSIVE RETIREMENT PROGRAM FOR THE EMPLOYEES OF THE CITY OF PHILADELPHIA. Philadelphia 7, Bureau of Municipal Research, 1954. 6 pp.

Salaries

1954 MICHIGAN MUNICIPAL WAGES AND SALARIES. Salary and Wage Data, Michigan Cities and Villages over 4,000 Population. Hours of Work, Overtime Pay Practices, Holiday Pay Practices, and Uniform Allowance Policy. Ann Arbor, Michigan Municipal League, April 1954. 121 pp. $3.50.

State Aid

WHAT IS STATE AID? Detroit 26, Citizens Research Council of Michigan, *Council Comments*, March 17, 1954. 2 pp.

Streets and Highways

WHAT OF GOVERNMENT'S ROLE IN HIGHWAY AID PROGRAMS? New Demands for Greater Federal Assistance Raise Many Questions Today. New York 20, The Tax Foundation, Inc., *Tax Review*, March 1954. 4 pp.

Surveys

THE CITY GETS A CHECK-UP. A Summary of the Reports of the Mayor's Committee on Management Survey and the Temporary State Commission to Study the Organizational Structure of the City of New York. With a Note on Progress. New York 38, Citizens Union Research Foundation, Inc., 1954. 15 pp.

Taxation and Finance

CALIFORNIA PROPERTY TAX BASE. I—TOTAL VALUATION. II—SECURED AND UNSECURED. III—KINDS OF EXEMPTIONS. By Richard Winter. Los Angeles 14, California Taxpayers' Association, *The Tax Digest*, February 1954. 7 pp.

FEDERAL LIMITATIONS ON THE TERRITORIAL TAXING POWER. By Henry T. Awans. Honolulu, University of Hawaii, Legislative Reference Bureau, December 1953. 28 pp.

FINANCING A NEW MUNICIPAL SERVICES BUILDING. Philadelphia 7, Bureau of Municipal Research, *Citizens' Business*, March 22, 1954. 4 pp.

FISCAL PROBLEMS OF URBAN GROWTH IN CALIFORNIA. Part Seven. Report of the Senate Interim Committee on State and Local Taxation. San Francisco, The Committee, June 1953. xyii, 253 pp.

$180,000,000 BUDGETED FOR 1954 BY 82 MILWAUKEE LOCAL TAXING BODIES COMPARES WITH $136,000,000 BUDGETED FOR 1951 BY 89 MILWAUKEE LOCAL TAXING BODIES. (Third in annual series on tax rates, assessments and budgets.) Milwaukee 2, Citizens' Governmental Research Bureau, Inc., *Bulletin*, April 23, 1954. 3 pp.

STATE AND LOCAL GOVERNMENT SPENDING: HOW FAST WILL IT RISE? Evidence Indicates Outlays Will Continue to Mount. By Roger A. Freeman. New York 20, Tax Foundation, Inc., *Tax Review*, February 1954. 4 pp.

TAX EXEMPTIONS AND LIABILITIES OF MUNICIPALITIES. A compilation showing federal taxes from which municipalities are exempt and for which they are liable with particular emphasis on excise taxes. By Randy H. Hamilton. Chicago 37, American Municipal Association, 1954. 8 pp. 50 cents.

Urban Redevelopment

SLUM CLEARANCE AND URBAN REDEVELOPMENT. By Gerald Gimre. Nashville, Tennessee Municipal League, *Tennessee Town & City*, March 1954. 2 pp.

Books in Review

LOCAL GOVERNMENT STRUCTURE IN THE UNITED STATES. By Bureau of the Census, Governments Division. Washington, D. C., Superintendent of Documents, U. S. Government Printing Office, 1954. 91 pp. 50 Cents.

LOCAL GOVERNMENT IN METROPOLITAN AREAS. Washington, D. C., U. S. Department of Commerce, Bureau of the Census, Governments Division, 1954. 24 pp. 25 Cents.

With the publication of two new special studies in its state and local government series, the Governments Division of the Bureau of the Census has made another valuable contribution to the basic information available on local governments. These studies are companion pieces to the statistical report, *Governments in the United States in 1952*.

The earlier report provided a tabulation of all local governments broken down by states and county areas. *Local Government Structure* "describes the definitions, criteria and standards applied by the Census Bureau in classifying governmental units and provides for each state, the District of Columbia, Alaska, Hawaii and Puerto Rico a summary description of each kind of local governmental unit for which there is legal authorization."

Local Government in Metropolitan Areas provides a tabulation of the major types of governmental units in each of the 168 standard metropolitan areas with a breakdown of each by the component county areas. In addition it includes a listing of the local governments and governmental agencies serving cities of 250,000 or more. This section of the report brings up to date the listing for the larger cities which appeared in *Governmental Units Overlying City Areas* (1947).

The publication of the descriptions of the types of governmental units state by state in *Local Government Structure* goes

a long way to clarifying certain misimpressions which may be gained by the bare tabulations of the 1952 study. Although the introduction to that study indicated generally the variation in the status of units of the same name in different states, an explanation of specific variations requires the more complete treatment provided by the new study.

The almost impossible task of distinguishing between the several meanings of the word "township" as used in different states has been faced but not quite accomplished. In the next tabulation of units of government consideration should be given to the inclusion of some townships in the "municipality" category. For example, it is impossible to make a distinction in anything but the name between townships and units classed as "municipalities" in New Jersey.

Particularly useful features of the report on structure are the sections dealing with special districts and subordinate agencies and areas which make up some two-thirds of the total text. The legal status of the principal categories of special districts in all the states is defined. Many special districts are named individually and briefly described. Listing under each state of subordinate agencies and areas which are not classified for census purposes as separate governments emphasizes the increasing fragmentation of local government. It is hoped that the ready availability of this information will stimulate a thorough-going review of the problem of functional fragmentation and its effects upon responsible government.

WILLIAM N. CASSELLA, JR.

THE AMERICAN ELECTORAL COLLEGE. By Roger Lea MacBride. Caldwell (Idaho), The Caxton Printers, Ltd., 1953. 89 pp. 75 cents.

This is a compact review of this subject for laymen and students and a comparison of the disadvantages and hazards of various alternative reforms. The author favors election of presidential electors by congressional districts with two statewide electors chosen in the same way as senators plus due attention by Congress to the dangers of gerrymandering in congressional districts.

THE SELECTMEN-MANAGER FORM OF ADMINISTRATION FOR GREENWICH. Gre:n-wich (Connecticut), The League of Women Voters, Greenwich Chamber of Commerce, Greenwich Taxpayers Association, 1954. 45 pp. (Free to campaign committees from the National Municipal League.)

This pamphlet is a temporary campaign document widely distributed in Greenwich to arouse local citizen support for the creation of a city manager position under the board of selectmen. Its significance here is in the skill of this unique presentation in hooking and holding reader attention with only a few big-letter phrases on each page. The National Municipal League cornered 50 copies to dole out for the inspiration of campaign committees elsewhere.

R. S. C.

BUREAUCRACY AND DEMOCRATIC GOVERNMENT. Edited by James C. Charlesworth. Philadelphia, The American Academy of Political and Social Science, The Annals, March 1954. 157 pp. $2.00.

To all those who are concerned with controlling government and its size, this issue of The Annals will prove most interesting. The sixteen articles are addressed to such questions as these: how bureaucracies develop and function, their size and cost, how to make them responsible, recruitment and training of bureaucrats, and how the legislature can retain control of the bureaucracy.

Emphasis is placed on the American scene. However, generalizations on bureaucracy wherever found, as substantiated by both European and American ex-

perience, are made by Arnold Brecht. Taylor Cole devotes an article to recent European developments of interest to students of American bureaucracy.

Members of the National Municipal League will be particularly interested in "Citizen Organization for Control of Government" by Richard S. Childs. Authors of other articles are: Harry Flood Byrd, Peter H. Odegard, James L. McCamy, Wallace S. Sayre, O. Glenn Stahl, Marshall E. Dimock, Charles E. Gilbert and Max M. Kampelman, James Hart, Herbert A. Simon, Edgar Lane, Edwin O. Stene, William S. Carpenter and Paul H. Appleby.

JOHN P. KEITH

PUBLIC SCHOOL FINANCING IN NEW JERSEY. Seventh Report of The Commission on State Tax Policy. Trenton, the Commission, 1954. xii, 189 pp.

At the direction of the 1953 New Jersey legislature, the Commission on State Tax Policy reported the results of its extensive survey, Public School Financing, to the legislature in March of this year.

The tasks facing the commission were: to distribute equitably an amount of state funds among 550 school districts, many of which were facing financial hardship; to determine the scope of additional state funds necessary; to recommend a tax program for raising these funds.

The state distribution formula includes a foundation program of $200 per pupil in average resident enrollment, from which is deducted the local district share (50 cents per $100 on full value of real estate; 50 cents per $100 on assessed value of railroad property and tangible personal property; plus 25 per cent of non-property "shared" taxes). No school district, however, would receive less than the minimum program of $50 per pupil provided it expends $200 per pupil, or levies an amount equal to its share for the support of its schools.

Certain special aids outside the equalization formula would be eliminated, for example, aid for dependent children, manual training and adult education. Other features of the program are: a reduction of the local share of regional high schools for ten years; $50 per pupil payments to vocational schools; special class aid of $2,000 per class plus regular equalization aid.

Suggested sources of revenue are: an increase of corporation franchise tax from .8 of a mill to 1.6 mills on the first $100,000,000 of net worth yielding $9,000,000; an increase from three to four cents per gallon on gasoline yielding $14,000,000; an increase from 12 per cent to 15 per cent on pari-mutuel betting yielding $8,000,000. This total yield of $31,000,000 is more than adequate to implement the commission's program. If effected, this program will nearly double the amount of state financial assistance currently extended to public schools in New Jersey, bringing state aid to $58,333,000 as against a total expenditure for schools in 1952-53 of $265,406,939.

DONALD B. MOORE
Director of Research
State Federation of District Boards
of Education of New Jersey

Additional Books and Pamphlets

(See also Researcher's Digest and other departments)

Adult Education

ADULT EDUCATION. THE COMMUNITY APPROACH. By Paul H. Sheats, Clarence D. Jayne and Ralph B. Spence. New York 19, The Dryden Press, 1953. xiii, 530 pp. $5.75.

RURAL SOCIAL SYSTEMS AND ADULT EDUCATION. A Committee Report, Charles P. Loomis, Chairman. (Resulting from a Study Sponsored by The Association of Land Grant Colleges and Universities and The Fund for Adult Education Established by the Ford Foundation.) East Lansing, Michigan State College Press, 1953. viii, 392 pp. $5.00.

Census Bureau

APPRAISAL OF CENSUS PROGRAMS. Report of the Intensive Review Committee to the Secretary of Commerce. Washington, D. C., Superintendent of Documents, U. S. Government Printing Office, 1954. 119 pp. 45 cents.

Child Welfare

CHILDREN IN COURT. By Helen W. Puner. New York 16, Public Affairs Committee, 1954. 28 pp. 25 cents.

The Community

THE QUEST FOR COMMUNITY. A Study in the Ethics of Order and Freedom. By Robert A. Nisbet. New York, Oxford University Press, 1953. x, 303 pp. $5.00.

Congress

THE LEGISLATIVE STRUGGLE. A Study in Social Combat. By Bertram M. Gross. New York, McGraw-Hill Book Company, 1953. xviii, 472 pp. $6.50.

Constitution

AMERICAN CONSTITUTIONAL CUSTOM: A Forgotten Factor in the Founding. By Burleigh Cushing Rodick. New York, Philosophical Library, 1953. xx, 244 pp. $4.75.

Crime

FINAL REPORT OF THE CALIFORNIA SPECIAL CRIME STUDY COMMISSION ON ORGANIZED CRIME. Sacramento, The Commission, 1953. 131 pp.

Education

LET'S EXAMINE OUR SCHOOL DISTRICTS. Lincoln (Nebraska), State Committee for the Reorganization of School Districts, 1953. 12 pp.

Election Methods

THE WARD SYSTEM OF ELECTION OF CITY COUNCILMEN. Minneapolis 14, Municipal Reference Bureau and League of Minnesota Municipalities, December 1953. 6 pp.

Fire Departments

MANUAL FOR VOLUNTEER FIRE DEPARTMENTS IN WISCONSIN. (Revised.) Madison 3, League of Wisconsin Municipalities, 1954. 42 pp. $1.00.

Grading

BLOCK AND LOT GRADING. Washington, D. C., Urban Land Institute, *Urban Land*, February 1954. 7 pp.

Group Dynamics

GROUP DYNAMICS. Research and Theory. Edited by Dorwin Cartwright and Alvin Zander. Evanston, Illinois, Row, Peterson and Company, 1953. xiii, 642 pp.

Land Use

LAND USE TODAY IN SACRAMENTO. A Tentative Generalized Land Use Plan—a Part of the Master Plan. Sacramento, City Planning Commission, 1953. 34 pp. Illus. 75 Cents.

Legal Aid

THE LEGAL AID SOCIETY, NEW YORK CITY, 1876-1951. By Harrison Tweed. New York, The Legal Aid Society, 1954. ix, 122 pp.

Planning

CITY PLANNING IN THE SOUTH: THE FINDINGS AND RECOMMENDATIONS OF THE SOUTHERN REGIONAL CONGRESS ON CITY PLANNING, August 17-19, 1953, Roanoke, Virginia. Atlanta (Georgia), Southern Regional Education Board, 1954. 152 pp.

COMPREHENSIVE PLAN FOR THE CORPUS CHRISTI AREA. By Harland Bartholomew and Associates. Corpus Christi (Texas), Chamber of Commerce, Area Development Committee, 1953. 90 pp. $4.00.

Police

NEW GOALS IN POLICE MANAGEMENT. Edited by Bruce Smith. Philadelphia, American Academy of Political and Social Science, *The Annals*, January 1954. vi, 158 pp. $2.00.

Political Parties

THE WEST VIRGINIA DELEGATION TO THE REPUBLICAN NATIONAL CONVENTION 1952. By Franklin L. Burdette. College Park, University of Maryland, Department of Government and Politics, 1953. 21 pp.

Population

ESTIMATES OF THE POPULATION OF THE UNITED STATES, BY AGE, COLOR AND SEX, 1950 to 1953. Washington 25, D. C., U. S. Department of Commerce, Bureau of the Census, 1954. 12 pp.

Public Administration

PUBLIC POLICY. A Yearbook of the Graduate School of Public Administration, Harvard University. Part I. Subsidy Problems; Part II. Problems of the Bureaucracy; Part III. Studies in Comparative Government and Civil Rights; Part IV. Book Reviews. Edited by C. J. Friedrich and J. K. Galbraith. Cambridge, Massachusetts, Harvard University, Graduate School of Public Administration, 1953. xi, 292 pp.

Public Records

RECORDS RETENTION SCHEDULE FOR MUNICIPAL AND COUNTY OFFICES. Trenton 7, New Jersey Department of Education, Division of the State Library, Archives and History, 1953. 3 pp.

Public Works

THE ALASKA PUBLIC WORKS ACT. Anchorage, League of Alaskan Cities, 1954. 23 pp.

Purchasing

CENTRALIZED PURCHASING OF GAS, OIL AND TIRES IN IOWA CITY, IOWA. By Robert E. Myers. Iowa City, Office of City Manager, 1954. 10 pp.

Recession

DEFENSE AGAINST RECESSION: POLICY FOR GREATER ECONOMIC STABILITY. A Statement on National Policy by The Research and Policy Committee. New York 22, Committee for Economic Development, 1954. 53 pp.

Salaries

SALARIES OF STATE PUBLIC HEALTH WORKERS, August 1953. Washington, D. C., U. S. Department of Health, Education and Welfare, Public Health Service, Bureau of State Services, December 1953. 55 pp.

School Insurance
SCHOOL INSURANCE FACTS FOR SCHOOL BOARD MEMBERS. Part I: INSURING AGAINST MATERIAL DAMAGE; Part II: INSURING AGAINST LIABILITY. Trenton, State Federation of District Boards of Education of New Jersey (undated). 20 and 16 pp. respectively. 35 cents each.

Shopping Districts
CONSERVATION AND REHABILITATION OF MAJOR SHOPPING DISTRICTS. By Richard Lawrence Nelson and Frederick T. Aschman. Washington 6, D. C., Urban Land Institute, 1954. 44 pp. $5.00.

THE PERIMETER PLAN FOR REHABILITATION OF MAJOR SHOPPING CENTERS. Chicago, Plan Commission, 1953. 9 pp. Illus.

State Government
YOUR CALIFORNIA GOVERNMENTS IN ACTION. (A government textbook for use in California schools.) By Winston W. Crouch and John C. Bollens. Berkeley and Los Angeles, University of California Press, 1954. 296 pp. $2.75.

State-local Relations
ARE THE STATES DOMINATING THE CITIES? By James F. Murray, Jr., George N. Craig and David Lawrence. New York 36, The Town Hall, Inc., Town Meeting of the Air, February 16, 1954. 16 pp. 25 cents.

Toll Roads
TOLL HIGHWAYS ARE LEGISLATIVE ISSUE IN MANY STATES. By Editorial Staff. New Haven, Connecticut, Institute of Traffic Engineers, *Traffic Engineering*, July 1953. 4 pp. 40 cents.

TOLL ROAD BOOM. 10,000 Miles for $10,000,000,000. By Henry K. Evans. Washington, D. C., *Nation's Business*, March 1954. 6 pp. (For reprints apply Chamber of Commerce of the United States, Washington 6, D. C., $2.00 per hundred postpaid.)

YEAR-END ROUNDUP OF TOLL ROAD TRENDS. By Editorial Staff. New Haven,

Connecticut, Institute of Traffic Engineers, *Traffic Engineering*, January 1954. 3 pp. 40 cents.

Traffic
FACING UP TO CLEVELAND'S TRAFFIC PROBLEMS. An Appraisal of Street and Traffic Functions, with Recommendations for Positive Steps to Improve Administration. Cleveland, Office of the Mayor, 1953. 42 pp. Illus.

Traffic Safety
WHAT EVERY DRIVER AND PEDESTRIAN MUST KNOW! A Digest of Traffic Code, City of Milwaukee. Milwaukee 2, Safety Commission, 1954. 48 pp.

PLANNING FOR CIVIL DEFENSE
(Continued from page 283)
to the national interest, location decisions may have to be made by other than management."

The *Times* article (April 25, 1954) noted: "Some trouble was foreseen on the resolutions, since they conflict in some cases with promotional plans by which Chambers of Commerce in cities within recognized target areas are endeavoring to attract new industries. The recent slump in economic activity has intensified the efforts of many Chambers to draw industries to their areas."

The tug of war between local and national interests is a normal feature of our federal system in both the public and private sectors. Yet, it would seem that a greater degree of self-restraint on the one hand and a greater degree of federal (or national) leadership on the other are essential if the vital interests of the defense of all are to be advanced in the age of the atom.

INSIDE THE OFFICE . . .

Charles Edison, chairman of the League's Council, spent an afternoon in the office recently discussing the League's activities with Executive Director Alfred Willoughby. . . . **Thomas J. Graves,** liaison director of the federal Commission on Intergovernmental Relations, visited the staff to confer on aspects of the commission's work . . .

Charles Edison and Alfred Willoughby

"Citizens at Work," the NML weekly radio series at 1 p.m. Sundays over NBC, has brought in many favorable comments from listeners. The League has arranged to sell and rent recordings of the half-hour broadcasts for $7.50 and $3.50 respectively. Present line-up for upcoming programs are June 6 — Kansas City, Missouri; June 13 — Brookfield, Illinois; June 20 — New Orleans, and June 27 — Roanoke.

Authors **Karl Detzer,** League Council member, and **Frank Denman** visited the new NML offices. . . . **Robert M. Goodrich,** executive director of the Rhode Island Public Expenditure Council, talked over local problems with the staff. . . . **Donald B. Moore,** research director of the State Federation of District Boards of Education of New Jersey, called on John P. Keith and other staff members. . . . **Mrs. Siegel W.**

Judd, League regional vice president, talked with Alfred Willoughby and John Bebout about Michigan affairs.

Mrs. Pearl F. Richardson, of the General Federation of Women's Clubs, talked with the staff about problems in connection with a projected national conference on the community. . . . **Dr. Ernest S. Bradford** and **Stanley Renton** of the Charter League of New Rochelle, New York, and **Bernard Margolis,** president of the New Rochelle Taxpayers Association, conferred with the staff on local problems. Two new publications have been issued by the NML — a 64-page report for 1953 with a directory of officers and a 6-page membership invitation folder.

Karl Detzer, John Bebout and Alfred Willoughby.

Assistant Director **John Bebout** recently attended the session on "Federal Government: Its Character, Prestige and Problems," held under the auspices of Columbia University's American Assembly at Arden House, Harriman, New York. . . . Senior Associate **John P. Keith** addressed a meeting of the Woodbridge, New Jersey, Township Civic Association and discussed with the group a school building program and general town planning questions.

NML Moves

League spring cleaning was circumvented this year by leaving the offices in the city hall area and moving to midtown Manhattan at Fifth Avenue and 45th Street. The operation was carried out over the weekend of May 1. No casualties were reported.

The move involved more than 20,000 library volumes, 40-odd filing cabinets of pamphlets and clippings, tons of publications and office equipment and seventeen weary NML staff members.

On the morning of May 3 the staff reported at the new 542 Fifth Avenue office amid the toxic gas of fresh paint, the harassing action of telephone men and hammering carpenters still at work on bookcases and shelving. In a short time hundreds of boxes were unpacked and the office was shipshape to receive several officers and Council members who dropped in after the spring Council meeting on May 7.

Bruna Norsa, League research librarian, ch one of the 160 boxes which were filled with NML's book collection in the old office prio the move.

Gallup in New Post

George H. Gallup, League president, has been appointed to the Advisory Committee on Local Government for the federal Commission on Intergovernmental Relations.

Chairman of the committee is former governor of Louisiana, Sam H. Jones. Other members include Mayor Glenn S. Allen, Jr., Kalamazoo, Michigan; Mayor William E. Kemp of Kansas City, Missouri, president of the American Municipal Association; Tom Kleppe, former mayor of Bismarck, North Dakota; Mayor Henry Pirtle, Cleveland Heights, Ohio; Mayor Elmer E. Robinson of San Francisco, president. of the United States Conference of Mayors; Mayor Hubert Schouten, Keokuk, Iowa; G. A. Treakle, president of the National Association of County Officials; and Richard J. White, Jr., county commissioner of Milwaukee County, Wisconsin.

National Chamber Meeting Features NML Officers

Seven officers and Council members of the League took an active part in the 42nd annual meeting of the Chamber of Commerce of the United States, April 26-28, in Washington, D. C.

Hon. Barry M. Goldwater, regional vice president and U. S. Senator from Arizona, addressed the labor relations luncheon on "State and Community Developments."

Six of the participants were Council members. H. Bruce Palmer spoke at the annual dinner meeting of former national officers of the U. S. Junior Chamber of Commerce. Rob Roy Macleod spoke on "Business Meets the Challenge" in a panel discussion on intergovernmental relations. Thomas R. Reid addressed a Jaycee reunion meeting. Mark S. Matthews and E. Bartlett Brooks were delegates from the Greenwich, Connecticut, and Dayton, Ohio, chambers, respectively. Karl Detzer was on hand to obtain material for a *Reader's Digest* article.

W. M. Shepherd of Little Rock, Arkansas, member of the League's Finance Committee, was also present as was Allen H. Seed, Jr., League assistant director.

NEWS for League Members

Conference Gets Town Meeting of Air

America's Town Meeting of the Air will originate on November 9 at the League's 60th National Conference on Government which will be held November 7-10 at Kansas City.

The broadcast, main feature of the dinner meeting, will be over the national radio hookup of 325 stations affiliated with the American Broadcasting Company. Two speakers at the Conference will be selected to discuss ·a current issue in the field of local or state government. Moderator for the discussion, which will include a period of questions from the audience, will be James F. Murray, Jr. The program will run from 8:00 to 8:45 P.M., Central Standard Time.

Several topics have been tentatively suggested but League members and others are invited to submit additional ideas. Among the topics under consideration are "Crime and Politics," "State Legislature and City Relationships," "Is the Spoils System Necessary?," "Are Our Political Ethics Improving?" and "The People's Right to Know." The topic chosen will be announced shortly before the Conference.

Other plans for the Kansas City meeting have been moving forward. On Sunday, November 7, a tour of Kansas City for Conference delegates will take place followed by a buffet supper, weather permitting, at the Saddle and Sirloin Club. Otherwise, the supper will be held in the Little Theater at the Municipal Auditorium. A tour of the Nelson Art Gallery and tea are also being arranged for women delegates during the Conference period.

Gallup Appoints Nominating Committee

A nominating committee of five League members has been appointed by President George H. Gallup to recommend candidates for officers and Council members for election at the annual membership meeting to be held November 8 in connection with the 60th National Conference on Government in Kansas City.

John S. Linen

Members of the committee are: John S. Linen, League vice president, chairman; Frederick L. Bird, member of the Council; William Collins, regional vice president; Mark S. Matthews, member of the Council, and Carl H. Pforzheimer, treasurer.

The committee will make nominations to fill ten vacancies which occur annually on the Council and will recommend candidates for expiring terms among the League's officers. Mr. Linen has invited suggestions for candidates.

League Founder Dies

Charles Francis Adams, one of the League's founders, died recently in Boston. Mr. Adams, a lawyer and ex-secretary of the Navy, was one of the most distinguished Americans of his day to support the calling of the 1894 National Conference for Good City Government in Philadelphia.

Book to Be Based on NML Radio Series

As a result of the success of the "Citizens at Work" dramatized radio broadcasts by the League with the National Broadcasting Company, the Sterling Publishing Company, New York, proposes to publish a book based on the broadcasts.

The scripts, prepared by NBC writers, tell the stories of citizen accomplishments in communities which have competed in the All-America Cities contest co-sponsored by the League and *Look* magazine.

Tentatively entitled *Citizens in Action*, the book is scheduled to appear in the fall. The publishing company will aim it at teenage and adult readers, offering it especially to school systems as supplementary reading in civics, social science and government courses.

The book, which will be illustrated, will be prepared by Sterling staff writers in cooperation with the League staff and will have an introduction by Alfred Willoughby, League executive director.

Childs Appointed to Probe Medical Examiners

Richard S. Childs, chairman of the League's executive committee, was appointed on June 9 by Luther Gulick, city administrator, to look into operations of the office of the chief medical examiner of the city.

Mr. Childs supervised the preparation of the League's *Model State Medico-legal Investigative System,* which was a joint report by six leading national organizations in the fields of health, law and civil service. The New York *World Telegram and Sun* said of Mr. Childs' appointment: "With him in the driver's seat, the public may soon ex-pect the reforms that are so badly needed."

Work Begins on Model State Planning Law

The League has begun work on a model state planning law.

Planning for the conservation and optimum use of land and other resources and for meeting long-range needs for public works is recognized as an indispensable tool of modern government. Authorities agree that state planning laws generally need strengthening. The proposed model would provide for a state planning agency with adequate powers and machinery for technical assistance and guidance for regional and other local efforts.

Coleman Woodbury, author and planning consultant of South Kent, Connecticut, and the Legislative Drafting Research Fund of Columbia University have been engaged to proceed with the work.

The League has been assured of the active cooperation of public officials, professional planners and civic leaders. The decision to proceed with a model stems from a meeting on April 17 at which eleven authorities on the subject discussed the project and recommended that the League prepare model state planning legislation to be ready for consideration in 1955 legislatures.

Richard S. Childs at his desk in NML office

National Municipal Review

Volume XLIII, No. 7   Total Number 445

Published monthly except August

By NATIONAL MUNICIPAL LEAGUE

Contents for July 1954

The contents of the Review are indexed in *International Index to Periodicals*
and *Public Affairs Information Service.*

Entered as second class matter July 11, 1932, at the Post Office at Worcester,
Massachusetts. Publication office, 150 Fremont Street, Worcester 3; editorial
and business office, 542 Fifth Avenue, New York 36. Copyright 1954 by the
National Municipal League.

Subscription, $5 per year; Canadian, $5.25; foreign, $5.50;
single copies 50 cents.

Editorial Comment

The Nature of the Union

THERE has always been too much talk about the alleged conflict between state and federal governments. The original purpose and the true genius of the federal union are cooperation, not conflict.

This is not to deny the invigorating influence of competition within the system nor the salutary effects of a certain amount of checking and balancing among different governmental agencies.

But the great objects sought by the makers of the United States constitution were affirmative, to "establish justice, insure domestic tranquility, provide for the common defense, promote the general welfare, and secure the blessings of liberty." While these ends were to be served primarily by the new federal government, their achievement was to depend in large measure upon the vigor and cooperation of the states in "a more perfect Union."

Technological and economic progress has made these national objects even more vital than they were in 1787. Inevitably this has meant a very great increase in the tasks and responsibilities of government up and down the line, with a substantial increase in the relative importance of the national government. This development has naturally caused some alarm on the ground that it threatens to undermine the states as independent, self-acting elements in the system and tends toward bureaucratic centralization.

There is some justification for the alarm but too many have sought to reverse the trend by forbidding or checking government rather than by the affirmative method of strengthening state and local institutions. The corrective is to recognize the essentially cooperative nature of our federal union of 48 states. It is elementary that only the strong can cooperate. The weak are destined to be led, driven or destroyed. We know that America must be strong to survive in the modern world. The only hope for the states is for them to be strong cooperating elements in the American system.

These truths are strikingly illustrated, in two quite different but equally vital areas of governmental action, by two articles which appear in this issue of the REVIEW—"We're All in the Same Boat" and "Defense Against Recession." The first article demonstrates the necessity not only for federal-state but for federal-state-local cooperation in civil defense. The second demonstrates the need for similar cooperation in planning and financing governmental programs and activities so as to prevent or cushion unhealthy economic fluctuations.

In both fields it is apparent that a substantial amount of federal leadership and some federal financing are necessary in order to enable state and local governments to play their appointed roles. On the other hand, it is equally clear that the states and localities must be prepared to take initiatives and to exercise heavy political, financial and administrative responsibility.

Neither of these jobs can be done at all without federal participation and guidance. Neither of them can be done properly, safely or adequately without the energetic and wholehearted participation of state and local governments.

The extent and effectiveness of state and local participation and consequently the extent to which these and other modern responsibilities of government can be met without a further radical trend toward centralization will depend largely upon the states. This is true because the states occupy the strategic middle sector of our system and are the mediating element that determines to a large extent the relation between the citizen and his city, county, town or village on the one hand and the more remote central government in Washington, on the other.

The states have somewhat jeopardized their position by failing to adjust to the transformation of America from a nation of farmers and frontiersmen into the greatest urban and industrial power on earth. There are constitutional and political reasons why the federal government has in recent years often shown more responsiveness to urban needs than have most of the states. In civil defense, surely, and in defense against depression, probably, there must be some direct dealings between the federal government and local governments, particularly those in our great metropolitan areas.

There are limits, however, beyond which the states cannot be by-passed without threatening the transformation of our system from a union to a consolidation with all important political and governmental power focused at the center. One hundred and fifty years ago Jefferson pointed out that the only defense against this tendency is strong government in the states. Under modern conditions a strong state government must necessarily be one which commands the confidence of its urban citizens and responds to their legitimate needs as convincingly and as readily as it does to those of its rural citizens.

These considerations must inevitably concern the national Commission on Intergovernmental Relations and the numerous official and unofficial commissions in the states which are currently reviewing the basic responsibilities and relationships of our several levels of government. These same considerations have for some time been moving the National Municipal League to devote increasing attention to modernization of state governments and to the discovery of solutions for the complex and vexing problems of government in our metropolitan communities.

Defense Against Recession

*States, cities and groups have important part to play
in avoiding disastrous effects of boom and bust periods.*

EDITOR'S NOTE.—The article below
is made up of excerpts from *Defense
Against Recession: Policy for Greater
Economic Stability*, a statement on
national policy prepared by the Research and Policy Committee of the
Committee for Economic Development. Copies of the 49-page report
are available without charge from
CED, 444 Madison Avenue, New
York 22.

GOVERNMENT action to pro-
mote economic stability does
not require an expansion of government powers but only a better use
of the influence that government
traditionally and properly exercises
in a free society, for example,
through monetary policy. This will
not restrict the freedom of individuals and it will not restrict the
individual adjustments that are
necessary for economic efficiency
and growth. On the contrary, greater stability will give these adjustments a more favorable environment, permitting the individual to
make his own plans and adjustments
with less fear that these will be
upset by extreme fluctuations in
the economy as a whole.

The automatic tendency of government budgets to respond to an
economic decline in a stabilizing
manner is one of our main defenses
against recession. Additional steps
should be taken to confirm and
strengthen this tendency.

Some of our most important continuing backlogs of needs are for
services of state and local government such as education, health and
roads. State and local expenditures
have been rising and, in normal circumstances, would be expected to
rise further.

If there were a recession, however, the tax receipts of these governments would decline. Certain expenditures, as for relief, would rise.
Deficits would appear in current
account budgets. There would then
be pressure for retrenchment in current expenditures and for going slow
in capital outlays. This would be
unfortunate, not only from the
standpoint of stabilization but also
because of the community needs involved.

State and local governments are
ordinarily required—and it is good
practice—to balance their current
account in one-year budgets. Such
budgets should also make provision
in good times for future capital improvements. This is not normally
done and it is a great weakness in
state and municipal finance. A general surplus is difficult to accumulate and difficult to hold. It is feasible, however, to set aside annually
in good times amounts which can be
used for future capital improvements not presently required. Tax
rates adequate to do this would provide some cushion against the necessity to cut current expenditures in
a recession.

In many cases existing debt limits
would seriously restrict the ability
of state or local jurisdictions to carry on their budget programs in a
recession. These debt limits should
be reviewed and revised if justified.

If there were a serious economic decline, many governmental units would encounter great financial difficulty in carrying on their planned programs of capital expenditures. And especially, if it may become desirable to step up state and local expenditures still further as a recovery measure, steps will have to be taken not only to provide financial assistance but also to assure adequate advance planning.

Preparing for Public Works

Flexible use of state and local construction as an anti-depression instrument involves two interrelated problems, planning and finance. Apparently there is on hand a sufficient backlog of plans to keep the current rate of construction running for about a year. If state and local governments should encounter financial difficulties, however, appropriations for the preparation of drawings and specifications would be sharply cut, especially in view of the expectation, based on past experience, that at some point the federal government will step in and provide funds for planning. The interruption of the planning function at the outset of a recession would mean an interruption in actual construction after a year or so.

The development of long-run capital budgets by many cities and states and the growth of metropolitan planning techniques and staffs will help to maintain the continuity of state and local construction. These institutions could well be adopted more widely, not only for this reason but also because of their contribution to government efficiency.

At the end of World War II, and again in 1949, the federal government arranged for loans to enable state and local governments to prepare plans in advance of need. Such a program should be revived. There would probably be little activity under the program in prosperous times, but the funds would be drawn upon in time of recession and would help to sustain the volume of state and local construction.

To sustain the total volume of state and local construction in a serious recession and, even more, to bring about an increase, is likely to require federal financial aid. At least, the question of such aid will arise and it will be important to have a federal policy to deal with the situation formulated in advance. Uncertainty about federal policy in this respect would be a major obstacle to the prosecution of local projects, including projects that the local authorities could and would carry on by themselves if they were confident that no aid would be forthcoming.

We may encounter a situation in which a substantial expansion of public works is desirable, in which the most urgently needed projects are at the state-local level and in which, despite all efforts to encourage purchase of state and local securities by private investors, state-local construction would not rise and might even decline unless federal financial aid were provided. Faced with this choice, we believe that federal aid, in the form of extension of credit for state-local construction, is clearly preferable to the expansion of less urgent federal works. This aid could take the form of direct loans to the state and local governments or of the purchase of marketable securities, either directly or from other investors.

Local Problems of Recession

Every economic decline has important local aspects. Some communities and regions are hit harder than others. Even when the nation as a whole is enjoying high prosperity, some localities are depressed.

The measures we have discussed for preventing depressions and moderating recessions would, of course, help in avoiding or solving these local problems. But they are not in themselves sufficient. There is a whole area of special measures, in existence or needed, to deal with the local problems. Consideration of such measures is beyond the scope of this paper but we do wish to call attention to the need for further study and action in this field.

Steps to improve the mobility of labor illustrate one approach to this problem. In this connection the existing system of state and federal employment exchanges needs to be reexamined.

Even during the postwar boom some communities have been wrestling with a serious local unemployment problem. In some cases, voluntary cooperation of government, business, labor and civic groups has been highly effective in bringing new industries into the community and increasing local employment. Other communities have much to learn from these successful projects.

Of course it is better to foresee and forestall local unemployment problems than to wait until they become acute before trying to correct them. Communities should appraise their economic future in a systematic way, estimating the probable employment opportunities and the probable local labor force. Sometimes this will indicate a decline in certain industries. In other cases there may be insufficient growth in prospect for the expanding labor force. Discovering the facts will lay the basis for preventive action.

Unemployment Compensation

Unemployment compensation is not only a major assistance to unemployed workers but is also one of the most effective devices that can be built into the economy to make it more stable. The present unemployment compensation system could be strengthened in the three chief features that determine its effectiveness as a stabilizer—benefit rates, duration of benefits and coverage—without seriously adverse incentive effects.

The ratio of average weekly benefits to average weekly wages in covered employment has declined since 1939. The amount of weekly benefit received by an unemployed worker is higher the higher was his weekly wage, but subject to a dollar-and-cents limit on the weekly benefit. Since 1940 these top limits have risen only about half as much as weekly wages. As a result, the proportion of benefits limited by the maximum dollar-and-cents rate has greatly increased. Increasing the maximum benefit would increase the effectiveness of the system as a stabilizer of incomes.

While benefit amounts have deteriorated relative to earnings since before the war, benefit durations have improved. In 1940 there were only six states in which an unemployed worker could receive benefits for as long as twenty weeks; in 1952 there were only six states in which a worker could *not* receive twenty or more weeks of benefits, and nineteen states paid twenty-six weeks of benefits. Although the present benefit periods appear to be generally adequate for normal between-jobs unemployment and for moderate recessions, it would be desirable for the remaining states to lengthen theirs toward the benefit periods now provided by the leading states.

Unemployment Coverage

The unemployment compensation system now covers about 70 per cent of all wage and salary workers. The 30 per cent not covered includes government employees, farm hands, domestic servants, employees of non-profit organizations and employees of small firms.

For many of these categories, coverage under unemployment compensation would involve serious administrative difficulties. Some steps could be taken, however, toward increasing coverage. For example, the federal act which stimulated the establishment of state unemployment compensation systems applied to employers of eight or more persons.

Twenty-nine states have now gone beyond this and applied their systems to smaller firms and some states have no exemption based on size of firm. The experience of these states should be reviewed to see whether it may not be feasible to reduce the size-exclusion from eight to some smaller number in other states.

In total the reserves of the unemployment compensation system seem large—equal in mid-1952 to 8 per cent of annual taxable wages. For the United States as a whole, 44 per cent of covered workers could be paid all benefits due them. But in some important industrial states the reserves are quite low. If, as we suggest above, the benefit rates are increased, the margin of safety of the state funds may be reduced. In some cases unjustified drains upon the funds could be reduced by better administration and by reconsideration of eligibility rules. These benefits are, of course, paid for non-production. Every inducement should be made for the individual to seek work. Conserving the funds in these ways will offset, at least in part, the increased costs resulting from higher benefits and longer benefit periods.

Some states may find it desirable to strengthen the financial status of their funds by raising the average levels of contribution rates. In addition provision should be made for federal loans to states that are in danger of exhausting their reserves.

* * *

The determination to prevent depression is a national determination shared by all sectors of the community. The responsibility is also shared by all.

What State and Local Governments Can Do:

1. State and local governments should assess the needs for constructive, possibly revenue-producing, expenditures within their jurisdictions and should examine possible ways, including local authorities, for meeting these needs to a larger extent.

2. State and local governments should include in their annual budgets appropriate sums which are reserved for future capital improvements.

3. Many local governments operate under obsolete debt limits which would be severe obstacles to the continuity of their operations through a recession. These debt limits should be revised.

4. More jurisdictions should develop capital budgets of projects to be initiated over the next several years, a substantial part of which should be advanced to the blueprint stage. This will help maintain the volume of state and local construction, despite economic fluctuations, and would permit an increase of such construction if necessary as part of a national program in which the federal government would take the lead.

5. State governments should explore the possibility of reducing the obstacles that smaller subdivisions experience in raising funds in the national capital markets. This might be done by centralized marketing arrangements.

6. The maximum weekly amount of unemployment benefit should be raised in many states. The maximum duration of benefits should also be raised in many states toward the standards already reached in the leading states. Administration should be improved and eligibility rules reconsidered to reduce unjustified benefit payments. States that have not already done so should consider the possibility of extending unemployment compensation to workers in firms with less than eight employees.

What Local and Regional Community Organizations Can Do:

Voluntary organizations at the local level, including businessmen, local government officials and other civic leaders, can do much to stimulate constructive action by all sectors of the community. Getting the vigorous and able people in a community together generates ideas and action. In fact, all of the things we have mentioned above as desirable are more likely to get done if there is a local face-to-face group devoted to their promotion.

Where special local unemployment problems exist, voluntary groups can be effective in encouraging the development of new industries. And local groups can forestall the emergence of such problems by surveying their community's economic prospects and taking corrective action if a future deficiency of employment opportunities is revealed.

. A number of such groups already exist. During the past six years, for example, the CED has had a part in encouraging the formation and maintenance in various parts of the country of more than twenty college-community research centers. Businessmen and college professors work together on local and regional problems of current and long-range interest. Nine of these centers are currently working on problems relevant to the present report. Studies of this character are a constructive supplement to research conducted by national organizations.

What the Federal Government Can Do:

. . . . . .

6. The federal government should establish a fund for loans to state unemployment compensation funds that may be in danger of exhaustion.

7. The federal government should collect additional data on the economic situation and outlook and make the data available more promptly.

. . . . . .

11. The federal government should offer loans to state and local governments for planning construction.

12. The federal government should prepare in advance, for institution when needed, a program of credit support to state and local governments for construction.

* * *

We need confidence that the American economy will be much more stable than it has been in the past. Without such confidence, the maintenance of reasonable stability over any long period will be difficult. And, even if we succeed, the continuing thought that we will fail itself has serious consequences. It is not healthful to have the friendly part of the world awaiting the next U. S. depression with fear while the hostile part looks forward to it as the event that will turn the tide of history in its direction.

We face a challenge. Despite its many brilliant achievements, the future of our competitive enterprise system will not be secure unless we can avoid the devastating effects of boom and bust.

We face that challenge with confidence. Our economy can achieve its high potential without violent fluctuations. We base our confidence upon many facts—such as strengthening of our financial and economic structure, the longer-term perspective of business planning, the stabilizing influence of unemployment compensation and income taxation, the other powerful instruments now available and the improved understanding of their use. And, most important of all, we base our confidence upon the determination of the American people to meet the challenge.

(Official recognition by the Congressional Joint Committee on the Economic Report of one phase of the problem discussed by CED in this article appears on page 336.)

Public Works Planning

PUBLIC works is another field in which the combined efforts of the federal, state and local governments can clearly make a contribution to regularizing employment. A growing population and rising standards of living bring with them untold requirements for new public facilities of which highways, schools, hospitals and municipal facilities are only the more obvious examples. Programs for meeting these requirements can, in some measure, be accelerated in times of rising unemployment to overcome existing backlogs and, indeed, to take some forward-looking steps in advance of immediate pressing community needs. It is well, however, to keep public works in proper perspective lest they be over-rated as a ready tool quite capable of alone solving the problem of unemployment.

While it is sincerely to be hoped that at no time in the foreseeable future will the maintenance of full employment in this country be abnormally dependent upon increased public works expenditures, we are somewhat disturbed by some of the facts brought out in the President's Economic Report and in testimony before the committee. The report points out that, if it should become necessary, outlays for federal public works could be stepped up within a year by, say, two billion dollars, or one-half of federal expenditures on that account in 1953, and that similarly, if financial arrangements were adequate, state and local outlays might be expanded by another three and a half billion dollars. Expenditures in these amounts would, without question, be helpful if we should suddenly find ourselves in a seriously declining economy, but the attainment of even these moderate aggregates would be dependent upon the prompt action of the Congress and other authorizing bodies. The committee finds little confirmation for the hope that federal public works might be speeded up administratively alone in any important way.

Local communities will undoubtedly use their resources to the utmost when threatened with local unemployment, yet the fact is that most of them are bound by tax, debt or user-charge limitations. If public works are to make an important contribution in solving unemployment in a serious recession, it seems clear that the federal government's credit must be substantially relied upon. Whether this should take the pattern of loans or grants-in-aid is a problem which need not now be settled, although all will agree that reliance on federal credit must not be allowed to become a basis for encroachment upon the traditional rights of local and state communities. . . .

As an aid to getting the most possible out of public works as a device with which to counter recessions, the committee recommends proposals which would facilitate the immediate planning and coordination, through an administrator directly responsible to the president, of all federal public works and community development with the cooperation of the federal, state and local governments.

—From *Joint Economic Report* of the Joint Committee on the Economic Report, 83rd Congress, 2nd Session, House Report No. 1256.

We're All in the Same Boat

*Project East River calls for strong action at all levels
of government for defense of nation's metropolitan areas.*

EDITOR'S NOTE.—This article is
taken from the *General Report,* Part
I of the ten-volume *Report of Project
East River,* published under Signal
Corps contract by Associated Universities, New York City. Since only
1,500 copies were published, the report
is no longer available. Partly because
of this, the REVIEW is reproducing here
certain sections which it is believed
will be of particular interest to readers.

THE great strength of the American system of federalism lies in
its capacity to reconcile national
needs and central authority with diversity of local needs and conditions
and demands for local initiative
and autonomy. In the case of civil
defense, the reconciliation of national and local needs and the coordination of national and local resources must rest upon a predeter-
mined allocation of responsibilities
and the agreed-upon definition of
operating authority.

The problem of civil defense necessarily involves all levels of government. The national interest is obvious: an enemy attack upon a critical industrial city is an attack upon
the entire nation—in addition to
humanitarian considerations, the entire nation would be affected, particularly if that city were producing
some vital war material. In the
United States, transportation and
communications systems are organized on a national basis, so are
many of the great manufacturing industries. Yet attacks would be localized in their first impact and
initial operational responsibility in
the event of an attack would neces-

sarily rest with the locality (with
the personnel and other resources
immediately available).

The actual direction of disaster
operations under emergency conditions is the responsibility of the local governments. The major elements of manpower and facilities are
concentrated there and the final implementation of complete emergency
plans takes place at the local level.
Thus, operational organization for
civil defense is the first priority job
of local government. Except for reliance upon the general principle
that this organization should be developed from extensions of normal
governmental activities, adjusted according to technical information
provided from federal and state
sources, no attempt to blueprint a
uniformly applicable organizational
pattern should be made although
this should not preclude sensible
standardization.

In peacetime local governments
should receive technical and financial assistance and benefit from
national informational and educational programs undertaken at both
the state and federal level. The national programs must set the stage
for intelligent local planning and action but can never provide the essentials in manpower and organization, which remain a local function.

In an emergency, when a situation is beyond the capacity of local
government (city or county), then
the state should be expected to provide assistance, coordination and

337

direction. And, when a situation is beyond the capacity of state government, then the federal government should be expected to provide assistance, coordination and such supervisory direction as the situation dictates. This is, of course, a somewhat oversimplified concept. A more realistic view would consider a critical target as the center of a set of concentric circles covering the bulk of potential mutual aid and mobile support.

Calls for Assistance

Depending upon the intensity of the attack, calls for assistance and support would reach the inner ring of circles first and then move outward. Obviously, the implementation of this concept requires some adjustments to state and municipal jurisdictional lines. Such adjustments can be made in two ways: (1) through interstate and intermunicipal mutual aid compacts; and (2) by provision for federal coordination of support across state lines during a critical emergency. These devices can be made compatible and supplementary and are discussed below. As a general proposition, however, only essential responsibilities should be assumed by higher echelons of government; at the earliest possible moment the prerogatives of state and local governments should be restored.

The present basic civil defense organization places primary operating responsibility on state and local governments and puts the states in a position of authority that may exceed their capacity to act. The national and regional offices of the Federal Civil Defense Administration deal only with the governors and state civil defense directors. This procedure applies even with respect to the federal responsibility of assisting in the provision of basic equipment, which was a main purpose of the civil defense law. The states are in a dominant role and can either provide or deny aid to critical target municipalities.

Another feature of the present organization is an emphasis upon interstate and intermunicipal mutual-aid compacts. Such agreements are of value in that they provide for an orderly process in time of disaster when a situation does not require a governor to proclaim a state of extreme emergency. It must be recognized, however, that mutual-aid pacts are not the complete solution to mutual assistance. Their weakness lies in a situation where, because of real or anticipated local needs, a city or state would be reluctant to provide assistance even though an agreement exists. The agreements have no mandatory provisions, they contain no penalty clauses, and there is little recognition of the role that the federal government might have to play in a critical emergency. In the event of a severe enemy attack, they would be inadequate.

Other considerations—such as the national character of the transportation system, the nature of metropolitan areas that cross state lines and the need for effective control of mobile federal resources—point up the need for realistic planning for greater federal support responsibilities in a major emergency.

Civil defense is a part of national defense; it would hardly be in keeping with the war powers of the national government for federal agencies to sit idly by if some state and local governments were unable to cope with an emergency situation. It is also inconsistent for all parties concerned to make one set of plans based on the predominant authority of the states while the same parties adhere to the unspoken premise that "when the real thing comes the federal government (meaning the military) will have to take over." In fact, in the most extreme situation, if a military theater of operations were declared, the establishment of military control over civil affairs could best be effected through the permanent machinery of federal, state and local civil defense organizations rather than through separate machinery and disaster plans developed by the military.

Planning for federal-state-local action should also recognize that, although formal mechanisms may be desirable over the long term, in a critical emergency the dictates of the situation will prevail, formal channels of communication and command may be short-circuited, and a great deal of responsibility will rest upon the man on the scene. Thus, a realistic middle-ground position would provide for the greatest possible exercise of local initiative, backed up with potential federal civilian direction and control if and when necessary. It would seem desirable, for example, that the federal regional director of civil defense play a significant part in the development of interstate mutual-aid compacts, so that he could render a service in the determination of priorities and in the provision for federal support when state lines have to be crossed. In the civil defense function, full emphasis should be placed upon the elements of co-operation in the federal system; federal, state and local governments are partners in an enterprise of mutual benefit to all. Realistic planning will be based on the principle of teamwork.

Recommendations of PER

Project East River, therefore recommends that:

(1) The federal civil defense regional director should be prepared to provide additional support when the situation is beyond the capacity of state and local governments;

(2) The placing of unreasonable burdens upon state governments be avoided;

(3) The officials of fifteen top priority urban target areas be permitted to consult and plan with both federal, regional and state civil defense officials.

If implemented fully, these recommendations would go far toward achieving an effective civil defense program, particularly in terms of permitting peacetime planning that would recognize both the practical limitations and the inherent advantages of all three levels of government. Although primary operational responsibilities would still remain with state and local governments, such planning would tend to ensure a far more orderly and expeditious movement of mobile support forces across state lines to priority target areas. Certainly, in view of the analysis presented in Part III [of the report of Project East River], *The Destructive Threat of Atomic Weapons*, more immediate emphasis is needed on mobile support to cope with the problem where it is most difficult and where appropriate measures will bring the greatest return.

Critical Metropolitan Targets

The foregoing discussion can be focussed most sharply upon the metropolitan area problem, which is peculiarly difficult of solution. Even a metropolitan area completely contained within a single state presents a host of challenging problems. The use of traditional municipal corporate and/or county lines creates extraordinary complications when normal governmental functions are involved. The observance of the same boundaries creates even greater difficulties when an effort is made to develop an integrated operational plan for civil defense of a metropolitan area.

The treatment of metropolitan areas in the civil defense structure has thus far reflected the following difficulties:

(1) The traditional complexity of the metropolitan problem, including lack of a single political leadership over the entire area;

(2) The additional problems created when state boundary lines are involved;

(3) The current practice of treating all critical targets on a non-priority basis (virtually regardless of size, density of population, location, the critical nature of war industry involved, etc.);

(4) The tendency to place an unreasonable burden upon the states in a situation that might call for extensive interstate movements of supporting forces;

(5) The tendency of the states to follow jurisdictional, legalistic lines of authority and also municipal and county boundary lines; and

(6) The restrictions that prevent the federal government from dealing directly with the civil defense officials of the major cities.

The problem is well illustrated by the actual case of a large mid-western city (undoubtedly one of the first priority targets in the nation):

City X has recruited 25,000 wardens. Its officials have recruited and trained in their own facilities 7,000 police volunteers and 3,000 fire volunteers. They have requisitioned $1,000,000 worth of training equipment and organizational supplies; half of it on June 13 and December 12, 1951; have encumbered their share of the funds; but have received not one single delivery.

Two air-raid sirens have been mounted but they have been received only because the city asked the X Corporation, from which they expect to obtain their sirens, to make an advance delivery. Both the city and X Corporation hope that state and federal red tape gets cut so that the payment can be made and the warning system completed.

The warden and welfare training

manuals are all that have been received in spite of the fact that many more have been issued. Reprints have been at the city's expense. City officials have devised their own fire and police training manuals.

Administrative bulletins have been issued serially. At the time when a bulletin between No. 85 and No. 90 was the last numbered release received by the city, reference in a news release to No. 103 was noted. Upon checking with state officials, it was discovered that No. 110 was out.

Identification cards were recognized as being necessary to permit some essential movement by key personnel. After fruitless attempts to obtain state issuance, the city printed up its own. A few weeks later the state came out with a different identification card and made those devised and issued by the city useless.

Regional officials of the Federal Civil Defense Administration feel that they cannot talk with civil defense officials of City X unless the state suggests it or is present. The state office has expressed a desire to be completely cooperative and helpful, has expressed much interest in the problems of the city, but nothing has happened.

For fiscal 1952, the state had available $1,973,000, which provided some matching money and a staff of 71. In spite of this staff and a desire to be helpful, a requisition for $108,500 worth of fire equipment (boots, coats, helmets and hose), sent to the state capital in January 1952, did not get transmitted to the regional office until April 28. For fiscal 1953, the legislature appropriated $271,000, which will carry a staff of seventeen. City X's 1952 budget provided $1,500,000 and contemplates continuance of the present staff of 42 paid persons for fiscal

year 1953 although the budget for 1953 is only $779,000.

Thus City X is faced with a problem. Should it continue its efforts in the hope that something will happen that will make it possible for equipment—for which it has its share of the money on the line—to be delivered and make possible the continuance of training, exercises and drills? Or should it throw in the sponge, apologize to the volunteers who have been inconvenienced and trust to luck that there won't be any need for use of civil defense forces?

Bridging the Gap

In this atomic era some organizational means must be found to bridge the gap between the federal level and the level of the more critical target areas without impinging on the "sovereignty" of the state or the dignity of its governor. The controversial history of this problem is recognized and there may be some merit in doing informally that which would create additional difficulties if instituted formally. The danger is that the problem of metropolitan areas can never be handled on an informal basis. It is preferable, in our opinion, to face up to the problem by attempting a formal rather than an informal arrangement.

Let it be emphasized that this does not mean any diminution of the status of the state or its predominant place in the organizational hierarchy. The situation is analogous to that present in many business organizations where a new activity or one that is encountering special difficulty is dealt with directly by the head of the business even though this appears to be in direct violation of the organizational chart. It is not unusual in complex organizational structures to find both a major and minor basis governing organizational relationships. Thus, the issue of geographical versus the functional basis of organization is often resolved so that both play a role where circumstances dictate.

Project East River believes that, in view of the threat and in view of the complexity of the problem, organizational means should be devised to permit a more direct handling of the critical metropolitan areas. In spite of the controversial background, it is believed that this can be done without materially changing the dominant, organizational emphasis, which is properly on the existing federal-state basis. Project East River recommends that affirmative action be taken by all levels of government to facilitate the buildup of the civil defense of our major metropolitan areas.

Project East River specifically recommends:

(1) The establishment in the Federal Civil Defense Administration of an office or division of urban defense.

(2) Action by the states to facilitate federal-state metropolitan planning for logistics and operations.

Such federal and state action, it is believed, would represent a realistic recognition of the special problems created by our major metropolitan areas. It would greatly facilitate the solution of the situations typified by City X. It would eliminate the unworkable situation typified in one state by the placing of three urban communities (contiguous cities really forming one natural community) in three separate disaster regions that cannot be coordinated save at the remote state capital. Finally, such action would also facilitate realistic planning that would permit the states to act within the limits of their capacity and would not thrust unreasonable burdens upon them.

Illinois Faces Redistricting

People will have chance in November to end half-century old gross inequalities in representation in legislature.

By RUSSELL E. OLSON*

ILLINOIS voters will have an opportunity at the fall election to pass on a constitutional amendment calling for a much needed reapportionment of districts for the election of members of both houses of the legislature.

Despite a constitutional mandate to reapportion every ten years, Illinois legislative districts have not been changed since 1901. Illinois courts have held consistently that the meaning of the constitution is clear—the legislative branch is required to reapportion every decade —but the court has just as regularly said it has no power to force an equal and coordinate branch of the government to act. As a result, the situation is at a critical stage.

Cook County is grossly underrepresented and within the county itself there are great inequalities in the size of districts. The suburban sixth district contains 700,325 persons and receives the same representation as the heart of the west side bloc, the seventeenth district, with 39,368.

Perhaps even more serious is the fact that this city district sends Roland Libonati to the Senate. At the time of this writing Senator Libonati was being sued by Chicago for non-repair of his West Side slum holdings. In addition to Libo-

nati, the seventeenth sends Representatives Euzzino, De Tolve and Granata to the House. All are members of the west side bloc, the worst element in the legislature, according to Chicago newspapers and other legislators. This district and the fifteenth, twenty-seventh, first and twenty-ninth, constitute the state's five smallest, with a combined population of 256,000.

Such was the situation facing the newly inaugurated governor and legislature in 1953. Governor Stratton had asked for a redistricting in his inaugural address and numerous proposals were introduced.

Most of the proposals for change were resolutions calling for change in the constitution. Fifteen unsuccessful resolutions were introduced in the 1953 session, the majority calling for a redistricting which would leave Cook County slightly less than a majority in one or both houses.

The successful reapportionment bill was Senate Joint Resolution No. 32, which calls for a referendum on amending sections 6, 7 and 8 of article IV of the constitution. It had the necessary support throughout. Governor Stratton and his administrative assistants took an active part in the drafting. It was introduced on May 27, as HJR 61, by an impressive lineup of sponsors, including the majority leader, majority whip, and chairmen of the

*Mr. Olson is a teacher of history in the public schools of Crystal Lake, Illinois. He expects to complete work for his master's degree in political science at the University of Wisconsin in August.

major standing committees. On June 3, the Committee on Elections and Reapportionment recommended the resolution be adopted and it was laid on the speaker's table.

At the same time, Senate Joint Resolution No. 32, an identical measure, was introduced in the Senate by the president pro tempore and majority leader, assistant majority leader, and chairmen of Senate committees. One week later the Executive Committee reported the bill favorably.

Upon unanimous consent, the Senate set a special order of business on the resolution for June 16. At that time the majority leader offered two minor amendments which were adopted and the resolution was quickly passed 43-2.

Reasons for Opposition

The two negative votes were cast by Senators Wimbash and Collins, a Chicago Democrat and a downstate Republican. Senator Wimbash, a Negro, is believed to have felt that any redistricting would be gerrymandered to deprive his people of a just representation. Senator Collins was the only member of the majority party to go against the governor in the Senate vote. (His vote, however, had been promised the governor if it was absolutely needed to pass the measure.)

Senator Collins believes that his constituents, in the rural area surrounding DeKalb, are against the amendment. He feels it gives Cook County control over initiation of appropriations and would concentrate too much power in one place.

He argued that downstate political machines were on a county basis and amounted to 101 machines or political organizations, each independent of the others. With so many groups, many with divergent views, it would be virtually impossible to keep them together in one legislative bloc. In Cook County, however, Senator Collins felt that the situation is different, with tremendous patronage power in the hands of the sheriff, judges, Chicago's mayor and the like. A powerful political organization is easily built in such an area and could control the votes of its legislators.

The senator also answered the point of view that legislators should vote in favor of a referendum and let the people decide the wisdom of the proposal. He voted against the referendum because he felt it could benefit only one group of people—those from Cook County.

The House measure, in the meantime, had been tied up in committee, and Senate Joint Resolution 32 reached the House on June 16. Made a special order of business, the bill met its first real opposition the next day. The Democrats caucused prior to the session but reached no conclusion. However, Democratic Floor Leader Paul Powell, of Vienna, protested vigorously, objecting to the rushing of the bill, claiming it had not been discussed thoroughly with the minority. He also spoke against the idea of allowing Cook County to control one house of the legislature. "We downstaters know that the Cook County boys are good traders on legislation.

They practice a different brand of politics than we do downstate."

Majority Whip Lewis retaliated, speaking in favor of the amendment and telling downstaters that although they would lose nine representatives, they would gain two senators; a far better bill for them than any previous proposal.

The resulting vote was 92-29, 10 short of the necessary 102. Twenty-eight members did not vote. The non-voters, mostly Democrats, included virtually the entire West Side Bloc. Representative Sprague, acting as floor manager for the administration, secured a motion to postpone further consideration.

Governor Takes Action

Then Governor Stratton went into action. Some items in the governor's program had rolled along and others had been held back but on June 17, with reapportionment facing defeat, he decided it was time to trade. The governor threw his administrative assistants William Downey and Joseph Carey into a twenty-four hour drive for votes. He also received help from Auditor Orville Hodge.

Votes and favors were apparently traded at a late session in the Executive Mansion. One legislator was promised a long desired bridge over "Apple Creek," another got route so-and-so resurfaced, etc. It was also reported that the governor had relieved some members from obligation to vote for other legislation in order to get support for reapportionment.

The *Chicago Tribune*, on June 19, quoted the governor as saying, "Pass reapportionment and pledges on other matters will not be considered as ironclad." Even the Democrats were told that support for reapportionment would ease pressure on bills objectionable to them. It is apparent that downstate went along on reapportionment only because of gubernatorial pressure.

Speaker of the House Warren Wood also felt the pressure of the governor. He had been vehemently opposed to reapportionment but on the day of the final vote he took the floor for the first time in the session and spoke in favor of the amendment. "Let us take this action to give concrete proof that our form of representative government in the end does solve all problems, and throw the lie in the teeth of those who would detract from it."

The reasons for Governor Stratton making reapportionment the keystone of his legislative arch has been a point of conjecture. The most logical is that the governor had a two-fold purpose. First, he believed that Illinois was badly in need of reapportionment and it was the just thing to do; secondly, it was probably the right thing to do politically.

Governor Stratton needs more support in Cook County and success in his endeavor to secure reapportionment should win him additional support in the county that stands to benefit most by redistricting. Republicans on a statewide ticket must get strong support in suburban Cook County to offset the usually heavy Democratic majorities piled up in Chicago. After

Stratton's nomination the ranks did not close behind him as satisfactorily as he may have desired. It may have been to get this suburban support that the governor fought so for reapportionment. Passage could also give him some inroads in traditionally Democratic Chicago. The downstaters had no place else to turn (the governor handles all patronage personally) and had to follow the governor's lead. This also explains why the legislative battle wasn't stronger.

Other political factors may have also determined the governor's stand. It has been said repeatedly that he is seeking nationwide attention. His support for reapportionment has also been classified as an effort to build up popularity for the next gubernatorial election.

Regardless of future intentions, the governor did give the resolution his utmost in the legislature. His drive for votes began on June 17, when the resolution fell 10 votes short of the necessary 102. On a vote taken the next day the measure passed easily 120-17. It had been a do-or-die situation and Governor Stratton did not die.

Let the People Decide

Although 120 favorable votes were cast, that should not be interpreted as meaning that 120 House members favor the proposed reapportionment. Some, such as Representative Stengel of Rock Island, had been opposed but voted "yes" to give the people a chance to decide the issue. He, for one, thought the people would not approve the measure.

Others, too, voted favorably so that the people could decide. Of this number, some will actually campaign against it. Noble Lee of Chicago is one. He feels that cities are more spendthrift by nature and should not control the treasury.

The proposed amendment will be submitted at the general election on November 2, 1954, and shall be effective upon adoption. However, the General Assembly meeting in 1955 shall consist of the legislators elected under the present constitutional provisions.

The schedule provides for the replacement of senators to provide a full quota of members by 1957-1958. It also provides that senators eliminated from their offices by redistricting, and not re-elected, shall receive all salary and benefits as would have accrued if they had served through the 1957-1958 term.

Since the passage of a "Gateway" amendment in 1950,[1] it has been much easier to pass an amendment than previously. It makes it possible for proposed amendments to be ratified either by a favorable two-thirds majority of the votes on the amendment itself or, as in the past, by a majority of all votes cast in the election, whichever is smaller. The reapportionment amendment will be voted under this system.

The proposal, if approved by the people, will give Cook County a slim margin in the House and downstate a substantial majority in the Senate. It follows the same general pattern as that of Congress, where

[1]See "Chicago Votes the Blue Ballot," the REVIEW, February 1951, page 88.

representatives are elected on a basis of population and two senators are chosen from each state regardless of population.

In the lower house, Cook County will be given thirty representative districts, while the remaining 101 counties will receive twenty-nine. With three representatives to be chosen from each district, Cook County will have a 90-87 majority in the House. This does not mean that either the Democrats or Chicagoans will control the lower chamber since the amendment stipulates that Chicago is to receive twenty-three and suburban Cook County seven districts. This suburban area has been predominantly Republican and, on issues concerning Chicago, usually votes with downstate.

By combining these suburban districts with those of downstate, Chicago representatives will be outnumbered 108-69. That would provide a substantial margin if any conflicts arise. If downstate citizens make this differentiation between the two Cook County areas, their opposition to redistricting should be somewhat diminished.

At present 35 per cent of the House members are elected in Chicago. This will rise 4 per cent to a total of 39 per cent in a future apportionment. However, Chicago's Senate representation will drop from 35 per cent to 31 per cent, leaving the city a net gain of absolutely nothing except more seats in a larger legislature. This very significant fact is being exploited in the present downstate campaign on behalf of the amendment.

Under the proposal the House will be elected on a basis of population with no limit placed on the number of districts in any one county. Chicago, suburban Cook County and downstate are created as three permanent divisions of representation. Any future redistricting must be on the basis of population the three divisions bear to the total population of the state. The new districts will contain, as nearly as practicable, a population equal to the representative ratio. Districts must be bounded by county lines unless the population entitles it to more than one district. In any redistricting that follows county lines districts will not be equal in size. The only restriction is that no district shall contain less than four-fifths of the representative ratio.

Schedule for Apportioning

Future reapportionments will be carried out in 1955, 1963, and every ten years thereafter. The amendment provides that redistricting will be carried out by an alternate method if the legislature fails to reapportion by July 1 of each year designated. The Illinois Legislative Council described various means by which this could be done in a study for the legislature.[2] Missouri's example, one of those mentioned, apparently caught the fancy of Illinois legislators because the proposed alternate method for redistricting shows a striking resemblance to it.

If the legislature does not act by July 1 of a year in which redistrict-

[2] *Legislative Reapportionment in Illinois,* Illinois Legislative Council, December 1952, page 11.

ing should take place, a commission is to reapportion the state. Within thirty days after July 1, the state central committees of the two leading parties in the last gubernatorial election are to submit lists of ten persons to the governor. Within thirty days thereafter, the governor must name a commission of ten, chosen in equal numbers from each list. The governor is to name five persons of his choice from a party not submitting such a list within the required period. Each member will receive $25 a day up to a maximum of $2,000.

The commission will then redistrict the state's representative districts as outlined in the constitution and file a statement, approved by seven of the ten commissioners, of the numbers of districts and their boundaries with the secretary of state. Future elections will then be carried out in accordance with the statement of the commission.

If this group does not file a statement within four months after its appointment, it shall be discharged and all legislators are to be chosen from the state at large in the next election. This, of course, puts teeth into the law, since neither party would stand for the expense and uncertainty of at-large elections for every legislator. If this did happen, however, the same procedure would be carried out in the next legislature. A new commission would be chosen if the General Assembly again failed to act etc. This would be repeated session after session until reapportionment is an actuality.

The amendment is written in such a way that the governor must carry out his duty also. A writ of mandamus compelling him to act can be issued by the courts. Thus, virtually all loopholes to avoid reapportionment have been blocked quite effectively.

In the Senate, the reapportionment picture is quite different. The amendment calls for permanent districts formed of contiguous and compact territory. There is no provision for ever again redistricting senatorial districts after 1955. Of the proposed fifty-eight districts, eighteen will be in Chicago, six in suburban Cook County and thirty-four downstate. Downstate, then, will be given a permanent ten-seat majority in the Senate and its present quota of thirty-two will be increased by two. This permanency is a concession to downstate which had to get some benefit from the legislation.

Senate Based on Area

Senatorial districts shall be formed with area as the "prime" consideration. Representative Sprague, sponsor of the amendment who pushed it through the House, stated that area will be the prime consideration in actuality and that it is planned to follow it, if possible, by dividing the number of square miles in the state by the number of districts and apportioning without regard to population. This suggests that the plan calls for dividing the number of square miles downstate by thirty-four to provide a ratio of 1,631 square miles for each downstate district. A Senate quotient for Chica-

(Continued on page 363)

News in Review

Nebraska to Vote on Constitutional Changes

Legislature Submits Eight; Petitions May Add Others

THE Nebraska legislature in its 1953 regular session submitted three proposed constitutional amendments to popular vote on November 2, 1954, out of sixteen placed before it. In a special session in April 1954, called to consider amendments as to revenue and taxation, it approved five out of nine for submission at the same time. Approval of each of the eight amendments required a three-fifths vote of the unicameral legislature. The final adoption of an amendment by referendum calls for affirmative votes representing a majority of all votes cast on the proposal and at least 35 per cent of the total votes cast at the election.

The eight proposed amendments are summarized and explained in a May 1954 bulletin of the Nebraska Legislative Council. Their brief descriptions and a few comments follow, the three proposals of the regular session being given first:

1. To substitute for the present *ex officio* Board of Educational Lands and Funds a board of five members to be appointed by the governor, the qualifications, terms and compensation of the members of the new board to be fixed by the legislature.

The present board administers 1,635,-000 acres of land and over $14,000,000 of invested funds held in trust by the state for public schools. It is made up of the governor and four other elected or appointed state officers, all but one of whom (the commissioner of education) are also *ex officio* members of other boards.

2. To authorize the legislature to fix the salaries of executive officers without the present restriction that such salaries may not be changed more than once in any eight-year period.

The present restriction makes it impossible either to increase or decrease the salary of such an executive officer at less than eight-year intervals, even in the event of rapid inflation or deflation. The bulletin mentions the case of the director of banking, whose salary was set at $5,500 in 1947; in 1951 the legislature authorized an increase to $6,500 which could not, however, become effective until 1955, after which it could not again be changed until 1963.

3. To remove members of certain types of boards and commissions from the present constitutional requirement that all executive officers shall reside at the seat of the state government.

At present the constitution requires that all executive officers, except the lieutenant governor, shall reside at the seat of government during their terms of office; and this includes members of any board or commission that constitutes the head of an executive department. The proposed amendment excludes the members of such boards or commissions. The bulletin cites the case of the State Board of Health, established in 1953 as head of the Department of Health. The seven-man board appoints a director, who administers the functions of the department, while the board meets quarterly and at special times to adopt rules and determine policies. A member is paid $20 for each day he is engaged in the board's business. Thus no one but residents of Lincoln, the state capital, could afford to serve on the board.

4. To authorize the legislature to

349

provide for the appointment of a tax commissioner or a tax commission which could have jurisdiction over the administration of the revenue laws of the state and power to review and equalize assessments of property for tax purposes.

The constitution now provides for appointment of a tax commissioner by the governor, with Senate approval, to administer the revenue laws of the state. Together with the governor, secretary of state, auditor and treasurer, he is a member of the State Board of Equalization. Under the amendment the tax commissioner would no longer be a constitutional officer nor the Board of Equalization a constitutional body; the legislature could make such arrangements as it desired, possibly placing one or both functions under a single appointive commission.

A committee of the Legislative Council has devoted a year's study to the problem of assessments, authorized by the legislature in 1953, in which year the legislature enacted a 50 per cent assessment law. The Board of Equalization materially revised assessments in most counties, following a direction from the Nebraska Supreme Court to equalize assessments among counties at full value.

5. To authorize the legislature to provide for the appointment of county assessors and boards of equalization and assessment for counties and other taxing districts.

At present all county officers are considered to be elective under the constitution.

6. To authorize the legislature to exempt household goods and personal effects from taxation in whole or in part as may be provided by general law.

The constitution at present exempts household goods to the extent of $200.

7. To authorize the legislature to prescribe standards and methods for the assessment and taxation of various classes and kinds of real and personal property, both tangible and intangible.

The present provision is that "taxes shall be levied by valuation uniformly and proportionately upon all tangible property and franchises," except for motor vehicles; and "taxes uniform as to class may be levied by valuation upon all other property." The amendment would give the legislature more leeway as to formulas of assessment, particularly as to farm property and merchandise.

8. To require that if a general sales tax or an income tax, or a combination of both is adopted by the legislature for state purposes the state shall be prohibited from levying a property tax for state purposes.

This would be a restriction on the legislature, whereas the other four amendments relating to revenues or taxation would enlarge its powers.

Petitions for Amendments

Besides the eight proposed amendments that the legislature has submitted, petitions for others have been circulated. One seeking to supersede the unicameral legislature by one of two chambers has evidently been abandoned in favor of one to enlarge it and to restore partisan elections for legislators.[1]

The Nebraska Bar Association and the League of Women Voters have been working together to obtain 60,000 signatures to petitions to place on the November ballot a proposed amendment instituting a variation of the Missouri plan for selection of judges. Instead of the present direct election of judges (on a nonpartisan basis) the governor would appoint a judge from a panel of three names submitted by specially selected committees. At the end of the term for which appointed, the judge

[1]See the REVIEW, March 1954, page 139.

would, if he desired, run for re-election on his record and not against another candidate; if he is defeated, the governor makes a new appointment. The plan would apply to the Supreme Court, district judges, county judges and municipal judges. The special committees would consist of three laymen (appointed by the governor) and three lawyers (chosen by the bar) from the district where a vacancy exists, except that for the Supreme Court the committee size is doubled. The Supreme Court in all cases would designate one of its members as committee chairman.

Arizona Hinders Annexations; Other New Legislation

Annexation programs of Arizona cities, particularly those of Phoenix and Tucson, received a setback as a consequence of two laws passed by the second regular session of the twenty-first Arizona legislature. Cities will not be permitted to compete with any privately-owned utility which is furnishing "adequate public utility service" in any area within or outside municipal boundaries, including newly annexed areas; instead, before extending their utility services, they must first acquire any portion of a private utility which is serving the area. Private water and garbage utilities supported the law as a means of circumventing the decision of the Arizona Supreme Court in 1953 which held that municipalities might compete with private utilities in newly annexed areas. At a rehearing early in 1954, the court ruled that the legislature might by law withdraw the privilege of competition.

Annexation petitions in the future must be signed by "the owners of not less than one-half in value of such real and personal property as would be subject to taxation by the city in the event of annexation. . . ." The old law required only owners of real property to sign. Because of the difficulty of arriving at the value of personal property in business and industrial areas, municipal officials anticipate that the new procedure will be difficult to operate and will lead to considerable litigation. Leaders of the recent session explained that the two houses had agreed to delete the personal property requirement but that it was inadvertently left in because of a mistake by an engrossing clerk.

The same law also requires that petitions submitted to property owners for signature must indicate the exterior boundaries of the area whose annexation is desired and must be accompanied by a map of the area. No additions in the area may be made but reductions are permissible. The Arizona Supreme Court had ruled in February 1954 that a complete description in the original petitions of the area to be annexed was not necessary.[1]

Cities and towns of Arizona may provide for the clearance and redevelopment of slums and blighted areas under provisions of another new law. Municipalities may create a slum clearance and redevelopment commission and may issue revenue bonds to finance projects. Redevelopment plans may be prepared by the municipality or submitted by "any person or agency, public or private . . . to a municipality."

Administration of state health activities was reorganized by a law which provides for the creation of a state department of health and the transfer to it of duties and responsibilities formerly performed by eight other agencies and officials. A commissioner appointed by a state board of health will serve as executive and administrative head of the new department. A five-member board of health, appointed by the governor with the advice and consent of the

[1] See the REVIEW, April 1954, page 199.

Senate, will exercise advisory and rule-making powers. The legislature also enacted a new income tax law, with withholding provisions, and new insurance and banking codes.

In the area of administrative law, the legislature authorized the judicial review by Superior Courts (on the county level) of the final decisions of agencies. The law, however, does not apply to the decisions of agencies already subject to judicial review under other statutes. Any action to review a final decision must be initiated within 35 days from the date of service of notice of the decision. Court review shall extend to all questions of law and fact presented by the entire record of the case. New or additional evidence in support of or in opposition to the agency decision may not be heard by the court, except in the event of a trial *de novo* or in cases where, in the discretion of the court, justice demands the admission of such evidence.

A person may ask for a trial *de novo* if the administrative agency failed to hold a hearing or if the proceedings before the agency were not stenographically reported so that a transcript could be made. Appeals from the decision of the Superior Court may be taken to the State Supreme Court.

The recent session, which met for ninety days, was the longest in the history of the Arizona legislature. The length of the session is attributed in part to the fact that each house, in an attempt to coerce the other to take favorable action upon certain bills which it had originated, frequently delayed action on bills which had reached it from the other chamber.　　　PAUL KELSO
University of Arizona

North Carolina to Vote on Constitutional Changes

At the November election the people of North Carolina will pass upon five proposed constitutional amendments. Their subject matter is summarized by the Winston-Salem League of Women Voters as follows:

1. Retirement of Supreme Court justices, and recall of retired justices to replace incapacitated ones;

2. To transfer parole power from the governor to the Board of Paroles; pardons, commuting of sentences and grants of reprieve to be left in the hands of the governor;

3. No county to have more than one senator;

4. To reduce requirement of length of residence in a voting precinct from four months to thirty days;

5. To give the governor certain powers to fill unexpired terms.

Louisiana Reapportionment Problem under Study

Both houses of the Louisiana legislature have voted in favor of the creation of a volunteer legislative study group to seek an acceptable plan of reapportionment of the state for legislative membership.

Although the present constitution, adopted in 1921, directs the legislature to reapportion after each federal census, the legislature has failed to do so. Three censuses have now occurred without a consequent reapportionment.

The Public Affairs Research Council of Louisiana points out that there are now four senatorial districts with a total population of 507,261 and only four senators while three other districts with a total population of only 115,988 also have four senators.

In the lower house, whereas there are eleven parishes (counties) with a total population of only 121,780 and eleven representatives the parish of East Baton Rouge (containing the city of Baton Rouge) has 158,236 people but only two representatives; Caddo (containing Shreveport) has 176,547 people and four representatives; and Jefferson (suburban to New Orleans) has 103,873 people and only one representative.

Four-Year Terms Furthered in Massachusetts

A joint constitutional convention of the Massachusetts House and Senate voted 183 to 69 on May 20 in favor of a proposed constitutional amendment to increase the terms of the governor and five other constitutional state officials from two years to four. The other five are the lieutenant governor, secretary of state, treasurer, auditor and attorney general.

The amendment must be approved by the 1955-56 legislature and then by the voters on referendum. If it is finally successful the governor elected in 1958 would be the first to be affected.

Attempts to place various other proposed amendments on the agenda of the convention were unsuccessful. In the preliminary debate on the four-year amendment a proposal to have it apply to legislators and to members of the executive council was ruled out of order. An amendment to allow for a recall vote after two years, on petition of 20,000 voters, and one to place two-term limits on officials with four-year terms were defeated.

Massachusetts Holds Pre-primary Conventions

In June the political parties of Massachusetts, under a new law (Chapter 406, 1953), held pre-primary state conventions to endorse nominees for U. S. senator, governor and two of the state offices for submission to the party voters at primaries in the fall. Opposing nominees, if any, will have until September 14 to get their names on party ballots by petition. The Democratic convention had 1,700 delegates, balloted for twenty hours and adjourned after the second day until a week later, leaving to an adjourned

session with a light attendance the task of designating a nominee for one remaining office, the state treasurer. The Republican convention, with 1,378 delegates, picked its slate without serious divisions, endorsing the incumbent governor and U. S. senator by acclamation.

The pre-primary convention device was tried in Massachusetts in 1934 and 1936 and abandoned although an informal one was held by the Republicans in 1952. The device differs from the National Municipal League's *Model Direct Primary Election System* in that a bulky short-lived convention writes the slate instead of the state central committee. So large a one-day assembly is susceptible to tight control, conceals the real sponsorship and diffuses responsibility for the slate. But like the *Model* it leaves time—in this case a long time—for opposition within the party to mobilize and file if the party managers behind the convention slate fail to cater deferentially to all factions, regions and elements, and, as in the *Model,* endorsees of the convention are identified as such on the primary ballots for the information of the voters, the label in this case being the words "Endorsed by ————— convention."

R. S. C.

Metropolitan Planning Agencies Form Organization

Representatives of eleven official and non-official metropolitan regional planning bodies met in Columbus, Ohio, on May 16 to consider a new Association of Metropolitan Regional Planning Organizations to represent the interests and activities of metropolitan regional planning throughout the United States. The meeting was held at the invitation of the American Planning and Civic Association in conjunction with that organization's annual planning conference. All present at the meeting voted to constitute themselves an organizing committee for an association, whose first formal meeting will be held on September 26 in Philadelphia at the time of the National Planning Conference of the American Society of Planning Officials.

The purposes of the new association will be: (1) to act as a national clearing house in the field of metropolitan regional planning; (2) to sponsor and conduct periodic conferences for citizens and professionals in this field; (3) to initiate or coordinate research on problems of metropolitan areas and to make the findings available in suitable form to persons and agencies holding membership in the association; and (4) to assist in the creation of metropolitan regional bodies, both official and unofficial, in areas where there are now none and to help strengthen the programs of existing agencies.

Provisional officers of the organizing committee are: president, T. Ledyard Blakeman, director of the Detroit Metropolitan Area Regional Planning Commission; vice president, Henry Fagin, planning director of the Regional Plan Association of New York; and secretary, Barbara Terrett, Washington, D. C. Frederick Gutheim, a member of the National Capital Regional Planning Council, who called the meeting on behalf of some twenty organizations in metropolitan areas, will act as adviser to the association.

Membership on the organizing committee and its steering committee is open to representatives of other official and non-official metropolitan regional organizations and to interested citizens. The address of the president is 1002 Cadillac Square Building, Detroit 26.

HENRY FAGIN
Regional Plan Association
of New York

Milwaukee Reduces Number of Wards by 30 Per Cent

The city of Milwaukee has reduced the number of its wards from 27 to 19— a 30 per cent decrease. One alderman is elected by the voters of each ward. Eight fewer aldermen will be elected on April 6, 1956, than are presently serving in the city council.

Eighteen of the new city wards are combined census tracts. Each ward includes approximately one per cent of the population of the state in accordance with an amendment to the city charter enacted by the city council in 1950. There are 100 members of the state assembly, and one assemblyman for each one per cent of the population therefore results in equitable representation. The automatic re-warding of the city on this formula is designed to facilitate the reapportionment of Milwaukee's representation in the state's Assembly and Senate, and in the county board of supervisors which is based on assembly districts.

The nineteenth new ward is the former town of Lake, with an area of nine and one-half square miles and a population of 13,000, which was consolidated with the city of Milwaukee as a result of a favorable referendum vote in each municipality on April 6, 1954. This consolidation and recent annexations have increased Milwaukee's area from 48 square miles the first of 1950 to 66 square miles at present.

PAULA LYNAGH
Citizens' Governmental Research
Bureau of Milwaukee

Council-manager Plan Developments

At a special town meeting in IPSWICH, MASSACHUSETTS, on May 24, it was voted 274 to 12 to present to the legislature for its approval a proposed new charter that would establish an executive secretary, with large administrative powers, under the board of selectmen. He would supervise all departments and activities, subject to the board, which would appoint him for a three-year term on the basis of training and experience. He would appoint various boards and officials, including the clerk, treasurer, counsel, collector, fire chief and superintendent of public works, subject to the approval of the board.

A special bill to allow BROCKTON, MASSACHUSETTS, to vote on council-manager Plan D next year was killed in the House of Representatives. The validity of a petition for such an election, filed last year, is now a subject of litigation.

The charter commission of MARION, OHIO, has drafted a proposed council-manager charter. The council would have nine members, six elected by wards and three at large. With growth of the city the number of councilmen would increase.

In JOLIET, ILLINOIS, a group of citizens favoring adoption of the council-manager plan have organized as the Better Joliet Committee, Inc. It intends to campaign for a popular referendum on the question of adopting the plan.

Citizens of HIGHLAND PARK, ILLINOIS, have formed an organization known as Highland Park Citizens for City Manager. It is working for a referendum in December of this year on the question of adopting the council-manager plan.

The executive committee of the DECATUR, ILLINOIS, Association of Commerce has gone on record as favoring adoption of the council-manager plan by the city.

In MEMPHIS, TENNESSEE, which now has the commission plan of government, a movement is on foot for change either to the council-manager plan or the strong mayor plan.

DE SOTO, MISSOURI, voted 1,016 to 841 on May 27 to retain the council-manager plan, which was adopted in 1948.

MARSHALL, MISSOURI, voted 1,506 to 1,293 on May 25 to abandon the manager plan, instituted six years ago. A mayor and eight councilmen will be elected in April 1955, and will take over the government of the city.

On June 3, LA JUNTA, COLORADO, voted more than three to one, 1,210 to 371, to retain the city's council-manager government.

The city commission of TULSA, OKLAHOMA, on June 2, directed Mayor L. C. Clark to call a special election for November 16 on the question of adopting a council-manager charter, drafted by the city's charter commission. A petition for the charter had been circulated in a drive headed by the League of Women Voters, and 21,863 signatures obtained.

In MINERAL WELLS, TEXAS, the charter commission has drafted a council-manager charter. It is expected to go to popular vote in August.

EL PASO, TEXAS, voted 6,369 to 2,997 on May 29 against a proposed council-manager plan.

Petitions for incorporation of MOUNTLAKE TERRACE, WASHINGTON, and calling for the council-manager plan, have been placed in circulation by the Mountlake Terrace Study Group.

In SAN CLEMENTE, CALIFORNIA, citizens voted overwhelmingly on April 13 in favor of hiring a city manager. The vote, which was advisory only, was 915 to 163.

Massachusetts and Connecticut managers met in Boston on May 20-21, with 18 of the 34 managers in the two states in attendance.

Five of the seven New Hampshire managers met in Concord on May 20.

Thirty-seven of the 50 North Carolina managers met in Greensboro on May 27-28.

The sixth annual conference of the Association of Municipal Managers of Pennsylvania was held at State College on May 14-15, with 31 of the 57 managers present.

Ten of the eighteen Vermont managers met in Randolph on May 19.

Thirty-nine of the 65 Virginia managers met in Natural Bridge on May 14-15.

In the 1953 national traffic safety contest, three council-manager cities won first place in their population groups: Phoenix, Arizona, Kalamazoo, Michigan, and Garden City, Kansas.

In the national fire waste contest the grand award for the United States was given to Hartford, a council-manager city, as are population group winners Dayton, Ohio, and Norfolk, Virginia.

Council Can Appoint City's Administrative Assistant

The voters of Willmar, Minnesota, recently approved a charter revision plan, 658 to 150, which includes an effort toward administrative betterment. One amendment provides that an administrative assistant may be appointed to assist in the administrative functions of the municipal government—but by the city council rather than the mayor.

Another change authorizes the council to combine the offices of clerk and treasurer. The clerk, now elected, will hereafter be appointed. A planning commission of nine members is provided; it will also control zoning. Maximum annual pay for the mayor and each council member is increased—from $108 to $300.

Mauch Chunk, Pa., Merges Neighbor under New Name

The adjacent municipalities of Mauch Chunk and East Mauch Chunk, on the Lehigh River in Pennsylvania, voted 2,203 to 199 on May 18 to combine into a single municipality. It is to be called Jim Thorpe, after the famous Indian athlete, who first won renown at the Carlisle Indian School in Pennsylvania.

Home Rule Bill Loses in Massachusetts

Although receiving a vote of 120 in favor to 102 against in the Massachusetts House of Representatives on May 19, a bill to limit the legislature's powers as to local legislation failed because a two-thirds affirmative vote was required. The Senate had voted 25 to 12 for the bill, which would have prevented legislative consideration of special bills for individual cities or towns without prior approval of the mayor and the city council or the selectmen.

Denver Seeks to Cure and Prevent Urban Blight

Organization and action to eliminate existing blight and prevent its recurrence have been urged upon Mayor Quigg Newton of Denver, Colorado, by his Housing Coordinating Committee, which has studied the problem pursuant to his request of July 22, 1953. Its leading recommendation was the establishment of a conservation-redevelopment board, with a director and clerical staff. This and other basic recommendations have been accepted by the mayor and the city council, and the conservation - redevelopment director is already appointed.

The Housing Coordinating Committee reported that, although Denver does not have widespread slum and blighted areas, they are developing and immediate steps should be taken to attack and control them. The conservation-redevelopment board is created to carry on both conservation and rehabilitation of existing housing and related facilities and the redevelopment of blighted areas by reconstruction. Administration of the present urban redevelopment program, now under the city's planning office, is to be transferred to the new board, which consists of the heads of the planning board, the housing authority, the board of health and hospitals, the building code revision committee, and six citizen members appointed by the mayor.

To assist in coordinating various city functions for purposes of conservation and redevelopment a city coordinating committee is included in the plan; it is made up of the directors or representatives of the housing authority and the following departments: building, planning, health, welfare, parks, law and conservation-redevelopment. It is to aid the new board in developing a program for the elimination of slums and blight.

The health department, which has given great attention to housing, is asked to prepare a new housing code with the aid of other departments and citizen groups, for early consideration by the city council. The planning department is similarly urged to draft a new zoning ordinance. Studies as to the need of a special housing court are recommended. It is also asked that the new board establish neighborhood projects committees for conservation and redevelopment.

N. Y. Village Officials May Serve Four Years

Villages in New York State are empowered to lengthen the terms of their mayors and boards of trustees from two years to four, by virtue of a new law effective July 1. A resolution increasing the term of office must be adopted, subject to approval of the voters at a referendum. Present officials will serve out their two-year terms.

Legislative Service Conference to Meet in California

The seventh annual meeting of the Legislative Service Conference will be held in San Francisco and Sacramento, California, September 8-11. Conference headquarters will be at the Palace Hotel in San Francisco. General sessions will be held on September 8. On the following day there will be workshop sessions on legislative research, legislative fiscal analysis, clerks and secretaries, statutory and code revision, and reference and library services. On September 10 there will be an all-day tour to the state capitol at Sacramento, with sessions there. Concluding general sessions will be on September 11.

The Council of State Governments, Chicago, acts as secretariat for the Conference.

Law and Public Administration Linked in New Cornell Course

A new four-year graduate program at the Law School and the School of Business and Public Administration of Cornell University, Ithaca, New York, enables students to combine work for the bachelor of laws and a master's degree in public or business administration. Ordinarily the LL.B. requires three years and the master's degree two.

County and Township · · · · Edited by Edward W. Weidner

Cities, Counties Continue to Cooperate

Buildings, Fire Reporting, Defense Activities Shared

THE ever present trend toward greater intergovernmental cooperation at the local level shows no sign of abating. For example, in Oneida County, New York, the various municipalities and other units which are members of the County Fire Chiefs Association have been instrumental in getting the county to develop a county-wide cooperative mutual aid fire protection system. The County Board of Supervisors appropriated some $60,000 to aid in establishing a single reporting center and this has been supplemented by nearly $30,000 put in by the cooperating local units. The result is that, throughout the county, improved fire protection without delay is available.

Knoxville and Knox County, Tennessee, are investigating the possibilities of consolidating their school systems.

At La Crosse, Wisconsin, the city council has unanimously approved a plan for a joint city-county building.

Construction of a community building, to be part of the public recreation facilities, has been approved by Lenoir County and the city of Kingston in North Carolina.

Wake County and the city of Raleigh, North Carolina, have a coordinator of civil defense whose office is jointly paid for on a 50-50 basis by the two units.

Manager Plan Advocated for Oklahoma Counties

A bill to be submitted to the Oklahoma Legislative Council calls for granting counties in that state permission to adopt either a county manager or a county executive form of government. At a meeting before the Canadian County Joint Advisory Committee, State Representative Hugh Sandlin of Holdenville and Dr. H. V. Thornton, of the University of Oklahoma's Bureau of Government Research, supported the bill.

Representative Sandlin commented that a number of Oklahoma counties are practically bankrupt and he believes the utilization of either of the proposed forms would enable them to get back to proper financial operation. Dr. Thornton cited the successful operation of the county manager plan in other states, notably Virginia.

Suffolk County Considers Forms of Government

A nonpartisan committee of five members will consider four forms of county government for possible application to Suffolk County, New York. They are the county administrator, county manager, county director and county president forms, as set forth in New York State's optional county charter law.[1] If one of these plans is recommended to the board of county supervisors by the committee, and is adopted by resolution of the board, it must then be submitted to the voters for majority approval.

The plan for a new form of government for Suffolk has recently been endorsed by Congressman Stuyvesant Wainwright of the county, who urges steps be taken to secure home rule.

The present ten-man board of supervisors acts as both legislative and executive branches of the county.

[1] See "New County Plans Offered," by Richard A. Atkins, the REVIEW, June 1952, page 288.

Clackamas County Voters Defeat Manager Plan

In an election on May 21, the voters of Clackamas County, Oregon, turned down a proposal for the county manager plan by a vote of 14,284 to 8,001. This was the third attempt to have a county manager charter adopted by the voters. The plan would have been a fairly extensive one and would have involved appointing most of the present independently elective county officers.

One of the most active groups behind the manager plan was the League of Women Voters. Arrayed against the plan were a variety of newspapers, public officials and ad hoc voters groups.

County Highway Engineer Plays Important Role

Professor John E. Stoner of Indiana University says the county highway engineer is somewhat of a general manager and professional leader. Writing in a recent issue of *The County Officer*, publication of the National Association of County Officials, Washington, D. C., Professor Stoner puts forth his conclusions as a result of a study of county highway engineers in Minnesota. He feels that the role of the county highway engineer is broader than merely supplying technical information and making purely engineering decisions. At the very least, the county engineer must gain a perspective of state-county relations and must be aware of the economic life of the county and developing trends that might be reflected in traffic congestion.

In conveying this information to the county board, he must understand public opinion in the county as a whole and seek to lead it as well.

In short, the engineer emerges as one of the most important and most trusted general officials in county government.

Proposals for Stronger Local Government in Pennsylvania

A number of specific proposals for securing stronger local government in Pennsylvania have been made by Professor H. F. Alderfer, executive secretary of the Institute of Local Government at the Pennsylvania State University. As set forth in the *County Officer*, these are: (1) reorganization of the structure of county government to eliminate most of the elective offices except the county commissioners, who would be the governing body of the county; (2) consolidation of the 1,500 townships of the second class to 500 townships; (3) development of a modern program for rural road building and maintenance under the leadership of the county; (4) development of a broader county health program; (5) continued modernization of assessment procedures in counties.

Taxpayer Group Recommends Coroner Be Made Appointive

The Contra Costa County Taxpayers' Association, California, has suggested to the board of supervisors that it recommend to the state legislature a bill permitting the office of coroner to be made appointive at the discretion of the board and requiring such appointee to be a licensed physician. County home rule, it was found, did not include power to shift a statutory elective office to appointive status and the association plans to press for extension of the appointive system to include the county clerk, recorder and public administrator if the supervisors so desire.

R.S.C.

Colorado Women Support Four-Year County Terms

The State Board of the League of Women Voters of Colorado is in favor of four-year terms for county officers.

(Continued on page 377)

Taxation and Finance • • • • *Edited by Wade S. Smith*

How Best Finance
Toll Highways

Bonds Guaranteed by State
Cheaper Than Revenue Bonds

PERHAPS the most popular innovation of the current period is the toll highway, constructed by a semi-autonomous state authority and financed by the issuance of bonds. These bonds are payable principally, and often solely, from tolls and incidental income derived from the operation or lease of such concessions as gas stations and restaurants located on the highway right-of-way. A formidable chain of such highways has already been provided by construction completed, under way or close to the financing stage, and the prospect of a coast-to-coast chain of toll roads within a decade or so no longer seems fantastic.

Basically, there is nothing new about toll roads in the United States nor publicly financed transportation arteries. The issuance of state and local bonds for toll roads and canals in the early 1800s played a significant part in the earliest wave of state and municipal bond defaults, and railroad aid bonds were a central feature of the defaults and debt repudiations of the later decades of the nineteenth century. The authority device was then unknown as a tool of state and local government in the United States, and most of the publicly issued bonds were used to aid private companies which constructed and operated the facilities. The subsequent failure of many of the enterprises and the damage to the public credit led directly to the inclusion in most state constitutions and many city charters of the present prohibitions against the use of the public credit in aid of private interests.

The modern toll road, however, is a far different creature, administratively and financially, than its ill-fated predecessors on this continent, although many observers fear that among the plethora of projects now undertaken or proposed some failures may occur. The opportunities for soundly conceived engineering and financial programs now are undoubtedly immeasurably greater than they were when we last experimented with toll highways and, more importantly, the twentieth century projects are wholly governmental in character, susceptible of public scrutiny in all their details if not wholly responsive to democratic control as practiced generally at the state and local level.

The first of the modern toll roads was the Pennsylvania Turnpike, constructed during the 1930s with federal emergency relief aid and now spanning the state from Philadelphia to Pittsburgh. Later, relatively short toll roads were constructed, or tolls were imposed to permit the improvement of existing routes, in Westchester County, New York, and southern Connecticut.

Postwar, New Jersey—a notorious laggard in the construction of modern traffic arteries because of its long adherence to a policy of limiting construction to that possible from current highway revenues—started the Jersey Turnpike, traversing the state north and south, New York State started the New York Thruway, to connect the metropolis with the Great Lakes, and Ohio began the Ohio Turnpike, to connect the western end of the Pennsylvania Turnpike with Cleveland and meet proposed toll roads in southern Michigan and across Indiana and Illinois.

An imposing link-up of toll roads is already in prospect, mainly in the eastern and midwestern sections. On the Atlantic coast toll roads are in existence or close to a reality in an almost unbroken chain from northern Maine to Delaware. Within another year or so, they will carry the motorist westward from New York City to Cleveland, and proposed links in the chain will, when financing plans have been perfected, extend to Chicago, thence to Kansas City, Oklahoma City and south into Gulf and central Texas. In the upper Mississippi Valley, proposals would extend toll roads from Chicago to Minneapolis and to Omaha. Authorized are connecting toll roads across southern West Virginia, western Virginia and North Carolina to connect Charleston and Charlotte, and from Fort Pierce to Miami in Florida. Denver and Boulder, Colorado, are already connected by a toll highway and plans are under consideration for a toll road along the western side of Puget Sound, Washington, from Tacoma through Seattle to Everett.

According to *Engineering News-Record,* toll road construction for 1954 definitely set includes nine projects with a length of nearly 1,100 miles, costing one and a half billion dollars, while half a dozen other projects, covering about 500 miles and costing close to a billion dollars, are likely starters during the year.

Financing

Toll roads have one major feature in common: construction and, generally, operating expenses are intended to be financed from the income from tolls and other charges imposed on the users of the highways. In fact, most of the projects are dependent for the repayment of their capital indebtedness exclusively on tolls and incidental concession income. Only a few major projects have been subsidized to any important extent with the general public credit: the Pennsylvania Turnpike, whose original highway was built partly with federal aid during the recovery years of the great depression; the New York State Thruway, about half of whose prospective indebtedness will be guaranteed by the state of New York; the Garden State Parkway

in New Jersey, the major portion of whose debt is guaranteed by the state of New Jersey; and the Connecticut Throughway, to which certain gas tax revenues have been pledged for debt service additional to the usual tolls.

The extraordinarily large sums of money involved in toll road construction —or, for that matter, in the construction of any modern limited access highway— and the fact that financing plans either require exclusive dependence on tolls or contemplate the substantial use of tolls to avoid dependence on the general credit of the state, make the toll road innovation of particular interest to all concerned with state-local fiscal affairs. Especial concern has been felt in some quarters because of the almost exclusive dependence on the revenue bond device in raising money to pay for construction. Revenue bonds, by their nature, are a more expensive type of financing than the general obligation or guaranteed bond backed not only by a pledge of tolls but also by the general credit of the state. Enabling legislation, and sometimes constitutional amendments, have been necessary to authorize virtually all the toll roads, and many students have felt that more liberal use of full faith and credit obligations in conjunction with the pledge of and covenant to collect tolls would materially lessen project financing costs as well as more adequately protect the public credit against temporary fluctuations in project earnings.

There can be little doubt that default on a toll road revenue bond will prove to be approximately as adverse in its effect on the credit of the state in which it is located and pursuant to whose laws it was issued as would a default on the state's general obligations, nor does it appear likely that the use of state general revenues can long be avoided in the eventuality that a revenue bond financed project fails over a prolonged period to meet its obligations in the manner originally contemplated. There may be no legal liability on the state's part, but, as a practical matter, the moral and political obligation of the state to stand behind its instrumentalities and provide all necessary implementation to maintain their integrity would seem to be overpowering. This being so, some observers argue, the state might better insist at the beginning that the means of financing used be the most economical available, in order that toll charges be as low as economically feasible.

Relative Costs

New York State's Thruway Authority provides an illustration of the relative costs of revenue bond financing. This project was originally expected to cost about half a billion dollars and the voters, by constitutional amendment, authorized the issuance of state-guaranteed bonds of that amount, secured by the state's credit and additionally by the revenues from tolls, etc. Cost increases (original estimates were made in 1950), the addition to the original project of several major extensions, and the decision to construct restaurant and service station centers as part of the project have about doubled the capital expense now prospective and, lacking authority to finance the entire project with bonds guaranteed by the state, the overrun of costs is being financed with bonds payable solely from revenues. A comparison of the interest costs and yield rates on $250,000,000 state-guaranteed bonds issued in 1953 with $300,000,000 revenue bonds issued early in June 1954 discloses that the authority will pay a material penalty for the use of revenue bonds.

The state-guaranteed bonds were issued in two installments, each of $125,000,000, in May and September 1953, and were identical as to maturity. Each issue was due serially in annual installments in 1958 through 1984, and had an average life of 22 1/6 years. Both issues were sold at par, with interest coupons so arranged that the net interest cost to the authority to maturity was 2.63827 per cent for the bonds sold in June and 2.6981 per cent for the bonds sold in September.

The revenue bonds, sold in June 1954, comprised $75,000,000 serials due in annual installments in 1964-79 and having an average life of eighteen years, and $225,000,000, 40-year term bonds due in 1994. The average life for the entire issue was 34 1/2 years. The bonds were taken by the underwriters at a price of 99.054, representing a net interest cost to maturity of 3.0716 per cent.

The prices and net interest costs do not disclose the full difference between the general and the revenue bonds, since material differences exist in the size of the issues, the term to maturity and market conditions at the time the bonds were sold. The June 1953 sale was made just as the money market was descending to a recent low and the September issuance before any material improvement had begun, while the recent sale enjoyed a more stable and improved market. Illustrative of the varied conditions is *The Bond Buyer's* index of yield on twenty representative state and municipal bonds; at the dates closest to the respective sales, it was 2.75 per cent in June 1953, 2.91 per cent in September 1953, and 2.51 per cent in June 1954.

Price Comparison

A good measure of the differential between the New York State Thruway state-guaranteed and revenue bonds may be made by a comparison of the prices at which corresponding bonds of the respective issues were reoffered to investors by the underwriters. Using bonds of twenty-year maturity, which corresponds to the maturities predominantly used in the construction of the index just cited, the June 1953 issue was reoffered to yield 2.45 per cent, the September 1953 issue to yield 2.50 per cent, and the June 1954 revenue issue to yield 2.75 per cent. The two state-guaranteed maturities were priced to yield respectively 30 and 41 basis points *less* than the index yield as it stood at the time of the reofferings, while the revenue bonds were priced to yield 24 basis points *more* than the index yield. The extreme spread was 65 basis points, or 65/100 of one per cent interest per annum, while the lower spread was just over 1/2 of one per cent. In dollars, the $300,000,000 revenue issue evidently costs at least $150,000 in interest per annum more than the authority would have been required to pay on state-guaranteed bonds. Over the term of the issue, the additional cost of having used revenue bonds might fairly be regarded as not less than $5,000,000.

It may be noted, further, that the spread between the cost of state-guaranteed and revenue bonds in the case of the New York project does not necessarily provide an extreme measure of the additional expense inherent in revenue bond financing. The New York Thruway is a highly regarded venture, connecting the nation's metropolis with other large urban centers, and the fact that part of the total project cost will be financed with state-guaranteed bonds additionally enhances the security of the strictly revenue-type obligations. In the case of less favored projects, the differential in favor of state-guaranteed financing might well be expected to be greater.

Evidently voters and taxpayers would be well advised to take a closer look at revenue bond versus general bond financing for their twentieth century highway systems; the using public is going to pay the bill in any event and the time may come when a nickle or a dime difference in tolls will seem more important than it does today.

ILLINOIS FACES REDISTRICTING

(Continued from page 348)

go will be obtained by dividing the eighteen districts into the number of city square miles and dividing the area of suburban Cook County by six will give the size of districts from that section.

Though little exists on paper to indicate how these districts will be organized, Governor Stratton has assured the author they will follow historic county lines. Thousands of such county combinations might be possible but it is probable that senatorial districts in the southern part of the state will contain less than 50,000 persons while suburban districts near and in Cook County will have populations in the vicinity of 300,000.

Despite this shortcoming, the amendment has much to be said in its behalf. First, it will reapportion the state in such a way as to reflect the latest population trends in Illinois—at least in one house. It will eliminate the gross under-representation of a majority of the people of the state and reduce the influence of the worst element in the legislature. The amendment also provides what should be an adequate provision to assure regular apportionments in the future. If the amendment is adopted Illinois need never have another fifty-year period pass without being redistricted.

Proportional Representation . . *Edited by George H. Hallett, Jr.*
and Wm. Redin Woodward
(This department is successor to the Proportional Representation Review)

Irish Elections Retire deValera

New Parliament Elected by Hare System of P. R.

A LOSS of eight seats in the Irish elections last May more than melted away the two-vote margin by which the Fianna Fail (Men of Destiny) party had held a majority in the Dail Eireann (Irish Parliament). In terms of first-choice votes—Ireland uses the Hare system of P. R.—Fianna Fail obtained only 43.4 per cent of the 1,335,-339 valid votes cast.

As a consequence of the election John Costello, whose Fine Gael (United Ireland) party stood second in first-choice votes and number of seats obtained, on June 2 succeeded Eamon deValera as prime minister, winning parliamentary leadership by a vote of 79 to 66. Except for Fianna Fail all the parties and most of the independent members backed Costello.

As usual in P. R. elections the principal leaders of the larger parties were easily elected in their constituencies whether their parties had local majorities or not.

The distribution of first-choice votes by parties was closely similar to the results of the election, as shown in the accompanying table.

P. R. Elections Held in New South Wales

The first elections under the law providing the Hare system for local elections in the Australian state of New South Wales were held on December 5, 1953.[1] In all municipal and shire (rural) elections in which three or more seats were to be filled, 137 communities, P. R. was used. In the remaining 103 places, mostly shires, where only one or two candidates were chosen from a ward or riding (rural electoral division), the al-

[1]See the REVIEW, March 1954, page 146.

IRISH NATIONAL ELECTION, MAY 1954

	First-choice Votes	Percentage of Votes	Seats Won	Percentage of Seats
Fianna Fail				
(Men of Destiny)	578,997	43.4	65	44.2
Fine Gael				
(United Ireland)	427,031	32.0	50	34.0
Labor	161,034	12.1	19	12.9
Clann na Talmhan				
(Farmers)	51,069	3.8		2.0
Clann na Poblachta				
(Republicans)	41,249	3.1	5	3.4
Independents	70,882	5.3	5	3.4
Others	5,077	0.4	0	0
	1,335,339		147	

ternative vote system was applied. At the time of adoption of the law on November 10, 1953, the method in effect for all local elections was ordinary plurality voting, save for the town of Armidale, which has used P. R. since 1928, and for the city of Newcastle, where the alternative vote system (Hare system applied to the election of one only) was in use.

The Hare system, the only form of P. R. ever adopted in Australia, was the method provided. The change to the new system resulted from action by the New South Wales state parliament. Provision was made in the law for local voters, by petition, to hold referenda on the question of continuing P. R., but prospects of any repeal efforts seem remote at this time.

P.R. Supported

In the course of the parliamentary debate on the issue of adopting P. R., the government, which sponsored the measure, stressed that democratic rule and effective voting required the use of P. R. and that efficiency and honesty in administration were impaired whenever one group of voters could monopolize all the seats. Under the former plurality system a minority of voters—sometimes as small as 35 per cent—often won a majority or even a monopoly of the seats. Furthermore, and more important, over a period of several months preceding the introduction of the P. R. bill, and occasionally in recent years, charges of corruption in several local councils, which were under the exclusive or near-exclusive control of only one party, received wide attention. The fact that A. G. Huie, the leading advocate of P. R. in that state, had kept the remedy for such electoral defects in the public eye over many years was an important factor in the adoption of P. R.

In the parliamentary debate on the bill, it is interesting to note, the oppo-

sition speakers expressed little objection to the principle of proportional representation. Many of them affirmed and emphasized their support of P. R. as such but challenged the government's motives for introducing it at the time. The opposition's primary attack was the charge that the government had designed the electoral changes to promote its own partisan interests in local elections.

The arguments so commonly expressed by American critics of P. R., namely, that it promotes splinter parties, causes instability in government, is difficult for the voter to understand and hard for electoral officers to administer, were not even mentioned by the opposition, perhaps because they knew that Australian experience with P. R. could not support such claims. The successful example of Armidale's use of P. R. was cited by government spokesmen and not challenged by the opposition.

About the only reference to the issue of P. R. and communism in all the parliamentary debates on the proposal was the following statement, made by a member of the opposition (Conservative) party:[2]

> Proportional representation seems to be a reasonable system of selecting representatives . . . and the principal disadvantage that can be suggested is that it provides an opportunity for all types of parties to be represented. Such might include the Communist party, but to my mind no danger lies here. If that party has a content in the community let it be brought into the open so that its strength can be known. Proportional representation, on that score alone, might have advantages over the present system.

No claim was expressed that P. R. would weaken political parties. On the

[2]Hon. H. D. Ahern, New South Wales Parliamentary Debates, 1953, No. 33, page 1468.

contrary, opposition speakers insisted that P. R. would unduly strengthen political parties and machines and hurt independents.[3] A large amount of opposition criticism to the P. R. proposal was not against "true proportional representation," to use their words, but against certain features of the "government's plan of hybrid proportional representation."

System Criticized

The chief criticisms in this connection were: (1) disapproval of the provision for the compulsory marking of preferences (see below), (2) opposition to provision for grouping candidates, whenever any of them so request, on the ballot according to party (a practice continued from the former plurality system) and (3) objection to the undue haste with which the new system was to be applied. Elections under the new proposal, which became law on November 10, were held on December 5. However, despite the short notice, the elections were apparently carried out smoothly by staffs without prior experience with P. R.

Although objections were made to the P. R. bill—of course an opposition party will usually object, if only as a matter of custom—it is interesting to note that no support was expressed for continuing plurality voting. Speakers of both parties described the "first-past-the-post system," as plurality voting is usually called in Australia, with such

---

[3] Actually what these speakers had in mind in denouncing what they called proportional representation was not P. R. itself but the alleged prospect that the government party (Labor) would combine the introduction of P. R. with an effort to establish state party politics in local affairs by running party tickets in council elections. Traditionally it was accepted that local affairs should not be connected with state politics, although departure from this view has increased in recent years.

terms as "this discredited system" and "this outmoded system of voting by crosses, which belongs more to an illiterate age." As all state and federal ballots in New South Wales are marked by numbers, the value of uniformity was advanced as argument for eliminating voting by means of X-marks.

Some differences between American and Australian P. R. election features were seen in the recent contests, in addition to the Australian practice of selecting surplus votes on an exact basis and of allowing "secondary" surpluses to accumulate.

Grouping of candidates. The P. R. election provisions, like those of the plurality system superseded, allow candidates, upon their request, to be placed on the ballot in groups, thus permitting all candidates of the same party to appear together in a separate block on the ballot. Arranged in a horizontal row, the groups were assigned by lot to positions on the ballot. When grouping was not requested, an alphabetical column was used. Names were not rotated.

The grouping feature, together with compulsory marking of preferences and the use of "how-to-vote" cards, explained below, enables political party managers to influence strongly the choice of which party candidates will be elected. If party supporters faithfully follow their party's recommendations, the effect of the grouping is to simulate the operation of a list system. However, as there is no obligation for the voter to observe the party's order of listing, the benefit of the full freedom of choice under the Hare system—to pick and choose individually among all candidates—is available whenever the voter wishes to use it.

The P. R. election in Sydney illustrated the voters' ability to "pick and choose" with success when they want to, notwithstanding party groups and how-to-vote cards. In this instance, Candidate Green was listed No. 15 on the ballot and on the Labor party how-to-vote card. As Mr. Green's party could not expect to win more than eleven or twelve of the twenty seats to be filled, it was assumed that the party candidates listed as No. 13, 14, and 15 had no hope of being elected. Supporters of Green, however, campaigned for No. 1 votes for him and he was elected as the eleventh and last successful candidate of his party. The candidate ranked as No. 11 on the endorsed party list was therefore not elected.

How-to-vote cards. Coupled with the provision for party grouping on the ballot is the use of how-to-vote cards. This card consists of what is roughly a sample version of the official ballot and lists the preference numbers for all candidates as recommended by the party sponsoring the voting card. These cards are distributed by party workers at the polling places where they are accepted and looked for by party supporters, who carry them into the booths and copy the preferences indicated by the sample marking onto the official ballot. Because of compulsory marking of preferences, together with the absence of party labels on the ballot, voting cards are welcomed and their advice observed in overwhelming numbers by party supporters.

Treatment of Surpluses

Unusual surpluses. As most voters of each party, following the voting card, will record their first choices for the same candidate, the No. 1 candidate receives a huge surplus. In the Sydney elections, in which the quota was 4,189, the No. 1 candidate on the Labor list received 38,920 votes; his counterpart in the other major party received 26,031. Because most of the ballots can be readily classified on the basis of the pattern of preferences indicated, the different types were "blocked" by the Sydney counting staff into respective

groups in accordance with similarity of pattern. This procedure, attended to before any transfers were made, greatly expedited the transfer of surplus.

Compulsory marking of preferences. Voters under the new law were required, at the penalty of having their ballots declared invalid, to mark preferences for twice the number of candidates to be elected, plus one, up to fifteen. Choices beyond fifteen were not required. This stipulation accounted for practically all invalidity other than blank ballots. In this land of compulsory voting the latter presumably are deposited by those few who, though not wishing to vote, are motivated by the wish to avoid the fine for non-voting.

GEORGE HOWATT, *Fulbright Scholar*
From University of Pennsylvania
to University of Melbourne

Italy Takes Steps to Return to P.R.

The Italian Chamber of Deputies, by a vote of 427 to 75 on June 9, acted to repeal the non-proportional amendment added in 1953 to Italy's P. R. electoral law of 1948. The provision of this amendment for increasing the representation of a majority party or combination of parties never came into play because the governing parties fell just slightly short of a popular vote majority in the 1953 elections.

Charges that the 1953 enactment was unfair were believed to have contributed to the disappointing poll of the governing parties in the 1953 election. Prime Minister Mario Scelba, who as interior minister endorsed the 1953 amendment, pledged himself, on the eve of the recent repeal, to replace the "bonus seat" law by a fair proportional representation statute. In the meanwhile the 1948 law would remain in effect.

At the writing of this report, the Senate had not concurred in the action of the Chamber of Deputies, but its endorsement was generally expected.

Albuquerque Voters 'Throw Rascals Out'

Newspaper Cites Need for a New Council-manager Charter

THE political career of one of the most colorful and controversial figures in New Mexico politics came to an end as a result of the April 6 city election in Albuquerque. Clyde Tingley, alderman, city commissioner, governor and most recently mayor under the council-manager plan, lost the majority control of the city commission (council) when an avalanche of votes elected the ticket of a newly organized Citizens' Committee. Although Mr. Tingley remains on the five-man commission for another seventeen months, his thirty-year control of city government collapsed with the staggering defeat of the pro-Tingley forces marshalled under the Albuquerque Unlimited banner.

The winning candidates, Richard Bice, Lars Halama and Maurice Sanchez, launched a vigorous and damaging attack against Mr. Tingley, the day-to-day meddling in administrative matters by the commission, the mishandling of public works projects and the deplorable condition of the city's finances. The voters marched to the polls in larger numbers than in any previous election to end Tingleyism.

A highlight of the election was the entrance into city politics of the first woman to wage a spirited campaign as an independent candidate and the first university professor to seek elective office. Miss Dorothy I. Cline, professor of government and author of a study on the operation of the council-manager plan in Albuquerque, supported the manager charter, denounced commission practices and condemned the use of slates and tickets in city manager elections. Although failing of election, she topped the list of independents and ran ahead of the Tingley ticket.

The Citizens' Committee, a guiding force in Albuquerque's government for the next four years, was an outgrowth of a citizens' council organized in December 1952 to study municipal problems, the charter and the council-manager plan. The council, reorganized into a larger Citizens' Committee, agreed that the city's critical problems could be solved only with the election of a commission majority pledged to observe the manager charter. As a consequence, the committee recruited a three-man ticket, opened headquarters in a downtown hotel and initiated a precinct organization. Three weeks prior to the election, the committee, backed by a number of civic and business groups as well as some key political figures, conducted an extensive publicity program via press, radio and television. Following the election, the chairman of the committee, C. L. Forsling, announced the Citizens' Committee would proceed with the establishment of a permanent organization.

The newly elected majority took immediate steps the second week in office to strengthen the city manager's position as chief executive and personnel director, locate additional revenues for the hard-pressed city, and assign to the executive departments the office formerly used by Mayor Tingley.

A severe setback for the new commissioners was the defeat of two tax proposals: a tax on cigarettes with the funds earmarked for recreation, and a gasoline tax to be used for streets. The cigarette tax lost by a slim margin of

376 out of 22,644 votes, whereas 50 per cent of the voters opposed the tax on gasoline.

The commissioners were heartened, on the other hand, by the passage of bond issues totaling $9,200,000 for libraries, streets, storm and sanitary sewers, water and additional money for an auditorium. The building of a municipal auditorium—theatre vs. convention hall, uptown vs. downtown—has been a major issue in city politics for 25 years.

The citizens of Albuquerque are hopeful for the first time in 37 years—since adoption of the manager plan—that a commission majority will be able to enforce the city charter while establishing responsible and serviceable government. It is generally conceded that the new commissioners will be harassed with the problem of obtaining sufficient revenues for a city that has been bursting its seams since the beginning of the defense program, and has been accustomed for years to pressure-group government.

Editorializing on the sweeping victory of the Citizens' Committee, the Albuquerque *Journal* cites the fact that provisions of the city's charter, adopted in 1917, "when the city manager form of government was just coming into vogue, appear to be inadequate to meet present-day needs. . . . Modern-day charters incorporate a number of things that are essential to good operation of a city manager form of government that are not touched on in the Albuquerque code. . . . Albuquerque did not have much precedent to go by when it drew the present charter. The city could profit now by a study of the newer codes and come up with revisions to meet present-day needs."

DOROTHY I. CLINE

●

University of Mexico

Citizens Defeat Pawtucket Machine

The first nonpartisan election in the history of Pawtucket, Rhode Island, was held January 4. The election was the culmination of a long uphill fight on the part of the Citizens' League for good government.[1]

Pawtucket adopted a new charter under the provisions of the state's 1951 home rule amendment, but the courts declared that such charters could not provide for nonpartisan election of council since only the legislature could regulate election matters. Later the legislature, at a special session called by the governor, gave the city permission to use its nonpartisan provisions.

The Citizens League supported a slate of candidates for council in the nonpartisan primary only three of whom were nominated. In the final election, however, the Democratic city administration that has held power for over twenty years "went down to smashing defeat under a landslide of votes." It secured only two members in the new, streamlined, nine-man city council which will inaugurate the city's new mayor-council government. A combination of five candidates endorsed by the Republican-Independent fusion and two supported by the Citizens League won the other seven.[2]

"Congratulations to the voters of Pawtucket," declared the Pawtucket *Times*. "To no one but the men and women of Pawtucket, the majority who swept the Democrat machine from office, are the congratulations due.

[1] See "Cities Rush Home Rule Gate," the REVIEW, February 1953, page 73; "Rhode Island Court Blocks Home Rule," November 1953, page 515; "Rhode Island Cities Win Nonpartisan Vote," December 1953, page 568.

[2] The Citizens League also supported candidates for the seven-member school committee, nominating five in the primary all of whom were elected.

"After years of striving for representative and responsible government they have accomplished their broad purpose, home rule, nonpartisan primaries and nonpartisan elections, a new charter, a strong mayor. They have a new foundation for better government and on it we hope the new city officials will build in the public interest. . . .

"But there is a particular group most worthy of commendation. They are the members of the Citizens League of Pawtucket, a comparative handful of men and women who in the interest of all the community gave unselfishly of themselves and of their time to keep burning the spark of representative government. . . .

"We can go forward to better things if the new city officials, the mayor and the city council and the school committee keep before them the message of yesterday's election, the desire of the people to have better things in a better city."

Connecticut Women Hold Mock Constitutional Convention

The League of Women Voters of Connecticut has come a long way and it still has far to go, but its mock constitutional convention at Hartford, May 18, was a giant step toward the goal of a modern constitution for Connecticut. Attended by 95 delegates from 48 local leagues, plus observers and members of the press—180 in all—the convention was the culmination of four years of intensive study on revising the state constitution and a long-standing effort by the league to bring about improved methods of state government operation. During the morning the delegates divided into four committees—direct citizen action, legislative, executive and judicial. After lengthy and searching discussion of the various changes needed in each of these areas, the groups adjourned for lunch

with the satisfaction of having approved, either by unanimous or large majority vote, the principles to be presented to the joint session in the afternoon.

Dr. Marjorie Dilley, chairman of the department of government at Connecticut College, New London, was chairman of the afternoon session. Twenty-five specific suggestions for revising the constitution were presented and voted upon by official delegates. A majority of the motions were passed without dissent.

Major recommendations included:

1. A constitutional provision guaranteeing home rule;

2. A constitutional provision for a mandatory, direct, closed primary for the nomination of state officials, U. S. senators and representatives, and state senators;

3. Mandatory provision requiring that the question of constitutional revision be put before the people every twenty years;

4. Representation for every town in the lower house of the General Assembly (the number of representatives per town to be determined by the town's population);

5. A mandatory provision for redistricting the Senate after each census;

6. Annual sessions for the General Assembly;

7. Restatement and strengthening of the ban on dual office-holding;

8. A short ballot for state officials, to include only the governor and lieutenant-governor;

9. Reduction of executive departments to a number not exceeding twenty;

10. Strengthening of the governor's powers of appointment and dismissal;

11. Placement of full administrative control over all courts of the state with the Supreme Court and the chief justice;

12. Appointment of all state judges by the governor from a list prepared by a commission established by law;

13. Provision for all compensation of judges to be established by law and paid by the state;

14. Deletion of all reference to county government from the constitution.

Two motions from the floor—for a unicameral legislature and to extend the primary to state representatives—were defeated, though minority feeling ran high on the latter question.

ELIZABETH H. HICKERSON
League of Women Voters of Connecticut

Sound Government Committee

The Sound Government Committee of Johnson and Johnson and Affiliate Companies continues its efforts to keep employees informed on local government.[1] Its weekly *Two Minutes Please*—a single sheet, easily read—bears such headlines as "Where Does the Money Go?" and "What Does Your Local Tax Dollar Mean to You?" *What Can I Do About It?*, a pocket-sized leaflet of sixteen pages, well illustrated, is "a five-point program that works: (1) I will get information about political candidates, taxes, budgets, etc.; (2) I will register and vote for the best candidates; (3) I will speak and write to public officials and agencies; (4) I will join political organizations, civic organizations; (5) I will serve in government."

A Helping Hand

Newest civic group in Hennepin County, Minnesota, according to the *News Bulletin* of the Citizens League of Greater Minneapolis, is the Richfield Citizens League. The new organization is patterned after the Minneapolis group, whose officers attended organization meetings as advisors and consultants. While the two leagues are completely independent of each other, it is expected they will work together on problems common to the suburban communities.

The Minneapolis league's annual program will be divided into county projects, Minneapolis projects and projects of other political subdivisions, according to a resolution passed by the board.

According to the *News Bulletin*, "Creation of the Richfield Citizens League pointed up the need for clarification of the league's policy and function as to the problems of suburbs and other political subdivisions. With 47 townships, villages and cities outside of Minneapolis and 55 school districts, the league cannot attempt to even catalogue the problems of all of these subdivisions, let alone work on them. It will endeavor to make a contribution to the solution of problems which are common to cities or villages or townships or school districts in the county. In addition, upon request, the league will give technical and advisory assistance to groups of citizens wanting to organize on a permanent basis for the study of local issues."

Support Pro-manager Candidates

Citizens for Council-manager, which worked for and secured adoption of a council-manager charter for Parsippany–Troy Hills, New Jersey, supported a slate of candidates for the township's first nonpartisan council under the new charter. Candidates for the Citizens for Council-manager published a thirteen-point pledge to govern their actions if elected to the council, among them: "We pledge ourselves to be truly independent, without commitment to any political group, boss, party or to anyone else"; and "to make council-manager form of government work to the full letter and spirit under which it was conceived; we have been in favor of this form of government since it was first advocated here."

Children Study State

Spring has brought to Tennessee's

[1]See "Employees Study City Forms," by David J. Galligan, the REVIEW, October 1953, page 450.

capital, Nashville, fleets of buses and automobiles filled with children studying the state and its government. They tour state offices and the hundred-year-old capitol building, according to *The Tennessee Planner* (Tennessee State Planning Commission), watching the legislature if it is in session. Teachers prepare for these field trips by discussing the state government with their pupils for several months previously. Libraries furnish books on the state for use by classes, and the State Planning Commission and the Division of Information of the Department of Conservation furnish maps, organization charts, lists of cities and pamphlets.

Aid on Sanitation Problem

At the invitation of the commissioners of Allen County, Indiana, to the Civic Association for assistance in drafting a "county private sewage installation ordinance,' the association has appointed a task force of home builders, engineers, health officials and representatives of several groups of citizens in the Citizens' Council. The volunteers will submit a tentative draft of an ordinance to the commissioners for possible approval.

Town Meetings on Planning

In Philadelphia the Citizens' Council on City Planning has reverted to the idea of holding town meetings and has received an enthusiastic response. The council has divided the city into districts and in each arranged a town meeting on the city's capital improvement program. Community groups which have been working with the council have joined it in sponsoring these meetings. In South Philadelphia over 300 people filled an auditorium and 235 people from Germantown, West Oak Lane, Chestnut Hill and Mount Airy attended a meeting covering those neighborhoods. In Northeast Philadelphia more than 300 citizens met at one of the elementary schools and in West Philadelphia 30 organizations worked together for the success of a meeting.

At each meeting Mayor Joseph Clark, Jr., and other top administrators are present to discuss the city's improvement program. After these officials have spoken, the moderator turns the meeting over to the audience by inviting questions on specific projects. Each member of the audience is familiar with the proposed improvements since he has received a booklet containing the capital program for his section of the city, reports the *News Letter* of the council. "Out of this exchange with the city representatives," says the *News Letter*, "has come a better citizen understanding of the city's planning program and a broader administrative knowledge of local problems."

The Passaic-Bergen (New Jersey) Community Planning Association heard a panel of experts discuss the President's Housing Program on April 20. Speakers included Emanuel M. Spiegel, past president of the National Association of Home Builders; Alexander Summer, past president of the National Association of Real Estate Boards and member of the President's Advisory Committee, and Wm. Charney Vladeck, president of the Citizens' Housing and Planning Council of New York.

Strictly Personal

Robert J. M. O'Hare, executive secretary of the Citizens League of Pawtucket, has been the recipient of two honors recently. The Citizens League, at a testimonial meeting, presented him with a gold watch "suitably inscribed." Chief speaker for the meeting was Hon. Chester A. Dolan, Jr., chairman of the Massachusetts "Baby Hoover Commission." who told of the commission's work. At a "Citizens in the News" breakfast, sponsored by the Pawtucket Business Chamber, Mr. O'Hare was presented with a plaque because of his election as president of the National Association of Civic Secretaries. In June Mr. O'Hare was appointed town manager of Stoughton, Massachusetts.

Researcher's Digest . . . . . *Edited by John E. Bebout*

Attack on Metropolitan Miami Problems Outlined

Research Foundation Urges Vigorous Citizen Support

IN JULY 1953, immediately following the referendum in which city-county consolidation was narrowly defeated in Dade County, Florida, (27,600 to 26,692) the Miami city commission created the Metropolitan Miami Municipal Board and ordered it: (1) to make a thorough study of all governments in Dade County, except Homestead and Florida City, and (2) to determine what consolidation, merger, federation or reorganization of governments is desirable in order to effect economies, improve efficiency and facilitate the solution of metropolitan problems.

The board was further directed to draft a plan for consolidation or other reorganization, together with proposed legislation to put it into effect, and to submit the proposed plan to the voters of Dade County and the affected municipalities for ratification or rejection prior to the 1955 legislative session. It was authorized to spend $50,000, all expense to be borne by the city.

This is a mighty big job. It will take a great deal of time, patience, open-mindedness and hard work by the members and staff of the survey board. And it will require the cooperation and understanding of a great many people. Here are the major steps or stages in this job:

Stage 1. Organization of subcommittees to study various phases of the subject, agreement on basic policies and procedures, selection of consultants and signing of a contract. This generally takes a month or two.

Stage 2. Initial hearings for officials, citizens and civic organizations in order to receive their suggestions as to problems which should be studied and possible solutions of these problems.

Stage 3. Field studies by the consultants covering the organization, activities and finances of each government concerned, with particular attention to possible conflict or duplication between governments.

Stage 4. Analysis by the consultants of the information and suggestions secured in Stages 2 and 3 and careful consideration of the pros and cons of various alternative solutions in the light of the particular conditions existing in Dade County. Stages 2, 3 and 4 can be done concurrently. Altogether, they take about eight months—some sort of preliminary report then.

Stage 5. Consideration of various alternative solutions by the survey board with the advice of consultants culminating in tentative decisions by the board as to the most desirable and satisfactory plan. It will take at least two months, probably longer, to resolve differences and secure substantial agreement on all major points.

Stage 6. Formulation by the consultants of the detailed plan, incorporating tentative decisions of the survey board. The detailed plan should outline a complete organization and major procedures, including a smooth transition to the new order of things. This plan must anticipate the complications and objections which will arise and provide a clear, convincing answer for each one. The plan will have to be cleared with the survey board. When completed, it will constitute the specifications for bill drafting. At least two months should be allowed for Stage 6.

Stage 7. Translation of the plan into legal language (legislation) by an attorney or attorneys of great competence, with the assistance of the consultants. This part of the project will include a careful check for constitutionality, because any plan, good or bad, is certain to be attacked in the courts. When the legislation has been completed and tentatively approved by the survey board, a preliminary report is generally published describing and carrying the full text of the proposed legislation. Estimated time for Stage 7, at least one month.

Stage 8. Hearings in all parts of the county in order to explain the tentative plan to officials, citizens and civic organizations, and to secure their comments, criticisms and suggestions culminating in reconsideration of the entire plan by the survey board in the light of objections received, and a final decision on each point. This will take from one to four months.

Stage 9. A well organized campaign to explain the proposed legislation to the citizens, answer objections and secure strong support for its adoption. At least three months should be allowed for this.

Progress to Date

The foregoing time schedule makes no allowance for vacations or for unusual delays, such as have already occurred. It is clear that the project cannot be completed until September 1955 at the earliest. As time rushes on, the temptation will be strong to "speed up" these operations and even omit some of them altogether. But short cuts would result in a half baked plan, full of "bugs," which would almost certainly be rejected by the voters. If this job is worth doing at all, it is worth doing well.

A year has elapsed since the Metropolitan Miami Municipal Board was created. Stage 1 has been completed and the following committees have been established:

fire and police; planning and zoning; sanitation and sewerage; streets and highways; taxes, assessing and collecting; transportation and public utilities. Stages 2 and 3 are under way.

When created by the Miami city commission, the board consisted of twenty members, twelve of whom were named in the resolution. The other eight members were to be designated by the following bodies: county commissioners, school board and city commissions of Miami Beach, Coral Gables, Miami Springs, Miami Shores, Hialeah, and North Miami. These bodies, except the school board, declined to appoint anyone.

The Dade County League of Municipalities urged its members to boycott the project on the ground that it should be conducted by the league and financed by all of the municipalities, not just the city of Miami. On October 25, however, the league voted to participate. Organization of the board was completed shortly thereafter.

On December 14, the full board met and approved a contract with the University of Miami under which the university's Department of Government will: (1) hire a nationally recognized consulting firm to conduct the fact-finding survey and furnish technical advice and assistance, (2) secure an executive secretary for the board, (3) build up a library on metropolitan problems, and (4) submit a report of findings with several possible solutions. The university will be paid $37,500 for these service as reimbursement for expense incurred.

At first, the contract was held invalid by Miami's city attorney. After several weeks of negotiation, a revised contract was drafted which is satisfactory to all parties. Under this contract, the survey board will receive two kinds of reports: (1) the findings and recommendations of the consultants, and (2) an analysis of possible alternative solutions by the University of Miami. Public Administration Service of Chicago has been engaged as the consultant for the fact-finding survey.

Later, the same or other consultants will be employed directly by the board to assist it in drafting and explaining the plan. These later stages (5 through 9) are not included in the university's contract. Cost of these services will be paid out of the remainder of the $50,000.

The Long Stretch Ahead

At the present rate, the project will not be completed until late 1955 or early 1956, but some recommendations may be ready before then. The original deadline (April 1955) is out of the question. This slow pace may be a blessing in disguise. It will afford time for public discussion and for allaying misunderstanding regarding an issue which has been highly controversial in the past.

Strong pressures will undoubtedly be exerted to delay and sabotage the project and to protect existing offices and powers against abolition or change of any sort. But if the survey board is sincere and determined, and if it takes the people of Dade County into full confidence at every stage, it will finally surmount all obstacles and will be able to submit a plan with such strong public support that it will be adopted.

Meanwhile the Dade County Research Foundation urges all civic organizations in the county to study this whole problem of metropolitan government and to support and assist the Metropolitan Miami Municipal Board in every possible way.

JOHN F. WILLMOTT
Executive Director
Dade County Research Foundation

GRA Announces
Conference Plans

The 40th annual meeting of the Governmental Research Association is set for September 13 through 15 at Shawnee Inn, Fred Waring's establishment at Shawnee-on-Delaware, Pennsylvania. The opening address will be delivered by Arthur S. Flemming, director of the Office of Defense Mobilization, Mayor Joseph S. Clark, Jr., of Philadelphia will speak at the annual dinner.

Between these opening and closing events a diversified program of recreation, entertainment and provocative workshop and general sessions have been scheduled. Divergent subjects of current importance to researchers highlight the program. Among these are intergovernmental relations, vocational education, tax and debt limits, fire administration, financing and publicizing governmental research, metropolitan government and administrative plans for large cities.

Full information regarding the conference can be obtained by writing Miss Elsie Haas, secretary, Governmental Research Association, 684 Park Avenue, New York 21, New York.

GRA Holds
Regional Conference

"Long Range Fiscal Programming in New York State" and "The Challenge of Rising Educational Costs" were the topics of discussion at the Governmental Research Association's Regional Conference in New York, May 15.

The discussion of fiscal programming centered largely on the report of the Temporary Commission on Fiscal Affairs of State Government (Bird Commission).[1] Homer E. Scace, director of the Department of Governmental Affairs, Empire State Chamber of Commerce, Albany, as chairman of the session, defined the broad requirements of sound fiscal planning and sketched out the

[1]See the REVIEW, April 1954, page 204.

chief obstacles that hinder the achievement of these in New York State. By an analysis of the state's financial reports and reporting procedures, he illustrated their inadequacy as instruments for budgetary planning and financial control.

The work of the commission's research staff was discussed by Lawrence S. Munson, of McKinsey and Company, the firm which conducted the bulk of the research. He listed as major accomplishments: (1) identification of areas where greatest financial benefits can be derived, and (2) the acceptance of specific recommendations by key state officials. The necessary tools for accomplishing sound fiscal planning as outlined by Mr. Munson, are: a comprehensive budget based on aims and purposes of government, a reporting structure that will enable department heads to make decisions, and an accounting system that reflects true costs.

The final speaker, A. E. Buck, who is serving as consultant to the commission, paid particular attention to specific aspects of fiscal planning and management. These include the need for competent staff service, the vital role of reporting to the whole process of government, and the role of the legislature in determining financial policy and in achieving financial responsibility. He pointed to the establishment of the Department of Administration in Kansas and the recommendations of the Pennsylvania State Government Survey Committee for a deputy to the governor to handle staff, management and housekeeping matters as being recent developments of significance, but deplored the failure of many states to develop adequate staff assistance for their chief executives.

The rising costs of education and the growing school population were discussed from three viewpoints, with Leigh B. Hebb, of the Philadelphia Bureau of Municipal Research, presiding. Dr. Paul R. Mort, professor of education at Teachers College, Columbia University, presented points of perspective for viewing this problem. He contended that the cost of buildings represented only a fraction of the total cost of educating the child, and that local citizen participation in education is not only healthy but it must be encouraged to prevent a division of our people into hostile groups of educators and lay citizens. Coupled with this viewpoint was a plea that separation of education from the traditional functional activities of government was desirable.

Allen H. Pike, of the Connecticut Public Expenditure Council, stressed the need for citizen research agency participation in solving education problems and suggested possible areas of investigation. These include questions of classroom size, teachers' salaries and the kind of education the citizens are getting for their tax dollars. Examination of postgraduate records and accomplishments of students was suggested as a possible means for investigating the quality of education.

Dr. W. Donald Walling, in light of his experience as educational consultant and former director of research for the New York Commission on School Buildings, offered practical suggestions for all citizens, to aid in the consideration of school building plans. Emphasis was placed on low cost construction with functional and standardized classroom planning being urged.

ROBERT H. KIRKWOOD
ALVIN K. PETERJOHN
Institute of Public Administration

Bureau Notes

A new statewide civic organization, the Washington State Research Council, has taken over the resources and fact-finding programs of the Washington State Taxpayers Association and the

Washington Bureau of Governmental Research, Inc. Moritz Milburn, who was president of the Taxpayers Association, and F. Bartow Fite, Jr., who headed the Research Bureau, are the president and vice-president, respectively, of the new group. Owen C. Dingwall, formerly with the Taxpayers Association, has been named executive director. The first number of the Research Council's new biweekly *Journal* appeared May 6, 1954. Offices of the council are 1059 Capitol Way, Olympia, and Arcade Building, Seattle.

(Beginning with this issue listings of research pamphlets and articles are being combined with the listings following Books in Review.)

COUNTY AND TOWNSHIP

(Continued from page 359)

Petitions are being circulated to have the proposal put on the ballot. Much of the interest comes from previous league recommendations for four-year terms for state and other officials in connection with a study of constitutional revision.

Erie County Adopts Pay Classification Plan

Another county has taken steps toward systematic personnel administration by adopting a modern salary and job classification plan for county employees. The Erie County Board of Supervisors adopted essentially the recommendations made by a New York City management consultant firm, Barrington Associates, following a five-month job evaluation survey.

The survey showed that average salary levels in many instances in supervisory, technical, professional and administrative jobs lagged while those in unskilled and less responsible positions generally were sufficient.

Regional Conferences Held in Wisconsin

Once again, the University of Wisconsin, through its Bureau of Government of the Extension Division, is carrying on a series of conferences with the Wisconsin County Boards Association. The boards of supervisors will attend a series of regional conferences which will stress the theme that county administrative control should rest primarily with the board of supervisors if the operation of vital departments is to be economical and effective.

The series will deal with problems of organization and operation of the boards of supervisors and the relations of the boards to county administration. In addition, evaluations of the past, present and future role of the county in Wisconsin government will be made.

The conferences will be under the general guidance of Professor Lloyd W. Woodruff.

North Carolina Holds School for Coroners

A school for coroners was held by the Institute of Government at the University of North Carolina in April. Main problems discussed concerned automotive fatalities by drunken drivers and the method of instruction was by the use of an imaginary case study.

Texas County Officials Hold Regional Meetings

Two of the regional associations of county judges and commissioners in Texas—south and west—have recently held annual meetings. At the West Texas Association meeting the problem of severe drought in the area was investigated and a demand was made that something be done to relieve it, perhaps in the direction of irrigation. Resolutions included such topics as the drought and the need for an improved system of grants in aid for highways.

Books in Review

GUIDE TO COMMUNITY ACTION, A SOURCE BOOK FOR CITIZEN VOLUNTEERS. By Mark S. Matthews. New York, Harper and Brothers, 1954. 434 pp. $4.

Someone has said that the National Municipal League's service to citizens is "as practical as a pair of army shoes." The same can be said of this book. There never was anything like it before, for the simple reason that nobody had ever come along who was prepared to invest the tremendous industry and patience required to produce this handy but comprehensive *Source Book for Citizen Volunteers*. It was assuredly a labor of love on Mr. Matthews' part, growing out of his own experiences with the U. S. Junior Chamber of Commerce, as a member of the Council of the National Municipal League and as a veteran of civic battles in his home town of Greenwich, Connecticut. The $4.00 price tag makes the result the book bargain of the year.

Mr. Matthews has assembled a few pages of well substantiated observations on practically every problem or project that may confront an American community, followed in each case by a verified list of sources, commercial or civic, that may be addressed for further information and advice. Sports and recreation, for instance—he sketches the activities that almost all communities provide and almost all the activities that some communities provide and then lists "Sources of Aid," six pages of them, from Academy of Model Aeronautics to Arthur Williams' book, *Recreation for the Aging,* and the U. S. Rubber Company's Soap Box Derby films.

He provides similar source materials on such programs as safety and fire protection, community arts, health, welfare, brotherhood, religion, vocational guidance, labor-management cooperation, government and community development.

One section overhauls exhaustively the details of the task of developing a live association and keeping it alive and finding funds for it. There are appendices entitled Special Days, Parliamentary Procedure, Sources of Films and Effective Speech.

If *Guide to Community Action* is "as practical as a pair of army shoes," its purpose is as fundamental as the causes for which armies sometimes fight. That purpose is to show the citizen how to stay on top of his job in a world of increasing complexity, specialization and reliance on experts.

Mr. Matthews recognizes the need for the expert but holds to the sound American doctrine that the good life is everybody's responsibility and that nobody can really enjoy the good life unless he is contributing to it as an active participating member of his community. This book will help the good citizen tap the experts for information and guidance and teach him how to translate his new knowledge into sound policy and constructive programs for community action.

J. E. B.

THE MUNICIPAL YEAR BOOK 1954. Edited by Clarence E. Ridley, Orin F. Nolting and David S. Arnold. Chicago, The International City Managers' Association, x, 613 pp. $10.

Every spring governmental researchers, public officials and others are re-equipped with the latest comparative municipal statistics when the new edition of *The Municipal Year Book* is off the press. In the 1954 edition, the 21st annual volume, the valuable tabulations on practically all aspects of municipal government, the carefully selected lists of references and model ordinances—all are brought up to date. The commentaries analyzing trends in each phase of municipal administration and the lead article, "Municipal Highlights of 1953" by George H. Deming, give a comprehensive picture of what has been happening on the municipal scene.

A significant innovation in the 1954 edition is the inclusion of a section on urban counties. Victor Jones, in his article introducing the section, comments: "The metropolitan county has been admitted at last to the family of urban governments." Recognition is given to the fact that an increasing number of municipal-type services are being provided by county governments. Two extremely useful tables present a variety of data on population, population density, land area, per cent of land in farms, county employment and payrolls as of October 1953, number of local government units within each county, kind of governing board and utilities owned and operated by the county. Inclusion of extensive data on county planning emphasizes the importance of the county as a planning unit.

Dr. Jones notes that "many urban counties have assumed functions that are administered over the entire county, . . . for example, health, welfare or parks." In the 1955 edition a tabulation of such functions would make this section even more useful.

In addition to the general report on "Metropolitan and Fringe Area Developments in 1953," John C. Bollens has prepared an analysis of "Controls and Services in Unincorporated Urban Fringes." The table on metropolitan areas and urbanized areas has been expanded to include the number and types of local government units within the standard metropolitan areas. These new features are valuable additions to the Year Book's coverage of metropolitan statistics.

A new section giving detailed data on refuse collection helps to round out the reporting of municipal activities.

The Municipal Year Book—1954 is an indispensable tool for all who are concerned with the operations of municipal government.

WILLIAM N. CASSELLA, JR.

AMERICAN DEMOCRACY IN THEORY AND PRACTICE: STATE AND LOCAL GOVERNMENT. By Joseph E. McLean. New York 16, Rinehart and Company, Inc., 1953. xii, 192 pp. $1.85.

Rarely has there been a better time for an expert to take a searching look at state and local governments in America. The president of the United States has announced that he favors returning to the states many functions taken over by the federal government during the past two decades. Already $100,000,000,000 worth of offshore oil reserves have been given to four states. Secretary of the Interior McKay has indicated that similar action ought to be taken with respect to water-power sites, timberlands and grazing valleys still under federal control.

If custody over these valuable assets is shifted, what will be the nature of the custodianship? The long, hard look taken by Professor McLean, of the Woodrow Wilson School of Public and International Affairs, of Princeton University, is scarcely encouraging. Dr. McLean, who also qualifies as a practical politician because he helped manage the successful gubernatorial campaign of Robert Meyner in New Jersey in 1953, believes that the 116,000 units of local government in America are in desperate need of reorganization.

State government is the umbrella over these plants. If it leaks, they will be in peril of inundation. One of Professor McLean's principal suggestions is for constitutional revision along the lines proposed by the National Municipal League. "Most state constitutions," says he, "suffer from the afflictions of old age—creaking joints, faulty coordination, a deaf ear (especially toward the urban populations), a fondness for quack remedies (patchwork of amendments as opposed to a complete overhaul), and a tendency to be garrulous at the expense of being relevant."

Because of his New Jersey background, the author prefers the convention method of amending or changing state constitutions to the old piecemeal system of separate clauses, voted upon one at a time. And he analyzes carefully the forces in New Jersey which worked for and against a complete overhaul of the state's basic charter, *viz.*, "petty partisan politics" against and "civic groups" in favor of the project.

This is a book which should be particularly valuable to men and women active in the realm of state and local governments. Professor McLean includes tables showing the salaries of state officials, disclosing the funds spent by each state on education at the various levels as well as other tables of immense importance. The salary schedule, for example, indicates that many states believe it safe to pay strategic office-holders far less than men of ability and training can earn in private industry.

As a member of an American state legislature, I am going to recommend that each member of our assembly be furnished with a copy of *State and Local Government* when we convene again in January of 1955. However, I feel sure my colleagues will agree, at most, with only 66 2/3 per cent of this conclusion by Professor McLean: "Present-day state legislators generally rank low in prestige, low in salaries and low in ability."

In spite of my admiration for this useful book, I have one complaint. As a westerner, I wish the author had included more information on state management and supervision of natural resources such as school lands and min-

eral reserves. Being one of those scholarly but provincial easterners, Professor McLean probably overlooked this phase of state responsibility which is so peculiar to those units of government that lie west of the Continental Divide.

RICHARD L. NEUBERGER
Member, Oregon State Senate

THE BOOK OF THE STATES. Chicago, Council of State Governments, 1954. 676 pp. $10.00. (Price includes 1955 supplement).

The Book of the States is the standard reference work for those concerned with state government. Each new issue is awaited by students of state government because of the wealth of facts that the *Book* contains. The data presented, such as rosters of state officials and tabular presentations of basic facts concerning each of the states, are indispensable to officials, legislators, schools, libraries and citizens interested in state government.

The current edition has sections devoted to interstate relations, constitutions and elections, legislators and legislation, administrative organization, finance, the judiciary and major state services such as education, highways, health and welfare, etc. Each of the sections is prepared by a leading student of the subject and is a succinct, definitive statement of recent developments and trends.

JOHN P. KEITH

PUBLIC AUTHORITIES IN THE STATES. Chicago 37, Council of State Governments, 1953. 158 pp. $3.

Public Authorities in the States, a report to the Governors' Conference of 1953, was prepared under the direction of Sidney Spector of the staff of the Council of State Governments.

At the 1952 meeting of the Governors' Conference, some concern was displayed over the increasing impact of the authority movement (particularly since World War II) on state government.

As a result, it adopted a resolution requesting the Council of State Governments to "make a study and submit recommendations with respect to the use, financing and responsibility of public authorities, as well as the philosophy underlying such governmental bodies."

This report is a response to that resolution. Its chief value lies in the enormous amount of up-to-date material it has gathered about the extensive use of local authorities. This information is assembled in usable form.

Mr. Spector and his associates grappled effectively with a variety of data which show that, since the end of World War II, the states and local governments are employing authorities for such purposes as "construction and operation of toll roads and bridges, airports, ports, terminal facilities, produce marketing centers, power, water and sewer systems and recreational centers. They are developing them as important instruments for constructing office buildings, armories, schools, hospitals and other institutional facilities."

The chief limitation of the report lies in its failure to come to grips with the question: Are authorities in many instances merely mechanisms to avoid coping with legal limitations rather than legitimate government forms, for example, in some instances the authority is being used as a dodge to avoid the debt limit.

It is undoubtedly true that the public corporation has a useful role to play at the local level. On the other hand, the proliferation of these agencies to fields normally handled by line departments raises serious questions. These authorities perform governmental functions and exercise great financial powers, but are only indirectly responsible to the voter. In certain instances, they have been set up contrary to the wishes of the general public. It is a question to what extent such authorities can be

multiplied without jeopardizing the democratic process. This question the report does not deal with.

RUTH WEINTRAUB
Hunter College, New York City

ANNEXATION? INCORPORATION? A GUIDE FOR COMMUNITY ACTION. (Second edition.) By Stanley Scott. Berkeley 4, University of California, Bureau of Public Administration, 1954. 163 pp.

This publication will be invaluable to citizens of unincorporated urban areas who are facing the question of what course they should follow—annex to a neighboring city or incorporate as an independent municipality? Although designed for use in California, the guide presents issues which must be resolved in fringe areas all over the nation.

CHOOSING THE PRESIDENT OF THE U. S. A. By Kathryn H. Stone. New York 16, Carrie Chapman Catt Memorial Fund, Inc., 1954. 44 pp. 25 cents.

This is a factual yet readable account of the whole quadrennial process of choosing a president, beginning with how the candidates emerge and going through the process of campaigning (in which the author played a personal part in 1952) to the struggle for nominations, the hurly-burly of the great conventions, the proposals for improvement in the process, presidential campaigns and the electoral college, winding up with a section "What Can the Citizen Do to Improve the Method."

In commenting on the process of selecting delegates, the pamphlet indulges in some critical commentary, for example:

> In recent years, and particularly in the Republican party in 1952, thousands of newer party members attended local and state conventions for the first time, with varying degrees of success and frustration. Sometimes the party machinery was working so smoothly that less experienced party

members did not know what was going on until it was over. At other times the newcomers had made special efforts to understand their local party procedures and were able to assert significant strength. Fresh partisans were highly successful in the Republican party in some states in 1952.

The pamphlet will be a valuable handbook for citizens in 1956 and in subsequent presidential years. It is written with the admirable clarity we have learned to expect from its author.

R. S. C.

5 YEARS OF PROGRESS 1948-1953. A Report to the Citizens of Richmond. Richmond (Virginia), Office of the City Manager, 1953. 64 pp. Illus.

After five years of council-manager government, the city manager's office produces this 64-page pictorial brochure proudly presenting, among other things, the high quality and caliber of the councils through three elections, enlistment of one hundred uncompensated public-spirited citizens on advisory boards, increased employee salaries of 25 per cent ($2,000,000), better retirement benefits to employees at lesser cost to them, performance budget with savings of hundreds of thousands of dollars, modern merit system, $2,900,000 from current revenues used for permanent public improvements instead of borrowing, expansion of many services and no increase in tax rates.

R.S.C.

Additional Books, Pamphlets and Articles

Absentee Voting

REDUCING FRAUD IN ABSENT VOTING IN VIRGINIA. A Report of the Virginia Advisory Legislative Council to the Governor and the General Assembly of Virginia. Richmond, Virginia Division of Purchase and Printing, 1953. 8 pp.

Air Pollution

LEGAL ASPECTS OF AIR POLLUTION— Parts I and II. By William Harris Bell. New York 1, Powell Magazines, Inc., *Modern Sanitation,* October and November 1953. 6 pp. each.

Annexation

ANNEXATION OF THE HEAVY INDUSTRIAL AREA OF CORPUS CHRISTI. By Stuart A. MacCorkle. Corpus Christi (Texas), Chamber of Commerce, 1953. 38 pp. $1.00.

Blighted Areas

WHAT CITIES CAN DO TO IMPROVE CLOSE-IN BLIGHTED AREAS. By George O. Consoer and Arthur W. Consoer. New York 16, *The American City,* April 1954. 2 pp.

Budgets

CONNECTICUT TOWN TRIES PROGRAM BUDGETING. By Hubert W. Stone. New York 21, Governmental Research Association, *GRA Reporter,* Second Quarter 1954. 3 pp.

DOES MISSOURI NEED A PERFORMANCE BUDGET? Jefferson City, Missouri State Chamber of Commerce, *Research Report,* February 9, 1954. 7 pp.

STATE BUDGETS—1954. By Leon Rothenberg. Chicago 37, Council of State Governments, *State Government,* May 1954. 6 pp.

Chief Administrative Officers

NEW YORK CITY INSTALLS CITY ADMINISTRATOR. By David Bernstein. New York 21, Governmental Research Association, *GRA Reporter,* Second Quarter 1954. 3 pp.

SAN FRANCISCO EXPERIENCE WITH CHIEF ADMINISTRATOR. By Alfred F. Smith. New York 21, Governmental Research Association, *GRA Reporter,* Second Quarter 1954. 3 pp.

City Councils

YOUR JOB AS COUNCILMAN. By Clayton L. Ringgenberg. Iowa City, State University of Iowa, Institute of Public Affairs, in cooperation with the League of Iowa Municipalities, 1954. 74 pp. $1.00.

City-county Consolidation

CONSOLIDATION STILL OFFERS CHANCE TO SHORTEN BALLOT. Philadelphia, Bureau of Municipal Research, *Citizens' Business,* May 24, 1954. 4 pp.

Civil Defense

H-BOMB—ZONES OF TOTAL AND PARTIAL DESTRUCTION IN PORTLAND AREA. New H-bombs Call for a Revised Look at Taxpayer Civil Defense Costs. Portland 4, Oregon Business & Tax Research, *Your Taxes,* May 1954. 4 pp.

SPOKANE SHOWS IT CAN BE DONE. First Mass Dispersal Test in Any American City Held April 26; Tenth of Population Evacuates Downtown Area; Civil Defense Based on Existing Municipal Agencies. By John J. Lenhart, Los Angeles 17, *Western City,* May 1954. 3 pp.

Congress

THE LEGISLATIVE PROCESS IN CONGRESS. By George B. Galloway. New York, Thomas Y. Crowell Company, 1953. xii, 689 pp. $6.00.

Corruption

SO THEY DID BUSINESS WITH SAMISH. Three important companies have lived close to a notorious political corruptionist, "Artie" Samish, czar of the California liquor industry. Two still do. But his conviction for tax fraud offers a chance to break the Samish power and to rid business of a damaging alliance. By Herbert Solow. Chicago 11, Time Inc., *Fortune,* April 1954. 7 pp.

County Government

YOUR WESTCHESTER COUNTY GOVERNMENT. By Jean S. Picker. White Plains (New York), Westchester County Government, 1954. 28 pp. Illus.

Crime

CRIME AND POLITICS IN CHICAGO. THE KOHN REPORT. A Preliminary Report of an Interrupted Investigation.

Popular Edition of the Famous Volume 6. By Aaron Kohn. Chicago, Independent Voters of Illinois, 1953. 128 pp. $1.00.

THIRD ANNUAL MEETING OF THE NEW YORK CITY ANTI-CRIME COMMITTEE. Transcript of Oral Report. By Spruille Braden. New York, the Committee, 1954. 20 pp.

Directories

DIRECTORY OF COUNTY OFFICIALS. 1953-54. Washington, D. C., National Association of County Officials, 1954. 247 pp. $5.00.

Economics

ECONOMIC INDICATORS OF MARYLAND COUNTIES. A Report Prepared for the Subcommittee on Financing of Maryland Health Activities of the Committee on Medical Care. College Park, University of Maryland, College of Business and Public Administration, Bureau of Governmental Research, 1954. 58 pp.

Education

TWELVE DISTRICTS GET TOGETHER IN SEEKING A SOLUTION TO SCHOOL PROBLEMS in Montgomery County and Chester County. Norristown, Pennsylvania Economy League, Inc., Montgomery Branch, 1954. 80 pp.

Elections

VERIFICATION OF ELECTION RESULTS. Springfield, Illinois Legislative Council, April 1954. 33 pp.

Federal-state Relations

FEDERAL-STATE RELATIONS. By Homer E. Scace. New York 21, Governmental Research Association, *GRA Reporter,* Second Quarter 1954. 4 pp.

Forms of Government

FORMS OF CITY GOVERNMENT. (Third edition.) Austin, University of Texas, Institute of Public Affairs, 1954. 33 pp. 50 cents.

THE STRUCTURE OF CITY GOVERNMENT IN WEST VIRGINIA. By Mavis Andree Mann. Morgantown, West Virginia University, Bureau for Government Research, 1953. 51 pp.

Home Rule

A DOZEN QUESTIONS AND ANSWERS ABOUT MUNICIPAL HOME RULE. College Park, Maryland Municipal League, 1954. 6 pp.

Housing

LOCAL DEVELOPMENT AND ENFORCEMENT OF HOUSING CODES. By Gilbert R. Barnhart. Washington 25, D. C., Housing and Home Finance Agency, Division of Housing Research, 1953. 60 pp. 40 cents.

THE SLUM, THE CITY, AND THE CITIZEN. By Albert M. Cole. Nashville 3, Tennessee Municipal League, *Tennessee Town & City*, May 1954. 4 pp.

Incentives to Industry

MUNICIPAL INITIATIVE IN INDUSTRIAL PROMOTION. By J. T. Benoit. Minneapolis 14, League of Minnesota Municipalities, *Minnesota Municipalities*, April 1954. 3 pp.

Legislation

GENERAL ASSEMBLY ACTION, 1954. A Staff Summary of Legislative Enactments. Frankfort, Kentucky Legislative Research Commission, 1954. 40 pp.

LEGISLATIVE REVIEW OF BILLS CONTAINING EXCEPTIONS TO GENERAL LAW. A Report of the Virginia Advisory Legislative Council to the Governor and the General Assembly of Virginia. Richmond, Virginia Division of Purchase and Printing, 1953. 5 pp.

Legislative Research

INTERIM STUDIES OF THE LEGISLATURES. Chicago 37, Council of State Governments, *State Government,* May 1954. 4 pp.

Local Government

SUMMARY OF GEORGIA LAWS AFFECTING LOCAL GOVERNMENT—November-December, 1953. By Olive Hall Shadgett. Athens, University of Georgia, Bureau of Public Administration, 1954. 32 pp. $1.00.

Metropolitan Areas

METROPOLITAN GOVERNMENT IN TORONTO. By Winston W. Crouch. Chicago 37, American Society for Public Administration, *Public Administration Review,* Spring 1954. 11 pp.

METROPOLITAN TORONTO. By Frederick G. Gardiner. (Address before the American Planning and Civic Association, Columbus, Ohio.) Washington, D. C., American Planning and Civic Association, 1954. 13 pp.

THE MUNICIPALITY OF METROPOLITAN TORONTO. Toronto, Metropolitan Council, 1954. 20 pp. Illus.

THE ROLE OF CITIZEN RESEARCH IN METROPOLITAN COMMUNITIES. Toronto 5, Bureau of Municipal Research and Citizens Research Institute of Canada, *Civic Affairs,* April 1954. 5 pp.

Municipal Government

KNOW YOUR CITY, YOUR ELECTIONS, YOUR SCHOOLS. By Aaron Simmons. New Rochelle, New York, 1954. 95 pp. (Apply author, City Manager, New Rochelle, N. Y.)

MUNICIPAL PROBLEMS, 1953. The Forty-fourth Annual Proceedings of the Conference of Mayors and Other Municipal Officials of the State of New York. Long Beach, June 17, 18, and 19. Albany, the Conference, 1954. 143 pp. $2.50.

THE 116TH ANNIVERSARY OF THE TOWN OF MILWAUKEE FINDS ITS ORIGINAL 106 SQUARE MILES REDUCED TO LESS THAN A MILE. Milwaukee 2, Citizens' Governmental Research Bureau, Inc., *Bulletin,* May 26, 1954. 7 pp.

Noise Abatement

QUIET, PLEASE! NOISE ABATEMENT FOR PHILADELPHIA. Philadelphia 7, Bureau of Municipal Research, 1954. 29 pp.

Parking

LOCATION FACTORS FOR OFF-STREET PARKING FACILITIES. By John F. Hendon and Howard D. Leake. Washington 6, D. C., Urban Land Institute, *Urban Land,* March 1954. 7 pp.

Personnel

THE MERIT SYSTEM. Our Continuing Responsibility. Providence 3, League of

Women Voters of Rhode Island, 1954. 13 pp. 15 cents.

Planning

IDEAS FOR A BETTER CITY. By Cecil Morgan. Knoxville, University of Tennessee, Division of University Extension, Municipal Technical Advisory Service, 1954. 42 pp.

PLANNING AND FINANCING CAPITAL IMPROVEMENTS. Chicago, Municipal Finance Officers Association of the United States and Canada, *Municipal Finance*, May 1954. 31 pp. 50 cents.

Public Works

ADVANCE PLANNING AND TIMING OF LOCAL PUBLIC WORKS. Still an Important Stabilization Device. By Robinson Newcomb. New York 16, *The American City*, April 1954. 2 pp.

Purchasing

COOPERATIVE GOVERNMENTAL PURCHASING. By James D. Kitchen. Los Angeles, University of California, Bureau of Governmental Research, March 1953. 25 pp.

Retirement

RETIREMENT PROVISIONS FOR FEDERAL PERSONNEL. Part II. The Relationships Between the Federal Staff Retirement Systems and the Old-Age and Survivors Insurance System. Proposal No. 2—The Civil Service Retirement System. Washington, D. C., Executive Office of the President, Committee on Retirement Policy for Federal Personnel, 1954. Variously paged.

Salaries

A SALARY SURVEY. Municipal Employment in Westchester County. Westchester County (New York), Municipal Administrators Association, 1954. 12 pp.

Shopping Centers

A NEW LOOK AT SHOPPING CENTERS. By Robert H. Armstrong. Washington 6, D. C., Urban Land Institute, *Urban Land*, May 1954. 4 pp.

State Government

NEVADA GOVERNMENT. A Study of the Administration and Politics of State,

County, Township and Cities. By Effie Mona Mack, Idel Anderson and Beulah E. Singleton. Caldwell, Idaho, The Caxton Printers, Ltd., 1953. xiv, 384 pp. $5.00.

State Reorganization

RECOMMENDATIONS TO THE STATE REORGANIZATION COMMISSION FROM THE MISSOURI PUBLIC EXPENDITURE SURVEY. By Edward Staples. Jefferson City, the Survey, 1954. 11 pp.

STATE ADMINISTRATIVE REORGANIZATION IN MICHIGAN: THE LEGISLATIVE APPROACH. By Frank M. Landers and Howard D. Hamilton. Chicago 37, American Society for Public Administration, *Public Administration Review*, Spring 1954. 13 pp.

Subdivision

REGULATING SUBDIVISIONS. The Control of Plats, Subdivisions, or Dedications. By Floyd M. Jennings and Ernest H. Campbell. Seattle 5, Association of Washington Cities in cooperation with the University of Washington, Bureau of Governmental Research and Services, 1954. 41 pp.

Surveys

THE CITY GETS A CHECK-UP. A Summary of the Reports of the Mayor's Committee on Management Survey and the Temporary State Commission to Study the Organizational Structure of the City of New York with a Note on Progress. New York 38, Citizens Union Research Foundation, Inc., 1954. 15 pp.

A COMMUNITY SURVEY. Newmarket Looks Ahead. By Bruce R. Dick, Marguerite M. Molloy, Shirley F. Price, James D. Reardon, Allan M. Towle and Rebecca B. Worcester under the supervision of David C. Knapp. Durham, University of New Hampshire, Department of Government, Public Administration Service, 1954. 101 pp.

DO YOU DARE TO RATE YOUR TOWN? *Town Journal's* tested questionnaire may touch off civic improvements you never dreamed possible. Look how Pennsboro,

West Virginia, used it. By Donald S. Stroetzel. Philadelphia 5, *Pathfinder* . . . *The Town Journal*, February 1954. 4 pp. 20 cents.

Taxation and Finance

ADDITIONAL POWERS OF TAXATION FOR ADOPTION BY COUNTIES. Report of the Virginia Advisory Legislative Council to the Governor and the General Assembly of Virginia. Richmond, Virginia Division of Purchase and Printing, 1953. 22 pp.

COMPENDIUM OF CITY GOVERNMENT FINANCES IN 1952. The 481 Cities Having More Than 25,000 Inhabitants in 1950. By U. S. Department of Commerce, Bureau of the Census. Washington, D. C., U. S. Government Printing Office, Superintendent of Documents, 1953. 163 pp. 65 cents.

FEDERAL AND STATE AID. Key Points Stressed at Tax Institute Symposium. Princeton, Tax Institute, Inc., *Tax Policy*, February-March 1954. 8 pp. 50 cents.

FEDERAL EXCISE TAXES. Exemptions Allowed Local and State Governments. Chicago 37, Municipal Finance Officers Association of the United States and Canada, April 1954. 4 pp. 50 cents.

FEDERAL FINANCES: 1. THE PROBLEM. 2. REDUCING EXPENDITURES. 3. THE TAX PROGRAM. New York 20, Committee on Federal Tax Policy, 1954. 27 pp., 30 pp. and 36 pp. respectively. $1.00 each.

FINANCIAL REPORT FOR 1953. New York 11, Port of New York Authority, 1954. 40 pp.

THE MICHIGAN BUSINESS RECEIPTS TAX—ITS BASIS AND ECONOMIC THEORY. By Alan L. Gornick. (Address before the University of Michigan Law School Institute.) Dearborn, Ford Motor Company, 1953. 24 pp.

MUNICIPAL RATING SYSTEMS. By A. R. Hutchinson. Melbourne (Australia), Municipal Association of Victoria, *Australian Municipal Journal*, March 1954. 3 pp.

A REPORT UPON THE 1953 OR EIGHTEENTH ANNUAL SURVEY OF COUNTY, CITY AND TOWN GOVERNMENT IN TENNESSEE. Nashville, Tennessee Taxpayers Association, 1954. 88 pp.

STATEMENT TO THE COMMISSION ON INTERGOVERNMENTAL RELATIONS ON FEDERAL GRANTS TO STATES AND TAX SOURCES. Jefferson City, Missouri Chamber of Commerce, January 1954. 27 pp.

STATE TAX LEGISLATION IN 1953. Princeton, New Jersey, Tax Institute, Inc., *Tax Policy*, November-December 1953. 40 pp. 50 cents.

THIS TAX PROBLEM. Lincoln 8 (Nebraska), Governmental Research Institute, Inc., *Bulletin*, April 1954. 6 pp.

Town Government

DIGEST OF 1954 LAWS AFFECTING TOWNS. Albany, Association of Towns of the State of New York, 1954. 48 pp.

Traffic

URBAN TRAFFIC. A FUNCTION OF LAND USE. By Robert B. Mitchell and Chester Rapkin. New York, Columbia University Press, 1954. 244 pp. $5.00.

Traffic Safety

OPERATION SAFETY. Program Kit on Traffic Safety Promotion. Theme for August 1954: SIGNS OF LIFE. Chicago 11, National Safety Council, 1954. Variously paged.

Waterworks

RECOMMENDED REORGANIZATION OF THE MUNICIPAL WATERWORKS SYSTEM, SAN ANTONIO, TEXAS. San Antonio, Southwest Research Institute, Department of Industrial Economics, 1954. 112 pp., charts.

Zoning

WE SHOULD BE REALISTIC ABOUT ZONING. Needs and Attitudes for Flexible Zoning. Philadelphia 4, University of Pennsylvania, Associated Institutes of Government of Pennsylvania Universities, *Horizons*, May 1954. 2 pp.

Inside the Office . . .

Howard P. Jones

Howard P. Jones, former executive director of the League and currently on leave between foreign assignments with the State Department, paid several calls at the new NML offices and held extensive conversations with Alfred Willoughby. Mrs. Jones accompanied him on one occasion. His most recent post was Counsellor of Embassy at Formosa.

John Shinn of the American Assembly discussed future assembly programming with the staff. . . . Edward Jones, executive director of the Springfield (Massachusetts) Taxpayers' Association, visited the office to review recent local governmental developments in various parts of the country.

Roger Freeman, special assistant to Governor Arthur B. Langlie of Washington, and Professor Weldon Cooper, of the University of Virginia, called to discuss state government problems and the 60th National Conference on Government. . . . Miss Belen Abreu, chief attorney to the Philippines Election Commission, called on John Bebout for advice on her tour of study in the United States.

Mrs. Maurice H. Noun, Council member from Des Moines, inspected the new League office in early June. . . . Albert Rudnick and L. Irving Smith, of Albany, New York, consulted

John Bebout and Belen Abreu

with staff on local governmental problems in Albany. . . . C. Bruce Smith, governmental consultant and son of Bruce Smith, director of the Institute of Public Administration, called on John Keith.

More than 30 preliminary inquiries about the 1954 All-America Cities Awards have been received thus far. . . . Dr. Robert E. Martin, of Howard University's Department of Government, consulted with John Bebout about civic education in colleges. . . . Henry Fagin, of the Regional Plan Association, discussed the NML's role in regional planning with several staff members. . . . Professor Joseph McLean of Princeton University, recently appointed Commissioner of Conservation and Economic Development by Governor Robert B. Meyner of New Jersey, visited the office recently to discuss the current series of excerpts from Project East River being run in the REVIEW. Dr. McLean, a consultant on Project East River, was author of the report appraising NML activities.

A. E. Buck, governmental consultant, author and leading authority on public budgeting, visited the office to discuss his manuscript of the revision of *Reorganization of State Governments in the United States*, published by the League in 1938.

(Continued on next page)

Women's Panel Report Published

A report entitled *Women As Campaigners* has been issued by the League. It is second in a series of mimeographed transcripts of panel sessions held in November during the 59th National Conference on Government at Richmond, Virginia.

Chairman of the panel, which discussed practical ways in which women can contribute to campaigns for candidates and issues, was Margaret Hickey of the *Ladies' Home Journal*. The panel included Mrs. John G. Lee, president, League of Women Voters of the United States; Mrs. Tom Ragland, Democratic National Committeewoman, Tennessee; Mrs. Maurice H. Noun, ex-president, League of Women Voters of Des Moines; Mrs. Cecil L. Brown, candidate, North Plainfield (New Jersey) Charter Commission; Mrs. Polly Cary Woodson, Republican chairman, Ridgewood, New Jersey; Mrs. Edward Kuhn, Women's Division, Cincinnati City Charter Committee; Mrs. Preston Farley, secretary, Illinois Committee for Constitutional Revision; Mrs. Shirley Wheeler, League of Women Voters of Arlington County, Virginia; Mrs. T. Jackson Waller, Women's Republican Club, Seaford, Delaware; Mrs. Martha Cheney, Republican district committeewoman, Stamford, Connecticut; Mrs. Charles Wilder, secretary, Citizens Association of Kansas City; Miss Phyllis Otey, vice chairman, Republican State Central Committee, Virginia; Mrs. Kathryn H. Stone, Virginia legislature, Arlington; Mrs. Dorothy Davis, mayor, Washington, Virginia.

The report covers 32 pages and is available from the League's office for 50 cents, or may be obtained on request without charge by sustaining members.

Seed to Speak in Seattle

Allen H. Seed, Jr., assistant director of the League, will attend the Institute of Government in Seattle, Washington, July 12-16. Mr. Seed will be the luncheon speaker on July 14 and will talk on the subject "Good Government Is No Accident." The Institute of Government is an annual summer conference sponsored by the University of Washington and attended by public officials, civic leaders and teachers from the Pacific Northwest.

Mr. Seed recently returned from a trip to Pittsburgh, Cincinnati and Dayton during which he conferred with League officers and representatives of citizen organizations.

Bromage Appointed

Arthur W. Bromage, League Council member and professor of political science at the University of Michigan, has been appointed a member of the Michigan Commission on Intergovernmental Relations by Governor G. Mennen Williams. Professor Bromage's latest book, *Councilmen at Work*, was published recently.

Inside the Office

(Continued from page 387)

Donald C. Wagner, executive director of the Greater Philadelphia Movement, visited the office recently.

Donald C. Wagner and Alfred Willough

NEWS for League Members

Californian Wins League Fellowship

Russell J. Cooney, city manager of Merced, California, is the first winner of the National Municipal League Fellowship at the Graduate School of Business Administration, Harvard University, and the nation's first municipal official who will attend the Advanced Management Program at Harvard.

The Advanced Management Program is a thirteen-week seminar in which 150 top executives from the business world, leading administrators from the federal government and senior officers from the armed forces take part. Mr. Cooney will attend the 26th session beginning this fall.

Inaugurated just after World War II, the program is an intensive course of study for mature, experienced executives who are expected to assume policy-making positions and posts of greater responsibility with their organizations.

Freed from their daily duties, those participating are able to take appropriate courses, exchange information and ideas with other students and with faculty members, and do some quiet thinking about administrative and management problems.

The new fellowship provides a $1,500 stipend contributed by Mr. and Mrs. Preston Farley of Evanston, Illinois, League members. Mr. Farley is a candy manufacturer and a graduate of the

Russell J. Cooney

Harvard Graduate School of Business Administration.

Not only did the far-sighted city council of Merced grant Mr. Cooney a leave of absence with pay, but it is allowing him up to $500 in expenses. In return Mr. Cooney agreed to remain at his Merced post for at least three years.

Chosen from numerous applicants, Mr. Cooney has been city manager at Merced, a city of 18,000 in central California, since November 1, 1951. Prior to that he was personnel director of Pasadena and of San Mateo County, California.

A graduate of Lincoln, Nebraska, High School, Mr. Cooney received his higher education as the opportunity presented itself. He took courses at Los Angeles City College, the University of California at Los Angeles and the University of Southern California, chiefly in the field of public administration.

The fellowship is open to public personnel on the state and local level.

Cash Foundation Prizes

The Albert D. Cash Foundation, named for a former member of the League's Council and former mayor of Cincinnati, will award four $300 prizes a year to employees of Cincinnati who make the best suggestions for improving the city's services.

2-Month Coast-to-Coast Trip Ended by Seed

Allen H. Seed, Jr., League assistant director, recently completed a two-month coast-to-coast tour in which he had speaking engagements and conferred with civic leaders in some twenty states.

Among other organizations, he addressed the Institute of Government of the University of Washington at Seattle, the Municipal League of Seattle and King County, Municipal League of Spokane and the Spokane Junior Chamber of Commerce, and the Colorado Springs Charter Committee.

Mr. Seed also stopped in Kansas City in connection with the League's National Conference on Government, November 7 to 10.

Bebout, Cassella Take Part in Chicago Parley

John E. Bebout, League assistant director, and William N. Cassella, Jr., staff member, are participating in the 50th annual meeting of the American Political Science Association in Chicago, September 9 to 11. The former is a member of a panel on "Recent Developments in the Forms of Local Government." Dr. Cassella, a member of the panel on "Current Problems in State and Local Government," will read a paper entitled, "Recent Trends in State-Local Relations: Some Fundamental Questions."

League Studies Presidential Primary Law

A project which may result in the publication of a new model law by the League is in its exploratory stages.

If completed, it will be called the *Model State Presidential Primary Law*. The project will be a topic for consideration at the National Conference on Government in Kansas City, if it is sufficiently advanced at that time.

Richard S. Childs, chairman of the League's Executive Committee, is in correspondence with some 50 political scientists, state legislators, congressmen and others and is circulating a draft for discussion.

According to Mr. Childs, delegates to the Republican and Democratic nominating conventions are sometimes hand-picked by party bosses without reference to the wishes of the voters enrolled in the party. The proposal would provide for submission to the parties' voters of slates of uninstructed delegates by each party's state committee. Independents and presidential candidates would have the opportunity to enter opposition slates to run in a June primary. If there were no opposition, there would be no primary.[1]

[1]See also page 413, this issue.

National Municipal Review

Volume XLIII, No. 8   Total Number 446

Published monthly except August

By NATIONAL MUNICIPAL LEAGUE

Contents for September 1954

The contents of the REVIEW are indexed in *International Index to Periodicals* and *Public Affairs Information Service.*

Entered as second class matter July 11, 1932, at the Post Office at Worcester, Massachusetts. Publication office, 150 Fremont Street, Worcester 3; editorial and business office, 542 Fifth Avenue, New York 36. Copyright 1954 by the National Municipal League.

Subscription, $5 per year; Canadian, $5.25; foreign, $5.50; single copies 50 cents.

Editorial Comment

Civil Defense Is Common Sense

COMMON sense is sometimes uncommon hard to live by. It is certainly common sense to spare no pains to protect our great cities from destruction in modern war. It is certainly common sense to protect these same cities from self-destruction in the toils of modern traffic and the swamp of urban blight.

Yet more people are running away from these problems than rallying to do something effective about them.

The article at page 403, "Defense of Metropolitan Areas," shows how closely and perhaps fatefully these two problems are tied together. It points out that effective civil defense cannot be had without effective areawide planning and action to guide future growth. Anyone who has been piloting an automobile for the last quarter century has long been painfully aware of the increasingly unpleasant effects of our failure to achieve metropolitan-wide planning and action to cope with the internal combustion engine. If we do not quickly rise to the challenge of nuclear fission and fusion there may be relatively few people left a quarter century hence to lament our lack of foresight.

Some of the things that need to be done to reduce urban vulnerability to attack would not make sense in an utterly peaceful world. Fortunately, many of the things called for by defense we should be doing anyway, to make our metropolitan areas more livable and more efficient.

The National Municipal League's work in the fields of state and metropolitan government is directed more and more to helping citizens and officials do these things. For example, the League is now preparing a model state planning law to help 1955 legislatures provide a legal basis for more realistic and more comprehensive state and regional planning for defense and for better communities.[1]

New Look at Pensions

THERE is a grim lesson for many cities and states in the recent report of the commission set up by the President and Congress to examine the various pension systems of the federal government. (See page 394.)

Pension systems generally have just grown, more often as a result of pressures than of careful study and planning.

Many are actuarily unsound, extravagant and inequitable. Furthermore, they have not been adjusted nor are they adjustable in recognition of the effect of inflation on those who retired some years ago after paying one-hundred-cent dollars into retirement funds.

How many cities and states actually know what their accrued lia-

[1]See page 440, this issue.

392

bilities are? Until the commission made its study, Congress and the executive department did not know that the United States had accrued liabilities of $30,000,000,000 in connection with various pension systems. Is that not part of the national debt?

While there has been increasing consideration of ability to pay and other basic requirements in debts contracted for public works, retirement programs in general have developed in a catch-as-catch-can manner with little thought of the burdens being wished on future generations.

For example, a bill currently before Congress gives employees of states and cities the power to decide whether their governments may coordinate retirement programs with social security, as if it were not the right of the people as a whole to decide how they wish to reward and provide for those working for them. This seems, on its face, entirely unreasonable and another bit of the kind of pressure group activity that has already made such a mess of things.

There will be serious trouble if cities and states fail to take advantage of the opportunity which the federal government offers to avail themselves of social security coverage to modernize their pension plans. When things get to the point, as they have in one large city, where the police and fire pension plan costs 30 per cent of the payroll for those services and the teachers' pension plan costs 18 per cent, it is easy to see how good intentions can be self-defeating.

It is none too early for cities and states to follow the example of the federal government in making a careful study of their own retirement programs. This should be done not only in the public interest but in the interest of fair and equal treatment of those who work for governments.

U. S. Studies Pension Plans

Conclusions of committee report on 23 retirement funds may serve as guide for state and local government units.

By H. ELIOT KAPLAN*

ADOPTION by Congress of the Reed bill authorizing broad social security coverage of state and local government employees focuses attention on the reports of the Federal Committee on Retirement Policy for Federal Personnel[1] which, after an extensive study of federal pension plans, advocated, among other recommendations to Congress, coordinating existing retirement plans with social security coverage.

The reports may serve as a guide for state and local governments which are facing similar problems of modernizing their pension plans and providing more adequate survivorship coverage. They hold out

*Mr. Kaplan, who served as chairman of the Committee on Retirement Policy for Federal Personnel, was New York State deputy comptroller from 1948 to 1952 and, for twenty years prior to 1948, executive director and counsel of the National Civil Service League. He is now counsel to the New York State Commission on Pensions and consultant on pensions of public utility companies for the New York State Public Service Commission.

[1]*Retirement Provisions for Federal Personnel*: Part I, 774 pp.; Part II, *The Relationships Between the Federal Staff Retirement Systems and the Old-age and Survivors Insurance System*, 225 pp.; Part III, *The Relationships Between the Federal Staff Retirement Systems and the Old-age and Survivors Insurance System*, 143 pp.; Part IV, (A) *The Financial Status of the Federal Retirement Plans*, (B) *Recommended Funding and Financing Policies*, 143 pp.; Part V, *Report on Special Benefit Provisions*, 478 pp. Executive Office of the President, Committee on Retirement Policy for Federal Personnel, Washington, D. C., 1954.

some promise and hope that rising costs of retirement benefits could, by economical and effective controls, be adjusted somehow to keep pace with the inflation spiral.

Since 1950 social security coverage could be extended only to state and local employees who were not eligible for membership in a public retirement plan. The new law authorizes extension of coverage to all state and local employees, subject to a referendum vote of the members of a retirement system where there is a pension plan in the jurisdiction. The recommendations of the federal committee, therefore, outlining the plan of extending social security coverage to federal employees, may prove of interest and substantial value to local governments seeking to take advantage of the new social security law.

Toward the end of the 1952 session, Congress, grappling with the problem of adjusting annuities of retired federal employees to meet the increased cost of living, was confronted with the problem of how properly to finance such increases.

In the course of committee hearings on the proposal there was evidently considerable misapprehension as to the accrued liabilities of the various federal pension plans. There also appeared to be lack of awareness of the relationship of the various federal retirement systems to each other, their relationships to

394

social security coverage, and benefits accorded under the Federal Employees' Compensation Act. Estimates, for example, of accrued liabilities of the various pension plans ranged from as low as $10,000,000,-000 to as much as $100,000,000,000.

Impressed by recommendations of the Bureau of the Budget that it was time a survey were made of all the federal pension plans to determine just what they involved and just where the government stood financially with respect to them, Congress enacted Public Law 555 of 1952, creating a Committee on Retirement Policy for Federal Personnel. It comprised the secretary of the treasury, secretary of defense, chairman of the Board of Governors of the Federal Reserve Bank, director of the budget, chairman of the Civil Service Commission and a chairman designated by the President.

All Plans Surveyed

The committee was directed to survey all existing federal retirement plans, both civil and military, involving about 5,200,000 employees, and report its findings and recommendations with respect to the following:

(1) The types and amounts of retirement and other related benefits provided to federal personnel, including their role in the compensation system as a whole;

(2) The necessity for special benefit provisions for selected employee groups, including overseas personnel and employees in hazardous occupations;

(3) The relationships of these retirement systems to one another, to the federal employees' compensation

system, and to such general systems as old-age and survivors insurance; and

(4) The current financial status of the several systems, the most desirable methods of cost determination and funding, the division of costs between the government and the members of the systems, and the policies that should be followed in meeting the government's portion of the cost of the various systems.

Originally the committee was to make its report by June 30, 1953. Because of delay in organization of the committee's work, due primarily to a change of administration, Congress extended the life of the committee to June 30, 1954. Congress appropriated $225,000 for its activities. A staff of about 24 employees was assembled, all recruited by the Civil Service Commission under its rules. Twenty-three federal retirement plans were surveyed.

The first report, submitted to Congress on January 22, 1954, comprised factual findings relating to all 23 retirement plans, comparing their benefit structures, methods of financing and other pertinent data. It was basically a description and comparative analysis of retirement and related provisions in effect on January 1, 1954.

The second report, submitted to Congress on May 13, 1954, dealt with a revision of the uniformed services retirement system and recommended a plan coordinating that system with old-age and survivor insurance benefits under the Social Security Act. The committee proposed that benefits for military personnel be confined to three sources:

(1) The Department of Defense would continue to administer the six months' death benefit on a somewhat revised basis;

(2) The Veterans Administration would administer newly designed service compensation and continuing monthly survivor benefit programs;

(3) The Department of Health, Education and Welfare would administer the old-age and survivors' insurance program for military personnel on the basis of contributory participation, the same as applies for employees in private industry.

Changes Would Cut Costs

The committee believes that its recommended changes would provide a measure of retirement protection for non-career personnel, improve the retirement protection of the career serviceman, and establish a sound and equitable program of survivor protection for all members of the services. Furthermore, the proposed plan would save over $100,000,000 a year.

The committee's third report, submitted to Congress on May 20, 1954, recommended coordination of the government's largest civil pension plan—Civil Service Retirement and Disability Fund—with old-age and survivor insurance coverage. The committee believed this would considerably improve the over-all survivor protection of federal employees, strengthen the civil service retirement system for the fulfillment of its essential role in the administration of the federal government, and eliminate serious inequities in benefit payments which now occur. In approaching the problem of coordinating the two plans, the committee agreed that for any such plan to be acceptable it would have to meet adequately the following specifications:

(1) Establish a rational relationship between retirement benefits and service for those whose work-lifetime may include employment in both the federal service and private industry.

(2) Maintain complete independence of the civil service retirement system;

(3) Assure continuance of the civil service retirement system as the primary means of providing adequate protection for career employees, while placing some of the cost on the old-age and survivors' insurance system for providing coverage — particularly for those shifting between federal and private employment;

(4) Provide at least the present level of retirement benefits based on federal employment;

(5) Maintain the total employee contribution at approximately the present level;   ·

(6) Maintain simplicity of formula and administration.

The committee's proposal was designed to carry out the President's program of extending old-age and survivors' benefits to areas of employment not now covered, among them the federal civil employees. About 550,000 federal employees holding non-permanent status positions, it was found, were already under social security coverage. They are not now eligible for membership in the federal retirement system. It was the committee's belief that its proposed plan "would establish a rational relationship between the benefits and length of employment in place of the present haphazard arrangement," and that generally immediate savings would accrue to both the government and to members of the retirement system. Specifically, costs would be immediately affected as follows:

(1) Reduction of 7.5 per cent in the total employee contribution rate (including the 2 per cent social security tax);

(2) Reduction of about one-third in both the "normal cost" and in the "unfunded accrued liability" of the civil service retirement system;

(3) Reduction of approximately 9 per cent in the over-all costs to government of providing retirement and survivor protection (including 2 per cent social security employer tax).

The existing level of retirement benefits would be payable prior to age 65. Retirement income to members of the system would be increased on the average by about 8 per cent after age 65. In addition, the wife or dependent husband of a retired employee could also qualify for a social security benefit.

Survivor protection for members of the civil service retirement system would be greatly improved. The widow of an employee would receive an annuity immediately, rather than at age 50 as provided at present. She would also become eligible for social security at age 65. The existing civil service benefits for dependent children would be replaced by the more adequate social security family benefits.

The committee believes that the over-all improvements in retirement and survivor protection which would be achieved by the proposal would restore the federal government to a position of leadership in the field of pensions.

Methods of Financing

The fourth report, submitted to Congress on June 29, 1954, deals with the method of funding and financing the Civil Service Retirement and Disability Fund and the military retirement system. The committee recommended a partial funding plan for the Civil Service Retirement and Disability Fund so as to provide a reasonable reserve fund at all times. In connection with the military retirement plan the committee concluded that it would be impractical to finance it other than on a "pay-as-you-go" basis, largely because of the large fluctuations from time to time in the military population.

The report reveals that the accrued liabilities of all existing federal pension plans now amount to about $30,000,000,000.

In its fifth and final report the committee reviewed the special benefit provisions in the various pension plans, including hazardous and arduous types of employment, disability and discontinued service retirement benefits, and federal employment compensation benefits for injuries or deaths occurring in the course of employment.

The committee completed its assigned task within the period directed by Congress. It also returned to the Treasury over 20 per cent of its original appropriation as an unexpended balance.

Commenting on the committee's

(Continued on page 402)

Court Settles Apportionment

Wisconsin achieves redistricting of legislature with help of judicial intervention reinstating 1951 law.

By WILLIAM H. YOUNG*

AFTER a struggle of more than three decades, the urban-industrial population of Wisconsin has achieved a reapportionment of the seats of the two houses of the legislature. This reapportionment substantially recognizes the major shifts of population in the state and is roughly equitable in representing people as such.

This is an achievement of no mean proportions. Reapportionments which accurately reflect the distribution of population have been extremely difficult to achieve politically and in many states are forbidden constitutionally. The unique feature of the Wisconsin achievement is rather, however, that it was accomplished only with the assistance of the State Supreme Court.

Most students of government have come to expect that courts will rarely, if ever, intervene in reapportionment contests. Generally speaking, the courts have pleaded want of power to enforce their decrees upon a recalcitrant legislature when invited to enforce various constitutional injunctions regarding reapportionment. Commonly, they have also ignored "minor deviations"

from constitutional rules governing reapportionment in an effort to give effect to the unmistakable intentions of legislative bodies.

The courts have not halted gerrymandering nor, typically, compelled a reluctant legislature to do its constitutional duty. Petitioners' arguments in support of constitutional directives, such as "as nearly equal as possible," "the equal protection of the laws" or "compact and contiguous districts," have commonly not been effective in persuading courts to upset legislative acts which demonstrably deviate from these requirements. It should, therefore, be of interest to examine the circumstances in which a high court effectively compelled a reapportionment on the basis of population.

The Wisconsin constitution provides: "At their first session after each enumeration made by the authority of the United States, the legislature shall apportion and district anew the members of the Senate and Assembly, according to the number of inhabitants." No consequential reapportionment of seats in either house, however, has occurred since 1921. The continuing urbanization of the population, therefore, has been inadequately reflected in the distribution of legislative representation. Assembly districts in 1951 ranged in size from 13,715 to 95,534 and Senate districts from 61,795 to 191,588. The under-rep-

*Professor Young, director of the Division of Departmental Research in the Wisconsin governor's office 1949-1951 and consultant to the governor of Wisconsin on state administration 1951-1952, has been with the University of Wisconsin since 1947 and chairman of its Department of Political Science since 1952.

resented populations were virtually all in the large urban and industrial regions of the state and the over-represented populations were in the agricultural and "cut-over" regions. The under-represented peoples had also shown a fondness for Democratic or Progressive candidates for office while the over-represented peoples, especially those in agricultural areas, preferred Republicans.

Thus, all the typical elements in state reapportionment controversies in industrial states were present in Wisconsin. The only mitigating factor was that even if reapportionment were made on a strict population basis, urban and industrial control of both houses of the legislature would not result.

Reapportionment Act Passed

In preparation for the post-census session of the legislature in 1951, both parties having pledged action on reapportionment, the Legislative Council appointed a committee to study the subject and prepare a report on it. This committee was headed by the former chief justice of the State Supreme Court, Marvin B. Rosenberry. The plan of reapportionment which it proposed became known thereafter as the Rosenberry plan. The judiciary here made its first contribution to reapportionment. The justice's substantial services on the committee gave the committee's report an air of judicious nonpartisanship.

After much study the committee prepared a new scheme of reapportionment in the spirit of the constitutional provision and provid-ing much fairer distribution of seats in both houses according to population. The Legislative Council forwarded the proposed reapportionment act to the legislature without comment. It also forwarded a proposed amendment to the constitution of Wisconsin which would, if adopted, allow area as well as population to be regarded in subsequent reapportionments of at least one house of the legislature.

The governor urged the legislature when it assembled to do its constitutional duty and pass the Rosenberry bill or some equitable version of it. He did not indicate that he would be adverse to amending the constitution to govern future reapportionments. In the legislative controversy that followed, the governor's influence, on the whole, was favorable to immediate passage of the Rosenberry plan. A rather unusual compromise plan was finally evolved at the price of a lot of midnight oil and the inhalation of large quantities of tobacco smoke. This plan accepted virtually the entire Rosenberry reapportionment plan but postponed its realization until 1954.

Meanwhile, a referendum, advisory in character, would be held in connection with the presidential election of 1952 in which the voters would be asked whether they favored a subsequent submission of a constitutional amendment which would make area as well as population a factor to be included in districting the state for legislative purposes. If the vote were affirmative on this proposition, the Rosenberry plan would not become effective. It should be noted in passing that the decision to submit the question in the presidential election in November 1952 was a concession won by the urban-industrial faction, for the turnout of urban voters is much heavier in general elections than in primaries or local elections.

The legislature of 1951 also passed—the first of two required endorsements—a constitutional amendment making area a factor in legislative districts. If the advisory referendum revealed popular approval for area, this amendment could then be considered at the next regular session of the unreapportioned legislature in 1953 and, if approved, submitted to the voters in 1953.

Court Intervenes

The court was invited formally to intervene in the reapportionment controversy for the first time when the advisory referendum provision was assailed in an original suit to compel the secretary of state to issue the election writs in 1952 in accordance with the Rosenberry law. In an original action before the Wisconsin Supreme Court[1] petitioners argued that the sections of the act effectuating the reapportionment fulfilled the mandate of the constitution and that the legislature was without power to qualify this fulfillment by making it contingent upon the outcome of a referendum. Furthermore, it was argued, the referendum was an invalid delegation of legislative power. The court

was not swayed by these arguments and sustained the act including the referendum and the delayed date of realization. The language of the opinion indicated that the court felt it was in fact expediting the reapportionment by its decision and that if it had found the referendum invalid it would have had to invalidate the whole act.

In the November election, the urban population gained a narrow victory—753,092 against 689,615—and thus pushed the state nearer to the realization of the Rosenberry population-only reapportionment.

When the legislators, elected largely in the same November election and from the old districts, met in the capitol for the session of 1953, the "areacrats," as they were now called, organized themselves to continue the struggle. Early in the session and in spite of the outcome of the referendum, they persuaded the legislature to pass the pending constitutional amendment providing for area as well as population to be considered in Senate districting. They were also successful in having the pending amendment placed before the voters in the April election (a nonpartisan municipal and judicial election). In this way the legislature, which usually meets for five or six months, would still be in session and still be able to repeal the Rosenberry Act and replace it with one based partially on area. In a light vote, the area amendment was approved 433,043 to 406,133. The rural leaders then proceeded to supersede the population reapportionment with a new reapportion-

---

[1]*State ex rel. Broughton* v. *Zimmerman*, 261 Wis. 398 (1952).

ment (the Rogan Act) which actually reduced urban representation in the Senate, the one house in which area was to be recognized. The legislature, anticipating a court test, recessed to October to await developments.

The secretary of state compelled judicial intervention at this juncture. He proclaimed his intention to issue writs of election for the 1954 legislative election on the basis of the repealed Rosenberry Act, contending that the constitutional amendment and the new reapportionment act based upon it were invalid. The attorney general brought an original action for a declaratory judgment before the State Supreme Court to compel the secretary of state to observe the new law. The court held for the secretary of state and thus reinstated the Rosenberry law and compelled the reapportionment which it provided.[2]

The argument of the court for this unusual action was substantially this. The legislature had exhausted its constitutional authority to reapportion again before 1961 by the passage of the Rosenberry Act. There was adequate precedent for the construction of the pertinent section of the Wisconsin constitution that only one reapportionment can be made in each decade between enumerations. In the second place, the court said, the question on the constitutional amendment was improperly submitted to the voters.[3]

The actual amendment changed not only the provision governing the basis of senatorial representation but also the provision governing the local boundary lines which are to be recognized in reapportionment—the village was added to town and ward as a unit whose boundary must be respected in laying out assembly districts and the county was eliminated as such a unit.

Furthermore, the amendment eliminated the existing provisions for excluding Indians and the military from population computations and this was not represented to the voters in the question put to them. Further, the amendment dropped from the constitution a prohibition against dividing Assembly districts in forming Senate districts and this was not included in the question submitted.

Several Amendments Needed

The court indicated that to accomplish these various changes in the constitution more than one amendment question would have to be submitted to the voters in order to comply with another constitutional provision that if more than one amendment is submitted they must be submitted separately so that the voters may consider them separately. None of these changes, said the court, were essential to achieve recognition of the area factor and, therefore, were not merely inciden-

---

[2] *State ex rel. Thomson* v. *Zimmerman,* 264 Wis. 644 (1953).
[3] The question +as submitted to the voters in April was: "Shall sections 3, 4

and 5 of Article IV of the constitution be amended so that the legislature shall apportion, along town, village or ward lines, the Senate districts on the basis of area and population and the Assembly districts according to population?"

tal to that question. More than this, the court said, the question placed before the voters actually misrepresented the contents of the amendment for it gave the impression that town, village and ward lines must be considered in Senate districts as well as Assembly districts and the actual amendment deletes all necessity to observe local boundaries in laying out Senate districts. The court, finally, said that the fact that certain publication requirements for amendments submitted in November were not observed was not significant.

It is possible to conclude from this that the "areacrats" bungled badly in their legal draftsmanship and certainly there were many private recriminations among them on this score. It is also possible to conclude that the court seized upon several relatively minor and technical errors to upset the most recent action of the voters and the nnquestioned intention of the legislature. And it did this in a field of legal controversy in which courts have traditionally supported legislative intentions, however grossly these may have departed from the letter and the spirit of the constitutions which govern them. The court, it should be observed, was staffed largely by appointees of Republican governors.

How does the matter now rest? The legislature met again in October and did the only thing it could do to save the "areacrat" cause. It passed for the first time a new constitutional amendment consistent with the letter of the court decision. The next action on this amendment will have to be taken by a new legislature elected from new districts on the basis of a bill repealed by the legislature and reinstated by the Supreme Court.

U. S. STUDIES PENSION PLANS
(Continued from page 397)
report, the President, on July 8, 1954, stated:

The reports of the committee reflect a thorough analysis and appraisal of federal employee retirement systems and provide an up-to-date base for the construction of forward-looking programs. In particular, the committee has explored the ramifications of extending old-age and survivors' insurance coverage to federal employees and to the personnel of the uniformed services on a regular contributory basis, an objective of great importance. The committee's findings as to costs and financial status of federal retirement systems should prove a significant contribution to future consideration of readjustments in those systems.

Defense of Metropolitan Areas

"Protection must be conceived on a scale which covers entire concentrations of population and industry."

EDITOR'S NOTE.—This article is taken from Part V, *Reduction of Urban Vulnerability,* of the *Report of Project East River,* published under Signal Corps contract by Associated Universities, New York City, 1952. This is the second of two articles taken from the report—see "We're All in the Same Boat," the REVIEW, July 1954, page 337.

IN ANY future war, the metropolitan areas of the industrialized nations will constitute primary targets for attack by modern weapons. Even though it may be economically and physically impossible to make these areas completely invulnerable to attack, a major objective in defense must be an increased chance for survival of people, industrial production, transportation and urban services. To keep pace with weapons development, it is essential to make urban targets less remunerative.

Targets for enemy attacks are found principally in the standard metropolitan areas of the United States where 60 per cent of the population live, where approximately two-thirds of all factory and wage earners are located and where skilled labor, technicians, scientists, management personnel and other key men are heavily concentrated.

From the point of view of civil defense the most important movement of population has been the continuous trend from non-metropolitan to metropolitan areas. The 1950 census showed a metropolitan area population gain of 22 per cent, three and one-half times the growth of non-metropolitan areas during the preceding decade. In fact, since the first census of 1790, the nation has gained steadily in urban concentrations.

The relative attractiveness of central cities as targets is still increasing despite metropolitan expansion. Suburban areas with a wider spacing of people and industry are growing rapidly—yet the equivalent of 37 cities the size of Flint, Michigan, was packed into the old central cities during the last census decade.

During the eighteen months prior to December 31, 1951, of a total of 246 industrial plants locating in metropolitan areas with a central city having 100,000 or more population, 105 plants were reported as being built in the central cities as compared with 141 in the suburbs. The construction awards for the 105 plants represent an estimated construction cost of $492,000,000 as compared with $1,162,000,000 invested in the suburbs.

Daytime Population

Daytime concentrations of people contribute to the problem of urban vulnerability. The flow of workers and shoppers to downtown areas adds over ten million persons to the prime target areas in 57 cities. This represents a daytime population gain of 75 per cent for these areas. The daytime gain for the central cities as a whole is 20 per cent. In the southern part of New York's Manhattan Island, to cite the na-

403

tion's most dramatic situation, three and three-quarter million persons enter each working day and leave each evening.

In general, while there is a marked trend of new residential and related retail development in suburban areas, industrial and commercial expansion is continuing in central areas. Although some industrial and commercial activities have been moving out of central areas at a slow rate during the past 50 years, a trend interrupted by World Wars I and II but now resumed, the rate of movement is low, affording no promise that dispersion will occur automatically on any large scale. The trends indicate, however, that dispersion of many industries and other job-producing activities from central to peripheral locations in metropolitan areas could be accomplished without major diseconomies. In relation to urban vulnerability, it is essential that these trends of dispersion be accelerated and guided on a metropolitan basis so as not to produce new or expanded target areas.

The task of building relative protection into existing urban development and current additions to it is not an impossible one. As to existing urban areas, it is estimated that casualties in the grey zones of partial damage could be reduced by as much as 75 per cent if a warning time of one hour and adequate shelters were available. The cost of an effective shelter program does not appear prohibitive.

American cities are growing and changing so rapidly that reasonable controls over new development could effect a large reduction in over-all vulnerability in a few years. It has been estimated that the total physical structure of the nation's major cities—the houses, streets, stores, schools, factories, water systems and other facilities that provide the physical basis for city living—increased about 25 per cent in size during the past decade, a net addition to the urban structure of 2.5 per cent a year.

The discussion has indicated that reduction of urban vulnerability can be achieved by two nonmilitary measures: (1) spacing (decongestion of existing cities and better standards of spacing of new urban developments) to reduce target attractiveness, and (2) structural protection (providing shelter in existing structures, developing fire-prevention standards and building new structures to bomb-resistant standards) to make urban areas more able to withstand attack.

Federal Leadership

While the federal government has long been directly involved in the development of long-range programs of soil conservation, irrigation and agricultural improvement in rural areas, there has been no major need prior to the advent of the atomic bomb for the federal government to be concerned with problems of congestion of industry and people in urban areas. It has therefore been difficult for the government to determine how it should proceed now that centers of population and industry have become the most lucrative targets for new weapons. As the authority on defense matters, the government is expected to provide leadership in this field. The program, however, should not substitute, under the guise of national defense, centralized federal control for traditional independence in local affairs.

The major defect in present policies seems to have been undue reliance on local volunteer committees in each metropolitan area to furnish the initiative for defense plant dispersion that can come only from the federal government. The slogan has been "Community responsibility—federal guidance." It would, of course, be highly desirable for dispersal to come as a "grass roots" movement. However, no community or local committee can carry out what is essentially a major responsibility of the federal government. Until the federal government precisely defines the standards and the program to be undertaken, local action can not be effective.

No one community, no single state, is in a position to adopt and enforce urban defense standards until other cities and states are subject to the same standards. Local communities and even states do not possess the facts on which to develop such standards. The outstanding authorities in the science of atomic warfare are associated with the federal government, and the security aspects of their work prevent the release of information upon which defense standards need to be based. The ability to assemble these facts and the duty of interpreting them clearly lie in the province of the federal government. Private business and local and state governments will implement their programs when the federal government demonstrates its leadership and establishes standards to govern its own activities in centers of population and industry. Until this is accomplished, the states, municipalities and private investors will assume that in so far as national defense is concerned, "building as usual" is the order of the day.

Developing Standards

Project East River believes that a set of standards for the decongestion of existing urban target areas (for example, the largest central cities) and the spacing of new urban development (for example, new suburban areas) should be established without further delay. While these standards will of necessity be oversimplified and crude at first, the direction of the program must be set immediately in order that progress may be made in developing and applying more refined standards, as well as to check the present dangerous trends toward increasing vulnerability.

a. *Urban Densities.* If civil defense were the only consideration, the greatest security could be achieved by the widest possible spacing of homes, factories and commercial establishments so as to eliminate target areas entirely. A modern industrialized society, however, requires urban concentrations. The problem, therefore, is one of achieving the best balance of dispersion or spacing within the practical limits of a properly functioning urban economy. In terms of population density, minimum limits appear to be between 2,000 and 8,000 persons per gross square mile with 5,000 to 6,000 persons per square mile as a theoretical optimum based on factors of labor supply, transportation, public services, balance of economic activity, provision of cultural functions, housing preference, housing economy and amenity.[1]

. . . .

Standards for U. S.

The standards for density and spacing developed[2] are applicable to a wide range of federal activities and, when properly used, the standards can have a strong effect in guiding future development so as to reduce urban vulnerability. While industrial and urban expansion is principally a function of private enterprise carried on under state police power regulations, the federal influence in city building is significant. For example, total building construction in all urban areas in 1950 is reported as amounting to $10,-400,000,000. During this same year, the federal government insured mortgages on building construction in urban areas in the amount of over $3,000,000,000, in addition to the $700,000,000 of contracts it awarded directly for such construction as public housing, schools, public build-

[1] See *Reduction of Urban Vulnerability*, Report of Project East River, Appendix V-B *Minimum Density and Spacing Standards for Metropolitan Dispersion*.
[2] For detailed statistics descriptive of Class I and Class II Vulnerable Urban Districts, see pages 21, 25 and 27-30 of Report V, Project East River.

ings and institutions, and public works.

a. *Residential Building*. The Housing and Home Finance Agency of the federal government probably has the greatest influence on the development of urban areas. The Federal Housing Administration and the Federal National Mortgage Association annually guarantee federal liability for hundreds of thousands of dwelling units, all of which should be subject to urban defense standards.

The direction of the present urban redevelopment and slum clearance program of the Housing and Home Finance Agency is generally toward reducing the density in central-city areas. This trend should be encouraged and all future redevelopment construction should be in accord with defense standards.

The activities of the Veterans Administration in home and business financing, as well as hospital construction, should likewise be subject to defense standards. Although veterans hospitals are being built in accordance with standards approved by the Federal Civil Defense Administration, the practice of locating many of these hospitals in highly congested urban centers should be discontinued.

. . . .

c. *Public Works*. Federal agencies such as the Post Office Department, the Federal Security Agency and the General Services Administration should comply with construction and density standards in their building programs. Post offices, schools of more than one story, hospitals and federal office buildings are some of the principal types of construction that should be made bomb-resistant. Federal agencies should not be permitted to lease space in office buildings that do not conform to defense standards.

Standards for States, Cities

a. *Public Works.* State and municipal (including county) agencies concerned with such construction as public office buildings, hospitals and schools should consider the defense advantages of location outside of Class I Vulnerable Urban Districts whenever it is practicable to do so.

b. *Highways.* State highway departments can contribute substantially to the reduction of urban densities by encouraging programs for circumferential highways at least ten miles from urban centers. Today, most state highway programs, backed by federal aid, are concentrated on building or improving radial routes into the centers of cities. Coupled with local zoning regulations which permit high-density building in the central areas of cities where land values are highest, these highway programs make further high-density development profitable even though it may increase target attractiveness.

Since the federal-aid highway funds are to a large degree allocated according to state recommendations and plans, state leadership is essential in construction of new expressways which will assist dispersion within metropolitan areas. Project East River recommends that federal-aid highway funds be directed

more intensively to the provision of circumferential expressways around central metropolitan areas located at least ten miles from the center of the city. Such expressways will not only act as important by-passes of congested sections through which traffic cannot be moved for some time after an attack, but will also tend to encourage the location of new industries and related development outside of central city areas.

. . . .

d. *Parks and Other Open Space.* Lack of large parks is common in most of the rapidly developing suburban areas today. Private golf courses, once a substantial source of open land, are being absorbed for large-scale housing developments. Civil defense requirements indicate the need of a vigorous revival of park acquisition programs by states and counties. Since the metropolitan areas are expanding rapidly into their surrounding countryside, a program of federal aid to states, counties and cities is essential for such areas. The problem of maintaining open space between urban communities is one of the most difficult to solve. Opportunities once missed, as a practical matter are almost always permanently lost.

e. *Administration.* Until the federal agencies act in accordance with defense standards of spacing and construction on a nation-wide basis, states and localities will be slow to impose standards which, in some instances, will appear to place them at a competitive disadvantage with other states or other municipalities. With federal acceptance of defense standards on any blanket, across-the-board basis, the advantage of organizing metropolitan district planning commissions in order to prepare a land use plan for each metropolitan area will become apparent.

Organization of such commissions and delegation of limited planning and land-use control powers to them will require state leadership and more local recognition of the metropolitan interdependence of central cities and their suburbs than now exist in most areas. The problem of local administration, however, is not insurmountable, as evidenced by the many metropolitan organizations already created to meet specific intercommunity problems. In fact, the creation of metropolitan planning commissions is advisable for reasons of sound peacetime metropolitan growth and development. Civil defense will give added impetus to a movement already under way in several metropolitan areas not only for metropolitan land use planning but also for zoning and building code revision.

Private Development

Private investment in urban buildings of all kinds constitutes the greatest force in city growth and development. In terms of building activity in urban areas, about six dollars of private funds are invested for every dollar of public construction.

Project East River believes that, if and when the federal government conducts its own construction and financing of construction activities

in accordance with defense standards, the states, municipalities and responsible private investors will follow suit as a matter of public responsibility and private self-interest.

No single set of standards, however helpful as a practical means to reverse the trend of increasing urban vulnerability and to set a ceiling on intensity of development generally, can be more than a stopgap substitute for a land-use plan of each individual metropolitan area. For this reason, Project East River recommends that the standards be modified for metropolitan areas having an approved metropolitan area plan which would make any of the recommended blanket requirements unnecessary in the interest of national defense.

Land-Use Plans

The modern city is rarely contained within the political boundaries of a single municipality. In 1950 the Census Bureau reported that nineteen metropolitan areas containing central cities of more than 500,000 population were surrounded by some 2,100 independent suburban municipalities.

During the past 40 years metropolitan area plans have been prepared for specific purposes as the necessity for such plans arose. For example, as central cities outgrew their local water supply sources, metropolitan water supply systems were planned and built. Similarly, metropolitan park plans and metropolitan park and parkway systems developed as a result of recreation needs. Highways, airports and trunk sewers have also been planned and constructed on a metropolitan basis.

The defense requirements of decongestion of central cities, limitation of densities of new urban developments, and location of new defense-supporting industries now make essential the preparation of metropolitan land-use plans. Such plans are necessary to determine how much any particular central city can be decongested and still perform its proper functions. They are needed to guide the new development in its suburban areas. Techniques now widely applied to individual cities in the preparation of land-use plans as the basis for zoning ordinances should be extended to metropolitan land-use plans to guide metropolitan development. In a number of metropolitan areas a beginning has already been made on such land-use plans by counties and unofficial metropolitan planning agencies.

Create Planning Commissions

Project East River recommends that the states, with federal encouragement and financial aid, if necessary, create and finance metropolitan district planning commissions to prepare, in cooperation with existing local planning authorities, metropolitan land-use plans.

Project East River recommends that metropolitan district planning commissions be given (by state delegation) power to review local zoning ordinances, local subdivision plans, local building codes and local permits to construct buildings and extend municipal services with whatever limitations on full local authority in these and related regulatory powers over land use as may be appropriate to make metropolitan land-use plans and defense standards of density and construction effective on a metropolitan basis.

It should be recognized that defense requirements will sometimes affect metropolitan land-use plans by adding requirements to urban development which differ from what might be called normal metropolitan growth and development.

Defense requirements of urban development must be supplied by the federal government to metropolitan planning authorities if intelligent metropolitan land-use plans are to be drawn up and made effective. If land should be reserved for suburban parks, farm lands or other protective belts, both metropolitan planning commissions and the public must be convinced that the setting aside of such open space from normal development is essential to security. Similarly, to open up congested central cities, with the great capital outlay involved and inevitable local opposition to be overcome, requires an authoritative appraisal of the security benefits derived from open space. For example, if expressways should be constructed through congested city areas to serve as rubble-free access roads and to decrease vulnerability from fire, the security benefits must be made clear.

The plans for immediately developing this program should be based on the guiding principles that central cities of highest concentrations of people and industry should gradually be decongested; that new developments in outlying areas should not exceed about 8,000 persons per gross square mile; that metropolitan development should not be susceptible to fire storms or large scale conflagrations unchecked by open space; and that a maximum of alternate transportation and utility facilities be achieved.

Closely tied in with the central-city density problem is the municipal tax base problem. Federal, state and local taxation has a profound effect on urban developments, arising from the fact that municipalities can raise revenue only from the land within their boundaries and the activities that take place on this land. To gain revenue it is necessary for each municipality to increase the assessed value of its land and the volume of business carried on within its city limits. This involves more intensive development, more concentration of people and industry, increased city density and added vulnerability.

Municipal Finances

Since a single municipality in a metropolitan area has no longer an adequate revenue area from which to collect its taxes, state and federal aid to municipalities is increasing. The effects of this trend require careful analysis to determine how significant the factor of taxation is in forcing municipalities to encourage intensive developments and whether federal and state local-aid policies could be shaped to make decongestion and dispersion more palatable to municipal officials.

The use of urban defense standards will bring increasing financial difficulties to municipalities which contain concentrated urban development or which may be subjected to new growth through operation of the standards. To meet these difficulties, there must be a readjustment in the present systems of taxing and spending by the local, state and federal governments.

At first glance it might appear that the central cities would be the portions of metropolitan areas hardest hit by application of urban defense standards which restrict further concentrations. Further analysis suggests, however, that the cities, counties or townships which contain the suburban fringe and the open country beyond may feel the heaviest impact of additional financial problems, as they seek to acquire community facilities and services in proportion to new residential, commercial and industrial development.

During recent years, the Hoover Commission, the United States Conference of Mayors, the Governors' Conference, the Congress, and many other organized groups have been interested in the problem of adjusting federal-state-local functional and fiscal relationships. Project East River recommends that the National Security Resources Board, in order to further the application of urban defense standards, give its strongest support to the proposal for a National Commission on Intergovernmental Relations, or to any alternative proposal which promises solutions to the urban financial problems arising out of defense requirements.

News in Review

Massachusetts Session Short but Effective

One of the 687 Bills Passed Creates Legislative Council

WHEN *legum latores Massachusett-enses* adjourned the 158th session of the General Court on June 11, they concluded the briefest session since 1937; but never before did the legislature have such a volume of bills and resolves to sort and dispose of. Six hundred eighty-seven bills and 128 resolves were passed out of a total of 4,395. Tight party leadership under the governor gave the chief executive little cause for complaint.

With an eye toward reducing the number of recess commissions, the legislature created the long-advocated Legislative Research Council and Research Bureau. The council—smaller than most state councils—will consist of two members of the Senate and four of the House, appointed by the presiding officers for one-year terms, each of the major parties to have equal representation. Council members will not receive salaries but will be reimbursed for expenses. The council is authorized to determine research policies and program and to appoint the research bureau director and assistants. The research bureau will be responsible for collecting facts and statistics for committees, recess commissions and individual legislators. State departments and local units are directed to furnish the information needed by the bureau.

The "Baby Hoover" Commission created in 1949 expired on December 31, 1953, in the midst of a study of salary classifications of state employees. The legislature took heed of the governor's plea to extend the life of the commission until March 15, 1954, so that it might complete the analysis of the general and labor service salary schedules, passing the necessary resolution early in the session. The commission's thirteenth and fourteenth reports, on public health agencies and personnel administration respectively, completed in 1953, were presented to the 1954 session. The legislature adopted a few minor recommendations from the thirteenth report and increased the power of the Division of Personnel in line with proposals in the fourteenth.

Only one of the more than 125 proposals to amend the state constitution received approval of the two houses. It would increase the term of six state officers from two to four years.[1]

Home Rule Loses

This year the number of special bills, of concern to particular cities, amounted to some 10 per cent of the total introduced, but an attempt to set up a measure of home rule via the constitution failed and an effort to approach the problem by a change of the General Court's joint rules pertaining to the manner in which local matters might be brought to the two houses was also unsuccessful.[2]

A Massachusetts Farm Bureau Federation bill to reorganize the State Department of Agriculture under a board drawn from different counties, most of whose members must be farmers, became law. The board will be responsible for the appointment of the commissioner who will administer the department.

A division on the employment of older

---

[1] See the REVIEW, July 1954, page 353.
[2] See the REVIEW, July 1954, page 356.

workers—probably the first in the country—was created and added to the Department of Labor and Industries. It is directed to encourage the employment of older workers by attacking age barriers to employment through research and education. To coordinate the various programs on the problems of the aging (10 per cent of the state's citizens are over 65 years of age) in state departments and in the communities, the legislature established a council of the aging comprising commissioners of labor and industries, public welfare, education, mental health and public health *ex officio*, and four members to be named by the governor. The State Health Department was given the job of cooperating with local authorities in organizing clinics for the aging. And, finally, two hospitals were set aside for the elderly—one for the care of senile cases and another for research in chronic diseases of older people.

A notable piece of legislation is the fair administrative procedures act which became law this session. The measure, an adaptation of the uniform procedures act of the Council of State Governments, provides uniform methods for the conduct of hearings in which individual rights or licenses are involved. The act spells out rules of evidence and sets forth procedures to be followed in the adoption of regulations and in adjudicatory proceedings. Provision is made for judicial review in county superior courts and the State Supreme Court. A controversial section to allow appointing authorities to appeal to courts in the same fashion as an individual aggrieved by an agency's decision was included in the final draft. Such units as the Department of Correction, the Youth Service Board, Parole Board and the Division of Industrial Accidents are excepted from the act.

The legislature approved and the gov-ernor signed a proposed compact between the commonwealth and other New England states setting up a New England Board of Higher Education with authority to establish a program for more medical and dental students in present schools.

Financial Measures

The 158th session will go down as the first to effect an income tax reduction, albeit slight, since world war I.

Two bond measures are worth noting: the first of $150,000,000 for the continuation of the highway construction program; the second of $15,000,-000 for local housing authorities ($5,000,000 was issued last year) to build homes for elderly people on low incomes.

Although there were no general salary increases for state employees, the sum of $4,250,000 in two bills was made available for salary adjustments affecting about two-thirds of the total number.

Early in the session a Fiscal Survey Commission was created; it is already at work on a far-reaching study of fiscal activities. The commission consists of three members appointed by the governor; one member from each party in the Senate and one member from each party in the House; the comptroller, commissioner of corporations and taxation and the budget commissioner are members *ex officio*. Among other matters they are authorized to recommend legislation concerning the number of funds, adequacy and fairness of taxes and fees, federal-state and state-local fiscal sharing programs, and the management of the state debt.

The Tax Commission originally created in 1948 and enlarged in 1951 is continued with power to study the general subject of taxation.

The legislature also established a state youth commission and continued existing commissions on child delinquency, public welfare legislation, communism and subversion, crime, educational television, retirement legislation, penal institutions and rents of veterans in state housing units.

Two bills, tagged by the governor as "musts" but eventually defeated, dealt with the state judicial system. The first would have revised the district court system by establishing 29 district courts (civil) with judges on a full-time basis. Judges in the smaller courts continuing on a part-time basis would have had charge of criminal cases only. The bill first passed both houses but was later killed because of attacks meted out by officeholders, the Taxpayers Association and others. It was not sufficiently a reform measure to attract the support of reformers and was easily open to cries of "patronage."

A juvenile court bill, recommended by a bipartisan commission, would have divided the state into nine juvenile districts with a full-time judge in each. After much argument it was defeated.

Delay in adjourning also came over two Boston bills: the first, had it passed, would have authorized Boston voters to ballot on whether to keep the present Plan A charter (mayor-council with councilmen elected at large) or to set up a borough system with election of council members from boroughs.

The second bill, one on which the Republican leadership was defeated, proposed to give to a state legislative commission the power to change ward lines in Boston.

The Republican plan to redistrict the state's fourteen congressional districts, to make it possible to gain from two to six of the seats now occupied by Democrats, attracted the ire of the Democrats, of course, but it also divided the Republicans. It fell by the wayside early in the session.

● VICTORIA SCHUCK
Mount Holyoke College

Connecticut Grants Leave to Employees for Study

Under a new policy announced by Frank M. Lynch, state finance commissioner, Connecticut state employees of "demonstrated ability" may secure a leave of absence with full pay to take technical or professional courses. These courses must be designed to aid them in their state work. Leaves may be granted by the State Personnel Division on the recommendation of department or agency heads that the state will benefit because of the further education of the employee. The leave permitted will usually be for one academic year but may be extended if the State Personnel Board, headed by the governor, approves.

Employees securing such leaves must have worked for the state for at least two years and must agree that they will return to state employment for at least two additional years after completing their courses. They will be required to pay their own tuition fees.

Employees may also be granted leaves of absence without pay for educational plans which receive approval of the Personnel Board. Such employees will be guaranteed their seniority and other benefits provided they pledge to return to the state's service for at least two years.

Montana to Vote on Presidential Primary Law

The legislature of Montana has submitted to referendum for vote in November 1954 a new presidential primary law, chapter 214, Laws of 1953.

Under the current law, as applied in 1952, precinct committeemen, elected two years before, assembled as county conventions in May to select delegates to the state convention, which in turn selected delegates to the national convention.

The proposed new law provides a late date for the primary, the first Tuesday after the first Monday in June of each presidential year, when voter opinion has probably matured. It allows a candidate for president, not later than 60 days before the primary, to file with the secretary of state an affidavit of candidacy, requesting that his name be printed on the primary ballot of his party and naming the slate of delegates whom he desires to represent him at the convention. No petition is required and the filing fee is only $25. During the next twenty days petitions may be filed for other candidates, who do not presumably solicit it as above, including a list of delegates and supported by a petition of one per cent of the votes cast at the last preceding presidential election, and a $25 filing fee. Four delegates will be elected at large and three in each congressional district. Delegates thus designated must sign a pledge to support their candidate at the convention on the first ballot and until released by the candidate or until the candidate receives less than 20 per cent of a convention poll.

A candidate for president named by petition may, before April 30, file an affidavit with the secretary of state stating that he is not a candidate for the nomination for president, and if nominated will not accept. In such case his name and that of his delegates will be left off the primary ballot. Voters will vote for the package consisting of candidate for president and delegates; voting for individual delegate candidates will not be permitted. Alternates to the national convention are allowed to be selected by the party state convention organized as now.

The proposed new law seemingly makes no provision for an uninstructed delegation and management activity will necessarily involve setting up a docile favorite son to head a petition filing if an uninstructed delegation is desired.

R.S.C.

Arizona Municipal League Enlarges Services

The Arizona Municipal League, at a special meeting in Mesa on July 8, adopted the report of a special committee on reorganization. It provided for the appointment of W. A. Moeur, city attorney of Tempe, as acting director, an increase in the salary of the director from $4,800 to $7,200, and funds for larger offices and a full-time secretary. The league asked its members to submit proposed legislation to the acting director before October 15, and instructed the latter to prepare a legislative program for referral to municipal officials before the fall meeting of the league. The acting director was instructed to develop an information service for Arizona cities, to visit each city at least once a year, and to endeavor to create a feeling of cooperation among league members. The committee on reorganization will remain on the scene to assist the acting director with the reorganization.

PAUL KELSO
University of Arizona

Most States, Cities Restrict Employee Political Activity

A recent survey of restraints on political activity of employees of state and local governments indicates that a great majority of the latter impose such restraints in some substantial degree. The survey was made by Richard Christopherson of the Personnel Department of the city of Philadelphia, and was related to Philadelphia's home rule charter provisions on employees' political activities. It is summarized in a report entitled *Political Activity Provisions in U. S. Cities and States*, published by the Civil Service Assembly.

The survey covered 119 civil service jurisdictions on the state and local level. Of these, 89 per cent were found to exercise at least some measure of restraint.

Over 90 per cent of the units that have rules against political activity forbid any public employee to use or threaten to use the authority of his job to persuade someone to vote a certain way. Most of the governments also bar their workers from soliciting money for a political purpose. Other controls cover membership on political committees, distributing campaign leaflets or buttons, and marching in political parades.

Most of the municipalities and states in the survey make a distinction between political activities of a partisan nature and those that are nonpartisan. Almost two-thirds of the units do not allow their employees to distribute partisan literature. Only 30 per cent forbid them to disseminate material on nonpartisan matters, such as the building of civic projects.

Two-fifths of those taking part in the survey answered that they had no problem with public employees entering into political action past the allowable point, and made the unsolicited comment that this was due to the existence of a long-standing, successful merit system of personnel management.

Mr. Christopherson concluded from his study that "a rational prohibition of detrimental political activities—clearly spelled out as to both nature and procedure—is essential to the full-time performance of skilled, experienced, able and efficient employees in the service of the entire citizenry."

Council-manager Plan Developments

There were 1,241 communities with the council-manager plan on June 30, 1954, according to a report issued by the International City Managers' Association. There are now more council-manager than mayor-council cities in two population groups—250,000 to 500,-000 and 50,000 to 100,000. The number and percentage of cities in each popu-

lation group with the manager plan are: 500,000 and over, 1 city (Cincinnati); 100,000-500,000, 33 cities (37.5 per cent); 50,000-100,000, 55 cities (43.6 per cent); 25,000-50,000, 105 cities (42.2 per cent); 10,000-25,000, 274 cities (36.4 per cent); 5,000-10,000, 269 cities (24.5 per cent); 2,500-5,000, 187 cities (12.0 per cent); and 1,000-2,500, 100 cities (2.9 per cent). In addition 217 council-manager communities are not included here because the Bureau of Census does not classify them as incorporated urban places, or because they have less than 1,000 population, or because they are outside the continental United States. On June 30, 1954, there were approximately 27,000,000 people living in communities with the manager plan.

MOUNT CLEMENS, MICHIGAN, (1950 population 17,027) has recently adopted the council-manager plan.

Other recent adoptions reported by the International City Managers' Association include BALDWIN BOROUGH (9,158) and McCANDLESS TOWNSHIP, Pennsylvania; BELLE GLADE, FLORIDA, (7,219); ELBERTON, GEORGIA, (6,772); and LAGUNA BEACH, CALIFORNIA, (6,661).

The city council of SANGER, CALIFORNIA, (6,400) on June 16 gave final approval to an ordinance establishing the position and duties for a city manager.

In SAN CLEMENTE, CALIFORNIA, (4,435) after a favorable advisory referendum in April, the city council on July 7 gave final approval to an ordinance creating the office.

CASA GRANDE, ARIZONA, (4,181) has adopted the manager plan.

A committee of five has been appointed by the town moderator in LEICESTER, MASSACHUSETTS, to investigate the advisability of adopting the town manager plan.

In HAMPTON, VIRGINIA, a council-manager city, a referendum on methods of council election, held on July 13, showed 1,837 votes for election at large,

1,017 for election by boroughs and 946 for a combination. As no plan received a majority, a run-off vote will be taken at the November 2 general election.

The PARKERSBURG, WEST VIRGINIA, Chamber of Commerce has adopted a program of action for a better community which includes the study, with other groups, of the council-manager plan for possible adoption in that city.

Proposed changes to the charter of MARTINSBURG, WEST VIRGINIA, one of which would have provided for the appointment of a city manager, were defeated at an election on June 8.

In ORLANDO, FLORIDA, a charter referendum on May 25, calling for expression of preferences between the council-manager plan, the mayor-executive plan and the present mayor-council form, resulted in a vote of 4,770 for the latter, with 4,232 for mayor-executive and 1,501 for council-manager. A run-off election on June 8 retained the present form.

In JACKSON, OHIO, a citizens' committee has been organized to promote the council-manager idea and circulate petitions calling for a referendum election. An educational campaign is being conducted by the *Herald* and *Sun-Journal*.

A total of 3,065 citizens of JOLIET, ILLINOIS, have signed petitions, circulated by the Better Joliet Committee, asking for a referendum on adoption of the council-manager plan. Only 2,400 are needed.

Petitions calling for a referendum election on the question of adopting the council-manager plan have been circulated in DECATUR, ILLINOIS, by the Junior Chamber of Commerce and the League of Women Voters. The movement is sponsored by a group called Friends of the Council-manager Form of Government, organized by the Association of Commerce and the League of Women Voters. The petitions, when completed, were to be submitted to the county court, which can order the city council to call the referendum if there are sufficient valid signatures.

A referendum to abandon the council-manager plan, held in SLATER, MISSOURI, on June 11, was defeated by a vote of 608 to 386.

An opinion poll of the PRATT, KANSAS, Chamber of Commerce, relating to various local issues, included a question as to a council-manager plan for Pratt. The chamber issued 324 questionnaires and 118 replies were received. Of those voting on the manager plan, 73 were in favor and 27 opposed.

An attempt to abandon the council-manager plan in CHADRON, NEBRASKA, on August 10, was defeated by the voters, 1,092 to 592.

A committee of six, including two councilmen, has been appointed by Mayor H. Paul Huss of SANTA FE, NEW MEXICO, to study the council-manager plan and make recommendations as to its adoption. It is reported that in the spring election campaign the manager idea was supported by the Democratic party and received partial support from the Republicans.

Mayor Floyd Atchison of RATON, NEW MEXICO, has appointed a committee of eight, including four councilmen, to study a proposal to change to the council-manager plan.

Voters of MINERAL WELLS, TEXAS, defeated a proposal for adoption of the council-manager plan on August 10. The vote was 1,159 to 564.

At the municipal election in LEWISTON, IDAHO, on June 14 a proposal for adoption of the council-manager plan was narrowly defeated, 1,311 to 1,256.

A board of fifteen freeholders in WALLA WALLA, WASHINGTON, has drafted a council-manager charter. It is expected to come to popular vote in November.

The city council of SOUTH GATE,

CALIFORNIA, has been studying the possibilities of the council-manager plan for more than a year, according to Mayor Charles Peckenpaugh.

· The 40th annual conference of the International City Managers' Association will be held in St. Petersburg, Florida, December 5 to 8.

Fort Lauderdale, Florida, Shrinks 27 Departments to 9

Prior to July 1 the rapidly expanding resort city of Fort Lauderdale (estimated permanent population, 57,000) on Florida's lower Atlantic coast provided municipal services through 27 separate operating units.

Of these thirteen reported to the city manager; five to the city commission; two to the utility manager; four to the city manager and engineer; two to the city commission, city manager and advisory boards; and one to the city manager and utility manager.

In addition, fifteen advisory boards and a citizens' traffic committee assisted the city commission on policy matters. Ten of the boards were charged with certain administrative duties as well.

It became increasingly apparent that this sprawling municipal setup was unwieldy. A streamlined government designed to provide more rigid financial control, end duplication of services and eliminate divided authority was proposed and ultimately adopted.

Under the reorganization, the number of departments and offices was reduced from 27 to nine, with three—offices of city manager, city attorney and city judge —continuing to report to the commission and six being responsible directly to the city manager.

The reduction was made possible by grouping all field operations under three major departments—police, fire, public works—and centralizing financial control under one, all under the manager.

The two remaining departments under the manager provide for staff services. One is responsible for internal controls including personnel, budgeting, administrative reporting, cost and performance records, public relations and investigation of complaints. The other is charged with liaison duty between the city manager's office and advisory boards dealing with the city's leisure-time facilities.

The city manager's office, on July 1, began issuing a monthly digest of items related to the city's administration.

DONALD P. WOLFER, *City Manager*
Fort Lauderdale, Florida

San Antonio De-annexation Held Void by Court

The Texas Third Court of Civil Appeals decided on July 21 that the city of San Antonio acted illegally in 1953 in detaching 65 square miles of territory, which was part of 79.7 square miles annexed in 1952. Under the law the city could detach unimproved territory, but the court held that the 65-mile tract could not be considered unimproved.

Incorporation of Suburban District Denied in Alaska

A petition for incorporation of an area known as Eastchester, surrounded by portions of the city of Anchorage, Alaska,[1] was denied on May 26 by Judge George W. Folta of the Alaska District Court, Third Division. In his written opinion the judge said: "The denial of the petition was based upon the facts that the area sought to be incorporated is a part of and indistinguishable from a large urban area which also embraces the city of Anchorage, and that experience teaches that an area of that kind is best served and administered by one municipality."

[1]See the REVIEW, May 1954, page 244.

Police and Firemen Combined for Quarter Century

Oakwood, Ohio, a suburb of Dayton, has completed 25 years with a single public safety department for police and fire protection. The department has 31 men to serve a population of 9,691.

The personnel includes a "property protection" crew, composed of men responsible for fire-fighting. They respond to major fire calls. Police cruisers go at once to the scene of a fire and in some cases extinguish it with equipment carried in each vehicle.

Uniform Laws Group Would Drop Coroners

The National Conference of Commissioners on Uniform State Laws voted 37 to 0 August 14 at its meeting in Chicago to recommend adoption by all state legislatures of laws that would abolish coroners.

In place of elected coroners the commissioners suggest a state operation headed by a chief medical examiner who would employ pathologists and other technicians to investigate all violent deaths and other deaths under suspicious circumstances.

The recommendations follow the general lines of the *Model State Medicolegal Investigative System* issued in 1952 by the National Municipal League in cooperation with the American Bar Association (Criminal Law Section), the American Medical Association, National Civil Service League, American Judicature Society and American Academy of Forensic Sciences.

Two New Governmental Publications in India

The Federation of All-India Local Authorities is inaugurating a new quarterly magazine entitled *Local Govern-*ment, edited by K. Narasimha Rao, with headquarters in Masulipatam (Andhra), India.

The Bombay Municipal Corporation began the publication of the monthly *Bombay Civic Journal* in March 1954. It is an attractive illustrated magazine, with a wide variety of articles. The editor is U. G. Rao.

PAS Completes Its Twentieth Year

This year the Public Administration Service marked its twentieth anniversary as an affiliate of the Public Administration Clearing House.

In two decades the organization has completed more than 1,000 consulting, research and publication projects at a cost of about $5,000,000. A permanent staff of about 30 experts has been augmented substantially by outside consultants for various projects.

The PAS is a major contributor to the literature of public administration, its publications having a combined circulation in excess of 250,000. It has conducted studies and surveys in many foreign lands.

Prior to 1934, the organization, known as the Municipal Administration Service, was constituted by the National Municipal League as a clearing house designed to give the published works of research agencies a wider audience.

New York Regional Plan Group Has 25th Anniversary

The Regional Plan Association, Inc., of New York City, which is devoted to the coordinated development of the New York–New Jersey–Connecticut metropolitan region, announces that the 25th anniversary Regional Plan Conference will be held on Wednesday, October 6, at the Hotel Roosevelt, New York City.

County and Township • • • • *Edited by Edward W. Weidner*

Administrative Officer Asked for Baltimore Co.

Commission Report Makes Five Main Recommendations

THE Commission to Study the Reorganization of Baltimore County, appointed in the spring of 1953 under a House Joint Resolution, has issued its report to the board of county commissioners,[1] suggesting that a chief administrative officer be appointed.

Five main conclusions were contained in the report:

(1) That the board of county commissioners be transformed into a body concerned primarily with local legislation and the over-all policy supervision of county government. As a consequence of this recommendation, it was felt that the county board should be increased in size and that its method of election be altered to reflect the interests of major community areas in the county.

(2) That the county take steps to achieve home rule under the appropriate provisions of the Maryland constitution. This recommendation would give the board of county commissioners a fairly wide scope of general policy formation and control.

(3) That the office of chief administrative officer be created. The CAO would take over the detailed tasks of county administration and would be appointed by and responsible to the county board or council.

(4) That the agencies now performing fiscal, purchasing, legal and personnel functions be consolidated into a single department of administration.

[1]*Report of the Commission to Study the Structure of Baltimore County.* Baltimore, The Johns Hopkins Press, 1954. 64 pp.

This department would act as the chief administrative staff to the CAO and its head would be the No. 2 man in county administration.

(5) That the chief administrative officer be charged with integrating the large number of independent departments now in existence into a smaller number of functionally organized agencies. As part of this proposal, the CAO, with the help of the department of administration, would present suggestions for continuing reorganization to the council as the need for these might arise.

In the primary election that took place during the past summer, candidates for the board of county commissioners pledged their support to the commission's report.

Recommend Manager Plan in Three States

Recommendations on the county manager plan have been made in three different states recently. In North Dakota, Dr. Ross Talbott, of the Department of Political Science, University of North Dakota, recommended the county manager plan in an article in the May issue of the *North Dakota Union Farmer.* Talbott emphasized that the county manager plan would provide an executive branch of government that would be professional in character, similar to the plan that has attracted so many cities in recent years. He felt that a county manager system could lower taxes or improve services or both and cited Petroleum County, Montana, as an example.

The *Hanford* (California) *Journal* has come out editorially in support of a county manager form of government for Kings County. It points out that county government is growing more and more complex and that the necessity of maintaining a skilled man to head it and to expedite services is ever greater; that supervisors, who are part-time public servants, are unable to keep their eyes on the numerous details of county government.

To back up its claims of better government under the manager plan, the *Journal* cites experiences of other California counties as well as studies made by the National Municipal League and the University of California.

Another newspaper, the *Gastonia* (North Carolina) *Gazette*, has suggested that its county, Gaston, should go in the direction of the county manager form of government. At a recent meeting of the county board, one of the commissioners suggested that the board visit some of the counties having such a form of government and that it should study the plans in use by them.

Citizens Establish Manager Plan in Maricopa County

Maricopa County, Arizona, has taken a number of steps recently toward awakened citizen interest and better county government. The citizens organized a Better Government Association two years ago which was successful in electing a majority of the board of supervisors.

As a result, a manager form of government was established in the county, but its existence depends upon a favorable majority on the governing body. There is no constitutional or legislative basis for the office of county manager, but the Better Government Association hopes within a few years to be able to persuade the legislature to pass such statutory authority because of the excellent record the manager plan is making.

Student County Employees Aid in Recruitment

Los Angeles County has established open competitive examinations for student employees (campus representatives) at the University of Southern California and the University of California at Los Angeles. These positions provide an opportunity for currently enrolled students to gain experience in work related to their fields of specialization. Each student worker will help the Los Angeles Civil Service Commission recruit for county employment by transmitting publicity about employment opportunities in the county to the student body and will serve as a contact person for recruitment information.

County Institutes Held in Wisconsin

A County Clerk and County Administrative Procedures Institute was held in June by the Bureau of Government of the University of Wisconsin in cooperation with the Wisconsin County Clerks Association and The Wisconsin County Boards Association. The institute included a section on recent developments in Wisconsin county government, including school district reorganization, civil defense, industrial development programs and parks and planning progress. A second section was devoted to improving administrative procedures and a third to problems of administration, such as finance and codification of the statutory duties of a county clerk.

Lloyd W. Woodruff, director of the institute, compiled an extensive manual which contained explanatory material for all sessions and which will serve in the future as a reference guide for county clerks on the subjects discussed.

Proportional Representation . . *Edited by George H. Hallett, Jr.*
and Wm. Redin Woodward
(This department is successor to the Proportional Representation Review)

P. R. Again Attacked in Cincinnati

Council Uses New Plan for Filling Council Vacancies

FOR the fifth time in eighteen years, proportional representation voting in Cincinnati has become the target of renewed attack. Petitions proposing an amendment to repeal P.R. and substitute the so-called limited vote have been filed under the initiative provisions of the Ohio constitution.

The plan proposed, while referred to in advance publicity as the "Indianapolis plan," is unlike the Indianapolis plan in that it contains no provision for a preferential primary, nor does it limit in any way the number of candidates that may be proposed by a political party or group. Its principal innovation is to provide for balloting with X-marks for six candidates, the nine candidates obtaining the largest number of X's being elected.

In their pronouncements, the sponsors of the change disavowed all political inspiration or associations. The City Charter Committee, traditional supporter of P.R., quickly exposed the past associations of most of the sponsors with previous attempts to kill P.R., all of which eventually traced back to the 70-year-old Republican machine which has fought P.R. ever since it was adopted.

Next it developed that virtually all the circulators of the petitions for amendment were either job holders in the county courthouse, the fortress of the old machine, or precinct workers for the machine.

In a belated effort to counteract these revelations, sponsors of the amendment dispatched a nominal number of blank petitions to each of the 26 ward executives of the Democratic party, with peremptory directions to circulate them at once and return them filled in less than a week. The chief inducement held out to the executives was "to establish the Democratic party in city of Cincinnati affairs." This maneuver in due course was also exposed by the Charter Committee as part of ultimate proof that the whole anti-P.R. movement is politically inspired.

Despite their vigilance, however, Charter Committee leaders are by no means complacent as to the result of this latest attack. The Charter group has called upon all responsible elements to join in rejecting this latest substitute for P.R., but is aware that the defection of even a small number of job-hungry Democrats, when linked with the work of the spoils politicians in the local Republican machine, could prove disastrous.

A full-scale campaign is planned and, as the Cincinnati *Post* remarked, "the fight will be hot."

Mayor's Vacancy

The seat in Cincinnati's city council made vacant in May by the death of Mayor Edward N. Waldvogel has been filled by appointment of his youthful campaign chairman, Vincent H. Beckman, Jr., attorney, in the first test of a procedure for filling vacancies adopted by popular vote last November.

The late mayor's title as chief ceremonial officer of the city, however, remains unfilled at this juncture, with the result that Vice Mayor Dorothy N. Dolbey, who had been substituting for Mr. Waldvogel since early March, continues in her unexpected assignment, thereby becoming *de facto* the first woman mayor in American history to serve a city of over 500,000.

The selection of Mr. Beckman for Mr. Waldvogel's council seat represents a notable step forward for Cincinnati's P.R.-elected councils. Filling vacancies previously, especially three of the past decade, had occasioned considerable acrimony and resentment. Charter supporters particularly were disturbed when such Charter leaders as former Mayor Russell Wilson, deceased, and Charles P. Taft, resigned, were replaced by the opposition machine councilmen, by majority vote of the council, on a strict political patronage basis.

Although the Charter Committee twice had recommended to the opposition joint action to enact as part of the city charter the P.R. council vacancy provisions of the National Municipal League's *Model City Charter*,[1] not until 1953 was there a hint of response. Last year, however, following widespread resentment over the action of the then machine majority in appointing one of its henchmen to the seat of the late Charter floor leader and former mayor, Albert D. Cash, Potter Stewart, a member of the majority, declared he would support a charter amendment designed to prevent such incidents in the future.

Mr. Stewart rejected, however, the Charter Committee's recommendation of the *Model Charter* provision, and instead proposed that each member of council, before taking the oath of office, be required to file with the clerk of council a certificate setting forth the names of one or more members of council who would thus be empowered to designate his successor in the event of death or retirement. The Charter Committee appointed a special committee headed by John J. Gilligan to attempt

to persuade Stewart to modify the proposal so as to ensure wider participation in the choice of the successor. This they felt important, particularly in the case of an independent member of council who might regard his colleagues as unsympathetic to his views.

Mr. Gilligan was not able to budge Mr. Stewart and ultimately the Charter Committee agreed, despite misgivings, to join in co-sponsoring a campaign for the adoption of the proposal. With both major groups thus aligned, approval was given as a matter of course.

Ironically, Mr. Gilligan became the first to exercise the authority granted under the new amendment. Elected to council for the first time in November, he was certified by Mayor Waldvogel to serve as Mr. Waldvogel's successor-designator. It was by his decision that Mr. Beckman was named to the vacancy.

FOREST FRANK, *Executive Director*
Cincinnati City Charter Committee

Worcester Newspaper Answers Labor Group

EDITOR'S NOTE.—The editorial below, titled "P.R. Attacked Again," is taken from the Worcester *Telegram* of August 7, 1954. Many labor groups have been strong supporters of proportional representation.

In attacking the proportional representation system of voting, the Massachusetts Federation of Labor repeated the familiar and weak arguments.

It called P.R. a European system. The charge is justified, but irrelevant. A large section of our population is of European origin. Many of our political institutions are of European origin, especially English. Our secret ballot system came from Australia.

The federation in its resolution said that P.R. "does violence to the American plurality system of voting." What of it? P.R. is a device under which groups of voters are sure of representa-

(Continued on page 429)

---

[1]This calls for the filling of all vacancies by a recount of the ballots cast for the outgoing member—as provided also for Massachusetts P.R. cities.

Taxation and Finance •   •   •   •   *Edited by Wade S. Smith*

St. Louis and Dayton
Renew Income Taxes

Phoenix Voters Adopt
Sales Tax Amendment

MUNICIPAL sales and income taxes received the attention of both voters and courts during the late spring and summer this year, again emphasizing the extent to which revenue from this type of excise has become a fixture in financing local budgets.

St. Louis, Missouri, on May 1 reimposed its local income tax of ½ of 1 per cent. The new act provides for the payroll withholding of the tax on salaries and wages and allows employers a 3 per cent discount to cover collection costs. The authorization runs to April 15, 1955. If the city submits a proposition for its continuance to the voters before that date, the tax will continue to April 15, 1956, if voted down and for an additional year if approved.

The city's first similar tax was enacted in 1946 but invalidated by the courts. Subsequent taxes were enacted in 1948 and 1952, with specified expiration dates also. Features of the old ordinance are reported to have been upheld by the United States Supreme Court, permitting differing treatment of individual and business income.

In Dayton, Ohio, the voters approved a renewal for five years of that city's ½ of 1 per cent income tax. The majority was 76.5 per cent, compared with 74 per cent when the tax was first adopted in 1950. The tax applies to salaries of persons living or working in the city and to net profits of businesses. One-fourth of the receipts are required, as under the previous charter amendment, to be allocated for capital improvements.

The tax yielded nearly four and a half million dollars in 1953.

In Phoenix, Arizona, where a local sales tax had been in use for five years but was invalidated by an adverse ruling in the state courts, an enabling charter amendment was adopted in July by a three-to-one majority to permit the city to levy a privilege license and sales tax. In the past, the rate of the tax had been ½ of 1 per cent. Following enactment of the enabling amendment, a citizens committee was appointed by the city council to recommend terms of the ordinance to be drafted pursuant to the new charter provision. The tax yielded over one and a half million dollars in 1952-53, and was estimated to produce $1,670,-000 for 1953-54, the equivalent of a property tax rate of $12.50 per $1,000.

Portland Officer Third Time
Winner of Louisville Award

The 1953 Louisville gold medal award of the Municipal Finance Officers' Association was presented to Will Gibson, city auditor of Portland, Oregon, for his development and preparation of a practical manual on *How to Account for, Preserve, and Dispose of Public Records.* Mr. Gibson was the recipient of the first gold medal awarded in 1940 in this annual cooperative recognition of outstanding service by the M.F.O.A. and the city of Louisville. In 1951, he received a certificate of merit and honorable mention.

The earlier award was for the installation of a modern accounting system in Portland, including the preparation of a comprehensive accounting manual covering procedural processes to be used by the staff of the city auditor who, under the charter in Portland, also serves as the city clerk. The 1951 award was for the installation of a new accounting system for the city's fire and police disability and retirement funds.

The 1953 award was announced and the presentation made at the association's 1954 annual conference at San Francisco.

Phoenix Introduces Performance Budget Features

The budget document of the city of Phoenix, Arizona, for 1954-1955, in addition to its general conformity to the pattern devised by the National Committee on Municipal Accounting of the Municipal Finance Officers' Association, contains a number of other noteworthy features.

It describes more completely the work programs of the coming year by including comparative work unit statistics for each activity when they are available. For example, comparative statistics for the division of accounts of the finance department include the number of payroll warrants issued, the amount of claims processed, the approximate number of internal audits and the man hours of internal auditings.

To show the true total cost of personal service, pension contributions, instead of being carried in lump sums classified as contractual services, are broken down and included under personal services in each separate activity. Estimates of the city's contributions under the federal insurance contribution act and for industrial insurance are entered in the same manner. The budget document also contains a page captioned "Phoenix Expansion," which gives outline maps and population figures since 1881, with the map for 1954 showing annexations since 1950.   PAUL KELSO
University of Arizona

Belsley, Elsbree Named by U. S. Commission

G. Lyle Belsley, associate director of the Public Administration Clearing House, has been appointed executive director of the federal Commission on Intergovernmental Relations. Hugh L. Elsbree, senior specialist in American government and public administration at the Library of Congress, has been made deputy director of research. Announcement of the appointments was made by the commission's chairman, Meyer Kestnbaum. The commission is scheduled to forward its final report to the President by March 1, 1955.

State-Local Borrowing at Record Rate

State and local long-term borrowing continued at record levels over the summer months this year, accumulating to more than four billion dollars of new bonds to August 1, 1954, an increase of nearly nine hundred million dollars over the 1953 period. At the same time effective interest rates, which had been abnormally high during the forepart of 1953 because of the federal government's "dear" money policies, returned to levels highly favorable to the borrowers.

For the first seven months of 1954, the total of state-local new long-term borrowing, as reported by *The Daily Bond Buyer*, was $4,013,851,111, as compared with $3,141,719,199 in the first seven months last year. There were 3,775 separate new issues this year, compared with 3,374 in the prior year's period. Revenue bonds (obligations payable solely from the proceeds of specified rates or charges for services and not entitled to support from general property taxes) were responsible for most of the over-all gain in this year's total. Revenue bonds included in this year's aggregate amounted to $1,602,411,100, compared with $739,449,570 in the first seven months of 1953.

Many of this year's new issues have been going, as to the shorter maturities, into the portfolios of the commercial
(Continued on page 429)

Pittsburgh First City with Educational TV

Families, Businessmen and Schools Contribute to WQED

"**E**VERYBODY talking about heaven ain't a goin' thar !" is the realistic but slightly pessimistic view set to music in an old spiritual. Regretfully, every community talking about a television station of its own isn't going to have one.

There are plenty of channels to go around in the reserved allocations for educational stations. There is enough money salted away to put stations on the air and keep them there. But what it takes, more than anything else, to put a community television station on the air and keep it there is a large number of dedicated, selfless, hardworking people who love their community, respect their fellow men, and keep a clear .eye on the future. This isn't so easy to find.

It hasn't been easy to make community television work in Pittsburgh, either. But it does have the first community sponsored television station in the world. Like all good things, the explanation is simply stated, only the accomplishment is difficult.

The pattern is this: One hundred thousand families in the Pittsburgh district subscribe two dollars a year to WQED, Channel 13, their community television station. This makes $200,000 net revenue to WQED. Interested individuals subscribe another $50,000. Most of this is in gifts of less than $50. School districts contribute to WQED on a pro rata basis of 30 cents per child, amounting to another $100,000. The operating budget for WQED for one year is $350,000.

Three foundations contributed the major part of the capital funds to build and equip WQED—the A. W. Mellon Educational and Charitable Trust ($100,000) ; the Arbuckle-Jamison Foundation ($100,000) ; and the Fund for Adult Education established by the Ford Foundation ($150,000). Westinghouse Radios Incorporated, a subsidiary of the Westinghouse Corporation, gave WQED the use of its FM tower as an antenna site and leased a portion of its transmitter house for the housing of WQED's transmitter.

The Pittsburgh Plate Glass Company gave a suitable building and grounds to the University of Pittsburgh, which in turn leased the property to WQED for a period of fifteen years at one dollar a year. With a minimum of remodeling, this strategically located building was converted into a large and adequate studio with conveniently located engineering and office facilities.

The first and requisite engineering equipment was purchased with the large initial capital grants of funds. The Howard Heinz Endowment purchased Vidicon projection equipment for films. Mrs. Edmund Mudge bought an organ for the studio. The community undertakes to support the station and to contribute its yearly operating funds.

WQED first went on the air in April 1954. During the spring the broadcast schedule included an hour each day of in-school programs, sponsored and produced by school people and educators. In-school service will be increased to two hours a day this fall and the programs are being carefully planned by a school committee of educators representing private, parochial and public schools so that the programs fit neatly into the established school curricula.

The "Children's Corner," from the

beginning Channel 13's important bid for popular support, has met with almost unprecedented response. Josie Carey, the hostess of the children's program, and Fred Rogers, its producer, now receive more than 1,300 letters each week from young fans.

This fall WQED will present the High School of the Air. Under the sponsorship of the adult education departments of the public schools and directed by Dr. Harry Snyder, veteran of many successful adult education programs, WQED will offer courses in basic subjects—mathematics, English, history, etc. Listeners who so desire may enroll for the complete course for five dollars and, at the end of the semester, take an examination. It is possible for thousands of residents of the ten-county area served by WQED to earn a high school diploma by participating in the High School of the Air.

The most important program of civic interest is WQED's "Community Portrait." Although the station is located in Pittsburgh, its signal area covers many communities of various sizes and interests. Each of these cities, counties, townships and boroughs has social problems and special accomplishments. On Community Portrait each has a chance to speak out. Rezoning, traffic, highway condemnation, plans for a new school library and public health are discussed and sometimes argued. All phases of civic development as related to specific communities find their way to Community Portrait.

Civic leaders are asked to be masters of ceremonies on the programs dealing with their localities. Bankers, mayors and labor leaders participate in these intimate visual portraits. Community Portrait has helped to solve some specific problems. It has given some communities the pat on the back that they deserve and it has helped one community to understand another and to unite the western Pennsylvania area in a common venture, community television.

In order to go to the 40-hour-a-week schedule anticipated for WQED in the fall, it is necessary to make the best use of good film. The Wherrett Memorial Fund has financed a research project in which available film on many subjects is being listed and programmed and made ready for future use.

WQED cannot sell time. It cannot promote the use or sale of products. It cannot influence legislation or sponsor candidates for election. It cannot permit the air waves on Channel 13 to be used for fund raising (other than its own) or money-getting gimmicks.

WQED can be used, however, to present two sides of a controversial issue. It can help the old to learn the uses of leisure and the young to understand the world and people about them. It can help one community in its signal area learn to know another.

Small Staff

The staff numbers only 33 and each member is skilled in some phase of community television operation. The station relies heavily on the help of amateur volunteers, students and the many other young people who contribute their services. Community television is a young person's business. They are quick to see its opportunities and its future.

It took a man of vision, Mayor David L. Lawrence, to get the idea for community television in Pittsburgh. It took Dr. Alfred W. Beattie, superintendent of Allegheny County Schools; Leland Hazard, president of the Metropolitan Pittsburgh Educational Television Station and vice president and general counsel of the Pittsburgh Plate Glass Company; John T. Ryan, Jr., vice president of MPETS and president of the Mine Safety Appliances Company; Leon Falk, Jr., also vice president of MPETS and chairman of the board of Falk &

Company; and others to make it work. It takes a lot of work—and worry. Ask anyone in Pittsburgh if it has been worth it.

DOROTHY DANIEL, *Editor*
WQED Program Previews, Pittsburgh

Winnetka Caucus System Spreads in Illinois

The Winnetka, Illinois, caucus, an informal nominating committee which chooses candidates to run for local office,[1] has been copied, with variations, in several other Illinois communities. The League of Women Voters of Elgin has canvassed those ·communities with a questionnaire, replies to which have developed the following facts:

Oak Park (population 63,529), soon after its adoption of the council-manager plan in 1953, developed a caucus committee composed of one representative from each civic organization, church group, patriotic club and school PTA, as well as the Republican and Democratic parties. The delegates asked for suggestions as to candidates for the city's new council and got a list of 225 names. These were carefully screened as to background and record of public service. Delegates selected six persons with geographic and occupational balance, none of whom had ever run for office, and promoted their election.

Wilmette (18,162) for many years has had what it calls a Harmony Convention, whose delegates are chosen by the so-called creative committee made up of delegates from recognized organizations. The convention consists of four delegates and one alternate from each district in the village, with the duty of enlisting citizens who have ability to be candidates for the village board, library board and park district board, without regard for political affiliations.

[1]For a description see the REVIEW, September 1949, page 416.

Hinsdale (9,846) since 1934 has had caucus committees with two classes of members, organizational and sectional. Organizational members are appointed by qualified and registered organizations. They invite suggestions of names of suitable sectional members and in combination with them develop a ticket of candidates through a nominating committee with careful provision for rotation of personnel every two years connected only by an interim committee of seven members.

Glencoe (6,980) elects a caucus committee for a two-year term through an informal election by ballots distributed to each family by mail. The committee consists of one man and one woman for each school district. It adds five members at large to its own number and develops a slate of candidates for the school board. Rotation of personnel of the caucus committees is provided.

The frequent result of such arrangements has been the unopposed election of caucus candidates in cooperation with the political parties. The device, of course, is facilitated by the absence of serious divisions of class or type of citizens in the communities using it.

R.S.C.

Cambridge Organization Surveys Civic Groups

The Cambridge Civic Association recently circularized good government groups in ten cities with a questionnaire on their local operations. Nine of them replied.

The questionnaire made inquiries on publicity: as to how publicity is handled —by a paid staff member or publicity director, by a volunteer chairman or committee assisted by paid secretary, by a volunteer chairman or committee; to what extent newspapers and radio are used in campaigns; how well the association's activities are handled by these media between elections. The questionnaire sought to establish whether there was ward and precinct organization, ward organization only at election time, neighborhood groups functioning between elections, no ward organization. Another question dealt with year-round and non-election year activities.

The groups responding to the questionnaire included the Cincinnati City Charter Committee, Municipal League of Seattle and King County (Washington), Des Moines (Iowa) Good Government Association, Citizens League of Pawtucket (Rhode Island), Citizens' Plan "E" Association of Worcester (Massachusetts), Richmond (Virginia) Citizens Association, Citizens Action of Grand Rapids (Michigan), Peorians for Council-Manager (Illinois) and the Hartford (Connecticut) Citizens Charter Committee.

The Cambridge association is using the replies to the questionnaire in making a reevaluation of its work. If the necessary funds become available it may publish a summary of its findings, omitting such information as is considered confidential.

District Planning Boards

The Citizens Union of New York City is advocating that Mayor Wagner redeem his election campaign promise to extend to the entire city the new institution of community district planning boards which he inaugurated in Manhattan while president of that borough. The Citizens Union feels that: (1) The establishment and operation of these boards should be a joint enterprise of the mayor and the five borough presidents; (2) the mayor's office should provide a small budget and staff for the organization of the new boards and the servicing of all the boards; (3) the city planning commission should be asked to review its maps of proposed community districts and stitution.[1] Among them are the Illinois Committee for Constitutional Revision, Illinois State Chamber of Commerce, League of Women Voters of Illinois and Citizens of Greater Chicago. All have issued literature explaining the amendment and urging voter support.

Aids in Adoption of Codes

The Municipal League of Spokane, Washington, reports that through its activities the league has influenced adoption of uniform building and fire codes for Spokane County and has helped to secure a larger staff in the county assessor's office for reevaluation of property taxes.

Richmond's First Councilwoman

The Richmond (Virginia) Citizens Association won six of the nine seats on the city council at the spring election. One of the winning candidates was the first woman ever elected to the council in the city's history, Mrs. Eleanor P. Sheppard.

Approves Annual Report

The Citizens Plan E Association of Worcester, Massachusetts, has commended its city council for planning publication of an annual report, to be in tabloid newspaper form. "Such an annual report," reads the commendation, "attractive in appearance and widely distributed, will give the citizens of Worcester an opportunity to receive a comprehensive, understandable annual report for the first time and enable them to appreciate more fully than is possible at present the functions and expenditures of our city government." Worcester has the council-manager plan with proportional representation for the election of its council.

---

[1]See the REVIEW, April 1954, page 195.

PROPORTIONAL REPRESENTATION

(Continued from page 422)
tion, on a council or school committee or other body, in proportion to their numbers. The goal is achieved by marking first-choice, second-choice, third-choice, and so down the line of candidates, on the ballots.

The federation said that P.R "destroys the bipartisan or two-party system." It does indeed seek to remove Republican-versus-Democratic partisanship from city government and city elections. But that does not mean "destroying" our two-party system in general. Further, P.R. in one sense is a protector of the two-party system, since it prevents any political party from having all of the seats in a council by winning a bare plurality of votes in an election.

TAXATION AND FINANCE

(Continued from page 424)
banks, which have sought replacement earning assets to offset the contraction in business loans. At June 30, 1954, for example, the dozen largest banks in New York City held roundly $413,000,-000 more state and municipal bonds than at the corresponding 1953 date. Individual investors have also been active buyers, particularly of the revenue issues, which combine the valuable tax exemption feature with price and coupon features which provide yields considerably above those to be secured after taxes from corporate bonds of anything like the corresponding quality.

As a result of the continuing strong investor demand, borrowing costs have materially bettered those of mid-1953. *The Bond Buyer's* index of yield on twenty representative bonds was 2.26 per cent the first week in August, compared with 2.90 per cent a year earlier. For eleven high-grade bonds, the spread was 2.10 per cent compared with 2.73 per cent.

Contra Costa Officials Coordinate Efforts

County's 130 Taxing Units Seek Functional Cooperation

CONTRA Costa County, California, is faced with a problem widespread throughout the United States but of special importance in the "Golden State." This is the problem of many governments with semi-autonomous powers serving the same taxpayers with no coordination of plans, programs or actions. Within the 700 square miles of the county are over 130 separate taxing jurisdictions with elected boards, administrative staffs and the other facilities of a governmental operation.

Because the concept of home rule for local government is so strongly instilled as a basic tenet of California political theory, cities, counties, school and special purpose districts have been given wider powers than in any other section of the country. The ease by which citizens can establish these units and the more than two hundred different laws under which they are set up has created such a welter of public agencies that the actual conditions are more nearly approaching anarchy than responsible government.

Some areas are governed by more than thirteen separate taxing jurisdictions with conflicting policies and considerable duplication in administrative functions, personnel, plant and equipment. Indeed, most of the counties of California resemble the conditions of prewar Europe with its many principalities and manifest similar characteristics of jealousy, competition and aggrandizement.

In the fall of 1951, the board of directors of the Contra Costa County Tax-

payers' Association decided that an approach to a solution of this problem must be found. The board developed a three-point program:

1. To work for greater coordination of special purpose district activities at the county level;

2. To promote an aggressive educational drive to convince legislators of the need to make a thorough study of the problem; and

3. Establishment of an organization to promote cooperation between public officials.

The first aim has been partially fulfilled by the county increasing its supervision of districts under the authority of the board of supervisors by assigning responsibility for the operation of these districts to regular county departments. Several interim committees of the state legislature are presently studying various aspects of the multiple government problem and, in September of 1951, the Contra Costa Intergovernmental Conference was sponsored by the Taxpayers' Association.

The membership of the conference was made up largely of the administrative officials of the cities, county, school and special districts who were most concerned with intergovernmental relations. This was because it is known by every student of government that a great deal of public policy is initiated by administrative officials. The first meeting was beset with suspicions, accusations and general timidity as to the aims of the Taxpayers' Association and the representatives of the other levels of government.

To explain the nature of the meeting the Taxpayers' Association representative related the following history of similar attempts in the field of intergovernmental cooperation:

"During World War II the conditions

Following this explanation, the group formally organized as the Contra Costa Intergovernmental Conference and elected the county administrator as the first chairman and the city manager of a small municipality as vice chairman. The representative of the Taxpayers' Association was named secretary.

Work of Conference

It was agreed by those present that the general aims of the conference should be to exchange information, coordinate programs and eliminate duplications in public services and expenditures wherever possible.

At the next meeting of the group it was decided to include as members all county and city department heads, the department heads of all large special districts and the superintendents of all school districts within the boundaries of Contra Costa County. The conference was organized into committees concerned with planning, personnel, finance, health, public works and an executive committee. The committees could meet at any time and place thought necessary for discussions of their assigned problems and to develop programs of operation. The committees were to have the right to choose their own subjects of discussion in addition to any assigned by the executive committee.

During the following five months, while the committees carried on discussions, speakers were heard on county-wide subjects. Such persons as the executive director of the League of California Cities, the western representative of a national management consulting firm, and the state controller brought information to the members on general methods of dealing with governmental problems which they would have had difficulty in obtaining individually.

While this was occurring, a subtle but immensely important change was taking place among members—personal friendships were being established. Officials, many for the first time, were beginning to call each other by their first names, and the informal relationships which grew enabled these men and women to phone or write each other for information and assistance with the easy assurance that comes only from personal friendships.

Committees Make Reports

At the end of a five-months period, the committees began to report on their discussions. A summary of the planning committee's study revealed that:

"(1) Upon the evidence so far available, it is estimated that the county population is growing at the rate of at least 3,000 per month and, with continuing and accelerated industrialization, this population increase will continue indefinitely;

"(2) In order to provide adequate public service, planning should be accelerated by all levels of local government in both the administrative and land use aspects;

"(3) Planning should be of a long range nature in all governmental jurisdictions within the county;

"(4) Methods of coordinating both the administrative and land use planning of local government jurisdictions should be found;

"(5) The present difficulty of coordinating the planning of local government jurisdictions points up the need for state legislation in the field of planning;

"(6) The first survey the committee should make is a population and economic survey of the entire county."

In the health committee marked progress was noted in its initiation of studies of a school health program, a mental health program, sewage disposal, garbage disposal, mosquito abatement and air pollution programs. In addition to these studies, immediate steps were taken to combine facilities between the hospital districts, county hospital and public health department so that common laboratories could be used and, in some instances, the services of some of the agencies were abandoned and carried on by contract with others. In this manner some duplication was eliminated and the citizen taxpayers received adequate services for several thousand tax dollars less.

The public works committee chose as its main project the inventory of all public works activities under way and planned for three years into the future. They surveyed by questionnaire over 80 political subdivisions in the county. They also recommended establishment of an informal committee to discuss and agree upon a priority of public works improvements to be made in designated areas and to recommend the means of financing these projects. This procedure was recommended because of public protest when two or more agencies serving the same taxpayers request bond elections at the same time.

The finance and personnel committees did much to bring about uniformity in the techniques of the various governmental units and exchanged large amounts of information on financial and personnel matters. The success of other committees in eliminating duplication and coordinating programs was not as marked because the nature of state law and the importance to legislative policy affected these efforts.

In most instances, the committees have become the clearing house of information within their individual fields among all the governments in the county. This has encouraged members and given prestige to the conference.

During the past three years the conference has had the county administrator, a city manager and presently a school superintendent as its chairman. The programs of the conference have instilled a new philosophy in the officials. The former concept of each unit of government as a separate principality, with its own sovereign powers and practical irresponsibility to other agencies of public service, has given way to realization of all governments as to the implications of their actions on each other and upon the citizen taxpayer.

Although much has been accomplished by the conference, there is a never-ending task ahead. The conference's major goals during the coming year are: to reappraise the system of local government in Contra Costa County; to attempt to develop principles by which this system may be fundamentally changed; and to ascertain how the informal cooperative arrangements established by the intergovernmental group may become institutionalized.

Democracy as a way of life and government is undergoing a test in the world today. If this way of life and government is to endure, it can only do so if men of good will in public and private life cooperate and coordinate their strength so that they are working together and not apart. The Contra Costa Intergovernmental Conference is a partial answer as to how this test can be met and overcome.

HENRY L. MORRISON, JR.
Executive Director
Contra Costa (California) County
Taxpayers' Association

Bibliography Available on Fire Administration

Surprisingly little has been published on the subject of fire department administration, although it is a matter of growing concern to municipal executives.

The fire chief or other city administrator concerned with sound fire administration quickly discovers the excellent text of the International City Managers' Association, *Municipal Fire Administration*. That text of over 400 pages explains the "how" of many fire problems but does not attempt to present the "what" of fire administration. To find more specific material to assist in the application of sound fire administration principles the administrator must reach beyond a single text.

Administrative survey reports of fire departments are a useful source of information. Their recommendations are specific to the municipality surveyed, of course, but other administrators will find the specific application of principles of interest. Recent fire surveys have been conducted by Robert E. Pickup, Earle W. Garrett and Bruce Smith, Jr.

Probably the best single source of up-to-date fire administration material is the International Association of Fire Chiefs (Hotel Martinique, New York). That organization periodically publishes useful information on fire department problems. Some is of a technical nature, perhaps of more interest to a fire prevention bureau than to a fire administrator. Among the important publications available from the association are reprints of bulletins of the National Board of Fire Underwriters and the proceedings of the Fire Department Instructors Conferences.

Bruce Smith, Jr., has provided the National Municipal League with a bibliography of available publications. Readers of the REVIEW may obtain copies from the League office.

Bureau Notes

The Texas Research League (213 West Fourteenth Street, Austin) has submitted its first study report, *The Child Care Program of the Texas State Orphans' Home* (40 pages), to the State Hospital Board. The report contains a proposal for a completely new type of program for care of children in the State Orphans' Home in Corsicana.

Books in Review

COUNCILMEN AT WORK. By Arthur W. Bromage. Ann Arbor, Michigan, George Wahr Publishing Co., 1954. v, 119 pp. $1.50.

Two-thirds of this little volume summarizes and evaluates the experiences of Professor Bromage while serving on the city council of Ann Arbor, Michigan.

Although he previously had written two other booklets on his councilmanic work, one as a freshman and another "when the glamor was wearing off," the third effort deals in retrospect with his four years of service.

The volume abounds with practical discussion of the workings of a weak-mayor form of government in a city of 50,000 persons. The author devotes a chapter to each of seven major fields of work of a councilman.

A councilman from almost any other city probably would find in the book considerable material of a familiar ring, and would nod agreement with many of the statements made. And many a newly elected councilman could profitably spend time in noting some of the sensible suggestions offered.

The author, while in office, apparently longed for a city manager or some other "common boss" to relieve the administrative load on the councilmen. Time and again he refers to the 300 to 500 hours per year that each conscientious (though unpaid) councilman was obliged to contribute.

In the latter part of the volume Professor Bromage compares the American local council with those in both England and Ireland. After noting the reform trends in the United States toward small councils, elections at large, non-partisan elections and city managers, he reports no such trends in England. The British remain happy with a system which is somewhat analogous to our weak-mayor strong-council form, and which does not make use of an "overall working executive."

The Irish, on the other hand, have experimented with a manager-council plan which is subject to central administrative control by the Minister of Local Government. City management in Ireland is "certainly more powerful and less subservient to councils than is the case in the United States."

Although the author generally supports the various "reform" trends in local government in the United States, he does not urge the same pattern for other countries. "Each to his own," he counsels. Even within the United States he wisely would not impose one form of government on all cities: "There are different models by which one can reach the destination of good government. Probably the time has come in the United States to emphasize good driving as well as good systems."

M. NELSON McGEARY
Pennsylvania State University

THE CORONER SYSTEM IN MINNESOTA. St. Paul, Legislative Research Committee, 1954. 66 pp.

Following a series of lurid articles entitled "Hidden Murder?" in the *Minneapolis Tribune* in February 1953, the Legislative Research Committee was directed by the legislature to make a study of the county coroner system and report its findings to the 1955 session. This is the study, and a very fine one, adducing the best experience of other states and revealing weakness of law and performance in Minnesota. It lines up the Hennepin County coroner with the Nassau County (N. Y.) medical examiner and finds the per capita costs to be 9.5 and 5.6 cents respectively for areas with a similar number of deaths per year; similar statewide comparisons favor the medical examiner system. No specific legislation is advanced.

PARTY POLITICS IN THE GOLDEN STATE. By Dean R. Cresap. Los Angeles (California), The Haynes Foundation, 1954. xi, 126 pp. $2.00.

In this pamphlet, the Haynes Foundation adds another important item to its list of documents which describe politics in California for the benefit of schools, colleges and citizens. The internal structure and operations of the two parties are described fully and frankly, including the effect of the unique primaries in which voters may participate at primaries of either party or both and in which candidates commonly indulge in cross-filing by getting their names on the ballot of both parties.

The author, curiously, seems to accept the long ballot as inevitable and argues, as party officers so often do, for voting by party tickets so that the management of a political party can seek the rewards of making good nominations even if the voters rarely scrutinize the nominees. The classic alternative of shortening the list of elective officers, to bring it within the comprehension and scrutiny of lay citizens, so that they will not have to place blind trust in the self-anointed party managers, is strangely neglected. It would seem to this distant observer a better remedy for the scramble of individuals and pressure groups which the pamphlet so ably describes.

R.S.C.

YOUR CALIFORNIA GOVERNMENTS IN ACTION. By Winston W. Crouch and John C. Bollens. Berkeley 4, University of California Press, 1954. 296 pp. $2.75.

Two of the four authors of the 1952 text *State and Local Government in California* (see the REVIEW, January 1953, page 55) have collaborated to prepare *Your California Governments in Action.*

The present book follows the general framework of the earlier one but several changes both in form and content have been made. The new book is more attractive and easier to read and, unlike its predecessor, it is illustrated with frequent photographs and line drawings. Certain chapters, as the ones dealing with California's constitution and the process of constitutional revision within and outside the state, have been expanded. Others have been extensively revised. The separate chapters on taxation and finance and on personnel in the earlier text have been omitted. At the end of each chapter the authors have included a list of questions as aids in stimulating classroom discussion and further research. It is regrettable that they did not make room for the bibliography included at the end of each chapter in the earlier book.

BRUNA NORSA

KNOW YOUR COUNTY. (Revised edition.) Washington 6, D. C., League of Women Voters of the United States, 1954. 47 pp. 35 cents.

In response to a previous edition under this title, many of the 969 local Leagues of Women Voters have in recent years gotten out "Know Your County" pamphlets, setting forth for voters a comprehensive description of their respective county governments, covering history, structure and services. ("Know Your City" and "Know Your State" manuals are also an important feature of life in the league.)

This pamphlet is essentially a questionnaire raising the whole range of incisive questions whose answers will constitute in any county a comprehensive local manual for stripping from any voter's mind the mystery and vagueness in which the county court house may be veiled.

R.S.C.

Additional Books, Pamphlets and Articles

Annexation

ARE ANNEXATION LAWS STRANGLING OUR CITIES? Indianapolis 4, Indiana Economic Council, *News Bulletin*, May 1954. 5 pp.

Assessments

ASSESSMENT LAWS. FORMS AND PROCEDURES. By A. C. Bakken. Bismarck, League of North Dakota Municipalities, *Bulletin*, May 1954. 5 pp.

HOW SHOULD A BOARD OF REVIEW FUNCTION? Madison 3, League of Wisconsin Municipalities, 1954. 14 pp. 25 cents.

Auditing

A BRIEF SURVEY OF MUNICIPAL AUDITING PRACTICES IN ALABAMA. By Robert T. Daland. University, University of Alabama, Bureau of Public Administration, 1954. 10 pp.

Bar Association

BAR ASSOCIATION ORGANIZATION AND ACTIVITIES. A Handbook for Bar Association Officers. By Glenn R. Winters. Ann Arbor, American Judicature Society, 1954. xx, 243 pp.

Budgeting

BUDGETING PROCEDURES FOR OHIO MUNICIPALITIES. Columbus 15, Ohio Municipal League, 1954. 23 pp. $2.00.

PERFORMANCE BUDGETING AND UNIT COST ACCOUNTING FOR GOVERNMENTAL UNITS. Discussions During a Workshop Session. Chicago 37, Municipal Finance Officers Association of the United States and Canada, 1954. 20 pp. $1.00.

County Government

THE CONNECTICUT COUNTY. A Description of Its Organization, Function and Relationship with Other Governmental Units. (Revised.) Storrs, University of Connecticut, Institute of Public Service, 1954. 40 pp. 35 cents.

1954-55 CALENDAR OF DUTIES FOR COUNTY OFFICIALS. Chapel Hill, University of North Carolina, Institute of Government, 1954. 12 pp. $1.00.

Disaster Plans

DISASTER PLAN FOR GRAND RAPIDS, MICHIGAN. Grand Rapids, City Manager, 1954. Variously paged, charts.

Education

EDUCATION DIRECTORY. Part 1: FEDERAL GOVERNMENT AND STATES; Part 2: COUNTIES AND CITIES. Washington, D. C., U. S. Department of Health, Education and Welfare, Office of Education, 1954. 55 and 92 pp. respectively.

FOUNDATION VALUES OF AMERICAN LIFE: for Major Emphasis in the Cincinnati Public Schools. Superintendent's Annual Report, 1952-53. Cincinnati 6, Public Schools, 1954. 38 pp. Illus.

HOW CAN WE HELP OUR SCHOOL BOARDS: A GUIDEBOOK FOR MUTUAL UNDERSTANDING. New York 36, National Citizens Commission for the Public Schools, 1954. 60 pp.

Efficiency

LIMITS TO ADMINISTRATIVE EFFICIENCY IN A DEMOCRACY. (Address at Fourth Annual Conference of the Victorian Regional Group, November 1953.) Sydney, Australian Regional Groups of the Institute of Public Administration, *Public Administration*, March 1954. 6 pp.

Fee System

THE FEES SYSTEM IN FLORIDA COUNTIES. Tallahassee, Florida State University, School of Public Administration, Bureau of Governmental Research and Service, 1953. 13 pp.

Government Text Books

DEMOCRACY IN THE UNITED STATES. By William H. Riker. New York, The Macmillan Company, 1953. xiv, 428 pp. $3.50.

PROBLEMS AND OPPORTUNITIES IN A DEMOCRACY. A Course in Government and Related Social Studies for Seniors in the Catholic High School. By Rev. John F. Cronin. Chicago, Mentzer, Bush and Company, 1954. xii, 755 pp.

YOUR AMERICAN GOVERNMENT. The Citizen's Approach. By Helen Miller Bailey, Eugene L. Lazare, and Conrad

H. Hawkins. New York, Longmans, Green and Company, 1952. x, 566 pp. $4.25.

Grants-in-Aid

FEDERAL GRANTS-IN-AID IN KANSAS. Lawrence, University of Kansas, Governmental Research Center, 1953. 47 pp., tables.

Leadership

EXECUTIVE DEVELOPMENT AND TRAINING IN INDUSTRY AND THE FEDERAL GOVERNMENT. By James C. Worthy. New York 16, National Civil Service League, *Good Government,* May-June 1954. 4 pp.

LEADERSHIP AND GROUP PARTICIPATION. An Analysis of the Discussion Group. By William Foote Whyte. Ithaca, Cornell University, New York State School of Industrial and Labor Relations, 1953. 52 pp.

Legislative Bodies

AMERICAN LEGISLATURES: STRUCTURE AND PROCEDURES. Summary and Tabulation of a 1953 Survey. Chicago 37, Council of State Governments, 1954. 85 pp. $2.00.

THE LEGISLATURE OF CALIFORNIA. By Arthur A. Ohnimus. Sacramento, California Legislature, Assembly, 1954. 47 pp.

Municipal Law

NIMLO MUNICIPAL LAW REVIEW. A RECORD OF MUNICIPAL LEGAL EXPERIENCE IN 1953. Proceedings of the 1953 Annual Conference of the National Institute of Municipal Law Officers. Edited by Charles S. Rhyne and Brice W. Rhyne. Washington 6, D. C., the Institute, 1954. 504 pp. $10.

Neighborhoods

C O M M U N I T Y ORGANIZATION FOR NEIGHBORHOOD DEVELOPMENT—PAST AND PRESENT. By Sidney Dillick. New York, William Morrow & Company, 1953. 198 pp. $4.00.

SOCIAL CHARACTERISTICS OF CAMBRIDGE NEIGHBORHOODS. C a m b r i d g e (Massachusetts), Planning Board, in co-

operation with Cambridge Social Agency Executives, 1953. 33 pp., tables.

Parking

PARSONS PARKING SURVEY. Lawrence, University of Kansas, Governmental Research Center, 1953. 35 pp.

Prisons

PRISONS IN TRANSFORMATION. Philadelphia, The American Academy of Political and Social Science, *The Annals,* May 1954. 162 pp. $2.00.

Public Administration

BALANCING GOOD POLITICS AND GOOD ADMINISTRATION. By David L. Lawrence. Chicago 37, American Society for Public Administration, *Public Administration Review,* Spring 1954. 3 pp.

THE EFFECTIVE LIMITS OF THE ADMINISTRATIVE PROCESS—A REEVALUATION. By Louis L. Jaffe. Cambridge (Massachusetts), Harvard University, *Harvard Law Review,* May 1954. 31 pp.

EXPERTS ON TAP (Editorial). Westminster, S. W. 1 (England), Institute of Municipal Treasurers and Accountants, *Local Government Finance,* May 1954. 2 pp.

Public Welfare

CAN AID TO NEEDY BE "RECOVERED"? Provisions in State Laws Reported. Los Angeles 14, California Taxpayers' Association, *The Tax Digest,* May 1954. 9 pp.

POLICIES AND PROCEDURES FOR VALID WELFARE ROLLS. Baton Rouge, Public Affairs Research Council, *PAR Reports on Welfare,* April 30, 1954. 16 pp.

WELFARE ORGANIZATION AND MANAGEMENT. Baton Rouge, Public Affairs Research Council of Louisiana, Inc., *PAR Reports on Welfare.* May 31, 1954. 15 pp.

Recreation

A CHANGE UNDER PRESSURE. The City Assumes the Public Schools Recreation Program. Pittsburgh 19, Pennsylvania Economy League, Inc., Western Division, *P. E. L. Newsletter,* April 1954. 7 pp.

PUBLIC RECREATION. A Study of Pub-

lic Recreation and Plan for Community
Action in Maryville, Alcoa and Blount
County. Nashville, Tennessee State
Planning Commission, May 1954. 45 pp.

RECREATION AND PARKS. (Vol. IX of
METROPOLITAN LOS ANGELES—A STUDY
IN INTEGRATION.) By Ellis McCune. Los
Angeles, The Haynes Foundation, 1954.
73 pp. $1.75 clothbound, $1.25 paper-
bound.

Retirement Systems

A SURVEY OF PUBLIC EMPLOYEE RE-
TIREMENT SYSTEMS ON THE SUBJECT OF
INVESTMENTS. Chicago 37, Municipal
Finance Officers Association of the
United States and Canada, 1954. 4 pp.
$1.00.

Salaries

MUNICIPAL WAGE SURVEY: SELECTED
KANSAS CITIES 1952. Lawrence, University of Kansas, Governmental Research Center, 1953. 34 pp.

School Districts

SELECTED CHARACTERISTICS OF REOR-
GANIZED SCHOOL DISTRICTS. By C. O.
Fitzwater. Washington, D. C., U. S.
Government Printing Office, Superin-
tendent of Documents, 1953. 49 pp. 20
cents.

State Government

AMERICAN GOVERNMENT FOR PENN-
SYLVANIANS. By H. F. Alderfer, An-
drew S. Sukel and John J. Serff. State
College (Pennsylvania), Penns Valley
Publishers, Inc., 1953. 276 pp. Illus.

Taxation and Finance

COMPENDIUM OF STATE GOVERNMENT
FINANCES IN 1953. By U. S. Department of Commerce, Bureau of the Census. Washington, D. C., U. S. Government Printing Office, Superintendent of
Documents, 1954. iii, 65 pp. 40 cents.

NEW YORK CITY FINANCES. A Re-
port to Governor Thomas E. Dewey.
By J. Raymond McGovern, Allen J.
Goodrich, T. Norman Hurd and George
M. Shapiro. Albany, Governor's Office,
1954. 30 pp.

1953 PROPERTY TAXES IN COLORADO

CITIES OVER 3,000 POPULATION. Denver
3, Colorado Public Expenditure Council, *Colorado Taxpayer,* April 1954. 8 pp.

THE OTHER SIDE OF THE FISCAL COIN.
By John W. Hanes. New York 20, Tax
Foundation, Inc., *Tax Outlook,* April
1954. 2 pp.

PENNSYLVANIA LOCAL GOVERNMENT
TAX CHART. Harrisburg, Pennsylvania
State Chamber of Commerce, Research
Bureau, 1954. 6 pp.

PROBLEMS IN CLASSIFYING PUBLIC EX-
PENDITURES. Princeton (New Jersey),
Tax Institute, Inc., *Tax Policy,* April-
May 1954. 12 pp.

PROPERTY VALUES, TAX LEVIES, RATES
FOR 1954. By R. A. Whitaker. Minneapolis 14, League of Minnesota Municipalities, *Minnesota Municipalities,* April
1954. 5 pp.

STATE SUPERVISION OF THE GENERAL
PROPERTY TAX. Tallahassee, Florida
State University, School of Public Ad-
ministration, Bureau of Governmental
Research and Service, 1953. 18 pp.

TAX OVERLAPS IN THE U. S. A. Trend
Since 1902 Outlined. (Excerpts from a
Study, *Overlapping Taxes in the United
States,* prepared for the Commission on
Intergovernmental Relations by the An-
alysis Staff, Tax Division, U. S. Treas-
ury Department, January 1, 1954.) Los
Angeles 14, California Taxpayers' Asso-
ciation, *The Tax Digest,* May 1954.
15 pp.

TWENTY-FIRST ANNUAL STUDY OF
DEBTS — TAXES — ASSESSMENTS. Sum-
mary. Chicago 2, The Civic Federation,
Bulletin, June 1954. 23 pp.

THE UNEASY CASE FOR PROGRESSIVE
TAXATION. By Walter J. Blum and
Harry Kalven, Jr. Chicago, University
of Chicago Press, 1953. viii, 107 pp.
$2.50.

Toll Roads

TOLL ROADS: A NEW SURVEY OF
PROGRESS AND TRENDS. New York City,
Engineering News Record, January 7,
1954. 8 pp.

Inside the Office . . .

Two foreign visitors called at League headquarters during the summer. **Miss Marietta Campos,** of the Brazilian Radio Ministry of Education, in Rio de Janeiro, gathered material for a program she produces on problems of public administration. . . . **Professor V. Joseph Kostka,** of the University of Manitoba Community Planning Division, Winnipeg, obtained source material for use by his students.

Gordon Clapp, assistant city administrator of New York City and former chairman of the board of the Tennessee Valley Authority, had a luncheon consultation with the staff in July regarding the National Conference on Government in November in Kansas City. . . . **Mrs. Siegel W. Judd,** League regional vice president, sought counsel on certain metropolitan area problems in Grand Rapids, Michigan, her home. . . **Philip H. Cornick,** consultant to the Intergovernmental Relations Com-

Charlton F. Chute   Gordon Clapp

problems. . . . **Charlton F. Chute,** director and vice president of the Eastern Division, Pennsylvania Economy League, called in connection with metropolitan area problems. . . . **Miss Jean Handley,** executive secretary of the Connecticut League of Women Voters, Hartford, checked the NML files on constitutional reform.

John P. Keith, League senior associate, has been nominated for reelection as a trustee of the Governmental Research Association.

John P. Keith   Mrs. Siegel W. Judd

mission and retired staff member of the Institute of Public Administration, called to discuss the *Model State Planning Law,* now in preparation.

An enterprising reporter, **Homer E. Dowdy,** of the Flint (Michigan) *Journal,* who recently completed a series on metropolitan area matters for his newspaper, enlisted the League's cooperation in another series, on survey

Council-Manager Plan Pamphlet Is Revised

The 25th edition of *The Story of the Council-Manager Plan,* one of the most popular pieces of League literature, is ready for distribution.

Revised and brought up to date by the League staff, the 36-page pamphlet sets forth the advantages of the council-manager system, its history, an outline of how it operates, some case histories from cities where it has worked successfully, and testimonials from prominent Americans. It also contains a directory of places where the plan is in effect.

First published about 35 years ago, hundreds of thousands of copies of *Story,* as it is called in the League office, have been distributed by the League and by civic committees advocating the council-manager plan.

Who's There? A Man With an Eviction Notice

It looks as though once again the League may be walking the streets, homeless, before very long. For the 12-story office building at 542 Fifth Avenue, at 45th Street, in which the staff of the organization was happily installed only last May, will be torn down.

The Bank of New York, whose offices at 530 Fifth Avenue, at 44th Street, are among the last vestiges of the mauve decade in midtown, announced that it will erect a twenty-story office building on the west side of Fifth Avenue between 44th Street and 45th Street. Among the structures to be supplanted is that in which the League is quartered.

Housing conditions being what they are in New York, the League has been forced to move three times in the last decade. Members of the staff have been inquiring wistfully whether the League will ever have a permanent home.

Model Planning Law Progressing Rapidly

Authorization of an expenditure of $5,000,000 in federal funds to provide technical and consultation services for local communities which wish to embark on a planning program has spurred the League's work on its *Model State Planning Law*.

This authorization, a section of the 1954 Housing Act, provides that in many cases funds for local communities will be available only through state planning agencies.

Because fewer than half a dozen states have adequate agencies, some observers fear that legislatures, in their desire to receive federal grants, will enact makeshift planning laws, thereby doing more harm than good.

Under the chairmanship of Dr. Coleman Woodbury, authority on planning, meetings on the model law were held in New York July 19 and July 26.

Dr. Woodbury presented his specifications on the League's proposed model law together with comments upon it which he had obtained from some 50 experts.

The League's objective is to complete the model law in time for use by state legislatures convening in 1955. Services of the Legislative Drafting Research Fund of Columbia University have been retained to pull the material into shape.

The plan is to submit the model to the Council of State Governments, which has expressed an interest in it. The Council's endorsement, if forthcoming, would bring the *Model State Planning Law* to the attention of top government officials in all states.

Among those who conferred on the model law were B. E. Crihfield, eastern representative, Council of State Governments; Henry Fagin, research director, Regional Plan Association; Hugh Pomeroy, executive director, Department of Planning, Westchester County, New York; Victor Jones, professor of government, Wesleyan University; John M. Kernochan and Frank P. Grad, Legislative Drafting Research Fund, Columbia University; Gerald Breese, director, Bureau of Urban Research, Princeton University; Herbert H. Smith, executive director, Community Planning Associates, Inc., Princeton, New Jersey, and members of the League staff.

Drafting Model Planning Law

Sixtieth Anniversary Issue
1894 — National Municipal League — 1954

A Permanent Home for the League

(Continued from preceding page)

An appeal to all League members to contribute to the building fund a sum at least equal to their normal annual subscription is being made according to Mr. Willoughby.

Mr. Willoughby noted that the purchase of the house would not only eliminate frequent, costly and disrupting moving, but would provide superior quarters and facilities for far less than they could be rented. Thus, in the long run, the building will be an economy, he said.

A letter from Mrs. Pforzheimer, vice president of the Carl and Lily Pforzheimer Foundation, Inc., stated that the bulk of the grant was to be applied to the purchase price of the building. The balance may be used for alterations or may be added to any fund created "to ensure the permanency of the work of the National Municipal League in its new headquarters."

It is hoped that renovations can be completed in time to permit removal from present headquarters at 542 Fifth Avenue to the new site early next year.

Commenting on the acquisition, Dr. Gallup declared:

"For the first time since Theodore Roosevelt, Carl Schurz, Louis D. Brandeis and others founded the organization 60 years ago, the League will have sufficient space to enable its personnel to operate at full efficiency.

"The library, for example, has heretofore been cramped. Now there will be ample space not only for its unusual collection of books, periodicals and source materials but also for scholars who wish to make use of this material.

"In the new building we shall have

Conference to Be Biggest Ever

The Sixtieth Annual National Conference on Government of the National Municipal League, to be held November 7 to 10 in Kansas City, Missouri, will be the largest in League history. It will also be the first time that the event is held in the Missouri metropolis.

A committee of leaders in the host city headed by John B. Gage, former mayor who played a leading role in breaking the hold of the Pendergast machine,[1] is rapidly completing arrangements for the conference.

Dr. George H. Gallup, League president and director of the American Institute of Public Opinion, will address the closing luncheon of the session, November 10, it was announced. And Thomas R. Reid, director, Office of Civic Affairs, Ford Motor Company, and long time League stalwart, is to be the speaker at a luncheon on November 8. On this occasion welcome addresses will be delivered by Governor Phil H. Donnelly of Missouri, Governor Edward F. Arn of Kansas and Mayor William E. Kemp, of Kansas City.

A luncheon on November 9 will be

Thomas R. Reid   John B. Gage

featured by an address by Mrs. Dorothy M. Dolbey, acting mayor of Cincinnati. Mrs. Dolbey is the only woman in the

---

[1]See also page 464.

United States to head the government of a large city.

A broad program covering twenty phases of governmental and citizen ac-

Frank C. Moore   Belle Zeller

tivity has been planned. Among the panels are the following:

"The Metropolitan County," with former Lieutenant Governor Frank C. Moore of New York State presiding. James A. Singer, member of the St. Louis County Council, Weldon Cooper, University of Virginia, and John D. Corcoran, Public Administration Service, and others will take part.

"State Legislatures: How Can They Operate More Effectively?" Dr. Belle Zeller, chairman of the Committee on American Legislatures, American Political Science Association, and professor of political science at Brooklyn College, will be chairman. Representative A. Clifford Jones, of the Missouri legislature, is among the members of the panel.

"Improving the Civil Service," with James W. Watson, executive director, National Civil Service League, as chairman.

"The Press as a Community Force," at which Roy Roberts, editor of the *Kansas City Star*, will preside. Others taking part include Edward E. Lindsay, editor of the Lindsay-Schaub chain of

(Continued on page 510)

443

Crime, Politics Topic of Forum

The topic, "How Can We Divorce Crime from Politics," will be the subject of discussion at the well known radio forum, "America's Town Meeting of the Air," which will emanate from the National Conference on Government November 9.

Robert E. Merriam

It will be the first time in League history that this program, heard over 325 stations affiliated with the American Broadcasting Company, will originate at a League function.

Robert E. Merriam, youthful member of the Chicago Board of Aldermen, who has made a nation-wide reputation in his battle against organized crime in the nation's second largest city, has accepted an invitation to be one of the two speakers who will take part. The name of the other has not been announced.

Moderator of the program will be James Murray.

Those attending the dinner meeting of the conference November 9 will constitute the audience and are invited to ask questions of the speakers. Usually the discussion and question period continues after the program goes off the air.

In his campaign against crime early this year, Alderman Merriam made a tape recording of a building inspector endeavoring to extort a bribe from the owner of a small apartment house in Chicago. He also arranged to have a *Life* photographer take a picture of the inspector while he was making his proposition.

Merriam found that getting the appropriate officials to prosecute was not as simple as might be imagined, despite the damning evidence. Four new building inspectors were sent to the apartment house and suddenly found a score of violations. And Merriam himself faced contempt charges for a time.

The 36-year-old alderman has successfully employed a regular television show in his fight against crime. It is this program which stirred the ire of many local and state officials. Merriam is therefore an ideal participant in any discussion of the relationship of crime and politics.

Day Is Coming When the Twain Shall Meet

The League's influence stretches half way round the world. Not long ago John E. Bebout, assistant director, sent information, suggestions and a series of publications to the Federation of All-India Local Authorities.

Expressing thanks for this material, K. Narasimha Rao, joint secretary, said, in part, "I shall try to take advantage of the . . . information furnished by you, and my heart opened up with gratitude at the elaborate pains you have taken to

John E. Bebout

convey the same. This really discloses how contacts do dispel prejudices and bring about understanding and sympathy, and I am sure the principle holds good in the case of nations as with individuals."

National Municipal Review

Volume XLIII, No. 9   Total Number 447

Published monthly except August

By NATIONAL MUNICIPAL LEAGUE

Contents for October 1954

The contents of the REVIEW are indexed in *International Index to Periodicals* and *Public Affairs Information Service.*

Entered as second class matter July 11, 1932, at the Post Office at Worcester, Massachusetts. Publication office, 150 Fremont Street, Worcester 3; editorial and business office, 542 Fifth Avenue, New York 36. Copyright 1954 by the National Municipal League.

Subscription, $5 per year; Canadian, $5.25; foreign, $5.50; single copies 50 cents.

Editorial Comment

Ahead of the Election Returns

THE opinions of the people on major public issues find their most authoritative expression in the ballot box. But long before this occurs, there is much frontier thinking, advance planning and evaluation of proposals within an ever widening circle. In its sphere, the National Municipal League, without ever engaging in a campaign, plays an important role in helping citizens prepare for basic decisions later registered at the ballot box or in action by official bodies.

For 60 years it has been the chosen instrument of determined people with a yearning for better government. Through it they have helped themselves formulate new civic goals and develop the means for attaining them. Just how this has been done and with what results is brilliantly told in the article by Dr. Thomas H. Reed starting at page 449 of this issue of the REVIEW.

There is ample evidence both in election returns and in the multitude of voluntary associations, built often on little more than good intentions, that the vast majority of the American people want good government and decent politics and are willing to make some personal effort to have them. The problem is to translate good intentions into sound and practical goals and set up clear direction signs for reaching them. Much of what is commonly lamented as citizen inertia is really citizen frustration resulting from good intentions that have found no outlet in good and effective works.

The League's essential mission is to liberate citizens from frustration. It does this by enlisting in their behalf the services of the soundest and most imaginative authorities to diagnose civic and governmental ills and prescribe practical remedies. It does this by providing a medium through which practicing citizens exchange experience and extend mutual aid in the common battle. It does this by serving as "Information Please" to any citizen or official who raises a legitimate question by mail, wire, phone or personal visit. It does this through an increasingly active program of applied civic education via the printed word, over the air, from the platform, in schools and colleges and by means of conferences and field and group activities.

The vitality and dynamic quality of the League are strikingly illustrated by the steady growth in recent years of the program, the attendance and the impact of its 60-year-old National Conference on Government, which meets this year in Kansas City, November 7 to 10. The League was born at such a Conference in Philadelphia in 1894. In a real sense, the League is born again at each succeeding Conference because at the Conference, as in all of its other activities, the League is invariably grappling with tomorrow's problems. That is how the League stays forever young and keeps constantly ahead of the election returns.

GEORGE H. GALLUP, *President*

National Municipal League

The Complete Citizen

CITIZENSHIP is a more exacting calling in the United States than it is in most other free countries. This is because of our complicated system of government.

Not only do we distribute responsibilities among more or less independent national, state and local governments, we also divide up the powers of a single government among separately elected legislative, executive and even judicial officers.

In addition, the national government and each of the states has its own distinctive constitution, while thousands of local governments have charters that display even greater diversity. Every constitution and charter imposes more or less detailed limitations and procedures on the exercise of governmental power. The interpretation of these has filled thousands of volumes with judicial decisions that make up a system of constitutional law so vast that the most studious lawyer can know only a small part of it.

As time has passed this system has become even more baffling both to the citizen and to the official eye by virtue of the growth of a more and more intricate web of intergovernmental relations. These relationships are a response to the fact that no matter how government may be fractured and parcelled out, on paper, it must achieve some unity and some consistency of purpose and direction if it is to be effective in an interdependent world.

The wonder is that, with this system to manage, American citizens do as well as they do. Surely they can be pardoned for an occasional sense of frustration. The point is that having, for essentially good reasons, saddled ourselves with an inherently complicated system of government, we have as citizens assumed the heavy obligation of carrying it successfully.

Next to the temptation to retreat into complete civic inertia, the nature of our system tempts citizens to concentrate on one level or one favored function of government to the neglect of equally important aspects or of the system as a whole. Despite the almost universal lip service to the doctrine of local self-government, the tendency in these times seems to be for more and more people to concentrate their attention, whether in love, hope or hate, on the national government.

This is noticeably true of many of those who most loudly decry "centralization in Washington." Many such people talk glibly about "turning back" functions to the states without troubling to inquire why the federal government has a hand in such functions or whether or how well the states are prepared to handle them. It should be as clear as crystal that if a substantial part of the job of government, including determination of policy on matters vitally affecting the safety, health, prosperity and general welfare of the people of the country, is to be confided to state and local governments, a substantial part of the attention of every citizen should be directed to those governments. Such attention will pay off even in Washington. It is the only safe way to lighten the load of a central government necessarily heavily burdened by defense, foreign relations and other inescapable national obligations. In addition, it insures better selection and in-service training of the national leaders who climb the ladder of local and state politics and government.

Of course, the individual citizen by his own unaided efforts cannot comprehend the whole range of complete and effective citizenship and make his influence felt as he might wish in every part of our government. Hence the imperative need exists not only for national parties but also for other national, state and local associations of citizens that permit individuals, while specializing to some degree in their own citizen activities, to enjoy the benefit of the specialization of others with similar purposes and ideals. Hence also the need for technical assistance for citizens, technical assistance of the kind supplied by the National Municipal League in its models, guides and consultant services. And hence the need for a more specific and more elaborate system of civic education for young and old than would be necessary in a country with a simpler system and lesser obligations.

No one seriously proposes that we abandon the basic division of powers among levels and departments of government. Experience abundantly justifies the belief of the founding fathers that all power of government should not be lodged in one place, particularly in a nation of continental dimensions and great regional differences. The very necessity which makes a starkly simple unitary government inappropriate enjoins us not to pile on needless complexities.

As Woodrow Wilson once put it, the imperative need is for simplification. This is the keynote of much of the National Municipal League's program for achieving more effective and more manageable state and local government.

The council-manager plan, the short ballot, the one-house legislature, the executive budget, permanent registration are but a few examples of innovations that in the last half century have simplified and clarified the task of the citizen.

Much of the needless complexity in modern government is due to exaggerated attachments for particular functions, agencies or procedures, to the detriment of balanced, responsible, effective, over-all government. One of the great dangers of complicated government lies in the fact that there are so many nooks and crannies in which citizens can hide out from their obligations as complete citizens while happily busying themselves with matters of minor importance or questionable merit. The first obligation of one who would be a complete citizen is to resist the temptation to be only a partial or special interest citizen. Complete citizenship is a high calling, but it is one that has room for every American.

An Old Master Speaks

Noted authority on governmental problems recalls early League days; sees no dearth of new worlds to conquer.

By THOMAS H. REED*

THERE is something very significant in the survival of any organization through 60 such changeful years as those from 1894 to 1954. Growing old gracefully is a ticklish business. For us humans it means not only a very disconcerting bodily degeneration but, what is worse, in most of us a stiffening of the mind—a more or less complete rejection of new ideas. We oldsters like to think that our conflicts with the young are the result of our greater experience and excess of wisdom. Unfortunately it is all too often due to our failure to keep in step with progress.

Institutions run a similar risk of creeping paralysis. Those which outlast more than one generation must not only be concerned with some principle of lasting value but must also have shown the capacity to adjust their activities to the conditions of a world which never stands still.

*Dr. Reed, noted governmental consultant, has made many studies of local governments, including Cincinnati (Ohio), Atlanta and Fulton County (Georgia) and Essex County (New Jersey). He drafted the council-manager charters of Hartford (Connecticut), Richmond (Virginia) and Augusta (Georgia), as well as the charter consolidating the city of Baton Rouge and East Baton Rouge Parish (Louisiana). Dr. Reed made a nation-wide survey of what universities and colleges are doing in citizenship training. Acting as consultant to the Citizenship Clearing House of New York University's School of Law, he is co-author, with Mrs. Reed, of two reports on the subject issued by the Clearing House.

In all institutions which have long survived, among which church and state are the most notable, there has always been a succession of young hearts and brains constantly challenging the "elder statesmen" whenever the latter have lost contact with the present.

The National Municipal League was at its formation in 1894 literally what its name implies, a league of organizations then engaged in uphill fights for better city government in their respective cities. They felt deeply the need of pooling their knowledge and experience in view of the absence of published materials on city government. The League, whose membership was soon after opened to individuals, thus started with the purpose of aiding groups and individuals interested in good government. After 60 years that is still its purpose. The importance of this service has not diminished. Though there is now an enormous literature relating to municipal affairs, most of it is highly technical, and the League continues to be the only organization of national scope devoted to supplying citizens and citizen groups with advice and usable information concerning the concrete problems of now not merely city but county and state government. It has thus satisfied the first condition of institutional longevity—concern with a principle of lasting value.

The League, however, would have

449

died long ago if it had not also been able to keep within hailing distance of the changing fronts on which the interminable campaign for good government has had to be waged. For good government, itself a changing concept, must be sought by means which alter from place to place and year to year. Good citizens need aid as much in 1954 as in 1894 but it may well be a different kind of aid and certainly will be related to different subjects.

The United States into which the League was born in 1894 differed vastly from the one we live in today —how different only the old can be expected to know for certain and even they have mostly forgotten. There were then no automobiles and no airplanes. The electric trolley car was something of a novelty. There were no radio, no motion pictures, no television, no electric stoves, no vacuum cleaners. On the other hand, there was no income tax, a billion-dollar Congress was a rarity, and you could hire a good housemaid for five dollars a week.

City Population Increases

Cities were much smaller than today. The 1890 census listed 124 cities of 25,000 or more, with a total population of 13,994,315, as against 481 such cities with a total population of 61,953,307 in 1950. Cities, however, were growing rapidly and their facilities and services compared unfavorably with those of old-world cities.

Only eight years earlier Bryce had justly characterized city government as our "one conspicuous failure." Nothing had happened in the mean-

time to alter the validity of this conclusion. Cities were dominated by machines allied with one or the other of the two great political parties. Except for the effect of recently adopted civil service laws in New York and Massachusetts, city offices were the spoils of the victor in each city election.

Direct primaries were unknown and the caucuses and conventions through which nominations were made were far from adequately r e g u l a t e d . Until Massachusetts adopted the "Australian" ballot in 1888 there had been no genuine protection to the voter's right to secrecy, and a party nomination for a city office generally carried with it the support of all that party's adherents on the ground that they did not wish to weaken the party's chances nationally by bolting its local ticket.

Responsibility for the bad conduct of city affairs was hard to fix. City councils were large and elected by wards. Through their committees they exercised a large share of what properly should be executive power, which was further divided among a number of elected heads of departments, leaving the mayor only a nominal chief executiveship. Finances were generally controlled by the council committees, regular budget procedure was unknown, and most cities had no better than a single-entry system of bookkeeping which might control the inflow and outflow of cash but nothing more.

Under such a setup jobs were held by political hacks, contracts went to political favorites, and outright corruption was common. But when the good citizens rebelled against waste and inefficiency they mostly butted their heads helplessly on the entrenchments of the machine. Their complaints were discounted by the professional politicians as what Dana in the *Sun* called the "infantile blubber of the goo-goos."

Such was the scene at the moment of the League's birth. The conditions which then prevailed and which have since been slowly, painfully and partially overcome have determined to a large degree the attitudes of advocates of better city government to the present day. The great obstacle to reform was the power of the political machines which stood right across the path of progress, entrenched behind a network of laws and traditions.

Political Reform Program

In the course of the first twenty years following the founding of the League a whole program of what can properly be called political reforms was evolved, the primary object of which was to give the people of a city the opportunity to have good government if they wanted it. It was a cardinal principle of this program that no rational relation existed between the issues of municipal politics and the real or alleged principles of the great national political parties. It followed that the national parties really had no business in municipal affairs, that to reduce their influence as far as possible municipal elections should be separated from state and national elections, and that party labels should be removed from the ballots used in municipal elections. Nomi-

nating and election machinery should be amended, according to the program, so as to ensure honest registration and an honest count. Still further, elections should be by proportional representation if possible and, failing that, should be preceded by a nonpartisan primary to reduce to two the number of candidates for any one office, thus ensuring a majority choice.

An equally important political reform was the merit system, advocated by the early reformers not so much as a means of promoting the efficiency of the civil service as of depriving the machine of the potent weapon of patronage. Home rule also was an integral plank of the reform platform. It was defended, of course, on abstract grounds as the inherent right to self-government possessed by every American community. It was sought chiefly as a means of further checkmating party influence—often that of the party opposed to the one in control of the city—at the state legislature and the infinite opportunities for chicanery in the backstairs politics of the state capitol.

The list of major political reforms also called for the reorganization of city government itself to provide the citizen a straight shot at those responsible for graft or mismanagement. This included abolition of two-chamber councils in favor of small councils elected at large, the disappearance of elected department heads and, at first, the concentration of executive power in an elected mayor with a veto and sole power to initiate the annual budget.

After the spectacular success of the Galveston commission in putting that hurricane-wrecked city on its feet, and the subsequent furor over the Des Moines plan, the reformers flirted briefly with the idea of commission government but gave it up enthusiastically for Richard S. Childs' council-manager plan. The initiative and referendum remained in the budget of reform measures as the permanent contribution of the Des Moines plan.

This whole program of "political" reforms was well launched by the time Dayton adopted the manager plan in 1913. Along with some provisions for budgeting and financial organization and procedures they have formed the gist of the League's *Model City Charter*. They have been supplemented by projects for the reorganization of county and state government and considerable talk but not much action anent the metropolitan problem. Home rule has made many advances in the constitutions and laws of the states. Innumerable local contests have been waged on the issues raised by the various parts of the program and many victories have been won. No foreign observer would today repeat Bryce's unfavorable judgment on city government. On the whole our cities today are better places to live in than most of their British and European contemporaries.

The improved quality of American city government, however, cannot be ascribed wholly to the adoption of these political reforms. A parallel influence of perhaps even greater importance has been the pro-

fessionalization of municipal administration. Our small cities of the eighteenth and early nineteenth centuries were operated on an almost purely amateur basis. It was assumed in those days, with reasonable justification, that any of the simple services then expected of a city could be performed by any citizen without previous training or experience. This idea, which fitted rather neatly with the methods of local machines and bosses, persisted long after most of the work was done by salaried employees. It still lurks in the minds of some reactionary politicians today.

The Merit System

The adoption of the merit system, even in its earliest and most primitive form, eliminated some of the worst political hacks from routine positions and prevented clean sweeps with each change of administration. Later the manager plan introduced a professional officer as chief executive. The most powerful inducement to professionalization lay in the growing volume, complexity and technical character of city business. The growth of cities and the equally rapid development of popular demand for services made possible by the progress of science in the first 50 years of the twentieth century, have made it politically suicidal for even the most strongly entrenched boss to trust the keeping of the city's books, the construction of its sewers, the direction of its water works, the protection of its public health, and even the command of its police and fire departments to any but professional hands.

There may be lucrative sinecures with high sounding titles for worthy politicos but the work, except in the smallest cities, is done by professionals. This trend has been supplemented by an enormous development of municipal administration as a field of scientific study, and of professional organizations of municipal officials.

A student at Harvard from 1897 to 1901, the writer had, as a preparation for a career in which city government has played a major part, the advantage of only a part of a one-semester course in that subject, and he would have got less in that field in almost any other university. Today every substantial institution of higher learning has at least one course in municipal government and administration, with one member of the faculty, at least, interested in municipal research. Several universities have elaborate graduate setups for work in public administration, including municipal administration. Some of these and other institutions have schools in which municipal administrators are trained for their jobs.

Citizen Agencies Grow

In 1906 the founding of the New York Bureau of Municipal Research started a long line of citizen-supported research agencies throughout the country, devoted to the continuing study of the administration of a particular city, and constant readiness to assist city officials with their administrative problems. Associations of city managers, finance officers, planning officers and the like, grouped together at the University of Chicago, perform important services in raising the professional standards of their members.

The result has been that along with the transfer of municipal services from amateurs to professionals has gone a steady improvement in the techniques of administration. No attempt has ever been made to compute the amount of money spent by colleges and universities, research agencies and organizations of municipal officials, but its aggregate would undoubtedly make the budgets of the National Municipal League over the past 50 years look modest indeed. Alongside of these generalized efforts to improve municipal administration have gone a great number of special studies, usually called surveys, of individual cities and counties, usually paid for by the governmental unit or units concerned, but sometimes by the voluntary contributions of citizens. The sums so spent over a half-century in the aggregate have been prodigious.

Throughout this era of professionalization and administrative progress the League has been consistently hospitable to all such endeavors. Stewart's history of the League[1] during this period is a rehearsal of one activity after another in cooperation with the rapidly increasing number of research projects, while at the same time the League continued its first and most vital activity of aiding citizens in their

---

[1] *A Half Century of Municipal Reform —The History of the National Municipal League,* by Frank Mann Stewart. University of California Press, Berkeley, 1950.

localities to secure political or administrative reforms. In so doing it developed to a high degree a procedure for extracting the consensus of expert opinion on various subjects through a series of committees. This resulted in not only a *Model City Charter* but also a *Model County Charter* and a *Model State Constitution*, as well as model laws on such subjects as bonds, budgets, election administration, registration, real property tax collection, state civil service and a state medico-legal investigative system. These models put into the hands of lay citizen groups throughout the country weapons they could by no means have forged by themselves and contributed greatly to the progress of good government.

League a Clearing House

Of this period it is enough here to say two things: first, the League was successful in living through two wars and an intervening depression, no mean achievement in itself for an organization wholly supported by voluntary subscriptions; second, the research organizations and those of municipal employees have gradually gone their own ways, leaving the League its original field as the clearing house for citizen action for better city and necessarily also state and county government.

It would be impossible to appraise accurately the relative importance of the further perfection of administrative techniques and the promotion of citizen action in the years ahead. There will always be conflicting views on this subject. It is

clear, however, that there are certain limitations in a democracy like ours on what can be done by research alone. For, if the results of research are to be adopted in most critical areas of the governmental spectrum, they must be supported by vigorous and decisive citizen action. Many of us have vivid recollections of the admirable research jobs done by some of the "little Hoover commissions" and what happened to their recommendations in default of warm and vigorous citizen support.

The helplessness of research by itself is further emphasized by the fact that college and university research agencies, the municipal research bureaus and the professional organizations of officials are by their very nature incapable of conducting any kind of campaign for any controversial policy other than by a simple publication of the facts. They frequently have to be careful how far they go in that direction. It must further be regretfully admitted that many researchers, all too well aware of these limitations, make a virtue of necessity and take to regarding research as an end in itself—which it is not. Municipal research depends for any immediate success on receptive city officials, and they are obviously a product of citizen action.

As one looks down the path of state and local government improvement for the next twenty years, one is impressed, of course, by the need for expanded research in many directions, but also by the extensive provision already made to supply it. One is further impressed by the imperative necessity of getting something practical and concrete done with the fruits not only of the things we will learn from the new research but also with truths we have known for years and which have so far been only partially applied. This is where the League has its work cut out for it —to interpret, as it has in the past, the conclusions of scholarship to the lay citizen, to arm him with model charters and laws embodying the consensus of expert opinion, and to inspire him by the examples of others who have done well. This is the role which the League was created to fill and which it has developed through thick and thin ever since. There is no stand-in or understudy to take over if the League should falter in its part.

Changing Scene

This does not mean, however, that the League must go on simply repeating itself like some old professor reading the lectures he prepared when his current class was still in diapers. The municipal scene is changing and new crises in municipal affairs are constantly arising. Programs for better government must be adapted to meet them. It is impossible to say just what municipal reformers will be advocating in 1994 but it is possible to point out certain changes of direction and emphasis which are imperatively called for by the conditions of today. They relate to the internal organization of local government, the relation of the state to

local affairs, and the means by which citizen action is to be carried out in the immediate future.

It has been a basic element in the creed of municipal reform that executive authority should be concentrated in the hands of a single individual, preferably a professional, nonpolitical official responsible to a small elective council—in other words, a city manager. This plan, to the tune of considerable self-congratulation on the part of its advocates, has achieved rather rapid acceptance until today over 1200 cities have embraced it. Its results have been, on the whole, very satisfactory. Candor, however, requires the admission, first, that it does not work well unless the city council is willing to let the manager manage and, second, that it has utterly failed to be adopted in the largest cities of the country.

It is not necessary to go into detail here as to what happens to the manager plan when the council steps out of its proper board-of-directors role. It has been demonstrated repeatedly that the conditions which make it possible for the manager plan to produce superior results require strong and unremitting defense which is all too often neglected. The nature of politicians is not changed by the adoption of the manager plan, and they have proved adept in finding their way around the provisions of the best charters. Defense of the manager plan where it has been adopted, not only against attempts to oust it but against the more frequently successful attempts to pervert it, must be an intensely serious preoccupation of citizen action.

According to the 1950 census, Cincinnati was the only manager plan city with more than 500,000 population, although San Antonio and Kansas City have now probably ·exceeded that mark. The only city with a population at the time of adoption of over 500,000 was Cleveland, where it was subsequently abandoned through the combined efforts of the Republican and Democratic machines. The reason for the reluctance of the big cities to adopt the manager plan is the subject of bitter dispute. Some assert that it is due to the inherent inadaptability of the plan to big city government. Others contend that the greater relative strength in large cities of the political party organizations, everywhere hostile to the plan, is responsible. Whatever the cause, the fact remains that more than a generation has passed since the manager plan was first widely publicized without its having made perceptible headway in the biggest cities where high class professional direction of administration is more poignantly needed than anywhere else.

The next prime objective in the field of internal municipal organization must be to find a solution of this "big city" problem. It may be found in the experiments now being tried in several cities in associating a professional administrator with an elective and intensely political mayor with almost unlimited executive power. There are excellent British precedents for professional officers at all levels of government who successfully guide the discretion of their lay superiors, just as there are German examples of an appointive city executive combining in one professional person the functions of a mayor and manager. The current experiments must be watched and their results analyzed in a spirit at once cordial and critical. If the results are negative still other experiments must be encouraged. Certainly the atmosphere in which an administrative coadjutor of a political mayor can attain any high level of success can be produced on a permanent basis only by continuous citizen pressure on that key figure.

Control of Personnel

Another spot in the internal organization of city government where changed conditions call for new strategy is in the control of personnel. Technical progress in personnel administration has been considerable but it is continually more and more evident that citizen pressure is essential to maintaining the integrity of any civil service system. The personnel experts cannot guarantee the good faith of the politicians with whom they must work, only the people can see to that. Moreover the increased numbers and unionization of municipal employees has created a new source of power in the employees themselves whose apparent interests are not always those of the community at large. Employee unions are apparently here to stay. How customary union policies are to be reconciled with the economical performance of city services in the face of the fact that the productivity of most city employees cannot be increased as pay is raised and hours of work shortened is already a crucial problem which cannot be solved by reference to any existing program.

The founders of the National Municipal League had a strong but negative interest in state-city relations. They saw in the constant meddling of the state legislature in city affairs a very fruitful source of bad and irresponsible government. They therefore went all out for a rather vaguely defined something called "home rule." The phrase had a great deal of popular appeal. It is impossible to deny that the people of any unit of local government should be free to determine their own form of government and their own policies, provided that in so doing they do not contravene the measures necessary for the welfare of the state as a whole. Considerable progress has been made toward the general recognition of this principle though there are states like Connecticut with no constitutional guarantees of home rule at all and others where such guarantees are frequently nullified by legislative intrusion supported by strained judicial interpretation.

Metropolitan Problem

There is also at least one field of activity which must occupy a major share of citizen attention in the immediate future, in which the principle of home rule has been stretched to block progress. The reader scarcely needs to be reminded that when Henry Ford and his competitors put almost everyone on wheels

they created a movement of population into the suburbs of cities which has produced vexatious problems of organization, finance and service, commonly lumped together as the "metropolitan problem." This problem is currently unsolved and, of all the issues of municipal existence, presents what can properly be called the greatest challenge to citizen open-mindedness, good sense and initiative. In every effort to bring about governmental integration in metropolitan areas, one is met by the alleged right of every existing unit in the area to a continued legal existence indefeasible except by its own act.

In other words, not only are the people entitled to govern themselves in such units as exist but also the state is assumed to have exhausted its authority to alter the boundaries of any such unit by the mere act of creating it. In Ohio, for example, an election on the subject of incorporation can be initiated by a petition signed by 30 citizens of an area which they describe in the petition. The county commissioners have no option but to call the election and, if a majority vote in favor of incorporation, a new municipal unit has been created which can stand until judgment day unless by vote of its own citizens it gives up this inalienable right to eternal existence. The absurdity of such a condition is obvious. We must be careful in our advocacy of home rule—and the principle is still a good one— to limit its meaning to the right of the people to govern themselves in whatever units the policy of the state provides. If we do not we shall be giving aid and comfort to the enemy in one of the most significant areas of conflict between stagnation and progress in the second half of the twentieth century.

Obviously the status of home rule must be settled at the state level. The same is true, though not necessarily to the same extent, of any constructive solution of the metropolitan problem. Most states have provided some procedure by which annexation of territory to a city may be carried out. Except in Virginia, where annexation is effected by a judicial proceeding in which a three-judge court settles the matter on its merits, and Texas and a few other states where annexation of unincorporated territory requires only a resolution of the city council, annexation calls for a majority vote in favor on the part of the area to be annexed. This means that annexations of unincorporated sections take place seldom and incorporated places almost never.

The general adoption of the essentials of the Virginia procedure would enable cities in general to keep their political boundaries in line with their economic and social boundaries. It would require a great effort on the part of interested citizens on a statewide scale. Several times in the last 25 years integration of particular metropolitan areas on a so-called "borough" plan have been suggested, only to be rejected.

Fresh interest in this type of metropolitan solution has been aroused by the recent creation of The Municipality of Metropolitan Toronto. More significant than the terms of this union of Toronto and twelve suburban municipalities is the fact that it was enacted without referendum of any kind by the legislature of the province of Ontario. Some form of integration had been more or less acrimoniously discussed for years. Separate proposals for consolidation by Toronto and one small suburb had been heard at great length by the Ontario Municipal Board with no sign of agreement. Then the provincial parliament took a hand and said, "This is it."

It seems too much to expect that the politicians in a dozen or twenty suburbs—large toads in small puddles—will voluntarily consent to their own extinction or to any serious curtailment of their powers. In any contest with the "big town" these local politicians usually have the sympathy of the suburban population afraid of increased taxes and distrustful of the kind of government to be expected from their larger neighbor. Where so many conflicting interests exist the state must in some way or other assume the role of arbiter.

Thus the battle for metropolitan integration must be fought on two fronts at once—local and state. Even to get a chance at a local referendum on a borough or other plan of consolidation in most states would require a constitutional amendment or statutory changes or both. It looks as if a great deal of citizen action will be necessary before the metropolitan problem ceases to be a mere subject of conversation and becomes an issue of practical politics.

Another field in which state action is imperatively necessary is that of local government finance. The days when the general property or real estate tax sufficed to provide comfortable city revenues have been gone so long as to create the suspicion in many people that they never existed. No local government can be good government unless it has the means to finance the services which modern municipal standards require. Most cities are short of money. Where can they get more? From the profits of municipal utilities? New taxes? State or federal grants? State-collected, locally-shared taxes? These are questions which can be settled only at the state level and with the concurrence of the federal government. They have got to be settled soon or else.

It is clear that a citizen interested in the welfare of his city has willy-nilly to be vitally interested in state government, its organization and procedures, and especially the working of the representative system in the state legislature, at this writing the weakest link in the governmental chain from town hall to White House. These things are vital to the citizen not only for what the state may do to him directly but also because an active, progressive and cooperative state government is essential to the vigor and efficiency of local institutions.

Finally, there must be some revision of the procedures by which citizen action takes place. We have

to give up expecting that the reflection of citizen will in city councils can be immediately secured by the wide adoption of proportional representation. The writer of this article, in the portion of the "Upson" survey of Cincinnati[2] relating to the council, recommended P.R. for that city and is proud of it. It has worked well there and everywhere else where it has had a fair trial, including New York City. There has, however, been a great deal of difficulty in selling P.R. to a municipal public too impatient to try to understand the details of the count. In view of this fact, and the constitutional obstacles to use of P.R. in some states, it is necessary to devise a "next best" method of election for recommendation where P.R. cannot be adopted.

"Nonpartisanship" has been a basic tenet of municipal reform doctrine from the League's origin on. It is based on the common-sense fact that there is no such thing as Republican asphalt or Democratic sewer pipe. The nonpartisan idea has been accepted at least to the extent of removing the party label from the municipal ballot in more than half the cities of the country. So far so good, because it has made independent candidacies and independent voting somewhat easier. However, not only are there still many localities in which there are no legal restrictions on party activity in local elections, but also many

(Continued on page 463)

[2]The Government of Cincinnati and Hamilton County, Survey Directed and Edited by Lent D. Upson. Cincinnati, 1924.

The League and the Future

Responsibilities and opportunities have not diminished;
they are greater now than they ever were in past years.

By CHARLES A. BEARD*

EDITOR'S NOTE.—The article below is made up of excerpts from an article by Dr. Beard appearing in the League's 50th anniversary issue of the NATIONAL MUNICIPAL REVIEW, November 1944, pages 503-510.

IN JANUARY 1894, the associational spirit, so long evident in American society, found expression in the formation of the National Municipal League, "composed of associations formed in American cities for the improvement of municipal government." The call for the first meeting was sponsored by many eminent leaders of the time, such as Theodore Roosevelt, Carl Schurz, Charles W. Eliot, Richard T. Ely and Charles J. Bonaparte.

But among the rank and file of men and women who carried the main burden of the work done by the League were innumerable persons whose names seldom if ever appear in written histories of the age and are utterly unknown to their beneficiaries. This anonymity is also a characteristic of most associational activities. Those who labor and bear burdens find their rewards

*Dean of American historians, Dr. Beard (now deceased) taught politics at Columbia University from 1907 to 1917, then became director of the Training School for Public Service in New York City. In 1922 he went to Tokyo as advisor to the Institute of Municipal Research. Dr. Beard, author of many well known books on American government and history, was former president of the American Historical Association, American Political Science Association and the National Association of Adult Education.

in good work conscientiously done, not in the prestige and emoluments sought by the ambitious.

Like many associations the League at first had no very comprehensive program of action. Perhaps the leading idea of the men who sponsored it was the belief that good government could be achieved if good men were elected to places of power in municipal government.

Broadly speaking, its development has fallen into three stages. At first it served as a kind of clearing house for information on municipal government and activities and as a point of contact for thousands of men and women in all parts of the country who were laboring to improve conditions in their own communities. At the annual conferences of the League papers on various phases of municipal government were read and discussed.

What may be called for convenience the second stage in the development of the League began in 1912 when a quarterly journal, the NATIONAL MUNICIPAL REVIEW, was substituted for the annual volume containing papers presented at the annual conference.

Two general ideas controlled this undertaking. The first was to reach a wider audience and maintain a more continuous discussion of municipal concerns than was possible by the publication of a bulky volume of proceedings each year. The second idea which the editors had in mind was to give extended consideration to municipal functions as well as to the machinery of city government.

Particularly under the leadership of Richard S. Childs, the National Municipal League entered upon the third stage of its career. The quarterly REVIEW was changed into a monthly REVIEW. Emphasis was laid again upon the machinery of city government and campaigns were launched to promote the adoption of the city manager form of government. The REVIEW no longer attempted to cover all the functions and services of city government. Model charters and other documents pertaining to government, administration and civil service were published; a consultant service was established.

In other words, the League continued and expanded its function as a clearing house for collecting and distributing information on the arts, sciences and methods of municipal improvement.

In the long course of the League's history, the position and functions of the city in American society have actually undergone a revolution. It is no longer a question of an autonomous municipality well governed within its borders. While the city has been gaining more home rule in respect to its form of government and many of its functions, its relations to state government have multiplied in many directions—financial, legal and operational, for instance. Furthermore new connections with the federal government and its numerous agencies have been established. Some of these connections are through the state government, others are direct. Was it not the federal government that came to the aid of cities during the great depression when they were threatened with bankruptcy?

It is no longer enough to consider municipal affairs mainly in terms of home rule, model charters and autonomous forms of government. Instead of easing the strain of thought about municipal government, the intense specialization of recent years has intensified it, has raised a new issue. Who is to do the general thinking about municipal government that encompasses all the disparate specialties, that gives unity to them, that considers the city as a self-governing body of citizens in its new relations to the state government and the federal government?

Herein lies, as I am given to see things, the opportunity of the National Municipal League to enter upon the fourth stage of its development, by taking leadership in fostering anew the general consideration of the whole art and science of municipal government in relation to state and federal affairs. This would, of course, be no sharp break in its history. It would be indeed a continuation and expansion of the general interest in municipal affairs that marked its first stage of development, combined with the several interests which were subsequently taken into account, and a new consideration of the whole field in the light of the present setting—as we face the future. If it be said that this is emphasis on theory, my answer is that all practice springs out of some theory, precise or muddled, and that without theory practice is rudderless.

In its membership and among its officials the National Municipal League has a body of citizens who, whatever their special concerns, have a general interest in the whole city— its place, role, functions and obligations in American society. No other association in the country is so constituted. No other organization is, in my opinion, so well fitted to look at the city as a whole, in relation to all its responsibilities. None is better prepared to promote the development and diffusion of knowledge pertaining thereunto, thereby more effectively equipping American citizens for those indispensable tasks which transcend, while making use of, each and every specialization—tasks which must be assumed if the ideal of the city just, efficient and beautiful is to be more than a shimmering mirage.

Many indefeasible tendencies of the times mark out for the League this more general opportunity and function in the years ahead. Although the League throughout its existence has laid emphasis on the methods, processes and mechanics of municipal improvement, leaders in the organization and, no doubt, most of the rank and file, have taken a double view of their work. The techniques of municipal improvement have been regarded as expressions of enlightened civic interest and as instruments for the accomplishment of civic ideals.

At the same time one of the supreme purposes of the League, from the beginning, has been the development of an informed, responsible and active citizenry capable of using such instrumentalities in the public interest. In short the League's model charters, model laws and other standards for guidance in municipal affairs have not been looked upon as ends in themselves but as agencies for the achievement of ends related to the good life in municipalities; to the preparation of citizens for efficient participation in public affairs and for the enjoyment of the activities associated with this participation.

In the experiences of social practice and of education is to be found one of the prime secrets of such success as Americans have achieved in the discharge of their civic responsibilities. No people can govern themselves on a large scale until they have acquired or developed the capacity to govern themselves on a small scale. From colonial times American society and political institutions have expressed this idea and have been so organized as to permit and encourage self-government in communities. On this basis rest the states and the union of states. And civic education in our schools now seeks to give youth knowledge of this complicated system and to encourage habits of participation.

Thus care for civic education merges in the growing consciousness of the American people that, apart from their individual interests, they are members of this great society and, as citizens, must function in groups—political and private. It is by the conduct of and coordination of such activities that they can keep alive the capacity for self-government and preserve those social decencies and liberties which are to be regarded as the prime values of American civilization.

To success in self-governing activities great bodies of workable knowledge and continuous readjustments in the light of "stubborn and irreducible facts" are indispensable. If this be true, and I believe it is, then the National Municipal League, as it enters upon a new stage in its long course, will face still greater challenges to the civic talents that it can muster.

AN OLD MASTER SPEAKS
(Continued from page 459)

others in which the absence of the party label on the ballot does not prevent the parties from vigorous and open participation.

The doctrine of nonpartisanship has also carried with it the idea that local citizen organizations must be organized across party lines. Some have been notably successful but most, it must be admitted regretfully, have been short-lived. This is not merely because citizens become weary but because "good government," once it has been attained, no longer in itself supplies a sufficient rallying cry for an active political group.

It is not suggested that we abandon ticket-splitting in municipal elections or restore party labels to the ballot. It is suggested, however, that a study be made of the procedures best adapted to influencing the result of elections in places where in law or fact nonpartisanship does not exist. This may prove to be some form of intra-party organization and activity or, again, it might be an organized plan of throwing weight from one party to the other, or the organization of a municipal party not dedicated exclusively to good government as an abstraction but with a vigorous attitude on local as contrasted with national issues.

However it is done, some means of vitally affecting the situation in party-ruled cities must be evolved or the scope of municipal reform is going to be limited to the relatively few places where genuine nonpartisanship prevails in city affairs. Moreover, if, as has been suggested, a wider field of activity in state government is to be anticipated, it is obvious that on that level the municipal reformer must contend with political parties on their native heath.

On the whole, no reader of this article needs, in the manner of Alexander, to weep because there is nothing new to be done in the arena of municipal affairs. As a rough-and-ready civil war general is reputed to have said to a fuss-and-feathers colonel of a brand new regiment who demanded to know where he "should go in," "Go in anywhere, Colonel, there's lovely fighting all along the line."

Citizens v. Boss: Citizens Win

Kansas City 20 years ago was one of nation's worst run communities; fearless leaders made it one of the best.

By LYMAN FIELD*

A CITY dying, losing population, its physical plant doomed to deliberate neglect and deterioration. . . . Intimidated citizens casting ballots under malevolent snouts of tommyguns. . . . "Ghosts," 65,000 of them, winning elections regularly. Prostitution, gambling and dope-peddling unchecked, often protected by city police. That was Kansas City, Missouri, through most of the 1930s. That was Kansas City, Missouri, under the domination and ruthless exploitation of the Pendergast political machine. That was "Tom's Town."

Today Kansas City has earned a new title. Three times winner of the All-America Cities Award, her city manager the first recipient of the La Guardia award for civic activities, Kansas City now enjoys a worldwide reputation for civic enterprise and administrative excellence. As recently as last August, her citizens trooped to the polls to approve, by a whopping six-to-one majority, a $57,500,000 bond improvement program covering such diverse items as trafficways, parks, acquisition of a

stadium for major league baseball and urban redevelopment. Approval of this program, in itself a startling display of pride and confidence, brought bond improvements authorized by the voters since the end of World War II to a total of $172,000,000.

Other cities have voted as much, or more, for postwar improvements; and other cities have writhed under the rule of corrupt political machines. Yet none of them has experienced such extremes in civic fear and pride as Kansas City, where voices raised in opposition once were muzzled by kidnappings, beatings or abusive use of "police powers," where the rebellious businessman once found his place of business declared a public hazard and closed upon orders of the building commissioner, where vocal women once were threatened with physical harm or with arbitrary tax increases, and where the cardinal sin in a democracy—the practical disfranchisement of the citizens by the wholesale use of ghost voters —was once common.

How has the complete reformation from such a quagmire been achieved? Who restored the sovereignty of the people? How can a people who voted $32,000,000 in bond improvements in 1931, only to find that more than $10,000,000 was utilized illegally for private gain, recover sufficient confidence in their municipal government to ap-

*Mr. Field is a partner in the law firm of Rogers, Field and Gentry. A member of the National Youth Movement since its inception in 1932, he took an active part in the bloody election battles of 1934 while still a student at Kansas University. Mr. Field has remained a leader in Kansas City's civic affairs. He served for five years as general chairman of the Citizens' Regional Planning Council and is now in his third term as president of the Council of Social Agencies.

prove with no apparent qualm further issues of $172,000,000?

It is often said that people in America get the kind of government they deserve. This is an over-simplification of a complex problem and completely ignores the possibility that a ruthless political machine may deny citizens the ability for—not the right of, but the ability for—self-determination. To understand and to appreciate the magnitude of the triumph in Kansas City, it is necessary to comprehend how utterly complete and overwhelming was the political machine's domination of the government, the economy, the law; indeed, of life itself.

Battling the Boss

The government was one in which the opinion of the man without "connections" was scorned, as was the law when it interfered with "The Boss" or his henchmen. In fact, after 1931 the local forces of "law and order," through "home rule" as opposed to state control of the Kansas City Police Department, were actually in unholy alliance with the criminal underworld—all under the dominance of Boss Pendergast. In 1934, gangsters were able to make a brazen, broad-daylight attempt to take a federal prisoner away from officers transporting him to the penitentiary in Leavenworth, Kansas. Four officers and the prisoner who was to have been rescued were slain by machine guns. The same day the director of police was playing golf in Kansas City with "Machine Gun Butch" Bailey, a notorious Oklahoma desperado and gang leader. It is believed that John Lazia, Pendergast's political leader and boss of the Kansas City underworld, escorted the killers who participated in the "Union Station Massacre" to the city limits and otherwise aided their escape.

This type of arrogance typified the attitude of city officials when, in 1932, Rabbi Samuel S. Mayerberg began his crusade for clean government in Kansas City. His dramatic spotlighting of the legal and moral wrongs of the machine struck a sympathetic chord, and the citizens' drive to obtain a citizens' government was on. Although the price of joining the fight might be the loss of home, business or even of life, these amateurs in politics went to work with an enthusiasm which machine politicians could not approach. With the election of 1934, the first offensive against the machine was culminated.

The 1934 campaign was conducted as a family crusade. Younger citizens founded, secretly at first, the National Youth Movement, which set up at ward level a vigorous organization to combat the machine. Women left their kitchens to labor side by side with their husbands in the often thankless, and sometimes dangerous, job of fostering opposition to the machine. Typical of the workers in the 1934 election were Mr. and Mrs. C. Paul Leathers, both political amateurs, who worked together in finding precinct workers, making speeches and doing the other jobs necessary in developing an effective vote-getting organization whose heartening efforts included the union of anti-machine Democrats and Republicans on a Citizens-Fusion ticket.

Other prominent workers included Kansas City's Mayor William E. Kemp and his wife, the late Margaret J. Kemp; Rev. D. A. Holmes, a Negro minister; Judge George S. Montgomery; Dr. A. Ross Hill; D. S. Adams; Joseph C. Fennelly; Harold W. Luhnow; Kenneth E. Midgley; Colonel Frederick Whitten; former Mayor John B. Gage and his wife, Marjorie Gage; Porter T. Hall; Charles Daniels; Russell F. Greiner; Hal Jones and the author.

Citizen Efforts Defeated

On March 27, 1934, "Bloody Tuesday," the voters went to the polls. The machine met the challenge in the only way it could—by a combination of force and fraud. Violence was centered at the polling places, where gangs of toughs acted to discourage independent voters from appearing. Anti-machine election workers were thrown into jail and held throughout the day. Tension mounted as the day wore on and it became obvious that the machine, protected by the police, was playing for keeps. The Citizens-Fusion group appealed to the governor of Missouri to call out the National Guard but their plea was ignored. And there was murder—four men slain as a result of election activity.

A tally of the votes gave the Pendergast forces a 40,000 lead over the nonpartisan ticket. Tales of fraudulent voting were as numerous as the bruises administered to the anti-machine campaigners, for the repeaters and the ghosts gave the machine an estimated 65,000 illegal votes. At this moment, the machine seemed unbeatable. The Citizens-Fusion party, disappointed and disillusioned, disintegrated; and again there was little or no organized opposition to the machine.

But the spark was there. The idealists and amateurs of the 1934 campaign had proved there was a deep-seated citizen feeling of disgust ready to combat the machine. The apathy of the man in the street toward his government was shaken. Although the first round had been lost, the citizens had exhibited a courage and a political restlessness which could be ignored no longer by outside forces—the state and federal governments.

In 1937, Governor Lloyd C. Stark appointed a nonpartisan election board, which completely reorganized the registration and voting system. Following the 1936 national election, an energetic federal district attorney, Maurice Milligan, moved into the picture and sent 259 machine workers to jail for vote fraud. And in 1939 the Kansas City police were placed under state control. A state grand jury, under fearless Judge Allen C. Southern, and federal grand jury, under Judge Albert L. Reeves, a distinguished and courageous jurist, went to work and returned wholesale indictments. A final symbolic blow to the tottering Pendergast empire came in the spring of 1939 when Tom himself was sent to jail for not including in his tax returns an amount he received in an insurance bribery case.

The crisis of 1939 meant danger to Kansas City, for she was a sick city threatened by bankruptcy and saddled with a government which for thirteen years had ignored the needs of the citizens. But the crisis also meant opportunity—a chance to reestablish the city.

The Clean-up

This opportunity was seized as numerous citizen organizations sprang to do their part in the rebuilding process. During the 30s, the Civic Research Institute, a privately-financed, nonpartisan, civic agency, had investigated and decried the machine administration's financial manipulations and violations of the city charter. Frank H. Backstrom, one of two Citizens' candidates elected in 1934, had endlessly —although hopelessly it seemed— protested the excesses of the machine. A Citizens' Audit Committee demanded of the holdover mayor that an independent audit be made. Businessmen started a clean-up committee known as the Forward Kansas City Committee. Within two months, 20,000 citizens, representing all elements in the city, had joined the organization and formed eighteen subcommittees, which conducted investigations and forced corrections to be made.

Revelations of machine misrule were featured by *The Kansas City Star* and *The Kansas City Journal Post*. The auditing firm designated to make the first independent check of city finances undertaken in thirteen years found fantastic shortages and improper expenditures. One sinking fund had a deficit of over eight million dollars. During the 1938-39 fiscal year, two million dollars in claims against the city were not even recorded.

Perhaps the most shocking of the auditors' discoveries had to do with a slush fund known as the city manager's emergency fund. Expenditures from this fund, which were illegal, were authorized solely by the city manager. Starting in 1931 with a deposit of $500, almost $6,000,000 passed through the fund during the next eight years.

Citizen investigators looked further than just fiscal matters. They found that there were no records stating how many employees were on the city payroll. The mayor estimated there were 3,500, but the citizens found the actual number to be 5,200 and forced a payroll reduction of 1,000.

The stage was set for the final ousting of the machine politicians. Although the next city election was not scheduled until 1942, the people were determined to rid themselves of machine rule. But recall petitions were "lost" and then blocked by legal maneuvering. The citizens finally were compelled to amend the charter to reduce council terms to two years, thus forcing an election in 1940.

Leading this citizen surge that forced an early election was Harold W. Luhnow, a dynamo behind much of the organized opposition to the machine. Baptized into warfare against the machine during the 1934 election, Luhnow received more bitter lessons in machine tactics during the 1938 campaign.

At a time when business interests feared the power of Pendergast, Luhnow, president of the far-flung William Volker and Company enterprises, was extremely vocal in denouncing the machine regime as a civic disgrace and a serious threat to Kansas City's economic strength. The machine answered by raising his personal property tax assessment eight-fold, and by quadrupling the Volker concern's assessment. Luhnow's stand against Pendergast domination, however, set an example for other business leaders to follow and had much to do with business's decision to add its resources to those of the citizen warriors.

In 1939 he became chairman of the newly formed Charter party which circulated the petitions that, when signed by over 100,000 disgusted Kansas Citians, led to the election of 1940. Luhnow then directed the 1940 campaign which brought about the demise of the machine. Initial victory did not dampen his enthusiasm for citizen government. After the election he was the spark in the organization of the nonpartisan Citizens Association and became its first chairman.

Playing a major part in the campaign were more than 6,000 women. In the beginning, machine politicians scoffed at the "woman's touch" as being too idealistic and impractical, but their derision soon turned to fear as the ladies proved intensely practical. Spurred on by such dynamic leaders as Mrs. George H. Gorton,[1] Mrs. J. W. Storms, Mrs.

---

[1] See "Cited for Service," page 498.

Williston P. Munger and Mrs. Leathers, the women organized with evangelical zeal. A ward and precinct organization spanning the city was set up. Women missionaries of good government conducted a door-to-door selling campaign which covered every part of the city.

As election day drew near, brooms, symbolizing the drive to sweep clean the city hall, appeared all over the city. Small brooms were pinned to lapels and large ones were carried like muskets on the shoulders of the citizen workers.

The crusade for charter government in Kansas City was not to be denied. The United Campaign ticket swept into office with John B. Gage, candidate for mayor, leading the way as seven of the eight anti-machine council candidates were elected. The sick city had found her road to recovery.

Government by the Citizens

History is replete with examples of reform groups which have turned the rascals out and then, through apathy, allowed victory to become defeat. Sustaining interest and support in a reform movement seems most difficult once the initial, most exciting victory is achieved. The sweat and toil of truly effectuating and perpetuating citizen control of government is, at best, humdrum compared with the excitement of wresting control from a political machine.

Therefore, it is noteworthy that Kansas City, since 1926, has had approximately fourteen years of the worst and fourteen years of the best in democratic municipal government.

Whereas much credit for this must be given to elected officials, such as former Mayor Gage and present Mayor Kemp, and to L. P. Cookingham, Kansas City's outstanding city manager, the lion's share of the credit must go to those citizens who have sustained an interest in municipal government since 1940.

Having won the initial victory, the citizens were determined to prevent the loss of all that had been gained. City business had to be open and aboveboard. Proper and complete records had to be maintained and open to public inspection at all times. Channels of communication from the citizens to the city government had to be established and maintained. Above all, reform alone was not enough. There had to be positive action and results.

To accomplish these ends, various techniques were resorted to and various types of citizen organizations were established. For example, the Citizens' Audit Committee, together with the independent auditors and the Civic Research Institute, compiled a list of 50 recommendations for improvement of the city government. Periodically the institute issued bulletins, known as *Kansas City's Scoreboard*, relating progress on these recommendations.

Perhaps the most important accomplishment, however, was the gradual breakdown of the fear and mistrust of city hall—the reestablishment of the citizens' confidence in their government.

The civic climate of Kansas City has undergone a complete metamorphosis since the dreary days of the 30s and the entire metropolitan area has reaped the benefits. Since 1940, Kansas City has had a government alert and willing to profit from citizen opinion. Given this favorable environment, there has been a renaissance of civic spirit and enthusiasm.

Population, which had decreased in the 1930s, has zoomed from 399,000 in 1940 to an estimated 481,000 at present. Bank clearings doubled from 1939 to 1940. Retail trade in 1942 was up 20 per cent over 1939. Over two hundred new industries came to Kansas City between 1939 and 1947; and the number of employees in downtown Kansas City nearly doubled from 1940 to 1950.

Sustaining Citizen Participation

To assure citizen control over municipal policies and to assure the propriety of city government activities, several citizen-type organizations have come into being in Kansas City.

Outstanding is the Citizens' Regional Planning Council. Operating with 6,000 committee members from all sections of the Greater Kansas City area, council membership represents local planning groups from a five-county, two-state area. Although the Regional Planning Council has no governmental powers, it has become most influential in long-range development simply because it is a citizens' organization.

Both the 1947 bond program of $41,000,000 and the 1954 bond program of $57,506,000 were strongly backed by the Regional Planning Council. In each case, the council

(Continued on page 507)

The National Municipal League . .

*Survey Committee examines its course and objectives
and finds that it is headed in the "right direction."*

EDITOR'S NOTE.—This is the major
portion of a report by a Survey Committee,[1] as amended and approved by
the League's Council on May 7, 1954.
The committee was appointed by President George Gallup to review *An Appraisal of the National Municipal
League,* made by Dr. Joseph E. Mc-
Lean of Princeton University.

AS MEMBERS of the Survey Committee analyze Dr. McLean's *Appraisal of the National Municipal League,*
its basic advice breaks down into four
main proposals: (1) that League objectives be restated; (2) that the Council become a more active participant in
League affairs; (3) that the League develop a more effective system of communication both within and without the
organization; (4) that new procedures
be established for a continuing review of
League program and policies.

We endorse these proposals unequivo-
cally.

1. *Restatement of Objectives.* The
draft of a proposed revised constitution[2]
for the League contains in Article II a
more explicit statement of objectives. The
wording will help sustain the League's
long standing position with the Internal
Revenue Bureau as an organization qualifying for tax deductible contributions.

2. *More Active Council Participation.*
We find that for the last several years
there has been a steady trend toward
greater participation by Council members
in League affairs. It is important that
this trend continue. We offer the following suggestions for strengthening it   :

[1]Members of the committee were:
Chairman, Cecil Morgan, counsel, Standard Oil Company (New Jersey); Bayard
H. Faulkner, vice president, Seaboard Oil
Company; Lloyd Hale, president, G. H.
Tennant Company; Frank C. Moore,
president, Government Affairs Foundation; and James M. Osborn, Yale University.
[2]See page 475.

a. The provisions of the proposed revision of the constitution which would:

(1) Enlarge the Executive Committee and make it more representative;

(2) Clearly fix the Council's right
to establish League committees and
determine how they shall be appointed;

(3) Require that minutes and reports of action by the Executive
Committee be transmitted promptly
to all members of the Council;

(4) Eliminate provisions regarding classes of membership and dues
from the constitution, thus making
them subject to by-laws which may
be adopted either at a meeting of the
Council or by majority of the Council
in a mail vote;

(5) Permit the Council or Executive Committee to designate the
chairman of any League committee to
serve as a member of the Council.

b. Continuation by the Council of
the precedent being set this year of having two all-day meetings, one at the
time of the National Conference on
Government, the other in the spring.

c. A policy of including as many
Council members as possible on each
of the working committees responsible
for development of the League's program in such fields as state government,
municipal government, county government, etc.

3. *More Effective Communication.*
This is extremely important not only to
insure orderly and responsible planning
and carrying out of League programs but
also to improve liaison with political scientists and other professional groups and
to obtain wider use and acceptance of
League services.

Internal communication within the
League, particularly communication that

. . . Where Is It Going?

Council endorses continuing review of program, more field work; proposes new areas for league activity.

will enable the Council to exercise its over-all responsibilities more confidently and effectively, will be greatly facilitated by the proposed changes in the constitution and by some of the other methods outlined above. In like manner the recommendations on the subject of continuing review of program and policies should substantially improve League relations with political scientists and other professionals and develop a closer rapport between the Council and the experts who contribute so vitally and generously of their time and talents to the League. Strengthening of existing communications media and the development of new ones, including films and TV, should be a major concern of the proposed Committee on Program and Policy suggested below.

Additional Recommendations

In the light of specific recommendations in the McLean Report, we make the following additional suggestions:

a. The League's field work should be stepped up as rapidly as resources permit. The use of properly qualified volunteers and the practice of sending regular headquarters staff into the field are the only practical methods of meeting the demand for field service until there is enough money to augment the headquarters staff itself. Without an adequate central organization, a field staff is ineffective and the selection and use of volunteers is necessarily limited. When funds permit, the League should consider the establishment of small field offices for better contact with citizen groups and political scientists and for better liaison with Council members and finance chairmen scattered around the country.

b. That a more regular system of communications with state correspondents and with others in the field be developed. In this connection members of the League's Council should, so far as their time and interest permit, serve as agents of communication between the League and the groups and areas with which they have helpful contacts.

c. That so far as practicable the League should encourage and cooperate with others in holding regional meetings, with a view to providing programs tailored to current civic needs in different parts of the country and to reaching people who are unable to attend the National Conference on Government. Since we have found that it would take substantially larger staff and resources for the League to organize its own regional meetings on any frequent or regular basis, we conclude that the best way to accomplish the desired objects is to take advantage of the regularly scheduled regional meetings of professional associations, universities and civic groups.

4. *Continuing Review of Program and Policies.* We find that the program and policies of the League and the political concepts underlying them have always been under continuous scrutiny and review by the League's working committees and staff and, ultimately, by the officers and Council. Tested by results and the growth of the League in prestige and influence, this has proved to be a basically sound and effective procedure. We believe, however, that it can and should be strengthened and supplemented to meet the requirements of a rapidly changing world and civic scene.

We find that steps in this direction have already been taken. For the last several years the National Conference on Government has been used as an occasion for scheduling sessions especially designed to get expert review and criticism of specific League models or doctrines or to

471

advise on possible new projects. Perhaps the best example is the Charter Clinic in which leading charter draftsmen and consultants have given critical examination to the *Model City Charter* and to preliminary drafts of the *Model County Charter*.

More recently, "a continuing seminar" on the application of basic political concepts to the League's program has been inaugurated. The seminar is a flexible plan for taking advantage of every opportunity to bring together a half dozen or more persons who can help the League keep the factual and theoretical basis of any of its programs in line with the latest knowledge and most authoritative thinking. We urge continuing and greater use of these procedures.

Advisory Committee

As a major addition to the facilities for continuing appraisal of the League's program and activities, we strongly endorse the recommendation in the McLean Report of a standing Advisory Committee on Program and Policy. The committee should be established by the Council in accordance with the constitution. The chairman of the committee should be a Council member and the committee should be composed of Council members and others, both laymen and professionals.

As the name implies, the committee would be an exploratory and advisory body. Partly in order to insure its complete freedom to explore any subject which it deems pertinent, and to evaluate objectively any phase of the League's work, it should be entirely free of operating or policy-*determining* responsibilities. It would report to and *advise* the Council, Executive Committee, officers and staff on both policy and operations.

The committee would have a roving commission to review any League doctrine or program, to explore possible new areas for League activity and to examine or audit the way in which various League services and activities, such as the NATIONAL MUNICIPAL REVIEW, the National

Conference on Government and publications generally are actually conducted. It should be especially helpful in coordinating the thinking and work of the various functional committees and in calling attention to possible points of over- or under-emphasis. It should be able to insure that the Council has at all times the kind of information that will enable it to satisfy itself as to the validity and soundness of the League's diverse operations.

At this point we think it should be noted that the nature of the League and the varied and sometimes rather technical aspects of its program make it impossible to expect every one connected with it to be in complete agreement on every subject upon which the League speaks. It is certain that there is not a single League model or guide upon all the details of which all of its authors agree. It is not, therefore, important, or even possible that every member of the Council should approve or be ready to go to bat personally for every League project. What is important is that the Council and its members have a good general understanding of what is going on, have confidence in the persons and processes that produce each League program and be satisfied that the programs themselves are consistent with the League's over-all philosophy and objectives as stated in the constitution.

The League in its 60 years of civic activity has built a huge fund of experience and tradition which should not be tampered with or radically changed without careful study. To the extent that change or departure from present practices and concepts is indicated, it should be accomplished in an evolutionary and orderly way.

Fortunately, as we have already indicated, we find that the process by which the League program has been developed is essentially sound, involving, as it always has, cooperation of the leading authorities recognized for their professional competence, their intellectual integrity and their ability to reflect the best and sanest thinking of the day on the subjects included in the League's program and arsenal of models and guides. If this were not the case, it would not have been possible for Dr. Frank Mann Stewart to conclude his careful study, *A Half Century of Municipal Reform—The History of the National Municipal League*,[3] with the following paragraph:

> The National Municipal League is a school of thought that stabilizes reform along sound and practical lines; it represents the consensus of opinion of thinking people as to what local government should be. It has been and is the heart of the municipal reform movement in the United States.

Program and Policy

In recommending creation of the Advisory Committee on Program and Policy, we do not propose that it should supersede the established procedure which has proved successful in the past. We see the committee simply as a logical extension of the procedure, to provide a mechanism through which the program as a whole can have the same kind of review that each of its parts has had and to help the Council inform itself on how each part relates to the League's total mission.

Project coordination, including coordination of research and inventions, and liaison with professional and civic groups, has always been, and should be, a primary responsibility of the League's professional staff. We find that the staff has done excellent work in broadening the League's outlook and influence and in keeping pace with developments in the field of political science. As funds permit, the staff should be broadened and strengthened so that it can meet more fully the growing demand for League services and provide the additional staff

———— •

[3]University of California Press, Berkeley, 1950.

assistance that will be required by an active Committee on Program and Policy.

Problem of Money

While Dr. McLean does not make any specific recommendation as to the size of the League's budget or the need for additional funds, it is clear that the program and operations envisioned by the report call for a substantial increase in the League's regular budget. This is in accordance with the thinking and plans that the League has developed during the last few years.

Much can be done along the lines already indicated to enhance the League's effectiveness and to increase participation in its work by Council members and others. However, we must emphasize the fact that the value of such an innovation as the Committee on Program and Policy and the rate at which it will be possible to improve communications will depend to a large extent on a continuation of the recent trend toward a larger annual budget.

Dr. McLean has mentioned as especially worthy of review from a program point of view the League's attitude toward the place of partisanship in local elections and the whole matter of party responsibility and organization, the developing experience with the so-called mayor-administrator plan of city government, proportional representation and other methods of election of city councils and state legislatures, the changing relations between federal, state and local governments with particular attention to the position of the states in our system and the problems of government and citizen control in burgeoning metropolitan areas.

As we have indicated earlier, questions of this sort should not be dealt with summarily. They should, as in the past, be subjected to continuing study and any decidedly new or changed position should be carefully considered. The continuing seminar of political scientists can be very helpful to the League in guiding the course of change involving basic political concepts.

There are, however, a few specific matters of program discussed by Dr. McLean to which we have given special attention.

1. *Proportional Representation.* We devoted one whole day to discussing P.R.

Our study confirmed the impression derived from the McLean Report that the issue for the Council to consider at this time is not the theoretical merits or demerits of P.R. The question is rather one of how to deal with it in a manner which will best serve the interests of those cities where P.R. is now or may be used and the interests of the communities where P.R. is not a desired or attainable civic objective.

We were impressed by emphatic testimony from Cincinnati, Worcester and Cambridge, where the leading advocates and supporters of good government appear to be convinced that proportional representation is essential to the general good government which they have long enjoyed with their P.R.–council-manager charters.

We make the following recommendations:

a. In future editions of the League's *Model Charters* and *Model State Constitution* spell out in draft form alternate election methods for the benefit of those communities where P.R. is not legally or politically feasible.

b. Issue a separate model set of rules, in the form of an enabling act, for the conduct of P.R. elections. With this document available the detailed rules could be left out of the *Model City Charter.*

c. Substitute for the P.R. department of the NATIONAL MUNICIPAL REVIEW a department on the broader subject of elections and representation. In this department and in occasional articles we could fulfill our agreement with the P.R. League to provide an outlet for legitimate news and writing on

P.R. in place of the old *Proportional Representation Review.* We believe this treatment of P.R. would be more effective than the single-purpose P.R. department. That P.R. gets more attention when treated along with other methods of election has been demonstrated at the last two National Conferences on Government in the sessions on broad problems of representation in local governments which have replaced the old sessions devoted exclusively to P.R.

Mayor-Administrator Form

2. *The Mayor-Administrator Form of Government in Big Cities.* Dr. McLean recommends that the League take the lead in assembling and evaluating recent experiments with this system. We find that the League has been watching closely the as yet rare experiments of this kind and has given extensive consultative and other assistance in connection with charter proposals for variations on the mayor-administrator plan in Philadelphia, New Orleans, Newark, New York and other places. We recommend that this be continued to the end that the League may so far as practicable carry out the recommendation of the McLean Report.

3. *A Model Municipal Optional Charter Law.* We endorse the recommendation in the McLean Report that such a model be scheduled as a high priority project.

4. *Intergovernmental Relations and the Federal System.* We endorse Dr. McLean's recommendation that the League accelerate its activities in this field and "assist in promoting a better understanding of the nature of our present day federal system." We also endorse his emphasis upon the crucial importance of state government and metropolitan area problems, including the status of urban counties.

We find that these matters have in recent years had increasing attention in the

(Continued on page 479)

Proposed New Constitution

Explanatory Memorandum

EDITOR'S NOTE.—The proposed revised constitution for the NATIONAL MUNICIPAL LEAGUE, set forth below, is hereby submitted to members as provided by the present constitution. It has been recommended by the Council for adoption at the annual membership meeting, to be held November 8 in conjunction with the National Conference on Government, Kansas City (Missouri), November 8-10.

IN ITS deliberations, the Survey Committee[1] considered the recommendations of *An Appraisal of the National Municipal League*, by Dr. Joseph E. McLean of Princeton University, and suggested a number of amendments to the League's constitution. There were two particular fields of inquiry, one with respect to the nature, objects and purposes of the League and the other with respect to adapting the constitution to the requirements of its everyday operation. The McLean report suggested a more active participation by members of the Council in the affairs of the League and an effort was made in the drafting of the proposed amendments to make possible such greater participation.

Nature and Purposes. The statement of objects contained in Article II has been rewritten under the title, "Nature and Purposes." The new statement reflects more clearly, fully and explicitly the extent and nature of the program. It puts greater emphasis on the educational nature of the League's work and on the fact that its service is primarily to citizens.

Membership. The new Article III includes specifically the provision that organizations as well as individual persons may be members. This is the intent of the present provision and has always been the case in practice. Details as to dues, classes and conditions of membership are

---

[1]For the report of the Survey Committee, see page 470.

deleted from the revised article as matters of detail which appropriately should be left to the discretion of the Council.

Government. Article IV—*Council and Officers*—and Article V—*Committees*—are combined in the proposed revision as a new Article IV—*Government.* It is felt that the content of the two present articles is so closely related it appropriately should be treated in a single article.

Specific provision is made that the president, vice presidents and treasurer be members of the Council. Actual practice has long assumed that this is the intent of the present constitution.

The 1938 amendment providing that members of the Council elected for three-year terms may not be eligible to succeed themselves before the lapse of one year has been incorporated in this article. A complication caused by this amendment is the situation in which a standing League committee is chaired by a Council member whose term expires. A new provision (section 8) permits the Council or the Executive Committee to designate a committee chairman as an *ex officio* member of the Council.

The membership of the Executive Committee has been increased to include the president, first and second vice presidents, chairman of the Council and treasurer. In practice officers must meet with the Executive Committee on particular matters. Further, the increased membership will provide for a more adequate deliberative group with a quorum set at five members (see Article VI-4).

In order to facilitate Council review and control on matters of policy, it is provided that minutes and reports of action by the Executive Committee shall be transmitted promptly to members of the Council.

Other proposed sections make provision for filling vacancies between meetings of the Council, for designating an acting treasurer or acting secretary if need be, and for clarifying the role of the Executive Committee and the executive director.

Elections and Referenda. No changes in substance are proposed in this article. A provision for the filling of unexpired terms on the Council is added.

Subsidiary Organizations. The proposed revision deletes the present Article VII, *Subsidiary Organizations,* as no longer required. Such organizations have not existed for a number of years and there is serious doubt as to the desirability of this arrangement.

Meetings, Liabilities and Disbursements, By-laws. Only minor changes in procedural provisions are proposed.

Amendments. Amendments to the constitution approved by mail vote of the Council are permitted under the revised article.

The present constitution was adopted at the annual meeting, September 20, 1932, in Washington, D. C., and amended November 1938.

Text of Proposed Constitution

Article I
NAME

The name of this association shall be the National Municipal League.

Article II
NATURE AND PURPOSES

1. The National Municipal League is a non-profit, non-partisan educational association of individuals and organizations dedicated to the proposition that informed, competent citizens, participating fully in public affairs in their home communities, are the key to good local, state and national government.

2. It is established in order to multiply the number, harmonize the methods and combine the forces of those who are interested in developing citizens who know how to work together for progressive improvement of our system of government with special attention to the need for more vigorous and responsible state and local institutions.

3. This objective shall be achieved through programs and activities designed for the following purposes:

To conduct and promote research and encourage creative thinking in the fields of government and administration, intergovernmental relations, public opinion and civic organization;

To hold and participate in conferences, institutes, workshops and seminars for the exploration and discussion of the application of the science, philosophy and art of government to the solution of current and emerging problems;

To sponsor and encourage formal and informal educational and training projects for civic leaders, public officials, teachers, students and other citizens;

To cooperate in efforts to enrich the content and improve the methods of civic education in schools, colleges and other institutions;

To develop and assemble informational and educational materials and to publish and disseminate them through the printed word or by any appropriate audio-visual means for the use of schools, colleges, journalists, citizens and citizen organizations;

To maintain an up-to-date library, information center and consultant service to serve the needs of educators, journalists, public officials and other citizens interested in public affairs;

To prepare practical guides, manuals, models and other working tools in the fields of government and administration, intergovernmental relations, civic education and citizen organization;

To provide media for communication and exchange of information and ideas among political scientists, public officials and lay citizens on matters of common concern;

To employ any appropriate educational means to raise the standards of citizenship, public administration and political ethics.

Article III
MEMBERSHIP

1. Individuals and organizations that support the purposes of the League shall be eligible for membership subject to approval by the Council or its authorized representative.

2. Dues, classes and conditions of membership shall be determined by the Council.

Article IV
GOVERNMENT

1. The government of the League, the direction of its work, the establishment of committees of the League and the control of its property shall be vested in a Council selected in the manner provided by this article.

2. Thirty Council members shall be elected by the League members to three-year terms, ten to be elected each year at the annual meeting of the League, provided that no member so elected shall be eligible to succeed himself before the lapse of one year. In addition, any unexpired terms of council members shall be filled by vote of the members at the annual meeting.

3. The officers of the League shall be a president, a first vice president, a second vice president, not more than twenty-five regional and honorary vice presidents, a treasurer and a secretary. The president and the vice presidents shall be elected for one-year terms by the members of the League at the annual meeting of the League. The secretary and treasurer shall be appointed by the Council. The president, the vice presidents and the treasurer shall be members of the Council by virtue of their offices and former League presidents shall be life members of the Council.

4. Officers and other members of the Council elected at the annual meeting shall assume office at the meeting of the Council next following their election and each shall serve until his successor shall be elected and assume office.

5. At its organization meeting the Council shall elect from among its members the chairman of the Council and six members to serve on the Executive Committee. The president, the first vice president, the second vice president, the chairman of the council, and the treasurer shall be ex officio members of the Executive Committee. The Executive Committee shall select its own chairman.

6. Subject to review by the Council, the Executive Committee shall act for it in the interim between meetings of the Council. Minutes and reports of action by the Executive Committee shall be transmitted promptly to all members of the Council.

7. Unless otherwise provided by the Council, the president shall appoint all committees of the League except the Executive Committee. No committee shall incur any indebtedness, make any expenditures or represent the League in advocacy of or opposition to any project or issue, without the specific approval of the Council or Executive Committee, or without such authority as may be clearly granted under general powers delegated to that committee by the Council.

8. By action of the Council or the Executive Committee the chairman of any League committee may be designated to serve as a member of the Council ex officio for the current year.

9. The Executive Committee may fill any vacancy on the Council or in any office. The term of any person appointed to fill a vacancy shall run only until the Council meeting next following the next annual meeting of the League. The Executive Committee may appoint an acting treasurer or an acting secretary to serve in the absence or disability of the treasurer or the secretary.

10. The secretary shall serve as executive director, shall be the chief administrative officer, shall have charge of the execution of the League's program, shall supervise the work of all members of the staff and employees and shall perform such other duties incident to the office as shall be required by the Council. Unless otherwise provided by the Council, he shall serve as secretary to all committees or shall designate another person so to serve.

Article V
ELECTIONS AND REFERENDA

1. *Nominations.* At least ninety days before the annual meeting of the League, a nominating committee consisting of five members shall be appointed by the president. At least thirty days before the annual meeting, the committee shall place one member in nomination for president, one member for first vice president, one member for second vice president, not more than twenty-five members for honorary and regional vice presidents, ten members for three-year terms on the Council and an additional number of members for any unexpired terms on the Council. Notice of such nominations shall be published to the membership at least thirty days before the annual meeting in a League publication, or by mail. Such notice shall include a statement that additional nominations from members of the League are in order. Such additional nominations may be made at the annual meeting at which the election shall take place.

2. *Referenda.* Provisions may be made by the Council for the submission to the members by mail, for approval or disapproval, of recommendations of the Council or any committee of the League on any question of organization policy.

Article VI
MEETINGS

1. Unless otherwise directed by the Council or the Executive Committee, the annual meeting of the League shall be held in November of each year. Special meetings of the League may be called at any time by the president, or the Council, or the Executive Committee.

2. A meeting of the Council shall be held in connection with each annual meeting of the League. Other meetings of Council and Executive Committee, and meetings of all other committees, shall be held when called by their respective chairmen or by the president or secretary. Meetings of the Executive Committee shall be called upon written request of at least three members thereof on two weeks notice.

3. Reasonable notice of all meetings shall be given.

4. The following quorums shall be established: at meetings of the League those present; at meetings of the Council, twelve members; at meetings of the Executive Committee, five members; and at meetings of all other committees a majority of the members. Whenever a quorum is lacking, the action of the majority of those present may be validated by the written approval of a sufficient number of the absentees to make up the deficiency.

Article VII
LIABILITIES AND DISBURSEMENTS

No disbursements of the funds of the League shall be made unless they shall have been authorized by the Council or Executive Committee. All checks shall be signed by the secretary and countersigned by the treasurer, provided, however, that for disbursements authorized by the Council or Executive Committee, the treasurer at his option may draw blanket checks in favor of the secretary, to be disbursed in turn through checks signed by the secretary or other person designated by the treasurer and secretary.

Article VIII
BY-LAWS

The Council may adopt such by-laws, not inconsistent with the provisions of this constitution, as shall be deemed necessary for the government of the League and the direction and control of its activities. Between meetings of the Council, by-laws proposed by the Executive Committee may be approved by a majority of the Council by a mail vote.

Article IX
AMENDMENTS

Amendments to this constitution may be adopted by a majority vote at any meeting of the League provided a notice of the proposed change shall have been published to the members in a League publication, or by mail, not less than thirty days before such meeting. The Council or the Executive Committee may submit amendments to the membership by mail for a referendum vote. Any amendment so submitted shall be accompanied by a ballot and an explanation. Approval by a majority of those voting on the question within a reasonable time set by the Council or Executive Committee shall be sufficient for adoption.

THE N.M.L. . . .
WHERE IS IT GOING?
(Continued from page 474)

NATIONAL MUNICIPAL REVIEW, at the National Conference on Government, in the League's educational and consultant service to citizens and in planning future activities.

The League always has recognized that its program deals with states, counties, cities and towns not in isolation but as vital elements in that larger entity, the United States of America. It feels that, in concentrating primarily on citizen understanding and action to strengthen state and local elements in our system, it is contributing substantially to the cause of sound government in Washington as well as at the state capitol and city hall.

As a national citizens' organization, the League is interested in our system as a whole and looks at it impartially without special professional or other attachment to a particular level or function of government. This being the case, we feel that it has a peculiar obligation to review and interpret current trends and proposals relating to the functions and responsibilities of the state and local elements in the system. We recommend that every effort be made to perform this service and at the same time to develop plans for more attention both to state and metropolitan area problems in so far as resources permit without detracting from the League's capacity to meet current needs for its established services.

In Conclusion

We concluded early in our deliberations that we could not exhaust the possibilities in the helpful ideas and suggestions in the McLean Report. This explains in part why we have concentrated on proposals which, if adopted, will facilitate continuing consideration not only of the McLean Report but of any other counsel or constructive criticism that the League may from time to time obtain.

We have necessarily concentrated on the parts of the McLean Report that have indicated the possibility of improvement. This should not lead us to lose sight of the most striking conclusion of Dr. McLean's study, which is that the League has an assured position in American life, is pointed in the right direction and is operating on basically sound principles. If his report and ours will more clearly define objectives, encourage more active interest and participation by the Council and better fit the League's work into the current panorama of local and world events, his efforts and ours will indeed have been worth while.

News in Review

City, State and Nation • • • •   *Edited by H. M. Olmsted*

Many State Constitution Amendments Put to Vote

People to Pass on Major and Minor Matters Alike

VOTERS in many states will be called upon at the general election on November 2 to pass upon a wide variety of proposed amendments to state constitutions. The number to be voted on in various states range from one to 31— the latter being in Louisiana, which has the longest and most amended constitution. Subjects range from minor local matters to proposals to abolish public education. In twelve states alone a total of a hundred amendments, many of which are hardly of constitutional caliber, have been submitted to the electorate.

Some proposals have been noted in these pages earlier in the year, including five in Georgia (March, page 138), one in Maryland (May, page 244), one in Colorado (June, page 294), eight in Nebraska (July, page 349) and five in North Carolina (July, page 352). Some 78 amendments submitted in various other states include the following:

California

Of twenty amendments being submitted, one, to increase maximum old-age pensions from $80 to $100 a month, was sponsored by pension advocates; the other nineteen, initiated by the 1953 and 1954 legislatures, include one to extend the terms of state assemblymen from two years to four and those of senators from four years to six, and to limit future governors to two terms; one to increase legislators' salaries from $300 to $500 a month; one to extend the time for preparation of proposed county charters by boards of freeholders from 120 days to six months; one providing $175,000,000

to help veterans acquire farms and homes; one for $100,000,000 in loans and grants to school districts for land, buildings and equipment, the districts being required to repay according to their ability; one permitting the use of state gas taxes and motor vehicle fees for construction of off-street parking facilities; and one authorizing the legislature to repeal the Torrens land title act.

Three proposals extend property tax exemption for churches, colleges, hospitals and charities, two do likewise for certain categories of California registered ships, and one authorizes $5,000 property tax exemption to veterans who lost both legs, or their use, in service. The remaining six are for various local or specialized purposes.

Florida

Seven proposed amendments would extend biennial legislative sessions 30 days beyond the present 60 and increase legislators' pay from $10 per session day to $1,200 per annum; prohibit use of state funds for toll roads extending into more than three counties; extend the governor's time limit for vetoes from ten to twenty days at the end of the legislative session; permit the consolidation of city and county tax assessing and collecting, after local referendum; require consolidated assessing in Monroe County (Key West); permit additional county judges in counties of over 125,000 population; and provide an additional judge of the Court of Record in Escambia County (Pensacola) and grant legislative authority for additional judges there, as needed.

Louisiana

About one-third of the 31 proposals, according to the Louisiana Public Affairs Research Council, involve local issues rather than basic statewide policy. Important items in the latter group include one prohibiting future state bond issues unless approved by popular vote; one providing for annual legislative sessions, those in odd-numbered years to be limited to 30 days and to budgetary and fiscal matters; one to continue segregation in public schools under the police power of the state; and one to permit absentee registration of military personnel.

Bills providing for comprehensive revision of the constitution by an elected convention, with or without a subsequent referendum, or by the legislature itself, subject to referendum, failed of passage.

Michigan

Three amendments proposed by joint resolutions of the 1953-54 legislature relate to the following: (1) permitting a registered qualified voter who moves within 30 days prior to an election to vote in the city or township from which he moved; (2) the return to local governments, on a population basis, of one-half cent per dollar of state sales taxes and the setting aside of two cents per dollar (less collection cost) for aid to school districts and school employee retirement systems; the total sales tax to be limited to three cents; and (3) authority for a bond issue of $80,000,000 for bonuses to persons in military service during the period June 27, 1950, to December 31, 1953.

Another amendment, proposed by initiative, permits lotteries for non-profit charitable organizations but not for other purposes.

Minnesota

Four proposed amendments provide: (1) legislative authority to prescribe qualifications for probate judges and, by two-thirds vote, to establish and extend their duties; (2) elimination of the present so-called double liability of bank stockholders, the legislature to have power to regulate stockholder liability in all kinds of corporations; (3) clearing the way for a constitutional convention

by specifying that any revision of the state constitution must be submitted to popular vote, that approval must be by three-fifths of those voting on the revision, and that state legislators shall be eligible for election as delegates to a constitutional convention; and (4) authority for the governor to fill a vacancy in certain state offices until the end of the term, or the first Monday in January following the next general election, whichever is sooner, and until a successor is chosen and qualified; the present requirement is for an appointment until the next annual election.

Mississippi

The legislature has submitted to the people privileged to vote an amendment giving the legislature power, by two-thirds vote, to abolish public schools in favor of state-subsidized segregated private education. This amendment will be voted on at an election on December 21. A somewhat similar amendment is being submitted in Georgia.

Texas

Eleven amendments are proposed. Among the topics are: a four-year term of office for elective district, county and precinct officers; increase in legislators' pay from $10 to $25 a day, and a grant of authority to the legislature of certain powers as to salaries of state constitutional officers; permitting the legislature to make agreements with the federal government to place employees of political subdivisions under federal social security; prohibiting pledge of state credit as to bonds for construction of toll roads; a requirement for women to serve on juries; and an increase from $45,000,000 to $52,000,000 in state spending for old-age pensions and other public aid.

Governors Discuss Federal-state Relations

At the 46th annual meeting of the Governors' Conference, held in July at Lake George, New York, one of the dominant topics, at a special round table and otherwise, was the proper relationship between the state and federal governments. At the round table Chairman A. B. Langlie, governor of Washington, stressed fiscal relations and urged a halt in federal grants-in-aid, with their related controls, a transfer of various taxes to the states, and adequate payments in lieu of taxes on federal property in the states.

Meyer Kestnbaum, chairman of the National Commission on Intergovernmental Relations, discussed its work and asked that each state indicate what programs it can take over from the federal government. Committees of various types—official or private—were reported to have been formed in 32 states to study intergovernmental relations and assist the national commission.

President Eisenhower, in an address read to the conference, emphasized the highway aspect of federal-state relations and the need of greatly increased efforts and expenditures for an adequate national highway network. He suggested the preparation of a "grand plan" for a properly articulated system to solve metropolitan, intercity and interstate highway problems; financing based on self-liquidation through gas taxes and tolls so far as possible, with federal aid where the national interest demands it; a cooperative alliance between federal and state governments, with emphasis on local control; and a program, probably to be initiated by the federal government with state cooperation, for the planning, financing and construction of a modern interstate highway system. He called for recommendations from the governors for cooperative action.

The conference adopted a resolution requesting the Council of State Governments, in cooperation with interstate governmental associations, to make a study and report on the status of highway programs and the position of the states with regard to highways, such program to be submitted to each governor and to the executive committee of the conference, and finally to President Eisenhower.

Federal Laws Contain Planning Aspects

The federal housing act of 1954 includes provisions to stimulate forward-looking municipal planning for slum elimination and to survey public works planning, efforts and accomplishments.

The act places major emphasis on the prevention of slums and urban blight and specifies that, as a condition to receiving federal assistance for slum clearance, urban redevelopment, public housing and certain housing insurance programs, municipalities must develop and place in operation a workable program for the prevention and elimination of slums and blight. Grants are authorized to state, metropolitan and regional planning agencies, to assist in surveys, land-use studies, redevelopment plans, etc.

The act authorizes a survey of the "status and extent of public works planning among the several states and their subdivisions." It is expected to be made by the Housing and Home Finance Agency, in collaboration with the Council of Economic Advisors and the Census Bureau, and to provide an index of the status of plans and the functional distribution of public works, and to be a guide to the size and cost of contemplated construction projects.

The federal aid highway act of 1954 authorizes a comprehensive study of highway financing, including toll roads, and a special study of the feasibility of the Great River Parkway for the Mississippi valley, and calls for consideration of the civil defense aspects of highways to be constructed and reconstructed. As noted elsewhere, President Eisenhower has also urged the preparation of broad plans for a national highway system.

Department of Urbiculture Proposed for U. S.

A bill to create a federal Department of Urbiculture was introduced in the last Congress by Representative J. Arthur Younger of California. Although not adopted, it attracted wide interest. The word "urbiculture" was coined by Congressman Younger as a name for a department that would do for the city population what the Department of Agriculture does for the farm population. He pointed out that when the latter department was established, in 1862, approximately 80 per cent of the nation lived on farms, whereas the situation now is reversed and most of our social and economic problems originate in city life.

AMA to Meet in Philadelphia

The American Municipal Association's 31st annual American Municipal Congress is scheduled for November 28-December 1 at the Bellevue-Stratford Hotel in Philadelphia. Afterwards President Eisenhower is expected to meet in Washington with the mayors and city managers of the 220 largest cities.

IULA Congress in Rome Next Year

The twelfth Congress of the International Union of Local Authorities is scheduled for September 26–October 1, 1955, in Rome, Italy. The main topic of discussion will be local government finance and its importance to local autonomy. The second topic is cultural activities of local authorities. The American Committee for International Municipal Cooperation, 1313 East 60th Street, Chicago, is assisting in arrangements.

New City Contracts for Governmental Services

Lakewood, California, a newly formed city in Los Angeles County, has a population of some 66,000 but only four paid city employees, receiving approximately $2,000 a month. Most of its governmental services are supplied by the county under contract. Some of these are charged to the city on a cost basis. Others pay for themselves through fees charged to private persons. Law enforcement is provided by the sheriff, the county keeping the city's share of fines and bail forfeitures. Tax assessing and collecting are paid for through a charge to the city based on assessed valuation.

Michigan League Sponsors Municipal Report Contest

The first annual report contest to be sponsored by the Michigan Municipal League for its 380 member cities and villages will be held in 1955. Any municipal annual report published between July 1, 1954, and May 31, 1955, will be eligible. The contest will be judged by three persons not connected with the league. Prizes will be given for the best reports in various population groups.

Norfolk Woos Prospective Residents

The city of Norfolk, Virginia, is annexing, effective January 1, 1955, a large adjacent area with some 55,000 residents and is conducting among them a campaign of education in municipal government. Marvin W. Lee, administrative assistant to City Manager H. H. George, 3rd, states:

"The city is embarking upon a program to orient these people before they become citizens of Norfolk. We are going to send eight newsletters, two weeks apart, to the residents of this to-be-annexed area, and in each issue we are going to explain various departments and their functions in the city. The newsletters will use many photos, charts and other graphic illustrations.

"Beyond this basic medium we are organizing a comprehensive public relations program using all the conventional media. We want these people to feel that they are being warmly welcomed by the city and we want them to become informed citizens."

Municipal Government Study Offered at the Hague

Under the Fulbright program in comparative municipal government it will be possible for a pre-doctoral fellow to spend the academic year 1955-56 in the Netherlands, serving chiefly at the headquarters of the International Union of Local Authorities at the Hague.

Normal conditions of Fulbright predoctoral candidacy apply. Applicants must be under age 35. The grant provides for living comfortably but not luxuriously for about nine months and for ocean round-trip transportation. There is no allowance for dependents. The working language of the IULA secretariat is English.

In outlining his proposed plan of study, the candidate should state his intention of working under the sponsorship of a professor at a Dutch university accredited by the Fulbright board, but with emphasis on field work at IULA headquarters. The names of available Dutch professors and additional information about IULA and its program can be obtained from Charles S. Ascher, associate director, Public Administration Clearing House, 45 East 65th Street, New York 21, New York.

Council Manager Plan Developments

On September 14 EDINA, MINNESOTA, (1950 population 9,744) adopted the village manager plan, 2,677 to 530.

The board of trustees of FARMINGTON, NEW MEXICO, (1950 population 3,637) has adopted the council-manager plan by ordinance and has appointed a manager.

TULIA, TEXAS, (3,222) voted 596 to 99 on April 6 in favor of the council-manager plan.

Mayor P. K. Hanson of GARDINER, MAINE, has appointed a city charter committee and is facilitating the discussion and drafting of charter changes particularly including the manager plan.

SEA GATE, a residential area in the borough of Brooklyn, New York City, controlled by a private corporation, now has a so-called city manager who will have various duties similar to those of a manager of an independent municipality. The newly appointed manager is from the staff of L. P. Cookingham, manager of Kansas City, Missouri, and is reported by the Kansas City Star to be the 24th member of the "Cookingham alumni association"—a group of young men who have taken city manager or similar positions after working under Mr. Cookingham.

In YONKERS, NEW YORK, a council-manager city, the Republican city committee is campaigning to change the city charter at a November 2 referendum so as to elect the city council at large instead of by wards. Six councilmen would be chosen at large for four-year terms, instead of one from each of twelve wards for two-year terms as at present.

The charter commission of the township of CEDAR GROVE, NEW JERSEY, has recommended the council-manager plan.

In CLARKESVILLE, GEORGIA, a council-manager charter approved by the legislature failed of adoption at the city election. It is expected to be voted on again within the next few months.

Voting on their preference for the manager plan, a "full-time mayor" plan or their present mayor-council system, the people of FOREST PARK, GEORGIA, chose to retain the present plan.

A citizens committee has been formed in the village of WORTHINGTON, OHIO, to study the pros and cons of the council-manager plan.

In JOLIET, ILLINOIS, a special election on the question of adopting the council-manager plan has been scheduled for November 2, the time of the general election, provided certain problems as to use of county election facilities and personnel for the special election can be worked out.

The Macon County Court on August 9 directed the city council of DECATUR, ILLINOIS, to call an election on the question of adopting the council-manager plan, to be held in not less than 30 days and not more than 120 days. Petitions bearing 2,775 names, requesting the election, were approved.

NORTH ST. PAUL, MINNESOTA, voted 831 to 511 on August 3 to retain the manager plan, which was adopted in 1951 by a vote of 660 to 511.

HOT SPRINGS, SOUTH DAKOTA, voted 783 to 284 on August 3 to retain the manager plan, adopted in 1951.

In KANSAS CITY, KANSAS, where the three city commissioners on March 4 created the position of administrative officer, with a salary of $8,292, the Citizens League points out that the commissioners receive more than $22,000 per annum and declares, "Either we should adopt the city manager plan or elect three city commissioners who will run the city."

The city council of HARTSHORNE, OKLAHOMA, has voted to join with local civic and fraternal organizations in making a study of the manager plan.

The Chamber of Commerce of CLAREMORE, OKLAHOMA, arranged a council-manager forum for mid-September.

In WATONGA, OKLAHOMA, the Chamber of Commerce and the Retail Merchants Association favor the manager plan. An election on the question of its adoption is sought.

ORANGE, TEXAS, voted for a city manager charter amendment on July 20 by a 291-vote margin but, at the same time, by 2,619 votes out of 3,093, elected a mayor who bitterly opposed the amendment. His supporters have challenged the election on the question and have filed a suit in district court, charging illegal votes were counted.

In what is described by civic leaders and newspapers in SAN ANTONIO, TEXAS,

as a campaign to discredit that city's council-manager charter, several events have occurred in rapid succession—discharge of the latest manager by the council majority controlled by "Boss" Jack White; resignation of White as mayor (but not necessarily from the council); and a proposal of the council majority to revert to the old commission form of government. Meanwhile there continues to be an active movement for the recall of five members of the White group in the council. Recall petitions bearing over 19,000 signatures were filed on September 2. It has been pointed out that White can see to it that one of his supporters is appointed to the vacancy caused by any resignation from the council and that a new appointee cannot be recalled for 90 days. The plan of the council majority to have an October 30 referendum on changing the charter is also considered to be an effort to confuse the public and divert attention from the recall movement.

In SANTA FE, NEW MEXICO, the chairman of the mayor's committee to study the manager plan predicted on August 5 that the plan would go into effect before the end of the year. An ordinance to that effect was being prepared.

Mayor Dayton Witten of AUBURN, WASHINGTON, in announcing his retirement, advocated adoption of the manager plan.

A proposed charter amendment providing the council-manager form of government will be submitted to the voters of MEDFORD, OREGON, at the November 2 election.

Clarence Arrasmith, city manager of FILLMORE, CALIFORNIA, died on July 21 after nearly 36 years in that office, which he assumed in October 1918 when 45 years old. His was the longest service of any city manager.

In CORDOVA, ALASKA, the people have voted in favor of the manager plan but the council has delayed action because of

(Continued on page 502)

County and Township   •   •   • *Edited by Edward W. Weidner*

Police Dept. Proposed for St. Louis County

Proposition to Be Voted on at November Election

IS THE traditional sheriff and constable system of police protection adequate for a metropolitan county of 485,000 population? Or should it be replaced by a non-political county police department, vested not only with the statutory law enforcement powers of the sheriff and constables but also with means of providing a higher level of police work throughout the entire county?

In brief, that is the issue to be decided by the voters of St. Louis County at the November election. Under an ordinance adopted by the County Council on August 25, the question of amending the county's 1950 home rule charter for the first time, in order to provide for a police department, will be on the ballot.

Action by the county council was the result of recommendations made by a Citizens Commission on Law Enforcement appointed by the county supervisor, with council approval, in mid-1953. The ten-member commission, headed by Arthur B. Shepley, Jr., prominent lawyer, and a similarly appointed fifteen-member Advisory Committee, with Victor D. Brannon, director of the Governmental Research Institute of St. Louis as chairman, were requested to study present provisions for police protection and the county's over-all structure of law enforcement and make such recommendations—including proposed legislation—as they believed would improve the system.

Public hearings were held, at which county and municipal officers most closely concerned with law enforcement—sheriff, constables and police chiefs of municipalities—gave their views and were questioned. Research reports on the operation of several eastern metropolitan county-wide police departments, on the sheriff's office and constables' offices of St. Louis County, and on the police departments of the 92 municipalities of the county, were received and discussed, together with a report of the commission's special counsel on the legal problems involved in alternative proposals for changing the present system. Bruce Smith, director of the Institute of Public Administration in New York City, was engaged as consultant to advise on these alternatives and suggest a workable county police organization.

The commission had determined that any proposals for improving the operation and organization of the sheriff's office "could not remedy the inherent weakness of that office or of the sheriff system generally—namely, its elective and inevitably political character . . . [and that] rather than attempt to repair [and patch the present basically unsound system, a wholly new police organization, removed from politics and modeled upon accepted present-day lines, should be established."

Two additional possibilities were rejected: a joint St. Louis City–St. Louis County police department, with jurisdiction over the entire metropolitan area, and a compulsory consolidated police department for St. Louis County only.[1] Under both proposals considerable time would have elapsed before the new system could go into effect.

The commission had grave doubt that either proposal would be adopted by the voters. Previous suggestions for uniting city and county into a single governmental unit had encountered much opposition. The possible establishment of a

[1] The city of St. Louis is not a part of St. Louis County.

metropolitan police department might well be construed as a "foot-in-the-door" approach. To propose setting up a single police unit for the entire county, on the other hand, would run counter to political and citizen opinion, especially in the more populous cities with well established police forces.

Final and unanimous recommendations of the Citizens Commission and its Advisory Committee were presented to the county council on April 28, 1954, with a draft of a proposed amendment to the county charter to put them into effect.

The basic charter change would transfer all police powers and duties from the elective sheriff and constables (who would continue as court officers and process-servers) to a new county police department. The department would have the same responsibility as the sheriff and constables now have for enforcing state laws throughout the county and county ordinances in its unincorporated areas. In addition, it would provide full-time police protection to those municipalities contracting with the county council for such service.

The department would be headed by a policy-making five-member bipartisan board of police commissioners appointed by the county supervisor, with the approval of the county council, for overlapping three-year terms. The board in turn would appoint a police superintendent, qualified in police administration and law enforcement, who would be responsible to the board for the complete operation of the department.

Although the Citizens Commission recommended that all police personnel come under the provisions of the merit system which the charter now provides for selected county departments, the proposed amendment provides that the superintendent appoint and promote personnel qualified in accordance with requirements of an ordinance to be adopted by the council no later than April 1955, which ordinance shall provide for authority in the board of police commissioners, upon recommendation of the superintendent, to establish minimum mental, character and physical qualifications for all personnel.

Amendment Far-reaching

The effect of the charter amendment, if adopted, would be far-reaching. The new provision which enables municipalities to contract with the county for police services should have an especially beneficial effect. It is believed that many of the small municipalities with tax resources too limited to provide their own police protection on an adequate basis would avail themselves of the full-time police services given by the well qualified and trained county police force—and at less cost than if each such city were to establish its own police system.

Another provision of the charter amendment permits the superintendent of police to deputize members of municipal police forces meeting minimum standards determined by the board of police commissioners. Such deputization is designed to permit municipal police to go beyond their city limits in pursuing a law violator, thus removing what has been a serious obstacle to effective law enforcement. But the proposed deputization should have the dual effect of raising the level of law enforcement throughout the county, since it is contemplated that deputization can be obtained only if the municipal police departments are operated efficiently and with freedom from partisan politics.

Should the charter amendment be adopted, it will become effective July 1, 1955. It is expected that a citizens group will wage an intensive campaign to assure that the voters of St. Louis County are acquainted with the issue and with the benefits accruing once the new department is established.

GRANT H. BUBY, *Assistant Director*
Governmental Research Institute
St. Louis, Missouri

Virginia Cities, Counties Cooperate on Hospital

City and county governments continue to cooperate in many different ways. Recently twelve counties and five cities in Virginia joined forces to operate a hospital for the chronically ill. Each one of the participating units pays twenty cents per capita toward the operating costs of the hospital.

City and county law officers in Columbus and Franklin County, Ohio, have completed plans for a blockade system to cover every road within 75 miles of Columbus in cases where bank robbers or other criminals are being pursued.

Manager Plan Recommended for Imperial County, Calif.

A recommendation for a county manager for Imperial County has been made editorially by the *El Centro* (California) *Press*. Noting that the county board of supervisors had sanctioned a change in the county employee group insurance program which appears ill-advised and wasteful of public funds and also that this action took place during general squabbling over county problems by the board and by the employees, the newspaper pointed out that such procedure is poor business in anybody's language. Since there has been much favorable experience with city managers in the state, it was felt that adoption of the manager form of government in county affairs was necessary so that full-time professional and efficient help might be secured.

South Texas Holds County Convention

Among the important issues discussed by the County Judges and Commission-ers Association of South Texas at its 1954 annual conference were those of reclamation, highway and road-users taxes and the possibility of four-year terms for county officials.

On reclamation the conference went on record as requesting the senators and representatives in Congress from Texas "to take steps to immediately get the services of the Bureau of Reclamation and/or any other state or federal agencies to, in cooperation with the Texas State Board of Water Engineers, make an investigation of the feasibility, both from an engineering and financial standpoint, of a project to include a canal from the Sabine to the Watershed of the Rio Grande." This project would include a multiple purpose system covering flood control, irrigation, power and especially water for industrial development and domestic use.

The association felt "that any future increase in the highway road-user taxes be based upon the fair and simple formula that each user pay a tax in accordance with the amount of use he derives from the roads and highways and further that the present sources of revenue for county roads and the farm-to-market program be continued without interruption."

Texas voters will make a decision this fall on a constitutional amendment to increase the term of county officials to four years. Instrumental in this move have been the State and County Judges and Commissioners Associations and the regional associations. The South Texas group, like its counterparts in other areas of the state, has gone on record as endorsing such four-year terms, encouraging each member to work toward its passage.

Proportional Representation . . *Edited by George H. Hallett, Jr.*
and Wm. Redin Woodward
(This department is successor to the Proportional Representation Review)

Limited Voting
No Substitute for P. R.

Requires Regimentation,
May Distort the Verdict

THE limited vote,[1] under which each voter votes for a smaller number than are to be elected, but without preferential voting, and those with most votes win, is a crude method of endeavoring to secure representation for minorities, to be accepted only when nothing better is available. It falls far short of the accuracy and freedom of P.R.

Here are a few examples indicating ways in which it can go astray. In each example there are 200,000 voters, who may cast six votes apiece in the election of nine. In most of these examples tickets of six will be assumed, because any group which nominates more under this plan ordinarily would be courting disaster. The dire results which may follow from having more on a ticket are illustrated in Example 9. One of the disadvantages of the system, as compared to P.R., is that, for success, it requires disciplined voting and subordination of the voter's choice to the decisions of a "boss" or organization headquarters.

Example 1: *Minority Rule.* Three slates, with all six candidates on each slate receiving a number of votes equal to the number of voters supporting it, as follows:

Slate	Voters	Elected	Probable P.R. Result
A	80,000	6	4
B	65,000	3	3
C	55,000	0	2
	200,000	9	9

[1] A proposal to substitute the limited

Here a 40 per cent minority elects two-thirds of the members, while a divided 60 per cent majority elects only one-third. The supporters of slates B and C might all agree in regarding the A candidates as the worst of the lot but, having no preferential vote, would have no way of registering this effectively if they could not agree on a single slate of candidates. The state of affairs indicated in this example is not at all unusual. A surplusage of candidates may be induced to run for the purpose of making such a result possible.

Example 2: *Exaggerated Minority Rule.* If there are many candidates and no effective effort is made to unite large groups of them behind agreed slates, a much smaller percentage may elect an undeserved majority. Although this is most likely to happen when there are no slates, it may be illustrated by supposing six slates, as follows:

Slate	Voters	Elected	Probable P.R. Result
A	45,000	6	2
B	35,000	3	2
C	33,000	0	2
D	32,000	0	1
E	30,000	0	1
F	25,000	0	1
	200,000	9	9

Here 22½ per cent elect two-thirds of the members, 17½ per cent elect the other third and 60 per cent elect nobody.

Example 3: *Majority Monopoly.* When there is considerable scattering of votes, it may be possible for a disciplined majority to divide its voters into two

vote for proportional representation will be on the November ballot in Cincinnati, Ohio. See the REVIEW, September 1954, page 451.

parts and win both the majority and the minority places. This actually happened a number of years back in a limited vote election of magistrates in Philadelphia. For example:

Slate	Voters	Elected	Probable P.R. Result
A1	55,000	6	3
A2	50,000	3	2
B	45,000	0	2
C	40,000	0	2
D	10,000	0	0
	200,000	9	9

Here a group with 52½ per cent of the votes elects all the members by dividing into two groups, each of which is larger than any of the remaining three.

Example 4: *Minority Monopoly.* The group that thus succeeds in monopolizing the seats may not even be a majority. For illustration, take Example 2 and suppose that slates A and B are divisions of the same group. In this case a 40 per cent minority succeeds in winning all the seats.

Example 5: *Majority Under-representation.* Even when there is no scattering of votes and all the voters are concentrated in two groups, there is no assurance that the groups will be fairly represented. The majority may even be under-represented. For example:

Slate	Voters	Elected	Probable P.R. Result
A	145,000	6	7
B	55,000	3	2
	200,000	9	9

Example 6: *Majority Over-representation.* The more likely result is majority over-representation, as in this example:

Slate	Voters	Elected	Probable P.R. Result
A	105,000	6	5
B	95,000	3	4
	200,000	9	9

Here a 52½ per cent group elects twice as many as a 47½ per cent group.

Example 7: *Necessity for Regimentation.* A group in a position to win a majority can only be sure to do so by uniting in support of all the group's candidates, whether personally liked or not. Any substantial defection from as many as two of the six candidates may deprive the group of its majority. For example, suppose that 15,000 of the voters in Example 6 cut two of the group's six candidates and either do not use their last two votes at all or give them to independent candidates with no chance of election. Then the two cut candidates will have only 90,000 votes each, instead of 105,000, and will run behind all the candidates on slate B. Thus group A, the majority, will elect four and group B, the minority, will elect five. Under P.R. each group normally has a choice of candidates and would not be likely to lose its rightful share because one or two of those nominated are personally unpopular with some voters.

Independent Action

Example 8: *Selection of Particular Candidates by Independents.* Although united support of a slate is essential for maximum representation of any group under this system, it is only those who disregard the maxim who determine the particular candidates to be elected on a slate unless they are all elected. The loyal voter who supports all six of his group's slate gives the one he favors least exactly the same support as the one he favors most. If the slate succeeds in electing only three, the three to win will be those voted for by those who do not support the other three. They may be very few in number and they may be voters who have no interest in the slate as a whole. In Example 6, suppose 1,000 voters of Group A, believing that their slate has a safe margin, decide to pick the three candidates on slate B whom they consider least objectionable and give them votes in addition to three of their own candidates, while all the other voters vote straight tickets. Then three of the A candidates will have 104,000 votes instead of 105,000, still ample to win, and three of the B candidates will have 96,000 instead of 95,000. These will be the three B candidates to win and they will have been selected by a group of A voters. The 95,000 B voters who put the slate in a position to win three places may largely prefer the three others.

Example 9: *Loss by Selecting Too Many Candidates.* It has been assumed so far that each group selects six candidates because that is what would ordinarily happen under this system. Concentration is necessary to assure results. If a group decides to support more than six in order not to offend some good candidates and their supporters, it may lose out by so doing. In Example 6, suppose that group A nominates nine candidates instead of six and that the group's votes are spread about evenly over the nine. Then each of the nine will have about 70,000 votes, instead of 105,000. (With six votes apiece, there are six times 105,000 or 630,000 votes in the group. If these are divided about evenly among nine candidates, each will have about one-ninth of 630,000 or 70,000.) Group B, with 95,000 votes for each of its six candidates, will elect all six, leaving only three places for the majority group. Under P.R., nine candidates can be nominated safely and the group's supporters given a choice of particular candidates.

Example 10: *Bullet Voting.* Because under limited voting a sixth choice counts as much as a first, a person, by voting all his choices, may help defeat the candidate he likes most of all. (See Example 8.) Those who care more about a particular candidate than the success of a slate may, therefore, vote bullet votes for their candidate and let the rest of their voting powers go to waste. This may help to produce distorted results. Suppose, for example, that in Example 6 group A has appealed to a particular mi-

nority by nominating one of its candidates, while group B has not done so. The members of the minority do not know whether group A can elect six or not. In case it elects only three, they want to be sure that their candidate is among the three who are successful. So they cast bullet votes for their candidate and neglect the other five on their slate. Assuming the minority has 15,000 voters who cast bullet votes in this way, this reduces the vote of the other five to 90,000, behind the six candidates of group B. Thus the group B minority will elect six of the nine candidates and group A will elect the candidate of the particular minority which wrecked its chances, and two others.

In Example 1 the possibility has been noted that, by connivance, so-called "independent" candidates may be induced, either singly or as tickets, to enter the race for the purpose of dividing the opposition. Here machination can outstrip the imagination. Suffice it to say that with this ballot, an adroit and powerful machine boss, by manipulating the candidacies of so-called "opposition" or "minority" representatives, can often cause votes to be wasted on them to a point where, with a cohesive machine bloc of 30 to 40 per cent, he can control the election of a majority of the members of council or perhaps even all of them. (Consider, for instance, the famous "bedsheet ballot" in the primary elections for Detroit's city council. With candidacies numbering from 150 to 200, Detroit's council would be determined by small, cohesive minorities were it not for Detroit's run-off elections, in which the eighteen candidates running highest in the primary fight it out for the nine council seats.)

The mere suggestion of the possibilities in this regard should suffice to warn the independent voter that a simple limitation in the number of X-marks he may use in voting cannot of itself assure either truly representative councils or fair minority participation.   G.H.H., Jr.

Taxation and Finance . . . . *Edited by Wade S. Smith*

Half-century
of State-local Debt

Period 1902-1952 Shows
Fifteen-fold Expansion

MAJOR changes in state and local government in the United States which have occurred in the 60 years since the founding of the National Municipal League are chronicled elsewhere in this anniversary issue of the REVIEW. It is appropriate here to note briefly something of the tremendous expansion in governmental operations which has occurred over the period. In attempting to do so, however, one fact becomes clear: we are infinitely better equipped today with factual information about the finances of state and local governments than we were when the League was founded. In fact, only one series of financial data on state and local governments is available with sufficient continuity to make it useful in a brief note such as this—that on government debt—and it extends back only to 1902 on a basis comparable with currently reported statistics.

Since debt expansion is both a result and a cause of expansion of governmental operations (growth and the addition of new services necessitate new improvements, while the new facilities themselves require additional personnel for their operation), the large increase in state-local debt over the years does afford a rough indicator of the attendant expansion of revenues and expenditures.

To the beginning of the current century, it will be recalled, state and local government debt had been of relatively modest proportions, although it had undergone rather large changes. State indebtedness had risen but gradually during the Civil War, then declined by about one-third during the ensuing three decades and, by 1902, was approximately a quarter of a billion dollars. Local government debt, on the other hand, experienced rapid increases, especially after the depression of the 1880s, and approximately tripled from 1870 to 1902, when it came close to equaling two billion dollars.

From 1902 to 1940 both state and local debt rose substantially and rapidly, except in the 1930s when depression influences sharply checked the expansion of local debt. During World War II the trend was downward, regaining levels of the late 1920s, but postwar borrowing, including veterans bonus loans incurred by the states and a large volume of public service enterprise borrowing by the local units, carried both state and local debts to successive new peaks after the 1946 low. By 1952, state and local debt aggregated more than thirty billions of dollars, fifteen times that of 1902.

Until World War I, state and local debts greatly exceeded that of the federal government in magnitude, except for a time during the Civil War. The financial responsibilities of the federal government in financing two world wars and the depression of the 1930s radically altered the relationship, however. By 1922, federal debt was more than twice the combined state-local debt. In the next decade, federal debt declined while state-local debt nearly doubled, and by 1932 federal debt represented just under half the total public debt. In 1932-40 federal expansion was much more rapid than state-local, and by 1940 the federal debt represented more than two-thirds of the public debt. Since 1940, federal and state-local debts have followed diverse trends, with the wartime

TOTAL DEBT (In Millions of Dollars)

	State	Local	State-Local	Federal	Grand Total[1]
1902	$ 270	$ 1,925	$ 2,195	$ 1,178	$ 3,373
1912	423	4,075	4,498	1,194	5,692
1922	1,163	9,093	10,256	22,963	33,219
1932	2,896	16,680	19,576	19,487	39,063
1940	3,526	16,720	20,246	42,968	63,214
1946	2,358	13,564	15,922	269,422	285,344
1952	6,874	23,236	30,100	259,105	289,205

increase in federal debt vastly outstripping the postwar rise in state-local indebtedness. The trend for selected years over the 50-year period 1902-52 is summarized above; data are from the current reports of the Governments Division of the U. S. Bureau of the Census.

Such debt figures, of course, take no account of the great increase in population over the half-century covered. In 1902, state debt equaled only $3 per capita, local debt $24 per capita, and federal debt $15 per capita, the combined state-local-federal per capita standing at $43.[1] At the prewar peak for state-local debt in 1940, the per capita figures were $27 for state debt, $127 for local debt and $326 for federal debt, a total of $480. Wartime reductions in state and local debt lowered the state debt to $17 per capita by 1946 and local debt to $96 per capita, combined state-local debt standing in 1946 at $113 per capita compared with $154 in 1940. Federal debt mounted to $1,908 per capita by 1946, however, and total public debt that year equaled $2,020 per capita.

By 1952, state debt was $44 per capita and local debt $148 per capita, the state-local combined figure thus standing at $192 per capita. Federal debt, however, was $1,651 per capita in 1952, and the total public debt $1,842 per capita. Both state-local and federal debts have risen further since 1952, the increase in local

debt in particular being somewhat faster than the increase in population.

Tax Institute Symposium Scheduled

The Tax Institute (formerly Tax Policy League) will hold a two-day symposium at Princeton, New Jersey, November 18 and 19, on the general subject "Financing Metropolitan Government." The preliminary program calls for two morning and two afternoon sessions, each concerned with specific phases of the subject. At the first morning session, Carl H. Chatters, who recently retired as director of the American Municipal Association to devote his time to municipal finance consultation, will preside at a discussion of economic trends affecting metropolitan government. At the afternoon session, specific problems affecting metropolitan finance will be considered, with Harold A. Caswell, tax manager for Sears, Roebuck and Company's eastern territory, presiding.

At the second morning session, the subject will be intergovernmental aspects of metropolitan finance and William F. Connelly, tax commissioner of Connecticut, will preside. At the final afternoon session Professor John F. Sly, director of Princeton Surveys, will preside. The subject will be taxation for metropolitan government. Details on all sessions, etc., may be obtained from the institute, Dr. Mabel L. Walker, executive director, at 457 Nassau Street, Princeton, New Jersey.

---

[1]Detailed figures may not necessarily add to totals because of rounding.

LWV Operates
Voters Service

*Its Goal — Education for
Intelligent Action at Polls*

ONE OF the most important activities of the nearly one thousand state and local Leagues of Women Voters in the United States is its "voters service." Now considered a year-round activity, it warms up during the late summer into a frenzy of activity as the November elections approach. An excellent description of this service appears in the July-August *Articulate Voter*, published by the League of Women Voters of Minnesota. Excerpts from the story, prepared by Mrs. Roger Klein, voters service chairman of the Minnesota League, follow:

"The history of the League of Women Voters is the history of service to the voters. In the beginning, it was to educate women who had won their fight for the privilege of real participation in government. This service has extended, through the years, to all voters—men, women, the 21-year-olds and the new citizens to this country. It is a history of which the league can be proud.

"The purpose of the league is to help the individual be an effective citizen. To this end, the responsibilities of voters service are: to build understanding of the essentials of representative government; to encourage an understanding of political parties, their processes and their relation to the citizen; to provide information on issues; to acquaint the community with candidates and their records; to educate the voters; and to encourage registration and get out the vote. We strive to accomplish this by distribution of nonpartisan information about government and the qualifications of those who hold the reins of government. By disseminating

this information, we give the individual opportunity to participate more intelligently in his government. Only through informed voting can we hope for sound democratic government.

"The party system is a valuable and integral part of our form of government. It has been said that government in the United States is government by political party. It is important to know what the parties stand for, why people work in them and why given candidates choose to run under one party label or another. The questionnaires[1] are means to these ends.

"Once having chosen, voters must be encouraged to follow through on the records of those officials to whom they have entrusted their government. The candidates meetings offer the voter the opportunity to meet the candidates personally, to question them about the issues of the election, and to discuss with them the necessary ingredients of good government. If the candidate knows the voter is interested in the issues and concerned enough to follow through on the record, we shall continue to improve government.

"The league's policy of nonpartisanship is one of its greatest strengths. The league tries to have no preconceived ideas—the issues are thoroughly studied before opinions are formed. As one national legislator said to a local league, 'We value letters from league members because they are informed and nonpartisan. They have studied the problem and know what they are talking about.'

"Every league member is, without appointment, a member of the voters service committee because she is an informed voter. She can inform others by talking about the responses to candidates' questionnaires, knowing the candidates' quali-

---

[1] Sent by leagues to candidates running for office.

fications, discussing the issues of government and taking the league program to the community. League members serve the public in a variety of ways. Here are some of the fine voters service projects that are being done by leagues throughout the state [Minnesota]:

"*Afton-Lakeland* publicized the party caucuses—the beginnings of grass roots party education. . . .

"*Brainerd* publishes a voters directory every two years with voting and registration information, listing names of all office holders from local to national, giving legislative and congressional districts of the community, and offering tips on how to write congressmen.

"*Excelsior* held a very successful candidates meeting using printed fliers and editorials to publicize it. . . .

"*Hibbing* attracted an attendance of over 300 for a recent candidates meeting and had the second highest voting percentage in the state for that election. . . .

"*Mound* tried a candidates meeting 'in the round' where the candidates and voters were seated informally in a manner which stimulated more spirited discussion. . . .

"*St. Paul* car stickers, 'Have your say —VOTE!' were seen all over the city."

Other Communities Active

Some Leagues of Women Voters actually aid in the registration of voters. This season Riverside and Bakersfield (California) league members acted as registrars, to whom voters applied for registration. . . . The Camas (Washington) league operated a "votemobile" which, accompanied by deputized and trained members, circulated around the county, registering 153 citizens.

An old-fashioned picnic rally was staged by the League of Women Voters of Atlanta so that members might meet candidates for Congress, the legislature and the county commission.

Glastonbury (Connecticut) members instruct new voters in the use of voting machines. . . . A "primary eve" session on voting problems was held by the Nyack (New York) league . . . while the Glynn County (Georgia) group held a unit meeting called "Let's Talk About Elections in Georgia."

Women voters in Lubbock (Texas) staged a "get-out-the-vote" rally prior to the August election, with a telephone committee spending the day previous reminding voters of their election day duties. . . . Each fall the New York City league conducts a telephone information service, made known to the public by spot announcements over the radio.

Many leagues seek information from candidates by way of questionnaires. The facts are published in a voters directory, which is usually widely circulated. While the league takes a stand for or against important questions before the voters, no league supports candidates. It is strictly nonpartisan.

This is but a brief sample of voters service activities. The list could be extended indefinitely. No one has ever tried to estimate the number of citizens which the league's activities have influenced.

LWV Publications

Recent publications of Leagues of Women Voters include *Kentucky Politics —A Primer* (31 pages), issued by the League of Women Voters of Kentucky at Louisville. *Nominations in Rhode Island* (six pages, six cents), *Organization of Political Parties in Rhode Island* (four pages, four cents), and *The Direct Primary* (five pages, five cents) are published by the Rhode Island league with headquarters in Providence. The league at Gainesville, Florida, has made a study of the city's hospital, reporting its findings in a 21-page document.

Striving for Citizenship in Schools and Colleges

Pomona College, at Claremont, California, has been granted $33,000 by the Falk Foundation of Pittsburgh for a three-year program to increase student observation and participation in civic affairs and practical politics. Dr. John A. Vieg, chairman of the Department of Government at the college, has been named director.

The grant will be used to provide two special courses for advanced students, stage annual Republican and Democratic rally days on the campus, and conduct summer projects for some students.

"This program of field work in politics is based on the theory that life itself is the best textbook in the social sciences," Dr. Vieg said. "It gives the student who demonstrates a *bona fide* interest in such problems an opportunity to check classroom theory by practical experience gained through service as a participant-observer in an actual campaign."

The Falk Foundation also sponsors the national Citizenship Clearing House Program which is designed to encourage greater participation by college men and women in practical politics as an avocation. A Southern California affiliate of the national organization was established several months ago with headquarters at Pomona College.

Workshop in Politics

A "Workshop in Practical Politics" will be held this fall and next spring by New York University's Division of General Education. Sydney S. Baron, political writer and director of public relations for the New York County Democratic Committee, will conduct the discussions. Mayor Robert F. Wagner of New York City and other prominent political figures —both Republican and Democratic—are to appear as guest lecturers. The program will be conducted in association with the Citizenship Clearing House for Southern New York.

The Action Program of the Citizenship Clearing House, affiliated with the Law Center of New York University, is an attractive 24-page pamphlet, well illustrated, setting forth the organization's objectives. The Clearing House

is working with many colleges and universities throughout the country:

1. To develop an interest in politics on the part of students;

2. To make it possible to continue this interest after graduation;

3. To provide the organizational framework that will make these goals possible.

During the past summer Professor Phillips Bradley, of Syracuse University, accompanied a class from the university on a six-weeks tour of American government. Two weeks each were spent in Washington, D. C., New York City and Albany, New York. Opportunity was given the students to confer with officials.

The Citizenship Education Project of Teachers College, Columbia University, which started five years ago with eight schools in the metropolitan area, now has affiliations with 1,500 institutions throughout the nation, reports the *New York Times.*

Among the volunteers who handled voting machine demonstrations prior to the July elections in Kansas City, Missouri, were 82 teenagers. These students manned 24 voting machines, giving nearly a thousand hours of volunteer service within a six-day period.

The Utah Foundation has distributed over three thousand copies of its book on state and local government to junior and senior high schools in all school districts of the state. The foundation reports that the First Security Bank purchased nearly a thousand copies for presentation to social science teachers, principals and libraries; other business firms and individuals presented quantities of books to various schools in their localities for classroom use.

Directors of the Rhode Island Home Rule Association have established a temporary committee, called the Civic Education Committee, to survey what secondary schools in the state are doing to cultivate an interest among students in the field of American history, civics and government. The committee has sent a questionnaire to principals and headmasters of all secondary schools, outlining areas of interest.

Last spring, students of Park College at Parkville, Missouri, who completed the course in American national government were offered a chance to sign a pledge card which read: "With a view to serving the public interest and regardless of the nature of my future vocation, I pledge that, upon leaving college, I will devote a portion of my time to active and definite participation in politics and public affairs."

Introduction of the Citizenship Volunteer Program at Park has been a means of making both students and graduates steadily aware of their responsibilities of citizenship.

East Cleveland Has Community Council

Founded about sixteen years ago, the Community Council of East Cleveland, Ohio, is made up of representatives from 44 organizations, as well as 26 members at large. The purposes of the council, as set forth in its code of regulations, are:

(1) To encourage voluntary cooperation of the various groups in matters of civic enterprise; (2) to foster a more effective understanding of the conditions and needs of the city; (3) to promote community welfare and progress, to make recommendations to member organizations and groups, and to take such action as may be necessary and proper to promulgate and give effect to its recommendations; (4) to improve the general conditions of living in East Cleveland.

The council is nonpartisan and provides an opportunity for leaders in every organization and other leading citizens to meet together and exchange ideas and be helpful to each other both in the community at large and in their own organizations.

More Cities Plan Educational TV

According to *Educational Television News*, published by the National Citizens Committee for Educational Television (Ring Building, Washington, D. C.) Cincinnati is the seventh city in the country to launch educational TV. Its station went on the air officially July 15. At least five other ETV stations expect to be in operation by the end of the year—St. Louis, Boston, Seattle, Consolidated University of North Carolina at Chapel Hill and Ohio State University at Columbus.

Several communities—Memphis, Champaign (Illinois), and Birmingham—are well advanced with fund raising and station plans. Fund drives are also slated in Minneapolis, New Orleans, Denver, Sacramento, St. Petersburg, Nashville, Philadelphia, Washington and Detroit. Organizations in Chicago, Oklahoma City, Tulsa and Athens (Georgia) are hoping to reach their goal in 1955.

The Citizens Committee has issued *A Speaker's Kit with Information on Educational Television*. It contains a wide variety of printed pamphlets and mimeographed material for those interested in securing a station for their own communities. Other publications by the committee include *What Educational TV Offers You* (28 pages) and *Tales of Seven Cities—And of Video That Teaches* (36 pages).

Civic Awards Offered to Youth Groups

Parents' Magazine is offering a $1,000 U. S. savings bond and 250 honor certificates to youth groups which have rendered the greatest public service during 1954. The Youth Group Achievement Awards will be made annually in order to encourage useful civic activity on the part of young people's organizations.

Eligible for the awards are all groups in the United States and its possessions and Canada with a minimum membership of ten. Members may be boys or girls or both, not exceeding high school age. Nominations may be made by the groups themselves, by teachers, principals, civic, school or church leaders, newspaper editors, parent-teacher associations and interested individuals.

Closing date for nominations for the 1954 awards is November 1, 1954. Application blanks are available from *Parents' Magazine*, 52 Vanderbilt Avenue, New York 17.

Boston Committee Dissolves

Dissension among its leaders has been given as one of the main causes for the demise of the New Boston Committee "after four controversial years as a civic organization dedicated to 'cleaning up politics'," reports the *Boston Daily Globe*. The organization was originally a youth movement which was credited with pushing "Boss" Curley out of the Boston political scene. It aided in securing a new charter for Boston to make the city's administration more efficient.

Cause of the dissension was the charge that the committee had come under the influence of political forces. Many officers resigned, leaving the organization without a chairman, executive secretary or an effective board of directors.

Some resigning directors appear to feel that a civic organization with good government principles is essential to the city and might be formed in the future under a new banner.

Foundation Fund

The City Club of Chicago has announced the establishment of a Foundation Fund the "purpose of which is to stimulate and strengthen the functioning of the club in the field of education for the responsibilities of citizenship and the techniques of democracy."

'Hats Off to Volunteers'

"Hats Off to Our Volunteers," headlines the Citizens Plan "E" Association of Worcester (Massachusetts) in a recent issue of its *CEA Planner*. "When CEA was organized," comments the bulletin, "a new field of opportunity for service opened for many Worcester citizens." The story lists the names of numerous volunteers who have given their services to the association, which has only a part-time paid staff. Volunteers cut and paste clippings, which are used as source material for various reports on the city's government released by CEA's research committees—members of which are also volunteers. After its preparation by the staff, volunteers assemble, fold and stuff the *CEA Planner* into envelopes; flyers and notices mailed from time to time are handled by them. One volunteer keeps an up-to-date list of club presidents for the use of the office staff; some do typing. "At campaign time," says the bulletin, "the number of volunteers becomes so large that a single sheet of paper cannot list them. This *Planner* is dedicated to all who have carried the load of responsibility for CEA's successes."

Cited for Service

Because of her years of outstanding civic service, the Citizens' Association of Kansas City (Missouri) has awarded Mrs. George H. Gorton a "citation of appreciation." Mrs. Gorton was "one of the founders of the cleanup movement in Kansas City," reports the *Kansas City Citizen*, "and a stalwart in the original organization of the association. She was one of the organizers of the 'broom campaign,' which was so effective in the movement which swept the Pendergast machine out of the city hall in 1940."[1]

[1]See "The Women in Public Affairs," the REVIEW, May 1940, page 334.

Flint Investigates
Fringe Area Problems

Citizens of City, Suburbs Organize to Seek Remedies

WHEN citizens of metropolitan Flint (Michigan) determined early this year to investigate the problems of their fast-growing area and try to do something about them, they thought they were in for a big job. Discussion didn't minimize the job ahead, but the natural optimism of this vibrant city seemed to say, if something as intricate as an eight-cylinder automobile can be turned out in mass production, surely integration of a metropolitan area of 300,000 persons can be devised.

Members of the Flint Area Study have found there's more plodding than running. They now know the digging, sweat, patience and persistence necessary in the first eight months are continuing elements of a metropolitan study.

Organization of the Flint Area Study has been completed and work started toward achievement of the purpose: "To identify and analyze the essential needs of the city of Flint and the surrounding communities and villages, and then make recommendations regarding the needs to the proper governmental authorities."

The Flint area is being studied for the same reason that practically every other metropolitan area is or should be. Some specific troubles: The state has threatened punitive action if fringe units don't control sewage. There is only one sewered area in the whole fringe. Young suburban families have overpopulated their schools and bonding limits are being reached. Individual and community wells outside the city are running dry. There are insufficient highways, sidewalks, street lighting, public transportation and zoning requirements and enforcement. Government adequate for rural communities 50 years ago still govern the four townships surrounding Flint.

The central city by no means escapes its problems of growth, not the least of which is the expense caused by workers and shoppers from the bedroom suburbs. Jurisdictional walls as impregnable as those of medieval fortresses separate city, county and township governments.

Since World War II there has been a growing awareness of the problems of metropolitan growth. The Flint Suburban Forum, a discussion group of fringe residents, devoted a portion of its 1953-54 program to governmental organization. Last fall, *The Flint Journal* ran a series of articles detailing area-wide problems, possible attacks against them and what some other communities were doing. One of the townships contiguous to the city attempted to incorporate as an independent city. Chiefly through these, the Flint metropolitan problem became articulate.

The incorporation vote failed. The newspaper stated in an editorial that nobody seemed to know what the metropolitan answer was, but it was high time somebody found out. A forum member volunteered to get the ball rolling toward establishment of an impartial study group.

In January, the temporary chairman—a suburban school superintendent—asked all other suburban superintendents to attend a meeting, bringing with them two or three of their communities' leading laymen. The Chamber of Commerce, labor officials and others in Flint were asked for names of likely representatives.

On January 26 the group met, heard the temporary chairman, Theodore J. Buell, and Sheldon H. LaTourette, who worked closely with him, explain the need for a cooperative approach to the problems shared by all the areas. The group decided to tackle the metropolitan problem. Representatives of each suburban area were asked to return home, call a public meeting for explanation of the project and elect from the grass roots a permanent delegate and alternate.

By the end of February, the elections were completed. Representative Flint delegates were chosen. The first formal meeting was held March 2. Subsequently, John W. Thomas, a Flint attorney living in the fringe, was elected chairman. Thomas D. Welch, an engineer and dairy farmer, representing one of the villages, and Arthur H. Sarvis, an industrialist, representing Flint, were named vice chairmen. A nine-member executive committee, with care given to geography, was selected.

Setup of FAS

The over-all Flint Area Study consists of one delegate and one alternate from each of ten suburban school districts, five small cities and villages and seven from the city of Flint. Buell and LaTourette were added as members at large. Two other communities, lying farther out from the central city, have requested membership and no doubt will be added. Except for voting, alternates have the same rights and duties as first-line delegates. They vote when their delegate is absent.

First order of business was to meet separately with the elected officials and department heads of Flint, Genesee County and the townships. Since it was decided FAS membership was to be citizen rather than official, this liaison was vital. Each promised cooperation.

With contact established, the members then turned to naming their problems. Again, they went to the grass roots to find out what people thought about sewage disposal, streets, schools, water supply and the like. Some 20 or 30 problems were grouped into seven fields. The entire membership was divided into seven working committees—sanitation, education, traffic, government, taxation and finance, zoning and planning, and public services. Each committee is headed by an executive committee member. The committees have started their individual studies. First, they intend to identify their specific problem by detailing its extent. Then, they expect to analyze it in terms of what can be done. With deliberations completed, each committee will report recommendations to the over-all group, which will work the seven segments into a final coordinated report.

On August 10 Dr. Basil G. Zimmer, resident director of the University of Michigan Social Science Research Project, was hired as consultant. He will have use of university and Flint Junior College students as part-time "leg men" to aid in research.

The Flint project has had the benefit of counsel from metropolitan authorities and a first-hand report of study committees at work in other metropolitan areas.

Good features appear to be:

1. *The open-end study to which the project is dedicated.* Each problem will be examined in the light of what consolidation, annexation, incorporation, special districts, federation and other alternatives have to offer. The final outcome may be recommending one of these, a combination of several, or working within the present framework by improving and updating existing forms of government.

2. *The practically spontaneous beginning and democratic representation on the study committee.* If the electorate feels it has a part in the decisions reached, it will be inclined to support the final recommendations, even if those are not to the liking of all officials.

3. *School representatives in at the beginning.* Because they helped launch FAS, school superintendents recognized their problems as part of a greater, over-all metropolitan problem.

4. *Open policy attitude.* All meetings are open to the public and press and are regularly reported.

Flint Area Study is not without its handicaps. Perhaps most serious is its relationship with government officials. At what point should they be brought in and when excluded in order to produce citizen thinking but at the same time have it practical and realistic?

Another possible danger is the lack of a time-table. With no deadlines to meet, committee actions can become sluggish. With the hiring of a consultant, however, there is good reason to believe most damaging pitfalls can be avoided.

FAS has operated to date from a small petty cash fund. Its real expenditures are yet to come. A finance committee now is drawing up a budget and expects to solicit Flint industry, labor, business and each community for token amounts, at least, to pay the bills.

Flint has contributed to making suburban living possible by helping give the world the automobile. No less than others, at least in proportion, it possesses the auto age's urban problems as well as its benefits. It would seem to have an obligation to contribute to the relief of urban problems, which have been brought on in large measure by suburban living.

With the Flint Area Study now in operation, it has an opportunity to make such a contribution. Except for the start in breaking down intercommunity suspicion among delegates, however, FAS has yet to prove itself.

The project may be significant in that it is one of the few in medium-sized areas to tackle in its own way its metropolitan problems and seek to come up with answers, not from the state capitol or academic halls but from the people themselves. It seems reasonable to assume that the final outcome will be of considerable benefit if the effort is carried through to completion with the thoroughness of professional consultation, the practicalness of official advice, the scholarly approach of academicians and the imagination and genuine interest of local citizen action. HOMER E. DOWDY
Staff Writer
The Flint Journal

Dr. Chute Receives
New Appointment

The Institute of Public Administration, New York City, pioneer organization in the field of governmental research, has announced the appointment of Charlton F. Chute as assistant director. Until October Dr. Chute was director and vice president of the Pennsylvania Economy League, Eastern Division. Former positions include: director of the Governmental Research Institute of St. Louis (1938-47), director of the Committee on Legislative Research of Missouri (1944-46), consultant to the Philadelphia Charter Commission (1949-51), and to the state commission appointed by the governor to study the government of New York City (1953-54).

GRA Holds
Fall Conference

Some two hundred governmental researchers and public officials met September 13-17 at Shawnee-on-Delaware for the 40th annual conference of the Governmental Research Association.

Joseph S. Clark, Jr., mayor of Philadelphia, delivered the address at the annual dinner. Mayor Clark issued a challenge to governmental researchers to assist in developing politically mature leaders for modern America.

H. Eliot Kaplan, chairman, Committee on Retirement Policy for Federal Personnel, in the opening address, discussed public retirement programs.

In addition to six workshops there were three general sessions. The first, with retiring GRA President Harland C. Stockwell presiding, was devoted to association problems. The second was on Metropolitan Government and was chaired by Frank C. Moore, president, Government Affairs Foundation. The third, presided over by Donald C. Wagner, personnel director of the city of Philadelphia, was on Intergovernmental Relations.

New GRA officers are: president, Harold L. Henderson, executive director, Minnesota Institute of Governmental Research; vice president, Howard Friend, Indiana State Chamber of Commerce; trustees, Henry W. Connor, John P. Keith, Leslie J. Reese, Estal E. Sparlin and Richard A. Ware.

Annual GRA award "for the most effective presentation of a subject" went to the Public Affairs Research Council of Louisiana for *PAR—Reports on Welfare.* The award "for the most noteworthy piece of research" was given to the Pennsylvania Economy League, Eastern Division, for *The Refuse Problem in Delaware County.*

CITY, STATE AND NATION
(Continued from page 485)

lack of funds and resultant difficulty in obtaining a manager. A mandamus suit has been threatened.

A proposal that the territory of ALASKA adopt a manager plan was made at a recent meeting of the Alaska Legislative Council by Representative Richard Greuel of Fairbanks.

Council-manager cities won first place awards from the International Association of Chiefs of Police in each of the seven population groups for cities of 10,000 to 750,000, for outstanding performance in traffic law enforcement in 1953. The seven cities are DALLAS, TEXAS; OAKLAND, CALIFORNIA; MIAMI, FLORIDA; PHOENIX, ARIZONA; COLUMBIA, SOUTH CAROLINA; EAST CLEVELAND, OHIO; and WINNETKA, ILLINOIS. Of 39 cities receiving honorable mention, 21 are governed by the manager plan. The awards were based on an evaluation of enforcement reports of cities in the annual inventory of traffic safety activities

conducted by the National Safety Council.

Urban Transportation:
A Committee and a Contest

Six national organizations of municipal officials have set up the National Committee on Urban Transportation to study problems in that field. The participating groups are the International City Managers' Association, American Municipal Association, American Public Works Association, American Society of Planning Officials, Municipal Finance Officers Association and National Institute of Law Officers. The U. S. Bureau of Public Roads and the Automotive Safety Foundation are cooperating. Orin F. Nolting, assistant director of the ICMA, is secretary.

The committee will determine the type of data needed by cities in dealing with transportation problems and will ascertain the best methods for obtaining such data. It will give attention to planning and financing street construction and maintenance, obtaining maximum efficiency and safety from the street system, mass transit, city-county-state relationships, and organization and management. A manual will be prepared as a guide to cities in developing broad transportation plans on an economical and continuing basis.

More than 140 municipal officials from all parts of the United States have been named to serve with the committee in gathering facts and preparing recommendations.

In an attack on urban traffic congestion, the Central Business District Council of the Urban Land Institute, Washington, D. C., is conducting a nation-wide contest for practical plans to make public transportation more attractive to the public and to stimulate more use thereof, thus reducing congestion and the size of outlays necessary to combat it in other ways, and also making redevelopment of central areas more feasible.

Books in Review

PROGRAM BUDGETING: THEORY AND PRACTICE WITH PARTICULAR REFERENCE TO THE U. S. DEPARTMENT OF THE ARMY. By Frederick C. Mosher. Chicago, Public Administration Service, 1954. xiii, 258 pp. $5.00.

The full title of this volume indicates clearly that it is devoted to program budgeting in the military organization of the United States government. But the blurb of the publisher gives the impression that the author has written a comprehensive treatment of program budgeting as developed and applied in this country. Those who read the book with this in mind will be disappointed. And it will not be the fault of the author, for he has taken pains to set out the scope of his treatment quite clearly.

The author makes a point of saying that he is concerned only with budgeting in the defense establishment of the national government, and that he has even excluded from consideration the nonmilitary functions such as the civil program of the corps of engineers. He has strictly limited himself to the budgetary practices of the Department of Defense, particularly those of the Army, with some attention to the Air Force and only occasional reference to the Navy.

The author is also fully aware that the defense establishment is not "typical" among public agencies, even in the field of federal budgeting; that it is unique in many respects because of its vast size, its astronomical fiscal requirements, its baffling administrative complexities (resulting from dual controls—both civilian and military), its perennial periods of "feast or famine" growing out of actual conflicts or international tensions, and its basic responsibility in an uncertain world—to defend America in any future struggle by outplanning, outbuilding, outmaneuvering and outperforming all attacking enemies. This responsibility is extremely difficult, if not impossible, to reconcile with the administrative and control processes which are normally applied to the ordinary governmental functions. Perhaps this is the most significant observation one gathers from reading this book.

The seven chapters are devoted to some general observations on the study of budgeting, mostly from the departmental standpoint; the unusual setting of military budgeting, including the "performance" legislation of 1949; the military plans, programs and budgets as they have developed since 1949; the military performance budgets, as envisaged by the Hoover Commission—"deceptively simple," yet "extremely difficult budgeting"; the budget process, as thus far developed by the defense establishment; the military comptrollers —postwar creations, supposedly emulating the practice in big business, mainly as conceived by Ferdinand Eberstadt— and their broad supervision of defense budgeting and fiscal management; and, finally, some conclusions and proposals.

Among the concluding observations are these: The author would unify military planning and program budgeting and then make it a top level operation, removed from the comptroller offices and assigned to appropriate program planning units in the three defense services. He would telescope the time span of the budgetary process for military estimating, thus reducing it by about a year and hitching it up to more recent thinking on military problems. After the President and the Congress have acted on the defense programs, an administrative budget constructed within the limits of authorized appropriations would be the primary means of internal planning and control. The author observes that the several devices used currently in the defense establishment to improve its organization and equipment requirements appear in many instances to make dubious contributions to combat efficiency. He remarks that "there are increasing charges that the military may be pricing and mechanizing itself out of the 'market' of the nation's economy, and out of the field of combat effectiveness." And he concludes that "in this area of dominant national as well as military importance, civilian control is at its weakest."

A. E. BUCK

THE ORIGIN OF THE CITY MANAGER PLAN IN STAUNTON, VIRGINIA. Staunton, Office of the Mayor, 1954. 40 pp.

Staunton enjoys the unchallenged distinction of being the first American city to have a manager. The official title was "general manager" although "city manager" became the colloquial local title and has been the one which has gone on to glory.

The Staunton city government has published this 40-page pamphlet describing the circumstances in 1906-1908 which after great labor resulted in the installation of the late C. E. Ashburner, the first city manager in the United States. This pamphlet becomes the source book of that episode. It carries the full texts of several abortive efforts in the city council to install a full-time executive in a community that was spending its money through unpaid committees of a two-house council. It includes the final text which went into effect and which served until the city moved on to the standard council-manager plan of today, in 1920, when a single five-man council replaced the old bicameral system of eight aldermen and fourteen councilmen and a separate mayor.

R.S.C.

POLITICAL PRIMER FOR NEW YORK CITY VOTERS. By Louise Burr Gerrard. New York City, Foundation for Citizen Education, 1954. 17 pp. 10 cents.

A readable review of what a conscientious citizen of New York City of either party needs to know about the local governmental structures, the party organizations and voting procedures.

The foundation is a new and small one whose publications are designed for use by members of the New York City League of Women Voters and similar civic groups.

THE COMMUNITY BUILDERS HANDBOOK (fourth edition). By the Community Builders' Council of the Urban Land Institute. Washington 6, D. C., Urban Land Institute, 1954. 314 pp. illus. $12.

It would be most unwise of one to build a residential subdivision of five hundred houses, with or without an adjoining shopping center, without checking the project against the remarkable mass of helpful experience in this compendium. Illustrated with photographs and plans, the book is obviously authoritative and fact-packed with data drawn from coast to coast.

Additional Books, Pamphlets and Articles

Assessments

MERITS AND PITFALLS OF ASSESSING AT CURRENT VALUES. By Ernest H. Johnson. (Extracts from address before Annual Meeting, Association of Towns, February 1954.) Albany (New York), Town and County Officers Training School of the State of New York, Board of Trustees, in cooperation with the Association of Towns, *Assessors Topics*, June 1954. 4 pp.

RURAL ASSESSMENT PROBLEMS. By Chester Hoyt. (Address before New York State Assessors Association, An-

nual Meeting Association of Towns.)
Albany, Association of Towns, *Assessors Topics,* May 1954. 4 pp.

City Managers
THE CHANGING ROLE OF THE CITY MANAGER. By D. G. Weiford. Richmond 19, League of Virginia Municipalities, *Virginia Municipal Review,* June 1954. 5 pp.

Community Development
LOOKING AT THE FUTURE. The First Midwinter Forum on Community Development, January 21-22, 1954. Lubbock, Texas Technological College, Department of Education, Adult Education Program, 1954. 78 pp. illus.

Constitutions
SUMMARIES OF LEADING CASES ON THE CONSTITUTION. By Paul C. Bartholomew. Ames (Iowa), Littlefield, Adams & Co., 1954. xxv, 334 pp. $1.75.

Education
MORE PUPILS AND HIGHER SCHOOL EXPENDITURES CALL FOR FISCAL PLANNING. Hartford 3, Connecticut Public Expenditure Council, Inc., *News and Views, Your State and Local Government,* May 3, 1954. 2 pp.

A NEW FOUNDATION FOR MISSISSIPPI SCHOOLS. By John E. Phay. University, University of Mississippi, Bureau of Public Administration, *Public Administration Survey,* May 1954. 4 pp.

PUBLIC EDUCATION UNDER CRITICISM. Presenting penetrative articles from leading magazines and educational journals dealing with criticisms of our public school system. Edited by C. Winfield Scott and Clyde M. Hill. New York, Prentice-Hall, Inc., 1954. xiv, 414 pp. $6.35.

THE REGIONAL SCHOOL PROGRAM IN MASSACHUSETTS. By John J. Desmond, Jr. Chicago 37, Council of State Governments, *State Government,* May 1954. 3 pp.

THE SCHOOL LOAD RISES. Chicago 37, Council of State Governments, *State Government,* May 1954. 7 pp.

Elections and Voting
ANONYMOUS ELECTION LITERATURE. Quotations from Pertinent State Statutes. Chicago 37, American Municipal Association, 1954. 7 pp. 50 cents.

THE HISTORY OF VOTING IN NEW JERSEY. A Study of the Development of Election Machinery 1664-1911. By Richard P. McCormick. New Brunswick (New Jersey), Rutgers University Press, 1953. xii, 228 pp.

THE RECORD SHOWS. (Twelfth consecutive analysis of the voting turnout and the sixth comparison between city and suburbs.) Toronto 5 (Canada), Bureau of Municipal Research, *Civic Affairs,* June 30, 1954. 4 pp.

REPORT OF GOVERNOR'S COMMITTEE ON ELECTION LAWS TO THE 1954 SESSION OF THE GENERAL ASSEMBLY. Columbia, South Carolina, The Committee, 1954. 83 pp.

Federal-State Relations
TENTATIVE REPORT OF KANSAS COMMISSION ON FEDERAL-STATE RELATIONS. Lawrence, University of Kansas, Governmental Research Center, 1954. 50 pp.

Fire Insurance
FEASIBILITY OF A STATE FIRE INSURANCE FUND. Report to the Colorado General Assembly. Denver, Colorado Legislative Council, 1954. 38 pp.

Functional Consolidation
ARE WE SITTING DUCKS FOR THE INTEGRATIONISTS? Best Defense Against Pressure for Combined Fire and Police Forces Is a Fire Protection Job Well Done. By Rod A. Porter. New York 18, *Fire Engineering,* May 1954. 3 pp. 10 cents.

Human Relations
EXPLORATIONS IN HUMAN RELATIONS TRAINING. An Assessment of Experience, 1947-1953. Ann Arbor, University of Michigan, Research Center for Group Dynamics, and Washington, D. C., National Education Association, 1954. 87 pp.

Industrial Development
THE COMMUNITY INDUSTRIAL DEVELOPMENT SURVEY. The First Step in a

Community Industrial Expansion Program. Washington 6, D. C., Chamber of Commerce of the United States, Department of Manufacture, 1954. 19 pp. 50 cents.

INDUSTRIAL SITE SELECTION—BURLINGTON COUNTY, N. J. A Case Study of Existing and Potential Industrial Location. By Gerald Breese. Princeton (New Jersey), Princeton University, Bureau of Urban Research, 1954. vii, 115 pp., maps. $2.00.

Land Subdivision

PLANNING RESIDENTIAL SUBDIVISION. By V. Joseph Kostka. Winnipeg, University of Manitoba, School of Architecture, 1954. 127 pp., illus. $3.50.

Legislation

SUGGESTIONS RELATIVE TO MEANS OF CURBING EXCESSIVE LOCAL, SPECIAL, AND PRIVATE LEGISLATION. Montgomery, Alabama Legislative Reference Service, 1954. 9 pp.

Local Government

REORGANISATION OF LOCAL GOVERNMENT. REORGANISATION OF LOCAL GOVERNMENT IN ENGLAND AND WALES. London (England), Association of Municipal Corporations, 1954. 7 and 12 pp. respectively.

Metropolitan Areas

REGIONAL ANALYSIS. TRENTON-CAMDEN METROPOLITAN AREA. A Study of the Economic Factors Affecting Development in New Jersey Along the Delaware River. Trenton, New Jersey Department of Conservation and Economic Development, Division of Planning and Development, 1954. 117 pp. $3.00.

Municipal Government

MAIN ROADS TO CITY GOVERNMENT. By Arthur W. Bromage. Ann Arbor, Alumni Association of the University of Michigan, *Michigan Alumnus*, Spring 1954. 6 pp.

Personnel

FRINGE BENEFITS IN MUNICIPAL EMPLOYMENT. A Survey of Practices in Oregon Cities Having Over 1000 Population. Eugene, University of Oregon, Bureau of Municipal Research and Service, in cooperation with The League of Oregon Cities, 1954. 44 pp. $1.00.

PRESCRIPTION FOR THE PUBLIC SERVICE. By E. S. Wengert, G. Lyle Belsley and Charles H. Bland. Chicago 37, Civil Service Assembly, 1954. 20 pp. $2.00 (Price to members, $1.50.)

Planning

THE JOINT PLANNING COMMISSION. By Clare E. Clark. Toronto, Canadian Association for Adult Education, 1954. 31 pp.

A PLANNING SURVEY FOR IOLA, KANSAS. By Lyle C. Kyle, Marvin Meade and Horace Mason. Lawrence, University of Kansas, Governmental Research Center, 1954. 149 pp., charts. $2.00.

PROCESS OF RENEWAL. South East Chicago Commission, 2nd Annual Meeting. Chicago, The Commission, 1954. 12 pp.

Police

REPORT OF THE CITIZENS COMMISSION ON LAW ENFORCEMENT IN ST. LOUIS COUNTY.[1] St. Louis, the Commission, 1954. 48 pp.

STATE POLICE COOPERATION IN PROVIDING PROTECTION IN THE RURAL AREAS. (Address before Township Officials at the League of Municipalities Convention, Atlantic City, New Jersey, November 18, 1953.) By Russell A. Snook. Trenton, New Jersey State League of Municipalities, *New Jersey Municipalities*, June 1954. 4 pp.

Politics

WHAT IT COSTS TO RUN FOR OFFICE. By Henry V. Poor. New York, *Harper's Magazine*, May 1954. 8 pp.

Primaries

KANSAS PRIMARIES—OUR NOMINATING PROCESS. By Marcene Grimes. Lawrence, University of Kansas, Governmental Research Center, 1954. 35 pp.

---

[1]For a review of this publication see page 486, this issue.

Public Health

GOOD HEALTH TO YOU. An Administrative Study of the Department of Public Health of the City of Springfield, Massachusetts. Springfield, Future Springfield, Inc., 1954. 7 pp., table. 35 cents.

Public Relations

THE GOVERNMENT PUBLIC RELATIONS BOOKSHELF. By Eric Carlson. Chicago, Government Public Relations Association, June 1954. 11 pp. $1.00.

NEWARK AIRPORT PUBLIC RELATIONS. A Case History. By Lee K. Jaffe. (Address before Public Relations Society of America.) New York City 11, Port of New York Authority, 1954. 13 pp.

Taxation and Finance

IT ISN'T JUST MONEY—A STUDY OF ST. PAUL'S FINANCIAL PROBLEMS. St. Paul 2, League of Women Voters, 1954. 11 pp. 10 cents.

LOCAL GOVERNMENT FINANCES IN MARYLAND 1952-1953. Baltimore 1, State Fiscal Research Bureau, 1954. 46 pp.

LOCAL TAXING UNITS: THE ILLINOIS EXPERIENCE. By Clyde F. Snider, Gilbert Y. Steiner and Lois Langdon. Urbana, University of Illinois, Institute of Government and Public Affairs, and Illinois Department of Revenue, Property Tax Division, 1954. 93 pp. $1.00.

LOUISIANA STATE TAX HANDBOOK 1953. Supplement. Baton Rouge, Public Affairs Research Council of Louisiana, 1954. 44 pp. 25 cents.

THE REPORT OF THE GOVERNOR'S ADVISORY COMMITTEE ON TAXATION—Territory of Hawaii. Honolulu, The Committee, 1954. 61 pp.

REPORT ON ECONOMY. The City of New York. By Luther Gulick. New York, Office of City Administration, May 1954. 42 pp.

REVALUATION PROGRAM TO INCREASE REVENUES. By Joseph J. Lennox. Chicago 37, Municipal Finance Officers Association of the United States and Canada, 1954. 4 pp. 50 cents.

CITIZENS v. BOSS:
CITIZENS WIN
(Continued from page 469)

organized committees to study the proposals of the city government and to recommend a program. This program was explained to the voters by members of the Regional Planning Council.

Typical of the people who have made the Planning Council such a success are William M. Symon, Delos C. Johns, Jess N. Gittinger, Dowdal H. Davis, Grover Milam, Mrs. Robert Casebolt, Mrs. Gorton, Mrs. Storms and the author. For these men and women, it was not enough that the bonds be approved. In order to assure proper utilization of the bond funds, they also were instrumental in establishing and operating citizens' watchdog committees that actually functioned.

Everyday Citizen Action

"Where do I get a building permit?" . . . "What does this zoning mean?" . . . "We need a small playground." These are but a few of the citizen problems which arise daily, and there is a citizen organization devoted to the day-after-day prosaic matters of municipal government. This is the Association of Community Councils.

First organized with the assistance of the city government, the Association of Community Councils is now divided into 38 neighborhood councils, which merge into fourteen community councils. These councils are two-way streets, since citizens can formally express their opinions on any municipal matter to the city government and city officials may attend community and neighborhood council meetings to explain municipal programs and to answer questions.

Each year representatives from each Community Council study the city's proposed budget for the coming fiscal year. They then report to their councils, which take a formal position on the budget. Of the true grass-roots variety, the Association of Community Councils has been highly important in recreating citizen confidence in municipal government.

If a citizen government is to be effective, merely providing an opportunity for expression of opinion is not enough. This must be complemented by a means of taking action. To bring this about, the Citizens Association was organized in December 1941. It is the heir of all the various groups which banded together to overthrow machine rule and its primary purpose is the continuation of nonpartisan government in Kansas City.

Operating on a full-time basis, the Citizens Association contains representatives of both major political parties as well as independents. Its policies are determined by an executive committee subject to review by a 200-member board of governors. The association's major function is selecting a slate of municipal candidates for each election and conducting a successful campaign to elect these nominees. It accents youth and is continually recruiting younger citizens. The present chairman, who is in his second term, is Clinton W. Kanaga, Jr., a prominent Kansas City insurance executive in his middle 30s.

Typical of the association's other activities was the recent sponsoring of "Town Hall" meetings in various districts of the city. At these meetings elected officials answered questions directed to them by the audience.

Conclusion

Kansas City furnishes an example of the best and the worst in municipal democracy. For fourteen years, ending in 1940, the city was ruled by a despotic machine. In 1940 the atmosphere cleared as if a dense fog had lifted. For the past fourteen years, Kansas City has had an enlightened, progressive government. New services have been added, badly needed improvements have been built, and the best in technical developments have been utilized.

Why has Kansas City undergone this complete change? The key lies in citizen interest and dynamic participation in governmental affairs. The sun peeked through the clouds in 1932 and again in 1934. It shone brightly in 1940 and has continued to illumine the city. It has done so because the forces of citizen pride and citizen participation have been too powerful to permit darkness to fall. An eclipse will come only if Kansas Citians lose the idealism and drive which has carried them so far.

Inside the Office . . .

Dr. Roger H. Wells, director of the Commission on Intergovernmental Relations Project, Governmental Affairs Institute, conferred recently with **Richard S. Childs,** chairman of the League Executive Committee, and staff members **John E. Bebout** and **John P. Keith** on federal-state-local relationships. . . . Mr. Childs, incidentally, is consultant to the Brookings Institution on research concerning national political convention delegates. Recently he was moderator of the Citizens Union Searchlight radio and television program, in New York, on which occasion he cross-examined Carmine De Sapio, Tammany leader, about the New York State political situation.

Herbert Emmerich, director of the Public Administration Clearing House, and **Patrick Healy, Jr.,** the new executive director of the American Municipal Association, lunched recently with **Alfred Willoughby,** League executive director. . . . **Dr. A. M. Hillhouse,** of the Cornell University School of Business and Public Administration, recently delivered the final manuscript on the *Model Investment of State Funds Law,* soon to be published by the League. . . . Members of the staff reviewed a number of films on public affairs with **Paul Bernard** and **Dr. Lillian W. Kay,** of the Citizens Com-

A. M. Hillhouse   Guthrie S. Birkhead

mittee for the Hoover Report. The League is studying the possibility of producing a number of films in its field for use on television and otherwise.

Guthrie S. Birkhead, the first League staff fellow, is making a study of research projects conducted by the State of New York. The purpose is to make sure that useful research is being conducted, that duplication is eliminated, and that results are made available to those who can use them. Dr. Birkhead is associate professor of political science at Syracuse University. . . . **Norman Blacher,** the new community manager of Sea Gate, Brooklyn,[1] called at the office. . . . Messrs. Bebout and Keith of the League staff conferred with New York City Administrator **Luther Gulick** about the possibility of inaugurating a continuing program on the impact of technology upon state and local government.

Carrol M. Shanks, president of the Prudential Insurance Company and former League Council member, won the 1954 Outstanding Citizen award of the New Jersey Advertising Club. . . . **Francis W. Rogers** of Thomas Y. Crowell Company discussed the American Commonwealth series of books on government and administration in the 48 states at League headquarters. His company is publishing one volume on each state.

Carrol M. Shanks   Richard S. Childs

---

[1] See page 484.

509

Experts in 20 Panels to Cover Wide Area

(Continued from page 443)

newspapers in Illinois, and Dowdal Davis, of the *Kansas City Call*.

"Industry's Responsibility for Achieving Sound Government." Cecil Morgan, counsel for the Standard Oil Co. (N.J.) and member of the League's Council, is chairman, and William H. Baumer, assistant to the president of Johnson & Johnson, is among the participants.

"State Legislatures: Do They Represent the People?" The chairman is Lashley G. Harvey, of Boston University, and Gus Tyler, political director of the International Ladies Garment Workers Union, is one of the panel members.

"Public Relations of the Council and the City Manager," with Ethan P. Allen, director, Government Research Center, University of Kansas, in the chair, and Elder Gunter, city manager of University City, Missouri, and Hugo Wall, University of Kansas, taking part.

"A New Look at Home Rule," with Martin L. Faust, University of Missouri, presiding. Among the other panel members are Bayard H. Faulkner, chairman, New Jersey Commission on Municipal Government (1950), Jefferson B. Fordham, dean of the Law School, University of Pennsylvania, and Arthur W. Bromage, University of Michigan.

"State and Regional Planning."

Cecil Morgan   Bayard H. Faulkner

Tract on Manager Plan Abandonments Revised

To keep its publications up to date in a fast-changing world, the League is continually making appropriate revisions. The latest work to undergo this treatment is *Manager Plan Abandonments*, prepared for the League by Professor Arthur W. Bromage of the University of Michigan. The fourth edition, now available for distribution, explains why 51 communities out of the 1,300 which have tried the council-manager system have rejected it. This 40-page booklet costs 50 cents.

Arthur W. Bromage   Joseph E. McLean

Joseph E. McLean, New Jersey Commissioner of Conservation and Economic Development, will be chairman. Others taking part include Hugh R. Pomeroy, director of the Westchester County (New York) Department of Planning, Coleman Woodbury, well known planning consultant, and T. Ledyard Blakeman, of the Detroit Metropolitan Area Regional Planning Commission.

"Organized Citizens At Work," with Clinton W. Kanaga, Jr., president, Citizens Association of Kansas City, presiding. Participating are Forest Frank, executive director, Cincinnati City Charter Committee, Guy C. Larcom, Jr., member of the board of the Cleve-

(Continued on following page)

Record Set in All-America Cities Contest

Indications are that the Sixth Annual All-America Cities Contest will draw a greater number of entries than ever before.

Requests for the formal entry blanks which competitors must execute to be considered in the contest, which is jointly sponsored by the National Municipal League and *Look* Magazine, exceeded 200. It is anticipated that by the October 1 deadline between 75 and 100, a record, will be returned to League headquarters.

A screening committee, as in the past, will narrow the entries down to 22, which will be given the opportunity to present their cases to a jury during the National Conference on Government in Kansas City, November 7 to 10.

The foreman of the jury will be Dr. George H. Gallup, president of the League and director of the American Institute of Public Opinion, who held the same office in previous contests.

Others who have been named to the jury include Mark Matthews, former president of the U. S. Junior Chamber of Commerce and member of the League's Council, Vernon Myers, pub-

George H. Gallup

lisher of *Look*, Dean William L. Bradshaw, University of Missouri, Professor Donald Webster, University of Washington, and Leo Perlis, National Community Services Director of the CIO.

The balance of the twelve-member jury will be announced at a later date.

Meeting

(Continued from preceding page)

land Citizens League, and Stanley H. Renton, Charter League of New Rochelle (New York), and others.

"Women in Public Affairs," at which Mrs. Martha Sharp, special assistant to the chairman, National Security Resources Board, 1950-53, will preside.

"Education for Political Participation" (primarily in colleges and universities). James W. Miller, Michigan State College, is chairman.

"Going to Town — Metropolis on

Wheels," chaired by Lee M. Sharrar, attorney, Humble Oil & Refining Company. Among the others on the panel are Mayor Roy Hofheinz, of Houston, and John W. Giesecke, of the Transit Board of Freeholders, St. Louis.

"State-local Fiscal Relations." John S. Linen, vice president of the Chase National Bank, will preside.

"Clinic on the Organization of a Statewide Civic Campaign," with Robert H. Rawson, former chairman of the Citizens Committee on the Ohio Constitution, as chairman.

(Continued on following page)

Another Reason for Attending K.C. Conference

In addition to profiting from the many sessions on topics of broad importance at the 60th Annual Conference on Government in Kansas City, those who attend the meeting will have an opportunity to see modern municipal government working effectively.

Recently Walter Blucher, one of the country's foremost planners, studied Kansas City which, fourteen years ago, was generally one of the worst-run cities in the nation. Until 1940, the municipality was in the grip of the notorious Pendergast machine.[1]

"What impresses one in Kansas City," Mr. Blucher declared, "is the vitality of the area, its aliveness, its optimism, the sureness of its residents and public officials."

Mr. Blucher called attention to bridges, parking facilities, expressways, slum clearance and many other public improvements which had been and are being made in the city. He noted with respect to planning that other cities in the area, and indeed in another state (Kansas), are all considered together as a single integrated metropolitan unit.

Kansas City has a planning staff of 28 persons, Mr. Blucher said, compared with twenty in Seattle, fifteen in Denver, and eleven in Indianapolis. This staff has better economic information than the average market analyst in the region, he continued.

"The smart market analyst in the Kansas City area will go to the Plan Commission for assistance," he asserted.

[1]See page 464.

If you want to be sure of staying at the conference hotel, the President, shown here, while attending the National Conference on Government in Kansas City, be sure to make your reservations early. With a record attendance anticipated, the hotel may not be able to accommodate everyone.

Meeting

(Continued from preceding page)

"The Water Problem: A Challenge to the States." Edward Ackerman, assistant general manager, Tennessee Valley Authority, is slated for the chairmanship. Arthur Lloyd, head of the Legislative Reference Bureau, Kentucky, Guthrie Birkhead, Syracuse University, and M. Turner Wallis, Central and Southern Florida Flood Control District, will be among those on the panel.

"Representative City Councils" (a clinic on methods of representation). Mrs. Albert D. Cash, former member of the Cincinnati city council, will serve on the panel.

Other panels will be held on "Youth in Civic Affairs," which will be primarily concerned with students in secondary schools, "Business and Professional Men As Civic Leaders", and "State Reorganization: Where Do We Go From Here?"

All Set for Conference

As final arrangements for the 60th annual National Conference on Government in Kansas City, Missouri, November 7 to 10, neared completion, a bigger and more fruitful meeting than ever before seemed assured.

In the All-America Cities Contest jury sessions, a feature of the Conference for the last six years, a record 225 nominations, twice the total in 1953, have been received.

A screening committee recently selected 22 finalists which will present their cases to the jury in Kansas City. Its members were Richard S. Childs, chairman of the League's executive committee; Bayard H. Faulkner, business executive and New Jersey civic leader; and Mrs. Edith P. Welty, former mayor of Yonkers, New York. The committee was assisted by staff member William F. Larsen, who is in charge of the contest.

James F. Murray, Jr., moderator of Town Meeting radio program.

Mrs. Dorothy N. Dolbey, acting mayor of Cincinnati, whose speech, "Conscripts for a Dream," will be heard by luncheon guests at the National Conference on Government, November 9.

The second speaker on the *America's Town Meeting of the Air* radio program, which will emanate from the National Municipal League's 60th anniversary dinner on November 9, has been announced. He will be Norton Mockridge, crime reporter for the New York *World-Telegram and The Sun*. Mr. Mockridge, well known author, will join Robert E. Merriam, crime-busting Chicago alderman, in a discussion of "How Can We Divorce Crime from Politics?"

Mr. Mockridge, a newspaperman for more than twenty years, is co-author of two books, *This Is Costello*, published in 1951, and *The Big Fix*, which will appear this month. The latter work sets forth how Kings County (Brooklyn) District Attorney Miles McDonald broke up the $20,000,000 Harry Gross bookmaking combine which, according to the writers, resulted in the departure of Mayor William O'Dwyer from New York's City Hall.

Radio commentator and master of

(Continued on page 559)

Five members of the jury which will select winners of the All-America Cities Contest, 1954. Left to right: Leo Perlis, national community services director, CIO; Mrs. Maurice H. Noun, member of the Des Moines Plan and Zoning Commission; Mark S. Matthews, civic leader and author of "Guide to Community Action"; Mrs. Albert D. Cash, former member, Cincinnati City Council; and Vernon Myers, publisher, "Look" magazine. Mrs. Noun, Mr. Matthews and Mrs. Cash are members of the League Council. Jury convenes on the afternoons of November 8 and 9 during the National Conference.

THE WHITE HOUSE
WASHINGTON

Denver, Colorado
September 21, 1954

Dear Mr. Willoughby:

I am happy to extend congratulations to members
of the National Municipal League on its sixtieth
anniversary and upon the occasion of the Sixtieth
Annual National Conference on Government. In
its long history, this organization has encouraged
citizens to play a more active, more intelligent
role in civic affairs. It has urged higher standards
in State and local government. In doing so, it has
helped to remind the American people of a central
fact about our American system of government:
that its effectiveness, at every level, depends upon
enlightened citizen interest and participation. I
sincerely hope that the League will carry this
message to more and more of our people and thus
do an even greater national service in the years
ahead.

Sincerely,

Dwight D. Eisenhower.

Mr. Alfred Willoughby
Executive Director
National Municipal League
542 Fifth Avenue
New York 36, N. Y.

National Municipal Review

Volume XLIII, No. 10   Total Number 448

Published monthly except August
By NATIONAL MUNICIPAL LEAGUE

Contents for November 1954

The contents of the REVIEW are indexed in *International Index to Periodicals* and *Public Affairs Information Service.*

Entered as second class matter July 11, 1932, at the Post Office at Worcester, Massachusetts. Publication office, 150 Fremont Street, Worcester 3; editorial and business office, 542 Fifth Avenue, New York 36. Copyright 1954 by the National-Municipal League.

Subscription, $5 per year; Canadian, $5.25; foreign, $5.50; single copies 50 cents.

Editorial Comment

Spotlight on State Legislatures

FORTY-four state legislatures will meet in regular session in 1955. Seven thousand of our fellow-citizens will spend hectic days and sleepless nights enacting approximately 25,000 new laws. They will authorize some twelve billions of expenditures for state and local services, not counting capital outlay, for the ensuing year. Thirty-four of these legislatures, which meet only every other year, will double their appropriations to cover two years.

No doubt about it, big business of far-reaching importance to every citizen will be transacted under the capitol domes during the next few months. In each state, hundreds of organizations, including corporations, trade and professional associations, labor unions, educational and charitable institutions and civic bodies will descend on the legislative halls along with thousands of individual citizens. Officials of hundreds of state agencies and over 100,000 subordinate units of government—counties, municipalities, school districts, special districts and authorities—will look to the legislatures for money or for renewed 'or extended authority.

For every bill enacted into law, five or ten will be thrown into legislative hoppers and an unknown number of other projects to add to the law will be sidetracked without finding legislators to introduce them for printing at public expense.

Nowhere else in the world is there anything like this biennial legislative carnival. The 7,000 men and women who are the featured performers are key figures in our society. It is important to every citizen and to the general welfare that we understand them and help them to play constructive, responsible roles.

Unfortunately, membership in the legislature does not carry prestige or working conditions commensurate with its potential for good or evil. Here are just a few of the reasons why the public seldom gets and no longer expects the kind of service it ought to demand from its state legislatures: nominal or totally inadequate pay, insufficient research and staff aids, limits on length of sessions which force hasty action in end of session log jams, constitutional provisions which unwisely cramp legislative discretion on the one hand and divert precious time to matters better left to administrative agencies or local governments on the other, long ballots which frequently put candidates for the state legislature at the tail of a ticket dominated by candidates for national office, the one-party system that prevails in large sections of a majority of the states, the failure of representation to reflect the growth of cities.

These conditions can be blamed partly on past legislatures; but basically they are the responsibility of the people themselves. Whatever the cause, they put serious handicaps on the men and women who will be making substantial sacrifices to serve in the 1955 legislatures.

Obviously, therefore, it behooves good citizens to approach the forthcoming sessions with some appreciation of the difficulties as well as the importance of the jobs that will be done in their name in Augusta and Columbus and Austin and Bismarck and Olympia and other capitals.

It should be equally obvious that if we wish to preserve healthy government in our states, government that can fairly compete for prestige and power with Washington, we had better improve conditions in our state legislatures. The basic need is not for different legislators but for making the job of legislator such that good people can do a consistently good job.[1]

Wane of the Commission Plan

STATISTICS for 1953 recently published in the *Municipal Year Book*[1] provide a logical opportunity to examine the commission plan, which began (as an elective government) in Galveston in 1903.

The 50th anniversary of the commission plan is no jubilee, for it moves steadily and deservedly toward oblivion.

An emergency commission of five appointed by the governor took over the government after Galveston was swept by a tidal wave in 1900. The commission did well, thanks to the quality of its members, but it could not legally be retained after normality was restored and, by a judicial decision, it became elective.

Nobody had designed it to be an elective government and authorities on public administration generally did not cheer the subsequent series of adoptions by other cities.

By 1913 the unofficial tally of the National Short Ballot Organization listed 316 commission plan communities. Two years later 465 were reported. How much further the movement went is curiously unknown, there being no census figures of such facts for some years. In 1923, a count limited to communities of over 5,000 population was 301 "plus 200 or 300 smaller places." In 1933, 26 per cent of cities over 30,000 population (no statistics for smaller places) had it. In 1943, it was in 16.1 per cent of the cities over 5,000 population and the 1953 figure is 372 out of 2,527—14.7 per cent, just half the number of cities over 5,000 having the council-manager plan.

Charter commissions nowadays simply do not consider the commission plan. There have been only four adoptions since 1942—Vancouver, Washington; Bessemer, Alabama; Marshall, Michigan; and Aurora, Illinois. Des Moines, co-leader of the movement with Galveston, abandoned the plan in 1949.

So the commission plan, in the light of abundant experience, dwindles out.

But it did accomplish one thing. It cracked the universal assumption that a two-headed mayor and council setup was the only conceivable structure for a city government and made a breach for the coming of the council-manager plan.

[1]International City Managers' Association, Chicago, 1954.

[1]See also review of *American State Legislatures*, Report of the Committee on American Legislatures of the American Political Science Association, and *Adventures in Politics*, We Go to the Legislature, by Richard L. Neuberger, page 553, this issue.

A Home Town Is Born

Crossett, Arkansas, company town, blossomed into thriving community when citizens gained chance to own their homes.

By LLEWELLYN MILLER*

THE Crossett Lumber Company was formed in 1899, when three Iowa investors bought a vast forest in Arkansas—920 square miles of tall, whispering pines laced only by wandering wagon trails and deer paths. The company hauled in a sawmill and imported workers to fell the trees and for these loggers' families they built dwellings, a store and a school. Gradually a little town took shape. They called it Crossett.

By 1946 the sawmill, a kraft-paper plant and a chemical factory were supporting a population of 3,000. At first glance it looked like any other small community in southern Arkansas, but it wasn't. Every dwelling and inch of land, with the solitary exception of where the post office stood, was owned by the company.

In many ways it was a pleasant place to live. Rents were low. The company gave each building a fresh coat of gray and white paint at regular intervals. If a tap dripped or a roof leaked, repairs were made in a hurry—no charge. Medical services were virtually free. Work was steady. Wages were good.

But something was wrong.

Crossett wasn't anyone's home town, not even the owners'. Most of the young people who went away to college never came back. There was no place for them unless they contented themselves with working for the company. A few employees who started with the logging camp stayed and reared their families. More people worked a few years and drifted away. Labor turnover was high.

The company made a steady profit from the mills and from rents and services but as the years went by the mood of their town worried them. In deepest secrecy they made elaborate plans for an experiment. Crossett was rocked with surprise on the morning of December 5, 1946, when the postmen delivered identical letters to each of the 967 homes announcing that the whole town was for sale to the people who lived there.

The news swept through the streets like a spring wind. It whirled women together in spontaneous meetings in their homes. At the company mills and plants, at the company bank, inn and service stations, men gathered in astounded conference. For years people had tried to buy homes in Crossett without success. What was behind this sudden, sweeping reversal of company policy?

Some tenants were delighted. Others were suspicious. "What's in this for the company?" they asked. "Why are they unloading the houses? Are they shutting down? Is this going to be a ghost town?" The company was asking questions also.

*Miss Miller, born in Louisville, Kentucky, but now a New Yorker, writer and author of a book on diet, has had many articles published in *Collier's, Cosmopolitan, Redbook, Woman's Home Companion, Coronet, American Weekly,* and other magazines of national circulation.

"Will the people want to buy? If they do, will they keep up the streets? Will they paint the houses? Will there be slums before long in our spic-and-span town?"

What happened astonished both groups.

Guesses as to how many homes would be sold had wavered from 10 to 50 per cent of the tenants. The first surprise was when every single renter except one bought. A few families paid cash, sold within weeks and cheerily moved away with several thousand dollars of quick profit jingling in their pockets. On the other hand, there was eager inquiry from scores of employees who commuted from neighboring towns. "What about us?" they asked. "Now that we can buy homes, we want to live in Crossett, too." So the company laid out new streets in the forest at the edge of town, and Crossett began its extraordinary growth in size.

Paint Up, Fix Up

Other surprises came fast. Half the town rushed to buy paint—white, yellow, pink, green, anything but Crossett gray. Hammers rang through the town on weekends as new owners added rooms and porches. Blocks of identical houses lost the look of tidy barracks.

There was a raid on seed stores. Flowers and shrubs went in. Lawns unwatered for years turned green. There was a boom in furniture buying. New rugs, draperies, stoves and refrigerators were delivered by the truckload. Water consumption per house jumped on an average of 1,300 gallons a month because of the increase in washers, air-conditioning and gardening.

Most significantly, the prim picket fences that cut each house off from the next came down in one contagious community impulse. They were in the way of the new neighborly trading of tools, advice and comment on scores of new problems of civic responsibility that other towns take for granted. "The place was electrified by private ownership. Overnight it even smelled better," said Paul Kays, appointed by the company to handle the complicated details of change-over from company-owned settlement to normal town.

Crossett had been incorporated as a town in 1902, mainly to get recognition for mail delivery. Technically the inhabitants had been choosing their own officials, but actually there was little interest. Frequently candidates ran unopposed. Why bother to vote when the company owned the town—and paid the taxes?

"I had served as election judge when not more than 25 voters turned out," said Ovid Switzer, former state senator, "but at the first city election after the change-over they turned out in droves. For almost the first time there was competition for office."

What they did about taxes was an eye-opener. Instead of being dismayed at the new, painful experience of taxes, the new home owners raised the rate by overwhelming vote. They wanted, and built, two handsome new schools and later a $200,000 municipal building. The airport had been only a cow pasture; they expanded and improved it. The fire department had been on an unpaid basis; this seemed an offense to newborn civic pride so the citizens voted to pay each volunteer $2.50 for each alarm answered.

Hardly any aspect of Crossett did not see a quick change. Before the people owned their town there were two small churches, both more than 40 years old. Today there are nine, all new. "The people fixed up their Sunday homes, too," said "Brother Dan" Robinson, pastor of the new $170,000 Methodist church built by a congregation of six hundred.

The little two-room jail stood idle. "People were too busy to get into trouble," said Police Chief Dempsey Polk. "My biggest troubles used to be fights and petty pilfering. When everything belonged to the company some people didn't think so much of property and 'borrowed' what they needed. Now when a man lays out good money for a saw, he respects the next fellow's lawn mower. Same with kids; we get ordinary kid mischief but no more vandalism."

Business Expands

Main Street expanded and thrived on a brand new thing in Crossett's business life—competition. Formerly, when the town wanted groceries, coats, cars, layettes or caskets it had been served only by the company store. Now that land and buildings could be bought, independent merchants opened shop; furniture, hardware, dress, jewelry, drug and flower shops prospered. Rates continued to be low at the company hospital but independent doctors ventured into practice and were busy. A radio station came in.

Crossett always had been a man's town but now things began to open up for women too. For the first time a woman ran for the school board. Mrs. Scott Campbell took over her husband's insurance business after his death and made a substantial success of it.

Before the company offered Crossett for sale it had called in a town planner to set aside generous park, playground and school sites for a model town of 6,000. But it was thought that the population would never grow to more than double current size. Within a year private enterprise had caused such a boom that they quietly ordered another plan—for a future town of 10,000.

The busier the town became, the more the citizens seemed able to do for it and themselves. Social activities increased. A community chorus was started. A branch of the American Association of University Women was organized. A concert club sold enough memberships to underwrite a series of musical attractions each winter. A civil air patrol was started. A riding club was formed and the members built a 3,500-seat arena. Various organizations ran benefits and raised money for new instruments and uniforms for the school band, for Teen Town and Scout club houses and a small zoo for the youngsters.

A curious change came over the company as well. Instead of losing interest in the town it no longer owned, it was inspired to even more generous gestures. When congregations formed to bring in new ministers the company matched privately raised building funds dollar for dollar. When Negro citizens cleared land, poured tennis courts and built a playground, the company built them a swimming pool and dedicated it to the city.

And the whole town joined in one

big, spontaneous community effort to save Miss Carrie Calhoun, principal of the elementary school, for Crossett.

Miss Carrie was the one tenant who did not buy her home. She couldn't afford to. She had started teaching in 1907 and her salary had taken care of younger brothers and sisters. When they were educated she was so in the habit of caring for others that all her extra money went to aid children of migrant workers who helped on the forest farms and drifted through Crossett's schools.

"If a child is cold, or hungry, or sick, he can't learn—and learning won't wait," she said crisply. She saved no money.

Present for the Teacher

"Everybody who grew up in Crossett had taken her orders and was better for them," said William Norman, one of the few young men who came back after college to Crossett and rose to high position with the company. "We have a teachers' retirement fund in Arkansas, and the school board voted her an additional sum, but it didn't seem enough for all she had done for the town. No one person started the idea but suddenly everybody from kids to company officials was collecting money to buy her house and keep her here."

Crossett is a great town for keeping secrets. Miss Carrie had no hint as to what was going to happen on her last day at school. First there was a parade. Teachers and children marched by classes. So did old graduates. Some came from far away for the event and there were letters and telegrams from 23 states. At night there was a pageant with Miss

Carrie's life acted by her teachers. Then she was called to the stage and given the deed to her house, paid for by contributions of from ten cents to $100 from virtually everyone in town. For once Miss Carrie was speechless, but the roar of applause spoke the whole town's emotion for her.

The biggest surprise to the company was that Crossett did not settle down after its first expansion but continues to grow. New industry came in, attracted by the chance to buy and build near plentiful power and raw materials and a newly stable labor supply. Chase Bag, Simplex Paper Corporation and Bemis Brothers Bag Company attracted hundreds of workers to Crossett; so many new citizens that the Crosset Company tore up the second town plan and ordered another—for a town of an expected 25,000.

Had the original owners seen any part of this they would not have believed their eyes. When they started they planned to follow standard practice of those days—slash down the trees and move on, leaving a ghost town among the stumps. They gave the village twenty years at the outside. But they were God-fearing men and while they were responsible for the settlement named after their company they were determined to keep it a safe and decent place to live in. Everyone was expected to obey the curfew, a blinking of all lights from the main switch at 10:55 each night. Time to go to bed! The company not only gave the town its buildings but also set the pattern for their use.

So, very early, two marked attitudes were established. One was a generous, somewhat fatherly, but quite strict control of private lives as well as of working conditions by the company. The second was almost total dependence of employees on the company for all civic and most social decisions. The man who was out of step with company ideas left town. There was no place to live except in company houses. The man who was fired or who quit left his house when he left his job. There was no problem about old folks ready to retire. All the workers were young. The town would be gone by the time they could no longer work.

"There are four important elements in industry," said Peter Watzek, grandson of one of the founders and president of the Crossett Company. "Raw materials, capital, customers—and people. We had the first three but we realized early that there was something wrong with the way we were dealing with the fourth. It took years of worrying before we came up with the answer, which is simple: Americans prefer freedom to paternalistic government, which is what the company had become."

Crossett was not changed overnight and all was not sweetness and light. There were growing pains. Most of the streets today are better than they ever were, but some few districts have let theirs run down. Nearly 50 years of depending on the company has left its mark. The company's gift of the auditorium was not received without criticism. "Why an auditorium when we need streets and another school?" said a portion of the town.

"That's normal too," said Robert Fisher, new owner and editor of the weekly Crossett *News Observer*. "It's the American spirit, reserving the right to bite the hand that feeds you."

There were scandals. Ashley County voted itself dry in 1942 and bootleggers lurked in the woods. "I've preached all over," said Brother Dan. "This is the cleanest town I've ever seen, but you'll always find some who live in hog heaven—vote dry and drink wet."

Steady Progress

Some citizens wanted to forge ahead too fast for the rest. The bond issue for the new municipal building, dedicated this year, was defeated twice before passing by a comfortable majority.

But progress is steady. The town, and the company too, have absorbed wisdom from the forest.

"When you work with nature you become very patient," said Peter Watzek. "When you plant a tree today that your children will not harvest for 50 years, you learn that all growing things need their own time—forests, people, towns. We tried to give Crossett the same chance we give our forests. When we gave nature a chance it replenished the forest. Now we know that we made no mistake in trusting human nature to do the same for Crossett and make it a town that all of us can call home."

Home Rule Still a Farce

Restrictions imposed by West Virginia legislature weaken powers of cities, undermine constitutional provisions.

By HAROLD J. SHAMBERGER*

THE WEST Virginia constitution contains a home rule provision but the municipalities do not enjoy home rule. Almost two decades have elapsed since the people of the state ratified such an amendment but to date home rule has yet to emerge from the realm of theory. Since 1937 cities with populations in excess of 2,000 have been free to draft, adopt and amend charters locally and, as a consequence, alter or change the structure of government, but at this point home rule privileges cease.

The amendment, drafted by Jefferson B. Fordham, now dean of the Law School, University of Pennsylvania, is basically sound. It seems to confer upon the municipalities authority which would enable them to determine locally powers and procedures for their own government with a minimum of state interference. Certainly this is in accordance with basic concepts of home rule.

The amendment contains three main divisions. The first prohibits special legislative acts incorporating municipalities and permits cities over 2,000 population to adopt and amend charters. The second provides for the restriction of powers of cities through general laws to borrow money, contract debts and to tax property. In each case, however, specific limitations are contained in

other older sections of the constitution. The third division grants to a municipality authority "to pass all laws and ordinances relating to its municipal affairs" which are not "inconsistent or in conflict" with the constitution or present or future laws of the state. The amendment was not self-executing, however, but required passage of enabling legislation.

While the amendment indicates that cities might take action in matters relating to their "municipal affairs" unless prohibited from doing so by general law, it has not been so interpreted by the legislature. The enabling act to the home rule amendment enumerates in considerable detail the powers of cities, prefaced with the caution that charters adopted locally are not to enlarge those powers specified by law.

Under the original act cities which had adopted home rule charters secured some advantages in the form of enumerated sources of taxation not available to special-act and general-charter cities, but subsequent action by the legislature has extended equal taxing privileges to all municipalities, thereby nullifying the only real advantage offered to a city adopting a home rule charter.

The home rule powers enumerated by the legislature extend to such matters of minute detail as authority to use a common seal, to "appropriate and expend not exceeding 25 cents per capita per annum for advertising the city and the entertain-

*Mr. Shamberger is executive director of the West Virginia League of Municipalities as well as research associate of the Bureau for Government Research at West Virginia University.

523

ment of visitors," and other areas which logically might be interpreted to relate to "municipal affairs" under the most conservative interpretation by the courts.

In addition to restricting the exercise of power by home rule cities to those specifically enumerated in the home rule act, the authority of municipalities is further limited by substantive and procedural provisions of other general laws, foremost of which pertain to fiscal affairs. Under general laws in force since 1933, strict control of budgetary and finance matters has been lodged in the office of the state tax commissioner. Approval by the commissioner is required before a municipal budget may be executed and he may at his discretion strike from the budget items which he may consider to be "unnecessary."

Legislative Policy

In all instances save one, prior to and since the advent of constitutional home rule, the established legislative policy has consistently adhered to the control of municipal authority through an enumeration of the powers which are extended to municipalities.

The one exception throws considerable light upon the view which the State Supreme Court of Appeals is likely to take of any attempt by the legislature to deviate from the enumeration and necessarily implied doctrine to which the court has tenaciously held. Much could be accomplished to clarify the legal position of home rule cities if the wording of the home rule amendment had been construed by the court; unfortunately this has never occurred.

Prior to the amendment, the court had been completely immersed in the Dillon Rule.[1]

Subsequent opinions regarding municipal powers indicate no deviation from that view. In one instance the city of Mullens, after adopting a portion of the home rule act, attempted to condemn utility property. This, the court held, the city was without power to do since nothing in the home rule statute or elsewhere authorized such action against an electric power company.[2] In the one instance in which the legislature attempted to alter its policy by bestowing upon a city a blanket grant of power, it was hauled up short by the court and severely reprimanded. While the grant of power was incorporated in a special-act charter passed prior to the ratification of the home rule amendment, the court's attitude toward this action is of great significance because the question appeared before it in 1945.

The charter of the city of Wheeling, granted in 1935, contains a remarkably broad grant of power which extends to that city all powers then available or which thereafter might have been conferred upon all cities, as well as "other powers possible for a municipality to have, *whether such powers be expressly enumerated in this charter or not, and without any further action on the part of the legislature.*"[3] With a

---

[1]That a city has no power not expressly given to it by the legislature and which is absolutely indispensable, not merely convenient, to its functioning. *Hyre* v. *Brown*, 102 W. Va. 505, 135 S.E. 656, 49 A.L.R. 1230 (1926).
[2]*Mullens* v. *Union Power Co.*, 122 W. Va. 179, 7 S.E. (2nd) 870 (1940).
[3]Italics mine.

slap on the wrists the court unanimously declared this action to be an exercise of power beyond the scope of legislative authority, although the court offered no demonstration of the constitutional provision which is purportedly contravened. Since there appears to be nothing contained in the constitution which prohibits such use of legislative discretion in formulating policy, this action seems only to violate the common law holdings surrounding Dillon's interpretation of state-municipal legal relations. The legislature was counseled by the court to enact statutes in the future which "cover specific and current intents and purposes, so defined that the public may know what laws to obey and what practices to avoid."[4]

While here the court was not directly concerned with the home rule amendment, its conclusions are sufficiently strong to serve notice of its attitude toward any future attempt by the legislature to endow the cities with the means of adjusting municipal affairs according to the divergent needs of their residents. Until that is accomplished, however, "home rule" will continue to mean only a reprieve for the legislature from the time-consuming task of enacting individual charters without a surrender of its traditional methods of stringent control.

What channels then remain which can lead to an unshackling of municipal government to the extent visualized by the framers of the home rule amendment? A portion of the answer should rest with the municipalities themselves. Yet, while municipal officials give lip service to

[4]*Tucker* v. *Wheeling*, 128 W. Va. 47, 35 S.E. (2d) 681 (1945).

the desirability of greater local authority, their actions belie their words.

Approximately two-thirds of the population of West Virginia is classified as rural. Therefore, it would appear to be exceedingly difficult for the cities to receive favorable consideration from a representative legislature. This could be accepted as fact if, in the past, municipal interests had pursued a concerted effort to gain greater independence and had been resoundingly rebuked. The record does not bear this out fully. During the seventeen years in which charter-making privileges have been available to them, only twelve of 68 cities have initiated action leading to a home rule charter and only six have been able to carry the movement to its conclusion. Of these six, none can be considered a major city.

Officials Should Act

A great reluctance has been demonstrated by some leading municipal officials to delve into what they consider the great unknown which surrounds home rule. The "hands-off" policy which they have consciously adopted has contributed nothing toward a clarification of the position of municipalities under the constitution. An unwillingness on the part of the cities to experiment, to test new ideas and new devices, or to pursue a concerted effort fostering a policy of less state intervention and greater local responsibility, has given no cause for presentation of the issues for public scrutiny.

As pointed out by Rodney L. Mott, home rule has made its greatest inroads in those states which

(Continued on page 545)

Learning to Work Together

*Philadelphia study reveals interjurisdictional pact is
a device more extensively used than has been supposed.*

By JEPTHA J. CARRELL*

INTERJURISDICTIONAL agreements are an integrating device and as such are the subject of increasing interest among those searching for a workable solution to the metropolitan problem.

A recent study[1] of the Philadelphia metropolitan area shows that a surprisingly large number of these compacts—some 756—have been formulated to meet the myriad difficulties which arise from the existence of an excessive number of governmental units in what is essentially a single service area.

It is evident from studies of metropolitan problems that the foremost objective in the endless quest for solutions is integration. That this is a problem which affects a large segment of the population is shown by the 1950 census, which lists 168 metropolitan areas with populations ranging from fifty thousand to almost thirteen million. These districts contain more than 55 per cent of the nation's population, and almost 30 per cent of the population total is concentrated in fourteen super-metropolitan communities, each having at least a million inhabitants.

Each of the five largest metropolitan areas embraces 500 or more units of government. In the Philadelphia district there are 686 cities, counties, boroughs, townships and school districts. The mere existence of several hundred independent units of government in one compact, urban area suggests at once the need for integration. Surveys[2] of metropolitan problems have revealed conflicts of authority, unnecessary duplications of facilities and personnel, uneven distribution of governmental services and pronounced inequities in revenue-raising capacities of the units involved.

Possible methods of integration are many and varied.[3] When structural changes are proposed, one or more of the following, or a combination of them, is usually suggested: (1) City-county consolidation and separation; (2) expansion of the functions of the county in urban areas; (3) municipal annexation and consolidation; (4) federation; (5) merger of special authorities with the central city or the county; and (6) creation of a new political entity—a metropolitan city-state.

---

*Dr. Carrell, formerly assistant dean of men at Swarthmore College (Pennsylvania) and later administrative assistant to the manager of Montgomery County, Maryland, is city manager of Xenia, Ohio.

[1] Doctoral thesis by Jeptha J. Carrell, "Interjurisdictional Agreements As an Integrating Device in Metropolitan Philadelphia," University of Pennsylvania, Philadelphia, 1953.

[2] To name a few: Victor Jones, *Metropolitan Government,* University of Chicago Press, Chicago, 1942; J. M. Leonard and Lent D. Upson, *The Government of the Detroit Metropolitan Area,* Detroit Bureau of Governmental Research (now Citizens Research Council of Michigan), Detroit, 1934; and Leonard V. Harrison, *Police Administration in Boston,* Cambridge, 1934.

[3] The classifications which follow are taken in large part from Jones, op. cit., chapters IV and V.

Most of the proposals which involve little or no change in the organization of government in the units of the district constitute a piecemeal approach, but are generally more easily achieved than are structural changes. The most important are: (1) Creation of special metropolitan authorities; (2) grant of powers to the central city to provide services and exercise jurisdiction outside the boundaries of the city; (3) transfer of metropolitan functions to the state; (4) extension of federal administration to assume metropolitan functions; and (5) interjurisdictional agreements.

The device used most extensively in the Philadelphia area, and considered most promising, is the interjurisdictional agreement.

The scope of this investigation is the Philadelphia metropolitan district as identified by the United States Census Bureau in 1950. It comprises eight counties: Philadelphia, Bucks, Chester, Delaware and Montgomery in Pennsylvania, and Burlington, Camden and Gloucester in New Jersey. Interjurisdictional agreements are taken to mean written, or clearly understood unwritten, compacts between local units. Agreements concerning the purchase of services or the rental of equipment by one jurisdiction from another are not included unless the service is one usually available only from governmental agencies.

Legal Bases for Agreements

Political subdivisions and school districts of Pennsylvania and New Jersey may exercise only those powers expressly assigned to them by the state, "those necessarily or fairly implied in or incident to the powers expressly granted," and "those essential to the accomplishment of the declared objects and purposes of the corporation not simply convenient, but indispensable."[4] Even though the power to deal with sewage problems, for example, is a local power, it does not carry with it the inherent power to cooperate with an adjacent unit in handling sewage problems jointly.

Various classes of municipalities in the Philadelphia metropolitan area have been granted express powers of agreement on such matters as airports, bridges, garbage and trash collection, health, joint purchasing, police, road construction and sewage. There are some significant omissions, however. On the Pennsylvania side, for example, there is no authorization for any political subdivision to enter into agreements for civil service and pension and retirement purposes, functions which would seem to lend themselves to interjurisdictional agreements. In none of the communities is there express provision for agreements in the joint hiring of personnel, which offer some real possibilities for sizeable savings. In building codes and planning and zoning there is a great need for inter-unit coordination but there is no express permission for such agreements in any jurisdiction other than counties of Pennsylvania.

However, the range of functions in relation to which interunit agreements may be made is a broad one.

---

[4] The "Dillon Rule," stated in J. F. Dillon, *Commentaries on the Law of Municipal Corporations*, 5th Edition, Little, Brown and Co., Boston, 1911, Vol. I, Sec. 237.

Indeed, if the potentialities of inter-jurisdictional agreements as an integrating device were exploited to the full extent permitted by law, much of the chaos, conflict and wasteful duplication now existing would be eliminated and more adequate and effective government services could be provided.

Clearly, Philadelphia area municipalities enjoy a wide range of authority to enter into interjurisdictional agreements. The "$64 question" concerns the extent to which this power is exercised. Existing agreements can be grouped under four headings: public works and utilities, protection to persons and property, education and miscellaneous functions.

Of the agreements which concern public works and utilities functions 102 deal with road construction and repair, 59 with sewage disposal, 51 with bridges, four with water supply and two with transportation.

Public Works and Utilities

Road Construction and Repair. Forty-four per cent of the municipalities on the Pennsylvania side of the metropolitan district and 31 per cent on the New Jersey side are parties to road pacts. Taking municipalities on both sides as a single group, of those having such agreements, two-thirds are signatories to only one agreement and slightly more than 27 per cent are parties to two agreements.

The integrative effect of road construction and repair agreements is somewhat limited in spite of the great number of pacts, since the bulk arises from the need to pave roads where the center line constitutes the boundary between municipalities. Approximately 40 per cent of the municipalities have one or more agreements of this nature.

Sewage Disposal. Agreements on sewage disposal have been consummated by 66 communities, or 19.5 per cent of the 339 municipalities in the district. About one-third of these 66 municipalities are parties to agreements involving the creation of an authority. Only thirteen are found in New Jersey.

Perhaps the most striking fact brought out by this part of the study is the high correlation between the degree of urbanization of a particular sector of the district and the number of sewage disposal agreements in that area. Part of that correlation is, of course, due to lack of public sewage facilities in many semi-rural sectors. The prevalence of sewage disposal agreements varies directly with population, as is shown in Table I.

Water Supply. In the Philadelphia suburban area, water supply is largely in the hands of private enterprise. Of the four agreements in this field, two concern water works jointly owned and operated by different municipalities, one deals with the joint hiring of a sanitary engineer by two municipalities and the other involves the city-county of Philadelphia and the Philadelphia Authority in development of the city's water facilities.

Bridge Construction and Maintenance. Counties are parties to 45 out of 51 agreements for construction and maintenance of bridges. This follows naturally from the fact that nearly all important construction and

TABLE I
SEWAGE DISPOSAL AGREEMENTS IN THE PHILADELPHIA METROPOLITAN DISTRICT
BY POPULATION OF MUNICIPALITIES

Population	Number of Municipalities	Number Having Agreements	Number of Agreements to Which Municipalities Are Parties
Under 1000	71	2	2
1000-5000	188	27	30
5000-10,000	47	15	22
10,000-20,000	22	11	26
Over 20,000	11	11	68
Total	339	66	a

aFigures in this column include duplications, hence total by addition is not significant.

maintenance of bridges within a county is done directly by the county. There are, however, four intertown bridge agreements and two other pacts to which a county and one or more municipalities are signatories. In the case of the Delaware River Bridge joining Camden, New Jersey, and Philadelphia, Pennsylvania, the two states are parties to an agreement.

Transportation and Other Utilities. Agreements in this field are almost unknown in the Philadelphia metropolitan district. At the time this study was made, the only transportation agreements, other than those involving school transportation, concerned the high-speed transit line which crosses the Delaware River Bridge. Both agreements involved the city-county of Philadelphia and the Delaware River Joint Commission.

It is impossible to determine the exact number of interjurisdictional agreements in the fields of public works and public utilities which have been consummated since, for example, 1930, because many municipal officials reporting agreements do not themselves have information as to the original dates of some of them. It is evident, however, from the dates of pacts which are known, that the bulk of agreements has arisen since the middle 1930s. Despite its recency, the interjurisdictional agreement has been rather extensively employed in the public works and public utilities fields.

Persons and Property Protected

Of 139 agreements relating to protection of persons and property, 134 concerned traffic lights and police protection, three public health administration and one refuse collection and disposal. Agreements in this field have facilitated the improvement of police, health and related activities in a number of cases and, in other instances, have made possible the extension of police protection and health and sanitation activities to local government areas which could not provide such services themselves. Under the agreements functional integration has been effected in some measure without disturbing the separate identity of the local governments involved.

Fire protection is an activity not directly under the control of the vast majority of local governments in the Philadelphia area. It is a semi-governmental activity carried on almost entirely by private companies. Although interjurisdictional agreements are not found in this field, the present state of intercompany coordination shows some degree of integration.

The most important agreements concern police radio communication (101). Through the use of cooperative action in this field a significant degree of coordination of the metropolitan district has been attained. Except in Montgomery County, where the county network is dominant, the largest part of interjurisdictional police radio broadcasting on the Pennsylvania side is handled by small groups of municipalities. The pattern normally shows one fairly well-to-do community operating a station and selling the service to others within radio range. The New Jersey side follows a somewhat different method. There, too, the coordination is through radio broadcasting but, instead of purchased service, the pattern is a series of interlocking monitoring arrangements, with no exchange of funds between municipalities.

Traffic light agreements, which account for the next largest number of pacts in the field of protection to persons and property, are all of a simple nature, involving the equal sharing of expenses by two municipalities for the installation, operation and maintenance of a border traffic light.

Generally speaking, municipalities of relatively small population have fewer agreements in the field of protection to persons and property than do municipalities of relatively large size.

Education

School district boundaries in Pennsylvania and New Jersey are coterminous with municipal boundaries and this has not worked satisfactorily. The excessive number of small municipalities, and municipalities with an insufficient tax base in relation to governmental needs, has been reflected in the large number of poorly equipped, inadequately staffed elementary and junior and senior high schools in suburban areas. Although the school district has power to levy its own taxes, tax money must be secured from the same tax base which is in so many cases insufficient for municipal needs.

In the last few years parents' groups, civic organizations and the Pennsylvania State Department of Public Instruction have been pressing for consolidated schools and joint schools, especially on the junior-senior high school level. Some consolidations and a substantial number of jointures (joint schools— schools which are operated by two or more districts acting together) have been effected on the Pennsylvania side. There appears to be less interest in jointures in New Jersey counties but there are examples in that sector.

Operation of joint schools is by far the most significant form of school district integration achieved by interjurisdictional agreement. However, there are other less extensive, but still important, cooperative arrangements between school districts which do not involve full

TABLE II[a]
SCHOOL DISTRICT AGREEMENTS IN THE PHILADELPHIA METROPOLITAN DISTRICT BY TYPES

Between School Districts	Number of Agreements	Number of Districts Involved
Jointures	34	124
Receiving districts	304	88
Hiring staff	10	13
Joint purchasing	1	2
Transportation	2	4
Film library	1	10
Adult classes	1	2
Between School Districts and Municipality or other Jurisdiction		
Recreation	31	31
Library	0	0
Joint purchasing	2	2
Parking	1	1
Building	2	2
Total	389[b]	200[c]

[a]Source: raw data collected in the field.
[b]There are three other agreements in which school districts are signatories, but which for various reasons are more appropriately tabulated in another way.
[c]Adjusted to eliminate duplications where one district is engaged in more than one type of agreement.

jointure. These include the joint hiring of part-time teaching specialists or administrative personnel, exchange of students for particular courses, acceptance of students in certain grades by one district in return for acceptance of that district's students in another grade or grades, and other similar agreements. Table II shows the numbers and types of school district agreements in the Philadelphia metropolitan district.

The interjurisdictional agreement as an integrating device in the field of public education has been used to a much greater extent than in any other field. Through the operation of joint schools covering all primary and secondary grades complete integration of a number of districts has been successfully carried out. Partial, but important, integration has been achieved through jointures for

junior-senior high school and for other groups of grades. What has been achieved is not likely to be dissipated for agreements are normally written compacts covering an initial period of 30 years or longer. There is relatively little cooperation, however, in the hiring of school staff members and the purchase of supplies and equipment.

There are a number of agreements between school districts and municipalities but most of them are concerned with recreation or library services. Nearly all such agreements are between a school district and its coterminous municipality.

Miscellaneous Agreements

There are some agreements in other functional fields as shown in Table III.

The relatively recent appointment

TABLE III
MISCELLANEOUS AGREEMENTS

Recreation	— 1 between 2 units of government
Airports	— 1 between 5 units of government
Housing[a]	— 5 involving 3 units of government
Joint Purchasing	— 2 involving 4 units of government
Personnel Administration and Retirement	— 1 between 2 units of government
Taxation	— 1 between 2 units of government
Zoning	— 1 between 2 units of government

[a]These may not now be operative.

of planning commissions for Delaware and Montgomery Counties, Pennsylvania, may lead in a few years to interunit cooperation in this field, but there is no immediate prospect of such action. Little increase in the number of agreements in other miscellaneous functions can be expected during the next several years, since they elicit only a minimum of official interest and little or no interest is manifest from other sources.

In spite of the excellent opportunity for savings which joint purchasing offers, municipal officials are not favorably disposed toward the practice. They claim that a joint purchasing arrangement would be "cumbersome" and would not save enough money to warrant the effort. Many seem to think, wrongly, that buying in quantity necessitates large municipal storage facilities. Some officials hesitate to enter into joint purchasing arrangements because the credit rating of their own municipality is good and they do not want it adversely affected by arrangements with financially weaker communities. The real deterrent to joint purchasing, as evidenced in a number of interviews, is the official's unwillingness to relinquish control of one of his important functions. Perhaps, if the public were better informed of the possibilities of savings through joint purchasing, there would be greater pressure on public officials to make savings in this way.

In the metropolitan district of Philadelphia there are 756 agreements in functional fields in 427 jurisdictions (including all eight counties, 218 cities, townships and boroughs, 200 school districts and one authority). Sixty-four per cent of the cities, townships and boroughs and 59 per cent of the school districts are parties to one or more agreements.

Of 686 local government units in the area the greatest number of participants in any one agreement is 49 (police radio) and most of the significant agreements involve no more than three or four parties.

Conclusions

On the basis of the record, the following conclusions may be drawn:

1. Interjurisdictional agreements for purposes of functional integration are widely used and meet with the approval of many local officials. Further exploitation of the device appears likely in a number of fields, such as sewage disposal, schools and police radio.

2. Functional integration has been achieved on a limited scale with greatest frequency in four main fields: sewage disposal (59 agree-

ments), road and bridge construction and maintenance (153 agreements), education (389 agreements) and police protection (134 agreements).

3. In the fields of garbage and trash collection and disposal, health, housing, purchasing and zoning—fields in which cooperation could provide real benefits—there is little or no integration.

4. While agreements for purposes of functional integration have been employed with increasing frequency in recent years, the record of achievement when related to the total problem is, at this time, a modest one.

The interjurisdictional agreement as an integrating device possesses certain characteristics and values:

1. It enables many jurisdictions to provide people with services through joint action which could not have been provided at all by the individual units with their limited financial resources.

2. Some jurisdictions have been able to expand and improve their services.

3. Certain economies, through reduction of overhead, elimination of wasteful duplication of equipment and large scale purchasing have been made possible.

4. A single agency is set up to provide a certain service where a number of agencies would be required to perform the same type of service in the absence of agreements. This obviously eliminates possible conflicts of authority and results in simplification of governmental machinery.

5. The optimum number of parties to an agreement varies with the subject of the agreement, population density, geography and other factors.

6. The interjurisdictional agreement is a flexible integrating device in that it may be used, within the limits of the law, for any functional purpose deemed advisable.

7. Functional integration through the interjurisdictional agreement has an unusual popular appeal because there is nothing compulsory about its use. The people and their local representatives and administrators decide in each case when and under what conditions it will be used.

It can hardly be said that the interjurisdictional agreement is an ideal solution to the metropolitan problem but, if Philadelphia is typical of other metropolitan areas, this is a device that is much more extensively used than has been supposed.

News in Review

Constitutional Revision Urged in South Dakota

Little Hoover Committee Submits Many Proposals

FIRST in a list of 29 recommendations of South Dakota's Little Hoover Committee[1] is the creation of a constitutional convention for comprehensive revision of the state's 65-year-old. constitution, which has been amended 57 times and has become long and confusing. The committee points out, however, that the procedure for establishing such a convention needs official clarification and that a period of four years or more will elapse before a convention can actually start work.

As the constitution requires that, after two-thirds of each branch of the legislature decide that a convention is necessary, the convention call must be approved by a majority of the people voting at an election for members of the legislature, the committee recommends that preparatory studies be made "to serve as a basis for action by a convention and as a means of acquainting the public with the need for constitutional revision."

The 28 other recommendations include several constitutional amendments for adoption whether or not a convention is called. Prominent among them is one to lengthen the term of the governor, lieutenant-governor and other constitutional officers from two to four years and to elect them midway between presidential elections. It is also suggested that legislative terms might well be lengthened from two years to four.

[1] *Report of the Little Hoover Committee,* (Legislative Research Council) Pierre, South Dakota, August 2, 1954. 48 pages.

The committee was appointed in 1953 by Representative Nils A. Boe, chairman of the Legislative Research Council, upon authorization by the executive board which, in turn, was charged with the responsibility of making a survey of state institutions, departments and commissions in an attempt to increase the efficiency of the state government. The 1953 legislature appropriated $20,000 for this purpose.

The board engaged Griffenhagen and Associates as consultants, to render reports on three subjects: (1) over-all administrative organization, (2) higher education and (3) the Divisions of Taxation and Licensing. Funds did not permit a detailed examination of all state departments and agencies.

Under date of August 2, 1954, the committee transmitted its 48-page report to the executive board of the Legislative Research Council.

Although South Dakota became debt-free in August of this year, the cost of its government has increased rapidly; the last general biennial appropriation act is seven times that of 1937-39. The increase is partially attributed to outmoded administrative organization. The last comprehensive organization study was made 32 years ago.

Departments Reorganized

There are now some 125 state departments, boards, commissions, agencies and institutions, with illogical grouping or overlapping of functions and dispersion of executive authority, according to the consultants, who advised that central direction could be attained by organizing state administration into fifteen basic departments. This would involve constitutional changes, especially in the field of finance. The committee made thirteen general recommendations (aside from those proposing a convention and four-year terms) as to administrative reorganization, representing a more limited amount of consolidation, as a foundation for future development.

A recommended Department of Education would be headed by a commissioner chosen by and responsible to a proposed Board of Education of seven members, appointed by the governor, with Senate approval, for seven-year overlapping terms. The present elective constitutional office of superintendent of public instruction would be eliminated by amendment to the constitution. The new department would include the State Library and the Service to the Blind, now separate agencies, and, by another amendment, the Schools for the Blind and the Deaf.

A Department of Commerce would be created, to be headed by a commissioner appointed for four years by the governor with Senate approval; it would assume the functions of the Banking and Insurance Departments, the fire marshal, the Securities Commission, supervision of incorporation (from the secretary of state) and the administrative activities of the Aeronautics Commission.

A Department of Natural Resources, likewise headed by a commissioner, would take over the conservation and regulation of oil, gas and water from existing agencies, with other functions to be determined by the legislature from time to time.

The staff and functions of the Divisions of Taxation and Licensing of the Department of Finance would be transferred to a new Department of Revenue, headed by a commissioner.

A Highway Department would be established, with a single head appointed by and responsible to the Highway Commission.

A Division of ●Administration would be created in the Department of Finance

to supervise central administrative services.

It was urged that continuous study of administrative organization matters be made by the State Affairs Committee of the legislature and an appropriate committee of the Legislative Research Council and that the legislature be given adequate professional assistance for analyzing state building, budgetary and fiscal needs.

Among eight separate recommendations on higher education a leading one proposes the consolidation of all state institutions of higher learning into a South Dakota State University system with a president as administrative head and as a contact with the legislature and the state administration. Another calls upon the legislature to authorize the Board of Regents to contract with boards of education in other states for professional education in certain specialized fields, on a reciprocal basis if possible.

The special study of the Divisions of Taxation and Licensing resulted in six recommendations for specific changes, primarily legislative, to increase efficiency and prevent abuses.

Kentucky League Stresses Legislative Program

At the 25th annual conference, held at Cumberland Falls State Park late in September, the Kentucky Municipal League adopted a series of resolutions designed to enlarge the service rendered by the league to Kentucky cities. A leading resolution called upon league officers and directors to have a proposed legislative program ready for discussion at next year's conference. Although such programs have been developed to some extent by the officers, staff and committees in the past, with specific suggestions for legislation being taken up at the conference, no broad program has been submitted in advance.

Another resolution establishes a new committee which will circulate in advance of the conference information on matters to be discussed, including the legislative program. Another directed that future conferences include special sessions for representatives of municipalities according to class—representatives of Louisville, the only first-class city, probably to meet with those of second-class cities.

A monthly news letter is to be published in place of the present quarterly, *The Kentucky City;* and special bulletins on current developments affecting cities will be prepared.

The delegates referred to the board of directors a proposal to study all state laws governing municipalities, with a view to modernization, the law schools of the Universities of Kentucky and Louisville being asked to conduct the study.

David Aronberg, mayor of Ashland, was elected president, succeeding Mayor J. J. Maloney of Covington. Mayor Andrew Broaddus of Louisville, chairman of the resolutions committee, was elected vice president.

'The Name's the Same' — Obscure Candidate Nominated

In the first primary contest (September 14) under the new Massachusetts law reviving pre-primary state conventions for the nomination of state party candidates,[1] one candidate, John F. Kennedy, described by local newspapers as an "obscure Democrat," employed at the Gillette Safety Razor plant in Canton, won the Democratic nomination for state treasurer because, the newspapers pointed out, the voters confused him with United States Senator John F. Kennedy, who was not up for election, Mr. Kennedy from Canton was the only successful candidate of those placed on the Democratic ballot by petition. Con-

[1]See the REVIEW, July 1954, page 353.

vention-designated candidates for governor and United States senator won over petition-nominated opponents. Other offices were uncontested.

The Republican slate as designated by that party's convention was uncontested.

Massachusetts' new nominating procedure differs from the National Municipal League's *Model Direct Primary Election System* in that it provides for submission of candidates by a big one-session convention instead of by a permanent state central committee of the responsible party managers.   R. S. C.

Legislative Service Conference Adopts New Name

At its seventh annual meeting, in San Francisco September 8-11, the Legislative Service Conference changed its name to National Association of Legislative Service Agencies. More than 275 state legislators and heads of staff agencies serving 39 states and two territorial legislatures participated in the meeting. according to *State Government.*

Workshop sessions dealt with legislative research, reference and library services, legislative fiscal analysis, operations of legislative clerks and secretaries, formal and substantive revision, bill drafting and legislative procedures.

Officers elected for the coming year are Ralph N. Kleps, California Legislative Counsel, president, and Robert A. Ainsworth, Jr., Louisiana state senator, vice president.

Council-Manager Plan Developments

The borough council of DANVILLE, PENNSYLVANIA, (1950 population, 6,994) has adopted the council-manager plan, according to the Danville *News* of September 15, which editorially applauds the action.

NARBERTH, PENNSYLVANIA, (5,407) has recently adopted the manager plan by ordinance.

The BENNINGTON, VERMONT, village committee for city government is drafting a charter and has been urged to adopt the manager plan.

GREENWICH, CONNECTICUT, by a vote of its representative town meeting, moved toward the council-manager plan on September 13 by voting to support a legislative bill creating a trained chief administrator who will be appointive and removable by the board of selectmen and who will be empowered to appoint and remove the heads of most of the operating departments subject to the approval of the board.

A proposed council-manager charter for MARION, OHIO, to be voted on at the November 2 election, is vigorously opposed by a group called the Independent Citizens Committee for Constitutional Government, which desires to have the offices of mayor, solicitor, auditor and treasurer remain elective.

GRAND ISLAND, NEBRASKA, voted on August 10 to retain the council-manager plan, 2,674 to 2,369.

In GARDEN CITY, KANSAS, petitions bearing 718 signatures were filed in September, asking for a popular vote on abandoning the council-manager plan in favor of the former mayor-commission plan. It was expected that the question would be on the November 2 ballot.

WATONGA, OKLAHOMA, voted 522 to 372 on September 14 against adoption of the council-manager plan.

The home rule commission of EL CAMPO, TEXAS, has adopted a tentative charter providing for the council-manager plan, to replace the present mayor-council form. Seven council members would be the only elected officials.

In ORANGE, TEXAS, the July election at which the council-manager plan was approved by the voters has been held valid by the district court. Although an appeal is pending, the *Orange Leader* states editorially that the chance of reversal is remote and urges the city council to take immediate steps to set up the council-manager plan.

In SAN ANTONIO, TEXAS, the council voted unanimously on September 23 to rescind a previous notice of intent to call an election on October 30 for the purpose of voting on proposed charter amendments for abolishing the council-manager plan. The council unofficially expressed its intention to name a commission to revise the present charter. On the same day the council declined to order a recall election, involving four councilmen, as sought by petitions that had been filed. A suit for an injunction to prevent the city clerk from certifying the sufficiency of signatures on the petitions was lost in district court on September 22. The court ordered the council to set the recall election and, on October 9, the council, with five members present (two of whom had previously attempted to resign), set it for November 16.

FORT COLLINS, COLORADO, on October 5 voted 2,133 to 1,834 for a council-manager charter in place of an existing commission-manager charter, adopted in 1939. A council of five will replace the present three commissioners.

Sixty managers, 48 from Maine and twelve from other New England states, attended the eighth New England Managers' Institute held at the University of Maine in Orono, August 22 to 26. Topic highlights included: The Job of Management, Delegation of Work, Do's and Don't's for Managers, Municipal Insurance, What Councils and Managers Expect of Each Other, Citizen Participation, Economic Status of Managers, Accounting for Small Communities, Annual Municipal Reports and Hints for Better Management.

Denver Provides for Career Service

An amendment to the charter of the city and county of Denver, creating a "career service" and Career Service Authority, was adopted by the voters at a special election on September 14, in conjunction with the primary election. The vote was 24,031 to 20,551.

The career service includes all city and county employees, with various exceptions such as city and county officers, judges, policemen, firemen, employees of the council, the auditor's office, the courts and several commissions.

The amendment creates a Career Service Authority directed by a Career Service Board of five members appointed by the mayor for five-year staggered terms, to serve without compensation. The board is authorized to make rules to govern the career service; and these must provide that: (1) appointments shall be made solely upon merit and fitness; (2) dismissals shall be only for cause, including the good of the service; (3) no discrimination shall be made because of race, color, creed, national origin or political opinion or affiliation; and (4) employees may designate agents to represent them in dealing with their superiors, the Career Service Board, the council or the mayor.

A classification and pay plan is directed to be enacted by the council after recommendations are made by the Career Service Authority, with pay rates, including fringe benefits, equal to "general prevailing rates."

The council is directed to appropriate for the authority at least one per cent of the payroll in the career service.

Present employees retain their positions without tests and shall be dismissed only in accordance with the provisions of the amendment.

Minneapolis Aldermen Retain Two-year Terms

At a special election on September 14 in Minneapolis, Minnesota, a proposed charter amendment to establish four-year staggered terms for members of the board of aldermen received 53,614 favorable votes as against 45,922 unfavorable votes, but failed to obtain the requisite 60 per cent of the total vote thereon. The total city registration was reported as 276,997, and the total vote at the election, 107,426.

The amendment, proposed by the city's charter commission, specified that aldermen from odd-numbered wards would be chosen at the next election for four-year terms and those from other wards for two-year terms, with four-year terms for all aldermen thereafter.

The Citizens League of Greater Minneapolis, which has favored four-year terms but not on a staggered basis, took no definite position on the amendments.

Dead Candidate Polls 2,435 Votes

In Spokane, Washington, one John F. McKay, a candidate for Congress, died August 25, 1954, too late for the removal of his name from most election ballots in his congressional district. The death was well publicized by press and radio but the Associated Press reports that with 463 of the district's 620 precincts counted, about one-third of the votes, 2,435, were nevertheless cast for the dead man.

College Students Prepare City's Annual Report

The current annual report for the city of Cortland, New York, has been prepared by ten graduate students from Cornell University at nearby Ithaca. The students were enrolled in municipal administration courses at the Cornell School of Business and Public Administration and worked as a staff for the mayor of Cortland in preparing the report.

The project was part of a two-year program during which architecture students are scheduled to prepare a master

(Continued on page 552)

County and Township .   .   .   . *Edited by Edward W. Weidner*

Houston to Study
City-county Merger

Fulton County Voters
Support Consolidation

MAYOR Roy Hofheinz of Houston, Texas, has appointed a committee of three city councilmen to map plans for possible merger of the governments of the city of Houston and Harris County. Chairman of the committee is Councilman George Marquette, who requested that the committee be appointed. He has asked the city attorney for a formal ruling which would outline the procedure necessary to effect a merger.

"I realize the actual merger may take some time, inasmuch as it will take a constitutional amendment," said Mr. Marquette, according to the Houston *Chronicle*, "but we have to start some time and now is as good a time as any." Both Mayor Hofheinz and County Judge Bob Casey have stated they are in favor of such a merger. Judge Casey comments, however, that he has no plans for bringing the matter before the county commissioners. "I think the action should stem from the citizens rather than governmental agencies," he said.

Fulton County Vote

Voters of Fulton County, Georgia, at the September 8 primary election, were asked to express their opinion on the question, "Do you favor a complete consolidation of Fulton County and City of Atlanta governments?" The vote was advisory only and about one-seventh of those who went to the polls expressed an opinion, according to the Atlanta *Journal*. But a majority of those who did so are in favor of consolidation. The unofficial count on the question was 6,659 "yes" and 4,814 "no."

This is the second time in recent years such a question has been on the Fulton County ballot. In 1952 the question was, "Do you favor one government for all citizens of Fulton County?", which was overwhelmingly approved.

County Official Offers
Good Advice

"Sound advice was given to county officials everywhere by William R. MacDougall," reports *Better Roads* for August in an editorial titled "Good Medicine for Counties." Mr. MacDougall, general manager of the County Supervisors Association of California, offered his advice in a talk before Colorado county commissioners at the University of Colorado. Quoting from the *Better Roads* editorial:

Increase the power of the board of supervisors or its equivalent in the management of county affairs, he counseled. Consolidate existing independent county offices and reduce the number of elected county officials. Create the position of county administrative officer in all medium and large-size counties. Centralize administration of county roads as a county-wide operation. Practice functional consolidation of services now performed separately by counties, cities and special districts to a larger extent.

These are not proposals drawn from the papers of theorists, Mr. MacDougall said; they are all developments that have been tested in actual practice in California.

Florida Attorney General
Holds County Manager Illegal

According to Attorney General Richard Ervin of Florida, answering a question raised by State Representative Henry S. Bartholomew of Sarasota, a county commission may not delegate its powers to a county manager. He added, however, that it would appear the legislature could authorize the county board to employ a person whose duties would be to act as the agent of the board, to supervise only the business affairs of the county which are under the board's control. As reported in the Sarasota *Journal,* Representative Bartholomew asked the attorney general for a ruling because of inquiries from numerous Sarasota County residents interested in the plan.

County Officials
Hold Annual Meeting

The 1954 annual meeting of the National Association of County Officials was held in Omaha in June. It resulted in recommendations on a number of issues confronting county government.

In the field of intergovernmental relations, and with special reference to the national Commission on Intergovernmental Relations, it was recommended that at least two days of hearings be held by the Commission's study committee on payments in lieu of taxes so that members of the association might have an opportunity to present to the committee results of their studies on the subject. It was recommended that association members contact their congressional delegations, urging that such hearings be held, that county government had not yet been adequately heard by the commission or its study groups. The association pledged its aid to the commission.

A second set of resolutions concerned welfare. Here again grants-in-aid were uppermost in the association's mind. For example, it was suggested that an endeavor to secure a just and equitable distribution of grant-in-aid funds, without the necessity of increasing federal appropriations for this purpose, be made and also that counties be aided in minimizing

the shock caused by abrupt cessation of any type of federal service given to Indians, particularly in the fields of health, welfare and hospitalization.

Among the resolutions adopted was one approving the continuing efforts of the counties of western states to obtain permission for national forest cutting receipts to be used as directed by each county's governing body for schools, roads or other governmental functions in the proportion that the public interest in each county may require from time to time.

The conference felt that there should be no change made in existing provisions of law for payment by the federal government of half the cost of administering public assistance programs.

Civil defense provided the central discussion for another set of resolutions. In this area the officials urged the Federal Civil Defense Administration to give immediate and special study to the problems of the American rural counties near urban areas, including the problems of emergency highways and policing.

Noting that reevaluation of civil defense plans is now in order and that the international situation has assumed an intensely threatening character, the association went on record as favoring renewed efforts to support the Federal Civil Defense Administration and all the local civil defense agencies wherever and whenever possible. The entire program of civil defense as now carried on must be strengthened.

One of the highlights of the meeting was an address by Dr. George C. S. Benson, research director of the Commission on Intergovernmental Relations, who reviewed the problems before the commission. Other addresses were on highway development, reviewing the objectives of a rather extensive study by the Highway Research Board Committee on highway laws, and on "The Drift Toward Socialism."

Taxation and Finance　　•　　•　　•　　•　　*Edited by Wade S. Smith*

Legislatures Amend Tax Laws in 1954

None of 20 States Holding Sessions Adopt New Taxes

ALTHOUGH the twenty state legislatures holding sessions in 1954 did not adopt any new taxes, more than half amended existing laws in one or more respects, according to a round-up of the off-year sessions made by the Federation of Tax Administrators.

Arizona completely revised its income tax legislation, raising rates in the $1,000 to $10,000 brackets by ½ of 1 per cent to 1 per cent, providing a standard optional deduction of 10 per cent of adjusted gross income up to $500, and changing the form of the personal exemptions from credits against the tax liability to allowances against taxable income. Income taxpayers in Kentucky were granted extended use of optional tax tables and of a standard deduction. Both these states and Colorado provided for withholding of the tax by employers.

Massachusetts lowered its normal tax on earned income of individuals, while Rhode Island extended a previously enacted temporary increase in corporation income tax rates. Virginia, which has a tax credit feature geared to the overrun of revenues as compared with budget estimates affecting both individuals and corporate income taxpayers, raised the levels at which the credit is allowed. Previously enacted temporary decreases in individual income tax rates were extended another year by New York and Colorado.

Four states revised taxes affecting motor vehicle transportation. Louisiana amended its special fuels tax to place collection responsibility on the distributor instead of on the dealer, and imposed additional motor vehicle tax fees for overweight vehicles. Kentucky revised its motor fuel tax laws to provide a use tax on interstate carriers while New Jersey raised the gasoline tax from three cents to four cents per gallon. Mississippi raised its maximum weight limitations and adjusted the motor vehicle license rates for the heavier vehicles.

Cigarette taxes were raised to three cents per pack in Kentucky, compared with a previous rate of one cent per ten cents of selling price. Utah taxes went from two cents to four cents per pack. Kentucky also raised its tax on wine from 25 cents to 50 cents per gallon and on beer from $1.50 to $2.50 per barrel. Maryland increased the tax on distilled spirits from $1.25 to $1.50 per gallon and prohibited local imposition of alcoholic beverage taxes. In Texas, the beer tax was increased from $1.37 to $2 per barrel. New Jersey increased liquor license fees.

No state changed its sales tax rates in 1954 but Rhode Island extended through May 31, 1955, a temporary 1 per cent tax imposed earlier. Procedural changes were made in the sales tax laws in Louisiana, Maryland, South Carolina and Mississippi, the latter extending to all cities the privilege of imposing a ½ of 1 per cent sales tax formerly extended to a limited group of cities.

Extensive changes were also made in taxes in the District of Columbia. Individual income tax rates were raised to a range of 2.5 per cent to 4 per cent compared with 1.5 per cent to 3 per cent previously, while the 1 per cent retail sales tax was extended to certain foods previously exempted. The gas tax was increased from five cents to six cents per gallon and motor vehicle license fees were increased. The tax on distilled spirits was raised also, from 75 cents to $1.00 per gallon, while the beer tax went from $1 to $1.25 per barrel and the tax on wine from fifteen cents to twenty cents per gallon.

State-local Voters Faced Heavy Election Calendar

Despite the fact that 1954 is an "off-year," state and local voters found no dearth of fiscal proposals on their ballots when they went to the voting precincts in November. Constitutional amendments, according to preliminary indications, were fewer than in most recent years, but the volume of new bond proposals was half again as high as in 1953, with state and local issues aggregating roundly $1,500,000,000 compared with about $1,000,000,000 last year.

A few bond proposals were of substantial size and large authorizations in general were more numerous than in recent years. New York State voters faced the largest individual propositions —one for issuance of $350,000,000 for mental hospitals and another of $200,000,000 for slum clearance. California voters were called on to decide on two big proposals also. One was of $175,000,000 for veterans' loans and the other of $100,000,000 for state school building aid loan bonds. Both were to provide additional money for programs already in operation, California voters having approved $80,000,000 of veterans' loan bonds following World War I and $380,000,000 following World War II, as well as $435,000,000 school building aid loan bonds in 1949 and 1952. In Michigan, an $80,000,000 veterans' bonus issue was on the ballot, augmenting $230,000,000 previously voted in 1947.

At least half a dozen cities submitted bond proposals in the $20,000,000 and over range. These included submission of $74,630,000 in Philadelphia, $39,900,000 in Cleveland, $32,500,000 for school

district purposes in Long Beach, California, $25,308,000 for building purposes in Los Angeles County, California, $25,100,000 in Seattle, and $19,580,000 for various purposes in San Francisco.

Local units also submitted a variety of special propositions to their citizens. Sacramento voters were called on to choose whether to acquire a privately owned bus system while Omaha voters considered granting a 25-year exclusive franchise to a bus company. In Denver, where financing has already been secured for a municipal parking project, a referendum was held on a proposal to authorize a permit to a private company to extend a parking lot under a city street. In Texas, a constitutional amendment was up for consideration to permit creation of county hospital districts, a device sought by civic leaders in Houston and some other centers to circumvent present limitations on city and county taxes.

Kansas Counties Heavy Users of Fiscal Aid

County governments in Kansas receive more than one-third of their current revenues from state and federal aid, according to a recent study of the League of Kansas Municipalities. By far the largest allocations were for social welfare; according to the league, county revenues in the fiscal year ended June 30, 1954, for this purpose included $18,485,000 from federal funds and $12,142,000 from the state welfare accounts, a total of $30,627,000. For county roads and bridges a total of $7,100,000 of fiscal aid was received, $3,600,000 from the state's county and township road funds and $3,500,000 from state gas tax allocation. In addition, $3,755,000 of federal highway funds were expended on approved county secondary road projects during the year, but not handled by counties. General county funds benefited by receipt of $1,311,000 from the cig-

(Continued on page 545)

Proportional Representation • •

Edited by George H. Hallett, Jr. and Wm. Redin Woodward

(This department is successor to the Proportional Representation Review)

Cincinnati Committee Formed to Uphold P. R.

Hare System Supported by Leading Citizens

THE Committee to Protect the Charter, composed of sixteen prominent persons associated with various civic, social and economic groups in Cincinnati, was formed recently to assist in the campaign opposing a proposed charter amendment seeking to substitute a form of limited vote for the proportional representation method of electing councilmen. Cincinnati has used P.R. since 1927.

Former Mayor Murray Seasongood, nationally known authority on municipal law, is honorary chairman. Mrs. Albert D. Cash and Mrs. Russell Wilson, both widows of former mayors, are honorary vice chairmen.

Active co-chairmen are Charles P. Taft and William A. Geoghegan, who, shortly after the committee was constituted, issued a statement denouncing the limited vote proposal as a monstrosity. They referred to it as an English scheme abandoned there 75 years ago and abandoned also in New York in 1882 after nine years' trial and in Boston in 1898 after four years' trial. As reported in the Cincinnati *Times Star,* they remarked:

P.R. has an outstanding record in Cincinnati. It has produced good councils, which have conducted the city's business on a basis designed to give Cincinnati the best streets, the best sewer system, the best lighting, the best traffic control, the soundest financial base, the best personnel operation, the best master plan and the best manager in the United States.

P.R. also insures that no minority machine can elect more than a minority of the council. This is what the self-styled "improvers" of the so-called Charter Improvement League don't like.

A vote on the substitute proposal was scheduled for the general election on November 2.[1]

Swedish Cities Hold P. R. Elections

Municipal and district council elections were held in Sweden on September 19 by the list system of proportional representation. Only the Conservatives were able to increase their number of votes, according to reports from the American-Swedish News Exchange. Attendance at the polls reached nearly 80 per cent, somewhat less than in the previous municipal elections, held in 1950.

According to preliminary figures for the entire country, not including absentee ballots, the Social Democrats polled 47.8 per cent of the votes as compared with 48.6 per cent in the 1950 elections. Corresponding figures for the other parties were: Liberals, 21.6 per cent, compared with 21.7 per cent in 1950; Conservatives, 15.2 per cent, compared with 13.2 per cent in 1950; Agrarians, 10.4 per cent, as against 12.3 per cent in 1950; and Communists, 4.9 per cent in both 1954 and 1950.

Both of the two largest parties lost ground slightly in the capital city of Stockholm. In the 100-member city council the Social Democrats now hold 41 seats and the Liberals 31 as the result of polling the equivalent percentage of the vote. This is a loss of two seats for the Social Democrats and a loss of four for the Liberals.

---

[1] See the REVIEW, September 1954, page 421.

The Conservatives gained three seats for a total of twenty and the Communists also gained three for a total of eight. The distribution of seats corresponds closely to the vote by party tickets, as the party list system of P.R. normally assures, but the Communist gain represents only a slight increase in the vote because that party failed to get fully proportional representation in the 1950 election (as may happen when a party is very small and the election is conducted in districts).

In the following table, in the column of percentage of votes, the change over the 1950 percentage is shown by the parenthetical figures.

Party	Votes Cast	Percentage of Votes	Seats Obtained
Social Democratic	177,413	40.8(—1.7)	41
Liberal	135,218	31.1(—1.8)	31
Conservative	88,639	20.4(+3.5)	20
Communist	33,430	7.7(+0.2)	8
Agrarian	265	.06	—

Combination System Used in Schleswig-Holstein

In the election of a provincial legislature by the state of Schleswig-Holstein on September 12, a modified form of proportional representation, similar to that used by other West German states and by the West German Federal Republic, was used. This system is based on district majority elections followed by a distribution of additional seats at large in such a way as to make the total results approach proportionality.[1] In the Schleswig-Holstein version of the system 42 of the 69 members of the legislature were elected by single-member districts, while the remaining 27 were chosen from party tickets on a proportionalizing basis.

The Social Democrats made a substantial gain over the previous election a year earlier, climbing from 26.5 per cent to 33.2 per cent in popular votes. They elected the largest number of single-member district seats, 22, and obtained three more on the proportionalizing distribution, for a total of 25.

The Christian Democrats, with almost as many votes, also obtained 25 seats, but only 20 of these were obtained by districts, and the proportionalizing feature of the electoral system was needed to give them the parity with the Social Democrats which they deserved because of their popular vote. The 32.2 per cent of the vote obtained by the Christian Democrats was a come-down for that party, however, as it had obtained 47 per cent of the poll in 1953.

The All-German Refugee party, the next in size, polled 14 per cent of the vote and obtained ten seats in the legislature, all of them by virtue of the proportional feature of the electoral system.

[1]For a description of the system see the REVIEW, October 1949, page 460.

SCHLESWIG-HOLSTEIN, ELECTION OF SEPTEMBER 12, 1954

Party	Votes Cast	Percentage of Votes	Seats Obtained	Percentage of Seats
Social Democratic	396,067	33.2	25	36.2
Christian Democratic	384,874	32.2	25	36.2
All-German Refugee	157,319	14.	10	14.5
Free Democratic	89,414	7.5	5	7.2
Schleswig-Holstein Bloc	61,270	5.1	4	5.7
Communist	24,730	2.3	—	—
German Reich	17,318	1.5	—	—
Federal German	10,009	0.8	—	—
Land	1,028	0.1	—	—

This party is allied with the Christian Democrats in Schleswig-Holstein, so that these two parties are preponderant in the state government with their slight majority in the legislature.

Although the Free Democrats, who received 7.5 per cent of the votes and five seats, are allied with the Christian Democrats in the federal parliament, they are in the opposition group in the Schleswig-Holstein legislature. The results of the election as reported in the *New York Times,* accounting for all but about 3 per cent of the vote, which may have been cast for scattered independent candidacies, are given in the table on page 544.

HOME RULE STILL A FARCE
(Continued from page 525)

sponsor aggressive associations of municipalities.[5] The most vivid example in recent years of the validity of this statement has been portrayed in Tennessee.

The League of West Virginia Municipalities had its inception during the early '30s, although the formal authorization of such action was extended by the legislature twelve years later. Restrictions contained in the law have never permitted adequate financing of league activities. A municipality is prohibited from contributing to the league an annual sum in excess of one cent per capita. As a result, the league has never been financially capable of sustaining a staff adequate to conduct the research necessary to

---

[5]*Home Rule for America's Cities,* Chicago, American Municipal Association, 1949, page 18.

buttress a realistic program. Instead, municipal officials must be content to stand hat in hand in legislative halls begging for bread in hopes that an occasional crumb will be cast their way.

Some members of the legislature have voiced concern over the need for documented facts as a basic requirement for a more intelligent solution to the current problems of municipal government. The legislature, however, has no regular research arm, although some attention has been directed to general problems of municipalities by interim committees. Under the circumstances, responsibility for the presentation of facts rests heavily upon the municipalities themselves and, until this is fully recognized and undertaken, few constructive results can be anticipated.

TAXATION AND FINANCE
(Continued from page 542)

arette tax and $426,000 from the liquor tax.

All these direct aids, which aggregated $39,464,000, exclude the county share of the state sales tax, which functions under the Kansas setup as a replacement for general property taxes, the individual units being eligible to share in the allotment only if and to the extent that their several fund tax levies are within the respective legal limitations set by statute. This aid included $615,000 for the welfare funds and $1,560,000 for county road and bridge funds. The total budget estimate of all county government expenditures for 1954 was $107,517,000.

Citizen Action .   .   .   .   .   .   *Edited by Elsie S. Parker*

Citizen Committees Render Reports

Cover Budgets, Police, Taxation and Economics

THE Citizens Advisory Tax Commission of Alexandria, Virginia, has published its report to the city council, *Alexandria's Tax System* (80 pages), as well as a summary report, *Alexandria's Taxes* (16 pages). Fifteen thousand copies of the latter have been distributed on a door-to-door basis by off-duty firemen, reports the city manager's office. Citizen response has been good and, during the consideration of the current budget program, there appears to have been a greater understanding on the part of the citizens that demands for services and improvements must be financed by taxes. The committee of seven members was appointed by the city council in March 1952.

The Report of Findings of the 25-member Citizens Advisory Committee on the Civil City Budget for 1955 was submitted to Mayor Alex M. Clark of Indianapolis in August. In addition to a "Summary of Budget and Tax Levy Reductions" recommended by the committee, and "General Observations," there are reports of four subcommittees—for the general fund and administration, park department, department of sanitation and department of health and hospitals.

The Citizens' Police Advisory Committee of San Jose, California, has completed three years of work, reports *Public Management* for September. The 32-member group was formed to study specific police problems and to foster a closer relationship between the police department and the citizenry. "The committee is broadly representative of the community and includes representatives of trade associa-

tions, parent-teacher groups, the press, radio, labor, veterans' organizations and other groups," reports *Public Management*. Among the problems discussed at its meetings are vice conditions, including certain forms of amusement and liquor licenses, police department man power and the possible construction of a new police headquarters building.

Citizen committees, with technical assistance from the University of Wisconsin, have completed a comprehensive economic survey of Kenosha, Wisconsin, reports Richard H. Custer, city manager, in *Public Management*. Purposes of the survey were "to inventory and appraise the strong and weak points of Kenosha's industrial and commercial life and to determine how the weak points can be strengthened." The report, *Kenosha—Its Economic Life and Related Aspects,* is divided into three parts: Part I, *Findings* (70 pages), Part II, *Findings* (113

©*The Des Moines Register and Tribune*

"Gad, when I think of the power the people have . . . it just isn't fair."

pages) and Part III, *Conclusions and Recommendations* (48 pages).

Albuquerque Citizens Group Reorganizes

The Citizens Committee of Albuquerque, New Mexico, organized in 1952, has reorganized on a somewhat more formal basis and adopted a new constitution. In its original form the committee confined itself to the study of various municipal problems, presenting its report to the city government. Finding that this approach was not productive of results, the committee, in the fall of 1953, decided to support candidates for the three vacancies in the city commission to be filled at the April 1954 election.[1] The efforts of the committee were so successful that the organization made its decision to reorganize with a larger program.

According to the new constitution, the purposes of the committee are:

1. To study municipal problems;
2. To ascertain public opinion on municipal affairs;
3. To disseminate information on municipal affairs;
4. To support and encourage sound practices in municipal government;
5. To formulate and promote city ordinances and state legislation bearing on municipal affairs;
6. To select and support suitable candidates for municipal offices;
7. To take such other actions as may contribute to the furtherance of good municipal government in Albuquerque.

The committee is completely nonpartisan in nature.

Citizen Planning Group Activities

The Citizens' Council on City Planning of Philadelphia acted as co-sponsor of the National Planning Conference of the American Society of Planning Offi-

[1]See the REVIEW, July 1954, page 368.

cials, held in Philadelphia in September. Earlier a large steering committee was formed, under the chairmanship of the council's executive director, which handled the many local details of the conference. Topics ranged from "Preservation of Historical Areas" to "New Communities—Lessons to Be Learned." A joint luncheon attended by CCCP delegates and planners was addressed by Mayor Joseph S. Clark, Jr., on "Local Government and the Next Decades." Citizens' Council president, John W. Bodine, presided.

The city-county planning committee of the Municipal League of Spokane, Washington, held a special dinner meeting in September to discuss "Planning for Spokane." City Plan Director Harry Aumack was the speaker.

The Greater Dallas Planning Council has just distinguished itself by having its budget of $50,000 oversubscribed, according to *Planning and Civic Comment,* official organ of the American Planning and Civic Association. . . . The Wheeling Area Conference on Community Planning has published *Today and Tomorrow in the Wheeling Area,* outlining planning projects under way in that city as well as tasks ahead. . . . The Buffalo and Erie County Planning Association, organized 34 years ago, is issuing a new publication, *The Planner.*

Membership Drive Success

For the second consecutive year, reports *Greater Cleveland,* bulletin of the Citizens League of Cleveland, the number of new members joining the league in its annual membership drive has exceeded 500. The 1954 drive added 598 members, exceeding the 501 for 1953. Success of the campaign is attributed to the drive and enthusiasm of Vice President Earl M. Richards, chairman of the membership committee, and Bernard H. Schulist, league board member and chairman of the general committee.

Know Your Government

Sponsored jointly by the Citizens League of Greater Minneapolis and the League of Women Voters of that city is a "Know Your Local Governments" course, taught by teams of university professors and government officials. The course, covering seven Thursday evenings, was offered through the adult education program at the YMCA.

Government Charts

The Hamilton County Research Foundation has published a four-page *Organization of Government in Cincinnati and Hamilton County*, which should be of value to local citizens. Accompanying a brief description of the two governments are charts for both city and county.

New Publications

Here are some recent publications which should be of interest to civic workers and groups.

So, You've Been Elected Publicity Chairman—Or, How to Make Friends with the Editor (22 pages) has been published by the Occidental Life Insurance Company of California at Los Angeles.

Recreation in the City of Worcester (17 pages), published by the Citizens' Plan E Association of Worcester, Massachusetts, has been presented to the Parks and Recreation Commission of the city.

Participation in Organized Activities in a Kentucky Rural Community (28 pages), by Paul D. Richardson and Ward W. Bauder, has been published by the Kentucky Agricultural Experiment Station at the University of Kentucky, Lexington.

The Church Federation of Greater Chicago has prepared *The Role of the Church in Community Conservation* (10 pages) in cooperation with the Office of the Housing and Redevelopment Coordinator of the City of Chicago. It is a report of a special conference on neighborhood conservation with a supplement recording developments in community conservation as of January 1954.

Emory J. Brown is author of *Who Take Part in Rural Organizations?* (36 pages), published by the Agricultural Experiment Station of the Pennsylvania State University at State College.

Young People and Citizenship (230 pages), by Edward B. Olds and Eric Josephson, is available from the National Social Welfare Assembly, 345 East 46th Street, New York 17, at $1.50. The report represents a cooperative effort on the part of many organizations, social workers, educators and social scientists and is concerned with the manner in which young people are prepared for responsible citizenship.

Citizens Report

The Citizens' Civic Association, Inc., and Citizens Council of Allen County, Indiana, tell of their activities in *1950—4 Years of Stimulus to Citizen Initiative and Helpful Service to Local Citizens—1954* (16 pages).

New Organization

A Citizens League has been inaugurated in Ketchikan, Alaska. Emery F. Tobin is chairman of publicity.

Strictly Personal

The executive committee of Citizens of Greater Chicago has announced the resignation of its executive director, Fred K. Hoehler. Mr. Hoehler's assistant, Robert Farwell, has been appointed acting director.

Mrs. Charles H. Wood has been named the new president of the Santa Fe Citizens Union; Eppie Chavez is vice president and Albert K. Nohl, secretary-treasurer. Principal project of the union is the securing of the council-manager plan for Santa Fe.

Researcher's Digest .   .   .   .   .   *Edited by John E. Bebout*

Time to Attack
Metropolitan Confusion

Pennsylvania Cities Need
Enabling Legislation to Act

EDITOR'S NOTE.—The article below is taken from "Time to Attack Metropolitan Confusion," appearing in the September 1954 issue of *Horizons for Modern Pennsylvania Local Government,* issued by the Associated Institutes of Government of Pennsylvania Universities—Pennsylvania State University, University of Pennsylvania and University of Pittsburgh.

METROPOLITANITIS, a condition arising from clusters of people in and around cities, is resulting in numerous governmental problems for cities throughout Pennsylvania. Showing no favorites, this condition is producing confusion and problems for eastern Pennsylvania cities including Allentown and Scranton, encompassing Harrisburg and Altoona among cities in middle Pennsylvania, and stretching to such cities as Johnstown and McKeesport in western Pennsylvania. Although a more serious problem calling for remedial legislation will not face the 1955 session of the Pennsylvania General Assembly, it has received little consideration in pre-assembly literature and discussion.

The complexities of modern living and citizen demands for governmental services have thrust upon municipalities the responsibility for maintaining public safety, guarding public health, providing needed utilities, building highways, constructing housing, developing recreational facilities, caring for the diseased, disabled and the poor, and a multitude of other services. The problems faced by a governmental unit in providing these services adequately and economically are staggering in any municipality, but they become multiplied many times where large num-

bers of people aggregate to form heavily populated areas. If the population has sprawled beyond the legally recognized limits of the central city into unincorporated areas or suburban cities, the need and demand for such services does not stop at the artificial and man-made boundaries of the central city even though the legal authority for providing these services does stop at such boundary lines.

Such aggregations of people are metropolitan areas—areas of urban population which are economically interdependent upon one or more central cities but which are politically independent of the central city. This condition of overlapping interdependence in economic and social matters and restricting independence in political matters is resulting in governmental confusion. The legal authority to provide the necessary governmental services demanded by the citizens of the area is splintered among a number of separate municipalities; as a result, the level and adequacy of services varies considerably from one unit to another.

Such a condition is a characteristic symptom of the metropolitan problem, which may be described as involving the need for providing services for a large population scattered over an area of land under the jurisdiction of many units of local government, a number of which are too small, are crippled by limited power to act, or are handicapped by inadequate tax resources to provide a larger number of services or more adequate services.

The types of problems described above are common to most growing municipalities in Pennsylvania. The same problems exist in small commercial and industrial communities but are less acute than in the large cities recognized as metropolitan centers. A city of 10,000 encircled by five or six small suburban communities has essentially the same problems in providing adequate and uniform services to its outlying neighbors as does a city of 100,000 with ten to twenty fringe communities. The number of citizens to be served and the number of governmental units involved is smaller, but the problems are identical in kind if not in degree.

Expanding Populations

The trend toward citizen concentration in cities has been a continuing phenomenon in Pennsylvania throughout its history. Seven out of every ten persons (70.5 per cent) in Pennsylvania in 1950 were residents of a municipality of 2,500 population or more compared to an average of 64 per cent for the nation as a whole. Of more pertinent interest, however, is the continuing tendency of Pennsylvania's population to cluster in and around a small number of large cities. Pennsylvania had fifteen cities of 50,000 or more population in 1950 and contained twelve standard metropolitan areas, as such areas are designated by the United States Bureau of the Census, embracing 81.8 per cent of the state's total population.

The big growth in the last two decades has been occurring in the fringe communities of large cities rather than in the center cities. For the decade 1930-1940, populations of central cities in the twelve metropolitan areas increased only 0.7 per cent in comparison with a growth of 38.4 per cent in outlying communities. In the last decade, the comparative growths were 155,815 persons, or 4.3 per cent, for central cities and 426,830 persons, or 9.9 per cent, for the fringe communities. By 1950, 56 per cent of the total population in these twelve areas resided in suburban communities. Five center cities actually declined in population in the last decade.

It is evident from this brief analysis that the state is burdened with the growing problem of declining cities and expanding fringe communities. This is the source of numerous problems for both the central cities and for the outlying areas arising from the disproportion be-

tween population distribution and the artificial boundaries of municipal corporations. Since many of these problems arise from the complex governmental structure within these metropolitan areas, it is pertinent at this point to take a look at the number of governmental units in the officially recognized metropolitan areas of Pennsylvania.

The combined twelve metropolitan areas contain a total of 2,627 governmental units including 1,257 school districts, 25 counties, 691 townships, 438 municipalities of over 1,000 population, 173 municipalities of under 1,000 population and 43 special districts. Such large numbers are not so revealing when lumped together so the number of governmental units in two of the metropolitan areas are given below to indicate the true complexity of the problem.

Complex Structure

The Lancaster metropolitan area, covering Lancaster County in central Pennsylvania, embraces 59 school districts, one county, 41 townships, nineteen municipalities of over 1,000 population, one municipality of under 1,000 population, and one special district—a total of 122 governmental units. The Reading metropolitan area in eastern Pennsylvania is limited to Berks County and yet it extends over 142 governmental units including 66 school districts, one county, 43 townships, 21 municipalities of over 1,000 population, ten municipalities of under 1,000 population and one special district. These numerous and overlapping local governmental units try to cope with the problems of providing municipal services for their citizens, but their best efforts result in much duplication of effort, uneven levels of service, often inadequate service, and unequal charges for similar services rendered from community to community.

The continued growth of a large number of governmental units in and around major population centers stems primarily from a concept of democracy that implies that government is best which is closest to the scrutiny and control of the people governed. This is still an important and generally true concept, but the complexity of governmental problems and the inability of many small units of government to cope with them defeats the theory of popular control. Local popular control is effective only if the citizenry is adequately served by its unit of government. Inadequate services and continued failure of neighboring governmental units to solve mutual problems jointly will only result in the continued encroachment of higher levels of government into areas which are rightfully functions of local government.

The problems of metropolitan populations are area-wide, and it is becoming recognized that the problems faced by local governments within a metropolitan area are also area-wide. A smoke abatement program in outlying communities is of little value on days when the wind blows in smoke from the central city unless the central city has a similar program. A system of highways and traffic feeder streets is a matter of area-wide concern so that people and goods can move freely and rapidly. Fleeing criminals can avoid capture by moving across the unmeaningful boundaries of one small unit into another, since the jurisdiction of the pursuing policeman stops at the sign reading "city limits."

While there is a growing recognition that such problems as those listed above are area-wide problems of mutual concern to governmental units, there is not such wide acceptance of the idea that it would be mutually beneficial to work together in solving them. Further, there is no legislation in Pennsylvania authorizing or permitting such joint action upon common problems, a void which should be bridged in the next legislative session by passage of a bill allowing the voluntary creation of metropolitan districts to carry on the governmental functions which the

member municipalities would voluntarily give to them.

A bill providing for such authorization was introduced and passed by the Pennsylvania Senate in 1949. It was sponsored by the Senate Local Government Committee and became known as the Pennsylvania Metropolitan Bill. After passage in the Senate, it was sent to the House of Representatives during the last two days of the session and was lost in the shuffle of activity characteristic of the closing of any legislative session, although there was no opposition indicated in the House.

The bill was not revived during the sessions of 1951 and 1953 largely, we suppose, because there was no organized effort to arouse interest in it. We hope, however, that the bill will be re-introduced in the 1955 session and that it will be enacted into law since the problems of government in metropolitan areas are more complex and numerous than ever before.

Objectives of Bill

In general, the bill authorized the voluntary creation of metropolitan districts by cities of the third class, boroughs and townships as municipal corporations to carry on jointly governmental functions which the participating governmental units would voluntarily give to the metropolitan district to perform. The legislation provided that the governing body of such a metropolitan district should be composed of one representative from each of the member municipalities and should be called a metropolitan commission. This metropolitan commission could not levy taxes or collect revenues but could charge for its services or facilities; it would not be allowed to exercise any governmental functions except those specifically designated to it by the participating municipalities.

The governing body of each participating municipality would elect one representative to the commission, designate by ordinance which of its governmental functions the metropolitan commission would take over, approve the annual proposed budget of the metropolitan district, and assume a proportionate share of the expenses.

Legislation similar to the Pennsylvania Metropolitan Bill would strengthen the principle of home rule because it would make it possible to provide modern, efficient local government at the local level. It would establish a local governmental organization for the real economic community which would be able to take care of urban needs and provide a uniform level of municipal services for the area's citizens in the fields in which the local units voluntarily entrusted it to perform. Making local government more effective is the one sure means of curbing further state expansion into areas primarily of local concern.

Research Groups Merge

Merger of the Philadelphia Bureau of Municipal Research and the Eastern Division of the Pennsylvania Economy League became effective October 1. Lennox L. Moak, formerly director of the Philadelphia bureau, will head the joint operation.

The merger is a "merger of activities" rather than a "merger of organizations." Both the league and the bureau will keep their individual identities and have their own boards of directors. The two boards will name a joint operations committee which will keep a close supervision over the activities of the staff under the direction of Mr. Moak.

In announcing the merger it was stated that the combined operation would enlarge the scope of activity and operate with better coordination and efficiency to provide a more effective program on behalf of good government.

Baltimore Planning System

A special series of bulletins on *Baltimore's City Planning System* has been prepared by the Baltimore Commission on Governmental Efficiency and Economy. These bulletins appraise the organization and operations of the city's planning department and present recommendations on how to make planning and capital budgeting more effective instruments of government.

(Listings of research pamphlets and articles are combined with the listings at the end of Books in Review.)

CITY, STATE AND NATION
(Continued from page 538)
city plan for Cortland and business and public administration students are slated to formulate a capital budget to supplement the plan.

The 32-page booklet, which summarizes year-round activities of Cortland city departments, includes charts on the city organizations, expenditures and municipal bonds, types of fires, maps on zoning, traffic accidents, schools, and parks, as well as photographs of officials and places of interest in the community.

Japan Has Central Laboratory on Death Causes

The *Tokyo Municipal News*, published in English, relates that the American Occupation developed in Japan the first systematic examination of mysterious deaths with a central laboratory in Tokyo to assist the criminal and police authorities by supplying medical evidence in cases referred by the latter.

The single laboratory serves all Japan and, of course, falls far short of bringing the benefits of medical examiner service to all unattended deaths. It does only 4,000 cases a year and aids in determining the cause of death.

So far as it goes, it follows the best American practice as promoted by the National Municipal League.   R. S. C.

Books in Review

ADVENTURES IN POLITICS. We Go to the Legislature. By Richard L. Neuberger. New York, Oxford University Press, 1954. xi, 210 pp. $3.50.

The title of this book is a happy one. Obviously, the author, Oregon state senator, journalist, champion of the natural and human resources of his native northwest, has inherited the zest for adventure that helped build America. He rightly regards politics as one of the great adventures of free men.

A Democrat in a heavily Republican state, he takes evident satisfaction in surmounting obstacles that have discouraged less hardy spirits and makes political mountain climbing sound exciting, important and rewarding. The fact that Senator Neuberger has a wife who is his companion in politics, even to the extent of being a member of the lower house of the state legislature, is a special advantage that no one will begrudge him. In a 22-page appendix, entitled Politics and You, he gives practical answers to 33 questions that should help any political pioneer get his bearings and chart his course.

There are really two themes running through the book. One has to do with personal participation in political life. The other, somewhat more sombre, is suggested by the title of Chapter I, What's Really Wrong with State Governments?

State government, Mr. Neuberger observes, "has fallen upon sorry days when a substantial body of public opinion regards any natural resources entrusted to the care of the states as practically gone forever." He attributes "the decline of state government in the United States, a deterioration which has accumulated in recent years," to basic weaknesses in the states themselves. Specifically, he mentions a number of those listed in the editorial, "Spotlight on

State Legislatures," on page 516 of this issue. He puts particular emphasis on the deadening influence of the one-party system which prevails in so many portions of the country, and pays his respects to people who orate about the importance of the two-party system in Washington while doing their best to prevent the growth of such a system in their own state or community.

Mr. Neuberger feels that any state that adopted a constitution based on the National Municipal League's *Model State Constitution* would "have laid the foundation and erected the scaffolding for an effective new edifice of government." Throughout the book Mr. Neuberger shows a refreshing appreciation of the importance both of machinery and of men. He recognizes the necessity for sound plans and equipment, as well as personal courage and skill, for worthwhile adventures in politics.

J. E. B.

AMERICAN STATE LEGISLATURES. Report of the Committee on American Legislatures of the American Political Science Association. Belle Zeller, Editor. New York, Thomas Y. Crowell Company, 1954. ix, 294 pp. $3.50.

The latest evidence of increasing interest in our state legislatures is the recent excellent report, *American State Legislatures,* prepared after four years of study by a committee of the American Political Science Association under the able chairmanship of Professor Belle Zeller of Brooklyn College.

From their high position of leadership, power and prestige under the early state constitutions, our state legislatures have in the last century and a half passed into a kind of partial eclipse. Few would quarrel with Professor Zeller's statement that "the state legislatures are poorly equipped to serve as policy-making agencies in mid-twentieth-century America."[1]

But despite this situation and despite occasional murmurs of discontent, the conviction that our legislatures are the core of our representative democratic government remains general and firm. Most of us will assent whole-heartedly to the committee's belief that "the state legislatures can—and should—function as dynamic, coordinate, efficient policy-formulating bodies."[1]

Within the last three or four decades there have been gratifying signs of improvement. The growth of legislative services and the work, in this and related areas, of the Council of State Governments come to mind. But much remains to be done; and the new report provides a timely call to arms for one of the most important causes in the field of governmental reorganization.

The report is essentially a survey of facts, problems and current practical thinking regarding state legislatures. Its data and recommendations are intended to serve as a basis for reform and also to stimulate interest and further study. In keeping with its survey approach and practical orientation, the report does not undertake any extensive reexamination of basic theory—though it is to be hoped that it will encourage needed explorations of this fundamental kind.

The report considers the major aspects of legislative organization and operation. Many of the chapters, such as those on Legislative Sessions and Organization, Role of the Executive, and Pressure Groups, furnish a first-rate, concise review of their subject-matter. Recommendations for reform follow most of the chapters. The result is a volume which will make an ideal desk- or hand-book for legislators, teachers, students and other interested citizens.

In general, the recommendations are moderate and realistic. A few highlights

[1]Preface, page v.

are: a special administrative agency outside the legislature to deal with apportionment; a reappraisal of the merits of bicameralism as against unicameralism; removal of time, pay and frequency limitations on the length of sessions; reform of the committee system; establishment of legislative councils and expansion of legislative services. Some of the recommendations may stir controversy but the majority should command wide approval.

There are minor caveats to be entered. Not all chapters are on a par. That dealing with The Constitutional Basis of State Legislatures naturally reflects the fact that not enough studies are available with respect to the effect of state constitutional restrictions. The committee rightly pleads for more research on this topic. In at least one vital area, The Committee System, the committee might well have explored more deeply the implications and interrelations of subjects treated. Thus, this reviewer would have preferred a fuller consideration of the role of the state standing committees—a role so significantly different from that of the congressional standing committees—and of the relation between the standing committee system and interim committees. Also, might not that role and that relation, as well as the functions of the legislative council, be substantially affected by the advent of the longer and more frequent sessions advocated by the committee?

Beyond these matters, there is some reason to fear that the manner in which the committee's recommendations are presented may encourage confusion between major and minor reforms. The question of comparative emphasis—as between the recommendations of different chapters, for example—does not seem to have been given systematic attention. The texts of the various chapters afford some, but not enough, guidance. Is there not a danger that the want of highlighting will give aid and comfort to a "tinkering" approach in cases where much more is called for? In any case, a concluding chapter, setting the topics and recommendations of the report in a somewhat clearer perspective based upon their relative importance and urgency, would have been most helpful.

The few caveats noted are not intended to suggest any considerable doubts about the basic merits of the APSA committee report. It is my opinion that this report is a timely contribution, that a worthwhile task has been well done, and that all hands concerned are to be congratulated on their labors. It seems to me that there is ground too for realistic hope that this report may have unusual success in achieving its aims of providing a basis for reform and stimulating further thought and action on a vital problem. In doing so it will perform a major public service.

JOHN M. KERNOCHAN, *Director*
Legislative Drafting Research Fund
Columbia University

Additional Books, Pamphlets and Articles

Annexation

ANNEXATION? INCORPORATION? A Guide for Community Action (Second edition, revised.) By Stanley Scott. Berkeley 4, University of California, Bureau of Public Administration. March 1954. 163 pp. $1.50.

ANNEX OR SERVE YOUR SUBURBS? By Edmund W. Meisenhelder III. Nashville 3, Tennessee Municipal League, *Tennessee Town and City* (Section edited by Municipal Technical Advisory Service of University of Tennessee). July 1954. 5 pp.

TENNESSEE'S NEED FOR NEW STATUTES ON ANNEXATION. By Harlan Mathews. Nashville 3, Tennessee State Planning Association, *The Tennessee Planner,* June 1954. 7 pp.

Budgets

A BUDGET MANUAL FOR WISCONSIN CITIES AND VILLAGES. (Revised edition.) Madison 3, League of Wisconsin Municipalities, 1954. Variously paged. $1.00.

Census

A STATEWIDE CENSUS EVERY FIVE YEARS. By Dorothee Strauss Pealy. Ann Arbor, University of Michigan, Bureau of Government, Institute of Public Administration, April 1954. 54 pp.

Charters

IDEAS FOR CHARTER COMMISSIONS. By George R. Sidwell. Lansing (Michigan), 1954. 165 pp. $5.00. (Apply author, 1527 W. Ionia Street, Lansing 15.)

Corrupt Practices

FLORIDA'S NEW CAMPAIGN EXPENSE LAW AND THE 1952 DEMOCRATIC GUBERNATORIAL PRIMARIES. By Elston E. Roady. Washington 6, The American Political Science Association, *The American Political Science Review,* June 1954. 12 pp.

Council-Manager Plan

A MODEL CHARTER FOR CITIES OF OKLAHOMA INCLUDING A DIAGRAM OF COUNCIL-MANAGER GOVERNMENT. (Revised edition.) By Charles F. Spencer. Ada (Oklahoma), June 1954. 15 pp. mimeo.

Debt

CONSTITUTIONAL DEBT CONTROL IN THE STATES. New York, The Tax Foundation, 1954. 40 pp.

Decentralization

OFFICE BUILDINGS IN THE SUBURBS. By Frederick P. Clark. Washington 6, D. C., Urban Land Institute, *Urban Land,* July-August 1954. 8 pp.

Directories

CIVIC EDUCATION IN THE UNITED STATES. A Directory of Organizations. By Robert Horwitz and Carl Tjerandsen and the staff of the University of Chicago Committee on Education for American Citizenship. Chicago, University of Chicago, University College, 1954. xx, 219 pp.

DIRECTORY OF ORGANIZATIONS AND INDIVIDUALS PROFESSIONALLY ENGAGED IN GOVERNMENTAL RESEARCH AND RELATED ACTIVITIES 1954-1955. New York 21, Governmental Research Association, Inc. 60 pp. $5.00.

PUBLIC ADMINISTRATION ORGANIZATIONS. A Directory of Unofficial Organizations in the Field of Public Administration in the United States and Canada. Chicago, Public Administration Clearing House, 1954. xi, 150 pp. $2.50.

Education

EXPENDITURES FOR EDUCATION AT THE MID-CENTURY. By Clayton D. Hutchins and Albert R. Munse. Washington, D. C., U. S. Department of Health, Education and Welfare, Office of Education, 1953. vi, 136 pp. Charts and tables. 65 cents. (Apply U. S. Government Printing Office, Superintendent of Documents, Washington 25, D. C.)

NEW JERSEY PUBLIC SCHOOL FACILITIES SURVEY. Phase I. An Inventory of Existing Public School Facilities, Needs and Resources. Trenton, New Jersey State Department of Education, Bureau of School Building Services, Division of Business, April 1954. 74 pp.

PUBLIC SCHOOL FINANCING 1930-1954. The Need for Local Solution to Rising Costs. New York 20, The Tax Foundation, Inc. 1954. 52 pp.

SCHOOL BOARDS AND SUPERINTENDENTS. (Revised edition.) A Manual on Their Powers and Duties. By Ward G. Reeder. New York, The Macmillan Company, 1954. xi, 254 pp. $3.50.

TEXAS PUBLIC SCHOOLS 1854-1954. Centennial Handbook. Austin, Texas Education Agency, 1954. vii, 59 pp.

Elections and Voting

THE MICHIGAN STATE DIRECTOR OF ELECTIONS. By Glendon A. Schubert, Jr. University, University of Alabama Press, June 1954. 65 pp.

Federal Aid

FEDERAL GRANT-IN-AID PROGRAMS. Report of the Committee on Social Legislation. Washington 6, D. C., Chamber of Commerce of the United States, Economic Research Department, 1954. 36 pp. 50 cents.

Forms of Government

FORMS OF CITY GOVERNMENT IN CONNECTICUT. By Max R. White. Storrs, University of Connecticut, Institute of Public Service, February 1954. 54 pp. 50 cents.

Government and Business

THINKING AHEAD. Businessmen and Government. By Joseph W. Alsop, Jr. (Reprinted from Harvard Business Review, May-June, 1954.) Cambridge, Harvard University, 1954. 7 pp.

Industrial Development

ALASKA'S LARGEST CITY—ANCHORAGE. An Analysis of its Growth and Future Possibilities 1951-1952. By Ralph Browne. Juneau, Alaska, Alaska Development Board, December 1953. 90 pp.

Industrial Tax Exemption

LOUISIANA'S INDUSTRIAL TAX EXEMPTION PROGRAM. By William D. Ross. Baton Rouge, Louisiana State University, Division of Research, College of Commerce, 1953. 87 pp. Tables.

Land Use

URBAN LAND PROBLEMS AND POLICIES. By Charles Abrams. New York, United Nations, Housing and Town and Country Planning, Bulletin 7, 1953. 182 pp. $1.75.

Legislatures

THE LEGISLATURE OF CALIFORNIA. By Arthur A. Ohnimus. Sacramento, California Legislature, Assembly, 1954. 47 pp.

Metropolitan Areas

THE FRINGE PROBLEM. Many Cities Face Strangulation from Without Unless a Good City Services Policy is Followed. By Harlan Mathews. Charlotte 1, North Carolina, Clark-Smith Publishing Company, The Municipal South, June 1954. 3 pp.

METROPOLITAN GOVERNMENT AND PLANNING. A Selected Bibliography. By the Joint Reference Library. Chicago 37,

American Municipal Association, 1954. 33 pp. $1.00.

SUBDIVISION AND FRINGE AREA CONTROL. By Dennis O'Harrow. New York 19, American Public Health Association, *American Journal of Public Health.* 3 pp.

Pension Fund Investment

A SURVEY OF PENSION FUND INVESTMENT PROBLEMS. A discussion of some of the investment practices that might be considered by public retirement systems. Chicago 37, Municipal Finance Officers Association, June 1954. 4 pp. 75 cents.

Planning

CITY PLANNING IMPLICATIONS OF INDUSTRIAL LOCATION. By Francis A. Pitkin. Minneapolis 14, League of Minnesota Municipalities, *Minnesota Municipalities,* August 1954. 3 pp.

URBAN PLANNING EDUCATION IN THE UNITED STATES. By Frederick J. Adams. Cincinnati, The Alfred Bettman Foundation, 1954. 58 pp.

Political Parties

THE AMERICAN PARTY SYSTEMS. By Austin Ranney and Willmoore Kendall. Washington 6, The American Political Science Association, *The American Political Science Review,* June 1954. 9 pp.

PARTIES, PARTISANSHIP AND PUBLIC POLICY IN THE PENNSYLVANIA LEGISLATURE. By William J. Keefe. Washington 6, The American Political Science Association, *The American Political Science Review,* June 1954. 15 pp.

Refuse Disposal

THE REFUSE PROBLEM IN DELAWARE COUNTY. A Survey of Refuse Collection and Disposal. Philadelphia 7, Pennsylvania Economy League in Cooperation with the Delaware County Planning Commission, May 1954. 76 pp.

Roads

COUNTY UNIT ROAD ADMINISTRATION IN TEXAS. By T.·E. McMillan, Jr. Austin, The University of Texas, Institute of Public Affairs, 1954. vii, 54 pp.

State Government

A LAYMAN'S GUIDE TO THE TEXAS STATE AGENCIES. (Revised edition.) Austin, University of Texas, Institute of Public Affairs, 1954. 173 pp. $1.50.

NEW JERSEY—THE STATE AND ITS GOVERNMENT. (Revised edition.) By Leonard B. Irwin. New York, Oxford Book Company, 1953. iv, 124 pp. 90 cents.

Streets and Highways

AS A CITIZEN OF OKLAHOMA YOU SHOULD KNOW ABOUT COUNTY ROAD EXPENDITURES. (A series of articles reprinted from the Tulsa *Tribune.*) Oklahoma City 2, Oklahoma Public Expenditures Council, 1954. 14 pp.

THE FEDERAL AID HIGHWAY ACT OF 1954. How Municipalities Obtain $350,-000,000 Federal Aid. By Randy H. Hamilton. Chicago 37, American Municipal Association, May 1954. 8 pp. 50 cents.

PROBLEMS INVOLVED IN THE IMPROVEMENT OF CITY STREETS. By Philip N. Royal. (Excerpts from address before the Seventh Northwest Conference on Road Building, Seattle.) Seattle 5, Association of Washington Cities in cooperation with the University of Washington, Bureau of Governmental Research and Services, May 1954. 10 pp.

Taxation and Finance

A CRITIQUE OF SOME FEDERAL, STATE AND LOCAL TAX COORDINATION TECHNIQUES. By Burton W. Kanter. Reprinted from *Indiana Law Journal,* Vol. 29, No. 1. Indianapolis 4, Indiana State Bar Association. 17 pp.

FINANCING GOVERNMENT. (Fourth edition.) By Harold M. Groves. New York, Henry Holt and Company, 1954. ix, 618 pp. $6.00.

1954 CONFERENCE PROCEEDINGS. Chicago 37, Municipal Finance Officers Association, *Municipal Finance,* August 1954. 56 pp.

STATE TAX COLLECTIONS IN 1954.

Washington 25, D. C., Department of Commerce, Bureau of the Census, Governments Division, 1954. 10 pp. 10 cents.

STATE TAX LEGISLATION IN 1953. Princeton (New Jersey), Tax Institute, Inc., *Tax Policy*, November-December, 1953. 40 pp.

THE TAXATION OF INTANGIBLES IN SOUTH DAKOTA. By C. J. Whitlow. Vermillion, University of South Dakota, School of Business Administration, Business Research Bureau, *South Dakota Business Review*, May 1954. 3 pp.

Technical Assistance

FIFTY YEARS OF TECHNICAL ASSISTANCE. Some Administrative Experiences of U. S. Voluntary Agencies. By Edwin A. Bock. Chicago 37, Public Administration Clearing House, 1954. x, 65 pp. $1.50.

Text Books

ELEMENTS OF AMERICAN GOVERNMENT. (Second edition.) By John H. Ferguson and Dean E. McHenry. New York, McGraw-Hill Book Company, Inc., 1954. x, 649 pp. $5.00.

Tort Liability

COGITATIONS ON TORTS. (Third in the Roscoe Pound Lectureship Series.) By Warren A. Seavey. Lincoln, University of Nebraska Press, 1954. 72 pp.

Tourist Trade

HOW STATES FIND OUT ABOUT THEIR TOURIST TRADE. By Robert S. Friedman. College Park, University of Maryland, Bureau of Governmental Research, 1954. 43 pp.

Town Clerk

THE NEW HAMPSHIRE TOWN CLERK. By Gilbert Cantor. Durham, University of New Hampshire, Public Administration Service, 1954. 12 pp.

Town Meeting

THE CONNECTICUT TOWN MEETING. A Handbook for Moderators and Other Town Meeting Officials. (Revised.)

By Max R. White. Storrs, University of Connecticut, Institute of Public Service, 1954. 39 pp. 25 cents.

Township Government

TOWNSHIP GOVERNMENT IN KANSAS. By James W. Drury. Lawrence, University of Kansas, Governmental Research Center, 1954. 72 pp. Tables.

Transportation

JOINT REPORT ON THE PROBLEM OF PROVIDING IMPROVED MASS TRANSPORTATION BETWEEN THE CITY OF NEW YORK AND NEW JERSEY—WESTCHESTER—LONG ISLAND. New York, New York Metropolitan Rapid Transit Commission and New Jersey Metropolitan Rapid Transit Commission, March 1954. 102 pp.

Urban Redevelopment

A BRIGHTER FUTURE FOR AMERICA'S CITIES. A Complete Report on the Businessmen's Conference on Urban Problems, San Diego, California, March 4 and 5, 1954. Washington, D. C., U. S. Chamber of Commerce, 1954. 149 pp. $1.00.

A FIGHT-BLIGHT PLAN FOR BINGHAMTON, N. Y. Binghamton, Broome County Planning Board, December 1953. xi, 70 pp.

Utilities

HANDBOOK ON UTILITY FRANCHISES. Boulder, Colorado Municipal League, 1954. 50 pp. $2.50.

SOME ASPECTS OF MUNICIPAL UTILITY ADMINISTRATION IN ALABAMA. By Robert T. Daland. Montgomery, Alabama League of Municipalities, 1954. 26 pp.

Water

WATER SUPPLY AND WASTE WATER DISPOSAL. By Gordon Maskew Fair and John Charles Geyer. New York, John Wiley & Sons, Inc. 1954. ix, 973 pp. $15.

Zoning

ZONING FOR THE PLANNED COMMUNITY. By Fred W. Tuemmler. Washington, D. C., Urban Land Institute, *Urban Land*, April 1954. 8 pp.

tuted for a session on state and regional planning. Richard S. Childs, chairman of the League's executive committee, will preside.

Chairmen of panel sessions not announced in the October issue of the NATIONAL MUNICIPAL REVIEW are as follows:

"Youth in Civic Affairs"—Mark Bills, superintendent of schools in Kansas City.

"Business and Professional Men as Civic Leaders"—Alex R. Thomas, chairman, San Antonio Citizens' Committee and building materials executive.

"State Reorganization: Where Do We Go From Here?"—John A. Perkins, president of the University of Delaware.

On November 7, the Charter Clinic will hold a luncheon meeting at which further sessions will be arranged. John M. Kernochan, director, Legislative Research Drafting Fund of Columbia University, will be the chairman.

The annual membership meeting of the National Municipal League will be held at 4:30 P.M., November 8, with President George H. Gallup in the chair.

The Proportional Representation League will hold its annual meeting at 9:30 P.M. the same day.

The National Association of Civic Secretaries will have a reception and buffet dinner at 6:30 P.M., November 8. This function will be followed by a civic workshop.

tionally known experts in a meeting of the Advisory Committee on Federal-local Relations of the Commission on Intergovernmental Relations in Kalamazoo, Michigan. Shown clockwise from foreground are Bebout; William Coleman, of the commission staff; Richard J. White, Jr., county commissioner, Milwaukee County; L. P. Cookingham, city manager, Kansas City, Missouri; Henry Pirtle, mayor, Cleveland Heights; Sam Jones, former Governor, Louisiana; Billie Jo Tanner, secretary; Carl H. Chatters, consultant to the advisory committee; and G. A. Treakle, former president, National Association of County Officials.

League Makes Statement at U. S.'s Request

The National Municipal League in October forwarded a 54-page statement entitled "American Intergovernmental Relations as of 1954" to the Commission on Intergovernmental Relations, established last year by Congress. This document was prepared by the League staff at the request of the commission.

The statement points out that the only safe and certain way to retard or reverse the current trend toward centralization of authority in Washington is to make the states more responsive, more effective and more representative of rapidly expanding urban interests.

In stressing the need for strengthening state and local government, the necessity for modernizing state constitutions and the importance of coming to grips with metropolitan area problems, the statement takes a position long familiar to League members.

80 Contribute to Remodeling Fund

The campaign to raise funds for renovating the League's new headquarters at 47 East 68th Street, New York 21, has moved into high gear.

Ten days after President George H. Gallup invited League members to contribute to the Remodeling Fund, 80 checks totalling $2,646 had been received.

First response came from Joseph B. Milgram, of Brooklyn, New York, a member since 1930. Mr. Milgram's letter was postmarked the day he received the appeal from Dr. Gallup. His check was twice the amount of his membership dues.

The second contributor was Mrs. Olga McLaney, senior member of the League staff in terms of service.

The building, which was acquired last month and will be named for Carl H. Pforzheimer, League treasurer, must be remodeled to make it suitable for office use and to comply with the New York City building code. Partitions must be shifted, plumbing and electric lines relocated, a sprinkler system installed and the elevator altered. The entire interior must be painted.

Magazine Reprints Article

The article on page 518 of this issue of the REVIEW, "A Home Town Is Born," will be condensed in the current *Reader's Digest*. This is the second REVIEW article so honored by the popular monthly this year. The first, by Council member Karl Detzer, appeared in May under the pen name, Michael Costello.

The League was honored by the National Citizens Committee for Educational Television during a broadcast of America's Town Meeting of the Air last month. Raymond H. Wittcoff, chairman of the committee, presented a citation to Dr. George H. Gallup, League president, praising the League's support of educational TV. Photo shows Mr. Wittcoff reading the citation. Dr. Gallup is at his left.

News of the League

1955 Conference to Be in Seattle

For the first time since 1912, the National Conference on Government will be held on the west coast next year.

The National Municipal League Council has voted unanimously to hold the 61st Annual Conference in Seattle, Washington, July 24 to 27, 1955. Officers of the League and others who attend the annual session regularly are already making plans to combine attendance at the Seattle meeting with a vacation trip through the Pacific Northwest and the Canadian Rockies.

The 1955 conference will be held in conjunction with the Twentieth Annual Institute of Government of the University of Washington.

A large delegation from Seattle attended the 60th Annual National Conference on Government in Kansas City last month with a view to bringing the function, the only one of its kind in the United States, to their city. The formal invitation was extended by Ben B. Ehrlichman, president of the First National Corporation, Seattle, and regional vice president of the National Municipal League; C. A. Crosser, executive secretary of the Municipal League of Seattle and King County; and Donald Webster, director of the Bureau of Governmental Research, University of Washington. The Seattle group lobbied for the 1955 Conference by distributing "Delicious" apples, Indian-made totem poles, and six-inch Douglas firs advertised to grow to 80 feet.

Five other cities vied for the honor of playing host to the conference. They were: Cleveland, Ohio; Dayton, Ohio; Fort Wayne, Indiana; Phoenix, Arizona; and Washington, D. C.

Mr. Ehrlichman was named general conference chairman for 1955 by the League's Council.

The first National Conference on Government was held in Philadelphia in 1894. Since then the meeting has been held in the far west only once—in Los Angeles in 1912.

Conference in Pictu

The 60th Annual National Confere
Government, held last month in Kans
Missouri, broke several records. The reg
was larger than ever. The number of out
delegates exceeded that in previous yea
attendance at luncheon meetings attaine
high. Public interest, as manifested
coverage by newspapers, radio and televi
by the presence of more than twenty out
correspondents, reached a new peak. T
of the conference is told in pictures on t
pages and on pages 614 and 615. As i
years, those who framed the conference
have operated on the principle, "All work
play," etc., etc. One of the features
year's meeting was a steak roast at the r
Saddle & Sirloin Club, outside of Kans
Out-of-town visitors, guests of the local
ence committee, first repaired to the bar
received steaks of grand proportions (le
then did away with them in the club'
room (below). Entertainment followed.

OPPOSITE PAGE: An innovation
Kansas City conference was a daily b
meeting (top), at which members of ea
got together and planned their sessio
agreed that this preparation made for a
performance in each of the 21 panels
program. Addresses by the luncheon spe
the conference, Thomas R. Reid, Mrs. Do
Dolbey and Dr. George H. Gallup (left t
center), may be found in this issue
NATIONAL MUNICIPAL REVIEW.
gathering at the final luncheon of the co
(bottom) provided a suitable climax to th
four-day program.

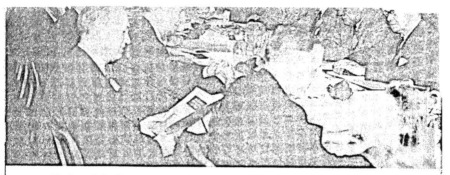

Members of the Council of the League held their annual meeting in Kansas City following the 60th Annual National Conference on Government. Sitting around the table from left to right are: Mark S. Matthews, Ben B. Ehrlichman, John Nuveen, Jac Chambliss, Lee M. Sharrar, John S. Linen, Bayard E. Faulkner, L. P. Cookingham, Mrs. Maurice H. Noun, Francis A. Harrington, Richard S. Childs, George H. Gallup, Alfred Willoughby, Carl H. Pforzheimer, Thomas Graham, Mrs. Albert D. Cash, John E. Bebout, L. E. Marlowe, E. Bartlett Brooks, Robert H. Rawson, Arthur W. Bromage, Alex B. Thomas, Lloyd Hale and Allen H. Seed, Jr.

League Names Gallup, Linen, Others

Dr. George H. Gallup, director of the American Institute of Public Opinion, was reelected president of the National Municipal League at its annual meeting in Kansas City, Missouri, last month.

John S. Linen, vice president of the Chase National Bank of New York, and George S. Van Schaick, counsel of Oliver and Donnally and former New York State Superintendent of Insurance, were reelected vice presidents.

The following were elected regional vice presidents:

Jac Chambliss, Chattanooga, Tennessee, lawyer and civic leader; Thomas R. Reid, Dearborn, Michigan, director of civic affairs, Ford Motor Company; and Mark S. Matthews, Greenwich, Connecticut, former president, United States Junior Chamber of Commerce.

Newly elected members of the Council are: Herbert Emmerich, Chicago, director, Public Administration Clearing House; Francis A. Harrington, Worcester, Massachusetts, former presi-

dent, Citizens' Plan "E" Association of Worcester; Arthur B. Richardson, New York City, president, Chesebrough Manufacturing Company; James M. Osborn, New Haven, Connecticut, research professor of English, Yale University; Major General Otto L. Nelson, Jr., USA retired, Princeton, New Jersey, vice president, New York Life Insurance Company.

Also Frank C. Moore, Kenmore, New York, former lieutenant governor and comptroller of New York State and president, Governmental Affairs Foundation; L. E. Marlowe, Richmond, Virginia, former president, Richmond Citizens Association; Mrs. Siegel W. Judd, Grand Rapids, Michigan, former president, League of Women Voters of Michigan and of Grand Rapids; Roscoe C. Martin, Syracuse, New York, former vice president, American Political Science Association; and Robert H. Rawson, Cleveland, Ohio, former chairman, Citizens Committee for the Ohio Constitution.

National Municipal Review

Volume XLIII, No. 11　　　　　　　　　　　　　　　Total Number 449

Published monthly except August

By NATIONAL MUNICIPAL LEAGUE

The contents of the REVIEW are indexed in *International Index to Periodicals*
and *Public Affairs Information Service*.

Entered as second class matter July 11, 1932, at the Post Office at Worcester,
Massachusetts. Publication office, 150 Fremont Street, Worcester 3; editorial
and business office, 542 Fifth Avenue, New York 36. Copyright 1954 by the
National Municipal League.

Subscription, $5 per year; Canadian, $5.25; foreign, $5.50;
single copies 50 cents.

Editorial Comment

Risks in the Two-party System

A GOOD deal was said during the recent campaign about the supposed apathy of the voters and the prospect of a light vote. Now that the late returns are in, it appears that the vote was light, the contrary statements of election night news analysts notwithstanding.

Other things being equal, a large vote is a good thing. The extent of chronic non-voting in our country is a danger signal that we ought to heed. The danger, however, cannot be disposed of by berating the non-voters. Unless they are driven to the polls as they are behind the iron curtain most people are not inclined to vote just for the fun of it or as a matter of form. Most of us need to have something to vote for or against to get us to the polls under our own power. Often what passes for apathy or indifference is really a considered conclusion either that a given election is unimportant or that it is impossible for the voter to tell which way his interest really lies.

It appears obvious that many voters decided to sit out the recent campaign because the candidates and their spokesmen had not given them a valid basis for the kind of convictions that take them to the polls. In some states and districts issues did become clearer and choices easier to make as election day drew near and some of the doubtful voters made up their minds.

On the other hand, some of the increased interest may have been due not so much to more light as to the greater heat generated during the closing days of the campaign by orators on both sides. People do respond to heat as well as to light. When their prejudices or dormant emotions are aroused, it is quite possible for them to develop a false sense of clarity and conviction. The closer the contest is, the more important the emotional reactions of a minority of the voters may be.

The elections of 1952 and 1954 seem to demonstrate that for the time being national elections and elections in an increasing number of states, both south and north, are likely to be close and energetically contested. This should be a good thing. It is generally taken for granted that democracy is best served by the two-party system. It certainly is true that voter participation is heavier where election contests are real and the outcome is not obvious before the votes are cast. The current trend should invigorate the parties and reduce the sharpness of old sectional divisions.

On the other hand, the two-party system involves risks and entails obligations which we ignore at our peril. A major risk is that, when contests are habitually close, campaigners are tempted to resort to cheap tricks and demagogic devices to corral votes that are for sale to the highest emotional bidder. This is a temptation to which spokesmen for both our parties have succumbed much too often for the good of the country.

Another temptation presents itself to the party which wins control of city, state or nation by a narrow margin. That is the temptation to visit reprisals on the opposition by misuse of the power to fire and hire and the power to investigate. It has been noted, for example, that while one-party states can maintain a fairly stable career service without a formal merit system, two-party states without such a system tend to observe the old rule, "to the victor belong the spoils."

We desperately need to develop a sense of political ethics and responsibility on the part of party leadership, candidates and elected officials that will reject methods that are destructive of the democratic system they exist to serve. Even more important, we must develop, by every method of civic and political education, a citizenry increasingly immune to spurious and narrowly selfish appeals. There will always be irresponsible minorities but it is not worth while for politicians to cater to them at the risk of alienating the solid core of their supporters.

There is mounting evidence that, while most Americans profess a basic attachment to one or the other of the major parties, more and more of them feel free to jump party lines whenever a valid reason is presented. When enough thoughtful voters are as ready to punish irresponsible action by their own party as some minorities are to respond to demagoguery, it is more worth while to cater to reason and to public interest than to passion, prejudice and greed.

A mere readiness to jump the party traces is not enough, however. More good citizens must get into the political act. They must vote in the party primaries which, by comparison with our general elections, are disgracefully neglected. They must also be ready to work in the party vineyards and to run for and accept party offices and the responsibilities for political leadership that go with them.

The NATIONAL MUNICIPAL REVIEW has always stressed the obligation to take part in party politics as well as in the nonpartisan citizen activity by which so much good has been wrought during the last 50 years in the modernization of city charters and the reform of local politics. At Kansas City, as at previous National Conferences on Government, there were sessions specifically devoted to political education and political participation by young people in schools and colleges, by women, by labor and management, by business and professional men— by all elements in our society.

As we move closer to a nationwide two-party system, we come closer to the democratic ideal of government by the expressed choice of all the people. Whether that will also mean responsible government for the good of the state or the nation as a whole will depend increasingly on our capacity for self-discipline, on our respect for one another and for the rules of fair play, and on the genuineness of our patriotism.

A Plea for High Standards

*Gallup, calling our system complicated and top-heavy,
hopes for solutions from current United States study.*

By GEORGE H. GALLUP*

ONE development that points toward growing political maturity in our country is the progress that has been made in disentangling strictly local issues and elections from state and national politics. About 60 per cent of the elections in municipalities over 5,000 are now on nonpartisan ballots. I realize that some people believe this trend will endanger the vitality of the two-party system. But their alarm is completely misdirected.

One reason why many of our most thoughtful citizens have found it distasteful to engage in party politics has been that they could not abide the entrenched local party machine nourished largely by patronage. We still have too many such machines but many of them have passed out of existence or have been seriously weakened.

In many cities like Cincinnati there never was a real two-party system at the local level until a charter had been adopted which encouraged voters to line up on local issues regardless of their national party attachments. Often when that condition has developed the local organizations of the national parties attract more citizens who are interested in principles and issues, with the result that the influence of the grass roots organizations of the state and national parties is more wholesome and constructive. That development has, I understand, been going on right here in Kansas City during the last few years. Now that the old machine no longer feeds at city hall, people like your mayor, who cooperate without regard to party in city affairs, find it possible to play much more effective roles in the local organizations of the national parties.

It was pointed out in an editorial in the October number of the NATIONAL MUNICIPAL REVIEW[1] that because of our complicated system of government "citizenship is a more exacting calling in the United States than it is in most other free countries." The facts behind this observation explain much of the non-voting and ill-advised and ineffective voting that occurs. No other country in the world has so many elections. In no other country are citizens asked to vote at the same time for so many offices at so many levels of government—national, state, county, municipal, school district and sometimes others. And in no other country are voters asked to say "yes" or "no" on so many issues, whether important or trivial, as are commonly presented by initiative or referendum action in many of our states.

*Dr. Gallup, president of the National Municipal League, is founder and director of the American Institute of Public Opinion. He is author of numerous books and articles on public opinion and citizenship. The article above was prepared for delivery by Dr. Gallup at the League's National Conference on Government, November 10, 1954.

[1]See "The Complete Citizen," page 447.

The people of California passed on twenty amendments to their state constitution as well as candidates for United States Senate, Congress, governor, state legislature and other offices, while the people of Louisiana were asked to vote on 31 proposals, one-third of which, according to the Louisiana Public Affairs Research Council, involved strictly local issues rather than statewide basic policy.

The conscientious voter may well conclude that if he has no basis for a valid opinion it is better not to kid himself and the public by decorating his ballot with every X he is allowed to make.

Short Ballot Aid to Voter

Thanks to the short ballot movement, inaugurated by Woodrow Wilson and our own Richard S. Childs almost a half century ago and carried on through the National Municipal League's *Model State Constitution, Model City Charter* and other publications, ballots in many parts of the country are less formidable than they used to be. We have a long way to go, however, before we can reasonably expect voters to deliver confident and well considered votes on all the candidates and public questions presented to them.

Even when we have achieved that goal we will still have one of the most complicated systems of government in the world and we will still be making heavier demands year in and year out on our voters than in any other country in the free world. This inescapable fact calls upon us to maintain the highest standards of responsibility in our political leadership and the highest level of civic and political understanding among our citizens.

These facts underline the importance of the work now being done by the Commission on Intergovernmental Relations under the chairmanship of Meyer Kestnbaum, and by similar commissions in nearly half our states. A basic reason for the establishment of this commission over a year ago by the President and the Congress was the conviction that our system of government was growing excessively complicated, top-heavy and unwieldy as a result of increasing concentration of functions and responsibility in Washington.

During the 1952 presidential campaign both General Eisenhower and Governor Stevenson spoke of the importance of strengthening our state and local institutions so that a larger share of the job of government could be handled and directed close to home. Charles Edison, chairman of the League's Council, spoke on this theme at the San Antonio conference in 1952. In that speech, and in his speech at last year's conference in Richmond,[2] he a s k e d for the strengthening and modernizing of state governments so that they might continue to play the part in the federal system envisaged by the founders of the republic.

It has been my privilege in recent months to serve as a member of a committee set up by the Commission on Intergovernmental Relations to advise it on national-local relations. I have been impressed by the progress that has been made on this complicated problem. We have rea-

[2] See tne REVIEW, December 1952, page 540, and December 1953, page 555.

son to hope that when the commission reports next March it will set before us one of the most important programs for the improvement of the working of our system of government that the American people have ever had to consider.

It is evident that we have to have more government today than we required 150 years ago or even 50 years ago. It is also evident that the power of the federal government to tax and to spend gives it a paramount position not anticipated by the founders. Some use of the so-called grant-in-aid system, by which the national taxing power finances some government functions that may best be carried out by state and local governments, is probably inevitable in view of the national, not to say international, character of much business and other enterprise today.

The questions are: How far should this system be permitted to go? And how can we curb the tendency of money from Washington to mean control from Washington?

The facts of modern life make it impossible to hope for an easy solution of the problem of maintaining a national government able to lead the free world and local institutions capable of preserving the essentials of freedom, democracy and responsible citizenship at home.

As Governor Edison pointed out at the Richmond conference last year, our state and local governments have an obligation to be strong. The weaker they are, the more dominant will be the role of the national government.

In the last analysis, the position of the states will depend largely on their own readiness to meet the need for government. A grant from Washington does not automatically convey the capacity to spend it wisely and effectively. The more fully the states meet the demands of their citizens, the less will be the tendency to by-pass them or simply to use them as local bureaus of a centralized system of government.

Remedial Action

Consequently, I do not see how the commission's report can fail to point to the need for remedial action not only by Congress and the national government but by the states and the localities as well.

If I am right about this, the report of the commission will lay a special obligation on the National Municipal League to provide information and guidance to citizens and officials who want to do something about it. I am sure the League will meet this challenge because ever since the war we have been consciously preparing for just this eventuality. We have been preparing by strengthening our organization and staff and by shaping our program along lines indicated in a series of speeches by Charles Edison at previous conferences and by recommendations in the recent survey and evaluation of the League by Professor Joseph E. McLean and by the League's survey committee under the chairmanship of Cecil Morgan. This explains why the program of this conference included an unusual number of sessions on strengthening state government and straightening out intergovernmental relations and responsibilities.

Of course the League must not and will not be alone in this effort. The United States Chamber of Commerce and many state chambers of commerce have been paying close attention to the work of the national and state commissions on intergovernmental relations and so have many other national and state organizations embracing citizens of diverse points of view.

Difficult Task Ahead

In some ways the task ahead of us is more difficult than the original task of laying down the broad outlines of our distinctive system of national, state and local government. The tasks and burdens of government are more numerous and more complex today than they were 175 years ago. Our whole economic and social structure is more complex and each part is more dependent not only on the whole but also on the world outside. Simple solutions that may have seemed fairly adequate in a simpler age just don't meet the needs of today. Yet we must keep our system of government as simple as we can. We must maintain clear lines of responsibility and open channels of communication and understanding between the citizen and each part and major function of his government. If we do not do this the citizen is bound to be overwhelmed by the extent of his responsibilities and the difficulty of discerning them clearly.

Consequently, it is imperative that there be a well planned, coordinated effort to follow through the constructive proposals that we anticipate will come from the Commission on Inter-governmental Relations. It is to be hoped that the commission itself will consider this problem and offer some guidance on the difficult task of moving from study and proposal to action. The membership of the commission, which includes persons of substantial experience in federal, state and local government, and in political and civic leadership, is well qualified for this role.

We recognize that it is necessary and proper for members of local charter commissions and state constitutional conventions to assume some leadership in carrying out their proposals. It is to be expected that the members of this commission will be prepared to follow through in like manner on the work they have started. In the long run, however, their efforts will mean little unless citizens, organized and unorganized, join in some such concert as has always been required to secure adoption of far-reaching proposals for the public good.

The great danger is that any fairly comprehensive plan for governmental improvement will be defeated for lack of organization of the general interest to counteract the inevitable attacks of special interests opposed to particular features. No comprehensive program is ever perfect or satisfactory to all groups. The very complexity of the problem attacked by the Commission on Intergovernmental Relations, together with the fact that its proposals must be addressed not only to the national Congress but also to the people and governments of the 48 states, makes the need for carefully planned affirmative action all the greater.

The high batting average of the first Hoover Commission in terms of the adoption of its proposals for reorganization of the federal administration can be attributed in large measure to the nation-wide campaign conducted by the National Citizens' Committee for the Hoover Report. The committee helped organizations and individuals all over the country to concentrate their attention on the major objectives of reorganization. In so doing, it mustered impressive support that would not have developed without careful planning. In this effort the committee had access to the great national media of information and communication.

Stress State, Local Needs

One reason why the task of carrying out recommendations of the Commission on Intergovernmental Relations will be more difficult is the greater difficulty of communication at the state and even at the local level. It may sound strange that it is often harder to get attention and informed action in the home state than on the national scene. The chief reason for this is that our newspapers, the air waves and other channels of communication are more and more crowded with national and international news and comment of interest to large audiences not confined by local or state boundaries.

Consequently, if we are to maintain state and local institutions in their full vigor, we must compensate for the tendency of national issues to overshadow state issues and monopolize the attention of voters and organized groups. This communication problem, therefore, is another compelling reason for not leaving the fate of the commission's recommendations to chance. It also indicates that a plan for concerted action must be both more complex and more flexible than that required to obtain support for the Hoover report. I am not prepared to suggest a blueprint. I am simply stressing the fact that this problem requires the same kind of study and consideration that is going into the work of the commission itself.

While we often seem to fall down on minor or relatively easy projects, our people have a record of rising to the most difficult tasks. It may well be that the very difficulty of this assignment with destiny will do more than one might imagine to counteract alarming tendencies toward confusion, division and political irresponsibility. Like other difficult tasks that we have mastered together, it may help us to forge a new unity in diversity by giving our voters a new understanding of their government and a renewed confidence in their own power to control it.

New Tasks for Citizens

More citizen committees, building of executive reserve pool on state and local levels suggested by businessman.

By THOMAS R. REID*

BACK in 1952, a few days after a great national election, I made the rather pessimistic comment that, after a glorious political binge and the inevitable hangover, Americans would probably swear off the stuff for another four years.[1] Well, we have just been through an off-year election which was closely fought right up to the time the polls were closed. It was really a pretty heartening and inspiring thing, whatever our personal political leanings may be.

One of the great lessons which that election should teach all Americans is the vital importance of one man's vote. I recall hearing that the mayor of one town in which several thousand people voted won by a single vote. Issues of national significance which will affect us all for years to come were determined by a few hundred or a few thousand votes. We have a House and Senate full of "Hair-breadth Harrys" and there

will be more scared running in 1956 than this country has ever seen. It all adds up to a tremendous potential boost to active citizenship. All of us who are interested in promoting that kind of citizenship have a really potent argument today.

Certainly the setting is auspicious. Among our hosts are many who took part in one of the really outstanding civic jobs of all time. The story of the courageous and finally triumphant fight waged by a handful of Kansas City citizens against a powerful, entrenched and corrupt political machine has been an inspiration to all who care about good government. What happened in Kansas City set an example and a pattern for the later clean-up of many other great American cities. The militant spirit of responsible citizenship clings to this city and creates an atmosphere of purpose and civic decency.

My subject is "New Tasks for Citizens." Instead of trying to sell private citizens on the fact that they have a job to do, I'm going to try to sell those who are in government the idea of making it their business to find jobs for them to do. Most of us know why citizens should exercise their civic responsibility. Many of us are convinced that Mr. Citizen is willing and eager to do his part. So I think a logical and important concern of the National Municipal League is the problem of how to translate some of that willing spirit into effective practical action.

*Mr. Reid, director of civic affairs for Ford Motor Company at Dearborn, Michigan, concurrently is a consultant to the director of the Office of Defense Mobilization in Washington, D.C., where he served in 1953 as assistant director of mobilization in charge of man power. He is also chairman of a Hoover Commission task force on special personnel problems in the Department of Defense. A member of the Council of the National Municipal League and a former member of the Baltimore city council, Mr. Reid also holds numerous local civic positions.

[1]See Mr. Reid's address before the 1952 National Conference on Government, "Businessmen and Government," the REVIEW, December 1952, page 546.

During the past decade or so we have seen the rampant growth in the business world of what has been variously described as an awakening of corporate responsibility or industrial citizenship. There seems to be some feeling that the businessman suddenly just got religion on this business of civic responsibility. Most of us would agree that what the businessman got was a dose of good common sense.

Business Citizenship

In the first blush of the new-found civic spirit, however, there was a great deal of flag-waving and inspirational exhortation. I don't mean to sell inspiration short. Anyone who has seen a blimp being inflated knows that it takes an awful lot of gas to get off the ground.

But underneath all the fanfare, somewhere along the line the businessman learned that good business citizenship was not just a matter of pious platitudes—not just gilding the commercial lily—but a matter of really serious importance to him as a businessman as well as a private citizen. Perhaps it was just that he grasped the fact that the great issue in modern American political life is the struggle between freedom and security, between democracy and statism.

In the span of a few brief decades we have seen bigness become characteristic of most of our institutions. We have big government, big labor, big business, big agriculture. While not an evil in itself, bigness has magnified the complexity of the relationship among these deep-rooted forces in our lives.

Big forces and big problems generate big pressures toward ever more centralized guidance of our lives. The continuing popular desire for social progress, for improvement in our living standards, is one such pressure. If it is not satisfied by private efforts it will seek satisfaction through other courses.

World conditions exert a heavy influence upon our freedom of choice. We have assumed vast burdens in support of the free world's defensive strength, which inevitably extend the influence of government through the whole fabric of our lives.

Living in this powder-keg world, we are acutely aware that the maintenance of American economic stability is a matter of life and death. We know that to a large extent wise governmental action is essential to that stability.

Fear of communist subversion has led at times to extremes which could endanger our personal freedom and our democratic institutions.

Again and again we find ourselves facing up to the same question: At just what point in our search for security and stability do we reach a decisive surrender of private control over private matters?

Maintaining freedom in the face of all these intense pressures obviously puts a high premium on private citizenship responsibility. It's up to private citizens to do as much as possible of the jobs that need to be done. If many of the things which must be done are not accomplished by private means, the supposition is that sooner or later they will be done by government.

Conversely, it seems clear that the

quality of our citizenship, even more than our economic or military strength, will determine our survival value—our fitness to meet the challenges of our time.

The strengthening of our citizenship, our national moral and political fibre, can't start at the top and percolate down. It's got to be built up slowly and steadily from ground level in our local communities.

Those of us who are accustomed to thinking of active private citizenship mainly from a viewpoint of utility—of getting things done cheaply and efficiently and privately—need to give a little more thought to its great importance in strengthening democracy. In effect, our local communities can and should serve as schools of democracy and self-government. We need a greater awareness of what might be called the "bonus benefits" of greater citizen participation in local, civic, economic and humanitarian activities.

Detroit's Record

Just for example, you are all familiar with the United Foundation idea which had its genesis in Detroit and has since spread to many other cities. We are exceedingly proud of the record of Detroit industry and labor and other organizations in making the foundation the success that it has been. But we tend to take for granted an extraordinary side effect of this program.

One man who perhaps more than any other was reponsible for launching the United Foundation, Henry Ford II, put it this way:

We live in a day of immense national and world problems which can only be solved, in the long run, by mutual friendship and cooperation and understanding among human beings of diverse races, creeds, nationalities and political beliefs. That kind of cooperation . . . must evolve naturally; it must come up from the grass roots. People must first learn to get along together at the local community level.

Here in Detroit, each year hundreds of thousands of Detroiters reach across the lines of race and creed and nationality to help each other. Tens of thousands of volunteers work together with a common goal and purpose. This must mean, in my opinion, a real growth in tolerance and understanding among our Detroit people based on practical cooperation. Someone has made the point, for example, that labor-management relations in our town have benefited very directly as a result of management and labor leaders working shoulder to shoulder year after year for the United Foundation.

All in all, then, it seems to me that the United Foundation has brought a wide range of benefits above and beyond the direct purposes which it was intended to serve.

What Mr. Ford has to say about the foundation applies in large measure to all citizen participation in all sorts of civic affairs. It tends to bring about an elevation of the whole moral tone of our political life. And ultimately, it seems to me that the way of self-disciplined, responsible citizenship is the only good road to survival in a world that balances precariously over the pit.

A moment ago I made the statement that there is a considerable desire on the part of Americans, whether in industry or labor or the professions, to be active, constructive citizens. The great problem is how to translate that willing spirit into effective practical civic action and how to bring it out where it is still largely dormant.

Citizen Task-forces

I suppose that an outstanding contribution of federal government to active citizenship has been the development of the citizen task-force idea. In recent years we have, of course, had dozens of citizen advisory groups on a vast variety of subjects and problems. The foremost value of these task forces has been the bringing together of leaders of diverse national groups, promoting not uniformity but a sense of unity and broad common purposes and interests. The general effect has been to broaden the viewpoints of all concerned, to temper special interests and point the way to greater national solidarity.

During my own service as assistant and presently consultant on man power to the Director of Defense Mobilization, I have been particularly concerned with the problem of bringing competent business and professional people into broader participatiou in government affairs. After considerable study of the problem, we have come up with several notions which I think are relevant to our subject.

In general, the recruitment of private leaders for national citizen commissions and the like has not posed serious problems. The prestige attached to such appointments, and the opportunity for important public service without pulling up stakes at home, provide sufficient incentive to assure acceptance in most cases.

When it comes to persuading competent people to take actual working posts, even on a short-term basis, we run into all sorts of difficulties. In the Office of Defense Mobilization we recently worked up a plan to build an executive reserve of non-government personnel for positions in government during periods of emergency. The general idea was to set up a trained executive nucleus ready to step into key government spots if the need should ever arise. Actually the need has arisen five times in the last twenty years, and we never had an orderly system to meet it. The executive reserve plan has just recently been put into effect and a pilot group is being recruited.

We were looking to the future and therefore wanted to bring in relatively young men, from about 35 to 55 years of age, most of whom would be in the middle ranks of management and the professions—the leaders of tomorrow. In order to attract that kind of man, we had to do several things. We wanted to assure the man and his employer that selection for the executive reserve would reflect some real prestige upon both. A man's career should be materially advanced and not hindered by taking on the job. We had to try to make the indoctrination period long enough to be really effective and short enough to avoid any serious personal or job disruption.

To assure maximum prestige, the program contemplates a high-level approach to the organization employing the executive, and the development of good and thorough press coverage of the problem and of specific appointments.

In a related sense, the problem of recruiting outstanding men for such reserve positions is affected by the general conditions of government service. In October I participated in the Sixth American Assembly on the Federal Government Service — Its Character, Prestige and Problems. Among the recommendations of that advisory group was one which called for a program to bring younger men in industry, labor, education and the professions into federal departments for relatively short assignments. It was even suggested that the exchange principle be established, giving middle-level government employees a chance at similar assignments in private enterprise. That's an idea which I think should be given some real thought; it might also have some application at the state and local government level.

Tap Local Talent

Thus far I have discussed practices of the national government which I think apply directly to our problem of encouraging more active citizenship at the state and municipal levels. As I see it, the problem in most communities is one of tapping more effectively a vast local reservoir of talents and know-how and enthusiasm—putting them to work for the whole community.

There is no doubt that a whole lot can be done to improve our performance in this area. As you go from place to place, you find a tremendous variation in the extent and effectiveness of citizen participation in civic affairs. Where it is strong, you al-

most always find a bustling, live-wire community, with vigorous civic pride, where things are being done to make life more pleasant, progressive and prosperous. Where it is weak, you often find general political apathy and costly, inefficient government.

It seems to me that the mobilization of effective citizenship is largely a problem of effective organization.

In communities where civic participation is ineffectively organized you generally find one or more of the following conditions: C i v i c action largely concentrated among a small group of top business leaders who lend their names as window-dressing for worthy causes and whose efforts are confined largely to fund-raising. You find little or no civic incentive for the second or third levels of management. If there is any work to be done, the boss may breezily pass the buck to some anonymous subordinate, who does the job grudgingly because he has to do it.

Resounding protestations of responsible citizenship are launched into an atmosphere of general public cynicism or indifference. As Herbert Hoover once said: "Words without deeds are death to ideals." And I can think of no greater civic sin than the assassination of public idealism through ineptness or indifference.

Aroused citizens can accomplish great things by private efforts where the stimulus is sufficiently great and that usually means where local conditions have become intolerable. But effective citizenship must be encouraged and developed under the intelligent guidance of local government.

I have two proposals to offer which I think would go a long way toward improving the record of civic participation in any community.

First, the development and more effective use of the citizens' committee or commission at the local level, patterned on the national commissions with which we are all familiar. Those of us who live in cities or states where citizens' commissions are widely employed know how tremendously effective they can be.

We in Detroit have been drawn extensively into this type of civic action under programs inspired by Mayor Albert E. Cobo. This year, for example, the city set up a group known as the Detroit-Tomorrow Committee, which brings together more than a hundred outstanding leaders of every conceivable group interested in the future of the city. Subcommittees have been set up to consider a broad group of the city's development problems, ranging from traffic and highways to slum clearance and waterfront development. From past experience, we know that all the members of those committees have a considerable job outlined for them, and we are sure that real and measurable accomplishments will result from their work.

Because the commission idea has not yet caught on in a great many communities, I would like to mention briefly what seem to be some necessary attributes of such commissions.

As a rule, they should be established by the governor, the mayor or other local officials. They should be composed of top-level leaders of the community, business and the professions. Their primary job is one of policy guidance, of study and analysis of the local problems and needs with particular emphasis on seeking out and bringing private resources to bear upon them.

In an important sense, then, the commission acts as a two-way channel of communication between local government and private resources and as a central point for the mobilization and coordination of private efforts. The citizens' commission can often be a really effective means for enlisting the top-level support of local industry and the professions—lawyers, educators, engineers, architects, accountants, doctors and so on —for civic enterprises.

Establish Reserve System

Once we have established our citizens' commission, we've broken the ice and made a real stride toward effective civic action. We need to take a further step in order to develop a really effective program—one which has not to my knowledge been adequately explored. Thus far we've pretty much limited civic responsibilities and action to what might be described as the senior executive group. We've got to do a better job of bringing the younger operational people into action.

Second, therefore, I propose establishment of the executive reserve system and the specialist task force idea at state and municipal levels. Briefly, the idea would be to set up a reserve of operational people at the secondary levels of management, skilled specialists in a variety of fields, who would be given active consulting jobs to do, without compensation, in problems of their local governments. Ideally, we would anticipate needs and explore the resources of our community so thoroughly that, whenever we have. a special task to do, we know right where to put our finger on the fellow for the job.

In order to make this system work, the enthusiastic support of senior management must be enlisted. Care must be taken to spread the load so as to avoid unreasonable burdening of any one firm or individual. Every effort should be made to endow the executive reserve with prestige. Appropriate public recognition should be given to members of the reserve and their work, so that they and their employers will find their prestige materially enhanced.

Once set up, the executive reserve would be a tremendously valuable asset to the community and local government, since it would provide capable professional advice and assistance over the whole range of civic activities and government administration.

In my opinion, this double-barreled combination of the senior citizen commission and the operational executive reserve would be just about unbeatable as a means of getting really effective civic action.

Once such an effort is launched, I believe it would rapidly pick up real momentum and draw inactive groups of the community into the fray. I know that in the space of five or six years we have brought about a situation in Detroit where we have really hot competition for posts on our various commissions. If we are not

asked to take part in one job or another, we begin to wonder what's wrong with us. And I can assure you that the kind of civic spirit we now have is sincere and thorough-going.

Enthusiasm Will Grow

Once you get rolling, you seem to develop a circle that's just the opposite of vicious. You get into a snowballing of civic enthusiasm. As more and more young people are drawn into the civic orbit, there is a rapid growth of informed and intelligent citizenship. Other young fellows coming along decide that maybe they better get into the swim too.

I don't believe we're headed for Utopia, and I don't know where it will all end. But I am convinced of this: By building effective citizenship at home in our communities, we can make perhaps our most effective contribution possible to our national moral and political fibre, to the strengthening of democratic institutions, and ultimately to the cause of world peace and progress.

American industry and private citizens have come a long way in developing a strong sense of civic responsibility. Today, a great many of our private leaders are ready to do a real job of public service. It's up to those of us who are in or associated directly with local government to help them translate that urge into effective action.

With cooperation and understanding between government and citizens, all things are possible.

Faith Is Base of Freedom

Cincinnati's vice mayor asks greater concern by pulpit for support of honest, efficient government.

By DOROTHY N. DOLBEY*

OUT of great need this land produced some of the world's finest leaders. And the world is in desperate need of leadership today. Not just a handful of top elected leaders but millions of men and women who remember their heritage—those who lived and died to make us free; who are mindful of the future, determined to hand down to coming generations a land of freedom and hope.

Today we need a leadership conscious of its spiritual power and determined that it will not lose the historical significance of its founding. Too many of us have forgotten that we are a country founded on religious faith. This thought was expressed by President Eisenhower recently at a meeting with leaders of the National Council of Churches of Christ in America: "The people of America must realize their spiritual power — it is the only power which can save the world. This nation's government must be based on a firm foundation of religious faith or it makes no sense."

Only periodically does the church

*Mrs. Dolbey, city councilwoman in Cincinnati since 1953, was acting mayor of the city from March of this year until a successor to Mayor Waldvogel (deceased) was chosen last month. She is a member of the Cincinnati Planning Commission, chairman of the city's Retirement Pension Board and chairman of the Hamilton County Civil Defense Committee. This article is made up of excerpts from her address on November 9 before the National Municipal League's National Conference on Government.

awaken to its responsibility and sound the clarion call for decent, honest and efficient government in local communities. Committees for good government in Chicago, Boston, Philadelphia and other cities have been c o m p o s e d of consecrated churchmen determined to bring an end to the disgraceful governments of their various cities.

It happened in Cincinnati almost three decades ago. Those early reformers included men and women of all faiths dedicated to the task of making Cincinnati the best governed city in the United States instead of the worst. I am told that we are unique, that, somehow or other, we have been able through the years to keep the spirit of that first reform group operating and effective in our local government. How have we done it? I would suggest that perhaps one answer is that we have been able to challenge men and women of high principles, of deep religious faith, to the ideal that in a democracy politics is everybody's business; to the ideal that city or national government must meet the needs of the individual citizens in such a way that the best interests of all are served.

I firmly believe that America's pulpits must inspire its citizens with the ideal that running a government of, by and for the people is a basic religious tenet of our faith. Today we need a leadership who will proudly proclaim its religious heritage. We need citizens for good gov-

580

ernment recruited from Protestant, Roman Catholic and Jewish churches, who will place the best interests of all above those of a few.

Secondly, we need a leadership today that is informed. It is imperative that we educate the average citizen to know the actual conditions of his community. Over and over again we find slum clearance, urban redevelopment, modern expressway programs voted down, either by citizens who were not acquainted with the true facts or by those who selfishly thought that that particular improvement would not affect them. Each of us must realize that the belief "no man is an island, no man lives alone" is as true for us in our local communities as it is in our country in a world of nations.

Education for Citizenship

We need to educate the average citizen in the individual role which he must play if "right" is to prevail. We need to challenge women to take their rightful place in their political government. Any citizen voluntary group for good government which does not include an active women's division is licked before it has started. In Cincinnati the backbone of the City Charter Committee ward and precinct organization is its Women's Division. The committee knows that with 8,000 more women voters in the area than men it must challenge each woman citizen to her individual responsibility for good government, efficient government.

How do we in Cincinnati get information to the average voter? First, we start with the realization of the miracle of mass communica-

tion. We are determined to use this powerful weapon for good. We know full well that it can be used for evil. The repetition over and over again of material without a true basis of fact can give the voter the wrong impression.

In the fight to take away the use of proportional representation for the election of the Cincinnati city council in this last election,[1] the opposing faction took for the name of its group "Charter Improvement League." This was deliberate for, to many a voter who listened to the advertising on the air, this appeared to be the City Charter Committee, a strong supporter of P.R., endorsing the amendment. Fluoridation in Cincinnati was defeated by one man on one radio station. We live in an age of digests. Too many of us don't take the time to read the original speech or story or basic research material. We let someone else do our reading for us and give his interpretation of the original.

Secondly, we get information to the average voter by presenting the facts in a door-to-door, block-by-block organization. Politically, this country is organized on a ward and precinct basis. Any good government group must do a similar job if it wishes to be successful. And how do you get enough recruits to do the necessary block work?

Today we are going through the second great industrial revolution. We have more leisure than any generation which has preceded us. The director of the National Recreation Association brought out this fact when he spoke to a group of Cincin-

[1]See page 595, this issue.

natians recently. The garment workers in New York will obtain a 35-hour week in 1955. He stated that it would not be too many years before the 30-hour week would be established. What are we going to do with our leisure time? The challenge is there.

We give a lot of lip service to fighting communism. Our most effective tool is to fight for good government on the local level.

Thirdly, we get recruits by the example of our top leadership. Two of the best volunteers that we have in the City Charter Committee in Cincinnati are Forest Frank, our executive secretary, and Mrs. Louise Hobart, secretary for the Women's Division. They and two others constitute our paid staff. Yet they do not work on an hourly basis. They give their time, their energy and their devotion in every waking moment. The rest of our organization is composed of volunteers—men and women who think it is their responsibility and who believe it to be worthwhile to spend their leisure in this fashion.

We do not have any patronage political organization. It is a historical fact that mercenary troops never do as well as volunteers. The Battle of Trenton was lost for the British because the paid Hessian troops were sleeping when Washington's forces surrounded them. I am not implying that a good government group can win all its battles. There will be victories and losses. I am saying that ultimately the war can be won.

If you doubt the ability and interest of such a volunteer group, I can point to the last P.R. fight in Cincinnati in November. There was a million-dollar insurance man filing cards and raising money; there were top lawyers and businessmen debating, doing block work, witnessing the count on election day. There were hundreds of women ringing doorbells, handing out literature, working at the polls. You cannot buy that kind of devotion and I believe that thousands of American citizens will do a similar job if they are informed of the facts—if they realize what is at stake.

Bravery Called For

Finally, we need a leadership with courage to act. If ever we needed people who are willing to stand up and be counted, we need them today. Our ancestors fought and died that we might inherit a free land. There are too many today who fear to speak out and, as a result, we have the attention of our whole country focused on what one man in Congress has or has not done. Senator McCarthy is not solely responsible for our state of jitters. McCarthyism is a state of being and it never could have become a household word if the average citizen had been determined to look at the problem in its entirety and not be stampeded through fear.

McCarthyism was possible only because as individuals you and I became insecure and fear-ridden.

In the 1953 Cincinnati councilmanic election, the City Charter Committee was damned with the words "pink" and "communistic" and what did we do? We carried our story over the radio, through the press and neighborhood meetings. We

(Continued on page 612)

News in Review

November Elections Swell Manager List

Eleven Cities Vote to Adopt New Government

THE council-manager plan was the subject of numerous referenda in November. Of the cities voting on the plan eleven have adopted it. Five others have also recently secured the plan.

JOLIET, ILLINOIS, (1950 population 51,390) voted 11,390 to 9,251 on November 2 to replace its commission government by the council-manager plan.

EAST PROVIDENCE, RHODE ISLAND, (35,871) voted 9,294 to 7,837 on November 2 in favor of a council-manager charter, superseding town meeting government. If its provisions for choosing the five-member council at nonpartisan off-year elections are not ratified by the state legislature, the council will be chosen at regular partisan elections according to state law. NORTH KINGSTOWN, RHODE ISLAND, (14,810) voted 1,468 to 974 on November 2 for a council-manager charter, although it was opposed by a majority of the Republican town committee and although the Republicans were returned to office.

In SANTA FE (27,998), capital of NEW MEXICO, the council-manager plan was adopted by ordinance on October 27. The plan had been recommended by a committee, appointed by the mayor, comprising representatives of the Citizens Union, the League of Women Voters and other civic organizations.

MEDFORD, OREGON, (17,305) adopted the manager plan by charter amendment by a vote of 6,086 to 1,812 on November 2. It becomes effective January 1, 1955.

On November 9 KENNEWICK, WASHINGTON, (10,106) adopted the state's optional manager law by a vote of 877 to 213. The plan will go into effect June 6, 1955.

RANDOLPH, MASSACHUSETTS, (9,982) adopted the town manager plan, under the optional state law, by a vote of 2,457 to 1,857 on November 2. It takes effect after March 1955.

ALTUS (9,735) and CLAREMORE (5,494), OKLAHOMA, adopted the statutory council-manager plan on November 2. The vote in Altus was 1,393 to 584; that in Claremore, 1,037 to 740. The plan will go into effect in both cities in May 1955.

The township of CEDAR GROVE (8,022) in Essex County, NEW JERSEY, voted 1,433 to 1,376 on November 2 to replace the commission plan by the council-manager plan, effective July 1, 1955, as recommended by a charter commission. A council of five will be elected at large in May 1955.

BROWNFIELD, TEXAS, (6,161) voted 109 to 50 on November 16 to adopt the statutory council-manager plan. It went into effect December 9, 1954.

VACAVILLE, CALIFORNIA, (4,803) recently adopted the council-manager plan.

Voters of GULFPORT, FLORIDA, (3,702) adopted the council-manager plan 1,458 to 514 on November 9. The plan went into effect December 9.

The following four municipalities have adopted the council-manager plan since July 1: CAMP HILL, PENNSYLVANIA, (5,934); NORTH LAS VEGAS, NEVADA, (3,875); SEAL BEACH, CALIFORNIA, (3,553); and POLK CITY, FLORIDA, (195).

At a special town meeting in NEWCASTLE, MAINE, on September 27, a proposition for adoption of the town manager plan was postponed indefinitely.

MILFORD, CONNECTICUT, voted to retain its town manager government 2,274 to 2,002.

Two NEW JERSEY municipalities now

583

under the commission plan rejected the council-manager plan at the November 2 election. In WEST ORANGE the vote was 7,496 to 4,967; in BELLEVILLE it was 6,254 to 2,771. In both towns the incumbent commissioners fought the proposed change.

NORTH PLAINFIELD, NEW JERSEY, which has a mayor-council form of government, voted 2,459 to 2,288 on November 2 against changing to the council-manager plan. The charter commission had split three to two on the issue.

HAMPTON, VIRGINIA, which comprises a former county, city and town, which became boroughs under a consolidation plan, has voted for a city-wide council rather than one elected by boroughs.

Voters of NORTH WILKESBORO, NORTH CAROLINA, on November 2 defeated a proposal to adopt the state's optional Plan D, providing the council-manager plan.

MARION, OHIO, voted 9,018 to 2,814 on November 2 against adoption of the manager plan. KENT, OHIO, did likewise, 3,097 to 1,109.

JACKSON, OHIO, voted 1,409 to 857 against a proposal to elect a charter commission.

The charter study commission of ST. IGNACE, MICHIGAN, has indicated approval of the council-manager idea.

A joint committee of the PRINCETON, ILLINOIS, Chamber of Commerce and Junior Chamber of Commerce has undertaken a study to determine the most effective and economical form of municipal government for the city. The joint committee has been subdivided into four groups. A survey group has employed Griffenhagen & Associates to make a survey of the present commission government and make recommendations. A reading group will compile data on the various forms of government. A traveling group will visit cities of similar size in northern Illinois to get first-hand knowledge of how well the several plans are working. A lec-

Whoever Hires Me

G. F. Alcott, a member of the All Bloomington (Illinois) Committee which backed the successful campaign for council-manager government in Bloomington three years ago, spoke Halloween evening at Joliet, Illinois, three nights before that city's election on the plan, over WJOL, the Joliet radio station.

Driving down town after the broadcast, he passed a large lot where several hundred children, dressed in Halloween costumes, were gathering for the annual parade.

At the curb was a pushcart bearing large signs reading, "Be a citizen, not a subject—Vote 'NO' on council-manager." Beside the cart stood a man dressed in clown costume and with painted face.

Mr. Alcott parked and approached the man, saying, "I'm surprised that you'd be against council-manager. It works fine down in my town at Bloomington."

The man looked puzzled for a moment and then replied, "Mister, I don't know nothin' about it. I am a professional clown. I works for whoever hires me."

On November 2 Joliet voters ADOPTED the council-manager plan.

ture group will arrange for public presentation and discussion of the committee's recommendations.

In MANKATO, MINNESOTA, an attempt to discard the manager plan failed on November 2. The vote was 3,688 for and 3,340 against a change, but a 60 per cent vote was necessary for that purpose.

The city council of AUDUBON, IOWA, has voted to employ a city supervisor to direct all departments of the city government.

SCOTTSBLUFF, NEBRASKA, voted 2,193 to 1,457 on November 2 to retain its council-manager plan.

As a result of a petition filed in WEISER, IDAHO, an election has been set for December 7 on the question of adopting the manager plan.

DUNCAN, OKLAHOMA, on November 2, adopted a new and up-to-date council-manager charter by a vote of 2,335 to 856. The city has had a manager plan charter since 1920.

ELK CITY, OKLAHOMA, defeated a proposed charter amendment to abolish the council-manager plan, 1,153 to 726.

TULSA, OKLAHOMA, voting on November 16, defeated a proposed new charter providing the council-manager plan, 24,846 to 15,488.

Sufficient signatures have been secured to petitions to call an election in LAWTON, OKLAHOMA, on adopting the statutory council-manager form of government. ENID, in the same state, is working on a proposed new council-manager charter to replace the manager charter under which it has been operating since 1947.

A referendum election as to adoption of the manager plan is scheduled for January 18 in SPARKS, NEVADA.

WALLA WALLA, WASHINGTON, defeated a proposal to adopt the council-manager plan on November 2.

Seven of the nine city managers in NEBRASKA met in Grand Island on September 16 and organized a Nebraska city managers' association.

Recent city manager meetings have been held in IOWA, at Iowa City, September 24-25, with eleven of the state's eighteen managers present; in OHIO, at Columbus, September 30-October 1, with eighteen of 28 managers; and in KANSAS, at Parsons, October 7-8, with 25 of 36 managers.

Voters Struggle with Many Propositions

Proposed constitutional amendments and items of direct legislation to the number of 232 confronted the voters of 37 states on November 2, along with the problem of choosing United States senators and congressmen, state legislators and administrative officers, and local officials, throughout the nation. As the dust of the conflict settled, some of the results as to constitutional amendments appeared to be as follows:

School Segregation

An issue that attracted wide attention beyond the two southern states where it was voted upon was the attempt to overcome the recent Supreme Court decision adverse to segregation of white and colored school children.

Louisiana overwhelmingly approved an

"Alfred wanted to vote for the forces of decency and good government against the forces of evil and corruption, but the printed ballot didn't say which was which."
—Reproduced by permission from COLLIER'S
Cartoon by Foster Humfreville

amendment (to Article XII) which requires separate public elementary and secondary schools for white and negro children "in the exercise of the state police power to promote and protect public health, morals, better education and the peace and good order in the state, and not because of race." The legislature is authorized to submit additional proposed amendments to Article XII at special elections (now possible only at general elections).

In Georgia the proposal was to permit the state to grant funds to individuals for educational purposes; thus it would be possible to abolish non-segregated public schools in favor of segregated private schools. This amendment carried by a rather small margin (about 29,000 out of 391,000 votes). Although heavily supported in rural areas, it was largely opposed in the cities.

Election Matters

Mississippi voters approved an amendment tending to restrict Negro voting. It requires that an applicant must be able to read and write and to write an interpretation of any section of the constitution required by the county registrar. Heretofore an applicant was qualified if he could read the constitution or understand it if read to him.

Michigan made voting easier for a person who has moved within the state 30 days or less before an election to vote in his prior district, if qualified there and if filing an affidavit with the election board of that district.

In California a proposal to remove the voting disqualification of persons convicted of "infamous crimes," after having paid the penalty for such, was defeated by a narrow margin.

Minnesota adopted an amendment to eliminate "short-term elections" by permitting the governor to fill vacancies in offices until the end of the term or until the first Monday in January following the next general election, whichever is sooner.

North Carolina approved a reduction from four months to 30 days in the length of residence of a voter prior to an election, in a precinct, ward or other election district.

The same state approved a provision that the governor can fill vacancies in executive and judicial elective offices, instead of requiring election, if the vacancy is only until January following the next general election.

Apportionment

In Illinois the "Blue Ballot amendment" prescribing legislative reapportionment for the state—last accomplished in 1901—carried overwhelmingly, especially in Chicago and the rest of Cook County, even though "downstate" control of the State Senate is increased by assigning only 24 permanent Senate districts to Cook County (eighteen in Chicago) out of a total of 58. The House of Representatives, however, is to be apportioned on a population basis, but Cook County is limited to 30 out of 59 districts; Chicago will have 23. If the legislature fails to reapportion a special commission is to do so.

Colorado defeated a proposal for legislative reapportionment with fixed districts specified for the Senate, while the House districting would be on a population basis.

North Carolina rejected a proposal for limitation of one senator to a county regardless of population.

Length of Terms

An amendment in Ohio to lengthen the terms of elective state officials from two to four years, and to limit governors after 1958 to two consecutive terms, appeared to have a large majority—while Governor Frank L. Lausche was winning his fifth two-year term. A proposal to double the two-year term of state legislators apparently lost.

In Colorado a proposed amendment to lengthen the term of elective state officers to four years, with elections in non-presidential years, and permitting salaries to be increased or decreased during terms of office, was defeated, while one to lengthen the term of county officers to four years, with elections in non-presidential years, was adopted—the margin being close in both cases.

Texas voted by a substantial margin to lengthen the present two-year terms of elective district, county and precinct officials to four years.

In Illinois the state treasurer's term was extended from two to four years.

California heavily defeated a proposal to raise the term of assemblymen from two to four years and the term of senators from four to six years, and to limit future governors to two successive terms.

In Kansas proposals to remove the present limit of two successive terms as to county treasurers and sheriffs were defeated.

Annual Legislative Sessions

Kansas approved a proposal for annual sessions of the state legislature, beginning in 1956, the session in odd-numbered years to be limited to consideration of budget matters.

West Virginia adopted an amendment providing annual sessions, those in even-numbered years to be for 30 days and limited to budget matters, unless the governor proclaims otherwise at least ten days before the session, or unless the legislature by two-thirds vote on a concurrent resolution decides to consider additional business.

Georgia approved an amendment for annual 40-day sessions of the legislature.

Legislator's Pay

Texas raised the pay of state legislators from $10 to $25 per day, for 120 days, and now allows the legislature to set salaries of state elective officers.

In California a proposal to increase state legislative salaries from $300 to $500 a month was approved by a narrow margin.

West Virginia approved an increase from $500 to $1,500 per annum for legislators, with an additional $10 per day for extended or extraordinary sessions.

Home Rule

In Kansas an amendment looking toward home rule in urban areas was adopted. The constitution has required that general state laws shall have uniform application and that special laws shall not be enacted where a general law can be made applicable (Article 2, Section 17). The amendment adds, "Provided, the legislature may designate areas in counties that have become urban in character as 'urban areas' and enact special laws giving to such counties or urban areas such powers of local government and consolidation of local government as the legislature may deem proper." Although the amendment is permissive, the hope is held out that it will bring increasing home rule for the larger cities and will relieve the legislature of a heavy load of local legislation.

Georgia adopted an amendment authorizing the legislature to provide by general law for the self-government of municipalities and to delegate its powers to that end.

Maryland adopted an amendment conferring the general powers of home rule on towns and cities, including the power to amend their charters on matters relating to incorporation, organization, government and affairs, without action by the legislature. The powers to fix a maximum tax rate and to levy any type of tax is reserved to the legislature. Other restrictions forbid municipalities to repeal statewide laws or laws pertaining to their class, or to change existing laws concerning Sunday observance or alcoholic beverages. The amendment excludes Baltimore, which already has such powers. Legislative action will be necessary to provide a classification of municipalities, procedures for amending charters, etc.

Local Charters

In California one proposed amendment, which was defeated, would have authorized the city of Vernon, in Los Angeles County, to submit a charter to local vote, despite lack of the general population minimum of 3,500. Such charter could permit non-resident property owners to vote. Vernon is an industrial community with a small and dwindling residential population.

Another California proposal, to extend the time given boards of freeholders to prepare county charters from 120 days to six months, was approved by a large margin.

Old Age Pensions

A proposed California amendment, submitted by popular initiative, to increase the maximum old age pension from $80 to $100 per month, was defeated by a substantial margin.

In Colorado a proposal to permit the legislature to eliminate an existing provision that a pensioner's income from other sources must be deducted from the amount of old-age pension was heavily defeated.

Public Utility Regulation

Colorado approved by a large majority an amendment authorizing the state Public Utilities Commission to regulate the facilities, service and rates of all privately owned public utilities. The power of municipalities to exercise reasonable police and licensing powers and to grant franchises is not affected.

Miscellaneous Amendments

Bonus payments to veterans of the Korean conflict were authorized in Michigan. An attempt to legalize bingo and other lotteries conducted by charitable organizations was defeated in that state.

Texas voters were in an affirmative mood, and approved eleven amendments,

two of which have been noted above. For others see the October Review, page 481.

A constitutional amendment establishing a Department of Alcoholic Beverage Control to administer liquor licensing laws, removing such administration from the State Board of Equalization, was passed in California.

In California eighteen amendments were voted on, twelve of which were approved. Seven have been referred to above. Several others are financial in character (see the October Review, page 480).

In Nebraska the voters authorized the governor to appoint the five members of the Board of Educational Lands and Funds, now an *ex officio* body made up of state officers. Most of seven other proposed amendments deal with taxation and finance (see that department).

Georgia adopted an amendment declaring slum clearance to be a governmental function and authorizing the exercise of the powers of taxation and eminent domain for that purpose.

Minnesota approved an amendment that will help to clear the way for a constitutional convention. It provides that any revisions adopted by such a convention must be submitted to the voters for approval—a point that has not been clear. It also permits state legislators to serve as delegates to such conventions.

Minnesota also adopted an amendment authorizing the legislature to set qualifications for probate judges and to establish and extend the duties of probate courts; and another which eliminates double liability of stockholders in state banks and some other institutions. All the amendments received affirmative votes in excess of the necessary 50 per cent of all ballots cast and counted.

Other State Propositions

Montana became the twentieth state to adopt presidential primaries. A proposition approved by a vote of 93,000 to 43,000 authorizes such a primary to be held in June 1956 and each four years thereafter.

New Jersey defeated a proposal to finance a state medical-dental college and health center. The move was supported by most medical and dental groups, the C.I.O. and the New Jersey Taxpayers' Association. It was fought by the Roman Catholic church, the Hudson County Democratic organization and some medical groups.

Wisconsin rejected a plan for a tax-supported non-commercial educational television network.

City Voters Decide Varied Questions

A wide variety of local matters was passed upon by the voters of many cities at the November 2 election. Many concerned bond issues, a subject dealt with elsewhere.[1]

Among charter matters, Hartford, Connecticut, defeated a proposal for salaries of $2,000 per annum to be paid to members of the city council, and one of $3,000 to the member who is also the mayor. In Hartford the city manager, appointed by the council, is in charge of administration. The vote was 6,033 in favor, 16,650 against.

In Yonkers, New York, a proposal for a city council of six members and a mayor, all elected at large for four-year terms, was defeated, 25,897 to 19,110, with 21,043 voters not acting on the proposal. Yonkers now has a council of twelve, elected from wards for two-year terms, with a mayor elected at large for two years as presiding officer. The council appoints a city manager.

In eleven communities voting on the question of fluoridation of city water in the hope of reducing tooth decay, seven rejected the idea. Palo Alto, California, and Mountain Home, Arkansas, approved it.

[1]See page 598, this issue.

In San Francisco, where cable-car lines on some of its hills had been reduced by half last January, the voters rejected a proposal to restore the eliminated portion.

Although Pennsylvania State College is now called a university, the town of State College voted 2,434 to 1,475 to retain its old name, rather than adopt the designation of Mount Nittany.

New Jersey Municipalities Vote for Charter Commissions

At least five municipalities in New Jersey voted on November 2 in favor of charter studies and elected charter commissions. The largest is the city of Passaic, where the proposal carried by 6,473 to 3,137 (unofficial). It stems from a movement started five years ago to replace the present commission plan by a strong-mayor form. The new charter commission is not limited to the latter plan, however. It must submit its recommendations by August 1955.

Bloomfield, which has a weak-mayor form, voted 8,137 to 5,020 for a charter study. In Newton, county seat of Sussex County, the vote was 1,392 to 192, and in nearby Pequannock it was 1,629 to 665. Livingston township, in Essex County, voted 4,124 to 615 for the study and elected to the commission the slate of the proponents. In Warren township a charter study was authorized 565 to 381.

Several municipalities voted on council-manager proposals, as noted elsewhere.

Irvington, in Essex County, voted 10,316 to 5,718 against a proposal to replace the commission form by a strong mayor and council. The latter plan was actively opposed by four of the five commissioners and by the Republican and Democratic county committees.

Charter commissions in New Jersey are not authorized to draft new charters but may select one of various options offered to cities and villages in the state under the so-called Faulkner Act.

Three Rhode Island Cities
Keep Nonpartisan Elections

The voters of Pawtucket, Newport and Central Falls, Rhode Island, reaffirmed on November 2 their desire for nonpartisan elections. Pawtucket, in an advisory referendum, voted 16,541 to 7,888 against a proposal of the legislature that the city revert to partisan city elections to be held at the same time as the state and national elections. Central Falls did likewise, 3,902 to 1,726.

In Newport retention of nonpartisan elections was approved 4,605 to 2,604, and city elections in off years 4,587 to 2,554.

Dead Man Elected
County Clerk

In Salem, New Jersey, W. P. Ballinger, a Republican, was reelected on November 2 to a five-year term as clerk of Salem County, although he died on the preceding Thursday. He was unopposed. Under state law Governor Meyner appoints a successor belonging to the same political party as the predecessor. Another clerk will be chosen at the next general election.

Why Is a Constable?

A proposal to abolish the office of constable in Detroit appears likely to be submitted to the voters of the city next spring. Perhaps then there will be an answer to the long-standing question: "Why is a constable?"

In 1941 the Michigan legislature created the office of bailiff in connection with the Common Pleas Court (formerly the Justice Court) of the city of Detroit. By that act all constables in Detroit (two per ward or 44) also became bailiffs. No work out of Common Pleas Court went to them thereafter as constables, and the judges of the court were given a greater measure of control over them as bailiffs than had previously been the case. The only work remaining for constables was out of Circuit Court

Commissioners Court; it could be and was handled by ten or twelve.

The 1953 legislature established a bailiff system for Circuit Court Commissioners Court, whereby twelve bailiffs are appointed by the commissioners to handle process issued out of that court. No work goes to a constable, as such. A bailiff cannot be a member of both bailiff systems.

The way is now open for repeal of the charter provision requiring the election of constables.   CHESTER J. MORSE
Executive Secretary
Detroit Citizens League

Phoenix Department Head
Chosen by Modern Methods

Modern scientific testing methods have again been used to select a department head in the city of Phoenix, Arizona. On October 1 an acting assistant fire chief was named fire chief as the result of a carefully prepared testing program.

Phoenix' first experience with the use of intensive examining techniques in selecting a department head was in August 1952, when a police lieutenant was promoted to police chief, a position which under the law is in the unclassified civil service and requires no examination.

While the fire chief position is under classified civil service, and has for years been subject to its rules, the examination which resulted in the selection went considerably beyond the civil service requirements.

The results of using these techniques indicate that procedures of the classified civil service can be valuable tools for top management in the selection of department heads.

RAY W. WILSON, *City Manager*
Phoenix, Arizona

Granville, Ohio, Merges
Clerk and Treasurer Offices

The village council of Granville, Ohio, took action on September 1 to combine the offices of clerk and treasurer as permitted by a state law sponsored by the Ohio Municipal League and adopted by the legislature last year. Granville is reported to be the first village to take advantage of the statute.

An earlier statute permits a township clerk to act as treasurer. The offices may also be combined by a municipality in adopting a charter.

International Municipal Groups Join in Membership Offer

Cities in the United States are being offered a combined membership in the International Union of Local Authorities and the Inter-American Municipal Organization, at a schedule of annual dues ranging from $50 for cities up to 100,-000 population to $400 for cities with more than 1,000,000 population.

The IULA, whose headquarters are in The Hague, the Netherlands, unites national leagues of municipalities from 26 countries in all parts of the world. Its publications include an illustrated quarterly bulletin printed in three editions—English, French and German. The IMO has a membership open to all the countries of the Western Hemisphere and issues publications in English and Spanish. Both organizations hold congresses which are attended by municipal officials from all over the world. The IULA holds its twelfth congress in Rome in September 1955; the fifth Inter-American Congress of Municipalities is in San Juan, Puerto Rico, December 2-7, 1954.

Further information about the membership offer may be obtained from the American Committee for International Municipal Cooperation, 1313 East 60th Street, Chicago 37. Among the seventeen member organizations of the Committee are the American Municipal Association, National Municipal League, International City Managers' Association and United States Conference of Mayors.

Rhode Island Primary System Shows Virtues and Defect

In Rhode Island's new primary election system, which had its fourth trial three months ago, the party managements submit candidates for confirmation by the party members at primaries, such "endorsees" being identified by asterisks on the ballots. Other candidates get on the party primary ballots by petition. The system is closer to the National Municipal League's *Model Direct Primary Election System* than that of any other state.

The Democratic and Republican primaries are, needlessly, held on different days, alternating in priority from year to year.

The 1954 endorsed statewide nominees were uncontested in both parties and contests appeared only in local partisan elections.

In the Democratic primaries, September 20, only one out of 29 memberships in the Assembly was won by an unendorsed candidate. In the Senate three incumbents who lacked the endorsement tried but failed reelection, and all nominations were won by endorsees, although there were some close and bitter contests.

In the municipal elections there were many contests for nominations for public and party office, victory going to endorsees with few exceptions.

The Republicans on September 29 accepted endorsed slates for public office in thirteen of the fifteen cities and towns where primaries were held. Six unendorsed candidates, three in East Providence and three in Westerly, won places on Republican town committees.

The *Providence Journal* of September 22 editorialized under the headline "The Odds Are Still Rigged for the Endorsed Candidates. . . . With a liberalized primary law there would be more unendorsed candidates running for office and there would be a higher rate of victory for their campaigns." It complained: "Endorsed candidates on a primary ballot are listed vertically in the first left-hand column of the voting machines. By simply running a finger down the line of butterfly levers opposite each name, it is possible to cast a quick ballot for every endorsed candidate. Names of unendorsed candidates, however, must be strung out horizontally by alphabet for each office at stake. A voter must pick his way through a frequently confusing list of names if he wants to back an unendorsed candidate.

"By law, too, there is no provision for appointment of polling place supervisors representing the interests of unendorsed candidates. The state primary act specifies that the supervisors are to be appointed from lists furnished by the local party committee and unendorsed candidates get short shrift from party machines. Yet supervisors are key personnel at any voting place. They may enter the polling booth at the request of a voter to give him help in operating the machine or expressing his choice. The area of their influence is considerable . . . The primary is a tremendous improvement on the old caucus method of picking candidates but it can be further improved whenever the General Assembly is willing to face up to the chore."

The Rhode Island League of Women Voters singles out an added major complaint, namely, that, unlike the *Model*, no time is reserved for unendorsed candidates to file after the organization slate is announced. Another deficiency is that unendorsed candidates may not combine to seek signatures on a joint petition. The league also asserts that the first column position and the asterisks on the ballot give endorsees the advantage, "placing the unendorsed candidate under a great handicap, which is difficult to overcome except under unusual circumstances."

The National Municipal League *Model* does not support giving endorsees a more convenient position on the voting machine but does favor identifying them by asterisks or in some other way on the supposition that all voters are entitled to the information.

R. S. C.

Contest Held for Good Canadian City Reports

The Canadian Federation of Mayors and Municipalities has granted awards to thirteen cities for outstanding municipal annual reports. The federation's contest was announced in 1953 and 42 reports were received up to May 31, 1954, the closing date.

Gold seal awards were made for the most outstanding report in each of four population groups (two such awards being made in one group), and red seal awards were given to eight cities receiving honorable mention. All reports were judged for content, understandability and attractiveness, by a group of three judges outside the federation.

Tokyo Has Municipal Matrimonial Bureau

Municipal functions steadily multiply everywhere throughout the world but Tokyo must be ahead of the procession in that, according to the *Tokyo Municipal News*, it has a matrimonial agency in its Public Welfare Bureau managed by a woman chief who studied sociology for ten years in the United States.

She has accumulated a list of 5,000 persons who are looking for wives or husbands and by various social devices brings together couples that might be congenial and, if nothing comes of the first attempt, she supplies another potential match.

The agency has been running twenty years and is described as unique in Japan.

R. S. C.

County and Township .   •   . •   • *Edited by Edward W. Weidner*

Butte County, Calif., Seeks New Charter

Taxpayers Group Leads Campaign for Revision

A N INTENSIVE campaign is being launched in Butte County, California, under the leadership of the County Taxpayers Association, to revise the county's charter, adopted in 1917. The association has interested several county-wide organizations in the need for a thorough examination and revision of the charter. These groups are conducting their own studies. They will be prepared to assist a citizens charter review committee which it is planned to ask the county board of supervisors to appoint soon after February 1, 1955. The groups will later become the nucleus of a broad and representative base of public support for adoption of a revised charter.

Major points to be considered in the study are: (1) A county manager or executive in lieu of a county administrative officer with limited authority; (2) a centralized fiscal management under a county controller; (3) a personnel management program under a limited civil service system; (4) centralized management of non-expendable property; and (5) the extent to which offices should be filled by election.

Butte was the third county in the state to adopt a home rule charter. Today only eleven of the 58 counties have such charters.

THOMAS H. SWEENEY
Executive Secretary
Butte County Taxpayers Association

Baltimore County Elects Charter Board

The voters of Baltimore County, Maryland, on November 2, approved overwhelmingly the election of a charter board. The board must draw up a charter within the next six months, to be presented to the voters in 1956.

St. Louis County Votes for Police Consolidation

By an overwhelming vote of 117,157 to 24,091, voters of St. Louis County, Missouri, adopted an amendment to the county's charter to replace the traditional sheriff and constable system of police protection with a consolidated non-political county police system. (For a full account of the amendment's provisions, see the REVIEW for October, page 486).

Michigan Counties Replace Coroner with Medical Examiner

A bill to permit the board of supervisors of Wayne County (Detroit), the most populous area of Michigan, to abolish the office of coroner was passed by the 1953 legislature and signed by the governor. The law, by its terms, was not to become effective until January 1, 1954. So great was the pressure exerted by and on behalf of the incumbent coroners, however, that a referendum section was included to the end that the bill would not become effective until approved by a majority of those voting on the proposition in the county at any general or special election at which the question might be submitted by the supervisors.

One would have expected the question to be submitted at the November 2 election. An opinion sought by the supervisors from the county's prosecuting attorney, however, questioned the advisability of submission at that election, when the two coroners would be chosen for two-year terms—two inconsistent matters would confront the voters, causing confusion. The opinion further stated that it would be proper to submit the question at the April 1955 election and, if approved by the voters, the act would become effective in ten days after the official declaration of the yote by the secretary of state. The board of supervisors could then abolish the office and appoint a county medical examiner as provided in the act.

Wayne County would then join with Kent, Oakland, Genesee and St. Joseph Counties, each of which has replaced coroners with a medical examiner. The first three took action under special legislative acts. St. Joseph County is the first to abolish its elective coroner under the state's 1953 optional law.[1] His replacement with an appointive medical examiner, chosen by the county supervisors, will take place January 1, 1955.

CHESTER J. MORSE
Executive Secretary
Detroit Citizens League

Milwaukee County to Make Administrative Survey

A survey of Milwaukee County, similar in nature to that of the city of Milwaukee started in 1949, is about to be launched. Important changes to bring about efficiency and economy are expected as a result of the survey.

Milwaukee County currently has a budget of $54,000,000, which represents a 57 per cent increase in a period of about five years. The county has 52 elected county and judicial officers and these, together with its many boards and commissions and other organizations,

[1]See the REVIEW, July 1953, page 348.

render over 200 governmental activities. In a recent issue of its *Bulletin,* the Citizens' Governmental Research Bureau of Milwaukee included an organization chart of Milwaukee County government showing the complicated nature of the present system.

Intergovernmental Relations Between Cities and Counties

A number of counties have participated in moves to enlarge the area of administration by inter-unit cooperation. In Colorado, Aspen City and Pitkin County have created a city-county planning and zoning commission. Both city and county officials look forward to increased direction and control of areas where ill-planned building and development have threatened existing property values. The new regional plan should lead to area-wide control.

The new St. Clair County–Port Huron, Michigan, joint governmental building was dedicated at ceremonies recently. The building, which will house offices of both the city and the county, cost $3,200,000.

In South Carolina a housing authority has been enlarged to include eighteen counties. Administrative economy was the goal in setting up the centralized authority which administers some 718 low-rent public housing units in 22 localities in the eighteen counties. The commission is composed of one member from each of the counties and one commissioner at large.

Proportional Representation • • *Edited by George H. Hallett, Jr. and Wm. Redin Woodward*
(This department is successor to the Proportional Representation Review)

P. R. Wins Again in Cincinnati

Recount Proves Voters Want Hare System in Use 30 Years

FOR the fourth time in the past eighteen years, Cincinnati voters on November 2 reaffirmed their support of the city's proportional representation system of electing members of city council. An amendment to the Cincinnati charter designed to eliminate the P.R. election provision and substitute a limited vote plurality system was defeated by the narrow margin of 672 votes in a total of 149,964 polled on the issue.

The slimness of the margin is not new in Cincinnati's history. In the 1936 May primary elections, when the first attempt to kill P.R. was made, P.R. won by 831 votes; in a special election in June 1939, the second attempt was defeated by 742; and in November 1947, in conjunction with the regular council election, the third attempt was rejected by a margin of 7,602.

This latest repeal effort presented the most formidable array yet to confront the City Charter Committee, sponsors and traditional supporters of P.R. In addition to the Hamilton County Republican machine, which has fought P.R. bitterly from the time of its first proposal in 1924, the opposition included a loud section — though of uncertain strength—of the Hamilton County Democratic party, numbering among others the chairmen of both the Democratic central and Democratic executive committees.

The campaign was made all the more ominous by the deceptive stratagem of the anti-P.R. forces which marshalled their various elements under the misleading cognomen, "Charter Improvement League." Anti-P.R. workers preyed upon less well informed voters throughout the city by representing themselves as "charter" workers. Even precinct election officials were confused by the deception and by the ambiguous wording of the ballot proposal itself into concluding that a "yes" vote was a vote *for* P.R. rather than *against*.

Two other factors militated against P.R. supporters. The proposal itself—substituting a simple "X" ballot with the voter restricted to marking for six candidates or less (with nine to be elected) —was solemnly held forth as a complete guarantee of the maintenance of minority representation, one of the principal arguments in the P.R. arsenal.

The second factor had to do with the mayoralty situation existing in Cincinnati's city council from May until eight days after the November election. The death of Mayor Waldvogel in May found the Charter majority elected in 1953 no longer a majority, the fifth Charter councilman, Albert Jordan, a steelworker union official, having resigned from the group in a rage over the imposition of a temporary 1 per cent earnings tax levied to balance the city's budget. Jordan declined to vote for Vice Mayor Dorothy N. Dolbey, whose promotion to the mayoralty office, which she had filled most creditably during Waldvogel's two-months illness prior to his death, seemed to Charter supporters generally as the most natural and advisable solution. The deadlock that resulted—though clearly not ascribable to P.R.—nevertheless was seized upon by the "Charter Improvement League" as evidence of P.R.'s deficiencies. (The cynicism of the argument was revealed on November 3—the day after election—when it became known that Jordan would cast his vote for the Republican machine floor leader in council, Carl W. Rich. This he did one week later, November 10.)

In the face of this adverse combination of forces and events, the City Charter Committee mustered its most vigorous campaign in recent years. Although handicapped by having at its disposal less than half the funds of the anti-P.R. forces, the Charter group made the anti-P.R. amendment the hottest issue in an election in which voters were confronted by seven separate ballots, seventeen questions and issues, and 62 candidates ranging from governor and U. S. senator to county commissioners and common pleas judges.

Newspaper, television and radio coverage—much of it necessarily on a commercial basis—blanketed the community. Scores of speaking engagements and house meetings were scheduled and nearly 600,000 pieces of literature were distributed. So pressing became the issue that even the Hamilton County Board of Elections informally broke a long-standing rule requiring counting of the ballots for governor first, to permit a counting of the ballots on the P.R. issue as soon as the polls closed.

Actually the elections board return on November 3 proclaimed P.R. dead and the amendment carried by 596 votes. But the Charter Committee wisely had recruited witnesses for the election count in the great majority of the city's 723 polling places. As a result, Charter leaders with their own reports of the precinct voting felt able to predict election night that P.R. would be found saved by several hundred votes.

When the adverse "unofficial" return of the election board was made "official" November 10, the Charter Committee promptly challenged the result and set about getting the evidence and the funds ($10 per precinct) on which to base a demand for a recount. This ultimately they were able to do and, on November 18, a recount of ballots in 497 of the city's 723 precincts resulted in a reversal of the "official" return. The amendment was declared defeated by 792 votes. For the first time in Hamilton County history, an election result had been reversed by recount.

The anti-P.R. elements then exercised their rights by advancing funds for a recount of the remaining 226 precincts not included in the Charter Committee's recount. In all but a few of these Charter witnesses were present on election night and confirmed election board returns. The opposition did pick up 120 votes, however, leaving the final margin of victory for P.R. on the recount of all precincts at 672.

Newspaper Coverage

The *Cincinnati Post,* which has always supported P.R., again gave effective aid in the campaign. In addition, the *Cincinnati Times-Star* for the first time took a position defending P.R.—declaring that "while we still dislike P.R. on a number of grounds, we dislike the proposed alternative even more." Support also came from many responsible Democrats who, disapproving the position of the party's titular leadership, organized as "Democrats for P.R." and mustered help from a large majority of the party's ward leaders.

Murray Seasongood, Charles P. Taft, Mrs. Albert D. Cash, Miss M. Julia Bentley (sister of the Charter Committee's first president, deceased), and many other noted figures of the Charter movement came forward to occupy key roles in the campaign. In the final analysis, however, victory lay as much in the P.R. record of good, able councilmen, elected over a period of 30 years, as in any other factor. For most Cincinnatians, even though their majority is a small one,

P.R. obviously still remains synonymous with the effort for good government.

FOREST FRANK, *Executive Director*
Cincinnati City Charter Committee

P. R. League Meets in Kansas City

The Proportional Representation League, Inc., now operating as a department of the National Municipal League, held its annual meeting at the latter's National Conference on Government in Kansas City, Missouri, November 8, 1954. Richard S. Childs of New York City, a member of the board of trustees and former president of the P.R. League, presided. Delegates from six cities and five states attended.

The entire board of trustees was reelected for the coming year: Mr. Childs; Robert P. Goldman of Cincinnati; C. G. Hoag of Haverford, Pennsylvania; Andrew B. Holmstrom, former mayor of Worcester, Massachusetts; Thomas H. Reed, municipal consultant, of Wethersfield, Connecticut; Oxie Reichler, editor of the Yonkers (New York) *Herald Statesman;* and Thomas Raeburn White of Philadelphia.

The meeting recommended to the trustees the election of Robert P. Goldman, president of the Cincinnati Bar Association and law associate of former Mayor Murray Seasongood, as president to succeed Mr. Holmstrom, who had asked to be relieved of the position's responsibilities for lack of time. It also recommended the reelection of all the other officers: Thomas Raeburn White, vice president; C. G. Hoag, honorary secretary; George H. Hallett, Jr., executive secretary of the New York Citizens Union, executive secretary; Elsie S. Parker, assistant editor of the NATIONAL MUNICIPAL REVIEW, assistant secretary and treasurer.

Mrs. Albert D. Cash, former member of the Cincinnati City Council, reported briefly on the campaign to retain P.R. in her city, the results of which were still inconclusive, and on the plans under way for a partial recount on the strength of discrepancies between the official figures and the reports of election witnesses. (See the first article in this department above.)

The meeting discussed and recommended a plan by which special funds would be sought for traveling expenses, stenographic help and materials for continuing educational and field work out of Cincinnati as a center, with a well grounded volunteer in charge locally and general cooperation and oversight from the central office in New York.

Plans were also discussed with Thomas S. Green, Jr., and Francis A. Harrington, of the Citizens' Plan E Association of Worcester, for a revival of the Massachusetts Plan E Association under local auspices, to do educational work on P.R. throughout Massachusetts and to campaign for a repeal of the ban on new P.R. adoptions in that state.

Those attending the meeting regarded the present low ebb of the P.R. movement in the United States as a serious but temporary reverse, due primarily to the accurate representation of a Communist minority on the P.R.-elected New New York City Council at a time when the United States and Soviet Russia were friendly allies. Belief was expressed that P.R. is bound to spread again because it offers the only answer to some of the most serious problems of representative democracy. The discussion emphasized the desirability of being alert for every opportunity for new adoptions so as to secure the benefits of P.R. with the least possible delay.

G. H. H., Jr.

Taxation and Finance . . . . *Edited by Wade S. Smith*

Federal Highway Bonds Proposed

Would Raise by 50 Per Cent 1955-64 Decade Expenditures

ONE OF the toughest problems likely to face the 84th Congress will, like similar problems of state and local governing bodies, revolve around highway improvements and their financing. The president's advisory committee on a national highway program, headed by General Lucius D. Clay, chairman of the Continental Can Company, has already recommended a ten-year improvement program to cost an estimated $50,000,-000.

At a meeting of the American Petroleum Institute in Chicago in early November, the general, according to press reports, stated that an additional $26,-000,000,000 would be needed, $23,000,-000,000 for improvement of existing interstate highways and $3,000,000,000 for new construction. The $76,000,000,000 total would be additional to existing highway expenditures, now running at about $6,000,000,000 annually and including about $1,000,000,000 of federal motor fuel taxes and the remainder state and local revenues and borrowings.

Controversy may be expected to center in the means of financing the proposed comprehensive program. Committee recommendations have not yet taken final form, but suggestions range from 100 per cent federal assumption of interstate highway costs to proposals that the whole program be financed with revenue bonds on a limited access toll road basis. At the Chicago conference, General Clay is reported to have called attention to the fact that of the present $1,000,000,000 of federal highway revenues, about $550,-000 is turned back to the states, leaving some $450,000,000 which could be used to service federal highway bonds to meet part of the ten-year program expenditures.

Big Issues Carry at November Election

State and local voters, called on to consider proposals to issue about $1,500,-000,000 in new bonds at the election November 2, evidently approved a majority of the propositions, although the unusual interest in close contests for elected offices throughout the nation contributed to slowness in reporting results on propositions.

The largest bond authorizations secured their needed majorities: New York State voters authorized two issues, for mental hospitals and slum clearance, aggregating $550,000,000, while California voters authorized $275,000,000, also comprising two issues and to be used for the veterans' loan and school building aid programs. Other large issues approved included: $54,530,000 by Philadelphia voters, $35,300,000 by Cleveland voters, $35,000,000 for roads by Colorado electors, $32,500,000 by voters of the Long Beach, California, unified school district, $19,500,000 by San Francisco voters, $14,800,000 sewer bonds by voters of Westchester County, New York, $11,500,000 by voters of Cincinnati, and $11,000,000 by Hamilton County, in which the city is located, and $11,400,000 by voters of New Orleans. Seattle voters, faced with $23,100,000 of proposed city issues, approved only $10,000,000.

Nebraska voters evidently approved a constitutional amendment prohibiting the state from levying a property tax for state purposes in the event the legislature adopts either a general sales tax or an income tax, or both. Also approved, according to preliminary returns, is an amendment authorizing the legislature to prescribe standards for assessing real and tangible personal property. An amendment which would have provided for an appointive tax commission with jurisdiction over administration of the revenue laws of the state and power to review and equalize assessments was narrowly defeated by a vote of 149,134 against the amendment to 149,108 for it.

Among eleven constitutional amendments submitted to the voters in Texas, four pertained specifically to state or local fiscal problems and were approved by large majorities. One authorized the creation of county-wide hospital districts in the counties of Dallas, Bexar, El Paso, Harris, Jefferson, Tarrant and Galveston, with separate borrowing powers and the right to levy general property taxes up to 75 cents per $100 of assessed valuation. Another implemented existing legislation intended to authorize the construction of toll roads with revenue bonds by prohibiting the lending of the state's credit to support toll highways. Another raised the limit on the state's public welfare expenditures from $35,000,000 to $42,000,-000, and the fourth provided for the election of assessors-collectors in counties of 10,000 population or less.

California voters, in addition to approving the two bond proposals, approved a group of amendments writing into the constitution various exemptions from property taxes for properties of educational, religious and charitable organizations. An amendment authorizing the use of state highway revenues for construction of parking facilities was defeated.

Interesting also were the results on special tax propositions in Cincinnati. Earlier this year the city council there had enacted a 1 per cent income tax, to be used for seven months of 1954 and based on seven-twelfths of estimated 1954 income. As an alternative, there was submitted at the November 2 election a proposal to authorize a special property tax levy of 6.22 mills for 1955 and 1956. Voters approved substitution of the special property levy for the income tax. In the suburban community of Norwood, which to protect its residents from "double taxation" had adopted a payroll tax last spring and also submitted as an alternative on November 2 a proposal for a special operating tax levy, the voters failed to approve the special levy. So, while the central city's income tax lapses and a special property tax takes its place, in the suburb the income tax will continue.

Bond-free Program Succeeds in Greenwich

On August 1, 1954, the town of Greenwich, Connecticut, realized one of the objectives of a financial program inaugurated 21 years earlier. It paid off the last of its outstanding bonded debt, under a program begun in 1933 to substitute annual budget appropriations for borrowing in financing recurring capital improvements.

Like many communities, the town had financed its capital requirements through the lush 1920s by the issuance of bonds, a procedure supported by substantial and continued increases in assessed valuations. By the end of 1931 the borrowing program was brought to a halt by inability to sell additional bonds in the sick financial markets of the period, and a small operating deficit was evident, caused by mounting relief requirements. Conditions worsened in 1932, with rising tax delinquency curtailing revenues and budget flexibility handicapped by the fact that more than one-fifth of the appropriations were for debt service.

Pay-as-you-go as a means of eliminating interest costs and adding to budget flexibility was suggested and, in 1933, with the aid of special legislation providing for substitution of a representative town meeting for the old open town meeting, the first budget on the new plan was adopted. The budget was raised 10

(Continued on page 604)

Citizen Action .   .   .   .   .   . *Edited by Elsie S. Parker*

What Is Civic 'Production'?

Citizen Groups Should Each Year Complete Some Projects

ONE OF the best things that could happen to a civic organization would be to have its contributors dole out its revenues only when it wraps up a solid project bettering its community which it originated and pushed through to completion.

This would place it on a parity with the ordinary business establishment which "doesn't eat" unless it makes sales. This may be impractical but it certainly would ensure greater production by our many civic agencies which yearly collect hundreds of thousands of dollars from their supporters.

Contributors to these organizations are far more lenient about demanding results than they are for their own businesses or for enterprises in which they own stock. True, they are dutifully provided with annual reports of activities by the secretaries of these civic agencies. But close analysis would disclose that some of these reports sound like a roaring motor in a car which is standing still.

Without discounting the accomplishments of the scores of hard-working secretaries all over the country, probably every civic league and similar organization could greatly increase its present "production" by changes in procedure and a reappraisal of its goals.

Here are some reasons.

Not too many civic secretaries have gone through a tough enough internship during which the need for "production" was beaten into them as it is into many young men in the business world.

Civic secretaries are not under the harsh compulsion to "produce or else," because their supporters mail in their checks year after year without quibbling. Of course, if the organization is actually ineffectual, members will quit.

Some secretaries don't have too clear an idea as to what "production" is expected of them. Some regard surveys or reports, which are decked with copious footnotes and appendices, as terminal depots when in fact they are only way stations. Actual installation of the project is the important thing, not its recommendation.

Ask a businessman supporter what he expects from his civic organization. In all likelihood he will say something like this.

"I can't be too specific because I'm a manufacturer—not a civic secretary. But I expect our civic organization to wind up the year with a few jobs accomplished which will result in a tax savings which can be approximately measured; and other jobs completed which will improve public services even though they may not show a money savings. I expect our secretary to originate such projects or to have sense enough to pick up a good project which is started by a public official. I expect him to keep a close watch on all important public transactions in our community and to assume the responsibility for sounding a Paul Revere alarm if he detects something serious on the make which should be blocked. Also, I realize the responsibility of our board or committee members to assist our secretary in doing these things."

Sometime, a Joe DiMaggio of a civic secretary is going to appear on the municipal scene and knock out so many home runs of money-saving and service-improving jobs as to set a new standard toward which other agencies will have to strive. Also, these jobs will bring him

hundreds of new members with little effort, because that is basically what the
citizen wants—to save money and get
better public service. We are still under
the strong impression that this type of
civic job will attract more new members
than a long research report which traces
the lines of administrative command from
the mayor to dog-catcher.

Here are three types of production
jobs by a civic agency:

1. Projects with immediately measurable results which save money and provide better public service;

2. Projects which are obviously beneficial but whose results cannot be immediately measured;

3. Projects in civic education.

The first type of project is the hardest
to achieve, which is the reason why so
few appear in annual reports of civic
agencies. They arouse more opposition
because saving money usually means that
some present employees will not be
needed under the new plan. A sample of
this kind of project is the installation of
complete mechanical accounting in the
county assessor's and treasurer's offices
to simplify and speed up writing the annual tax rolls and the tax bills. Another
would be to secure the passage of an
act taking away from the sheriff his per
diem fee for feeding prisoners in the
county jail. Another would be to persuade the county commissioners on good
grounds to lop off several million dollars
in a proposed road bond issue.

The second type of project is similar
to the first except that the results are not
immediately measurable. An example
would be passage by the legislature of a
joint resolution to submit a constitutional
amendment to the voters permitting
counties to adopt home rule charters.
Another which would earn public gratitude, although it might not save money,
would be to secure a law requiring the
titles of ballot propositions to be crisply
descriptive and in large type.

Easiest projects to put over are those
under the heading of citizens' education.
One of these could be a series of television shows. A weekly newsletter to
all the members would come under this
category.

How many jobs a year should a civic
secretary put across? Experience of
veteran civic secretaries shows that if
he has one assistant to do much of the
leg work, he should be able to complete
not less than twenty large and small jobs
a year.

Emphasize the 'Pay Dirt'

That this sense of production—of completing jobs with tangible results—is not
especially keen in some civic agencies
can be discerned from their annual reports. Their annual statements do not
start out listing, with the emphasis of a
page one murder story, their one or two
big jobs of the year as though they were
proud of them and wanted their members
to hear about them. One fails to sense
the satisfaction of the man who has
"brought home the bacon."

Some reports contain such comments
as, "We studied the city's classification
plan" or "We reviewed the county's
purchasing procedure." This is fine as
far as it goes but it fails to mention the
pay-dirt discovered or tangible results
ensuing from recommendations.

This type of report would be similar to
the annual statement of a large automobile manufacturing plant which emphasized a laborious research job on a
new spring and mentioned only incidentally the number of cars sold last year,
which, after all, is the main goal of its
existence.

The civic secretary can profitably
spend some of his time while shaving or
mowing his lawn in thinking up profitable jobs for his agency. It is surprising
how many good ideas will pop into a
mind which is open to receive them in
the tensionless hours away from the
office. This off-hours mental prospecting

for nuggets of ideas won't bring on any nervous prostration either. Rather, it will refresh him like his morning calisthenics. As a word of caution, it should not be carried on to the extent that wives will complain about abstracted husbands.

Then what a rewarding glow will be his when, a year or two later, he hears the final and clinching "aye" from a city council member which puts his idea into official effect.

Of course, he should be equally alert to recognize and come to the support of some meritorious proposal by someone else—say a city or county official. He should rally to it the help of his organization even though such "we too" support doesn't give him the satisfaction of a job which he originated.

Inventory of Accomplishments

Here is a stimulating little exercise for a civic secretary which will have as good an effect on his morale as deep breathing has on his physical being. He should keep an accumulative inventory of his more important accomplishments over the years. Each year, he should be able to add several to a half dozen from the list of the past year's jobs. The force of this list would be diluted by including minor jobs which, while they may have been significant this year, are hardly important enough to be transmitted to posterity.

This inventory of accomplishments will serve several purposes. It will furnish a list of worthwhile accomplishments to reinforce the sales-arguments of a member of your finance committee when trying to get a prospect to subscribe. Also, on a blue day, the secretary can restore his self-confidence by running his eyes over these past jobs which he had a major share in putting through, as the miser runs his fingers through the jewels in his casket. Lastly, it will give the secretary a measure as to whether he is increasing his "production" over the years or is slipping.

tion and material about the Blue Ballot," reports a bulletin of CGC. Tens of thousands of Blue Ballot tags were distributed on tag day, October 29.[1]

'I Have Voted'

Instead of distributing gold feathers to citizens who went to the polls in the state of Washington this November, the office of the Secretary of State distributed badges stating: "State Seal Citizen—I Have Voted." Some 800,000 badges, made available by the Citizens' Voting Committee, composed of representatives of both major political parties, labor and civic groups, were distributed to voting precincts throughout the state.

Quarter Million Use Report

The Municipal League of Seattle and King County, Washington, reports that by the time November 2 rolled around nearly a quarter of a million people had read the league's fall election report. So great was the demand for the *Report on Candidates and Issues* that a second press run was necessary. Other thousands read the report in Seattle's two daily newspapers. All this, says the league's *Municipal News,* "is gratifying evidence that voters want an unbiased, nonpartisan election report to help them make their decisions before they go to the polls."

De Soto Jaycees Get Award

Associated Industries of Missouri, a statewide organization, at its 35th annual meeting in October, presented the De Soto (Missouri) Junior Chamber of Commerce with its 1954 Community Relations Award for communities of 5,000-10,000. The Jaycees were given a plaque, according to *The Jefferson Republic,* "in recognition of their vigorous program to interest citizens in their city government, to acquaint them with their re-

---

[1]See page 586, this issue.

sponsibilities as citizens, and to encourage them to vote in city elections." Basis for the award was the successful campaign which the Jaycees conducted early this year for retention of the council-manager plan, adopted in 1948.

Gordon T. Beaham, Jr., president of AIM, commented: "While De Soto is the smallest community represented, the program of its Junior Chamber of Commerce rates our highest commendations. If America is to remain free we must all of us live up to our individual responsibilities as free men and women. The De Soto Junior Chamber of Commerce program vividly demonstrates the tangible good which can be accomplished when groups of businessmen speak out publicly for their firm convictions."

De Soto, one of five Missouri communities honored by AIM, was an All-America City in the 1953 contest of the National Municipal League and *Look* magazine.

Citizen Welfare Committees

"Citizen Boards and Advisory Committees in Public Welfare Administration," by Kittye Clyde Austin, is the title of an article appearing in the October 1954 issue of *Public Welfare,* journal of the American Public Welfare Association. "Citizen boards are important in public welfare administration and more thought needs to be given to their potentialities," says a secondary head.

Students in Politics

During the campaign leading up to the November 2 elections, twenty Barnard College (women's college at Columbia University) students aided at the headquarters of some fourteen state and local candidates as part of their study of practical politics. Duties of the volunteers included helping to write platforms and speeches, canvassing districts and supervising other volunteers doing such chores as addressing, stuffing and mailing of envelopes. Each student devoted from five to fifteen hours weekly to the campaign, in conjunction with a course in practical politics under American Political Parties and Practice.

Some 25 University of Minnesota students, early in October, worked for Republican and Democratic-Farmer-Labor candidates for the Minnesota legislature. They rang doorbells, posted placards, mailed literature and spoke before audiences. The students are enrolled in a course on Field Work in Government and Politics, the purpose of which is to teach citizenship through active and often arduous participation.[1]

Teaching Local Government

An eight-weeks school on the governments of Minneapolis and Hennepin County has been arranged by the Citizens' League of Greater Minneapolis and the League of Women Voters. It offers some unusual insights into the way our local government machinery works, reports the Citizens League *News Bulletin.* "Sessions will stress the influence of interests and pressures on the city council and the county board, the importance of committees and committee chairmanship, and will dissect both the existing and the alternative ways of organizing and financing the governments." Professors of political science, public officials and civic leaders will be among those addressing the sessions.

Xavier University, in cooperation with the city of Cincinnati, is conducting an adult course in city government "to provide interested citizens an opportunity to better know the organization, functioning, objectives and problems of their city government." City officials will address those in attendance and liberal use

[1]See also the REVIEW, February 1953, page 96.

will be made of motion pictures, slides, maps, charts, etc.

TAXATION AND FINANCE

• (Continued from page 599)

per cent, to provide for full debt service and the repayment of the accumulated operating deficiencies, but only the provision for relief was increased among the operating appropriations, all others being cut. Foreclosure proceedings were instituted for the first time in years to collect delinquent taxes. The result was to reduce the town's total debt from $6,085,-000 at the beginning of the year to $5,-718,000 at the end of the year, and replace the deficit with an operating cash surplus of $36,268.

Succeeding budgets continued adherence to a policy of providing current revenues to meet anticipated requirements, including debt service which in 1935 took nearly 28 per cent of total expenditures. That same year, the town completed construction of a school for which it had been unable to sell bonds in 1931, and with the total debt down to less than $5,000,000. In 1939 short-term borrowing was introduced to provide for short-term financing of major projects, and since 1943 a reserve fund has been accumulated to provide for capital and non-recurring outlays.

The town's story is told in a little booklet, *Greenwich, 1954: The Year of Jubilee,* which bears the notation "Published at no expense to the Greenwich taxpayers," and was prepared by Mrs. C. Y. Belknap and Reynolds Girdler. "Significantly," it states, "the last bond retired had originally been created to refund a debt contracted during the Civil War—a fitting reminder of the blithe spirit with which one generation could impose its debt on posterity during the days of the Town's grasshopper financing."

Fifty Years of Citizen Research

Bureaus Have Done Much to Raise Government Standards

EDITOR'S NOTE.—The article below, by JOHN F. WILLMOTT, executive director of the Dade County Research Foundation, Miami, Florida, is made up of excerpts from his September 11 address before the American Political Science Association at Chicago.

CITIZEN research in state and local government has been going on in this country for almost 50 years. It started in 1905 when a group of civic leaders in New York City decided to find out *why* the city was so badly governed, *what* specific things were wrong with it, and *how* they could help officials get better results with the taxpayer's dollar. So they formed an association called the Bureau of City Betterment, which was later renamed the Bureau of Municipal Research.

Since then, the citizen research movement has spread until now there are more than one hundred such organizations in all parts of the United States. They are called citizens' research bureaus, councils, institutes and taxpayers' leagues. In this paper all these agencies are called citizen research associations. All have a common objective: better government through fact-finding, through citizen education and through cooperation with public officials.

The surveys and reports of the various citizen research associations touch every function and activity of government. In the beginning, of course, almost every research agency delves into budgeting and accounting because proper budgeting and accounting are indispensable for financial planning and administrative control of every public function. Other basic subjects, such as over-all organization, purchasing, planning and personnel administration, are generally treated during the early years of a research unit and appear again and again in its reports.

In addition, the various operating functions have been surveyed. Proposed bond issues, budgets and tax levies, initiative and referendum measures, proposed legislation, new charters and charter amendments, and other proposals which are pending before state and local bodies or which await the voters' decision are analyzed by citizen research bodies in published reports.

Organization of Research Agency

Citizen research associations are local, autonomous organizations, but the basic organization structure is the same in practically every case. It consists of a membership, a governing board and a research staff headed by an executive director. The board of trustees or board of directors sets general policies, hires the executive director, determines the program of activities, exercises general control over operations, reviews major reports in final draft, approves the budget and raises money to finance the organization.

Is there any danger that the board's thinking on any given subject will be influenced by personal or business bias or by the political connections of individual directors? That does happen, of course. To expect otherwise would be more than a little naive. But such occurrences are extremely rare and of short duration. If the board is well balanced with representation of different interests and viewpoints, other directors will raise an outcry if one board member attempts to steer the ship around to his own dock for his own selfish benefit.

The day-to-day work of a research association is carried on by the executive director and his staff. They are in close touch with the process of government. They attend meetings of public bodies. They talk constantly with officials. You will find them at police headquarters, in the finance department, at a school, out at the incinerator or in the city hospital. You may even see them at a fire. Everywhere they go, they are observing and analyzing the work of government. And they are constantly asking themselves, "How can this particular job be done more efficiently?"

Work with Officials

We have said that the principal objective of a citizen research association is to help officials improve government. How can that best be done? Well that all depends upon the attitude and outlook of the officials.

Let us consider first the most favorable situation—which we will call Type 1—where the officials are intelligent, alert, forward-looking. In that case, the citizen research agency is accepted by officials and a cordial relationship develops. In fact, the association is frequently at its wit's end to keep up with the insistent demands of officeholders for information and advice.

Much of the association's work will be carried on quietly and without publicity unless the official concerned desires to publicize it. The association seeks no public credit. It will, of course, report its activities to its members, but such a report will not be publicized. In that sort of situation, a research association is almost never militant or sharply critical; it doesn't have to be.

Now let us consider the second type of situation, one in which most of the officials are honest and devoted to good government in the abstract but have never had much contact with any other system except the one which they have been using for many years and which they believe to be perfect.

Officials with such an outlook will generally welcome the research association and will assume that its surveys will be favorable, even flattering. However, the association's first X-rays of the department or institution in question may show a diseased condition which not even the researchers had suspected. A complete reorganization is obviously in order with installation of controls and modern methods. No other recommendation is possible.

No matter how mild the research recommendations, no matter how well supported by facts, and no matter how tactful the presentation, officials will be shocked, hurt and angry. Some of them will explode and go right up through the courthouse roof. And, of course, that is what courthouse roofs are for, as any architect will tell you.

What can the research association do under such circumstances to win official support for needed changes? One good way is to wait. Six months from now, a tactful researcher may be able to sell some of those recommendations to the very same officials, particularly if the researcher can relate the recommendations to official problems and headaches which have developed in the meantime.

If, after waiting and negotiating with the officials immediately concerned and with their superiors, it appears that nothing is going to happen, the research association will probably resort to publicity.

If the research association's recommendations are sound, effectively presented, and widely disseminated and persistently followed up, the association will ultimately win. And if it has competent staff, sound leadership and strong membership support, it will ultimately transform its community into the type of environment previously described as Type 1.

We come now to the third type of community, one in which government is backward, permeated with politics, waste and inefficiency, and the target of public it and the truculent officials will soon find that they are not just fighting the research association but a large group of decent citizens who are fed up with official racketeering and tax waste.

If the research association sticks to its guns, meets hysterical counter charges and accusations with calm facts tactfully presented, officials will ultimately find themselves in a vulnerable position where their continuance in office and their hold on public confidence is slipping. Ultimately, the citizen research agency's work will bear fruit. Slowly but surely, the political climate of the community will change. Official hostility will cease. Higher standards of public morals and official behavior will be established. And the community will ultimately become a Type 2 or even Type 1 environment. The research agency will then be able to work harmoniously and effectively with all elements in the community.

Citizen research associations have now had almost half a century of existence and fruitful achievement. Dr. John M. Gaus, in *A Study of Research in Public Administration*, points out that, although not all advances in the field of public administration can be attributed to organized citizen concern with government, yet it was the governmental research bureaus which initiated and developed modern methods of administration across the country.

I believe you will agree with me that these citizen research associations, working quietly and helpfully where possible and courageously and openly where necessary, have done much to raise the standards of state and local government. Let us hope that their number and usefulness will richly increase in the years to come.

(Listings of research pamphlets and articles are combined with the listings at the end of Books in Review.)

Books in Review

THE MAYOR'S WIFE—CRUSADE IN KANSAS CITY. By Marjorie Beach. New York City, Vantage Press, Inc., 1953. x, 210 pp. $3.

Machine politics in American cities have received fairly thorough treatment in books before, but Marjorie Beach's story of her husband's fight against the Pendergast machine in Kansas City during the 1920s has a personal and dramatic note which will bring its message home to a wide variety of readers.

The personal documentation in the book is what lifts it above the ordinary run of books on the subject. One of the humorous—and at the same time maddening—scenes revolves about the experience of four women who ventured into Kansas City's notorious Twelfth Street district to make a poll to weed out fraudulent voters. In one day the women, disguised as Red Cross workers searching for missing relatives, turned up over 200 fraudulent votes, among them Tom Muffet, Peter Piper and Simon Blue, three tropical fish.

Among the many interesting tales recounted in the book, one of particular interest to readers of the REVIEW will be the story of how a machine politician was picked in 1925 by a five-to-four Pendergast majority on the Kansas City council to be city manager.

Albert Beach, then entering his second term as a reform mayor, was faced with an impossible situation, and the frustrations he experienced as the city's chief executive with the politically picked city manager are at once interesting and frightening. It is a living illustration of a council-manager charter being voted on at the wrong time—in this case, when the good government groups had not consolidated their forces sufficiently to have a good council elected in the first place.

Mrs. Beach concludes her narrative before the sweeping changes of the 1940 were accomplished, changes which hav righted the wrongs of the city's mal administration during the years when he husband was fighting for clean, efficient government.

ANDREW J. LAZARU

URBAN TRAFFIC — A FUNCTION o LAND USE. By Robert B. Mitchell and Chester Rapkin. New York 27, Colum bia University Press, 1954. xviii, 22 pp. $5.00.

This important book is a milestone in the quest to place urban planning on a scientific footing. Its reasoning and conclusions are indispensable for understanding traffic problems, for evaluating existing transportation planning theories and methods, and for developing a more adequate approach to transportation.

It has been recognized for many years that activities using land and the transportation facilities serving them are completely interdependent. But the exact interrelation of transportation and land usage has remained largely uncharted to the present day.

Urban Traffic presents the first rounded framework of concepts and terminology to link the two aspects of man's activity. It furnishes a theoretical system for understanding traffic as part of the general productive living pattern of the urban area, and suggests ways of forecasting one from the other.

There is one major criticism of *Urban Traffic*, a reservation appropriate only because the book comes so close to encompassing an entire field. The text establishes beyond argument the impossibility of adequately considering traffic without at the same time considering land use. But strangely enough there is little consideration of another sector of the transportation problem that is just as closely nterrelated with urban traffic and very much more obviously so: the other modes of transportation such as rail, rapid transit and air. It is to be hoped that the authors in another book will integrate these additional forms of travel into their framework so as to complete their comprehensive statement on the movement of people and goods.

HENRY FAGIN

Regional Plan Association
New York City

THE DOCTRINE OF RESPONSIBLE PARTY GOVERNMENT—ITS ORIGINS AND PRESENT STATE. By Austin Ranney. Urbana, The University of Illinois Press, 1954. xi, 176 pp. Clothbound, $4.00; paperbound, $3.00.

This is a scholarly and competent analysis and comparison of the American Political Science Association's study, *Toward a More Responsible Two-party System,* and the concepts of leading writers of a generation ago—Woodrow Wilson, A. Lawrence Lowell, Henry Jones Ford, Frank J. Goodnow and Herbert Croly. The writer complains that these writers gave different meanings to key words like democracy and party membership and that such uncertainties plague the discussions of today. He argues also that modern political science should venture to define what a model party would be anyway!

R.S.C.

THE ADVICE AND CONSENT OF THE SENATE. By Joseph P. Harris. Berkeley, University of California Press, 1953. xii, 457 pp. $5.00.

Here is an important study dealing with a major problem of American national government—senatorial confirmation of presidential appointments—which may be read with profit by students of state and local government. It is a comprehensive and scholarly account of this aspect of executive-legislative relations from the debates of the Constitutional Convention to Senator McCarthy's opposition to Ambassador Bohlen. Students of state politics will benefit from the revealing account of struggles for senatorial confirmation which often reflected various state and local issues, and always reflected the dilemma of "balance of power." Those who urge more or diminished power for state legislatures in the matter of confirming appointments will ponder with profit the author's criticisms of the U. S. Senate. Readers of the REVIEW may be interested to compare Professor Harris' excellent study of this matter in the federal structure with the *Model State Constitution* which nowhere provides for legislative control of executive appointments.

WILLIAM F. LARSEN

SUGGESTED STATE LEGISLATION. Program for 1955. By The Drafting Committee of State Officials. Chicago, The Council of State Governments, 1954. viii, 158 pp. $1.50.

This program of suggested state legislation is an annual feature of the Council of State Governments. Leading off with a summary of its proposed laws, it covers some 38 subjects from accident prevention to weights and measures. Included are recently promulgated uniform acts of the National Conference of Commissioners on Uniform State Laws, which deal with such subjects as a uniform disposition of unclaimed property act, a uniform aircraft financial responsibility act and the National Municipal League's *Model State Medico-legal Investigative System* converted to the text of a model post-mortem examinations act.

In addition are included descriptions of the National Municipal League's new *Model State and Regional Planning Law, Model Election Administration System, Model Voter Registration System, Model Direct Primary Election System* and its four fiscal models—*Accrual Budget Law,*

Cash Basis Budget Law, County and Municipal Bond Law and *Real Property Tax Collection Law.*

Additional Books, Pamphlets and Articles

Administrative History

THE JACKSONIANS. A Study in Administrative History 1829-1861. By Leonard D. White. New York, The Macmillan Company, 1954. xii, 593 pp. $8.00.

Airports

AIRPORT AGENCIES IN METROPOLITAN AREAS. Springfield, Illinois Legislative Council, September 1954. 36 pp.

Civil Defense and Education

CIVIL DEFENSE AND HIGHER EDUCATION. Washington 6, D. C., American Council on Education, Committee on Civil Defense and Higher Education, March 1954. 18 pp.

Civil Service

BETTER GOVERNMENT NEEDS BETTER CIVIL SERVICE. By Harold L. Henderson. New York, National Civil Service League, *Good Government*, July-August 1954. 5 pp.

STATE CIVIL SERVICE IN KANSAS. By William H. Cape and Edwin O. Stene. Lawrence, University of Kansas, Governmental Research Center, 1954. 160 pp.

Constitutions

FROM THE DECLARATION OF INDEPENDENCE TO THE CONSTITUTION. The Roots of American Constitutionalism. Edited by C. J. Friedrich and Robert G. McCloskey. New York, The Liberal Arts Press, 1954. 139 pp. Paper, 75 cents; cloth, $2.00.

METHODS OF STATE CONSTITUTIONAL REFORM. By Albert L. Sturm. Ann Arbor, University of Michigan, Institute of Public Administration, Bureau of Government, 1954. xii, 175 pp.

Education

A COOPERATIVE STUDY OF SCHOOL BUILDING NEEDS. NEWCASTLE-HENRY TOWNSHIP SCHOOL CORPORATION. Lafayette, Purdue University, Division of Education and Applied Psychology, 1953. 70 pp.

LAKE COUNTY HIGH SCHOOL FINANCIAL AND BUILDING PROBLEMS 1954 TO 1961-62. Waukegan (Illinois), Lake County Civic League, 1954. 21 pp.

A SURVEY OF THE INDIANAPOLIS PUBLIC SCHOOL. Indianapolis, Chamber of Commerce, Bureau of Governmental Research, May 1954. 75 pp.

Elections and Voting

THE ELECTORAL SYSTEM IN BRITAIN, 1918-1951. By D. E. Butler. New York 11, Oxford University Press, 1953. xi, 222 pp. $3.40.

REPORT OF THE GOVERNOR'S STUDY COMMISSION ON ELECTIONS. Lansing, the commission, 1953. 33 pp.

Labor Relations

MUNICIPAL LABOUR RELATIONS IN CANADA. A Study of Some Problems Arising from Collective Bargaining Between Municipalities and Municipal Trade Unions. By S. J. Frankel and R. C. Pratt. Montreal, The Canadian Federation of Mayors and Municipalities and The Industrial Relations Centre, McGill University, 1954. v, 87 pp. $2.50.

Metropolitan Areas

METROPOLITAN GROWTH AND ITS EFFECT ON DALLAS. Dallas 5, Southern Methodist University, Business Executives' Research Committee, 1954. 60 pp. Illus. $1.00. (Apply Dr. Warren A. Law, Southern Methodist University, Box 157, Dallas 5.)

OUR CITIFIED COUNTY. A Study of Cuyahoga County and Its Land Use Now, and for the Future. Cleveland, Regional Planning Commission. 29 pp. Maps.

Municipal Fund Investment

TECHNIQUES AND PROCEDURES OF INVESTMENT IN U. S. TREASURY BILLS. By Robert H. Bethke. Chicago 37, Municipal Finance Officers Association. September 1954. 4 pp. 75 cents.

Municipal Government

THE CITY TRIES FOR BETTER MANAGE-MENT. An Exercise in Municipal Self-improvement. Pittsburgh 19, Pennsylvania Economy League, Inc., Western Division, *P.E.L. Newsletter,* June-July 1954. 9 pp.

HANDBOOK FOR ILLINOIS MUNICIPAL OFFICIALS. By Thomas A. Matthews. Springfield, Illinois Municipal League, 1954. 58 pp. $1.00.

Parking

AUTOMOBILE PARKING IN THE UNITED STATES. Selected References 1946-1952. Washington 25, Highway Research Board, 1953. v, 119 pp. $1.35.

Planning

OFFICIAL JOINT PLANNING IN THE UNITED STATES. By Robert J. Piper. Chicago 37, American Society of Planning Officials, Planning Advisory Service, November 1953. 41 pp. $2.00.

Police Public Relations

ROCKS IN THE ROADWAY. A Treatise on Police Public Relations—by a Police Officer—for Police Officers. By Dan Hollingsworth. Chicago, Northwestern University, The Traffic Institute, July 1954. 51 pp.

Political Parties

INHERITED DOMAIN—POLITICAL PARTIES IN TENNESSEE. By William Goodman. Knoxville, University of Tennessee, Bureau of Public Administration, 1954. ix, 95 pp. $1.50.

Public Employees

REGULATING POLITICAL ACTIVITIES OF PUBLIC EMPLOYEES. By Richard Christopherson. Chicago 37, Civil Service Assembly, 1954. 13 pp. $2.00. (Price to members, $1.50.)

Recreation

WASHINGTON STATUTES RELATING TO PARKS AND RECREATION WITH ANNOTATIONS. By Ernest H. Campbell and Henry D. Ambers. Seattle, University of Washington, Bureau of Governmental Research and Services, July 1954. xix, 121 pp. $2.00.

Research

CITIZEN RESEARCH: ITS VITAL ROLE TODAY. By Loren B. Miller. Toronto 2B, Canadian Tax Foundation, *Canadian Tax Journal,* May-June, 1954. 4 pp.

WISCONSIN RESEARCH INVENTORY. Madison, Wisconsin Legislative Reference Library, April 1954. 32 pp.

Retirement Systems

REPORT ON 1954 FEDERAL LEGISLATION RELATING TO PUBLIC EMPLOYEE RETIREMENT SYSTEM. By A. A. Weinberg. Chicago 37, Municipal Finance Officers Association, 1954. 4 pp. 50 cents.

Revenue Bonds

THE LAW OF REVENUE BONDS. By Lawrence E. Chermak. Washington 6, D. C., National Institute of Municipal Law Officers, 1954. 236 pp. $5.00.

Salaries

FIRE DEPARTMENT SALARIES. Salaries in Effect in Fire Departments of the United States and Canada, April 1954. Washington, D. C., International Association of Fire Fighters, 1954. 13 pp. of tables.

1954 MICHIGAN MUNICIPAL WAGES AND SALARIES: Supplement to Michigan Municipal League Bulletin 73. Ann Arbor, the league, August 1954. 9 pp.

Streets and Highways

HOW TO GET THE MOST OUT OF OUR STREETS. Washington 6, D. C., Chamber of Commerce of the United States, Transportation and Communication Department, 1954. 50 pp. Illus. $1.00.

Taxation and Finance

ADMISSIONS TAXES IN OHIO CITIES. Columbus 15, Ohio Municipal League, March 1954. 36 pp.

COMPENDIUM OF CITY GOVERNMENT FINANCES IN 1953. The 481 Cities Having More Than 25,000 Inhabitants in 1950. Washington, D. C., U. S. Department of Commerce, Bureau of the Census, 1954. vi, 139 pp. 70 cents.

COUNTY FISCAL PROBLEMS IN CALIFORNIA. By Vincent T. Cooper and Wm. R. MacDougall. Sacramento 14, County

Supervisors Association of California, May 1954. 10 pp. Tables.

CRITERIA FOR JUDGING A MUNICIPAL FINANCIAL REPORT. Chicago 37, Municipal Finance Officers Association, 1954. 4 pp. 50 cents.

LOCAL TAX LEGISLATION, 1952-1954. Princeton (New Jersey), Tax Institute, *Tax Policy*, July-August 1954. 14 pp. 50 cents.

STATE FUND STRUCTURE. Report to the Colorado General Assembly. Denver, Colorado Legislative Council, 1954. 13 pp., tables.

STATE GENERAL REVENUE WORKING BALANCE A NECESSITY—$15 Million Not Excessive. Jefferson City, Missouri Public Expenditure Survey, September 1954. 4 pp.

STATE SUPERVISION OF THE GENERAL PROPERTY TAX. Tallahassee, Florida State University, Bureau of Governmental Research and Service, 1953. 18 pp.

SUMMARY OF CITY GOVERNMENT FINANCES IN 1953. Washington 25, D. C., Department of Commerce, Bureau of the Census, August 1954. 19 pp. 15 cents.

SUMMARY OF STATE GOVERNMENT FINANCES IN 1953. Washington 25, D. C., Department of Commerce, Bureau of the Census, May 7, 1954. 21 pp. 15 cents.

TAX COMPARISON—JURISDICTIONS WITHIN THE WASHINGTON METROPOLITAN AREA. Arlington County (Virginia), Office of the County Manager, August 1954. 18 pp.

TRENDS IN STATE FINANCE: 1953. Chicago 37, Federation of Tax Administrators, January 1954. 44 pp.

UNANSWERED QUESTIONS IN MUNICIPAL FINANCE. Princeton (New Jersey), Tax Institute, *Tax Policy*, June 1954. 4 pp. 25 cents.

Townships

PROBLEMS OF URBAN TOWNS (TOWNSHIPS) IN MINNESOTA. St. Paul, Minnesota Legislative Research Committee, November 1953. 34 pp.

FAITH IS BASE OF FREEDOM

(Continued from page 582)

fought the issue fairly and squarely and won with 51 per cent of the voters' confidence.

I believe today's problems call for a kind of bravery. Bravery is a key to a state of mind—a state of national poise. Its result will be statesmanship. What matters most is that you and I act as we know we ought, even at the risk of unpleasant consequences.

Citizenship is a sacred trust. We need to be leaders who will proudly proclaim our religious heritage. We need to be leaders who will seek to know facts, to distinguish truth from lies. We need to be leaders who will be fearless in the face of criticism, to work for the betterment of all people.

On one Sunday in December many years ago, President Woodrow Wilson spoke on this common devotion while visiting England. He pointed out how the attempt to govern the world by a partnership of special interests had failed. And he concluded by saying that "there is only one thing that can bind peoples together and that is a common devotion to what is right."

This is "my land, my native land." Well, it isn't yours, not completely, until you lose yourself in its service.

We are the sons of sacred flame,
Our brows marked with a sacred
    name,
The company of souls supreme,
The conscripts of a mighty dream.

1955
All-America
Cities Awards
jury.

All-America Finalists Tell Jury Their Story

Eleven winners in the 1954 All-America Cities Awards competition, jointly sponsored by the National Municipal League and *Look* magazine, will be announced next month, climaxing the most successful operation of the contest in its six-year history.

Representatives of 22 finalists, which were winnowed from a record 225 cities, counties and villages nominated for Awards, stated their case before a jury of citizen leaders and experts in governmental affairs during the 60th Annual National Conference on Government in Kansas City last month. The finalists converged on Kansas City from points as distant as New Jersey and California.

Opening the hearings, Dr. George H. Gallup, League President and jury foreman, said: "The All-America Cities Awards . . . are given not for good government, efficient municipal administration or a specific improvement, as such, but rather for 'energetic, purposeful, intelligent citizen effort.'

"Some of the awards in other years have been made to communities where a remarkable record of courageous and well conceived citizen effort has been launched and aggressively pursued against entrenched forces which will require years to dislodge. In these cases, the awards have been a distinct aid to the citizen groups in furthering their good work.

"We hope citizens of the cities re-ceiving recognition will consider the award a challenge to demonstrate that their interest and concern for the well-being of their community will be sustained."

The 22 finalists were: Beatrice, Nebraska; Burbank, California; Chicago; Decatur, Arkansas; El Cerrito, California; Elmwood Park, Illinois; Fort Wayne, Indiana; Johnson County, Kansas; Kettering, Ohio; Maricopa County, Arizona; Mexico, Missouri; Modesto, California; Newark, Parsippany-Troy Hills, and Passaic, New Jersey; Pendleton, Oregon; Pueblo, Colorado; Richfield, Minnesota; Riverside, California; Rock Island, Illinois; Rockville, Maryland; and Warren, Ohio.

Serving with Dr. Gallup on the jury were: Mrs. Albert D. Cash, former member, City Council, Cincinnati; Mrs. Maurice H. Noun, former president, League of Women Voters, Des Moines, Iowa; Mrs. Ruth Robinson Roach, National Federation of Business and Professional Women's Clubs; Dean William L. Bradshaw, University of Missouri; Philip C. Ebeling, attorney, Dayton, Ohio; Leo Perlis, director of community services, CIO; Vernon Myers, publisher, *Look*; Mark S. Matthews, author and former president, U. S. Junior Chamber of Commerce; Professor Donald H. Webster, University of Washington; Lloyd Hale, member, National Municipal League Council and president, G. H. Tennant Company, Minneapolis; and Powell C. Groner, president, Kansas City Public Service Company, and former vice president, U. S. Chamber of Commerce.

Something New Is Added

For the first time in the history of the Nationa Conference on Government, America's Tow Meeting of the Air, heard over 325 ABC station formed a feature of the program. The topi "How Can We Divorce Crime From Politics?" was discussed by (left to right, above) Robert I Merriam, Chicago alderman, Thomas F. Murra Jr., moderator, and Norton Mockridge, crime r porter for the New York World-Telegram an The Sun. Mr. Mockridge advocated removal c law enforcement officials from political contre Mr. Merriam called upon citizens to devote mo attention to local government. During the que tion period, a platoon of visitors to the conferenc lined up (below) to quiz the speakers. After th program Dr. Gallup presented the League's annu Distinguished Citizen Award to John B. Gag former mayor of Kansas City (left). The citatio praised Mr. Gage "for his steadfast devotion an faithful service to his community."

OPPOSITE PAGE: As usual, panel meeting formed a major portion of the Conference pr gram. In a session on "The Urban County chaired by Frank C. Moore, New York State former lieutenant governor, Thomas H. Reed veteran municipal consultant, makes a poin (top). Another Council member, Lee M. Sharra chaired a session on traffic problems; he is show listening to Mayor Roy Hofheinz of Houstos Texas. Cecil Morgan, League Council member presided at "Industry's Responsibility for Achiev ing Sound Government," in which representative of management and labor participated. Hig school students from the Kansas City area g into the act in "Youth in Civic Affairs" (nex to bottom). A group of women discussed problem faced by their sex in government, politics an civic affairs (bottom).

REED   MR. MOORE   MR. EDWARDS

MR. RIEDL   MR. YOUNG   MR. MORGAN   MR. BAUMER   MR. EHRHARDT

R. S. Childs Wins LaGuardia Award

Richard S. Childs, chairman of the League Executive Committee, will receive the LaGuardia Memorial Award "for outstanding achievement in municipal government" at the fourth annual award luncheon of the LaGuardia Memorial Association at the Hotel Astor, New York City, December 11.

The award will be made on the 72nd anniversary of the birth of the late Fiorello H. LaGuardia, former mayor of New York City. It is presented by a group of his friends and associates who gather annually "to renew faith in his philosophy and rededicate ourselves to the ideal to which he devoted his life."

Mr. Childs was chosen recipient of the award from a group of nominees screened by the Graduate School of Public Administration and Social Service of New York University. The committee's selections were then submitted to an advisory panel consisting of de-Lesseps Morrison, mayor of New

Orleans; Paul G. Hoffman, former ch of the Economic Corporation Admir tration; Harold S. Buttenheim, edit *The American City*; John Nuve former U. S. Minister to Greece; a Mrs. Millicent McIntosh, preside Barnard College.

Known as the father of the coun manager plan, Mr. Childs will be ci for his efforts in the reform of st and local government and for numerous unselfish contributions civic improvement.

Dr. Buell G. Gallagher, president City College, will be guest speaker.

New Constitution Adopted

A new constitution, the text of whi appeared in the October NATIONAL M NICIPAL REVIEW, was adopted at t League's annual membership meetin in Kansas City, November 8.

The new instrument, which replac one adopted September 20, 1932, is outgrowth of a report by a survey co mittee appointed by League Preside George Gallup. A summary of this port also appeared in the October R VIEW.

Three New Model Laws Published by League

Two revisions of existing model laws and a model law on a new subject are being published this month by the National Municipal League.

The revisions are entitled *Model Voter Registration System* and *Model Real Property Tax Collection Law*. The third publication is *Model Investment of State Funds Law*. Each is priced at $1.

L. Arnold Frye

The two fiscal publications were p pared under the supervision of t League's Committee on a Program Model Fiscal Legislation, of which Arnold Frye is chairman. Mr. Frye, lawyer, is an authority in the municip bond and debt field.

Dr. Joseph P. Harris, of the Univ sity of California, is chairman of t committee responsible for the registr tion law, and is author of the origin text of this edition as he was of the thr previous ones. The League first issu its *Model Voter Registration System* January 1927.

Tools for Achieving Better Government

Citizen groups often turn to the League for help in achieving better government in their locality. Listed below are some of the tools available to them:

Campaign Pamphlets

Story of the Council-Manager Plan, 36 pages (1954).........................$ .20
Charts: Council-manager Form, Commission Form, Mayor-council Form
    (17½ x 22½"), 50 cents each, set of three.. 1.00
County Manager Plan, 24 pages (1950)... .20
Forms of Municipal Government—How Have They Worked?
    20 pages (1953).. .25
Facts About the Council-Manager Plan, 8 pages (1954)........................... .05
City Employees and the Manager Plan, 4 pages (1952)........................... .05
Labor Unions and the Council-Manager Plan, 8 pages (1953)................. .05
P. R., 12 pages (1952).. .05
The Citizen Association—How to Organize and Run It, 64 pages (1953) .75
The Citizen Association—How to Win Civic Campaigns, 64 pages
    (1953) .... .75
    (The two pamphlets above may be purchased together for $1.20)

Model Laws

Model Accrual Budget Law, 40 pages (1946)... .75
Model Cash Basis Budget Law, 42 pages (1948)....................................... .75
Model City Charter, 173 pages (1941)... 1.50
Model County and Municipal Bond Law, 54 pages (1953)........................ 1.00
Model County Charter (New edition in preparation.).............................. 1.00
Model Direct Primary Election System, 48 pages (1951).......................... 1.00
Model Investment of State Funds Law, 23 pages (1954) 1.00
Model Real Property Tax Collection Law, 40 pages (1954) 1.00
Model State and Regional Planning Law (1954)....................................... 1.00
Model State Civil Service Law, 32 pages (1953)....................................... .75
Model State Constitution, 72 pages (1948).. 1.00
Model State Medico-legal Investigative System, 39 pages (1954)............ .50
Model Voter Registration System, 56 pages (1954).................................. 1.00

Other Pamphlets and Books

American County—Patchwork of Boards, 24 pages (1946)....................... .35
Best Practice Under the Manager Plan, 8 pages (1954)........................... .15
Civic Victories, by Richard S. Childs, 367 pages (1952)........................... 3.50
Citizen Organization for Political Activity: The Cincinnati Plan.
    32 pages (1949).. .50
Coroners in 1953—A Symposium of Legal Bases and Actual Practices,
    90 pages, mimeographed (1954).. 2.00
Digest of County Manager Charters and Laws, 70 pages (1954)............. 2.00
Guide for Charter Commissions, 44 pages (1952)..................................... .75
Manager Plan Abandonments, by Arthur W. Bromage, 36 pages (1954) .50
The Metropolitan Problem—Current Research, Opinion, Action, by
    Guthrie S. Birkhead (reprinted from NATIONAL MUNICIPAL RE-
    VIEW), 12 pages (1953).. .25
More Responsible States. Panel Discussion, National Conference on
    Government, Richmond, Virginia, 33 pages, mimeographed (1953) .50
Proportional Representation—Illustrative Election, 8 pages (1951).......... .10
Proportional Representation—Key to Democracy, by George H. Hallett,
    Jr., 177 pages (1940)... .25
Women as Campaigners. Panel Discussion, National Conference on
    Government, Richmond, Virginia, 32 pages, mimeographed (1954) .50

Discounts on Quantity Orders — Write for Complete List and Description.

National Municipal League

Lightning Source UK Ltd.
Milton Keynes UK
UKHW010617091218
333661UK00004B/494/P